Colonial America in an Atlantic World

From Colonies to Revolution

Second Edition

T. H. Breen
Northwestern University

Timothy Hall
Central Michigan University

PEARSON

Boston   Columbus   Indianapolis   New York   San Francisco   Upper Saddle River   Amsterdam
Cape Town   Dubai   London   Madrid   Milan   Munich   Paris   Montréal   Toronto   Delhi
Mexico City   São Paulo   Sydney   Hong Kong   Seoul   Singapore   Taipei   Tokyo

Editor in Chief: *Ashley Dodge*
Program Team Lead: *Amber Mackey*
Managing Editor: *Sutapa Mukherjee*
Program Manager: *Carly Czech*
Sponsoring Editor: *Neeraj Bhalla*
Editorial Project Manager: *Lindsay Bethone, Lumina Datamatics, Inc.*
Editorial Assistant: *Casseia Lewis*
Director, Content Strategy and Development: *Brita Nordin*
VP, Director of Marketing: *Maggie Moylan*
Director of Field Marketing: *Jonathan Cottrell*
Senior Marketing Coordinator: *Susan Osterlitz*
Director, Project Management Services: *Lisa Iarkowski*
Print Project Team Lead: *Melissa Feimer*

Operations Manager: *Mary Fischer*
Operations Specialist: *Carol Melville / Mary Ann Gloriande*
Associate Director of Design: *Blair Brown*
Interior Design: *Kathryn Foot*
Cover Art Director: *Maria Lange*
Cover Design: *Lumina Datamatics, Inc.*
Cover Art: *artida/Shutterstock*
Digital Studio Team Lead: *Peggy Bliss*
Digital Studio Project Manager: *Liz Roden Hall*
Digital Studio Project Manager: *Elissa Senra-Sargent*
Full-Service Project Management and Composition: *Murugesh Rajkumar Namasivayam, Lumina Datamatics, Inc.*
Printer/Binder: *RRD Harrisonburg*
Cover Printer: *RRD Harrisonburg*

Acknowledgements of third party content appear on page 409, which constitutes an extension of this copyright page.

Library of Congress Cataloging-in-Publication Data

Breen, T. H.
  Colonial America in an Atlantic world : from colonies to revolution / T.H. Breen (Northwestern University), Timothy Hall (Central Michigan University).
    pages cm
  Includes bibliographical references and index.
  ISBN 978-0-205-96867-1 (alkaline paper)—ISBN 0-205-96867-8 (alkaline paper)
  1. United States—History—Colonial period, ca. 1600-1775. 2. United States—Ethnic relations—History. 3. Acculturation—United States—History. 4. Cultural pluralism—United States—History. 5. United States—Social conditions—To 1865. 6. North America—Colonization. I. Hall, Timothy D., 1955- II. Title.
  E188.B79 2015
  973.2—dc23
                                                                                    2015028701

4 2021

ISBN 10:   0-205-96867-8
ISBN 13: 978-0-205-96867-1

Table of Contents

Preface

The second edition of *Colonial America in an Atlantic World*, like the first, responds to a growing interest among teachers and students in a broad and exciting field commonly known as Atlantic history. The approach greatly expands the human and physical boundaries of the subject, which once only looked at white settlers organizing new forms of religion and government. This traditional perspective left too many people out of the story. We have, therefore, tried to present the history of Colonial America in terms of dynamic interaction among the peoples of four continents over several centuries. The world in which these diverse peoples fought, traded, befriended, allied, betrayed one another, made love, married, and bore children was an extraordinarily complex and fluid multiplicity of communities, a vast region in which nations remained in constant flux from fifteenth century through the end of the eighteenth century and beyond.

Our narrative continues to center on the development of the North American region that became the United States. In this second edition, we carry that narrative through the ratification of the Constitution in three new chapters. While we wish to avoid treating the long colonial period as a mere prologue to the founding and development of the United States, we also want to avoid the sort of emphasis on the Atlantic and world contexts that risks fragmentation of the narrative into discreet treatment of topics with no attempt to identify a larger, unifying set of themes. To be sure, a variety of narratives may be teased out of the scattered documentary and archaeological traces of past historical experience. But one that surely emerges from an examination of colonial experience in what became British America is the development and eventual division of empire as the thirteen main-land colonies eventually came to declare and win their independence from British rule.

Approach and Themes

We set the story of colonial British America's development in a broader Atlantic narrative not simply for the sake of shifting the interpretive focus away from a familiar tale of intrepid settlers in the wilderness. The Atlantic context exposes more clearly themes that are often overlooked. After all, it constituted the very atmosphere within which ordinary men and women made crucial decisions about work and religion, about families and communities, and about warfare and exploitation. The first European settlers brought with them a bundle of social and religious ideas that shaped how they behaved in the New World—both for good (e.g., setting up governments that allowed for greater participation than had been known in the Old World) and for ill (removing Native Americans and promoting slavery). So, studying Early America without a background that includes European and Africa misses the significance of the flow of ideas and customs across the ocean.

Moreover, from the very beginning, the Europeans saw that Atlantic commerce was essential to their prosperity. Massachusetts governor John Winthrop and his friends traded with planters in the Caribbean; early Virginians sold their tobacco on the European market. Without understanding the movement of goods—incentives for work and entrepreneurial efforts—we are left with a narrow, parochial, and truncated understanding of the development of these communities. The frontier was always in close contact with distant markets and imperial capitals. Our approach, therefore, dismisses the long-discredited notion that white

Americans were merely plotting for independence and democracy from the first landing. This is wrong. They were trying to carve a place within this larger commercial world, and on the ships that carried trade, came new religious, literary, and scientific ideas from Europe as well as Creole languages, music, and art from Africa, and combined both with borrowed ideas, practices, and bits of language borrowed from the indigenous peoples they encountered in this world they called new.

No inhabitant of North America remained unchanged from this experience, and the European colonists in particular did much more than simply echo European thought, art, and architecture. They turned these influences into something different—not degenerate, as some aristocratic eighteenth-century European *philosophes* charged—just different. Anglo-American political experiences were based on English law and practice, but the particularities of life in the North American colonies required adaptations that produced different institutions. Architecture made use of readily available local materials and fitted local needs.

It was this creative aspect of the Atlantic World—a borrowing and recasting—that many historical treatments tend to overlook. And this process of creative adaptation characterized not just the first generation of colonization, but continued to shape the development of colonial American society and culture throughout the eighteenth century. The wars that defined the entire period from 1690 to 1763 were driven in large part by competition for markets among European powers. But here again, there were unintended consequences. The Americans were not cut off from Great Britain, but they had their own ambitions for land, which in turn exacerbated white-Indian relations. The creative process of constitution writing that occupied leaders of the newly independent states reflected the same process of creative borrowing and refiguring. Seen in this light, the Federal Constitution ratified in 1788 was yet another product of the process of creative adaptation that made America at once a part of the larger Atlantic World and a collection of particular local communities with their own distinct cultures.

Structure and Features

The structure and features of *Colonial America in an Atlantic World* are intended to stimulate student interest and curiosity about a complex, multiracial past. The book traces the theme of creative adaptations—a key argument throughout the work—within a three-part structure organized chronologically. The first edition's three chapters of Part I, "Three Worlds Meet," have been condensed to two. The first chapter of this section reviews the pre-Columbian background of European conquest Europe and explores the earliest years of European discovery and encounter within a complex story of trade and bondage throughout the African and American worlds. The next chapter surveys sixteenth-century Iberian colonization of the Caribbean and North America and the contest among other European powers for entry into this lucrative Atlantic system. Unlike other titles in the field, we insist that imperial power in the New World—battle ships and trained soldiers—figured centrally in how people formed and maintained political identities over the entire period. Together, these chapters provide an indispensable historical context for understanding the specific shape taken by English, Dutch, and French colonization of North America during the following century.

The five chapters of Part II, "The Contest for Seventeenth-Century Settlement," focus more closely on English and Dutch colonization of the Caribbean and North America while continuing to trace Spanish and French development on the continent. The varieties of adaptation that took place in each colonial region help explain both the striking diversity that appeared—even among colonies established by the same European nation—and the course of imperial conflict that emerged among various European and native rivals for North America. The five chapters of Part III, "Provinces in a Contested Empire: The Eighteenth Century" survey the growth of Anglo-American colonies through an ongoing process of political and cultural adaptation. It sets this process within a context of an accelerating struggle among the British and French for control of the North Atlantic world as Spanish influence in the region waned. A new Part IV, "Revolution in Atlantic America," offers an overview of the rapid alienation of the thirteen mainland colonies in response to sweeping changes in Britain imperial policy, which eventuated in the division of the first British Empire when armed conflict erupted and the thirteen mainland colonies declared independence. The final chapter reviews steps the newly independent United States took to establish itself as an Atlantic power in its own right.

Each chapter of *Colonial America in an Atlantic World* opens with an account of human experience written to raise one or more significant questions about the chapter topics and provide a concrete example of how actual men and women—many of them obscure people—experienced the great historical changes of their era, the conquest of the Native Americans, the expansion of world markets, the demands of imperial competition and warfare, the spread of evangelical region, and the growth of slavery. Chapters are organized chronologically and by colonial region, incorporating the main themes of the text in the appropriate context. Each chapter includes brief chronology and a bibliographic essay, which summarizes works consulted in preparation of the chapter and offers suggestions for further investigation. We believe that the organization and length will make the text especially useful for providing students of history a comprehensive overview of colonial development, which they can deepen through further investigation of specialized works like those included in each chapter's bibliographic essays.

New to This Edition

- In response to a rapidly expanding student interest in Atlantic History, *Colonial America* draws on the latest scholarship and develops a broad comparative story of New World Conquest and Imperial Rivalry in North America and the Caribbean.
- The new edition adds chapters on the American Revolution, an event covered only superficially by other products in the market.
- Provides much fuller coverage of Native American history from before European Conquest through the 18th century.
- Offers enhanced discussion of the African Diaspora and Development of African American culture in the New World.
- Includes updated bibliographies for each chapter so that students can locate the best current scholarship in Atlantic and Colonial American history.
- Each chapter has been thoroughly revised and updated to incorporate new developments and interpretations in colonial American history.

Part I

Creating an Atlantic World

Three Worlds Meet

"I have found a continent more densely peopled and abounding in animals than our Europe or Asia or Africa," the explorer Amerigo Vespucci reported to his Florentine sponsors in 1503. "These we may rightly call a new world, because our ancestors had no knowledge of them, and it will be a matter wholly new to all those who hear about them."

Vespucci's new world soon came to bear his name as word of its existence spread throughout Europe. The news stimulated a rush of explorers across the Atlantic: intrepid, idealistic, and often unscrupulous men who set out in search of treasure, converts to Christianity, and opportunities for enterprise and transatlantic empire. Within a few decades after Columbus first set foot on the island of Hispañola, the Americas were undergoing cataclysmic change that made their worlds equally new to the remnants of once-great peoples who had originally inhabited them. The transformation quickly swept Africa into its wake as America's new overlords brought Africans in chains to replenish a native labor supply unexpectedly decimated by the introduction of epidemic disease to the Americas.

Iberian adventurers and missionaries dominated the sixteenth-century New World. Spain took possession of vast territories rich in precious metals, which enriched the entire European economy as they entered circulation through the port of Seville. Spanish rulers initially hoped to secure all lands discovered in the western Atlantic through the Treaty of Tordesillas in 1494. Yet the subsequent discovery that the Brazilian coast lay east of the treaty line allowed Portugal to stake its own claim to New World territory that was rich in dyewood and soil suitable for sugar cultivation.

Ambitious European rivals viewed the burgeoning Iberian empires with a mixture of envy and fear. By the 1560s, both England and France were mounting vigorous challenges to Iberian hegemony in the New World. Soon Spain's rebellious northern provinces in the Netherlands entered the fray. The ensuing contest for treasure and territory brought a fresh wave of contact and exchange as northern Europeans raided Spanish and Portuguese possessions and probed for resources and trading partners not yet exploited by the Iberians.

Spanish authorities found themselves increasingly pressed. They strengthened the armed escorts of their treasure fleet. They seized foreign vessels in American waters and enslaved the crews in galleys or on plantations. They patrolled the North American coastline, searching out rival settlements, razing the buildings, and enslaving or killing the inhabitants. They sent out missionaries to win converts, establish missions, and strengthen ties with native peoples in hopes of shutting their rivals out. Yet English, French, and Dutch raiders kept striking at the edges of Spain's mighty but increasingly brittle empire, exploiting every weakness they could find and growing more effective with every success. By the end of the sixteenth century, the widening cracks in Iberian hegemony were creating new opportunities for rivals to gain permanent colonial footholds in the New World.

Chapter 1
Origins of an Atlantic World

 ## Learning Objectives

1.1 Recognize the presence of Indians in America before Columbus' discovery of it

1.2 Describe the early Portugese and Spanish sea ventures to America

1.3 Report the conflict that occurred when the voyagers tried to settle in America

1.4 Explain how coastal North America came to be conquered by European countries other than Spain

1.5 Examine the effect of the Europeans invasion on the indigenous traditions of America and Africa

1.6 Explain how the encounters between the invaders and the invaded transformed the landscape of North America

On August 7, 1498, inhabitants of the María Peninsula on the northern coast of South America welcomed Admiral Christopher Columbus to their shores with presents of "bread and maize and things to eat and pitchers of a beverage." According to his custom, the Spanish Admiral brought the Native Americans on board his ship and laid out samples of trade goods for their inspection. His guests proved discriminating customers, giving "nothing for the beads, but all they had for hawks' bells. . . . They esteemed brass very highly." In return the Indians offered him "parrots of two or three species" and "kerchiefs of cotton carefully embroidered and woven in colors and workmanship exactly like those . . . from the rivers of Sierra Leone [West Africa]." The Indians left Columbus's vessel before nightfall, thwarting his desire to take "half a dozen" New World souvenirs with him.

The account of this brief exchange during Columbus's third voyage reminds us that the story of cultural encounter involved much more than simply discovery and conquest. Yet the native voice in this exchange was quickly drowned out by a familiar European narrative in which intrepid explorers brought glory to the Christian faith, to the Spanish monarchs, and, not least, to the conquerors themselves. In a letter circulated throughout Europe at the end of his first voyage—the new print technology spread knowledge of the New World to an eager public—Columbus announced,

"As I know that you will be pleased at the great victory with which Our Lord has crowned my voyage, I write this to you, from which you will learn how in thirty-three days, I passed from the Canary Islands to the Indies. . . . And there I found very many islands filled with people innumerable, and of them all I have taken possession for their highnesses [King Ferdinand and Queen Isabella]."

Columbus and the adventurers who sailed in his wake wove a tale of discovery that survived in Western memory long after many of the Indians he encountered had become extinct. The story recounted first in Europe and then in the United States depicted visionary captains, selfless missionaries, and intrepid settlers carrying civilization to the peoples of the New World and opening a vast virgin land to economic progress. This tale celebrated the inevitable triumph of European values over peoples and cultures viewed as primitive and inferior. It was a history populated by the victors that silenced the voices of the conquered, ignored a horrific record of untold millions dead or enslaved, and overwrote the pasts of their victims with a woefully partial and inadequate explanation of how Europe's descendants had come to dominate the world we know today.

Yet the newcomers established settlements on the ruins of an ancient America whose majestic archaeological remains constitute only part of a huge body of evidence that suggests a much different story line. Historians, anthropologists, and archaeologists since the 1960s have tapped these sources to reconstruct long, complex histories of American Indian and African civilizations along with much more balanced accounts of early encounters among the inhabitants of four Atlantic continents. Far from being passive victims of Columbian Conquest or Atlantic slavery, Indians and Africans brought sophisticated cultural traditions to the exchanges with Europeans, influencing powerfully the character of interracial societies that developed in the New World.

By placing these complex, often unsettling events within a framework of encounters shaped by the past and present cultures of the various participants—rather than exploration, colonization, or settlement—we can begin to recapture the full human dimensions of these early exchanges. At the same time, we must recognize that the manifold settings of encounter, which historians have variously described as "cultural frontiers," "zones of exchange," or "middle grounds," were extremely precarious. Like environmental ecotones or border areas between two ecological systems, New World settings of encounter were fraught with opportunity and danger. Too often, the New World was the scene of tragic violence and systematic exploitation. Yet it also presented ordinary people with opportunities to exercise extraordinary creativity in shaping their own lives; neither the Native Americans nor the Africans were passive victims of European colonization. Nor, for that matter, were the poor whites who took their chances on the New World.

Within their own families and communities, these obscure men and women made choices, sometimes rebelling, sometimes accommodating. Yet always they labored to make sense in their own terms out of what was happening to them, taking advantages and minimizing costs as they were able. Although they sometimes failed to preserve dignity and often lost independence, their efforts poignantly reveal that the history of the New World—be it from the perspective of the Native American, the African American, or the European—is above all else a story of human agency.

1.1: Diverse Historical Experiences

1.1 Recognize the presence of Indians in America before Columbus' discovery of it

A recent outpouring of scholarship reminds us that African and American Indian cultures possessed pasts as lengthy and distinguished as the cultures of Europeans who came into sustained contact with them in the sixteenth century. Inhabitants of Africa and the Americas as well as Europe were divided into a multiplicity of nations and peoples embroiled in intense and constantly shifting conflicts and alliances. Each brought to the New World encounter conflicting cultural beliefs, assumptions, aspirations, customs, and practices that had been shaped by long historical development. The diverse perspectives each group brought to encounter sometimes overlapped, allowing them to find common ground for cooperation. On other occasions conflicting agendas sparked deadly clashes, which engulfed neighboring peoples as well. Whatever the outcome, the processes of conflict, adaptation, resistance, and accommodation that marked colonial American history were conditioned by histories that had been shaping each group long before Columbus plotted his westward course in 1492.

Most North American Indian origin stories have taught that their ancestors have always been on the continent, a belief that many continue to hold today. Most modern archaeologists, on the other hand, believe that America's indigenous peoples arrived in successive waves of migration during the last Ice Age, beginning at least thirty thousand years ago and perhaps much longer. They theorize that the vast glaciers of the period lowered ocean levels by hundreds of feet, creating- the subcontinent of Beringia in the region of what is now the Bering Sea as well as a much longer Aleutian Island chain, which supported travel by small boats. Ancient hunters fished along the Aleutian coastline or tracked large game animals such as mastodons and wooly mammoths across the land bridge from the Asian steppes to North America, eventually pressing into South America as well.

Traditional Indian and modern archaeological accounts agree that the first American peoples were highly migratory, dispersing widely across both Americas in waves. Local populations developed distinct languages, distinct cultures, and often even distinct physical features such as stature. Some lineage groups continued to rely on hunting and gathering for thousands of years, while others began cultivating agricultural crops on a scale that eventually supported large and powerful civilizations. Evidence suggests that some such civilizations existed in South America over four thousand years ago and in North America by the first few centuries C.E. In Mesoamerica, the highly complex Olmec civilization flourished more than two thousand years ago, giving rise to a succession of large-scale civilizations whose massive ruins dot the landscape from central Mexico through Central America. By the first few centuries C.E., inhabitants were constructing the sophisticated Mayan centers of the Yucatán, the highland city of Monte Albán, and the great Mesoamerican metropolis of Teotihuacán. Like the Incas who lived in what is now known as Peru, Mayan and Toltec peoples ruled their great city-states through government bureaucracies that controlled large tributary populations. The Mayans also developed hieroglyphic writing and a solar calendar that predicted eclipses as accurately as any Old World systems. In size and population, Mesoamerican cities often exceeded those of medieval and early modern Europe. The Aztecs and Tlaxcalans encountered by Cortés were only the latest of several such civilizations.

Further north, the Anasazi people of what is now the U.S. Southwest lived in large cities of stone connected by a network of well-surveyed and well-constructed roads for communication and trade. The area encompassed more than 25,000 square miles, linking central towns with straight, well-made roads up to 40 feet wide and as much as 60 miles long. At its height in 1150 C.E., the principal settlement at Chaco Canyon supported a population of at least 15,000 people, while another center at Mesa Verde sustained a population of at least 2,500 in dwellings

CAHOKIA

dramatically situated among almost inaccessible cliffs, while a cluster of settlements in nearby Montezuma Canyon was home to as many as 30,000. In the Ohio and Mississippi River valleys of central North America, a succession of mound-building civilizations such as the Adena, Hopewell, and Mississippian cultures flourished over a similar range of time, conducting trade that ranged from the shores of Lake Superior to the north, Yellowstone to the west, and the Appalachians and Gulf to the south.

Like the Americas, sixteenth-century Africa boasted a great variety of states and societies with long and distinguished histories. As with American Indians before Columbus, the work of archaeologists, ethnographers, and anthropologists over the past hundred years has done much to uncover the rich complexity of sub-Saharan Africa's ancient past. Trans-Sahara trade flourished for millennia, supporting a succession of populous, and powerful states and empires. By the fifteenth century, these trans-Saharan routes provided rich sources of gold and salt for the Mediterranean trade, further enriching the African states while sparking competition among them. Great rivers of West and Central Africa such as the Gambia, the Niger, and the Congo enabled merchants to extend trade networks deep into the interior. Skilled boatmen also plied the African coast with valuable cargos of iron bars and implements, rich varieties of cloth, gold, silver, kola, gum, and slaves.

The multiplicity of African states and societies obscured some important overarching unities among the peoples of various regions. Scholars now identify three broad cultural zones within which West and Central Africans lived out their lives. The Upper Guinea cultural zone encompassed the region from the Senegal River to modern Liberia and incorporated the dialects of two great linguistic families, the Wolof and the Mande. The Lower Guinea cultural zone stretched from the Ivory Coast to modern-day Cameroon. Little interaction took place between Lower and Upper Guinea, but trade and travel flourished among the two major cultural and linguistic groups, the Akan of the west, many of whom mined gold, and the Aja farmers, fishermen, and salt traders of the east. The zone of central Africa's Angola coast extended north and south from the mouth of the Congo River and stretched hundreds of miles inland throughout the Congo's vast network of tributaries. Most coastal peoples spoke either Kikongo or Kimbundu, two western Bantu languages as similar as Spanish and Portuguese. One or the other of these "Angola" tongues also served as a lingua franca among the more linguistically diverse interior groups. Like the peoples of the two culture zones to the north, these peoples shared many religious concepts, artistic forms, social customs, and religious beliefs. In political life, however, sharp rivalries marked relations between the elite leaders of the many states, especially the powerful Kongo and Ndongo kingdoms. Yet ordinary people cared little for their rulers' stance toward other states and interacted readily with one another during war as well as peace.

In fifteenth-century Europe, several important developments began converging to provide powerful new impulses that pushed European adventures southward along the African coast and westward into the open Atlantic. Europe became more prosperous; political authority became more centralized; and the overlapping movements of the Renaissance and the Reformation fostered an extraordinary intellectual ferment, religious reform, and political change. A major element in this shift was the slow but steady growth of population after 1450. Historians are uncertain about the cause of this increase—after all, neither the quality of medicine nor personal sanitation improved much—but the result was a substantial rise in the price of land, since there were more mouths to feed. Landlords profited from these trends, and as their income expanded, they demanded more of the consumer goods, often luxury items such as spices, silks, and jewels, that came from distant ports. Economic prosperity created powerful new incentives for exploration and trade even as new political and religious developments presented new opportunities to ambitious, talented persons of ordinary birth.

1.2: First European Ventures across the Atlantic

1.2 **Describe the early Portugese and Spanish sea ventures to America**

In ancient times, the West possessed mythical appeal to people living along the shores of the Mediterranean Sea. Classical writers speculated about the fate of Atlantis, a fabled civilization said to have sunk beneath the ocean. Fallen Greek warriors allegedly spent eternity in an uncharted western paradise. But because Greek and Roman ships were ill-designed to navigate the open Atlantic, the lands to the west remained the stuff of legend. In the fifth century, the inventive Irish monk St. Brendan reported visiting enchanted islands far out in the Atlantic. He even claimed to have met a talking whale named Jasconius, who allowed the famished voyager to cook a meal on his back.

In the tenth century, Scandinavian seafarers known as Norsemen or Vikings established settlements in the New World. In the year 984, a band of Vikings led by Eric the Red sailed west from Iceland to a large island in the North Atlantic. Eric, a master of public relations, named the island Greenland, reasoning that others would more willingly colonize this icebound region "if the country had a good name." A few years later, Eric's son Leif founded a small settlement called Vinland at a location in northern Newfoundland now known as L'Anse aux Meadows. At the time, the Norse voyages went unnoticed by other Europeans. The hostility of Native Americans, poor lines of communication, and political upheavals in Scandinavia made maintenance of these tenuous outposts impossible. The Vikings abandoned the settlements, though Greenland's inhabitants maintained sporadic contact with North America into the fourteenth century. At the time of his first voyage in 1492, Columbus seemed to have been unaware that other Europeans had preceded him.

The inhabitants of Europe's Iberian Peninsula led the way to permanent European contact with the Americas. The Iberians' seafaring impulse sprang from a potent combination of religious and economic motives bound up with their long struggle to reclaim Iberian territory long ruled by North African Muslims and unify it under Catholic rule. This effort, known as the *Reconquista*, not only shaped the internal cultures of Spain and Portugal, but their efforts at exploration and colonization as well.

1.2.1: The Atlantic Route to Gold, Slaves, and Spices

The Iberian path to America took a circuitous route along the coast of West Africa. Strong winds and currents along the Atlantic coast moved southward, which meant a ship could sail with the wind from Portugal to West Africa without difficulty. The problem was returning, and the Portuguese solution was to invent a sailing technology that eventually carried Columbus to Hispaniola. Not surprisingly, the earliest Portuguese explorers were reluctant to venture too far south. Yet the lure of African riches, coupled with a passion to press Portugal's anti-Islamic crusade southward, prompted Portuguese rulers and merchants to push further down the African coast.

Backed by the steady funding and encouragement of Prince Henry the Navigator (1394–1460), Portuguese seafarers solved the problems of Atlantic navigation as they encountered them. Their experimentation culminated in the caravel, a vessel that combined a northern European hull design with lateen (triangular) sails and rigging borrowed from North African shipwrights. The caravel's sturdy hull could withstand heavy seas, while the lateen sails allowed seamen to tack

much closer to contrary winds than traditional European ships. During the fifteenth century, Portuguese sailors also discovered that by sailing far to the west, often as far as the Azores, they could, on their return trips to Europe, catch a reliable westerly wind. Columbus was evidently familiar with this technique. Before attempting to cross the Atlantic Ocean, he sailed to the Gold Coast (modern Ghana), and on the way, he undoubtedly studied the wind patterns that would carry his famed caravels to the New World and back again.

Decades of Portuguese investment and experimentation began paying off in 1443 when Nuno Tristão pushed past the Muslim strongholds of the North African coast and returned to Portugal with a cargo of slaves from Argium (modern Arguin on the coast of Mauritania). Tristão returned to the area twice to raid the coastal fishing villages for slaves before pressing even further south to the mouth of a large river, perhaps the Saloum or the Gambia. There he met his match when local natives surrounded his launch and killed Tristão and his crew. The unfortunate raiders had reached sub-Saharan Africa, where large, prosperous kingdoms and empires vied for the control of the West African river systems while keeping the Portuguese at bay through military might. Thereafter, the Portuguese had increasingly to accommodate themselves to West African laws and regulations governing trade to turn a profit.

The potential for profit was great in both natural resources and human labor. North African caravans had long traversed the Sahara laden with goods such as gold and salt along with slaves whom they sold along the Mediterranean coast. The Portuguese soon learned to wring great profits from the Atlantic trade by tapping into a robust and widespread West African demand for slaves. In African societies where all land was corporately owned, slavery functioned much differently than in the plantation colonies of the Americas. In Africa, slaves "were the only form of private, revenue-producing property recognized in African law," according to the historian John Thornton. Because of slaves' role within the African economy, ruling elites prized them highly, and rival states often went to war over slaves for the same reason that European powers battled over territory. Indeed, the quest for slaves made conflict among African states endemic long before Europeans entered the scene. The Portuguese capitalized on this economy by transporting slaves from one part of coastal Africa to another where they could exchange them for African gold and goods sought in Europe.

Before long, the Portuguese also began adapting slavery for use in plantation production of staple crops on various islands they had claimed such as Madeira, Príncipe, and São Tomé. Slavery on Portuguese plantations became a much different institution. Unfree West Africans had often led lives similar to European peasants, working the land at their own direction and providing a small percentage of the crop to their master as a sort of rent. Others performed domestic service. In the eyes of local law, wives and concubines were often slaves. Warrior slaves bore arms in military service, sometimes commanding a king's armies. Other slaves exercised great authority as deputies of a royal master or served in the court as scribes and scholars. The laws of some states extended ownership by ruling families or clans over all inhabitants of their dominions.

Other African slaves had become such by capture and were held by right of conquest in lieu of death. The Portuguese tapped primarily into trade in such captive slaves rather than the "settled" variety and served the captors' interest by transporting them long distances for trade to make escape or rescue more difficult. Such "trade" slaves arriving at a final African destination might often be assimilated into the local society, gaining protection of local law and even being incorporated into their masters' kinship networks. Those carried to Portuguese plantation colonies, on the other hand, usually found themselves chained to short, miserable lives of backbreaking labor in abject conditions, struggling to rebuild what community they could from fragments of the cultures and traditions they brought with them.

No matter where they found themselves, Africans experienced slavery as loss and injustice. The eighteenth-century freedman Olaudah Equiano, who published a fascinating account of his experiences in Africa and America, no doubt spoke for millions of earlier slaves whose memories went unrecorded when he described spending his first months of slavery in Africa "oppressed and weighed down by grief after my mother and friends." Though the apparent kindness of some African masters sometimes tempted him to "forget I was a slave," Equiano regarded the loss of his freedom as slavery's defining characteristic in Africa and America alike. In Africa, he remained vulnerable to the caprice of masters who might treat him as an adopted son one day and sell him into "hardship and cruelty" the next. Slavery among the Europeans sometimes reduced him to "grieving and pining, and wishing for death rather than anything else." Yet Equiano's "love of liberty" empowered him to join other slaves in creating resilient African American cultures that sustained them through the harsh experience of slavery, providing strategies of survival, resistance, and sometimes escape from bondage.

The Portuguese ability to tap into African trade slavery contributed to growing profits and ever further ventures south along the African coast. The Portuguese accepted the trade regulations enforced by officials of West African states such as Mali and Joloff, paying tolls and other fees for permission to enter ports and trade. Local rulers usually restricted the foreign traders to conducting their business in small "factories," forts or castles located at the mouths of the major rivers. Local merchants acquired slaves and gold in the interior and transported them to the coastal traders in exchange for European manufactures. Merchants calculated transactions in terms of local African currencies: a slave, for example, would be offered to a European trader for so many bars of iron or ounces of gold.

The Portuguese were only too ready to leave the control of interior trade to Africans on a continent where the virulence of local diseases commonly condemned six out of ten Europeans to die within a single year's stay in Africa. There is tragic irony in this exchange, for when the Portuguese and other Europeans carried Africans to the New World, the captives died at rates that paralleled those of Europeans in Africa. Portuguese agents remained at their factories on the coast, where they cultivated the favor of local rulers and traders to build networks of mutual obligation and exchange. Some who survived the initial onslaught of disease sought to strengthen their ties by adopting African customs, settling in African villages, and taking African wives. Some who adopted African ways of life completely became known as *lançados* or *tangos-maos*, and the mulatto families they established often served for generations as powerful intermediaries between Europeans and Africans. Their position gave *lançados* leverage against the Portuguese crown's efforts to regulate and levy taxes on trade.

Portuguese mariners pressed further south along the African coast during the later fifteenth century, establishing factories along the way. In 1487, Bartolomé Dias rounded the Cape of Good Hope, and in 1498 Vasco da Gama returned from India with a fortune in spices and other luxury goods. Da Gama secured a Portuguese monopoly on trade with Africa and the East, which endured into the seventeenth century.

The birth of these exploratory efforts in the Portuguese *Reconquista* infused in them a religious as well as commercial purpose that persisted throughout the period of discovery and encounter. Portuguese Catholics regarded Moslems as infidels and potential enemies wherever they encountered them along the African coast and in the Indian Ocean as well. Catholic missionaries traveled with the mariners to provide them spiritual guidance and to propagate Christianity among the peoples they encountered. Most Africans resisted, especially the Moslems who had experienced a long history of antagonism with Portuguese Catholics. Missionaries did manage to establish a few enclaves of Catholic believers near the trading posts of West and Central Africa. In the 1490s, a series of revelations prompted Kongo's King Nzinga a Nkuwu to lead his people in conversion to Christianity. The new religion flourished in Kongo throughout the sixteenth century as priests trained native catechists to propagate the faith. Several of Kongo's princes and children of royal officials also sailed to Portugal, where they resided in the royal court while studying theology and the arts.

By the 1480s, Portuguese traders were diverting so much African gold from the trans-Sahara trade that their Genoese rivals were beginning to suffer. The Genoese traders' Moorish partners charged higher prices than the Portuguese could obtain, and the center of international commerce began a crucial shift from the Mediterranean to the Atlantic. The flow of gold to the coast increased even more when in 1482, the Portuguese obtained permission from Akan authorities to build a castle at Elmina on the coast of modern Ghana. This fort further strengthened their position, giving them a reliable supply of African gold which they obtained in exchange for European iron and slaves brought from other places along the coast. The resulting squeeze on the Mediterranean trade prompted other merchants and rulers to seek an Atlantic route to wealth.

1.2.2: Spain's "Admiral of the Ocean Sea"

If it had not been for Christopher Columbus (Cristoforo Colombo), of course, Spain might never have gained an American empire. Little is known about his early life. Born in Genoa in 1451 of humble parentage, Columbus devoured the Renaissance learning that had so recently become available in printed form. Like other humanists, he combined the study of classical texts with the latest scientific and spiritual developments of his age. He mastered geography, and—perhaps while exploring the coast of West Africa—he seems to have convinced himself that God had called him to sail west across the Atlantic Ocean to reach Cathay, as China was then known.

In 1484, Columbus presented an ambitious plan to King John II of Portugal. However, while the Portuguese were just as eager as Columbus to reach Cathay, their discoveries had already convinced them that the way to the riches of the East lay around the continent of Africa rather than across the Atlantic as Columbus suggested. Contrary to popular modern myth, neither they nor other Europeans doubted the earth was round. Yet they rightly suspected that Columbus's enthusiasm had outrun his mathematical ability. He had substantially underestimated the earth's circumference at 3,000 nautical miles, more than 7,000 miles short of its actual distance, one agreed upon by contemporary navigators and Church scholars. As the Portuguese reminded Columbus, no ship then known could carry enough food and water for such a long voyage. Columbus was clever, but his sailors would surely starve. The Portuguese alternative route around the Cape of Good Hope seemed much more promising even before da Gama reached India, and the king declined to sponsor him.

Like a modern inventor looking for capital, Columbus turned to European monarchs for financial backing. Henry VII of England rebuffed him in 1489, as did the French regent, Anne de Beaujeu. Undaunted by rejection, Columbus ventured to the court of Isabella and Ferdinand. The Spanish were initially no more interested in his grand design than other European monarchs had been. But time was on Columbus's side. Spain's aggressive New Monarchs envied Portugal's recent success in oceangoing trade. Columbus boldly played on the competition between these countries, talking constantly of wealth and empire. Indeed, for a person with so few contacts with those in power, he seemed brazenly confident. One contemporary reported that when Columbus "made up his mind, he was as sure he would discover what he did discover, and find what he did find, as if he held it in a chamber under lock and key."

Columbus's stubborn lobbying on behalf of his "Enterprise of the Indies" gradually wore down opposition in the Spanish court. The two sovereigns provided him with a small fleet containing two of the most famous caravels ever constructed, the *Niña* and the *Pinta*, as well as the square-rigged *nao Santa Maria*. Without the slightest knowledge that America stood between Spain and China, Columbus demanded that Isabella and Ferdinand grant him grand titles and broad authority over any new islands or mainland territories he might discover. The indomitable admiral set sail for Cathay in August 1492, the year of Spain's unification. But had the New World not been in his way, he and his crew would have run out of food and water long before they reached China, as the Portuguese had predicted.

After putting in at the Canary Islands to refit the ships, Columbus continued his westward voyage in early September. When the tiny Spanish fleet sighted an island in the Bahamas after only thirty-three days at sea, the admiral announced he had reached Asia. Since his mathematical calculations had apparently been correct, Columbus began looking for the Chinese. It never occurred to him that he had stumbled upon a world hitherto unknown to most Europeans. Columbus assured his men, his patrons, and perhaps himself that these islands were indeed part of the fabled "Indies," or at least an extension of the great Asian landmass. He searched for the splendid cities Marco Polo had described. Instead of meeting wealthy Chinese, however, Columbus encountered bands of indigenous American Taínos whom he called "Indians," a triumph of theory over fact.

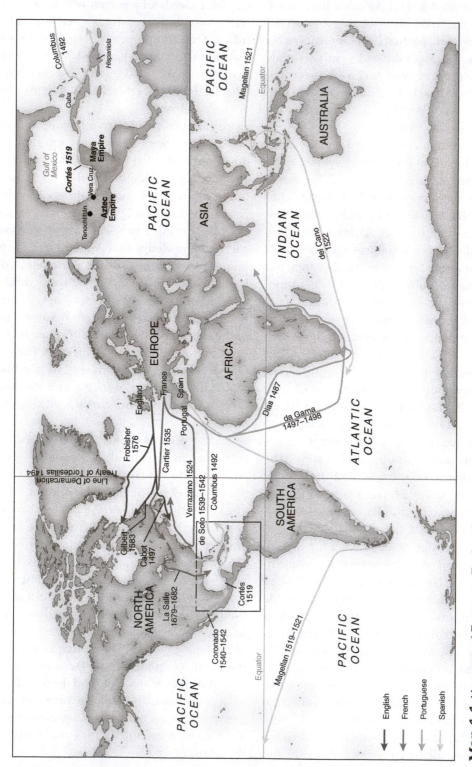

Map 1.1 Voyages of European Exploration

After his first voyage of discovery, Columbus returned to the New World three more times. But despite his stubborn courage, he could never find the treasure his financial supporters in Spain demanded with ever-increasing impatience. Columbus had oversold his dream. Indeed, his third voyage of 1498 was brought to an abrupt end when a royal commissioner charged Columbus and his brothers with maladministration of Spanish claims and sent them to Madrid in chains. His influence at court plummeted. Columbus died in 1506, a frustrated but wealthy visionary, unaware to the very end of his life that he had reached a previously unknown continent separating Asia from Europe. The final disgrace came in December 1500 when an ambitious falsifier, Amerigo Vespucci, fabricated a sensational account of his travels across the Atlantic, convincing German mapmakers that he, not Columbus, had discovered a completely new continent. Before Amerigo's claim could be corrected, his name had spread throughout Europe on the latest published maps.

1.2.3: The World Divided in Two

Only two years after Columbus's first voyage, Spain and Portugal almost went to war over the anticipated treasure of Asia. Pope Alexander VI negotiated a settlement that pleased both kingdoms. Portugal wanted to exclude the Spanish from the west coast of Africa and, what was more important, from Columbus's new route to "India." Spain insisted on maintaining complete control over lands discovered by Columbus, then still regarded as an extension of China. In 1493 Alexander had initially supported the Spanish effort by issuing two bulls, *Inter Caetera* and *Dudum Siquidem*. Both seemed to threaten Portuguese interests in Africa by dividing the entire world along a line only one hundred leagues west of the Azores. The Treaty of Tordesillas (1494) averted conflict by moving the line another 170 leagues

west. Any new lands discovered west of the line belonged to Spain. At the time, no European had ever seen Brazil, which turned out to be on Portugal's side of the line (a fact that explains why, to this day, Brazilians speak Portuguese). The treaty cut any other European power from trying their luck in the New World, at least in theory.

1.3: Encounter and Conflict

1.3 Report the conflict that occurred when the voyagers tried to settle in America

Spain's new discoveries unleashed a horde of entrepreneurial conquistadores on the Caribbean. History once depicted these ambitious figures as heroic explorers, but the conquistadores merit only tepid regard. Following procedures developed during the *Reconquista*, the conquistadores received a license to extend Spanish dominions in the pursuit of their own interests. These *adelantados* or independent proprietors were not interested in creating a permanent society in the New World. Rather, they risked their own resources to pursue instant wealth, power, and honor. They preferred to take their profits in gold and were not squeamish about the means they used to obtain it. Bernal Díaz, one of the first Spaniards to migrate to this region, explained he had traveled to America "to serve God and His Majesty, to give light to those who were in darkness, and to grow rich, as all men desire to do." Even by the values of their own time, their quest for wealth brought violence and suffering wherever they went.

Yet Native Americans were not hapless victims of the Spanish. The earliest encounters often occasioned surprise and unexpected opportunity for trade and alliance. When relations turned hostile, Indians could exact a terrible price for European aggression. No conquistador found them pushovers in battle. Europeans may have possessed tremendous firepower with cannons and cumbersome matchlock firearms, but Indians wielded their own weapons with deadly effect. Native soldiers were formidable fighters in hand-to-hand combat. Their longbows enabled their users to strike with stealth, hitting a distant target without revealing their position as a matchlock's report inevitably did. Longbows could also be reloaded faster than matchlock guns, were more reliable, more accurate, less cumbersome, required far less maintenance, and still worked after the powder ran out. Indians knew the terrain much better than Europeans, and they initially enjoyed a significant—sometimes overwhelming—numerical advantage over the small groups of European explorers, traders, and settlers.

1.3.1: The Caribbean

For a quarter century, the conquistadores concentrated their actions on the major Caribbean islands. For the first seven years Columbus himself oversaw Spanish exploration and settlement, but he proved utterly incompetent to wield the unprecedented administrative powers the Spanish monarchs had granted him. In 1499, Francisco de Bobadilla superseded him and reorganized Spanish colonial rule. From the port of Santo Domingo, which served as capital of Spain's American dominions for half a century, Crown officials continued the exploration and settlement of Caribbean islands including Cuba, Jamaica, and Puerto Rico. In 1501, settlement began in earnest with the arrival of a new governor, Frey Nicolás de Ovando, and 2,500 colonists. Spanish settlement expanded steadily throughout the West Indian archipelago, led by ruthless adventurers in search of gold. Expeditionary forces took each new Caribbean island by storm, terrorizing native inhabitants and brutally crushing any attempts at rebellion.

Indigenous bands of Taínos, Arawaks, and Caribs (from whom the Caribbean derives its name) had hunted, cultivated, and fished in the islands for centuries prior to the arrival of Columbus. Each band governed informally and independently of others. In times of conflict, bands from neighboring islands might join forces for raids against rivals, disbanding the raiding parties to return to their own autonomous communities as soon as their aims were achieved. Their loose organization and limited weaponry made it difficult for these peoples to withstand the Spanish assault as it proceeded island by island across the Caribbean. Yet it gave those on the more remote islands an ability to move quickly to avoid capture and to organize sporadic raids which harassed European newcomers and gave the Caribs, in particular, a reputation as fierce fighters.

Even so, most indigenous inhabitants fell victim to enslavement and distribution among the leading adventurers of the Spanish expeditions of conquest. "One got thirty, another forty, a third as many as a hundred or twice that number," the Spanish observer Bartolomé de Las Casas reported; "everything depended on how far one was in the good books of the despot who went by the title of governor." Colonists put their Indian slaves to work panning for gold in island streams or pasturing herds of pigs and cattle. When the gold ran out on smaller islands, the colonists abandoned them to the surviving livestock, which quickly overran them. On larger islands such as Cuba and Hispaniola, the Spanish put the Indians to work on sugar plantations. In less than two decades, the Arawaks and Caribs who originally inhabited the Caribbean islands had been decimated, victims of exploitation and disease. The Spanish planters sought to meet the consequent labor shortage with African slaves (see Chapter 2).

1.3.2: The Conquest of Mexico

As the Caribbean settlements expanded, rumors of fabulous wealth in Mexico stirred the avarice of many Spaniards. The great city-states of central Mexico were only the latest of a succession of powerful indigenous civilizations whose origins lay in the development of sedentary farming communities more than four thousand years earlier. By the first centuries C.E., inhabitants were constructing the sophisticated Mayan centers of the Yucatán, the highland city of Monte Albán, and the great Mesoamerican metropolis of Teotihuacán. Like the Incas who lived in what is now known as Peru, Mayan and Toltec peoples ruled their great city-states through government bureaucracies that controlled large tributary populations, and developed hieroglyphic writing as well as a solar calendar that predicted eclipses as accurately as any Old World systems. In size and population, Mesoamerican cities often exceeded those of medieval and early modern Europe.

The Toltec and Mayan civilizations had faded to distant memory by 1250 C.E., when the Mexica migrated into the Valley of Mexico to begin their rapid rise to dominance. An aggressive, warlike people, this group of late Aztec arrivals established themselves in the region by occupying swampy, snake-infested territory no one else wanted. In 1325 the Mexica founded Tenochtitlan on an island in the center of marshy Lake Texcoco and began transforming the swamps into a system of dikes, canals, and productive raised fields. Tenochtitlan's nobles extended the city-state's wealth and territorial influence by forging shrewd alliances with neighboring city states, which they supplied with mercenary soldiers. By 1400, Lake Texcoco's swamps had become a ring of lush raised fields surrounding a beautiful lake, in the center of which rose the splendid capital city of Tenochtitlan. The city attracted migrants from all over the Valley of Mexico, and its population eventually reached 250,000. Aztec princes and nobles secured alliances with neighboring city-states through diplomacy and intermarriage, while Aztec warriors extended Tenochtitlan's dominance through conquest. It is no wonder that when the Spanish conquistadores first saw Aztec "towns and villages built in the water," they asked "whether it was not all a dream?"

The Aztecs ruled by force, reducing defeated rivals to tributary status. When Hernán Cortés arrived in 1519, Aztec rule extended outward from Tenochtitlan to the Pacific coast as well as the Gulf of Mexico. Elaborate human sacrifice associated with Huitzilopochtli, the Aztec sun god, horrified Europeans, who seldom questioned the savagery of their own civilization. These Aztec ritual killings were connected to the agricultural cycle. The Indians believed the blood of their victims possessed extraordinary fertility powers and that daily human sacrifice ensured the return of the sun each morning. A fragment of an Aztec song-poem captures the fiercely self-confident spirit that once pervaded this militant culture:

> Proud of itself
> is the city of Mexico-Tenochtitlan. Here no one fears to die in war.
> This is our glory . . . .
> Who could conquer Tenochtitlan?
> Who could shake the foundation of heaven?

On November 18, 1518, a minor government functionary in Cuba named Hernán Cortés embarked with a small army from Havana to verify the stories of Mexico's treasure. Like so many members of his class, he dreamed of glory, military adventure, and riches that would transform him from an ambitious court clerk into a preeminent *adelantado*. Events soon demonstrated that in this context Cortés possessed extraordinary ability as a leader.

Cortés's adversary was the legendary Aztec emperor, Montezuma. The confrontation between these two powerful personalities is one of the more dramatic of early American history. A fear of competition from rival conquistadores coupled with a burning desire to conquer a vast new empire drove Cortés forward. Determined to push his men to their imagined rendezvous with glory, he scuttled the ships that had carried them to Mexico, preventing them from retreating in the face of danger. Cortés led his band of six hundred followers across rugged mountains and on the way gathered allies from among the Tlaxcalans, a tributary people eager to gain freedom from Aztec domination.

Cortés possessed obvious technological superiority over the Aztecs. The sound of gunfire initially frightened the Indians. Moreover, Aztec troops had never seen horses, much less armored ones carrying sword-wielding Spaniards. But these elements would have counted for little had Cortés not also gained a psychological advantage. For some reason, the emperor hesitated to mount full resistance. Some early accounts state that at first, Montezuma thought that the Spaniards were gods, representatives of the fearful plumed serpent, Quetzalcoatl. Many scholars now believe that Aztec survivors invented this self-serving explanation after the fact and that the emperor simply needed time to assess the strength of his alien adversary. When the Montezuma's resolve finally hardened, it was too late. Cortés seized the Aztec ruler as a hostage, setting in motion a chain of tragic and bloody events culminating in the utter destruction of Tenochtitlan. Cortés shrewdly retained the symbolic power of the site by building the colonial capital of Mexico City on the ruins of the Aztec metropolis. Spanish victory in the Valley of Mexico, coupled with other conquests in South America, made Spain the wealthiest state in Europe.

Cortés could not have hoped to conquer the Aztec empire without the cooperation of the Aztecs' own rebellious subject peoples, who paid a heavy price in wartime casualties for their actions. In a culture where subject peoples commonly paid tribute to their overlords in labor, goods, and even human sacrifice, many of these groups may well have understood that terms of alliance with Cortés included replacing Aztec with Spanish overlords. Whatever their initial arrangement, the outbreak of hostilities committed tributary groups to fight to victory with the Spanish or face the gruesome vengeance of their former Aztec rulers. By allying with Cortés, the Indians of central Mexico ensured that they would make their way in their new world from a position of dependence.

The conquest of Tenochtitlan became a model for Spanish conquest elsewhere in North America. Later conquistadores such as Hernando de Soto sought to replicate Cortés' methods. When Spanish governors extended authority over the Pueblos and others who had once maintained diplomatic relations with the Aztecs, they communicated their intentions through symbolic plays portraying Spanish destruction of the great city. Indians who watched the plays soon came to understand that a similar fate awaited all who refused to submit to the Spanish conquerors.

1.3.3: Early Encounter in the Southwest and Florida

Inspired by tales of Cortés's conquests, other ambitious and now jealous conquistadores ventured to mainland North America in search of fabled wealth and glory. Some set out to the north and west from Cortés's New Spain, while others headed for Florida and the Gulf Coast. In both areas, large indigenous civilizations drew the avaricious adventurers in search of their own fortunes.

In what is now known as the U.S. Southwest, a large network of indigenous peoples collectively termed the "Pueblos" lived a sedentary existence sustained by cultivation of maize. Before the arrival of the Spanish, many had engaged in trade and diplomatic relations with the Aztecs and were rumored to possess great wealth in their own right. By the sixteenth century, the sophisticated Anasazi civilization known to historians as the "Chaco Phenomenon" was a distant memory, with most of the old towns abandoned to the desert as climate change reduced rainfalls and poor yields made it no longer possible to sustain their large population centers. Descendants of the Anasazi along with later arrivals lived in smaller villages (*pueblos* in Spanish). The native inhabitants built their adobe dwellings in a style similar to earlier Anasazi structures and continued to build round, subterranean kivas characteristic of earlier Anasazi ceremonial structures. They also continued to rely on maize as their staple crop, adapting earlier Anasazi agricultural techniques to farm in the arid climate.

Still further west across the Sierra Nevada mountain range, an exceedingly diverse population of indigenous peoples plied coastal waterways and hunted, fished, and cultivated the fertile valleys of what is now California and the Pacific Northwest. Many of these western peoples were bound closely to the lands of their birth and spoke languages viewed as mystically tied to those locations. In the region of California alone, sixty-seven languages were spoken, most of which differed from each other as widely as Korean from English.

Pacific coastal peoples experienced only brief contact with Europeans in the sixteenth century. Two of Cortés's men, Fortún Jiménez and Francisco de Ulloa, sailed colony-built vessels north from the port of Zacatula to explore the peninsula of Lower California. Cortés's rival, Viceroy Antonio de Mendoza, sent his protégé Juan Rodríguez Cabrillo with a small expeditionary force which pressed north to Santa Catalina Island before Cabrillo died there of infection. His chief pilot, Bartolomé Ferrer, sailed further to the region of the present-day California-Oregon boundary before turning back. These voyages were significant only inasmuch as they formed the basis of Spanish claims to the Pacific Coast. Sustained efforts to colonize much of that coastline did not occur until the eighteenth century.

The Pueblo peoples, by contrast, experienced great change as a result of sustained Spanish presence. In 1538, only two years before Hernán Cortés departed Mexico never to return, Cortés's rival Antonio Mendoza quietly sent Fray Marcos de Niza to reconnoiter the former Anasazi homeland. Although the region was rumored to harbor a civilization greater than the Aztecs, the friar found only a few small adobe-built pueblos.

Before he returned home, however, Fray Marcos received assurances from the inhabitants that the fabled city of Cibola was not far away. The news prompted Mendoza to commission Francisco Vásquez de Coronado to lead an elaborate expedition into the North American interior. Fray Marcos's Cibola turned out to be a small pueblo of about one hundred families, and Coronado sent the imaginative friar home to Mexico. Nevertheless, the conquistador captured the Zuñi city, the center of sixteenth-century Pueblo power, and made Cibola his headquarters for further exploration. Coronado spent the next three years in a fruitless quest for wealth and empire that carried him all the way to the Arkansas River at the site of present-day Lyons in central Kansas. Coronado returned to Mexico City empty-handed in 1542. Spanish settlement proceeded slowly northward over the next six decades, culminating in the submission of the Pueblos to Juan de Oñate in 1598 and the establishment of Santa Fe as the capital of New Mexico.

Even before Cortéz sailed to Mexico, Spanish adventurers were reconnoitering Florida and the Gulf Coast. The region supported many coastal tribes as well as significant population centers further inland, several of which were direct heirs to a "Mississippian" civilization that had dominated the great Mississippi River drainage system over four hundred years earlier from the great city of Cahokia near present-day St. Louis. Cahokia's complex of flat-topped, pyramid-shaped earthen mounds—the largest of which was over 100 feet tall—formed a template for the design of smaller Mississippian cities of the Southeast. Cahokia had supported a population of between twenty and forty thousand, nearly as large as that of medieval London. The city went into decline and was largely abandoned by 1400 C.E., permitting Mississippian cultures elsewhere to expand. Rival chiefdoms vied for preeminence in the Southeast throughout the following century, producing nations such as the Natchez, Choctaw, and Cherokee, which endure to the present day.

The Mississippian chiefdom of Coosa, centered on the site now known as Little Egypt in northwest Georgia, achieved regional supremacy by the sixteenth century.

Mississippian peoples themselves had little knowledge of the first Spanish expedition to eastern North America under Juan Ponce de León in 1513. No surviving firsthand evidence supports the idea that he hoped to find a fabled "fountain of youth," but he certainly hoped to bring gold and slaves back to his home base on Puerto Rico. Ponce's initial voyage to the Florida coast netted him little, but Cortés's exploits in Mexico prompted him to try again in 1521. Ponce met his death in Florida during a fierce battle with Calusa Indians.

Almost twenty years later as Coronado was exploring the Southwest, another even less appealing conquistador, Hernando de Soto, was wreaking havoc among the Mississippian peoples of the Southeast. From his starting point near Tampa Bay, De Soto led a force of more than six hundred adventurers on a sanguinary quest for gold and slaves. His route took him north into what is now North Carolina, across the Appalachians into Tennessee, down the Tennessee River valley into Alabama, overland to the Mississippi and across that "Rio Grande" into present-day Arkansas. The Spanish reputation for cruelty preceded De Soto, sparking fierce Indian resistance to his progress. The conquistador, whom one observer described as "much given to the sport of hunting Indians on horseback," exceeded the Indian's worst fears. He slaughtered his Indian foes mercilessly, plundered Indian crops to feed his troops and livestock, and mounted vicious attacks on peaceful Indian towns with little or no provocation. The Mississippians of the Southeast responded in kind. Local leaders deployed expert longbowmen against De Soto's forces—marksmen who could sink an arrow 6 inches into a poplar trunk and shoot more accurately than any European archers. Indian enemies slowly whittled down his troops, and in May 1542, De

Soto himself took ill and died. The three hundred survivors of his expedition wandered another year from the Mississippi to Texas and back before finding their way down the river and along the Gulf coast to a small Spanish settlement at the mouth of the Pánuco River.

Later explorers pressed Spanish dominion over Florida but left much of the Southeast to its native inhabitants, contenting themselves with a few small outposts along the Gulf Coast. In 1565 Pedro Menéndez de Avilés established the municipality of St. Augustine on Florida's Atlantic coast. The town's impressive fortress discouraged European rivals from entering the region until 1763.

1.3.4: Managing an Empire

From the earliest days of New World colonization, the Spanish crown confronted a difficult problem. Ambitious adelantados, semi-independent entrepreneurs interested chiefly in their own wealth and glory, had to be brought effectively under royal authority, a task easier imagined than accomplished. Adventurers such as Cortés were stubbornly independent, quick to take offense, and thousands of miles away from the seat of imperial government. Their brutality toward indigenous populations provoked endemic conflict, making government of the colonies even more difficult and costly.

The crown found a partial solution in the *encomienda* system, an adaptation of the *repartimiento* system which the Spanish had developed to govern the Canary Islands. Like earlier conquering peoples such as the Normans of medieval England, Spanish rulers treated the New World's native inhabitants as a valuable source of tribute labor and rewarded the conquering military leaders with Indian villages. The people who lived in these settlements provided the *encomenderos* with labor tribute in exchange for legal protection and religious guidance. In Mexico the system combined Spanish methods with older Aztec mechanisms for levying labor tribute. Wherever it was imposed, the *encomienda* subjected Indians to cruel exploitation. One historian concluded, "The first *encomenderos*, without known exception, understood Spanish authority as provision for unlimited personal opportunism." Cortés alone was granted the services of more than twenty-three thousand Indian workers. The *encomienda* system made the colonizers more dependent on the king, for it was he who legitimized their title. In the words of one scholar, the new economic structure helped to transform "a frontier of plunder into a frontier of settlement." For native peoples, the *encomienda* system permitted them to continue the annual cycle of planting and harvest while paying a tribute to the *encomendero* in a manner similar to what they had practiced under Aztec or Tlaxcalan overlords. The rapid decline of the native population eventually gave rise to a modified *repartmiento* where scarce Indian labor was allocated to wage-paying employers for limited periods on the basis of need.

Spain's rulers attempted to maintain tight personal control over their American possessions. The volume of correspondence between the two continents, much of it concerning mundane matters, was staggering. All documents were duplicated several times by hand. Because the trip to Madrid took many months, a year often passed before receipt of an answer to a simple request. But the cumbersome system took on a life of its own. In Mexico, officials appointed in Spain established a rigid hierarchical order, directing the affairs of the countryside from urban centers. The practice of building these cities on the sites of former centers of native administration helped officials to transfer Indian obedience from indigenous overlords to Spanish ones. Spanish and Indian populations of these cities mingled, producing the rich admixture of European and native cultures that remains characteristic of Mexico and other Latin American nations.

The Spanish also brought Catholicism to the New World. The Dominicans and Franciscans, the two largest monastic traditions or "orders"

of Catholic clergy, established Indian missions throughout New Spain. Some barefoot friars tried to protect the Native Americans from the worst forms of exploitation. One Dominican, Fray Bartolomé de Las Casas, published an eloquent defense of Indian rights, *Historia de las Indias*, which among other things questioned the legitimacy of European conquest of the New World. Las Casas deplored "the violence, the oppression, the despotism, the killing, the plunder, the depopulation, the outrages, the agonies, and the calamities" which Spanish conquistadores had inflicted on the Indians of the Americas. He suggested sweeping reforms in Crown policy toward native peoples, including the replacement of Indian laborers with African slaves. Las Casas's work provoked heated debate in Spain. The king had no intention of repudiating his vast American empire, but did initiate new measures designed to bring greater "love and moderation" to Spanish-Indian relations.

To ascertain how many converts these friars made is impossible, though one observer placed the total at 9,000,000 baptisms by 1536. Some conversions, especially in the early years of settlement, took place at the point of a sword. Many early Spanish governors were also priests who authorized their missionaries to build churches and shrines on sites held sacred by indigenous peoples. In Puerto Rico, for example, settlers carved a chapel for celebrating Mass into the trunk of an enormous sacred tree. In Mexico, Cortés built the cathedral in Mexico City on the site of the principal Aztec temple, refashioning the temple treasures into Christian icons and artifacts. Elsewhere in Mexico, Catholic churches also sprang up on traditional indigenous temple sites. Such practices gained at least the external conformity of many Indians.

Indigenous converts throughout New Spain also began making Catholicism an Indian religion or giving traditional beliefs and practices a Catholic mask. In other words, accommodation did not signal the eradication of traditional

Indian cultures. The Native Americans made compromises when compelled to do so, then resisted domination through half measures. They fashioned statues of Mary with native features and dress and adapted processions and rituals to traditional agricultural cycles for traditional religious purposes. Statues of native gods sometimes assumed a place in processions beside those of Catholic saints, and the saints were eventually made to absorb the characteristics of various local deities. The gods of war had proved impotent and were abandoned, but the priest Bernardino de Sahagún found that when his Indian informants knelt in a church built on ancient temple ruins, many secretly venerated the old gods of that site. In 1531, a newly converted Christian reported a vision of the Virgin, a dark-skinned woman of obvious Indian ancestry, who became known throughout the region as the Virgin of Guadalupe. This figure—the result of a creative blending of Indian and European cultures—served as a powerful symbol of Mexican nationalism in the wars for independence fought against Spain almost three centuries later.

In frontier areas where the Spanish were fewer, Indians could sometimes exercise more leverage in negotiating the terms of encounter even when the Europeans insisted on holding the reins of power. Rather than suffer the high cost of armed resistance, many sixteenth-century Pueblos of the Southwest cautiously accepted the terms of Spanish rule which the conquerors communicated through a commemorative dramatization of the conquest of Tenochtitlan. Some Pueblo chiefs embraced Christianity as charismatic Franciscan missionaries convinced them of its spiritual power, sparking factionalism as others resisted the new ways. Inhabitants of the pueblos selectively appropriated Spanish goods and Spanish became the lingua franca among Zuñis, Hopis, Acomas, and other Pueblo groups. Pueblos offered varying degrees of outward conformity to Catholicism, but traditional religion remained strong. Many of the baptized embraced Catholic words and rituals as new names for traditional beliefs and new ways to access traditional sacred powers. Worship in the circular kivas continued, often secretly when Franciscan missionaries attempted to stamp it out.

In the Southeast, repeated depredations by conquistadores such as Ponce de Leon and Hernando De Soto taught the Indians to keep the Spanish at arm's length whenever possible. Throughout the sixteenth century, St. Augustine and other Spanish garrisons encountered resistance from groups such as the Cusabos, who resented the Spanish presence and attempts to extend its authority over them. Yet the outposts did present enticing opportunities to barter for European goods, eventually persuading southeastern groups to forge trading partnerships with the Spanish. Here too, some Indians embraced Catholic Christianity. Other groups favored the Spanish missionaries who came their way with the grisly gift of martyrdom, highly prized by the Catholic clergy—in theory at least—for the glory and divine favor its victims could anticipate when they died for their faith.

The New World attracted hundreds of thousands of Spanish colonists in the first hundred years after conquest. About 250,000 Spaniards migrated to the New World during the sixteenth century. Another 200,000 made the journey between 1600 and 1650. Most colonists were impoverished single males in their late twenties seeking economic opportunities. They generally came from the poorest agricultural regions of southern Spain, almost 40 percent migrating from Andalusia alone. Since so few Spanish women migrated, especially in the sixteenth century, the men often married Indians and blacks, unions which produced mestizos and mulattos. The frequency of interracial marriage indicated that, among other things, the people of New Spain tolerated racial differences more readily than the English who settled in North America. Economic worth affected the people of New Spain's social standing as much, or more, as color. The Spanish regarded persons born in the New World, even those of Spanish parentage (*criollos*), as socially inferior to those born in the mother country (*peninsulares*).

1.4: The American Northeast and Northern Europeans

1.4 **Explain how coastal North America came to be conquered by European countries other than Spain**

Ferdinand and Isabella's sponsorship of Columbus gave Spain an early lead in exploring and colonizing the Americas, but coastal North America held less appeal for the Spanish. Rulers of other nations readily stepped into the gap. They were reluctant to accept a Spanish monopoly over the Americas even if a papal treaty had granted it. Northern European explorers were eager to explore possibilities for trade with North America's native inhabitants and to probe for a Northwest Passage to the Pacific and access to Asian wealth. Many also found North America's indigenous peoples indifferent to claims of rulers an ocean away and ready to trade with any partner who could offer them bargains in European goods.

1.4.1: Eastern Woodland Cultures

The historian Colin Calloway has observed that the Europeans who laid claim to eastern North America arrived at the back door of an Indian America whose major exchange networks had been centered on the Mississippi Valley and the Gulf Coast for much of the previous millennium. By 1500, however, Atlantic coastal Indians lived on the fringes of a system that was in severe decline. The causes of this decline remain unknown, but the collapse of the great Mississippian trading network threw much of

eastern North America into flux as various groups competed for territory and influence. Indians of the Northeast did not practice the type of intensive agriculture common among inhabitants of the Gulf Coast and Southwest, but generally supplemented mixed farming with seasonal hunting and gathering. Conservative estimates put the total population at less than a million before the arrival of Europeans, and most belonged to what ethnographers term the Eastern Woodland Cultures. Small bands formed villages during the warm summer months. The women cultivated maize and other crops while the men hunted and fished. During the winter, difficulties associated with feeding so many people forced these communities to disperse. Each family lived off the land as best it could.

The northeastern woodlands were nevertheless home to a number of nations and confederacies which were coming to exert considerable influence in their own right. A vast exchange network stretched from the western Lake Superior to the St. Lawrence River valley, bringing meat and skins from groups such as the western Ojibway in exchange for maize produced by Iroquoian-speaking Huron farmers of southern Ontario.

To the south of Lake Ontario lay the settlements of the Huron's powerful enemies, the Hodenosaunee, or People of the Long House. More than a century before their first contact with Europeans, the Five Nations of this people—the Mohawks, Oneidas, Onondagas, Cayugas, and Senecas—formed what European observers termed the "Iroquois League." According to oral traditions, the league originated during a time of constant feuding among the five nations and surrounding groups. This state continued until an Onondaga chieftain remembered as Hayenwatha or Hiawatha lost three of his daughters in a conflict. Rather than seeking blood vengeance as the Iroquois "mourning war" tradition demanded, Hiawatha determined to break the cycle of violence. A stranger named Deganawidah met Hiawatha in the forest and assuaged his grief with comforting words and wampum beads. Together Hiawatha and Deganawidah, who became known as the Peacemaker, traveled from village to village, persuading the Five Nations to adopt laws and teachings of peace, each of which they had woven onto a string of wampum for posterity to remember. The nations agreed to unite for common defense. The Seneca became Keepers of the Western Door, the Mohawk Keepers of the Eastern Door, and the Onondaga Keepers of the Council Fire. The Cayuga and Oneida comprised the League's younger moiety.

Confederation generated strength. The League of Peace made the Iroquois a powerful military force capable of holding its own against other Indian groups as well as Europeans. While the Five Nations apparently did not establish sustained diplomatic or trade relations with surrounding groups, they did view their league as a great shelter for other peoples. They could extend protection to client groups through treaty, and they augmented their own population and increased the league's ethnic diversity by taking in refugees and adopting captives.

To the east of the Iroquois League lived many bands of Algonquian-speaking peoples, the Indians whom most seventeenth-century English settlers first encountered as they explored and settled the Atlantic coast from North Carolina to Maine. Included in this large linguistic family were the Powhatans of Tidewater Virginia, the Narragansetts of Rhode Island, and the Abenakis of northern New England, as well as the Ojibwe- and Odawa-speakers of the Great Lakes.

Despite common linguistic roots, however, these scattered Algonquian communities would have found communication with each other extremely difficult. In their separate, often isolated environments, they had developed very different dialects. A sixteenth-century Narragansett, for example, could not have understood a Powhatan. Linguistic ties, moreover, had little effect on Indian politics. Algonquian groups who lived in different regions, exploited different resources, and spoke different dialects did not develop strong ties of mutual identity. When their own interests were involved, Algonquian leaders were more than willing to ally themselves with Europeans or "foreign" Indians against other Algonquians. This is an important point. These Indians did not see themselves as representatives of a single racial group, but as Narragansetts or Powhatans. Divisions among Indian groups would in time facilitate European conquest. Local Native American peoples greatly outnumbered the first settlers, and had the Europeans not forged strategic alliances, they could not so easily have gained a foothold on the continent.

However divided the Indians of eastern North America may have been, they shared many cultural values and assumptions. Most Native Americans, for example, defined their place in society through kinship. These personal bonds determined the character of economic and political relations. As historian James Axtell explains, "The basic unit of social membership in all tribes was the exogamous clan, a lineal descent group determined through one parent." The farming bands living in areas eventually claimed by England were often matrilineal, which meant in effect that the women owned the planting fields and houses, maintained tribal customs, and had a role in tribal government. Among the native communities of Canada and the northern Great Lakes, patrilineal forms were much more common. In these groups, the men owned the hunting grounds that the family needed to survive.

Eastern Woodland communities organized diplomacy, trade, and war around reciprocal relationships that impressed Europeans as being extraordinarily egalitarian, even democratic. Chains of authority were loosely structured. Native leaders were renowned public speakers because persuasive rhetoric was often their only effective source of power. It required considerable oratorical skills for an Indian leader to persuade independent-minded warriors to support a certain policy.

Before the arrival of the white settlers, wars among Eastern Woodlands peoples took place on a small scale and were seldom very lethal. Young warriors attacked neighboring bands largely to exact revenge for a previous insult or the death of a relative, or to secure captives. Fatalities, when they did occur, sparked cycles of revenge. Avengers tortured some captives to death, while adopting others into the community as replacements for fallen relatives.

1.4.2: Early English Encounters in North America

The first English visit to North America remains shrouded in mystery. Fishermen working out of Bristol and other western English ports began working their way across the Atlantic in search of new cod fisheries in the fourteenth century and were fishing off the coast of Iceland by 1400. English merchantmen soon struck a prosperous trade with Icelanders while the fishermen pressed even further west. The knowledge they gained of navigating North Atlantic winds and currents may have enabled them to land in Nova Scotia and Newfoundland as early as the 1480s. There they began fishing regularly for codfish along the Grand Banks.

The Bristol fishermen's knowledge of North Atlantic navigation proved valuable to John Cabot (Giovanni Caboto), a Venetian sea captain commissioned by Henry VII to search out a new trade route to Asia in 1497. Cabot's main contribution on this voyage was to publicize the location of the Grand Bank fisheries. Soon ships of other nations such as France, Portugal, and Spain began appearing annually to cast their nets in North American waters alongside the veteran Bristol fishermen. Cabot himself died during a second attempt to find a direct route to Cathay in 1498, but the English fishermen continued venturing further into the Gulf of St. Lawrence. English merchantmen also explored the coast between Labrador and New England between 1498 and 1505, but their failure to establish profitable trade brought formal efforts to a halt. Sebastian Cabot continued his father's exploration in the Hudson's Bay region in 1508–1509, after which English interest in such ventures subsided.

The Newfoundland cod fishery, however, attracted the growing attention of English investors from Bristol, Plymouth, and even London itself throughout the sixteenth century. By mid-century it became one of the largest multinational European business ventures in the New World, attracting investors across national boundaries and annually drawing to the Grand Banks ships from all over Europe. Each year between March and May, fleets of vessels would depart from England's western ports for the coast of Newfoundland, where they arrived in early June just about the time the cod began to come inshore. While one portion of the crew fished, another setup operations on shore for gutting and drying the cod. Once dried, the cod was carefully packed in the holds. English vessels commonly rendezvoused in St. John's Harbor or Placentia Harbor to return in convoy to Europe, often joining ships of other nations there to trade for commodities and surplus fish. Fishermen also engaged in casual trade for furs with coastal Indians.

For the next half-century, the English people were preoccupied with more pressing domestic and religious concerns, and the crown sponsored only a few minor ventures into the Atlantic. When interest in the New World revived, however (see Chapter 2), Cabot's voyages established England's belated legal and diplomatic claim to American territory, and the valuable Grand Banks fishery excited Elizabethan greed to monopolize that claim.

1.4.3: Initial French Ventures

Official French interest in the New World developed more slowly than in England, although individual French mariners were quick to recognize the potential of the North American fisheries. Indeed, soon after the Portuguese explorers Gaspar and

Miguel Corte-Real publicized their discoveries of Labrador and Newfoundland, Norman and Breton fishermen began flocking to the Grand Banks each summer. In 1506, the French navigator Jean Denys of Honfleur explored the eastern coast of Newfoundland. In 1508, another Frenchman, Thomas Aubert of Dieppe, retraced Denys's route, returning to Rouen, France, with seven Indians he had captured from the region. Only in 1524, however, did King Francis I commit French royal backing to a voyage of exploration by sponsoring Giovanni de Verrazano's quest for a short water route to China.

Verrazano's quest initiated a series of sixteenth-century French exploratory efforts along the North American coast. Verrazano himself concluded that North America blocked the route to China and that it held no treasures comparable to those of Mexico. He nevertheless claimed the coast from present-day South Carolina to Maine for the King of France. Despite their apparent lack of value, these claims proved useful to Francis in persuading Pope Clement VII that an earlier papal division of the world between Spain and Portugal applied only to lands known in 1493, not to those discovered later by other nations.

In 1534, Francis I attempted to build on this diplomatic triumph by commissioning the French explorer Jacques Cartier to renew the quest for a route to China. Cartier's first voyage led him to the Gulf of St. Lawrence, where he found the rocky, barren coast of Labrador depressing. "I am rather inclined to believe that this is the land God gave to Cain," he grumbled. Yet Cartier reported to the king promising signs both in the eagerness of local Indians to trade and in the discovery of a large, promising waterway to the interior. The next year he returned to reconnoiter the Saint Lawrence, traveling up the magnificent river as far as modern Montreal. Despite his high expectations, Cartier got no closer to China. He did, however, bring back to France several captive Indians who assured Francis I that a kingdom of fabulous wealth lay within reach of the St. Lawrence. In 1541, the king sent Cartier and the French nobleman Jean-François de la Rocque de Roberval to establish a settlement that would secure France's exclusive title to the hoped-for wealth of Canada. The explorers failed to find any treasure, however, and the harsh Canadian winter made the land seem uninhabitable. In 1542, Cartier gave up the effort to establish a permanent settlement and returned to the comforts of France.

Despite these early failures, French fishermen carried on sporadic trade with North American coastal peoples throughout the sixteenth century. Indeed, Cartier discovered during his first voyage that this trade was already going on when he encountered a French merchant vessel in the Gulf of St. Lawrence. Cartier's voyages helped to ensure the gradual increase of such trade by enabling Francis I win trade concessions in the New World from Spain and Portugal. By 1550, both kingdoms grudgingly accepted the right of French subjects to trade peaceably in territories such as Canada which remained unoccupied by Europeans. The unofficial French presence on the St. Lawrence grew as a result. By the 1570s, traders were establishing small, permanent settlements along the riverbanks to secure a share of the growing market for beaver pelts.

1.4.4: Patterns of Encounter in the Eastern Woodlands

When the French and English began establishing official trading partnerships with North American Indians in the later sixteenth century, native peoples could often draw on a long history of contact with Europeans that had taught them how volatile encounter could be. Some acted on this knowledge in ways similar to a group of Chesapeake Indians who paddled out to a French trading vessel in "over thirty canoes, in each of which were fifteen or twenty persons with bows and arrows." The Indians would not permit "more than two to come on board," but struck a deal satisfying to both sides. The French went home with "a thousand marten skins" for which they gave "knives, fishhooks and shirts."

Like other coastal groups during the early years of contact, these Indians bargained with European traders from positions of strength. Heavy French reliance on their native trading partners allowed the Indians to set many terms of cultural as well as economic exchange. By the 1580s, the benefits of European trade were beginning to entice Indian groups to concede the French "Father" preeminence within a long-existing system of trade alliances. Yet native acknowledgment of French authority remained little more than a formality well into the seventeenth century. Micmac, Abenaki, and Huron allies still held the balance of power in exchange. To secure their position within trade alliances, Frenchmen often married native wives and went to live in native villages, adopting many Indian ways in the process. Early French governors often found they could only preserve a commercial alliance by joining their trading partners in battle against traditional enemies.

Benign though it was in comparison with Spanish rule, French trade and settlement introduced its own set of cultural upheavals. Jacques Cartier described the St. Lawrence of his 1534 visit as a lush river lined with populous towns and fertile fields. Decades of intermittent contact brought about the abandonment of those fields and villages as various groups competed for European trade and as epidemic disease, inadvertently introduced by French traders, ravaged local populations.

1.5: New Worlds for All

1.5 **Examine the effect of the Europeans invasion on the indigenous traditions of America and Africa**

The arrival of Europeans in Africa and the Americas confronted inhabitants of each continent with a world which, as historian James Merrell has reminded us, was just as "new" as those that greeted European invaders. In the Americas and the Caribbean, the encounters presented unprecedented opportunities and dangers while profoundly altering indigenous American cultures. Coastal Africans also encountered new opportunities for trade and exchange. The rates and depth of change varied from place to place around the Atlantic shorelines. American Indian villages located on the Atlantic coast came under severe pressure almost immediately; inland groups had more time to adjust. African coastal peoples experienced a rapid growth in trade and exchange as well as in the volumes of enslaved peoples transported from port to port and across the ocean. Africans confined their European partners largely to coastal towns and factories, but wrought changes in the dynamics of intertribal warfare and capture in order to supply an ever-growing European demand for slaves. For many Atlantic peoples, European arrival, trade, and conquest strained traditional ways of life. As daily patterns of experience changed almost beyond recognition, native and captive peoples had to devise new answers, new responses, and new ways to survive in physical and social environments that eroded tradition.

1.5.1: The Columbian Exchange and Cultural Transformation

Epidemic disease was the most devastating result of the contact sixteenth-century Europeans initiated among previously separate biological environments. The Columbian Exchange of plants, animals, and microbes continues even today, and the contagious diseases it introduced destroyed the cultural integrity of many sixteenth-century North American tribes. New arrivals from Europe and Africa exposed the Indians to bacteria and viruses which spread like wildfire in "virgin soil epidemics" among populations with no natural immunity. Smallpox, measles, and influenza decimated the Native American population. Other diseases such as alcoholism took a terrible toll.

Within a generation of initial contact with Europeans, Native American populations were usually decimated. One Massachusetts colonist reported in 1630 that the Indian peoples of his region "above twelve yeares since were swept away by a great & grievous Plague . . . so that there are verie few left to inhabit the Country." Since the earliest settlers possessed no knowledge of germ theory, they speculated that a Christian God had providentially cleared the wilderness of heathens. Historical demographers now estimate that some tribes suffered a 90 to 95 percent population loss within the first century of European contact. The death of so many Indians decreased the supply of indigenous laborers, who were needed by the Europeans to work the mines and to grow staple crops such as sugar and tobacco. The decimation of native populations helped persuade colonists throughout the New World to seek a substitute labor force in Africa. Indeed, the enslavement of blacks has been described as an effort by Europeans to "repopulate" the New World, one that ironically brought with it African strains of virulent diseases such as yellow fever and malaria.

Indians who survived the epidemics often found that the fabric of traditional culture had come unraveled, in a way very similar to the toll AIDS has recently taken in many African nations. Whole villages, bands, and even nations could be wiped out in a single epidemic, obliterating all memory of a people's customs, beliefs, and way of life. The enormity of the death toll and the agony that accompanied it called traditional religious beliefs and practices into question. The living remnant lost not only members of their families, but also elders who might have told them how properly to bury the dead and give spiritual comfort to the living. Nevertheless, survivors struggled to reconstitute tribal groups and customs and, when that failed, to create new communities made up of people from different tribes

who supported one another by pooling resources and cultural traditions. The biological devastation that followed in the wake of De Soto's rampage through the Southeast gave rise to the groups eighteenth-century colonists knew as Catawbas, Cherokees, and Natchez. Such groups often combined a variety of dialects into distinctive new tongues and drew upon various traditions to shape the beliefs, rituals, and customs that would bind them together as a people.

Inland native peoples often withstood the crisis better than did those who immediately confronted Europeans and Africans. The distance of Iroquois lands from the northeastern coast gave them more time to respond to the challenge, as did the situation of the Chickasaws and Choctaws of the Southeast. Refugee Indians from the hardest hit eastern communities were absorbed into healthier western groups. Nonetheless, the cultural and physical shock that the dwindling Native American population experienced is beyond the historian's power ever fully to comprehend.

Europeans visitors to Africa proved similarly vulnerable to the diseases they encountered there. Virulent strains of diseases such as malaria and yellow fever killed Europeans by the scores, helping to make sixteenth- and seventeenth-century Africa an unattractive place for potential colonization. Survivors of these visits did manage to marry and reproduce, introducing new mixed populations into coastal societies, but Africans remained largely in control of their own futures.

On balance, the results of the Columbian Exchange were mixed. Native American populations hosted few diseases that threatened either Europeans or Africans who crossed the Atlantic. However, native crops such as beans, squash, potatoes, tomatoes, cassava, and maize supplemented European as well as African diets and helped fuel the rapid growth of the European population and economy. Europeans also brought to the Americas crops such as sugarcane and bananas which flourished in the fertile American soils, as did European weeds such as dandelions. European and African livestock also thrived. Pigs escaped into the surrounding forests from the herds that accompanied De Soto's southeastern expedition, multiplying into herds of dangerous razorbacks that supplemented native supplies of game.

No European introduction transformed native life more than the horse, which Spanish explorers reintroduced to a land where it had been extinct for thousands of years. Indians acquired horses by capturing them directly from Spanish troops, rounding up strays from expeditions or supply trains, or capturing animals from the wild herds that multiplied from stray Spanish stock. Horses permanently changed the cultures of those groups that employed them by making possible long-distance travel. Plains Indians could now track buffalo herds much more effectively over their entire range. They also gained the speed needed to kill buffalo in large numbers, and the increased food supply permitted large mobile villages to supplant the small roving bands of earlier times. Pawnees, Wichitas, and Comanches rose to dominate the plains north of Texas and New Mexico, far from the effective reach of Spanish military might. Groups such as the Apache found themselves caught in a deadly three-way struggle as Comanches swept south from the Rockies, Wichitas moved west from the Arkansas River, and Spanish pushed north from the pueblos.

1.6: A World Transformed

1.6 **Explain how the encounters between the invaders and the invaded transformed the landscape of North America**

By the time the first Virginia Company colonists left England for the Chesapeake Bay in 1607, the wrenching, complex processes of encounter had already transformed much of the North American landscape. Disease had wiped out whole peoples who once boasted a long and glorious past. Yet Native Americans had displayed a remarkable tenacity and resilience, a fierce determination to survive. New groups had arisen from the ashes of conquest, weaving together elements of ancient and disparate traditions into a culture adapted to this unprecedented world of opportunity and danger. Experience had made every party wary of the others, but had also taught all how to navigate the treacherous shoals of encounter, seeking out opportunities to mitigate unfavorable circumstances, survive in an adverse environment, and sometimes prosper beyond expectations. American Indians and Africans proved themselves resourceful participants along with Europeans in the creation of the Atlantic World that emerged from the sixteenth-century process of encounter, trade, and conquest.

Chronology

30,000–12,000 B.C.	Migrants cross the Bering Strait from Asia into North America
1000 B.C.–A.D. 400	Adena and Hopewell cultures flourish in North America
A.D. 1001	Norsemen establish a small settlement in Vinland (Newfoundland)
1100	Mississippian society flourishes
1150	Anasazi center at Chaco Canyon begins decline
1324	Mali ruler Mansa Musa takes pilgrimage to Mecca
1325	Tenochtitlán founded by Aztecs
1469	Marriage of Isabella and Ferdinand leads to the unification of Spain

ca. 1480	Iroquois Great League of Peace established
1481	Portuguese build castle at Elmina on the Gold Coast of Africa
1492	Columbus lands at San Salvador
1494	Treaty of Tordesillas establishes dividing line 270 leagues west of the Azores between Spanish and Portugese claims
1500	Pedro Cabral discovers Brazilian coast
1513	Juan Ponce de León leads first expedition to Florida
1521	Cortés defeats the Aztecs at Tenochtitlán
1534	Cartier claims Canada for France
1540	Coronado explores the Southwest for Spain
1536	Pedro Menéndez de Avilés establishes St. Augustine on Florida's Atlantic coast

Chapter 2
Trade and Violence in An Emerging Atlantic World, 1500–1625

 ## Learning Objectives

2.1 Recount the decades of monopoly of Spain and Portugal over the Americas, Africa, and East India

2.2 Examine the impact of slavery on the New World

2.3 Summarize the conflict between the European nations to control the wealth of the emerging Atlantic world

2.4 Recall England's rise to power in the Atlantic

2.5 Examine the continuous human suffering and ecological disaster of the 17th century

Anthony Knivet survived in a harsh seafaring world. His extraordinary adventure began in 1591, when he sailed with the English navigator Thomas Cavendish on an ill-fated attempt to circumnavigate the globe in search of plunder and glory. Knivet fell into Portuguese hands during a raid on the Brazilian coast. His captors put him to work as a slave on the governor's sugar plantation, and his varied tasks brought the Englishman into contact with a diverse range of fellow slaves from Africa, Brazil, and Europe. Knivet oversaw gangs of African and Native American fishermen who caught fish for the plantation labor force and beat paths into the interior, where he gained knowledge of native Brazilian customs.

Knivet remained alert for opportunities to escape, listening eagerly to the rumors that flew among fellow slaves about the appearance of ships from England, Holland, and France as well as Spain and Portugal. On one occasion, Knivet heard that the English seafarer Sir John Hawkins had anchored at a nearby island. Knivet stole a rowboat and tried to slip away to Hawkins's vessel, but was recaptured after crashing on the rocks. Another time, Knivet managed to board undetected a Portuguese vessel bound for Angola, where he hoped to get away to an African port open to English or Dutch vessels that might take him home. In Angola, however, a Portuguese captain reported him to the governor, who sent him back to Brazil. Knivet worked there several more years before his master eventually brought him to Portugal, where his skill as an interpreter enabled Knivet to make connections with influential English patrons who finally helped him get home nearly a decade after he had departed.

Anthony Knivet was an English Protestant caught up in an ongoing struggle for religious and political control of a new Atlantic World, one that embroiled peoples from Africa, Europe, and the Americas in a series of brutal, far-flung conflicts over trade and plunder. This world began to emerge within a decade after Columbus's first voyage to America as Spanish adventurers sailed west to exploit New World possessions, while other nations launched their own efforts to find westward routes to Asia. By 1510, Spanish vessels were plying regular trade routes from the Caribbean to Seville. The Portuguese likewise began developing trade along the Brazilian coastline they first discovered in 1500.

Not until Spain's conquests of Mexico and Peru, however, did America begin producing the fabulous wealth that sparked the vicious competition for control of this emerging Atlantic World. The conquests not only prompted Spain to organize a system for securing its American riches but also fired the imaginations of competing nations, which mounted stiff challenges to Iberian dominance as the century advanced. By 1570, the Spanish and the Portuguese found themselves increasingly pressed by English, French, and Dutch competitors who sought alternative sources of New World riches even as they tried to siphon off a share of colonial Iberian wealth through unofficial warfare and piracy.

The rivals found ready cooperation among American Indian and African traders for whom increased competition meant leverage for negotiating more favorable terms of exchange. Though these efforts did not immediately displace the Iberians, English, French, and Dutch challengers did manage by 1600 to gain a toehold in Atlantic commerce. In the process, they helped create a volatile, exploitative world that held great dangers for the powerless and unwary but promised fabulous returns for those who thought they possessed sufficient resources, daring, and good fortune to risk in New World ventures.

2.1: The Iberian Atlantic

2.1   **Recount the decades of monopoly of Spain and Portugal over the Americas, Africa, and East India**

Spain and Portugal entered the sixteenth century with claims to exclusive control of the Atlantic World, but they soon found themselves waging a doomed defensive struggle to preserve their tenuous monopoly. The Treaty of Tordesillas in 1494 granted Spain control of all non-Christian lands discovered south and west of an imaginary Line of Demarcation drawn approximately 1,100 miles west of the Azores. Portugal gained rights to non-Christian lands east of that line. Other European nations refused to acknowledge the treaty's terms, but the Iberian powers remained best positioned during the early 1500s to turn their paper claims into the reality of transatlantic empires. Spain's energetic exploration of the Americas (see Chapter 1) made it the most formidable territorial power of the age, while Portugal was able to build on its valuable African and East Indian trade to become the century's great maritime commercial power. It took several decades for European rivals to overcome the Iberians' head start. When they began to do so by the mid-sixteenth century, the cumbersome Atlantic system that the Spanish had constructed proved extremely vulnerable.

LA CARRERA DE INDIAS   From the beginning of transatlantic navigation, Spain's dominance rested on precious metals extracted from New World sources mines. Caribbean islands such as

Cuba and Hispañola contained significant gold deposits. By 1510, Spanish seafarers were averaging over fifty voyages per year on its east-west "Indies Run," carrying grain, supplies, missionaries, and colonists to the Caribbean and bringing precious metals and colonial products back to Seville. Despite this steady traffic, the yield from the first quarter-century of Spanish commerce in the New World seemed disappointing in comparison with Spain's own trade with European partners, let alone Portugal's enormously profitable African and East India routes.

Cortés's conquest of Tenochtitlán in 1519 marked a dramatic shift toward Spain in the balance of Atlantic commerce as ships laden with Mexican gold plied annual routes from Vera Cruz to Seville. Francisco Pizarro's conquest of Peru in the 1530s and the opening of Peru's rich Potosí silver mines in 1545 extended Spain's lead even further. Peruvian silver, like Mexican gold, passed through the Caribbean after being transported up the Pacific coast of South America and across the Isthmus of Panama to the region's Caribbean port of Nombre de Dios. Once loaded, the ships left the swampy, exposed coastline of Nombre de Dios for the well-defended harbor of Cartagena on the coast of Colombia, where they waited for favorable winds that would carry them back across the Atlantic. Through the remainder of the sixteenth century, precious metals flowed from Vera Cruz and Nombre de Dios to Seville. By 1610, Spain was importing nearly fourteen times as much New World treasure annually as it had a century before.

As the artery of Spain's New World wealth, the *Carrera de Indias* enriched several important ports through which it passed on its way to Seville. Chief among these were San Jaun, Puerto Rico, the first Caribbean call of port for convoys from Seville, and Havana, Cuba, where treasure-laden ships from both Vera Cruz and Cartagena regrouped into convoys for the return voyage to Spain. Havana's harbor could accommodate up to a thousand vessels at once, and a chain of fortifications kept the treasure fleets formidably secure. Havana's superior shipyards not only repaired Spanish vessels for the return voyage to Seville but also produced creole ships—ones built in Spanish colonial shipyards—whose quality rivaled that of vessels produced in the best Spanish yards. The French explorer Samuel de Champlain admired Havana in 1599 as the "warehouse where all the riches of America are held."

This great current of New World wealth flowed into the cosmopolitan port of Seville, stimulating the city's rapid growth as people from the surrounding countryside moved to take advantage of new commercial opportunities. Merchants from other European commercial centers established residence in Seville to sell such items as English wool, Flemish textiles, German iron, and French trade goods for Spanish gold and silver. Banking families from the Italian city of Genoa helped make Seville a center of European finance. The transactions made by these merchants and bankers directed Spanish wealth through powerful mercantile networks, which stimulated production and commerce in many other parts of Europe.

New World gold made Spain a military as well as a commercial threat to other maritime powers. It enabled Spanish monarchs to buy the navy, artillery, and armaments needed to make their dominion the most powerful in Europe. After the Spanish crown passed to the Emperor Charles V, the first of the powerful Hapsburg dynasty to rule Spain, he used its wealth and power aggressively to extend his influence over Continental Europe. Charles's successor, Philip II of Spain, continued his father's expansive policies. Other European nations feared the growing Spanish threat. The English promoter Richard Hakluyt the Younger, for example, warned that "the contynuall commynge of . . . threasure" from Spanish America to Philip II would enable the monarch to finance international "mischief" that could destroy England.

2.1.1: Treasure for Some, Oppression for Many

Spanish colonists depended heavily on indigenous American workers to keep the treasure flowing into Seville. The *repartmiento* system established in the first decades of conquest harnessed Indian labor to produce profits for the Spanish colonists (see Chapter 1). In the earliest years of colonization, Columbus sanctioned the enslavement of Carib and Arawak Indians, many of whom panned gold for Spanish masters from the rivers and streams of Caribbean islands such as Hispañola, Cuba, and Puerto Rico. The crown soon halted indiscriminate enslavement of Indians, permitting colonists to enslave only hostile "cannibals" on whom they had declared war. Colonists often circumvented this restriction by defining as "cannibals" whatever Indians they wanted to enslave. Nevertheless, the restriction prevented them from fulfilling their need for labor with native slaves. Instead, they had to develop or adapt various traditional forms of obtaining labor by tribute.

In Mexico, Cortés and his successors initially extended a form of *encomienda*, which gave the new Spanish aristocrats almost absolute control over the Indians within their borders. *Encomenderos* often enslaved, branded, rented, and sold their native laborers or put them to work on estates to produce goods or mine ore for export. Soon after the discovery of rich silver lodes at Zacatecas in 1546, the Spanish crown introduced to Mexico a reformed *repartmiento* system of labor tribute. New laws prohibited enslavement of Indians except captives of war and adapted previous Aztec methods of exacting labor from the resident population on a rotating basis. In distant mining zones like Zacatecas, however, the owners and managers had to rely primarily on free wage labor to attract sedentary Indian workers from distant centers of Spanish dominion. The Spanish supplemented the wage-labor force with Indian slaves captured in frontier warfare as well as smaller numbers of slaves transported from Africa.

Indians also comprised the bulk of the mineworkers in early Peru. As in Mexico, the Spanish adapted an earlier indigenous system of labor tribute, the *mita*, to supply the earliest Peruvian mining operations with forced workers. The discovery of silver in the high Andean region of Potosí in 1545, however, brought about a shift to free contract labor as Quechua-speaking Indians flocked to the mines in search of opportunity. The Spanish depended on Indians not only to mine the ore but also to refine it using smelting technology that Inca craftsmen had developed for oxygen-poor high altitudes. For twenty years, Spanish and Indian alike profited from mining and refining the abundant, high-quality ore. After 1570, Indian contract laborers began to drift away as depletion of the purest ore made the task of mining and processing much less profitable. Spanish officials responded by instituting the *mita* system of forced tribute labor once again to sustain production in the Potosí mines.

The various forms of forced labor that the Spanish imposed on their conquered peoples enriched colonists and crown alike. Yet the catastrophic decline in Spanish America's native population—through disease and oppressive work conditions—soon produced a chronic labor shortage, precipitating a search for new sources of workers. The Spanish turned increasingly to African slaves during the sixteenth century, augmenting the economic power of the Portuguese who controlled the transatlantic slave trade.

2.1.2: The Portuguese Atlantic: Another Story of Unfree Labor

While the Spanish were busy using the wealth of the *Carrera de Indias* to expand their economic and political might, the Portuguese were building a worldwide commercial empire that profoundly shaped the Atlantic World. Although the English promoter Sir Thomas Peckham regarded Portugal as "scarce comparable to some three shires of Englande," he marveled at its leaders' resourcefulness in "fortifying, peopling, and planting" the coasts of "the West, the South, and the East partes of Africa, and also at Calicute (Calcutta) and in the East Indies, and in America." Until Portuguese planters began settling Brazil after 1530, however, their far-flung empire consisted mainly of fortified trading depots strategically located where their commodities would command favorable returns in spices, textiles, gold, and slaves. Until 1530, Portugal imported more gold through its Africa trade than Spain imported from the Caribbean and Mexico combined. Portugal's control of the lucrative Asian spice routes continued to make it the envy of Spain and other European nations even after imports of New World gold began outpacing imports from Africa.

Portugal began extending its trading empire to the New World shortly after Pedro Cabral discovered the Brazilian coast in 1500. Cabral was not primarily interested in discovering New World territory, but rather in finding a way to avoid sailing into the teeth of the southeast trade winds that made navigation to the Cape of Good Hope so difficult. In this he succeeded. Brazil soon became a stop for Portuguese vessels to take on fresh fruit and water en route to the Indian Ocean. Brazil's location east of the Line of Demarcation gave Portugal the exclusive right to exploit its resources, and the Portuguese crown claimed a monopoly on coastal trade in brazilwood, a source of valuable dye.

For three decades Portuguese merchants remained content to use Brazil's coast primarily as a provisioning stop on the route to more profitable ports. The minor trade in brazilwood and logwood (both used for making dyes) did bring the Portuguese into contact with indigenous peoples who bartered their labor for European commodities, cutting the wood that grew wild in the forest and piling it on the shore for loading. During this period, French merchants also traded regularly with Brazilian Indians for dyewood with little opposition from the Portuguese. Only in 1530 did the Portuguese begin to view its American territory as a place for permanent settlement of traders who could secure the monopoly on brazilwood and begin developing other resources.

In the 1550s, Brazilian settlers began shifting attention from the dyewood trade to sugar planting, a fateful change both for their relations with their native neighbors and for the larger history of the Atlantic World. Early planters obtained financing from Antwerp's traditional sugar investors to purchase cane and expensive mills. They brought the sugar-producing supplies and technology from the well-established Portuguese sugar islands of Madeira off the coast of Morocco and São Tomé in the Gulf of Guinea. More importantly, Brazilian planters transferred from those islands the plantation system based on slave labor. While the east Atlantic sugar planters had long relied on the labor of African slaves, Brazilian planters initially enslaved neighboring Indians to work their cane fields and mills. As in other parts of America, however, epidemic diseases soon began taking their toll on Brazil's indigenous population. As the Indian labor supply declined, planters increasingly turned to slaves shipped from Africa.

Brazil's sugar plantations proved highly successful, stimulating rapid expansion of transatlantic Portuguese shipping between Europe, Africa, and America. The abundance of fertile land near the coast made it possible to produce sugar on a much larger scale than ever before. While a Madeira sugar mill could produce a yearly average of around 15 metric tons of sugar, the average mill in Brazil was producing better than double that amount only two decades after large-scale planting began. By 1600, the average Brazilian sugar mill was producing 130 metric tons per year. The wealth that circulated the Atlantic from Brazilian sugar and African slaves stirred European rivals to envy Portugal as much as they did Spain. Indeed, mid-sixteenth century English promoters commonly referred to the wealth of the "King of Spaine and the King of Portingal" in the same breath.

Shrewd—often cruel—exploitation of their New World possessions enabled Spain and Portugal to transform the sixteenth-century Atlantic into a greater Iberian world. Spanish ships dominated the central east-west route from southern Europe to the Caribbean and Spanish Main, while a growing stream of Portuguese vessels dominated the triangular route between Africa, Brazil, and Europe. Other European seafarers navigated on the margins of this great Atlantic World, gleaning what profits they could at the sufferance of Spain and Portugal or from pockets of trade and plunder neglected by the Iberian lords of the sea. By 1580, when Spain's Philip II seized the Portuguese crown, the combined wealth of the united kingdoms made Iberian power seem invincible.

Spain's apparent strength masked deep flaws in its imperial system, which was soon undone by its own success. The sudden acquisition of so much American gold and silver triggered a huge inflation in the price of necessary goods. This hurt ordinary Spaniards who had no desire to emigrate to America. They were hurt further by long, debilitating European wars funded by American gold and silver. Moreover, instead of developing its own industry, Spain became dependent on the annual shipment of bullion from America. In 1603, one insightful Spaniard declared, "The New World conquered by you, has conquered you in its turn."

2.2: The Sixteenth-Century Atlantic: The African Experience

2.2 Examine the impact of slavery on the New World

The ability of the Portuguese to extend African slavery to the Americas flowed out of nearly a century of well-developed trade relations with powerful African commercial interests

(see Chapter 1). Too often, historians have ignored Africa in their haste to tell the story of colonial American development. This is a mistake. One should not allow the enormity of the slave trade to obscure either the diversity of Africa's transatlantic commerce or the active role that African leaders themselves took in developing the Atlantic economy.

The expansion of slavery represented a continuous process of change in Africa as new slavers carried the trade to new recruitment areas. Europeans did not dictate the terms of exchange in this developing commerce in human beings. Coastal African rulers and merchant communities brought sophisticated bargaining skills and discriminating preferences to the Atlantic market. In most ports, African law governed the terms of trade. Europeans had to do business using African weights and measures. European rulers often had to lubricate the wheels of commerce with generous gifts to local African rulers. Europeans who balked at or tried to circumvent these constraints often ran afoul of African laws backed by formidable military force. European merchants depended on their African partners to develop the sustained supply and demand—in goods as well as humans—that made Africa a vital link in the emerging Atlantic World economy. The story of New World slavery remains incomplete without understanding how it set in motion transformative processes on both sides of the Atlantic.

2.2.1: Competition and Conspicuous Consumption

Africa's entry into the Atlantic market did not come about because Europeans arrived on the coast with superior goods that Africans could not produce for themselves. Indeed, the reverse often proved true, as early Portuguese traders on the Gold Coast discovered when their Akkan partners demanded African slaves rather than European goods as the price of their gold. African ironworkers possessed the technology to produce

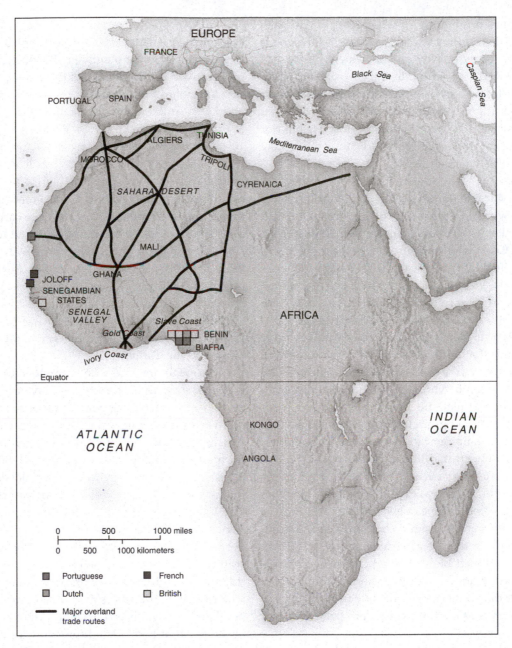

Map 2.1 Trade Routes in Africa

the best steel in the sixteenth-century world. African weavers could produce cloth as fine as any available in Europe.

To break into this sophisticated African market, European traders had to identify and meet specific market demands as well as create new demand by appealing to their customers' instinct for a bargain and taste for variety. Europeans managed this in a variety of ways. Sometimes they supplied Africans' demand for products originating in other parts of Africa by using their sailing vessels to transport the goods more cheaply, quickly, and in greater volume than could African traders. In the case of iron, Europeans found a market niche in supplying poorer grades at prices far cheaper than those of African producers. African craftsmen could use inferior European iron selectively to produce everyday utensils for which it was adequate, while preferring higher-grade African steel for stronger, more durable items such as metalworking tools and swords. European textiles eventually found a market as well, even among the Akkan of the Gold Coast who were already well-supplied with beautiful cloth of African make. European fabrics offered a greater range of texture, beauty, and design, and large collections of cloth became a mark of wealth and status for their African owners.

African merchants also offered a wide variety of goods that Europeans valued, besides the gold that served as the basis of Portugal's fifteenth and early-sixteenth-century African trade. Sixteenth-century Spanish and Portuguese traders regularly purchased grain from several parts of West Africa for shipment to their plantation colonies. Exquisitely crafted items made from native African materials such as ivory fetched high prices in Europe, as did raw ivory itself. Senegambian mats covered European beds. Some types of African cloth enjoyed a significant European demand. Weavers in the West African region of Allada produced their highly prized fabrics by unraveling the threads from cloth imported from Europe, which they rewove in distinctive patterns for sale to markets as distant as the Caribbean island of Barbados.

2.2.2: Africans and the Atlantic Slave Trade

The European market for African minerals and manufactured goods always existed alongside a strong European demand for slaves. The demand rose steadily even before 1492 as the Portuguese and Spanish sought workers for the sugar plantations on their Atlantic islands (see Chapter 1). The introduction of sugar planting in Brazil after 1550, coupled with the decimation of the native population throughout the sixteenth-century Caribbean and Latin America, brought a dramatic increase in the trade in African slaves. Between 1550 and 1600, the number of Atlantic slave exports from West Africa rose to over 200,000, at least 30,000 more slaves than were exported during the previous hundred years. During the seventeenth century, nearly two million Africans were carried to the New World, and the number soared to over six million in the eighteenth century. By the time Brazil became the last Atlantic nation to abolish slavery in 1880, over eleven million Africans had crossed the Atlantic in chains. The vast majority of those who survived the Atlantic crossing— around 80 percent—wound up on plantations in Brazil and the Caribbean.

European demand alone cannot account for the rapid growth of the Atlantic slave trade, for no early modern European state wielded the military or economic power sufficient to coerce African rulers into supplying slaves. Indeed, the Portuguese concluded as early as the 1450s that it was far more practical to trade for slaves than to risk war with powerful West African coastal states by attempting to capture them in raids. African authorities remained firmly in control over all but a few regions such as the Portuguese colony of Angola, and even there European traders depended heavily on African suppliers who readily exchanged slaves for the commodities they desired. Europeans tapped into systems of slavery that had existed for centuries among these African states (see Chapter 1). The victims in most cases were prisoners of war—casualties in the endemic conflict that raged constantly among Africa's many fractious states. Captives were taken in a variety of ways: some during pitched battles, others during lightning raids on villages or fields, still others as tribute from defeated territories. The captors did not regard their slaves as members of a common racial group, but as alien peoples who had forfeited their freedom by right of conquest and could be put to work or sold as circumstances demanded.

Captives of wars or raids often traveled long distances overland, chained or yoked together, and marched in single columns that could be easily guarded. The marching distances increased as the coastal supply of slaves dwindled, prompting traders to offer higher prices that made it worthwhile for inland rulers to bear the cost of transport. Slaves might change hands between traders several times during transit. A buyer might put a newly acquired slave to work for a while before reselling him. The eighteenth-century slave Olaudah Equiano, for example, recorded how he spent time working temporarily for various masters who exchanged him along the route from his homeland to the West African coast. African masters living in port towns often put newly arrived slaves to work in fields or on projects for several months while waiting for a European slave trader to arrive.

Over time, the slave trade shifted to different centers along the African coast as states responded to new internal demands and pressures as well as new commercial opportunities. During the fifteenth and early sixteenth centuries, for example, Portuguese merchants purchased many slaves from the coast of Benin for resale on the Gold Coast or for transport to their sugar islands of Madeira and São Tomé. By 1550, however, Benin's rulers cut off the supply, possibly because they needed slave laborers themselves to support the brisk export trade they had developed in cloth and pepper. The Kingdom of Kongo, on the other hand, continued to deal in slaves until the early seventeenth century, when war with neighboring states disrupted the trade. As some states pulled out of the trade, others entered, enticed by rising prices or the desire for specific goods. Still other regions, such as the Portuguese colony of Angola with its many links to the continent's interior, continued supplying slaves to the Atlantic market from the late sixteenth through the seventeenth centuries.

The European demand for slaves produced a seismic shift in the direction of the long-distance African trade. Before the sixteenth century, many slaves remained in the region where they were captured. Others were transported to more distant regions along the coast, and a large number were carried north across the Sahara to the Mediterranean and Middle East, where most masters purchased them as domestic servants and concubines. The growing demand for laborers in America, however, redirected the trade to the Atlantic during the seventeenth century.

The Atlantic trade also produced a shift in the demographic impact of slavery in Africa. Not only did it draw off many more slaves than had the trans-Sahara trade, it also demanded a much higher proportion of males. The earlier long-distance trade had drawn a higher proportion of female slaves to satisfy the demand for concubines. European buyers, by contrast, preferred male slaves for heavy plantation labor, although they also put slave women to work in the fields. The sexual imbalance in the Atlantic trade contributed to the ongoing demand for new slaves from Africa by making it difficult in most areas for the New World slave population to sustain itself through natural increase.

2.2.3: The Horror of the Middle Passage

Portuguese dominance of the sixteenth-century African coast ensured that their vessels carried the vast majority of slaves to the New World until the 1620s, when Dutch competitors began to break their monopoly. Portuguese ships could make the trip from West Africa to Brazil in approximately six weeks, making large-scale transport of Africans to their American colony practical and cost-effective. Portuguese vessels also carried Africans to the Spanish American mainland ports of Cartagena and Vera Cruz as well as Spanish Caribbean ports such as Havana and San Juan, where the much longer voyages took a heavy toll in mortality, disease, and profits.

This voyage across the Atlantic united the slaves that endured it in a shared experience of trauma and deprivation. Mortality during the Middle Passage was high, often killing as much as a third of a ship's slaves during the voyage. Long chains bound slaves together in groups of six or more, and many captains took the additional precaution of shackling captives by the ankles in pairs to prevent escape. Slaves spent much of the voyage locked below decks, where the stifling heat and poor circulation made the air so bad that a candle would not remain lit. The stench of vomit, urine, and feces soon became intolerable, even on vessels whose crews periodically cleaned the holds. A port's inhabitants often knew when a slave ship had arrived by the foul smell near the harbor. On some vessels, the captains gave the sufferers temporary relief from these horrific conditions by bringing them on deck for a short period each day in small, closely watched groups.

Slaves on the Middle Passage also endured malnourishment, dehydration, and illness that only worsened as the voyage grew longer. After 1520, the Portuguese crown required crews to load royal vessels with adequate food and water supplies. The regulations did not bind private traders, however, who commonly overloaded their vessels with slaves and skimped on supplies in an effort to make as much profit as possible. Alonso de Sandoval, an early-seventeenth-century observer of the Portuguese trade, reported that slaves usually received only a "small jar of water" and one meal of millet gruel per day. Sandoval wrote that slaves arriving at the end of the long voyages to Cartagena or Vera Cruz were typically "reduced to skeletons." Poor nutrition made the captives especially susceptible to epidemic diseases such as typhoid fever, measles, yellow fever, and smallpox. These diseases sometimes claimed entire shiploads of slaves along with their crews, and infected ships sometimes spread their epidemics to the ports where they anchored.

The Middle Passage marked its survivors with enduring scars of unspeakable psychological and physical trauma. Yet contrary to the assertions of some modern historians, it neither stripped Africans of their cultural memory nor reduced them to a state of fawning dependence on their European masters. Abundant evidence testifies that the Middle Passage began the process of forging new African communities bound together by a common experience on which they could build coherent cultural traditions. In doing so, Africans drew on their past for the resources to cope with their experience in the New World and to create communities that could provide support and nurture in the midst of a harsh experience. Africans also exhibited a persistent determination to resist bondage when opportunity arose, and some escaped to forge independent societies of "maroons," escaped slaves who lived in areas beyond the control of Latin American authorities.

2.2.4: The African Diaspora: Sixteenth-Century Beginnings

African slaves were part of the process of New World conquest from Columbus's first voyage onward. As their numbers grew in Spanish and Portuguese America, so did their power to contribute distinctive African elements to the emerging Atlantic World. Africans served as seamen on the early voyages of discovery as well as servants in the households and estates of early Spanish conquistadores and royal officials. Spanish colonists soon came to rely on African labor for mining and agricultural enterprises as well, especially after epidemic disease killed so many Native American workers. Portuguese colonists in Brazil likewise turned to African labor to supplement indigenous labor on the colony's sugar plantations. These laborers brought with them knowledge of plants and cultivation, which proved indispensable to their masters. They also brought patterns of community life; ideas of the sacred; and ways of feasting, marrying, celebration, and mourning that permanently shaped the societies they inhabited.

African slaves filled an important niche in the Spanish American labor system even before the devastating declines in the native population. The limitations that the crown placed on Indian slavery, coupled with the *repartmiento* system's restrictions on the use of Indian labor, created a need for a permanent labor force to sustain and coordinate crucial operations. *Encomenderos* used African slaves to fill the gaps. Throughout Spanish America, African slaves provided the domestic labor force as permanent members of colonial households. Africans occupied supervisory and administrative roles in Spanish mining operations both in the Caribbean and on the Mexican and Peruvian mainland. Slaves from Senegambia, who brought to the Americas cattle-herding skills unknown among the Indians, tended herds on Spanish American *haciendas*. Expert divers from the Gold Coast fished pearls for Spanish masters off the coasts of Venezuela and Trinidad. Skilled African craftsmen worked as blacksmiths, barrel makers, carpenters, and cabinetmakers. African slaves worked in the cane fields and sugar mills of the Spanish Caribbean. They also harvested mahogany trees throughout the region. In many of these operations, they worked alongside or supervised indigenous American slaves, tribute laborers, and wage earners. As disease decimated the supply of native laborers, Spanish masters replaced them wherever possible with African slaves.

In Portuguese Brazil, enslaved Tupinambá Indians provided most of the labor on the early sugar plantations. Even so, Portuguese masters preferred to employ African slaves in domestic service and skilled tasks. The rapid expansion of the plantation economy soon created a demand for African slaves in the fields and mills as well, one that was only exacerbated as epidemic disease began to take its toll on the Tupinambá population. By the early 1600s, African slaves almost completely replaced the Tupinambá in all aspects of plantation labor.

Africans' experiences in Colonial Latin America varied widely according to the type of labor they performed and the conditions in which they lived. Most slaves in the Spanish mining regions, for instance, were male. Though they enjoyed some privileges associated with their supervisory and skilled positions, they usually could not marry African women or create the families and stable communities that could nurture their cultural traditions. The slave populations of plantation regions also suffered from an imbalanced sex ratio of two or more men for every woman. Nevertheless, the greater presence of women on some plantations did make it possible for African slaves to marry, have children, and form communities. Africans also forged a variety of relationships with Indian coworkers as well as Europeans. Both Spanish American and Brazilian colonists tolerated sexual unions among Europeans, Africans, and Indians. The resulting mulatto (offspring of African-European unions) and mustee (African-Indian offspring) populations were incorporated along with mestizos (European-Indian offspring) into Colonial Latin American societies.

Slave communities of Latin America rarely reproduced the culture of any specific African group; in other words, the creation of New World African American cultures drew upon the memories and customs of diverse African communities. Although the ethnic makeup of individual slave cargos was often homogenous, the slaves arrived into port only to be dispersed onto plantations where they encountered people from very different cultural backgrounds. Slaves living in the cities of Spanish and Portuguese America often overcame this separation by seeking out fellow countrymen with whom they formed ethnic secret societies. Slave communities on the plantations, however, had to combine features of diverse cultures they had known at home with European and Native American elements, producing new cultural forms. The resulting innovations in music, dress, language, religion, and customs of marriage and family life sustained the members of slave communities and eventually linked slaves of entire regions to one another through a shared cultural system. African seamen traveling from port to port on European vessels may have tapped into several of these regional cultural systems to provide even wider links among maritime Atlantic slave communities.

Not all Africans who came to Spanish and Portuguese America as slaves remained so throughout their lives. A master could manumit a slave in reward for particular services performed or as a show of magnanimity, or he might allow a slave to purchase his freedom through additional labor. Over time, significant communities of free blacks emerged in Colonial Latin America. Other slaves simply stole themselves, running away to remote areas where they formed maroon communities that resisted capture while preying on Iberian settlements and shipping. Maroons on Caribbean islands often pursued the time-honored coastal African tradition of piracy, ambushing unsuspecting vessels from canoes and open boats. Maroon communities in Brazil formed powerful, well-armed states that could effectively repel colonial militia units periodically dispatched to suppress them. Maroons of Central America, whom the Spanish called *Cimarrones*, staged periodic raids from their well-hidden jungle villages, harassing coastal communities and attacking the treasure convoys that carried Peruvian silver across the Isthmus of Panama.

The written history of the New World has tended to focus on European migrations. But this is a tale told by the winners, by those who profited from unfree black labor. In fact, during every single year between 1650 and 1831, more Africans than Europeans came to the Americas. As historian Davis Eltis writes, "In terms of immigration alone . . . America was an extension of Africa rather than Europe until late in the nineteenth century."

2.3: Northern Europeans Enter the Atlantic World

2.3 Summarize the conflict between the European nations to control the wealth of the emerging Atlantic world

By the mid-sixteenth century, Africa had become an indispensable part of the Iberian Atlantic system, thanks to a widespread African demand for European commodities and its role in supplying slaves to a growing New World market. African labor increasingly sustained the flow of precious metals from the Spanish Main as well as the growth in Brazilian sugar production. The transatlantic circulation of wealth excited the envy of Spain's and Portugal's rivals to the north, while growing Spanish military power aroused their fears.

In the later sixteenth century, challengers moved ever more boldly to wrest the Atlantic economy from Iberian control. Privateers raided colonial ports and seized vulnerable galleons. Traders intruded into African and New World networks of exchange. Explorers sought alternative routes to the riches of the East and laid claim to stretches of coast unoccupied by Spanish or Portuguese colonists. In most instances, they ignored the prior claims of native peoples, although a few such as the Dutch adventurer Peter Minuit sought to gain legal advantage by purchasing claims from the original inhabitants. The boundaries of the Atlantic World steadily expanded as northern Europeans secured new American beachheads to find new sources of wealth and "cutt off the common mischefes that commes to all Europe by the peculiar aboundance" of the Spanish king's "Indian Treasure."

2.3.1: The French

Spain and Portugal no sooner began consolidating their control of Atlantic shipping lanes between Africa, the New World, and Europe than the French monarch Francis I began challenging them. France and Spain were locked in almost perpetual warfare from 1521 to 1559, and King Francis viewed New World enterprise as a means of gaining advantage over his rival Charles V. This motive had driven the French crown's sponsorship of Verrazzano's and Cartier's quests for a Northwest Passage to Asia (see Chapter 1). It also prompted several direct challenges to Spanish and Portuguese claims in the Caribbean, the Gulf of Mexico, and the coast of Brazil. Although most early French attempts to wrest a toehold in the New World ended in failure, they nevertheless established a persistent French presence in the sixteenth-century Atlantic and laid the foundations for successful seventeenth-century colonial ventures.

EARLY FRENCH VENTURES IN THE CARIBBEAN AND BRAZIL France and Spain had barely been at war a year when in 1522 French squadrons belonging to the Norman nobleman Jean d'Ango captured four galleons returning to Spain laden with treasure from newly conquered Mexico. The richness of these prizes, which were taken near the Azores, soon emboldened French captains to seek "letters of marque," official documents from the French crown authorizing them to invade the Caribbean itself in search of Spanish plunder. By 1550, these French corsairs had established a fearsome reputation through their yearly raids on the coastal towns of Puerto Rico, Cuba, and Hispañola. In 1655, the corsair Jacques de Sores captured and burned Havana, the fortress of the Spanish Caribbean itself. The conclusion of peace between Spain and France in 1559 did little to diminish the French presence in the Caribbean, where corsairs continued raiding and smuggling operations into the seventeenth century.

The corsairs wasted little time in extending their activities to the coast of Brazil, where they competed with Portuguese merchants for dyewood. The Portuguese initially tolerated the trade out of fear that the French crown would issue letters of marque against their ships. As the tide of war turned against France in Europe, however, Portugal's King John III sent a fleet to round up French traders and execute them as pirates. In spite of this action, the French refused to surrender their contest for Brazil. By 1550, the corsairs controlled a significant stretch of the Brazilian coast, where they traded for dyewood and staged raids on Portuguese settlements. French traders established amicable relations with their Indian trading partners, often settling in native villages and intermarrying to cement alliances in a manner that became characteristic of French-native interaction throughout the Americas. These alliances helped the French hold out against Portuguese efforts to dislodge them from Brazil until 1603.

CHALLENGING SPANISH FLORIDA French adventurers also made sporadic attempts during the sixteenth century to compete with Spain for a foothold in southeastern North America near Florida. In 1562, a group of French Protestants established a settlement on what is now Parris Island in South Carolina's Port Royal Sound. This new colony of Charlesfort was the first European settlement in what would become Britain's thirteen mainland colonies. Its founders hoped it would become a refuge for French Protestants, or Huguenots, a center for exploiting new discoveries of American wealth, and a base for preying on Spanish shipping. Internal strife soon tore the colony apart, however, and Spanish forces from Havana burned Charlesfort's abandoned buildings in 1664. That same year the Huguenots attempted to found a second colony at Fort Caroline near the mouth of the St. Johns River on the Atlantic coast of Florida. It lasted less than a year. In 1565, the Spanish governor Pedro Menéndez de Avilés surprised the settlement, sparing women and children but systematically executing more than 130 male defenders of the "evil Lutheran sect."

This illustration produced by Jacques Le Moyne in 1564 depicts Native Americans of coastal Florida depositing gifts of food at the foot of a column erected by French explorers who had established a short-lived settlement in the region.

France's sixteenth-century efforts along the Florida coast succeeded mainly in spurring the Spanish crown to pour more funds into American defenses. During the 1560s, Florida's Governor Menéndez established St. Augustine along with six other Spanish forts to secure the coast of Florida and the Bahama Channel. He also devised a scheme to bypass Caribbean routes by transporting silver overland from Mexico's Zacatecas mines to the new fort of Santa Elena on Parris Island near the former site of the Huguenot's ill-fated Charlesfort. Menéndez's idea, though impractical, testified to Spain's growing fear of the French corsairs who infested Caribbean waters and to the rising costs of defending the Spain's New World empire.

NEW FRANCE ON THE ST. LAWRENCE While intrepid corsairs contended in the sixteenth-century Caribbean for a share of Spanish treasure, French merchants and fishermen were quietly pursuing a more peaceful and increasingly lucrative enterprise in the Gulf of Lawrence. By the 1550s, the Grand Banks were attracting large squadrons of French fishing vessels to supply a huge demand for fish during France's Lenten season, when consumption of meat and poultry was prohibited by church tradition. In addition, the growing popularity in Europe of wide-brimmed hats was boosting the demand for American beaver pelts, the soft underfur of which made excellent felt for hats. Each year, the abundant supply of pelts and fish enticed more Frenchmen to establish permanent outposts in the region, belying earlier Spanish predictions that Canada's frigid climate would soon force the French to abandon any colony they attempted there. Wherever they settled, the traders soon began farming their own crops and cultivating good relations with nearby native bands.

By the 1570s, these unofficial fishing and trading communities were producing healthy profits for French merchants, who pressed the crown to protect their American investments. Religious turmoil, however, diverted royal attention and resources from North America for another thirty years. Only in 1598 was King Henry IV able to begin securing the French foothold in Canada by appointing officials to organize government and supervise trade. During the next decade, these men made several abortive efforts to establish a seat of royal government in the region. Finally, in 1608, Samuel de Champlain succeeded in founding the city of Quebec on the banks of the St. Lawrence River.

Quebec proved an excellent strategic choice. From its site at a point where the St. Lawrence narrowed, French artillery could command both riverbanks and control all traffic to the interior. Its location near Huron population centers also enabled the French to forge an alliance with an important nation whose networks of exchange extended throughout the Great Lakes. The Hurons and other northern nations were eager to trade for European goods and readily accepted Champlain's new settlement as a center of commerce with France. To consolidate the native trade network, Champlain reciprocated by cementing an alliance with Hurons against their enemies the Iroquois. The alliance secured France reliable trading partners, while Quebec's strategic location insulated it from European competitors.

As was the case with other colonial powers, the French declared they had migrated to the New World in search of wealth as well as in hopes of converting the Indians to Christianity. As it turned out, these economic and spiritual goals required full cooperation between the French and the Native Americans. In contrast to the English settlers, who established independent farms and who regarded the Indians at best as obstacles to proper cultivation of the land, the French viewed the natives as necessary economic partners. Furs constituted Canada's most valuable export, and to obtain the pelts of beaver and other animals, the French depended completely on Indian hunters and trappers. French traders continued to live among the Indians throughout the colonial period, often taking native wives and studying local cultures.

Catholic missionaries also depended on Indian cooperation. Canadian priests came from two orders, the Jesuits and the Recollets. In 1618, Recollet missionaries laid out a plan to populate New France with settlers who could familiarize the natives with European ways of life to facilitate their conversion. Recollets and Jesuits also traveled far inland with their message, living among the Indians and learning to speak their languages as the fur traders did. Jesuit missionaries distinguished themselves by a careful study of native customs and beliefs in an effort to frame Christian teachings in terms intelligible to Indian cultures. Despite their unavoidable cultural bias, Jesuit accounts remain valuable sources of information on seventeenth-century native culture. This culturally sensitive approach appears to have helped French Catholic missionaries convert more Indians to Christianity than did their English Protestant counterparts to the south.

The establishment of Quebec secured France a permanent outpost in the Atlantic World, albeit one far removed from the great arteries of coveted Iberian wealth. Moreover, the French dream of expanding its northern claims into a vast American empire suffered from serious flaws. Political turmoil in France and Europe prevented the crown from giving much attention to Canadian affairs until late in the seventeenth century. Royal officials stationed in New France received limited and sporadic support from Paris. An even greater problem was the decision to settle what seemed to many rural peasants and urban artisans a cold, inhospitable land. Canada's European population grew very slowly throughout the period of French rule, which came to an end in 1763. A census of 1663 recorded a mere 3,035 French residents. By 1700, the figure had reached only fifteen thousand. Moreover, because of the colony's geography, all exports and imports had to go through Quebec. It was relatively easy, therefore, for crown officials to control that traffic, usually by awarding fur-trading monopolies to court favorites. Such practices created political tensions and hindered economic growth.

2.3.2: The Rise of the Dutch

The Dutch entered the competition for Atlantic wealth as an act of rebellion against the Spanish crown. King Philip II had sparked unrest in the provinces of Netherlands soon after his accession to the throne when he began revoking their ancient privileges, imposing a Spanish garrison, and instituting the Spanish Inquisition to stamp out the Calvinistic Protestantism that had taken root in the seven northern provinces called Holland. The war that broke out in 1572 wore on by fits and starts for eighty years, although it was interrupted in the early seventeenth century by the Twelve Years' Truce. The Catholic southern provinces of Belgium bore the brunt of war and were exhausted into complete submission by the early 1590s. The seven Protestant northern provinces, however, concluded the Union of Utrecht in 1579 and proclaimed their independence from Spain.

Despite warfare with Spain, the United Provinces enjoyed a security and fund of resources that enabled them to capture a significant share of transatlantic commerce very quickly. Holland's treacherous coastline was a curse to potential Spanish invaders, but a blessing to the Dutch navigators who knew the waters well and could take advantage of their strategic location near the center of northern European sea-lanes. During the previous century, Dutch navigators had captured the bulk of the carrying trade between the Baltic and southern Europe, while Dutch artisans had developed a burgeoning trade in export goods. The provinces also experienced a great influx of wealth and talent as refugees poured in from the war-torn south. By the 1590s, the merchants, financiers, and artisans that had once made Antwerp the economic center of northern Europe were poised to capture world markets from Amsterdam.

CHALLENGING THE PORTUGUESE Amsterdam investors began moving to capture Portuguese markets around the world during the last two decades of the sixteenth century. The sea battles of that period had disrupted the Portuguese trade with Africa and the Indian Ocean, creating an opportunity for the Dutch to move in. By 1602, the newly created United East India Company controlled a large share of the spice trade. Many of the company's investors financed voyages to the coast of Africa as well, where they quickly undercut Portuguese traders by offering cheaper, better cloth from Europe and India as well as superior iron ingots from Sweden. Out of this trade the Guinea Company emerged to contend with Portugal for the African slave trade. The company built forts at strategic points in Senegambia and the Gold Coast to double as trading posts and bases of operation against Portuguese slaving vessels.

The Dutch conquest of world markets would be incomplete without a rich American possession, and investors first set their sights on Portuguese Brazil. By the end of the sixteenth century, Dutch shippers regularly carried a large share of Brazilian sugar to European markets. Not content with this, the Dutch launched a struggle for possession of the territory itself. In 1621, the newly created West India Company began pouring its resources into a protracted effort to capture Brazil while continuing the now-defunct Guinea Company's contest for key Portuguese possessions in Africa. The company eventually captured Portugal's West African forts at Elmina and Axim (see Chapter 7), but failed in Brazil. The long struggle diverted resources away from Dutch colonization efforts in the Caribbean, where they gained possession of only a few islands in the Lesser Antilles including Curaçao and St. Eustatia.

NEW NETHERLANDS ON THE HUDSON The Dutch, like the French before them, ultimately found it most practical to establish a foothold on the North American periphery of the Iberian Atlantic. And like the French, they happened on the site of their North American colony while searching for the elusive Northwest Passage. In 1609, Henry Hudson, an English explorer employed by the Dutch East India Company, sailed up the river that now bears his name in search of a shorter and safer route to the Indian Ocean. Further voyages led to the establishment of trading posts in New Netherland, the most important of which was Fort Nassau on Castle Island near present-day Albany. The area also seemed an excellent staging ground for attacks on Spanish American ports and shipping.

Fort Nassau provided a base from which early Dutch traders fanned out into the surrounding countryside to search for mineral deposits and forge trade alliances with neighboring Indians. This proved difficult along the Hudson, where fierce rivalries among Mohawks, Mahicans, and Munsees threatened to divide Dutch interests. Conflict among the traders was frequent, and relations with one Indian nation could jeopardize trade with another. On one occasion, for instance, a group of traders risked a potentially devastating war with the powerful Iroquois Confederacy by joining Mahican allies in an attack on Mohawk villages. Dutch officials soon established the New Netherland Company to quell cutthroat trading practices and to impose a policy of strict neutrality in military affairs. In 1621, the Dutch West India Company assumed a monopoly over the Hudson River trade.

The directors of the Dutch West India Company sponsored the establishment of two permanent outposts on the Hudson in 1624. Fort Orange (Albany) replaced Fort Nassau, which a spring flood had washed away in 1618. New Amsterdam (New York City) on Manhattan Island provided an excellent harbor that remained free of ice year round. The company populated these settlements with salaried employees, and their superiors in Holland expected them to spend most of their time gathering animal furs. They did not receive land for their troubles. Needless to say, this arrangement attracted relatively few Dutch immigrants.

New Netherlands remained a small, struggling colony neglected by West India Company officials in their vain quest to conquer Brazil. It nevertheless secured the Dutch an important foothold in the New World, a base for staging forays into the Spanish Caribbean and the Brazilian coast, and a steady flow of profits from the fur trade. New Amsterdam soon became an integral port in the Dutch carrying trade which dominated the Atlantic by the mid-seventeenth century (see Chapter 7). The colony's Iroquois, Mahican, and Munsee trading partners also provided an eager transatlantic market for Dutch manufactured goods. Indeed, Dutch trade linked the Five Iroquois Nations to a transatlantic supply of arms which they used to extend their influence in all directions.

2.4: The Emerging English Atlantic

2.4   Recall England's rise to power in the Atlantic

As French corsairs preyed on Spanish gold shipments and revolt brewed in the Netherlands, English interest in the New World began to rebound after lying dormant for nearly half a century. In the 1560s, the realm emerged from decades of religious conflict and reformation to become a leader of Protestant Europe and one of Spain's most implacable foes. A rising group of English adventurers pointed out that the Spanish monarch owed the "mighty and marvelous" increase of his "territories and dominions" to his American possessions. They argued that England could best respond by challenging Spain's monopoly on New World treasure. Under the effective guidance of Elizabeth I and her councilors, English seafarers began carving out a niche for their nation in the later-sixteenth-century Atlantic. They interloped in Iberian trade, raided Spanish treasure shipments, made the first efforts to plant English colonies in America, and eventually launched an all-out war with Spain.

2.4.1: The Sea Dogs

Elizabethan mariners became the shock troops of English Protestant militancy. They plunged into the contest for New World wealth at a time when the lucrative trade in slaves to Brazil and the Caribbean was beginning to offer an attractive alternative to risky raids on Spanish gold shipments. English shipowners began interloping into the Portuguese-controlled slave trade as early as 1551. In 1662, the English captain John Hawkins made hefty profits for himself and his investors by capturing 300 slaves from Portuguese ships in Sierra Leone and carrying them to the Spanish Caribbean. Hawkins's piracy attracted the attention of wealthy Englishmen, including members of the court, who readily financed a second slaving voyage in 1564. This excursion, which included one of the queen's own ships, netted Hawkins and his investors a 60 percent profit and prompted Elizabeth I to honor him for his valor with the title and privileges of knighthood. A third expedition for gold and slaves ended in disaster for Hawkins when the Spanish viceroy captured him at San Juan, Puerto Rico, but the Sea Dog succeeded in making himself a *cause célèbre* by blaming the loss on Spanish treachery.

In the aftermath of Hawkins's disastrous third voyage, Queen Elizabeth herself challenged Spain's New World and Asian monopolies with increasing boldness, authorizing pirate raids against Spanish shipping. Soon royal sponsorship of daring Caribbean raiders such as Francis Drake became an open secret. When Drake led a force of Englishmen and *cimarrones* to capture a shipment of Spanish gold at Panama in 1673, Philip II fumed at Elizabeth but did nothing. The next year the Treaty of Bristol brought a temporary moratorium on English freebooting. Yet the expansionists had tasted opportunities for wealth in Spain's vulnerable empire, and the scheming, information gathering, and sorties into New World waters persisted.

The adventurers who directed Elizabethan expeditions remembered the early English explorer John Cabot's voyages only vaguely, and they had gained experience in settling distant outposts only in Ireland. Over the last three decades of the sixteenth century, English adventurers made almost every mistake one could imagine. They did, however, acquire valuable information about winds and currents, supplies, and finance.

2.4.2: Religion, War, and Nationalism

In the mid-1580s, Philip II, who had united the empires of Spain and Portugal in 1580, decided that he could tolerate England's arrogantly Protestant queen no longer. He ordered the construction of a mighty fleet, hundreds of transport vessels designed to carry Spain's finest infantry across the English Channel. When one of Philip's lieutenants viewed the Armada at Lisbon in May 1588, he described it as *la felicissima armada*, the invincible fleet. The king believed that with the support of England's oppressed Catholics, Spanish troops would sweep Elizabeth from power, restore England to the Catholic fold, and halt English depredations against Spain's Atlantic empire.

It was a grand scheme; it was an even grander failure. In 1588, a smaller, more maneuverable English navy dispersed Philip's Armada, and severe storms finished it off. Spanish hopes for Catholic England lay wrecked along the rocky coasts of Scotland and Ireland. Not surprisingly, English Protestants interpreted victory in providential terms: "God breathed and they were scattered."

However spectacular their defeat of the Spanish Armada, the English did not yet possess the sea power necessary to follow it up. Over the next few years, English naval officers made several large-scale attempts to strangle Iberian commerce by capturing Lisbon and Seville as well as the Azores, which were indispensable to Spanish treasure fleets. Spanish forces repelled each effort. By 1591, Spain rebuilt much of the naval fleet lost in the Armada, forcing the English to reduce the scale of their naval offensives. Instead they reverted to hit-and-run privateering operations, which inflicted heavy losses on Iberian trade in the Atlantic and the Caribbean.

2.4.3: Irish Rehearsal for American Colonization

During Elizabeth's reign, England's designs for a transatlantic empire became entwined with a renewed policy of colonizing the nearby island of Ireland. The experience of colonizing Ireland paralleled the Iberian conquest of the Canaries and Azores (see Chapter 1), powerfully shaping how later migrants would view the New World. It was not a happy precedent, for in Ireland ambitious Englishmen first learned to subdue a foreign population and to seize its lands. When Elizabeth assumed the throne, Ireland's one million inhabitants were scattered across the countryside. There were few villages, most of which were located along the coast. To the English eye, the Irish people seemed wild and barbaric. They were also fiercely independent and difficult to control. The English dominated a small region around Dublin by force of arms, but much of Ireland's territory remained in the hands of Gaelic-speaking Catholics who presumably managed to survive without English culture.

During the 1560s and 1570s, English adventurers—curious parallels to the Spanish conquistadores they claimed to hate—decided that considerable fortune could be made in Ireland. There were substantial risks, of course, not the least of which was the resistance of the Irish. Nevertheless, private "projectors"—a number of whom were also deeply involved in various schemes for raiding or colonizing in the New World—sponsored English settlements. In turn, these colonists forced the Irish either into tenancy or off the land altogether. During this period, the English planted semimilitary colonies in Ulster and Munster.

As one might expect, colonization was a disaster for the Irish. The English settlers, however humble their origins, felt superior to the Catholic Irish. After all, the English people had championed the Protestant religion. They had constructed a complex market economy and created a powerful nation-state. They saw the conquest of Ireland as part of one vast effort to humble the forces of Catholic Europe on both sides of the Atlantic. To the English settlers, the Irish appeared lazy, licentious, superstitious, even stupid—characteristics that they would project onto subjected peoples throughout the empire for centuries to come. English settlers ridiculed unfamiliar local customs, and it is not surprising that even educated representatives of the two cultures found communication almost impossible. English colonists, for example, criticized pastoral farming methods prevalent in sixteenth-century Ireland. It seemed perversely wasteful for the Irish to be forever moving about, because as any English person could see, such practices retarded the development of towns. Sir John Davies, a leading English colonizer, declared that if the Irish were left to themselves, they would "never (to the end of the world) build houses, make townships or villas or manure or improve the land as it ought to be." Such stubborn inefficiency—surely (the English reasoned) the Irish must have known better—became justification for the seizure of large tracts of land wherever the English established colonies.

English ethnocentrism remained relatively benign so long as the Irish accepted the subservient roles the colonizers assigned them. But when the indigenous population rebelled against the invaders, something it did with great frequency, English condescension turned to violence. The brutality of Sir Humphrey Gilbert in Ireland resembled that of the more unsavory Spanish conquistadores. Gilbert wrote treatises on geography, explored the coast of North America, and entertained Queen Elizabeth with witty conversation. But as a colonizer in a strange land—in what some historians now call England's "permissive frontier"—he became a military autocrat. In 1569, he was appointed military governor of Munster, and when the Irish in his district rose up, he executed everyone he could catch, "mane, woman and childe."

The Irish experiments served as models for English colonies in the New World. Indeed, one modern Irish scholar argues that "English colonization in Virginia was a logical continuation of the Elizabethan conquest of Ireland." Indeed, Gilbert himself projected a detailed scheme to colonize Newfoundland but was lost at sea in 1583 while attempting to carry it out. English adventurers to the New World commonly compared Native Americans with the "wild" Irish, a kind of ethnocentric shorthand that equated all alien races. This mental process was a central element in the transfer of English culture to America. The English, like the Spanish before them, did not perceive America in objective terms. Instead, they saw an America they had already constructed in their imaginations, and the people and objects that greeted them on the other side of the Atlantic were forced into Old World categories. Preconceived notions about strangers hardened into stereotypes, hurtful images that have sometimes survived into our own modern age.

2.4.4: Raleigh and Roanoke

Like Spain's French and Dutch challengers, English adventurers regarded it most practical to found a permanent American beachhead sufficiently distant from Spanish settlements to remain undetected but near enough to prey on Spanish galleons. To Sir Walter Raleigh, the coast of North Carolina seemed a likely spot. In 1584, he obtained from Queen Elizabeth a grant for the region and dispatched two English captains to search out a likely site for a settlement. The men returned with glowing reports aimed at opening the pockets of financial backers. "The soile," declared Captain Arthur Barlowe, "is the most plentifull, sweete, fruitfull, and wholesome of all the world."

Raleigh diplomatically renamed this marvelous region Virginia, in honor of his patron, the Virgin Queen. Indeed, one should note the highly gendered vocabulary that figured prominently in the European contest for Atlantic empire. As historian Kathleen M. Brown explains, "Associations of the land with virgin innocence reinforced the notion that Virginia had been saved from the Spaniard's lust to be conquered by the chaste English." Elizabeth encouraged Raleigh in private conversation but rejected his persistent requests for money. With rumors of war in the air, she did not want to alienate Philip II unnecessarily by sponsoring a colony on land long ago claimed by Spain.

Raleigh finally raised the funds for his adventure, but his enterprise seemed ill-fated from the start. Despite careful planning, everything went wrong. The settlement was poorly situated. Located inside the Outer Banks—perhaps to avoid detection by the Spanish—the Roanoke colony proved extremely difficult to reach. Even experienced navigators feared the treacherous currents and storms off Cape Hatteras. Sir Richard Grenville, the leader of the expedition, added to the colonists' troubles by destroying an entire Indian village in retaliation for the suspected theft of a silver cup, an often repeated scenario—then and now—in which authorities made a pathetic show of force in the name of principle only to create a far worse disaster.

Grenville hurried back to England in the autumn of 1585, leaving the colonists to fend for themselves. Although they coped quite well, a peculiar series of accidents transformed Raleigh's settlement into a ghost town. In the spring of 1586, Sir Francis Drake was returning from a Caribbean voyage and decided to visit Roanoke. The colonists, tired of waiting for an overdue shipment of supplies, climbed aboard Drake's ships and went home.

In 1587, Raleigh launched a second colony. This time he placed in charge John White, a veteran administrator and talented artist, who a few years earlier had produced a magnificent sketchbook of the Algonquian Indians who lived near Roanoke. For modern anthropologists, White's drawings remain a key source about early Native American culture. Once again, Raleigh's luck turned sour. The Spanish Armada severed communication between England and America. Every available English vessel was pressed into military service, and between 1587 and 1590, no ship visited the Roanoke colonists. When rescuers eventually reached the island, they found the village deserted. The fate of the "lost" colonists remains a mystery to this day. The best guess is that they were absorbed by neighboring groups of natives, some from as far away as the James River in Virginia.

2.4.5: Selling a Transatlantic Empire

Had it not been for Richard Hakluyt, the Younger, who publicized the Sea Dogs' Atlantic adventures, the dream of American colonization might have died in England. After all, North Carolina yielded no gold. Hakluyt, a supremely industrious man, never saw America. Nevertheless, his vision of the New World powerfully shaped English public opinion. He interviewed captains and sailors upon their return from distant voyages and carefully collected their stories in a massive book titled *The Principal Navigations, Voyages, and Discoveries of the English Nation* (1589). The work's strength lay in the fact that it seemed a straightforward description of what these sailors had seen across the sea. In reality, Hakluyt edited each piece so it would drive home the book's central point: England's freedom and prosperity depended on America. So did that of American Indians, who languished everywhere under the Spaniard's cruel yoke. In Hakluyt's America, there would be no losers.

The Indians would bask in light of Protestant Christianity, and English colonists would live by simply plucking fruit from the trees. "The earth bringeth fourth all things in aboundance, as in the first creations without toil or labour," he wrote of Virginia. Hakluyt's blend of piety, patriotism, and self-interest proved immensely popular, as evidenced by the frequent reprinting of his *Voyages*.

2.5: A Brave New World

2.5 **Examine the continuous human suffering and ecological disaster of the 17th century**

By the opening of the seventeenth century, the principal European contenders for New World wealth had created an Atlantic system of commerce, colonization, and plunder. The united kingdoms of Spain and Portugal still controlled the core of this vast oceangoing network, but their hold was beginning to slip under increasing pressure from French, Dutch, and English challengers. Iberian influence declined steadily in the following decades, transforming the Atlantic into a field of open competition as rival nations raced to capture trade and develop new American enterprises that could enrich European coffers and enhance national glory.

Yet the Atlantic World emerged through cooperation in addition to conflict, as colonists and seafarers of rival powers discovered ways to profit from overlapping interests. Spanish colonists benefited from northern European smugglers who skirted Spain's stifling navigation laws to bring desired goods at better prices. Portuguese, French, and English colonists eventually came to depend on Dutch vessels to carry their plantation goods to European markets. Spanish doubloons and "pieces of eight" circulated throughout the New World, lubricating the wheels of commerce in British, French, and Dutch as well as Latin America. This cooperation helped to make the Atlantic basin a place of great opportunity for those resourceful and lucky enough to become winners in the scramble for fortune. Yet most of those caught in its vast swirl—European as well as African and Native American—experienced the seventeenth-century Atlantic World as a place of continuous human suffering and ecological disaster.

Chronology

1530	Portuguese begin exporting dye wood from Brazil
1545	Potosí (Peru) silver mining begins
1546	Zacatecas (Mexico) silver mining begins
1550	Portuguese begin planting sugar in Brazil
1558	Ascension of Elizabeth I consolidates English Protestantism
1562	Captain John Hawkins captures 300 slaves from Portuguese
1564	Spanish burn newly-established French settlement at Charlesport in South Carolina
1573	Sir Francis Drake captures Spanish gold at Panama
1579	Dutch proclaim independence from Spain
1585	First Roanoke settlement established on the coast of South Carolina
1588	Spanish Armada defeated by the English
1602	Dutch United East India Company established
1608	Samuel de Champlain founds city of Quebec
1614	New Netherland Company established to license Hudson River traders
1624	Founding of New Amsterdam and Fort Orange (Albany) on the Hudson

Part II

The Contest for Seventeenth-Century Settlement

In 1584, Richard Hakluyt presented to Queen Elizabeth I his *Discourse on Western Planting*, a work urging "her Majestie . . . to take a hande in the westerne voyadge and plantinge" of "Norumbega." English maps of the period located this fabled land of wealth and natural resources near present-day New York and New England. Hakluyt argued that by planting a colony in Norumbega, the English could gain multiple advantages against their rivals. Such a colony would "staye the spanish kinge from flowinge over all the face of . . . America." It would generate new markets for English woolen goods. It would stimulate production of a "new navie of mightie new stronge shippes" for trade, defense, and conquest. A North American colony would allow English Protestants to "plant sincere religion" and provide a haven for Protestant refugees "from all partes of the worlde that are forced to flee for the truth of gods word." It would offer asylum to the native slaves of Spanish "pride and tyranie." And it would provide a second chance for English victims of poverty and debt. In short, Norumbega "offered the remedie" for a wide range of English economic, political, and military ills.

Hindsight makes Hakluyt's words sound prophetic to present-day readers, but they must have struck many of his contemporaries as crackbrained dreams. In a world seemingly dominated by Iberian gold and military might, risky colonization schemes threatened to divert scarce resources and manpower from the important tasks of securing a Protestant England against the forces of Catholic Europe.

Early colonial ventures only confirmed the difficulty of establishing even the most tenuous English presence overseas. Sir Walter Raleigh's Roanoke venture disappeared with scarcely a trace during the 1580s, while the ships that might have saved it were occupied instead with repelling Spain's "Invincible Armada" from the English coast. Colonists perished by the thousands during Virginia's early decades through their own folly in alienating potential native allies and in underestimating the arduous demands of establishing a viable settlement. Well into the last third of the century, English, Dutch, and French remained locked in an uncertain struggle for influence with the Iroquois League and control of territory in the American Northeast.

Only by recovering this sense of precarious contingency can we begin to understand a seventeenth-century world created through the vicious conflict, unexpected alliance, resourceful adaptation, and amazing resilience of its varied native and colonizing peoples. The nascent English Atlantic empire of the 1690s, far from a straightforward outcome of Richard Hakluyt's dream of colonizing "Norumbega," emerged through a contest whose outcome remained uncertain well into the eighteenth century.

Chapter 3

Winners and Losers on the Tobacco Coast, 1607–1660

 ## Learning Objectives

3.1 Describe the Powhatan way of life in the 1600s

3.2 Evaluate the result of anti- Catholism

3.3 Recall Maryland's rise to power as a Catholic stronghold

3.4 Report the hardships faced by the European planters who settled in Chesapeake

3.5 Review the model of cooperation between the natives and the settlers

3.6 Identify the deterioration in the quality of life that the planters faced

George Yeardley succeeded in Virginia beyond his wildest dreams. He was clever and ambitious, lucky and self-absorbed. Indeed, after only a few years in the New World, Yeardley amassed an impressive fortune and gained the governorship. In 1617, Yeardley returned to London, an obscure soldier who had taken a chance on Virginia and become a celebrity. During his visit, Yeardley spent a huge amount of money in an ostentatious show of wealth. His display commanded enough public acclaim to win him a knighthood from the king. Sir George, as he was now called, strutted the streets of London, followed by fourteen or fifteen fawning servants.

Yeardley's braggadocio masked the sorry state of Virginia. From the moment English adventurers had first sailed up the James River almost everything had gone wrong. During the so-called Starving Time of 1609–1610, the colony's population had dropped from over five hundred to about sixty within a few months. Despite massive assistance from England, the colonists seemed incapable of producing enough grain to feed themselves. They certainly made no progress in paying back English investors who had purchased shares of stock in the Virginia Company. Disease killed thousands. So too did local Indians who had been provoked by English intruders into almost perpetual hostilities. By 1618, Virginia appeared an experiment gone sour.

And yet, through it all Yeardley prospered. He and a few fellow adventurers figured out how to line their pockets, even though their callous greed brought death to ordinary migrants and bankruptcy to English investors. Theirs was an extraordinary tale, one repeated many times in Virginia and Maryland—indeed, throughout the New World. As governor, Yeardley persuaded the London officers of the Virginia Company to give him over 3,000 acres of prime land as well as one hundred servants. He looked out for himself. During his term of office, 3,570 colonists poured into Jamestown—ordinary men and women dreaming of a better life—but within a few years almost three thousand of these people had needlessly perished, victims of gross mismanagement. Their misfortune hardly affected Yeardley. The company sent him thirty new servants to replace those who had died. His self-serving policies invited massive Indian attack, and, in 1622, the local Native Americans killed another 347 colonists. The stench of corruption finally reached the king. In 1624, he revoked the company's charter. And still, Yeardley turned a profit. By the time of his death in 1627, he owned a huge estate that he successfully passed on to his wife and children.

In the scramble for wealth, Sir George knew how to be "a right worthie statesman, for his owne profit." In fact, as one historian observed, Virginians did not develop a meaningful sense of community, since everyone was so busy "looking out for number one." In this world, Yeardley was a winner. But for every Yeardley, thousands of cruelly disappointed settlers faced death and oppression. In their ignominy, they may have been more fortunate than those other losers, Indians and the Africans whose lives were forever transformed by the returns from a "stinking weed" known as tobacco.

3.1: A Native American Empire

3.1 Describe the Powhatan way of life in the 1600s

The Chesapeake Bay region for which English colonists set sail in December 1606 was firmly in control of the Powhatan chiefdom, one of coastal North America's most powerful Algonquian-speaking peoples. Early colonial writers reported that the Powhatan tribes had moved into the region some three hundred years before the Jamestown settlers, but archaeological evidence suggests that people with a similar culture had been living in the region much longer. Sometime during the early years of Elizabeth I's reign, an enterprising leader named Wahunsaunacock inherited authority over six Chesapeake tribes. He ruled as Powhatan, or paramount chief, until 1618. A capable and aggressive leader Powhatan expanded his rule throughout the Chesapeake region. By 1600, he controlled a loose association of some thirty tribes that may well have constituted the largest Native American empire east of the Mississippi River. Powhatan's influence extended over a region he called Tsenacommacah, probably meaning "densely inhabited territory." The core of Tsenacommacah included the coastal plain between the James and Mattaponi Rivers, while the fringes of Powhatan's influence extended across the bay to Virginia's Eastern Shore and as far north as the Potomac River. Powhatan governed a population of around 14,000 people, of whom 3,200 were warriors.

Powhatan's inherited authority and military conquests made him overlord to a cluster of lesser tribal chiefs called werowances. Werowances inherited rule from the mother's line. Inheritance passed first to the brothers of the chief who had died and then to his eldest sister and her sons. Some werowances such as Wowinchopunck, the chief of the Paspahegh tribe of the lower James River, had been born or elevated to power within their own tribes but acknowledged Powhatan's dominion in exchange for peace and security. Other werowances were Powhatan's own kinsmen. The Pamunkey chief Opechancanough, for example, was either brother or cousin to Powhatan and eventually assumed the paramount chief's mantle of leadership, while the werowance of the Kecoughtan tribe at the mouth of the James River was one of Powhatan's sons. Each of

Powhatan's werowances held sway over lesser werowances who owed them allegiance, tribute, and obedience.

Werowances enjoyed great advantages in Powhatan society. In theory, anyone could achieve status and wealth by great deeds in war or shrewd dealings in trade. The werowances' status, however, was assured by the tribute in corn, game, trade goods, and labor they received to support their families. Werowances usually held trade monopolies and channeled the profits to their own families. Powhatan himself, for example, held a monopoly on copper goods, which before Europeans arrived were available only from Native American trading partners far inland. Women could wield authority as *werowansquas* equal or even superior to their male counterparts. Ruling families regulated social mobility, rewarding achievement with wealth and status. Werowances shared power with advisers (*cockarouses, cronoccoes*) and priests (*quiyoughcosucks*), all of whom were men and enjoyed membership among Powhatan ruling families.

Like other Eastern Woodlands peoples, the tribes of the Powhatan chiefdom based their economy on a mixture of hunting and agriculture centering on the production of corn. The people lived in riverfront villages of semipermanent dwellings during the summer months, fishing and cultivating fields planted simultaneously with corn, beans, and squash. A portion of the cultivated crops went to Powhatan in tribute, but people paid no taxes on certain edible plants and herbs gathered from the wild such as tuber-producing tuckahoe. The Powhatans' mixed agriculture kept nutrients in the soil from depleting as quickly as they would have with a single crop. When a field became less productive, the cultivators moved to a new one that the men of the village cleared by girdling the trees and burning off the brush.

Women controlled agricultural production, giving them significant economic power and occupying their days with a variety of tasks. In the autumn, the men hunted as the communities prepared to disperse into small parties for the winter to reduce competition for foraging. Hunts were communal operations in which groups of men worked to surround game within a particular area and then set fire to the brush and shoot the animals as they ran from hiding to escape the flames. Later European colonists adopted this practice to supplement their own diets.

Maize cultivation formed the basis of wealth among Powhatan ruling families. Powhatan prized maize above all other commodities. His subjects cultivated the paramount chief's maize in special fields set aside for the purpose, while subordinate tribes paid much of their annual tribute in maize. Powhatan and his werowances stored their maize in raised scaffolds or "treasure houses" along with quantities of dried meat, fish, and oysters. These stored surpluses became valuable trade commodities for products of inland tribes and indirectly for European goods from Spanish Florida. Maize and other food products were never mere economic goods, however; when exchanged they also held profound social significance that bound the giver and receiver together in a relationship of mutual obligation. When the English arrived in the Chesapeake, the Powhatan wealth in agricultural commodities gave the great chief a powerful initial advantage in trade and diplomacy.

The Powhatan tribes gained firsthand experience of European ways when in 1560 a Spanish expedition kidnapped the son of a chief in the Chesapeake Bay area and carried him to Havana to learn Spanish and Christianity. There he received the Spanish name Don Luis de Velasco. He traveled to Spain, where he was presented to King Philip II and received instruction at the royal court. In 1570, Don Luis returned to the Chesapeake with several Jesuit missionaries who hoped to establish a permanent presence in the region and convert the local tribes to Roman Catholicism. Instead, Don Luis returned to his father's people and led a war party that wiped out the Jesuit mission in 1571. The Spanish partially avenged the Jesuits' martyrdom later that year in a punitive raid that claimed the lives of thirty Powhatan, but they did not make another attempt to settle the Chesapeake.

This episode of Spanish contact in the Chesapeake may have contributed in at least two ways to Powhatan's position of strength in subsequent dealings with the English. In the first place, a wave of epidemic disease that accompanied Spanish contact may have weakened many tribes' ability to resist Powhatan's efforts to consolidate power in the Chesapeake. When the English arrived in 1607, however, the Powhatan population had rebounded. The Powhatan continued to outnumber the English until the 1630s. The history of contact with the Spanish, and possibly with English survivors of Roanoke (see Chapter 2), may also have given Powhatan some knowledge of European cultures. He grasped very quickly the distinction between the English and the Spanish and exploited differences for his own advantage.

3.2: The ILL-Planned Settlement at Jamestown

3.2   Evaluate the result of anti- Catholism

After the Roanoke debacle in 1590, English interest in American settlement declined, and only a few propagandists such as Richard Hakluyt kept alive the dream of English colonies in the New World. These advocates argued that the North American mainland contained resources of incalculable value. An innovative group, they insisted, might reap great profits while supplying England with items that it would otherwise be forced to purchase from European rivals: Holland, France, and Spain.

Moreover, any English enterprise that annoyed Catholic Spain or revealed its weakness in America seemed a desirable end in itself to patriotic English Protestants. Anti-Catholicism and hatred of Spain became an integral part of English national identity during this period, and unless one appreciates just how deeply these sentiments ran in the English popular mind, one cannot fully understand why ordinary people who had no direct stake in the New World so generously supported English efforts to colonize America. Soon after James I ascended to the throne in 1603, adventurers were given an opportunity to put their theories into practice in the colonies of Virginia and Maryland, an area known as the Chesapeake.

3.2.1: Dreamers and Schemers: The Virginia Project

During Elizabeth's reign, the major obstacle to successful colonization of the New World had been raising capital. No single person, no matter how rich or well connected, could underwrite the vast expenses a New World settlement required. And the English government had no interest in footing the bill. The solution to this financial problem was the "joint-stock company," a new business organization in which scores of people could participate in a major project. A merchant or landowner could purchase a share of stock at a stated price, and at the end of several years the investor could anticipate recovering the initial amount plus a portion of whatever profits the company had made. Joint-stock ventures sprang up like mushrooms. Affluent English citizens, and even some of more modest incomes, rushed to invest. As a result, some projects were amassed large amounts of capital, enough certainly to launch a new colony in Virginia.

On April 10, 1606, James issued the first Virginia charter. This document authorized the London Company to establish plantations in Virginia. The London Company was an ambitious business venture. Its leader, Sir Thomas Smith, was reputedly London's wealthiest merchant. Smith and his partners gained possession of the territory lying between Cape Fear and the Hudson River. These generous but vague boundaries reflected ignorance about the details of American geography.

The Virginia Company—as the London Company soon called itself—set out immediately to find the natural resources Hakluyt had promised.

In December 1606, the *Susan Constant*, the *Godspeed*, and the *Discovery* sailed for America. The ships carried 104 men and boys who had been instructed to establish a fortified outpost some hundred miles up a large navigable river. The natural beauty and economic potential of the region was apparent to everyone. A voyager on this expedition reported seeing "faire meaddowes and goodly tall trees, with such fresh waters running through the woods, as almost ravished [us] at first sight."

The leaders of the colony selected—without consulting resident Powhatans—what the Europeans considered a promising location more than 30 miles from the mouth of the James River. A marshy peninsula jutting out into the river became the site for one of America's most unsuccessful villages, Jamestown. Modern historians have criticized this choice, for the low-lying ground proved to be a disease-ridden death trap; even the drinking water was contaminated with salt. But the first Virginians were neither stupid nor suicidal. Jamestown seemed the ideal place to build a fort, since surprise attack by the Spaniards rather than sickness appeared the more serious threat in the early months of settlement.

Early contacts with Powhatan tribes gave the settlers additional reason for apprehension, although not because native inhabitants seemed inherently hostile. Mistaken cultural assumptions on the part of both groups led to missteps which prompted each to remain wary of the other. Nearby tribes, for example, found it impossible to understand the English disregard for the social dimensions of gift-giving and exchange, while the English misunderstood the native conceptions of land use. A series of misadventures resulted as the English traveled up the James River during the first few weeks after their arrival, making contact with subordinate tribes and asking pointed questions about the region and its resources. On May 26, only thirteen days after the founding of Jamestown, a large force of warriors representing four Powhatan tribes attacked the settlement while Captain Christopher Newport was away exploring and laying claim to Powhatan territory further up the James. Powhatan observed from a distance as raids and sniping continued over the next three weeks. Finally, on June 15, the paramount chief himself intervened to restore peace and establish trade relations.

Almost immediately, greed and self-interest divided the Jamestown colonists in ways that gave the more unified Powhatans an enormous early advantage in trade and diplomacy. The adventurers were not prepared for the challenges that confronted them in America. Some men may have been depressed by conditions in Virginia; others may have assumed that lower-class people performed physical labor. But part of the problem was surely cultural.

Most colonists had grown up in a depressed agricultural economy that could not provide full-time employment for all who wanted it. In England, laborers shared what little work was available. One man, for example, might perform a certain chore while others simply watched. Later, the men who had been idle were given an opportunity to work for an hour or two. This labor system may have been appropriate for England, but in Virginia it nearly destroyed the colony. Adventurers sat around Jamestown while other men performed crucial agricultural tasks. It made little sense, of course, to share work in an environment where people were starving because too little labor was expended on the planting and harvesting of crops. Some modern historians branded the early Virginians as lazy, irresponsible beings who preferred to play while others labored. In fact, however, these first settlers were attempting to replicate a traditional work experience.

Avarice exacerbated these problems. The adventurers had traveled to the New World in search of the sort of instant wealth they imagined the Spaniards to have found in Mexico and

Peru. Tales of rubies and diamonds lying on the beach probably inflated their expectations. Even when it must have been apparent that these expectations were unfounded, the first settlers often behaved in Virginia as if they fully expected to become rich. Instead of cooperating for the common good—guarding or farming, for example—individuals pursued personal interests. They searched for gold when they might have helped plant maize. No one was willing to take orders, and those who were supposed to govern the colony looked after their private welfare while disease, war, and starvation ravaged the settlement.

The unified Powhatans capitalized on the colonists' self-interest and factionalism. The Jamestown settlers' reluctance to plant maize resulted in chronic food shortages that made Powhatan maize extremely valuable. When colonial leaders attempted to impose price controls on maize, colonists simply ignored them by paying their Indian neighbors as much as four times the official price. Colonists pilfered from each other and from common stores to obtain the goods needed for barter, exacerbating disunity within the colony. Jamestown's leadership changed hands three times in the first eighteen months, placing each new leader at a disadvantage in dealing with the stable leadership of Powhatan and his werowances. Indeed, members of the Jamestown council vied for Powhatan's favor and sought to undercut each other by offering the great chief gifts and trade concessions more generous than their rivals'.

3.2.2: Captain John Smith: Saving the Colonists from Greed

Virginia might have gone the way of Roanoke had it not been for Captain John Smith. By any standard, he was a resourceful man. Before coming to Jamestown, he had traveled throughout Europe and fought with the Hungarian army against the Turks—and, if Smith is to be believed, he was saved repeatedly from certain death by various beautiful women. Because of his reputation for boasting, historians have discounted Smith's account of his experience in early Virginia. Recent scholarship, however, has affirmed the essential truthfulness of his curious story. In Virginia, Smith brought order out of anarchy.

While members of the council in Jamestown debated petty politics, Smith negotiated with the local Indians for food and mapped the Chesapeake Bay as the colony's "cape merchant" in charge of trade. During the fall and winter of 1607, his efforts kept the colonists alive. At one point, Smith was taken captive by Powhatan's kinsman Opechancanough. The experience gave Smith the opportunity to observe Powhatan culture closely as Opechancanough escorted him through the central region of the empire. Smith eventually met Powhatan face to face in a series of ritual encounters and feasting

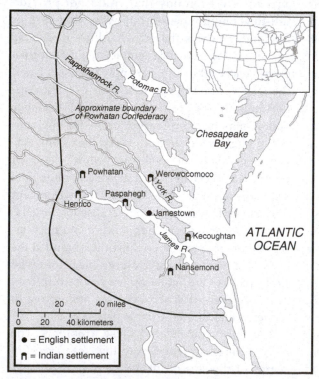

Map 3.1 Powhattan's Chesapeake Bay

lasting over three days. Historians still debate the truth of Smith's claim that he was in danger of execution during this encounter or that Powhatan's 12-year-old daughter, Pocahontas, rescued him. Those who accept the account regard Pocahontas's action as part of an elaborate ritual by which Powhatan adopted Smith and the English into his chiefdom. In the end, Smith did promise that the English would become Powhatan's vassals in exchange for sustenance throughout the winter.

Smith's pragmatic promise helped the English survive the winter of 1608–1609. The next fall, however, he joined Captain Christopher Newport in an attempt to turn the tables by conducting a coronation ceremony to make Powhatan a vassal of King James. Powhatan recognized what the English were attempting. He accepted his coronation Crown but refused submission to a foreign ruler.

Through encounters such as these, Powhatan and John Smith took each other's measure, developing increasingly sophisticated understandings of one another's cultural assumptions, political aims, and terms of exchange. In his later accounts of these years, Smith declared that the Spanish had the right idea in forcing "the treacherous and rebellious Infidels to doe all manner of drudgery worke and slavery for them, themselves living like Souldiers upon the fruits of their labours." He did not hesitate to browbeat or coerce Powhatan tribes into trading their maize when negotiation failed. Yet even with firearms, Smith's contingent of a few hundred colonists posed no serious threat to Powhatan's three thousand–man force in the early years. The colony's survival depended far more on negotiation than on English military might.

In addition to his dealings with the Powhatans, Smith moved to impose order on the colony itself. In the fall of 1608, he seized control of the ruling council and instituted a tough military discipline. Convinced that colonists would "starve and eat one another" if the council's indulgent policies continued, Smith organized the settlers into work gangs and marched them out to labor in the maize fields. Under Smith, no one enjoyed special privilege. He warned colonists that "every one that gathereth not every day as much as I doe, the next daie shall be set beyond the river, and for ever be banished from the fort, and live there or starve." To prevent a mass exodus from Jamestown to the surrounding tribal villages, he persuaded neighboring werowances to enforce the same discipline on any runaway settlers they found. Individuals whom he forced to work came to hate him. But he managed to keep them alive, no small achievement in such a deadly environment.

Leaders of the Virginia Company in London recognized the need to reform the entire enterprise. After all, they had spent considerable sums and had received nothing in return. In 1609, the company directors obtained a new charter from the king, which completely reorganized the Virginia government. Henceforth all commercial and political decisions affecting the colonists rested with the company, who ruled directly through the governor. The company stripped the colonial council of any other than a strictly advisory role and gave the governor absolute civil and military power. Moreover, in an effort to raise scarce capital, the original partners opened the "joint stock" to the general public. For a little more than £12—approximately one year's wages for an unskilled English laborer—a person or group of persons could purchase a stake in Virginia. Company officials anticipated that in 1616 the profits from the colony would be distributed among the shareholders. The company sponsored a publicity campaign; pamphlets and sermons extolled the colony's potential and exhorted patriotic English citizens to invest.

This burst of energy came to nothing. Bad luck, poor planning, and ongoing conflict with Powhatan plagued the Virginia Company. A vessel carrying additional settlers and supplies went aground in Bermuda, and while this misadventure did little to help the people at Jamestown, it provided Shakespeare with the idea for *The Tempest*. The new governor, Lord De La Warr, added to the confusion by postponing his departure for America. To make matters worse, English-Powhatan relations soured in the summer of 1609. Powhatan refused to trade any more maize to the colonists and ordered his subordinates to put Captain John Smith to death. Smith retaliated, using armed intimidation to extort tribal maize, surviving at least one attempt to poison him in the process. In the fall of 1609, the indomitable captain suffered a gunpowder accident that forced him to return to England.

Between 1609 and 1611, the remaining Virginia settlers suffered from lack of capable leadership. A poor harvest in the fall of 1609 combined with the cessation of the maize trade resulted in a severe food shortage. The terrible winter of 1609–1610 became known as the "Starving Time." A few desperate settlers engaged in cannibalism, an ironic behavior because Europeans had assumed that only savages would eat human flesh. In England, Smith heard that one colonist had killed his wife, powdered [salted] her, and "had eaten part of her before it was known; for which he was executed." A team of archaeologists recently recovered the woman's body after four hundred years. The captain, who possessed a curious sense of humor, observed, "Now, whether she was better roasted, broiled, or carbonadoed, I know not, but such a dish as powdered wife I never heard of." Other people simply lost the will to live.

In June 1610, the surviving settlers decided to abandon Virginia. Through a stroke of luck, however, they encountered De La Warr just as they commenced their voyage down the James River. The new governor and the deputy governors who succeeded him, Sir Thomas Dale and Sir Thomas Gates, veterans of England's wars against the Spanish, ruled by the mostly martial *Lawes Divine, Morall and Martial*. The new colonists, many of them male and female servants employed by the company, were marched to work by the beat of a drum. Gates and Dale also moved to expand English settlement in the region and to bring neighboring tribal peoples under English rule by military force. Guerrilla raids between colonists and Powhatan tribes became increasingly vicious. Such methods saved the colony but could not make it flourish. In 1616, company shareholders received no profits. Their only reward was the right to a piece of unsurveyed land located 3,000 miles from London.

3.3.3: The Tobacco Road to Riches and Slavery

The solution to Virginia's economic problems grew in the vacant lots of Jamestown. Only the Powhatan tribes bothered to cultivate tobacco in the Chesapeake until John Rolfe, a settler who arrived in 1610, realized this local weed might be a valuable export. Rolfe experimented with the crop, eventually growing in Virginia a milder variety that had been developed in the West Indies and was more appealing to European smokers.

Virginians suddenly possessed a means to make money. Tobacco proved relatively easy to grow, and settlers who had avoided work now threw themselves into its production with single-minded diligence. In 1617, one observer found that Jamestown's "streets and all other spare places [are] planted with tobacco . . . the Colony dispersed all about planting tobacco." Although King James I originally considered smoking immoral and unhealthy, he changed his mind when the taxes he collected on tobacco imports began to mount. He was neither the first nor the last ruler who decided a vice that generates revenue is not really so bad.

Tobacco cultivation eventually introduced a new source of tension into English-Powhatan relations as settlers spread beyond the negotiated boundaries of the colony to squat on Powhatan land. As tobacco production was first catching on, however, the marriage of John Rolfe to Pocahontas in 1614 helped briefly to foster positive diplomacy and trade. Ironically, Rolfe and Pocahontas fell in love while she was living in Jamestown as a hostage during a period historians have called "the first Powhatan war" (1610–1613). Pocahontas apparently entered English society and marriage willingly, however. In 1613, she converted to Christianity while living in the household of the Reverend Alexander Whitaker, submitting to baptism and taking the name "Rebecca." Two of her uncles attended the wedding on behalf of Powhatan, who regarded the ceremony an "assurance of [King James's] friendship."

The Rolfes' marriage demonstrates the possibility of English and Powhatan men and women overcoming cultural differences to form lasting unions. In fact, however, surviving records indicate that only two other couples took that road

in seventeenth-century Virginia. A few additional marriages, particularly any sealed by Powhatan authority, may have gone unrecorded, and many colonists engaged in brief sexual liaisons with Indian partners. Yet unlike the French or the Spanish, most English refused to take Indian spouses.

Pocahontas sailed to England in 1616 with Rolfe, their infant son Thomas, and a dozen other Powhatans, where she enjoyed the hospitality of leading Londoners. She died there of a respiratory illness in 1617. Her grave was destroyed during the German bombing of England in World War II. Pocahontas's conversion and marriage prompted the English to hope that other Powhatans could be won to Christian faith and English ways. The years after Pocahontas's death, however, witnessed the frustration of those hopes as changes in company policy offered even greater rewards to colonists, thus fueling the competitive drive to plant tobacco on more Powhatan lands.

In 1618, the company sponsored another aggressive effort to transform Virginia into a profitable enterprise. Sir Edwin Sandys (pronounced Sands) led a faction of stockholders that began to pump life into the dying organization by instituting a series of sweeping reforms and eventually ousting Virginia Company founder Sir Thomas Smith and his friends. Sandys wanted private investors to develop their own estates in Virginia. Before 1618, company policy had offered little incentive to do so, but by relaxing Dale's martial law and promising a representative assembly called the House of Burgesses, Sandys thought he could make the colony more attractive to wealthy speculators. Even more important was his method for distributing land. Colonists who covered their own transportation costs to America were guaranteed a "headright," a 50-acre lot for which they paid only a small annual rent. Adventurers could gain additional headrights for each servant they brought to the colony. This procedure allowed prosperous planters to build up huge estates at the same time as they acquired

This portrait of Powhatan's daughter Pocahontas was painted while visiting London in 1616 with her husband John Rolfe, an early Virginia settler who pioneered tobacco as a cash crop. Shortly before her marriage to Rolfe, she converted to Christianity and took the name of Rebeka.

dependent laborers. The headright system persisted long after the company's collapse. So too did the notion that the wealth of a few justified the exploitation of many others.

Sandys had only just begun. He also urged the settlers to diversify their economy. Tobacco alone, he argued, was not a sufficient base. He envisioned colonists busily producing iron and tar, silk and glass, sugar and cotton. There was no end to his suggestions. He scoured Europe for skilled artisans and exotic plant cuttings. To finance such a huge project, Sandys relied on a lottery, a game of chance that promised a continuous flow of capital into the company's treasury. The final element in the grand scheme was people. Sandys sent new English settlers by the thousand to Jamestown, men and women swept up by the same hopes that had carried the colonists of 1607 to the New World.

3.3.4: Deadly Harvest

Between 1619 and 1622, colonists arrived in Virginia in ever-larger waves. Company records reveal that during this period, 3,570 individuals embarked for the colony. These people seldom moved to Virginia in families. Although the first women arrived in Jamestown in 1608, most emigrants were single males in their teens or early twenties who came to the New World as indentured servants. In exchange for transportation across the Atlantic, they agreed to serve a master for a stated number of years. The length of service depended in part on the age of the servant. The younger the servant, the longer he or she served. In return, the master promised to give the laborers proper care and, at the conclusion of their contracts, to provide them with tools and clothes according to "the custom of the country." And the master, not the servant, received the headright for 50 more acres of tobacco land.

Whenever possible, planters in Virginia purchased able-bodied workers, in other words, persons capable of performing hard agricultural labor. This preference dramatically skewed the colony's sex ratio. In the early decades, men outnumbered women by as much as six to one. As one historian, Edmund S. Morgan, observed, "Women were scarcer than maize or liquor in Virginia and fetched a higher price." Such gender imbalance meant that even if a male servant lived to the end of his indenture—an unlikely prospect—he could not realistically expect to start a family. Moreover, despite apparent legal safeguards, masters could treat dependent workers as they pleased; after all, these people were legally considered property. Servants were sold, traded, or even gambled away in hands of cards. It does not require much imagination to see that a society that tolerated such an exploitative labor system might later embrace slavery.

Most Virginians did not live long enough to worry about marriage. Death was omnipresent in this society. Indeed, extraordinarily high mortality was a major reason the Chesapeake colonies developed so differently from those of New England (see Chapter 4). On the eve of the 1618 reforms, Virginia's population stood at approximately seven hundred. The company sent at least 3,000 more people, but by 1622 only 1,240 were still alive. "It Consequentilie followes," declared one angry shareholder, "that we had then lost 3,000 persons within those 3 yeares." The major killers were contagious diseases. Salt in the water supply also took a toll.

Conflict with the Powhatans exacerbated the insecurity of life in early Virginia. Between 1618 and 1622, colonists seized more and more Powhatan land to plant tobacco. Powhatan had passed the government of his kingdom to his kinsmen Opechancanough and Itoyatan. Opechancanough soon attained the paramount chiefdom. The new ruler grew increasingly concerned as the spread of English settlement threatened his control of the Chesapeake. On Good Friday, March 22, 1622, Opechancanough launched a well-coordinated surprise attack that claimed the lives of 347 Europeans. Most victims inhabited outlying settlements, while Jamestown itself escaped completely. One historian has recently argued that Opechancanough intended not to exterminate the English, but to drive them back into previously accepted boundaries where the Powhatans could control them more easily while continuing to benefit from English trade. Whatever Opechancanough planned, the English interpreted the attack as an effort to drive them out of the Chesapeake. Company officials retaliated with a counteroffensive to exterminate the Powhatans, ushering in a "policy of perpetual enmity" that took a horrendous toll on the tribes throughout the following decade.

No one knows for certain what impact such a mortality rate had on the Europeans who survived. At the very least, it must have exacerbated a sense of impermanence, a desire to escape Virginia with a little money before sickness or Indians ended the adventure. The settlers who drank to excess aboard the tavern ships anchored in the James River described the colony "not as a place of Habitacion but only of a short sojourninge."

3.3.5: Reinventing Virginia

On both sides of the Atlantic, people wondered who should be blamed for the failure of early Virginia. Why had so many colonists died in such a fertile land? The burden of responsibility lay in large measure with the Virginia Company. Sandys and his supporters were in too great a hurry to make a profit. Settlers were shipped to America, but neither housing nor food awaited them in Jamestown. Weakened by the long sea voyage, they quickly succumbed to contagious disease.

Company officials in Virginia also bore a share of guilt. Colonial leaders such as George Yeardley were so eager to look out for their own interests that they ignored the common good. Various governors and their councilors grabbed up the indentured servants owned by the company and sent them to their own private plantations to cultivate tobacco. As the 1622 attack demonstrated, officials also ignored the colony's crumbling defenses. Jamestown took on the characteristics of a boomtown, like those more familiar ones in Alaska and California. Colonists shared no sense of purpose, no common ideology—except perhaps unrestrained self-advancement—to keep the society from splintering into highly individualistic, competitive fragments.

The company's scandalous mismanagement embarrassed King James. In 1624, he dissolved the bankrupt enterprise declaring Virginia a royal colony. The Crown appointed a governor and a council. No provision was made, however, for continuing the local elected assembly, an institution the Crown heartily opposed. The House of Burgesses had first convened in 1619. While elections to the Burgesses were hardly democratic, the assembly did provide wealthy planters with a voice in government. Even without the king's authorization, the representatives gathered annually after 1629, and, in 1639, King Charles I recognized the body's existence.

He had no choice. The colonists who served on the council or in the assembly were strong-willed, ambitious survivors. They had no intention of surrendering control over local affairs. Since Charles was having political troubles of his own and lived 3,000 miles from Jamestown, he usually allowed the Virginians to have their own way. In 1634, the assembly divided the colony into eight counties. In each, a group of appointed justices of the peace—the wealthy planters of the area—sat as a court of law as well as a governing body. The "county court" was the most important institution of local government in Virginia, and long after the American Revolution, it served as a center for social, political, and commercial activities.

By the mid-1620s, white society in Virginia was growing somewhat more stable if no less exploitative. The regional balance of power was also shifting against the Powhatans, who found themselves increasingly on the defensive. By the

1630s, their numbers had declined to perhaps five thousand while the colonial population was on the rise, reaching eight thousand by 1640. During the 1620s and 1630s, the General Assembly conducted a sustained offensive, authorizing at least three major military expeditions per year against the Powhatans between 1629 and 1632. As the Indians were killed, made into tributaries, or pushed north and south, Virginians took up large tracts of land along the colony's many navigable rivers.

The Powhatans put up stiff resistance to English expansion, making strategic withdrawals from some regions to avoid attack but fiercely defending crucial territories. In spite of intermittent hostilities throughout the 1630s, Powhatans also found ways to trade furs to the English for the European cloth, metal tools, and even food that they now needed to survive. In the early 1640s, however, the English began contending for control over the strategic headwaters of the York River, the Powhatans' last bastion against English encroachment into the interior. In 1644, Opechancanough sought to push the English back by masterminding a well-coordinated surprise attack in which five hundred colonists died. The English responded by conducting retaliatory raids and building forts at the falls of the James, Chickahominy, and Appomattox Rivers.

In 1646, an expeditionary force under Governor William Berkeley captured Opechancanough. The great chief, now nearly 100 years old, was "so decrepit that he was not able to walk alone . . . his eyelids so heavy that he could not see, but as they were lifted up by his servants." Yet he remained defiant, convinced of his moral superiority over his English captors. Berkeley intended to send him to England "hoping to get reputation by presenting his Majesty with a royal captive," but a resentful English soldier "basely shot" Opechancanough in the back. An observer recorded that this "ancient prince" remained "brave to the last minute of his life, and showed not the least dejection at his captivity." Opechancanough's death

marked the end of open warfare between the English and Powhatans.

3.3: Maryland: A Catholic Refuge

3.3   Recall Maryland's rise to power as a Catholic stronghold

While Virginia authorities extended their hold on the rivers of the lower Chesapeake during the summer of 1632, Charles I inflicted on the colony what the eighteenth-century planter William Byrd II described as its "deepest wound" by "cutting off MARYLAND from it" in a grant to a royal favorite, Sir George Calvert. Byrd surmised that the grant marked "one fatal Instance among many of his Majesty's complaisance to the Queen" and observed that it "provd a Commodious Retreat" for seventeenth-century Roman Catholic refugees from England. By 1700, however, the colony Calvert had hoped to make a feudal haven for persecuted Catholics became a flourishing tobacco colony remarkably similar to Virginia.

Sir George Calvert, later Lord Baltimore, was a talented and well-educated man who enjoyed the patronage of James I. The king awarded him lucrative positions in the government, the most important being the secretary of state. In 1625, Calvert shocked almost everyone by publicly declaring his Catholicism. The memory of the Gunpowder Plot of November 1605, an abortive attempt by Roman Catholic conspirators to assassinate James I, "made England too hot for Papists to live in, without danger of being burnt with the Pope, every 5th of November," as William Byrd later put it. Persons who openly supported the Church of Rome were immediately stripped of civil office. Although forced to resign as secretary of state, Calvert retained the Crown's favor.

Before resigning, Calvert sponsored a settlement on the coast of Newfoundland. After visiting the place, however, the proprietor concluded that no English person, whatever his or her religion, would transfer to a place where the "ayre [is] so intolerably cold." He turned his attention to the Chesapeake, and on June 30, 1632, Charles I granted George Calvert's son, Cecilius, a charter for a colony to be located north of Virginia. The boundaries of the settlement, named Maryland in honor of Charles's French queen Mary, were so vaguely defined that they generated legal controversies not fully resolved until the mid-eighteenth century when Charles Mason and Jeremiah Dixon surveyed their famous line between Pennsylvania and Maryland.

Cecilius, the second Lord Baltimore, not only wanted to create a sanctuary for England's persecuted Catholics, he also intended to make money. Without Protestant settlers, it seemed unlikely Maryland would prosper, and Cecilius instructed his brother Leonard, the colony's governor, to do nothing that might frighten off Protestants. The governor was ordered to "cause all Acts of the Roman Catholic Religion to be done as privately as may be and . . . [to] instruct all Roman Catholics to be silent upon all occasions of discourse concerning matters of Religion." On March 25, 1634, the *Ark and Dove*, carrying about 150 settlers, landed safely at the mouth of the Potomac River.

The first Maryland settlers encountered a more complex situation among the Native Americans of the region than the Virginians had nearly three decades before. During the sixteenth century, the Algonquian-speaking Piscataways had ruled much of the northern Chesapeake from their ancient palisaded town of Moyaone on the Potomac River. By 1600, however, a new set of challenges confronted the Piscataways. Their former empire was divided; Maryland's Eastern Shore was given to the Naticokes and the western shore and Potomac to the Piscataways. Powhatan soon wrested control of the Potomac's southern bank, while Iroquoian Nacotchtanks pressed down from the upper Potomac onto Piscataway lands. Another Iroquoian tribe, the

Susquehannocks, moved down the Susquehanna River to challenge neighboring Yoacomacos. After the founding of Jamestown, English colonists also pushed northward to trade. Virginia-Piscataway relations eventually turned hostile. Thus, when Governor Leonard Calvert requested permission from Wannas, the Piscataway *tayac* or paramount chief, to "set downe in his Countrey," Wannas rebuffed him. Calvert instead purchased an abandoned Yoacomaco village at the mouth of the Potomac that became St. Mary's City, the capital of Maryland.

Within two years of Maryland's founding, however, the Piscataways forged an alliance with the new colonial government after Wannas's brother Kittamaquund murdered him to seize leadership of the tribe. Kittamaquund needed English support to hold on to power, and the whole tribe required the additional security that a military alliance and trading partnership could provide. Maryland also needed the alliance since officials were unsure of the disposition of other tribes and could not count on the support of Virginians, who resented the encroachment of a Roman Catholic colony on land they considered their own. Governor Calvert eventually negotiated the right to select Piscataway tayacs, making the tribe a vassal of the proprietor.

The Calverts also labored to convert the Piscataways to Roman Catholic Christianity by bringing Jesuit missionaries to the colony. Kittamaquund welcomed the Jesuit Andrew White into his own household in 1639 and delighted Maryland colonists by submitting to baptism along with several other Piscataways a year later. During the next three years, they baptized another 130 Indians in villages along the Potomac before Susquehannock raids forced them to abandon the mission. Archaeological and textual evidence from the period suggests that the converts likely accepted the new faith without relinquishing their old beliefs, but the conversions nevertheless formed a significant element of an ongoing cultural exchange between the two groups.

Leonard Calvert's success in negotiating Piscataway vassalage suggests how he and his brother, the proprietor, envisioned Native Americans' place within the larger feudal order they hoped to create in Maryland. The colony's charter transformed Baltimore into a "palatine lord," a proprietor with almost royal powers. Settlers swore an oath of allegiance not to the king of England but to Lord Baltimore. In England, such practices had long ago passed into obsolescence. As the proprietor, Lord Baltimore owned outright almost 6 million acres; he possessed absolute authority over anyone living in his domain.

On paper, at least, everyone in Baltimore's Maryland was assigned a place in an elaborate social hierarchy. Members of a colonial ruling class, persons who purchased 6,000 acres from Baltimore, were styled lords of the manor. These landed aristocrats were permitted to establish local courts of law. People holding less acreage enjoyed fewer privileges, particularly in government. Baltimore figured that land sales and rents would adequately finance the entire venture.

The Calverts probably intended to fit the Piscataways into this feudal system as well. Leonard Calvert's references to the tayac Kittamaquund as his "brother" and Baltimore's "friend and servant" suggest that the governor may have regarded the tayac as one of Baltimore's lords of the manor and treaties with the tribe imposed English law on them. In other ways, however, Maryland officials dealt with the Piscataways as a tributary people. Maryland courts, for example, often left them to conduct their internal affairs "according to their owne lawes and customs" so long as no interests of English colonists were at stake.

Baltimore's feudal system never took root in Chesapeake soil. Colonists and Indians alike simply refused to play the social roles the lord proprietor had assigned. These tensions affected the operation of Maryland's government. Baltimore assumed that his brother, acting as his deputy in America, and a small appointed council of local aristocrats would pass necessary laws and carry out routine administration. When an elected assembly first convened in 1635, Baltimore allowed delegates to discuss only those acts he had prepared. The members of the assembly bridled at such restrictions, insisting on exercising traditional parliamentary privileges. Neither side gained a clear victory in the assembly, and for almost twenty-five years, legislative squabbling contributed to the widespread political instability that almost destroyed Maryland.

The colony recruited both Protestants and Catholics. The two groups might have lived in harmony had civil war not broken out in England. When Oliver Cromwell and the Puritan faction executed Charles, transforming England briefly into a Protestant republic (see Chapter 5), it seemed Baltimore might lose his colony. To head off such an event and to placate Maryland's restless Protestants, in 1649, the proprietor drafted the famous "Act concerning Religion," extending toleration to all individuals who accepted the deity of Christ. At a time when European rulers regularly persecuted people for their religious beliefs, Baltimore—like Roger Williams in Rhode Island—championed liberty of conscience.

However laudable the act may have been, it did not heal religious divisions in Maryland. When local Puritans seized the colony's government, they promptly repealed the act. For almost two decades, vigilantes roamed the countryside. During the "Plundering Time" (1644–1646), one armed group temporarily drove Leonard Calvert out of Maryland. In 1655, civil war flared again.

The Piscataways, for their part, used the Calverts' new order for their own ends. Kittamaquund's conversion, for instance, strengthened his ties with the English and made them more willing to support his hold on tribal power. Piscataway converts probably accepted Roman Catholic faith while continuing to observe traditional beliefs and practices. When the Jesuits fled colonial unrest in 1645, most converts returned to the old ways. After Kittamaquund's death, the tribe simply ignored the Maryland governor's right to appoint a successor and continued to choose their own tayacs. They also obeyed or sought protection of English law when it benefited them and ignored it when it did not. For many years Maryland's need for a native trading and military alliance gave the Piscataways significant bargaining power to retain control of their own affairs.

Tobacco cultivation in this troubled sanctuary rapidly transformed the colony into a reflection of neighboring Virginia. Ordinary planters and their workers cultivated tobacco on plantations dispersed along the Potomac riverfront. In 1678, Baltimore complained that he could not find fifty houses in a space of 30 miles. Tobacco affected almost every aspect of local culture. "In Virginia and Maryland," one Calvert explained, "Tobacco, as our Staple, is our all, and indeed leaves no room for anything Else." A steady stream of indentured servants supplied the plantations with dependent laborers—that is, until they were replaced by African slaves at the end of the seventeenth century.

3.4: The Planters' Perspective

3.4   Report the hardships faced by the European planters who settled in Chesapeake

Europeans sacrificed much by coming to the Chesapeake. For most of the century, their standard of living was primitive when compared with that of people of the same social class who had remained in England. The focus of Chesapeake colonists' existence was the isolated plantation, a small cluster of buildings housing the planter's family and dependent workers. Two-thirds of the planters lived in wooden houses of only two rooms, a design associated with the poorest classes in contemporary English society. Not until the eighteenth century did the gentry construct the great Georgian mansions that attract modern tourists. The dispersed pattern of settlement retarded the development of institutions such as schools and churches. Besides Jamestown and St. Mary's no population centers developed, and as late as 1705, Robert Beverley, a leading planter, reported that Virginia did not have a single place "that may reasonably bear the Name of a Town."

This distinctive pattern of settlement owed much to tobacco cultivation and its associated labor system as contemporaries suggested, but demographic forces also played a role. The crop exhausted the soil quickly, spurring planters to move onto fresh land after only a few years. The many Chesapeake estuaries allowed planters to fan out along the waterfront where they built their own wharves for loading heavy hogsheads. This efficient arrangement saved the cost of transporting goods overland to middlemen in harbor towns. It gave riverfront planters a competitive advantage and a tidy side business from the loading and storage fees they charged inland planters. The practice also helped to scatter the population across the countryside. Historical demographers have argued, however, that the Chesapeake's death rate constituted the most important reason for the distinctive character of these early southern plantation societies. A frighteningly high mortality tore at the very fabric of traditional family life.

3.4.1: Family Life in a Perilous Environment

Unlike New England settlers, the men and women who emigrated to the Chesapeake region seldom moved in family units. Most traveled to the New World as young unmarried servants, youths cut off from the security of traditional kin relations. Although these immigrants came from a cross section of English society, most had been poor to middling farmers. It is now estimated that 70 to 85 percent of the white colonists who went to Virginia and Maryland during the seventeenth century were not free; that is, they owed four or five years' labor in exchange for the cost of passage to America. If the servant was under age 15, he or she had to serve a full seven years. The overwhelming majority of these laborers were males between the ages of 18 and 22. In fact, before 1640, the ratio of males to females stood at 6 to 1. This figure dropped to about 2 to 1 by the end of the century, but the sex ratio in the Chesapeake was never as balanced as it had been in early Massachusetts.

Most Chesapeake immigrants died soon after arriving. It is difficult to ascertain the exact cause of death in most cases, but malaria and other diseases took a frightful toll. Recent studies also indicate that drinking water contaminated with salt killed many colonists living in low-lying areas. Throughout the entire seventeenth century, high mortality rates had a profound effect on this society. Life expectancy for Chesapeake males was about 43, some ten to twenty years less than for men born in New England. For women, life was even shorter. A full 25 percent of all children died in infancy; another 25 percent did not see their twentieth birthdays. The survivors were often weak or ill, unable to perform hard physical labor.

These demographic conditions retarded normal population increase. Young women who might have become wives and mothers could not do so until they had completed their terms of servitude. They thus lost several reproductive years, and in a society in which so many children died in infancy, late marriage greatly restricted family size. Moreover, because of the unbalanced sex ratio, many adult males simply could not find wives. Migration not only cut them off from their English families but also deprived them of an opportunity to form new ones. Without a constant flow of immigrants, the population of Virginia and Maryland would have actually declined.

High mortality compressed the family life cycle into a few short years. One partner in a marriage usually died within seven years. Only one in three Chesapeake marriages survived as long as a decade. Not only did children not meet grandparents; they often did not even know their own parents. Widows and widowers quickly remarried, bringing children by former unions into their new homes, and it was not uncommon for a child to grow up with persons to whom he or she bore no blood relation.

The psychological effects of such experiences on Chesapeake settlers cannot be measured. People probably learned to cope with a high degree of personal insecurity. However they adjusted, it is clear family life in this region was vastly more impermanent than it was in either England itself or the New England colonies during the same period.

Women were obviously in great demand in the early southern colonies, a situation made even more acute by the common English refusal to take Indian spouses. Some historians have argued that scarcity heightened the woman's bargaining power in the marriage market. If she was an immigrant, she did not have to worry about obtaining parental consent. She was on her own in the New World and free to select whomever she pleased. If a woman lacked beauty or strength, if she were a person of low moral standards, she could still be confident of finding an American husband. Such negotiations may have provided Chesapeake women with a means of improving their social status.

Nevertheless, liberation from some traditional restraints on seventeenth-century women must not be exaggerated. As servants, women were vulnerable to sexual exploitation by their masters. Moreover, in this unhealthy environment, childbearing was extremely dangerous, and women in the Chesapeake usually died twenty years earlier than their New England counterparts.

3.4.2: Rank and Status in Plantation Society

Colonists who managed somehow to survive grew tobacco—as much tobacco as they possibly could. This crop became the Chesapeake staple, much like sugar in the Caribbean or rice in the

Carolinas. Because the plant was relatively easy to cultivate, anyone with a few acres of cleared land could harvest leaves for export.

Cultivation of tobacco did not, however, produce a society roughly equal in wealth and status. To the contrary, tobacco generated striking inequality. Some planters amassed large fortunes; others barely subsisted. Labor made the difference, for to succeed in this staple economy, one had to control the labor of other men and women. More workers in the fields meant larger harvests, and, of course, larger profits. Because free persons showed no interest in growing another man's tobacco, not even for wages, wealthy planters relied on white laborers who were not free, as well as on slaves. The social structure that developed in the seventeenth-century Chesapeake reflected a wild, often unscrupulous scramble to bring men and women of three races—black, white, and Indian—into various degrees of dependence.

Great planters dominated Chesapeake society. The group was small, only a trifling portion of the population of Virginia and Maryland. During the early decades of the seventeenth century, the composition of Chesapeake gentry was continually in flux. Some gentlemen died before they could establish a secure claim to high social status; others returned to England, thankful to have survived. Not until the 1650s did the family names of those who would become famous eighteenth-century gentry appear in the records. The first gentlemen were not—as genealogists sometimes discover to their dismay—dashing cavaliers who had fought in the English Civil War for King Charles I. Rather, such Chesapeake gentry as the Burwells, Byrds, Carters, and Beverleys consisted originally of the younger sons of English merchants and artisans, in other words, ambitious men with fortunes to make.

These favored sons arrived in America with capital. They invested immediately in laborers, and one way or another, they obtained huge tracts of the best tobacco-growing land. The members of Virginia's provincial gentry were not technically aristocrats, for they did not possess titles that could be passed from generation to generation. They gave themselves military titles, sat as justices of the peace on the county courts, and directed local (Anglican) church affairs as members of the vestry. Over time, these gentry families intermarried so frequently that they created a vast network of cousins. During the eighteenth century, it was not uncommon to find a half-dozen men with the same surname sitting simultaneously in the Virginia House of Burgesses.

Freemen formed the largest class in white society. Their origins were strikingly different from those of the gentry, or for that matter, from those of New England's yeomen farmers. Chesapeake freemen traveled to the New World as indentured servants. By sheer good fortune, they managed to remain alive to the end of their contracts. If they had dreamed of becoming great planters, they were gravely disappointed. Most seventeenth-century freemen lived on the edge of poverty. Some freemen, of course, did better in America than they would have in contemporary England, but in both Virginia and Maryland, historians have found a sharp economic division separating the gentry from the rest of white society.

Below the freemen came indentured servants. Membership in this group was not demeaning; after all, servitude was a temporary status. But servitude in the Chesapeake colonies was not the benign institution it was in New England. Great planters purchased servants to grow tobacco. No one seemed overly concerned whether these laborers received decent food and clothes, much less whether they acquired trade skills. Young people, thousands of them, cut off from family ties, sick often to the point of death, unable to obtain normal sexual release, regarded their servitude as a form of slavery. Not surprisingly, the gentry worried that unhappy servants and impoverished freemen, what the planters called the "giddy multitude," would rebel at the slightest provocation, a fear that turned out to be fully justified.

The character of social mobility—and this observation applies only to the whites—changed considerably during the seventeenth century. Until the 1680s, it was relatively easy for a newcomer who possessed capital to become a member of the planter elite. No one paid much attention to the reputation or social standing of one's English family. Only toward the end of the century did a "creole majority" or indigenous ruling elite emerge as life expectancy rates improved for those who survived childhood in the Chesapeake. For the first time in the history of Virginia and Maryland, important leadership positions went to men who had actually been born in America. Where earlier immigrant leaders had died without heirs or had returned as quickly as possible to England, the members of the new creole class took a greater interest in local government. Their activities helped give the tobacco colonies the kind of political and cultural stability that had eluded earlier generations of planter-adventurers.

Opportunities for advancement also decreased for the freemen in this region. Studies of mid-seventeenth-century Maryland reveal that some servants managed to become moderately prosperous farmers and small officeholders. But as the gentry consolidated its hold on political and economic institutions, ordinary people discovered it was much harder to rise in Chesapeake society. Those men and women with more ambitious dreams headed for Pennsylvania, North Carolina, or western Virginia.

3.4.3: Race and Freedom in the Chesapeake

In 1619, the first immigrants of African descent arrived in the Chesapeake when a Dutch merchant sailed up the James to sell "20. and odd Negroes" to Virginia planters. Surviving records provide no clear indication of their status, though they may well have been slaves for life. For the next fifty years, the status of the Chesapeake's black people remained unclear. English settlers classified some black laborers as lifetime slaves, chattel to be bought and sold at the master's will. But other Africans became servants, presumably for stated periods of time, and it was even possible for a few blacks to purchase their freedom.

Early relations between blacks and whites in the Chesapeake were complex. Although colonists certainly took note of differences in skin color and based some decisions on that difference, it remained only one of several factors that shaped black-white interaction. Black and white unfree laborers worked side by side in Chesapeake tobacco fields. They shared a similarly miserable existence on most plantations and often cooperated with one another in efforts to resist poor treatment or escape their bondage. Blacks who gained their freedom also faced challenges and opportunities similar to their white counterparts. They could work for wages or purchase property and set up their own tobacco plantations. Success proved elusive for poor freemen regardless of skin color, and blacks who failed found themselves pushed to the margins of settlement along with whites, where they again had to cooperate to survive.

Several seventeenth-century Africans did beat the odds to become successful planters. Anthony and Mary Johnson, for example, managed to gain their freedom and acquire a respectable estate of 250 acres on Pungoteague Creek of Virginia's Eastern Shore. There the Johnsons supported a family of four children by cultivating tobacco and raising cattle, horses, and hogs. Anthony Johnson's operation was large enough to demand the labor of indentured servants and one black slave, Casor. It also gave him sufficient resources to help his two sons set up their own plantations on adjacent land. Johnson traded with his white neighbors and hauled them into court when they attempted to take advantage of him. He also maintained close ties with other free blacks such as his neighbors Anthony Payne and Emmanuel Driggus. As family patriarch, Johnson led his clan to Somerset County, Maryland in the 1660s, where his grandson carried the Johnson legacy of freedom into its third generation by purchasing his own plantation which he named "Angola." The plantation name, like the pattern of associations and family arrangements, suggests that the Johnsons managed to incorporate substantial elements of their African cultural heritage into their new lives in America.

The Johnsons likely enjoyed the toleration to pursue their independence in large measure because the Chesapeake's black population remained very small. By 1660, fewer than 1,500 people of African origin lived in the entire colony (compared to a white population of twenty-six thousand), and it hardly seemed necessary for the legislature to draw up an elaborate slave code to control so few men and women.

If the planters could have obtained more black laborers they certainly would have done so. There is no evidence that the great planters preferred white indentured servants to black slaves. The problem was supply. During this period, slave traders sold their cargoes on Barbados or the other sugar islands of the West Indies, where they fetched higher prices than Virginians could afford. In fact, before 1680, most blacks who reached England's colonies on the North American mainland came from Barbados or through New Netherland rather than directly from Africa. Only after the Royal Africa Company emerged as a part of a new thrust to develop the British empire (see Chapter 5) did Africans begin to supply the bulk of labor needs in the Chesapeake.

3.5: Indians and Colonists Adjust to A New Order

3.5   **Review the model of cooperation between the natives and the settlers**

The history of relations among colonists and Indians in both Maryland and Virginia reveals complex patterns of interaction rather than simple conflict and English domination. To be sure, tension and competition characterized relations throughout the seventeenth century as each maneuvered to gain advantage over the other in trade, diplomacy, and territory. Neither Powhatan nor his successors hesitated to use military force when they considered it necessary to defend their interests and keep Virginia colonists. The English likewise resorted to armed force to achieve their aims. English planters, always on the lookout for laborers, did not hesitate to enslave Indians captured in combat and put them to work in tobacco fields. Yet colonists and Indians found that they could achieve certain aims more effectively by cooperation.

During Virginia's early years colonists and Powhatans often found themselves living side by side despite the potential for conflict. On various occasions this proved disastrous for both colonists and Indians, most notably during the Powhatan attacks and colonial reprisals in 1622 and 1644. Nevertheless, the pattern persisted as tribal groups continued to live in areas overtaken by English settlement. Some English colonists, especially servants, preferred life among the Indians to the miserable conditions on tobacco plantations. In both Virginia and Maryland, runaway servants caught living among various Chesapeake tribes were punished severely with flogging, branding, and extended terms of service, but this did not always deter others from making the attempt.

Indian and colonial neighbors came to know each other by name as they engaged in a variety of relationships and cooperative ventures. Piscataway leaders in Maryland regularly enjoyed hospitality in English households when they traveled to St. Mary's on business and reciprocated when colonial officials or agents traveled in Piscataway territory. Colonial Virginians learned Powhatan ways of hunting game by traveling with them in joint hunting expeditions. Colonists throughout the Chesapeake hired their Indian neighbors to hunt for them and to kill the wolves that preyed on colonial livestock. Virginians often risked prosecution to lend guns to the Powhatans they hired to hunt for them. After 1646, the colony entered an alliance with the Powhatans and relaxed prohibitions against arming them. Individual colonists and Indians traded with one another, even in regulated or prohibited goods. Planters also tried to control their bound labor force by negotiating agreements with neighboring tribes to control the capture and return of runaways.

As the century progressed, economic and social change among Indian tribes throughout the Northeast prompted both colonists and their nearby Indian neighbors to cooperate in military ventures. Population decline among the Iroquois, for example, prompted them to engage in "mourning wars" to gain captives from neighboring tribes which they could adopt to replace lost clan members. Such actions sparked a chain reaction of conflict that reached the Chesapeake as beleaguered groups pressed into the region to escape conquest elsewhere. Overtrapping also caused clashes as the Iroquois and others ranged far from their traditional lands to find new sources of valuable furs. Chesapeake colonists and tribes benefited from mutual military support against the "new-come" Indians that posed a threat to all.

Over time, the growing English population displaced Indians throughout the Chesapeake, pushing them off ancestral lands or confining them to reservations within English territory. Contemporary observers noted how trade made tribal peoples increasingly dependent on European goods while European disease caused the "numbers of the Indians in these parts [to] decrease very much." Europeans also noticed the toll taken by the Indians "being so devilishly given to drinking." Tribal people themselves complained that they were "miserable Poor" and "reduced to a small Number." Yet historians such as James Merrell have recently argued that these "supposed signs of decline provide evidence less of cultural disintegration than of cultural persistence." Chesapeake tribes proved remarkably resourceful in resisting cultural change, and their "importance as allies and as suppliers of maize and skins enabled them to retain much of their independence and cultural integrity despite their tributary status."

3.6: Escaping the Past

3.6 Identify the deterioration in the quality of life that the planters faced

The pattern of English colonization in the Chesapeake exacted heavy costs on all inhabitants of the region. Life became much harder for the original inhabitants of the land. The ethos of looking out for number one made life hard for the English and African immigrants as well, particularly the great majority who suffered exploitation at the hands of those who came out on top of the scramble for wealth. Even the winners faced a social life in the New World that was severely diminished by Old World standards.

Social institutions associated with stable family and community life were either weak or nonexistent in the Chesapeake colonies. In part, this sluggish development resulted from the continuation of high infant mortality rates. There was little incentive to build grammar schools, for example, if half the children would die before reaching adulthood. The great planters sent their sons to England or Scotland for their education. Even after the founding of Virginia's College of William and Mary in 1693, the gentry continued to patronize English schools. As a result of this practice, higher education in the South languished for much of the colonial period.

Tobacco influenced the spread of other institutions in this region. Planters were scattered along the rivers, often separated from their nearest neighbors by miles of poor roads. Because the major tobacco growers traded directly with

English merchants, they had no need for towns. Whatever items they required were either made on the plantation or imported from Europe. Other than the centers of colonial government, Jamestown (and later Williamsburg) and St. Mary's City (and later Annapolis), there were no villages capable of sustaining a rich community life before the late eighteenth century. Seventeenth-century Virginia did not even possess a printing press. In fact, Governor Sir William Berkeley bragged in 1671, "There are no free schools, nor printing in Virginia, for learning has brought disobedience, and heresy . . . into the world, and printing had divulged them . . . God keep us from both!"

Berkeley was making a virtue of necessity, as Virginians would continue to do for the remainder of the colonial period. Colonial Chesapeake chroniclers consistently lamented the colony's woeful history from a vantage point of privilege made possible by the ruthlessly competitive system their fathers created. Still, the planters always hoped for a fresh start. The land was rich and plentiful. Virginians needed only to "rouse . . . out of their lethargy . . . and make the most out of those happy Advantages which Nature had given them."

Chronology

1600	Powhatan controls large Native American empire in the Chesapeake
1605	Exposure of Gunpowder Plot to assassinate James I
1607	Jamestown established
1610	Lord De La War averts abandonment of Jamestown after "starving time," establishes Lawes Divine, Morall and Martial
1610	John Rolfe introduces West Indian tobacco to Virginia
1613	Pocahontas weds John Rolfe
1617	Pocahontas dies in London
1618	Reforms under Sir Edwin Sandys establishes House of Burgesses
1619	First blacks arrive in Virginia
1622	Opechancanough leads surprise attack, 347 Virginia colonists die
1624	James I dissolves Virginia charter
1632	Charles I grants Maryland to Sir George Calvert
1634	First colonists arrive in Maryland
1640	Colonial population reaches 8,000
1644–46	"Plundering Time" drives Leonard Calvert from Maryland
1646	Governor William Berkeley's force captures Opechancanough

Chapter 4
Sugar, Slaves, and Profits
The English Contest for a Caribbean Empire

 ## Learning Objectives

4.1 Report how the line of amity in the Atlantic marked the end of all European treaties

4.2 Describe how the sugarcane trade drove economic growth in the seventeenth and eighteenth centuries

4.3 Evaluate the fabric of society in English West Indies

4.4 Report the shift of slave traffic to the West Indies due to its abundant sugarcane output

One evening in 1624, an aged Carib woman made her way quietly to the quarters of Captain Thomas Warner, the leader of England's new tobacco colony on the tiny Caribbean island of St. Christopher. The warriors in her village, she warned the captain, had "made their drinking." They were preparing for battle in a traditional drinking ceremony that lasted another three or four days before they attacked Warner's small band of English colonists. The old woman advised the captain that if he and his men did not want to die a gruesome death, they should quickly "gett into his Cannoes and begonn."

The English thought that this Carib woman came to Warner out of "great affecion," but the warriors may also have sent her with an advance warning that would frighten the strangers off the island before the conflict came to blows. Either way, her visit disclosed the Caribs' conclusion that these newcomers constituted an unprecedented threat to their existence on this small island. Earlier generations of English privateers had merely used this island band's homeland as a temporary staging ground for raids on the Caribs' hated Spanish foes. In contrast, Warner's group was constructing a permanent settlement. Indeed, the fort they had begun building near the Carib village alarmed the headman, who became even more suspicious when the English coyly assured him that its defenses would only serve to "looke after those fowles they had about theire houses." The drinking ceremony therefore signaled the headman's decision that the time had come to drive these intruders from his territory.

If the Caribs intended the old woman's visit to warn the English off St. Christopher (also called St. Kitts), they miscalculated badly. Warner had already led one failed expedition to colonize Guiana on the Caribbean coast of South America, and he was determined not to fail again. This tiny island in the Leeward group of the Lesser Antilles held a steady supply of fresh water and sufficient arable land on its 68 square miles for plantations and subsistence farming. It had supported the Carib population; it could support aspiring English tobacco planters equally well. Less than 300 miles from Puerto Rico, it provided ready access to the heart of the Spanish Caribbean while remaining distant enough to help insulate the English settlement from attack. Warner would take any action necessary to secure this island for his investors. Late at night the captain and his men "tooke ye advantage of [the Indians'] being druncke" and attacked the Carib warriors, killing many and driving the survivors off St. Christopher to take refuge among Carib settlements on neighboring islands.

Warner had taken a great risk. Now, in addition to his Spanish foes, he had to worry about the vengeful Caribs. When they returned in force, as Warner knew by reputation that they would, his handful of gentlemen adventurers could not repel them. Thus, when the crew of a French privateer arrived early in 1625, Warner struck a bargain to occupy the island jointly in exchange for French assistance in arms against Caribs and Spanish. The French took the island's northern and southern ends, while the English remained in the middle. When the Caribs attacked later that year, the combined forces of French and English colonists easily repelled them. They had less success four years later against a concentrated Spanish attack, but survivors of both nations managed to rebuild

and live together in an uneasy peace for another three decades.

The tumultuous experience of St. Christopher's early English conquerors was not at all unusual for colonists in the seventeenth-century Caribbean. Yet the harsh and uncertain prospects of Caribbean life did not deter thousands of settlers from embarking for the English West Indies rather than the North American mainland during the first half of the century. Indeed, in 1635, the number of colonists departing London for the Caribbean outnumbered migrants to the recently established Massachusetts Bay Colony (see Chapter 5) by more than five hundred. Only Virginia attracted more. Most arrived as servants, and most fell victim to tropical disease or maltreatment before getting the chance to pursue their dreams of bettering their condition. Most who survived their terms of service saw their hopes cruelly dashed as they found themselves pushed to the hardscrabble margins of life in the island economies. But a few ruthless, calculating, and lucky planters eventually managed to strike it rich in sugar production, an enterprise that won them wealth beyond their wildest dreams and turned England's Caribbean possessions into dynamos of economic growth throughout the English Atlantic.

Virtually no leading colonist living anywhere in early America would have relegated the Caribbean to the margins of awareness as subsequent histories of this era have commonly done. To English colonists, the Caribbean was central—the front line in the struggle against Spain, the main market for agricultural staples from the mainland, the source of England's enormously profitable sugar trade, and the primary destination for English and colonial slave ships departing from Africa. Seventeenth- and eighteenth-century colonists understood implicitly how profound an influence the English Caribbean exerted on mainland colonial development. Early mainland colonists understood that their security rested in part on the ability of English privateers to keep Spanish ships occupied in the faraway Caribbean. They knew that the wealthy English sponsors of mainland colonial ventures backed colonizing efforts in the Caribbean as well. Leaders of early mainland colonies such as Massachusetts Bay's Governor John Winthrop (a friend and former neighbor in England of St. Christopher's Captain Thomas Warner) maintained friendships and alliances with English adventurers in the Caribbean and kept close tabs on developments there. As early as the 1640s, direct trade began to spring up between American mainland and Caribbean colonies of several nations, and this trade expanded dramatically during the following century (see Chapter 6). This budding commerce in turn stimulated the growth of a colonial carrying trade, which soon grew to transatlantic scope as New England sea captains began sailing to the coast of Africa in search of slaves for the Caribbean market (see Chapter 5).

If English Caribbean history contributed in important ways to the growth of northern mainland colonies, it was absolutely indispensable to the development of the colonial South. Virginia tobacco planters turned to slave labor on a large scale well after Barbadian sugar planters did, and many of the Africans who arrived in colonial Virginia passed through a period of "seasoning" in Barbados en route. Indeed, for much of the colonial period, shipments of slaves to North America constituted a mere side business for the main enterprise of supplying the Caribbean slave labor market. And South Carolina became a thriving plantation colony primarily through the efforts not of colonists from England, but of slaveholding planters from Barbados (see Chapter 7). By the eighteenth century, the economy of the English West Indies and England's mainland colonies had become so deeply intertwined that either would suffer greatly without the participation of the other. The story of colonial American growth is inseparable from that of the English Caribbean.

4.1: "No Peace beyond the Line"

4.1 Report how the line of amity in the Atlantic marked the end of all European treaties

At the opening of the seventeenth century, the Caribbean was a hornet's nest of privateers from every major seafaring nation in Europe who competed ruthlessly for Spanish silver, Carib slaves, and increasingly for possession of the islands themselves. The sixteenth-century conflict between Spain and other nations over rights to New World territory had resulted in the development of a "line of amity" that marked limits of European treaties. Once an English vessel passed west of the prime meridian in the mid-Atlantic or sailed south past the Tropic of Cancer, it became fair game for Spanish, French, or Dutch vessels, even when peace prevailed among those nations in Europe. Spain reserved the right to drive competing nations out of the Caribbean if they could marshal the strength to do it. Adventurers of other nations reserved the right to trade or raid among Spanish possessions as opportunity arose and to occupy any territory they could seize.

The decision of European rulers to suspend international law in the Caribbean created a scene of anarchy among the region's competing inhabitants. Colonists of rival nations might cooperate as need dictated even if their parent countries were at war. Spanish settlers, for example, readily dealt with English, French, and Dutch smugglers when they could get away with it to circumvent the artificially high prices and sluggish operation of Spain's cumbersome mercantile system. The Spanish held these traders at arms' length, well aware that the vessel that this year brought them illicit goods at discount rates might return next year to raid their coasts or capture their ships. Spain's European challengers often cooperated with each other against Iberian enterprise in the Caribbean, but they also readily took advantage of one another when opportunity arose. After the Spanish attacked St. Christopher in 1629, for instance, English survivors joined forces with a fresh group of English colonists who arrived a few weeks later to appropriate abandoned French lands as well as their own. When the French colonists who had fled the invasion returned to the island, they had to fight their way back onto their former possessions.

Despite the chaos that marked the seventeenth-century Caribbean, however, a variety of factors made it increasingly worth the risk for English adventurers to attempt new settlements in the islands. In the first place, Spain entered the seventeenth century as a wounded giant, still dangerous near the center of empire but weakened at its peripheries by decades of war. Spanish officials found it increasingly difficult to police their Caribbean claims, opening the chance for colonists of England and other nations to establish island settlements undetected. Many zealous Puritan gentry thought they detected in this weakness a chance to drive the English Protestant sword into the heart of Spain's popish empire.

Iberian tobacco and sugar planters had also shown their English rivals that a New World colonist could grow rich by means other than capturing a silver mine or finding El Dorado. All one needed was land, seed, and labor—large amounts of each. The sparsely inhabited islands of the Lesser Antilles offered an untapped source of arable land with the proper growing season for plantation staples. Dutch merchants were eager to expand their suppliers of staple goods by providing the seed, equipment, and know-how to launch a plantation. A surplus of young, underemployed English men and women were willing to provide labor in the early years. When the supply of English laborers began to dwindle, the Dutch were ready to step in with African slaves.

4.1.1: A West Indian City on a Hill

As inhabitants of the newly established Massachusetts Bay Colony struggled through their first winter in 1630–1631, the *Seaflower* carried one hundred colonists from London to a little-remembered Puritan colony in the very heart of the Spanish Caribbean. Providence Island had been settled a little more than a year earlier with the backing of a group of England's most powerful Puritan leaders, great lords, and gentlemen who were determined to press the cause of godly reform in the face of what they saw as a national decline into civil decay and religious error. They hoped to make the new colony a model of godly society for English leaders to emulate, a profitable enterprise that would shore up English wealth, and a base for advancing the Protestant cause against Catholic Spain—a cause they believed King Charles I was neglecting.

Providence Island seemed the perfect spot for achieving all three aims. Visitors reported that the island held rich agricultural potential and could support a large population of godly settlers. Its location a hundred miles from the coast of Nicaragua made it a promising base for launching trading ventures and new colonizing efforts on the mainland. Its strategic position "in the high way of the Spanish fleets" that carried silver from Cartagena and Portobelo (see Chapter 2) enabled Puritan privateers to disrupt the commerce of "popish Spain" for the glory of their Protestant God. The island was a natural fortress; its harbors were protected by treacherous sandbars and overlooked by high rock formations from which well-placed artillery could train murderous fire on enemy vessels and landing parties.

Peaceful relations between Spain and England in the 1630s delayed the initiation of Providence Island's privateering enterprise. Charles I refused to authorize military action against Spain's possessions except for targeted reprisals against Spanish raiders who attacked English possessions in the Caribbean. In the meantime, the colony's backers demonstrated their devotion to the cause by pouring vast sums into the project. Providence Island Company founders were determined to avoid the mistakes in planning and governance that had plagued earlier colonial enterprises in Roanoke and Virginia. Men such as the great Parliamentarian John Pym, an avid defender of local government and small property owners' rights during the English Civil War, concluded that the problems of earlier colonies had arisen through too much local control. The backers decided to govern Providence Island from London and retain ownership of all property.

This impractical scheme engendered tension and hampered the island's economic development. The decision makers remained too far distant to respond to urgent problems as they arose. Middling planters who sold out to go to Providence Island soon grew discontent with their status as tenants and company employees. They began to agitate for private ownership of their own plantations, a concession that the London adventurers remained reluctant to grant. The company had promised planters a steady supply of servants, whom they hoped would provide labor for three or four years before assuming a place among the island's free planters. Recruitment lagged, however, increasing the discontent of planters who needed more labor and servants whose terms were prolonged to compensate for the lack of replacements. Investors made matters even worse by directing colonists to experiment with too many unfamiliar crops at once, an effort that spread the labor too thin and resulted in a string of failures. Eventually, the London grandees had to permit planters to concentrate on tobacco, which grew well on Providence Island and helped stem the investors' losses for a time.

Providence Island's religious life disappointed its pious founders' hopes as well. Like inhabitants of Massachusetts Bay Colony (which many of Providence Island's backers also supported), the founders hoped to establish a society whose inhabitants would pursue lives of sincere Protestant faith and practice. They hoped to foster such a society by creating parallel civil and religious systems whose leaders would contribute to the common good by devoting themselves wholly to their respective spheres. Ministers would have no civil authority, but "spend their Times and pains in the service of [the colonists'] souls." They were expected to appear before the civil magistrates as humble petitioners, hats in hand, just as every other ordinary colonist on the island. By the same token, civil officials were strictly forbidden from meddling in the colony's religious affairs. Company officials, however, did retain the time-honored right of noble and gentry patrons to handpick ministers for the people under their authority.

The Providence Island plan instituted sweeping religious reforms, but the best emigrant ministers chose to go to the American mainland rather than the Caribbean. Despite their extensive connections with English Puritan clergy, the island's London investors had to content themselves with sending ministers of lesser experience or poorer qualifications, men who ultimately proved unable to unite Puritan colonists. Indeed, ministers such as Lewis Morgan and Hope Sherrard exacerbated tensions among pious colonists who brought with them conflicting ideas of worship and the life of faith. Morgan, for example, antagonized one of the leading colonists, Captain William Rudyerd, by encouraging his congregation to sing psalms in worship. When Rudyerd challenged the practice, Morgan excluded him from participating in communion. In the aftermath of this confrontation, Morgan's colonial followers coalesced into an opposition group and thrust him into the role of spokesperson for their grievances against company policies. The investors recalled Morgan to London in disgrace, but the religious life of the colony remained divided.

In 1635, the colony entered a promising but risky new phase of development after an unsuccessful Spanish assault on the island. The attack gave investors the excuse they needed to ask for letters of reprisal that would authorize English privateers to strike back at Spain. The Crown readily issued the letters, and Providence Island became a central base for staging English raids on Spanish colonial ports and shipping. The colony's London backers hoped that privateering would turn the money-draining settlement into a profitable enterprise, providing a firm fiscal foundation for future development. The island's pious middling planters, however, clashed with the rough seamen who poured into their settlement. They also objected that the turn to privateering would increase the costs and risks of life on the island, a concern that materialized as London investors demanded new defense expenditures in the face of escalating Anglo-Spanish tensions in the region.

By May 1640, the ongoing depredations of the Providence Island privateers had so disrupted Spanish shipping that colonial officials resolved exterminate this English Protestant "den of thieves." The island simply lay too close to vital Spanish treasure routes. Cartagena's sergeant-major Don Antonio Maldonado de Texeda attacked Providence Island with an amphibious force of thirteen Spanish ships carrying more than seven hundred infantrymen in addition to their crews. The English took excellent advantage of the island's natural defenses, however, and repelled the invasion with a force of around hundred fighting men.

Providence Islanders enjoyed their victory for only one year. In May 1641, General Francisco Díaz Pimienta organized a second invasion force of 1,400 infantrymen and more than 600 seamen who sailed to the island in seven large ships and four pinnaces. This time, the Spanish captured the island in a well-executed, multipronged attack. A few of the island's 350 English captives scattered among remaining English settlements in the Caribbean; the rest returned to London at their own expense. Spanish invaders also captured 381 African slaves, whom they sold in Cartagena.

Pimienta turned the island into a Spanish garrison to prevent English or Dutch corsairs from regaining control of a base that had proved so destructive to the colonies and shipping of the Spanish Caribbean. By July 1641, Pimienta was boasting that more merchant ships had entered Cartagena in the past two months than in the previous two years before the English fell.

The brevity of English Puritan settlement on Providence Island belies the colony's importance in the history of the seventeenth-century English Atlantic. Domestic unrest and civil war in England (see Chapter 6) demanded all the attention of the colony's great backers during the 1640s. Even so, they did not forsake the hope of making the Caribbean a theater of militant English Protestantism. Indeed, those who survived into the 1650s helped transform their vision into English national policy as the Western Design, a renewed effort to capture the Caribbean for England (see Chapter 6). The military dimension of English Caribbean policy persisted throughout the colonial period, as did the Protestant impulse in a less Puritan form. Yet a new road to fabulous wealth was beginning to emerge far off the path of Spain's treasure fleets, among the British sugar islands of the Lesser Antilles.

4.1.2: Barbados: Sugar and Broken Dreams

Sugar was a part of the plan for Barbados at the colony's beginning in 1626, when the Anglo-Dutch merchant Sir William Courteen fetched to the newly founded settlement "32 Indians from the [South American] mayne wth tobacco suger canes Cotton plantaines Potatoes Cassada pines & c . . . to assist and instruct the english to advance the said plantation." Courteen had chosen an island well suited to the type of plantation enterprise he had in mind. Barbados' location far away from the Spanish treasure routes afforded it shelter from England's enemies—indeed, throughout the seventeenth century Spain never once

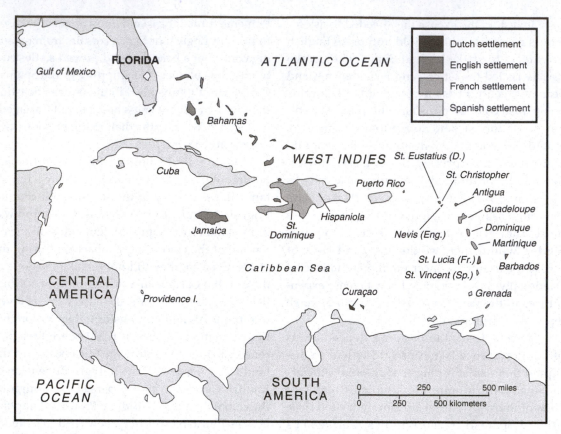

Map 4.1 Caribbean in the Seventeenth Century

attacked the island. English visitors thought Barbados resembled their homeland and was "more healthful than any of hir (Caribbean) Neighbors; and better agreeing with the temper of the English Nacion," despite the fact that many of its European inhabitants succumbed to tropical disease. The island enjoyed abundant rainfall, and a very high percentage of its 166 square miles consisted of gentle, rolling hills that provided excellent land for planting when cleared.

Despite Barbados' promise, unrest and mismanagement delayed the emergence of sugar as a major crop for over a decade. To be sure, Courteen followed up on his initial preparations quickly enough. By 1627, he obtained a patent for the island and dispatched seventy-four colonists to begin building, clearing, and planting under the direction of his newly appointed governor John Powell. Yet within a few months of the colonists' arrival, the earl of Carlisle, an influential courtier of Charles I, sent his henchman Charles Woolverston with sixty men to challenge Courteen's claim to Barbados. Woolverston soon "seduced the people, imprisoned the Governour & c., and tooke the gouerment upon himselfe for the Earle of Carlile." A two-year power struggle ensued in English courts and on Barbadian soil for control of the island. Carlisle's connections at court eventually enabled him to win a patent for all English possessions in the Lesser Antilles, and Courteen had to forfeit much of his enormous £10,000 investment in Barbados.

Unlike Courteen, who had planned to direct the development of his Barbados plantations from London, Carlisle was interested only in collecting annual quitrents on the land and cared little how the colonists went about generating them. Under his proprietorship, Barbados settlers received grants of land which Carlisle expected them to develop using their own funds and labor. During the 1630s, several hundred colonists obtained land from Carlisle and began recruiting servants to the island to help them develop their claims. The grants varied greatly in size, a few as large as 1,000 acres and many parcels no larger than 30 to 50 acres, establishing a pattern of inequality among landholders that would characterize Barbados throughout the colonial period.

The early planters on Barbados followed Virginia in producing tobacco for export, a choice that made the new colony similar to its mainland counterpart in many ways. Like Virginia, Barbados drew thousands of indentured servants to provide labor for the arduous task of clearing rain forest and cultivating tobacco plants among the stumps of the felled trees. During the 1630s, a little less than nine thousand English colonists embarked for the island, most of them single males in their teens or twenties. Though Barbados tobacco compared poorly with that grown in Virginia—Massachusetts governor John Winthrop declared one shipment of it "very ill conditioned, fowle, full of stalkes and evill coloured"—the colony nevertheless attracted young people on the make because it seemed likely to make them moderately prosperous yeoman planters once their terms of service were complete. Not only was the Barbados climate reportedly healthy by Caribbean standards, but crops were said to grow so well in its fertile soil that it quickly became known as "a granary of all the rest of the charybbies Isles."

The island's plantation economy failed to live up to its promise during the 1630s, however, delayed by low prices and the poor quality that kept Barbadian tobacco unprofitable throughout the decade. Planters responded by shifting to cotton for a short time, but it proved no more profitable. Finally, in the early 1640s, they experimented with sugar. The crop grew well—much better than either tobacco or cotton—and the first cargos, though too coarse, dark, and sticky for the finest European tastes, nevertheless reaped a tidy return. During the next few years, Barbadian planters learned how to improve production from visiting Dutch merchants or by traveling themselves to Dutch-controlled plantations in South America. By the mid-1640s, the Barbadian sugar boom had arrived in full force.

The turn to sugar cultivation made many Barbadian planters rich within a few years. In 1646, one Barbadian managed to sell his 500-acre plantation for £16,000, more than the value of the entire island a decade before. Some planters sold out and retired to England; others sold off excess lands to increase efficiency—the optimum size of a seventeenth-century sugar plantation proved to be around 200 acres—and a new group of aggressive, well-heeled investors moved onto the island or snapped up plantations from London to reap Barbadian profits as absentee landlords. Real-estate values soared, and planters moved quickly to put as much land as possible into sugar production. By the 1660s, Barbados' rain forests had disappeared, replaced by fields of cane that prompted one visitor to describe the island as a single "beautifully planted green garden" dotted with windmills where the sugar was processed.

Not all Barbadians prospered in the sugar boom, however. Small planters found themselves crowded onto ever-smaller plots of marginal soil, where they scrounged out a meager existence by farming a mixture of sugar, cotton, ginger, and provision crops. Poor nutrition made both hardscrabble farmers and indentured servants more vulnerable to the island's virulent tropical diseases. Those servants who survived their terms in the hope of becoming independent landowners found themselves shut out of the soaring real estate market, shunted into wage-earning jobs on great plantations or forced off the island to seek their fortunes elsewhere. The soaring demand for labor brought additional English servants to

Barbados after 1640, but word of the island's dim prospects for landless young men discouraged many others from coming. Planters increasingly had to rely on the labor of transported criminals, prisoners taken during the English Civil War, or hapless victims who had been "barbadosed," kidnapped, and taken to the island against their will.

The chronic labor shortage made it "fatally easy," as historian Richard S. Dunn has observed, for the English planters on Barbados to take the plunge into African slavery. Sugar cultivation demanded a large workforce. Seventeenth-century planters quickly came to regard as optimum a ratio of one worker for every acre of cane, although only the richest could afford to acquire and maintain such large numbers of slaves. English planters who traveled to Brazil observed firsthand how a handful of European masters and overseers could keep hundreds of Africans on task in the cane fields. They sought to replicate this system on Barbados almost as a matter of course. Dutch merchants were eager to expand their growing market for African slaves by supplying Barbados with as many as the island economy could absorb. The Dutch reaped a dual benefit, profiting not only from the slave trade but also from Barbadian sugar, which they transported to Europe for handsome profits.

The shift to African slavery brought about an explosion in population and prosperity for the planters on Barbados. African slaves multiplied very rapidly on the island after 1640, soaring to twenty thousand by 1655. By contrast, the total population of African slaves on all Virginia plantations numbered only three hundred in 1650. The European population of the island rose to around twenty-three thousand during the same period, making Barbados the most densely populated colony in English America. Most of the new European arrivals worked as servants alongside African slaves, and their combined labor in sugar production made Barbados one of England's most lucrative New World colonies.

4.1.3: Contested Tobacco Islands

The English who colonized the Leeward Islands— St. Christopher, Nevis, Antigua, and Montserrat —contended with chronic instability in their attempts to establish a viable plantation economy. Unlike Barbados, whose distance from other islands insulated it from conflict, the Leewards' location near the northern end of the Lesser Antilles placed them much closer to the center of European conflict in the Caribbean. In this region beyond the line, European inhabitants lived by "that common proverb at Sea, Oy por mi, mañana port ti . . . to day I have got what tomorrow I may lose again." The earliest settlers had to remain constantly on their guard against raids by Carib Indians and Spanish colonists. Indeed, the Spanish temporarily drove their enemies off both St. Christopher and Nevis in 1629. As the Carib and Spanish threat waned toward the middle of the century, both Anglo-French and Anglo-Dutch tensions began heating up. Between 1650 and 1713, Nevis was sacked once, Montserrat and Antigua twice, and St. Christopher changed hands seven times. They also rode out several devastating hurricanes that destroyed their buildings and wiped out their crops. Yet the English persisted in settling the Leewards despite these repeated setbacks.

English colonists fanned out to the other Leewards from their initial base on St. Christopher. In 1628, a planter named Anthony Hilton led 150 colonists to Nevis across the 3-mile channel that separated it from St. Christopher. Other colonists ventured to the more distant Antigua and Montserrat in 1632. Colonists found the gentle, rolling terrain of Antigua most suitable to their agricultural purposes, despite the island's shortage of fresh water. The mountainous, volcanic terrain, and dramatic coastal cliffs of the other three islands, which tourists find so beautiful today, struck the seventeenth-century planters as savage and inhospitable. Nevertheless, they poured great energy into carving fields of tobacco, cotton, and ginger out of the jungle-covered island slopes.

The earl of Carlisle confirmed Captain Thomas Warner as the governor of St. Christopher when that island and Nevis came into his possession in 1629, making Warner a deputy of the earl's lieutenant governor of Barbados. Each of the other three Leewards received its own deputy governor during the 1630s as well. Each also maintained its own council and assembly. The Leewards' distance from Barbados prevented the lieutenant governor there from exercising any real influence in their governance. Officials on each island remained extremely jealous of any outside authority, particularly from their wealthy rivals on Barbados, and they labored to strengthen local control. The restored monarchy of Charles II (see Chapter 6) eventually attempted to unite the four Leewards under a single government distinct from that of Barbados, but the islands remained virtually independent of one another throughout the seventeenth and eighteenth centuries.

In contrast to the relatively high percentage of wealthy planters on Barbados, the early Leeward planters were obscure men who lacked the capital to amass land, purchase slaves, or invest in expensive equipment such as sugar mills. The majority of free English planters on St. Christopher were former indentured servants who had managed to purchase one of the 10- to 12-acre plots that comprised most of the English sector's cultivated land. Prosperity eluded colonists on Antigua through the 1650s as they labored under a chronic burden of debt to the island's governor, Henry Ashton. Montserrat became a refuge for a majority population of Irish Catholics who managed to purchase small plantations after working off their indentures. Like their counterparts on other Leeward Islands, these planters "of an Ordinary and low rank" could not establish the credit needed to establish estates or attract investment. Only on Nevis did a sizable group of planters possess sufficient means to establish sugar plantations before 1650. Even there, a shortage of servants and African slaves limited the growth of sugar cultivation.

The Leewards thus remained preserves of mostly small planters with limited prospects and chronically frustrated hopes, yet they attracted a steady stream of immigrants through the 1650s. Tobacco grew better there than on Barbados, though not as well as in Virginia and Maryland. Leeward planters persisted in cultivating it and recruiting additional servants to the island to assist them. Population estimates for the early years are scarce and unreliable, but a traveler to St. Christopher in 1655 reported that the English sector comprising little more than half the island's 68 square miles was "almost worne out by reason of the multitudes that live upon it." In that same year, the population of Antigua stood at around 1,200, as did that of Montserrat.

Most who came to the Leewards had to eke out an existence in a rough frontier environment, building flimsy, thatch-roofed huts supported by a frame of forked stakes walled with reeds. Only a few brought with them or earned the capital necessary to build the more substantial plantation dwellings that began appearing on Barbados soon after its planters turned to sugar production. Their reputation for fractious behavior and love of idleness dogged Leeward islanders well after they began turning to sugar cultivation in the 1660s.

4.1.4: The Carib Challenge

Early English settlers in the Caribbean had to contend with the constant presence of Carib Indians, or Karifunas. Sixteenth-century Spanish colonists had all but exterminated the Caribs from the Greater Antilles (Puerto Rico, Hispañola, Cuba, and Jamaica) through warfare, enslavement, and epidemic disease (see Chapter 2). Caribs in the Lesser Antilles, however, managed to resist Spanish conquest and maintain an independent existence in a 500-mile chain of island societies that extended from Tobago off the coast of South America to the Leewards. The Caribs living on these islands developed an effective system of communication and cooperation that enabled faraway groups to come to the assistance of any Caribs under pressure from European interlopers. Carib reinforcements might not arrive in time to repel a particular attack, but they could soon amass a force large enough to exact devastating reprisals against any European expedition foolish enough to attack an apparently insignificant, isolated Carib settlement.

The Caribs resisted English attempts to settle the Lesser Antilles as they had resisted the Spanish before them. Captain Thomas Warner's effort to expel Caribs from St. Christopher in 1624 succeeded only temporarily. Although the English and French jointly staved off Carib reprisals against St. Christopher in 1625, small bands of Caribs soon managed to return to the island, where they lived in areas the Europeans found hard to reach. In the later 1620s and early 1630s, the French and English conducted several joint expeditions to search out and destroy persistent Carib settlements on St. Christopher.

English settlers on other Leeward Islands faced conflict with the Caribs as well, and the Indians managed to retain complete control of some islands well into the eighteenth century. In 1639, for example, Carib soldiers easily repelled an English effort to capture their stronghold on St. Lucia. The next year they retaliated with a full-scale attack on Antigua, capturing the governor's wife and children, killing fifty settlers, and destroying English crops and houses. Barbadian governors sought constantly for opportunities to defeat the Caribs on nearby St. Vincent, a common destination for runaway servants and slaves. The Indians always managed to stave off attacks, and governors of other English islands soon began taking a dim view of Barbadian raids on St. Vincent, which put their own communities at risk of Carib reprisals.

Despite persistent tensions between the Caribs and English, the two groups did find occasions for cooperation as well as conflict. During the earliest years of settlement, the English traded sporadically with Caribs on nearby islands. In 1638, Caribs astounded the English on St. Christopher with their seemingly uncanny ability to forecast a deadly hurricane. Their warning gave the English enough time to prepare, saving both lives and many goods. Carib headmen usually returned to the early planters any runaway servants or slaves they found. English and Caribs occasionally sought each other's assistance against rival European groups as well, though their mutual antagonism made most efforts short-lived. Caribs more often sided with the French or Dutch against the English.

The Carib presence in the Lesser Antilles complicated English efforts to develop sugar plantations there. They resisted settlement when possible and contributed to the instability that delayed sugar planting on the Leewards. As the sugar boom swept across the Caribbean, the Caribs fiercely defended their remaining islands of freedom against a rising sea of slavery. St. Vincent, St. Lucia, and Dominica emerged as Carib centers of resistance to a system of bondage and commerce that was being built on the foundation of a growing European taste for sweetness.

4.2: Cultivating Sweetness

4.2 **Describe how the sugarcane trade drove economic growth in the seventeenth and eighteenth centuries**

Sugar rapidly emerged as one of the main engines of economic development in the seventeenth- and eighteenth-century English Atlantic. It transformed Barbados, and eventually the Leewards and Jamaica as well, from struggling tobacco settlements to the richest plantation colonies in English America. The fabulous profits from sugar, even more than those from tobacco, prompted London policymakers to begin enacting the series of laws that gave shape to England's Atlantic commercial empire (see Chapter 7). Sugar transformed the diet of Europe as it made its way from docks to the kitchens and tables of consumers.

Sugar also transformed the lives of Atlantic peoples. Barbadian sugar planters created a society unlike any other in the colonial New World. They ruthlessly exploited the labor of thousands of English servants who embarked to better their condition in London or Bristol only to see their hopes dashed in the islands. The sugar planters led England's full-scale plunge into African slavery. The Caribbean sugar islands, not the Chesapeake tobacco plantations, first drew the Dutch and English into the circuit linking Africa with the English colonies, carrying hundreds of thousands of Africans in chains to toil and die far from home.

4.2.1: An Appetite for Sweetness

At the opening of the seventeenth century, sugar remained a costly luxury that mainly graced the tables of royalty and nobility, though a growing number of wealthy gentry and merchant elites were also beginning to consume it. Common people satisfied their palates on a diet of grain foods supplemented with meats and dairy products. If they wanted something sweet, they ate honey or fruits, and did so sparingly in the belief that fruit eaten in large quantities posed a danger to health. The gradual introduction of sugar into the everyday diet of ordinary Europeans took place over the course of the seventeenth and eighteenth centuries as a result of the boom in sugar production that took place in that period.

Seventeenth-century Europeans used sugar in many ways that later generations would find peculiar. Wealthy consumers thought of the product as a spice or condiment rather than a sweetener, sprinkling it lightly onto meats, fish, vegetables, or fruit and mixing it into recipes in quantities similar to other spices. Physicians prescribed it as a medicine for treating a variety of maladies such as indigestion, respiratory ailments, and eye infections. Some also sprinkled it onto cuts and scrapes to promote healing; others used it to clean teeth. Monarchs and noblemen used it lavishly to signify their power and status, decorating banqueting halls with large figures of trees, humans, animals, mythical beings, castles, or sailing ships armed with working cannons, all sculpted from pure hardened sugar. The powerful regarded sugar as a kind of edible precious stone and displayed their opulence by lavishing it on their guests when an important occasion such as a coronation or wedding demanded.

As the price of sugar gradually dropped within reach of the lesser gentry, the middling sorts, and eventually working people, its uses gradually changed. By the 1680s, the extravagant displays were falling out of fashion. Gentry consumers now used sugar to mark status in more subtle ways, most notably in combination with coffee, tea, and chocolate, three exotic tropical beverages that began to appear in Europe about this time. Sugar's growing affordability also stimulated the development of an ever-expanding array of sweetbreads, pastries, custards, cakes, and puddings that could complement a hot beverage at teatime or could make a dinner complete. An increasing number of aspiring gentry on mainland North America were also beginning to emulate the European example, spreading the demand for sugar to both sides of the Atlantic.

4.2.2: Sugar Production

It was demanding work to satisfy the growing European taste for sweetness. The complex process of sugar production required a hefty initial investment in workers and equipment, backbreaking, hazardous labor, and painstaking management. Yet sugar offered staggering returns to those willing to expend the necessary capital and to squeeze the maximum labor from their workforce.

Sugar plantations combined agricultural and mechanical procedures into a time-critical process that the historical anthropologist Sidney Mintz has seen as "the closest thing to industry that was typical of the seventeenth century." Sugar plant-ing began with the backbreaking task of clearing and tilling fields, a process accomplished almost exclusively with axes and hoes. Once the field was ready, servants and slaves dug trenches or holes in which they set fresh cuttings of cane, which would quickly sprout new roots. During the sixteen-month period of maturation, workers hoed the fields several times. They also spread manure ob-tained from large herds of sheep and cattle, which the planters kept mainly for generating fertilizer. When the cane ripened, gangs of workers har-vested it with heavy knives called "bills," stripping the leaves and bundling the stalks as they went.

The field harvest only began the arduous process of rendering the cane to sugar. Work-ers had to get the bundled stalks to the mills as quickly as possible to maximize the yield. There, operators fed the cane into the livestock- or wind-driven rollers, which pressed out the juice into a collecting trough. The cane was light, but the pace so quick and relentless that workers soon became exhausted. All too frequently, the rollers caught the hand of a tired worker and pulled in his arm. The overseer commonly amputated the mangled arm on the spot with a knife kept handy for the purpose, barely slacking the pace as the severed limb passed on through the mill with the cane.

From the mill, the freshly pressed cane juice flowed through a channel or pipe to the boiling house, where it passed through a series of kettles to boil off excess water. Sugar-boiling was an art performed under very difficult and hazardous con-ditions. The heat was stifling; the stench was over-powering; and the scalding syrup would "stick like Glew or Birdlime" to a worker who accidentally spilled it on a limb, inflicting serious and sometimes life-threatening injury. Skillful craftsmen tended the sugar through this process, skimming off impurities as the syrup boiled and "striking" or arresting boil-ing as soon as they judged it ready for cooling.

After cooling, the workers poured the par-tially granulated sugar into earthenware pots with a hole in the bottom and set the pots in the curing house on ceramic trays called "drips." Workers kept the curing houses as hot as pos-sible to promote the draining of molasses and drying of the sugar crystals. After curing, they knocked out the hardened loaves of brown "mus-covado" sugar and pressed them into hogsheads

Slaves on West Indian sugar plantations endured arduous labor during harvest, when the cane had to be cut quickly and processed into sugar at mills like the one depicted here.

for shipping. Some planters followed a somewhat different method to obtain "clayed" sugar, a white, soft product that needed no further processing and fetched a higher price on the English market. Both methods of curing yielded a large amount of molasses which the workers collected for sale or distilling into rum, an English invention that provided yet another source of profit.

The tasks of harvesting, milling, boiling, curing, and distilling kept Caribbean plantation laborers working at a continuous breakneck pace each year from January until May. The staff of the mill and boiling house worked in continuous shifts from dawn until well after sundown and often through the night, resting only on Sundays. A well-run sugar operation demanded careful management to synchronize the various tasks and keep the labor force on a strict production schedule. Few other enterprises required management or time discipline on such a scale until textile mills began appearing in England during the late eighteenth century.

4.2.3: Sweetness and Profits

Poor seventeenth-century records make it difficult to know exactly how much a planter could profit from sugar production, and profit margins fluctuated widely over the seventeenth century as prices fell, costs rose, and war disrupted trade. Nevertheless, historians agree that "only inept and unlucky planters actually lost money, even in the worst of times," while industrious and lucky planters such as the Barbadian Henry Drax did very well indeed. Drax himself was reported to have shipped home around £5,000 worth of sugar annually during the 1680s, a gross income matching that of the wealthiest landed aristocrats in England. While Drax and other planters had to plow much of their income back into the maintenance and expansion of their plantations and labor forces, the profits they cleared supported lives of extravagant luxury in the islands. Their accumulated wealth also enabled many retiring planters to purchase or build great estates in the English countryside, where they spent their remaining years in leisured opulence.

The sugar trade fueled English commercial expansion throughout the Atlantic during the later seventeenth century, prompting London pamphleteers and policymakers of the period to wax eloquent on its benefits to the nation. Some hoped that England's sugar colonies would soon corner the European sugar market, expanding opportunities for ownership and employment in shipping while bringing an influx of European trade commodities that would increase prosperity and improve the lives of English people. Others pointed out that prosperous sugar colonies themselves could provide significant markets for English manufactured goods. Wealthy planters wanted not only luxurious consumer goods such as table service, glassware, textiles, and household furnishings; they also needed great quantities of clothing and tools for their slaves along with supplies of many items such as nails, iron, and cordage used to keep the plantation in good working order.

The sugar colonies stimulated production not only in England, but on the North American mainland as well. Barbados planters found sugar so profitable that they quickly put every available plot of land into cane and began importing the grains needed to feed themselves and their workers. Massachusetts began supplying Barbadian planters with grain and salt pork as early as the 1640s (see Chapter 5). Farmers in coastal New England—and later New York, the Jerseys, and Pennsylvania—exported agricultural goods to the Caribbean throughout the colonial period, gleaning modest profits, which many used to purchase cheap English imported goods as they became increasingly available.

The fabulous profits, the transformation of the European diet, the expansion of Atlantic commerce, and the gradual emergence of a consumer society—all came at a cost far greater than what bookkeepers could measure in pounds and pence. Sugar production exacted a terrible price in human misery from thousands of European servants and hundreds of thousands of African slaves. Life in the tropics was filled with strain and peril even for the planters themselves. Society on England's Caribbean sugar islands bore the tragic marks of continual, violent exploitation, arduous toil, chronic malnutrition, virulent disease, and death.

4.3: Society in the English West Indies

4.3   Evaluate the fabric of society in English West Indies

Barbados "is divided into three sorts of men, *viz.*, Masters, Servants, and Slaves," the traveler Richard Ligon reported in 1657. Island life presented all three groups with peculiar challenges, but it was especially brutal for servants and slaves. By the time Ligon published his account, African slaves already comprised nearly 50 percent of the island's population. A few aspiring sugar planters on Nevis had begun purchasing slaves by this time as well, but the proportion of African slaves there was much smaller, and it remained negligible on the other Leeward Islands until the 1670s. Planters on Providence Island also rapidly turned to slaves to meet their labor demands, but their defeat in 1641 made Barbados the first successful English colony in America to develop a society based on the large-scale employment of African slaves. The social and cultural patterns that resulted there were peculiar to the specific demands of sugar cultivation, the hazards of life in the tropics, and the high percentage of African slaves in the island populations.

Society on the other sugar islands followed the pattern set on Barbados, taking a course distinct from social development on the North American mainland. English West Indian life took on a freewheeling, callous, impermanent quality as planters raced to accumulate the highest possible profits before they died or retired to England. Barbados hosted a diverse, multiethnic population that included, besides English and Africans, significant communities of French, Dutch, and Scots. The largest percentage of servants was Irish, and Bridgetown, the Barbados capital, also hosted a significant community of Portuguese Jews. Barbadians "have that liberty of conscience which we so long have in England fought for," the English visitor Henry Whistler commented in 1655, "but they do abuse it." The unique culture that emerged in the English Caribbean provides an instructive counterpoint to the development of mainland colonial society, as well as an important backdrop for understanding the peculiarities of the Lower South, where transplanted Barbadians exerted a direct influence.

4.3.1: Family and Population in the Tropics

The Barbadian planter gentry "live far better than ours do in England," commented one early visitor. Yet wealth could not buy the sugar barons long lives or stable families. Seventeenth-century Caribbean planters, great and small, lived hard, drank even harder, and died like flies. The early English population of the islands was, if anything, more distorted by gender imbalance and high death rates than that of the early Chesapeake. Most first-generation colonists who sailed to the Caribbean were male servants. All founding settlers of Barbados and St. Christopher were men. Almost a decade after its founding, males still constituted more than 90 percent of new arrivals to Barbados. As late as 1680, only one in every four English who arrived in Barbados was a woman. The sex ratio of whites in the islands became more balanced after 1710, but disease and death continued to destabilize family life throughout much of the eighteenth century.

Most English emigrants to the Caribbean succumbed quickly to virulent tropical diseases. Malaria was rampant on every island except

Barbados, and dysentery or the "bloody flux" was common everywhere. The turn to slavery brought the introduction of devastating diseases from Africa such as yellow fever, leprosy, and skin-ulcerating yaws, as well as deadly parasites such as hookworm and guinea worm. Chronic deficiencies in nutrition not only lowered resistance to such diseases among servants and slaves but also caused additional maladies such as scurvy and beriberi. Disease reduced the life expectancy of white colonists well below 35 years, and death carried off men at a higher rate than women. Masters constantly had to bring new shiploads of laborers to the islands to replace those who had died. Even the wealthiest members of the ruling gentry seldom escaped early death, opening the highest offices of government to unusually young men. Elected leaders typically secured their first seat in the legislature during their 20s and were elevated to the council in their early 30s. Comparable offices in New England seldom went to men under 40.

English colonists found traditional patterns of family life very difficult to sustain in this deadly environment. Many first- and second-generation English males entered into irregular unions with their female slaves. Offspring of such liaisons who survived infancy might sometimes be freed along with their mothers. More often both mother and child remained in bondage, though white fathers extended paternal favors to their mulatto offspring by giving them coveted positions as artisans or domestics.

The unbalanced sex ratio created a great demand for English women in the early years of Caribbean settlement. Planters recruited female servants to increase opportunities for marriage as well as to provide labor. Young women considering this move must have been apprehensive at the prospect of embarking for reputedly sickly tropical islands so far from traditional social supports. Yet surviving evidence suggests that many who accepted the risk had no better option. Indeed, women spirited or press-ganged from London's brothels onto Barbados-bound vessels gained a

chance for social betterment unheard of by their sisters who remained in England. One patronizing observer sneered that "a bawd brought over" to Barbados "puts on a demure comportment, and a whore if handsome makes a wife for some rich planter."

Not all English women managed to marry into the Caribbean planter elite, nor did marriage to a planter necessarily translate into other gains for women. West Indian widows rarely gained control of their deceased husband's estate as often happened in the early Chesapeake. Marriage remained a woman's primary means of not only achieving social advancement but also maintaining it thereafter. Until the 1680s, the preponderance of males in the white population made this feasible, at least for women who had already managed to marry into elite society. Yet wives of small planters or artisans saw their condition erode as the sex ratio became slowly more balanced and the gap between rich and poor more pronounced. Many poor husbands found themselves squeezed by rising prices and decreasing returns in the later seventeenth century and simply abandoned wives and children to seek their fortunes elsewhere. Destitute white women ended up on parish poor relief, supported by the charitable gifts of great planters so long as their willingness to provide care for orphans or the indigent kept them "deserving."

Marriage and child-rearing increased as the sex ratio among English colonists gradually became more balanced, yet family life remained unstable. Husbands tended to die young, leaving widows and fatherless children to carry on. Death might also spare the husband only to take his wife and children, and many masters poured their short lives into amassing rich estates only to die without legitimate heirs. Families often died out within a generation of their arrival in the islands or retired to England to escape the deadly environment, inhibiting the formation of creole gentry dynasties or kinship networks like those that came to unite the Chesapeake gentry.

4.3.2: Small Fortunes and Great Estates

The relative scarcity of land in the English West Indies limited a colonist's chance of rising from obscurity to great wealth and status. First-generation planters on Barbados tended to be the younger sons of English gentlemen, merchants, and artisans who possessed sufficient capital to secure the largest and choicest grants of land. To be sure, the introduction of sugar cultivation to the islands enabled some of these relatively obscure young men to rise from "small fortunes to great estates" during the 1640s, as Richard Ligon observed. But servants, who were drawn from the lower ranks of English society, found little remaining land to choose from if they managed to survive their terms. Indeed, the rapid inflation of land prices after 1640 squeezed even many middling planters out of the real estate market. Those with good land could sell out at a premium to larger planters or wealthy outside investors, but most who did so had to leave Barbados to find good, productive land at affordable rates. Antigua was a favorite spot for such persons who wanted to set up new sugar plantations during the later seventeenth century, but many also went on to establish other types of enterprise in England's North American colonies. Leeward colonists enjoyed greater equality until later in the century, when large-scale sugar planting brought about a replication of the Barbados pattern.

Land scarcity combined with sugar prices to create a yawning gulf between the islands' richest and poorest free inhabitants. Small landholders who lacked the capital to move off the islands had to grind out a precarious existence on arid, infertile plots of ground. A fortunate few might be able to secure a modest living with the help of a handful of servants or slaves, but most had to get by on whatever mixed crops they could raise by their own labor. Unlike the majority of the free population elsewhere in English America, the lower half of the property holders in Barbados could not vote.

The great nabobs at the other end of the social scale plowed much of their profit first into indentured servants and slaves, and only then into ostentatious displays of wealth. Indeed, first-generation sugar planters put very little into their houses and furnishings. Yet after 1660, these newly rich gentry began building splendid stone great houses, filling them with exquisitely crafted imported furnishings which they purchased by mortgaging future sugar crops. The sugar barons dined from costly silver plates, quaffed the best imported wines, sweltered under several layers of the finest English fashions, rode in elegant carriages drawn by beautifully matched teams of horses, and kept domestic servants constantly at their elbow. They rapidly achieved a standard of living far higher than that enjoyed anywhere else in English America.

The West Indian sugar barons created versions of English social institutions that advanced the planters' own interests in ways unthinkable for elites elsewhere in British dominions. They created legislative assemblies similar to those of the mainland colonies, but the gentry who filled those legislatures did not answer to a broad electorate as did their counterparts in Virginia and Massachusetts. They replicated the system of courts they had known in England, but the judges set aside the common-law rights of servants and freemen whenever needed to administer the planters' version of justice. They held pews in the Anglican parish churches as well as seats in the vestries, governing boards that oversaw local church affairs. Although masters allowed the slaves to rest on Sundays, they refused to let the clergy convert Africans to Christianity. They sometimes hired schoolmasters but made only minimal attempts to promote education among the islands' free inhabitants.

4.3.3: Riotous and Unruly Servants

Richard Ligon thought servants led "the worser lives" of all mid-seventeenth-century Barbados inhabitants, "for they are put to very hard labour, ill lodging, and their diet very slight." The harsh conditions of servitude on Barbados produced sharp tensions between planters and their indentured laborers. Ligon observed that as early as 1647 masters were responding to these tensions by building their houses "in the manner of Fortifications" that could repel the assaults of their bondsmen. They brutally punished the slightest gestures of insubordination, sometimes stringing up servants and lighting matches between their fingers, other times locking them in stocks to roast for hours in the tropical sun or beating them mercilessly over the head until the blood flowed. "Truly," Ligon declared, "I have seen such cruelty there done to Servants, as I did not think one Christian could have done to another."

The Irish origins of many servants only exacerbated tensions. Recruiters began enticing young Irish men and women to the islands as the sugar boom began in the 1640s, and the burgeoning demand for laborers soon prompted English officials to begin deporting large numbers of Irish "undesirables" to Barbados and the Leewards as well. The English planters despised their Irish Catholic servants, whom they considered as fit only for field labor. The Irish, conditioned by English oppression, dispossession, and the ongoing colonization of their homeland, cordially hated their masters. The absence of opportunity on the islands only increased their resentment, and planters fueled further discontent through systematic discrimination against the Irish. Masters shunted Irish servants into the most menial jobs, refused them any chance to learn a craft, meted them especially harsh treatment, and denied due process to any who had the temerity to seek redress for their injuries in a court of law.

These practices yielded only chronic unrest. Planters instituted increasingly harsh measures to keep a lid on the rebellious spirit that simmered constantly among the Irish population. Leeward planters worried that the Catholic convictions of their Irish servants would prompt them to join forces with the French against English rule of the islands, a fear that proved justified in 1667 when Irish servants assisted the French in seizing St. Christopher and Montserrat. Planters on Barbados constantly monitored relations between Irish and African laborers for signs of conspiracy to unite in revolt against their oppressors. Barbados officials eventually passed a strict servant code that restricted Irish movement between plantations and imposed harsh penalties for resistance, absenteeism, or disorderliness. Planters appealed to London to send them no more Irish, but their pleas availed little until late in the seventeenth century.

4.3.4: Africans in the English West Indies

The turn to sugar in the English West Indies brought a full-scale plunge into African slavery as well. Barbados planters purchased nearly twenty thousand slaves in the first decade of sugar production alone. They brought another fifty-one thousand slaves to the island during the next twenty-five years. Indeed, Africans comprised nearly 75 percent of Barbados' population by 1675. Planters on the Leewards and Jamaica began importing significant numbers of slaves during that period as well. By 1700, the number of enslaved Africans shipped to the English West Indies had soared to more than 260,000, the majority arriving on vessels belonging to the Royal Africa Company or to merchants from New England and New York. It was only the beginning. During the eighteenth century, the English sugar islands would absorb nearly 1.2 million additional slaves, most of whom would die of disease and overwork within a decade of arrival.

The horrific death rate of Africans in the West Indies defied English insistence that Africans were better suited than Europeans to tropical heat and disease. Most slaves arrived in the islands debilitated by their ordeal on the Middle Passage (see Chapter 3), making them much more susceptible to the deadly diseases to which they were commonly exposed during the first months of "seasoning." Those who survived seasoning often fell victim to deficiency diseases such as scurvy and beriberi, a bewildering illness stemming from chronic malnutrition which often stimulates a craving to eat dirt. Planters observed a percentage of dirt eaters on nearly every Barbados plantation, and beriberi likely caused many of the deaths attributed to "dropsy." Africans who survived seasoning and malnutrition could expect to live between 7 and 17 years after their arrival, their most productive years. Those whose bodies broke down through age or hard labor soon died from neglect and short rations. The annual rate of decline among West Indians of African descent was highest before 1750, but births did not begin exceeding deaths until after the 1790s.

Although men comprised 60 percent of Africans brought to the Caribbean, the sex ratio quickly balanced out as a greater number of women survived seasoning. Birth rates nevertheless remained low for a variety of reasons. Women commonly worked in the field alongside men, and the combination of hard labor and poor nutrition likely reduced fertility. Seventeenth-century planters gave few concessions to pregnant women in either work or discipline, producing a higher rate of miscarriage. Travelers often marveled how African women would stop to give birth beside the row they were hoeing, rarely acknowledging that women entered the field so near the end of their terms because of the master's determination to extract every possible moment of work from each slave. The work regime also contributed to higher infant mortality by forcing new mothers back to the fields within two to three weeks of giving birth, taxing their health and interfering with the care of their newborns. Some African neonatal practices, such as packing the umbilical stump with mud, exacerbated infant mortality by introducing deadly infections. Women may also have resisted bringing children into a life of slavery by practicing contraception or inducing abortion.

Economic considerations governed the planters' turn to slavery as well as their treatment of enslaved Africans, yet English masters seldom justified the practice purely in terms of planter profits. Indeed, they adopted a quite different pattern of rhetoric. English writers associated blacks in Africa with heathen religion, barbarous behavior, and sexual promiscuity—in fact, with evil itself. From such a racist perspective, the enslavement of Africans seemed unobjectionable, even defensible. West Indian sugar planters argued that the slaves' dark skin and their "brute natures" best suited them for field work, conveniently ignoring their equal susceptibility to exhaustion as well as their equal facility for acquiring difficult skills in craftsmanship. Masters claimed that even the slaves themselves "prefer their present slavery before their former liberty" in war-torn Africa, "the loss whereof they never afterwards regret."

The rapid expansion of the black population on Barbados frightened the white planters, prompting the passage of stringent laws to control their slaves. In 1661, the Barbadian legislature pulled these laws together into a comprehensive slave code that became the template for later slave codes passed in Jamaica, South Carolina, and Antigua. This code assumed a racial basis for slavery and drew a sharp line between how masters could treat European servants and how they could treat African slaves. Slaves were subject to much harsher penalties than servants, including maiming, castration, and branding. Masters could be prosecuted for manslaughter if they accidentally killed a servant while punishing him or her, but they suffered no penalty for accidental death of a slave. A planter who murdered his slave would incur a fine of £25, far less than the £80 it would cost him if he was caught keeping another planter's runaway slave. Capital offenses for slaves, by contrast, included rebellion, assault, rape, murder, and theft of any item worth more than a shilling.

Despite the severity of their slave codes and the harshness of their racism, Caribbean planters never drew racial lines as sharply as their counterparts on the North American mainland. On no island did the law prohibit sexual liaisons between white masters and black slaves as Virginians attempted to do in the early eighteenth century. To be sure, planters never fully approved "miscegenation," and they actively discouraged sexual relations between black men and white women by refusing poor relief to any white woman who bore a mulatto child. The offspring of slave mothers remained slaves for life no matter who the father was. Yet Caribbean mulattos did occupy a social rank above pure-blooded Africans, gaining access to favored positions in crafts and domestic service. English fathers sometimes freed their mulatto offspring and helped them establish a life in free society. Descendants of such persons could find full acceptance in white society after only three generations, a phenomenon unheard of in mainland society.

Relations between Europeans and Africans in the English West Indies remained tense throughout the period of slavery. Planters maintained tight surveillance over the black majority that emerged on each of the islands, searching their quarters for weapons every other week, requiring Africans to obtain a pass in order to travel, monitoring their movements and associations for any sign of conspiracy, and ruthlessly suppressing any signs of resistance. Masters gave their most despised Irish servants greater privileges in law and custom than their most valued slaves in an effort to drive a wedge between the two groups. Masters sought to divide the slaves against themselves by rewarding those who worked harder, cooperated more fully, or informed on their fellows. Masters also tried to divide slaves by language barriers, according to Richard Ligon,

purchasing them from "severall parts of *Africa* . . . some from . . . *Guinny* and *Binny*, some from *Cutchew*, some from *Angola*, and some from the River of *Gambra*."

Despite harsh slave codes and brutal suppression of dissent, masters could never establish total control over the lives of their slaves. Africans looked for openings to create a culture that could sustain them through the harsh experience of Caribbean slavery. They also found ways to negotiate concessions from their masters that could make their lives more bearable. First-generation slaves on Barbados, for instance, so protested their monotonous diet of the maize-based porridge "loblolly" that their masters provided them plantain instead. During sugar harvest, masters commonly conceded their slaves the right to drink as much as they wanted of the "hot liquor" from the "last copper" in the boiling house. The iron- and vitamin-rich mixture of brown sugar and molasses gave slaves better health during harvest than at any other time of the year. Masters also began importing a higher percentage of slave women during the early years in response to complaints of male slaves who wanted wives.

Slaves drew on elements of their various African traditions, combining them into new cultural forms they could adapt to conditions of life in the West Indian environment. They labored to bridge language barriers by developing a pidgin tongue that combined elements of English and several African dialects. In a similar way, Africans combined various European and African musical forms into unique West Indian patterns of song, instrumental music, and dance. The planters would not permit their slaves to make or play drums because the Africans could use them to communicate across great distances. Instead, slaves shook out rhythms from gourd rattles filled with beans or wrapped with a netting of beads.

Richard Ligon recorded an especially detailed instance of this intercultural creativity after watching an African slave named Macow develop a marimba-like musical instrument. Macow apparently conceived the idea while experimenting with a lute to learn the relationship between the length of the string and the pitch of the sound. He later applied what he had learned to fashion a very different invention, a series of six wooden bars whose progressive lengths produced six different pitches on the scale when struck. When Ligon introduced Macow to the concept of sharps and flats, the African cut additional wooden bars to produce the new pitches. In this way, Macow incorporated European and African features of form and tone into a distinctly new, West Indian instrument capable of producing a new kind of music.

Africans had to create new patterns of marriage and family life within the constraints of West Indian slavery as well. Slaves on Barbados replicated the practice of polygamy even before the sex ratio became balanced, with lower-status slaves conceding to those of higher rank the right to take multiple wives. Marriage patterns, however, varied over time from plantation to plantation and island to island according to the specific conditions of life and labor. Slave marriages were not formalized by law, though Africans respected the unions as long as they endured. The informality of marriage may have given women greater independence from their husbands within the slave community. Child-rearing patterns likewise varied as conditions on the plantations shifted over time. The widespread practice of sending mothers to work in the fields only two or three weeks after giving birth made rearing the children a communal affair. The children's status as property of the master also weakened the parents' power to offer protection and guidance to their children.

Slaves managed to create their own social, religious, and economic institutions within the constraints of plantation society. Slaves as well as masters rested on Sundays, and the slaves spent their discretionary time in dancing,

games of skill, and socializing. On these days and at other times, slaves also pursued a variety of economic activities. Where land was available, slaves cultivated and sold among one another a variety of provision crops. The scarcity of land on the small sugar islands prevented Africans there from sustaining such a market for long, but a vibrant internal market endured among Jamaican slaves into the nineteenth century. Sundays also gave slaves the opportunity to observe religious rituals and ceremonies adapted from their various African pasts. Slaves invoked supernatural powers for protection from malevolent forces and sought spiritual guidance through divination. They looked to religion for healing from disease or injury as well as for vengeance, all of which could be especially potent when combined with their knowledge of medicinal herbs. Religion also provided solace for the bereaved, and funerals tragically became one of the slaves' most important ritual occasions.

Despite their masters' claims to the contrary, Caribbean slaves were never content in chains. They protested their debasement in many ways: sometimes in passive acts of resistance such as work slowdowns or feigning illness, sometimes in individual acts of violence, sometimes in running away, and sometimes in plotting rebellion. Yet even though slaves comprised a majority on most islands by 1670, only Jamaica and Antigua experienced actual slave rebellions.

To be sure, the Barbadian planter minority experienced a number of scares. In 1675, an island-wide uprising was narrowly averted when a domestic slave named Fortuna alerted her master of the plot. Officials rounded up the ringleaders, burned six alive, beheaded eleven others, and dragged their bodies through the streets of Speightstown, Barbados, as a warning to their comrades. Planters subsequently ferreted out and executed another seventeen conspirators to satisfy themselves that they had thwarted the plot. Quick and ruthless suppression also characterized the Barbadian planters' response to four subsequent alarms in 1683, 1686, 1692, and 1702. On Barbados, and on the Leewards too, tight controls, constant surveillance, and the timely warning of a compassionate informer thwarted every attempt at revolt.

Slaves who resisted by flight enjoyed a somewhat higher rate of success, though that avenue proved very difficult as well. The dense settlement on Barbados made leaving the island by boat the only real hope for runaways. Most who attempted this course headed for Carib-controlled St. Lucia or St. Vincent, where they attempted to enter Indian society. Caribs at first returned most runaways to their masters. As Anglo-Carib tensions increased, however, the Indians provided safe haven for runaway blacks to form maroon communities of "Garifunias" who could help defend Carib territory. Runaways on the Leewards could hide in the forested hills, but the planter militia usually managed to recapture them before long. Only on Antigua did a significant maroon community emerge during the 1680s to foment rebellion among plantation slaves, but in 1687, the planter militia rounded up its members and executed the leaders.

Jamaica's size, its mountainous terrain, and the presence of a Spanish maroon community on the island made control of its slave population a much more difficult matter. Sparser population and a more widely scattered pattern of plantation settlement made it easier for runaways to steal into virtually inaccessible mountainous regions such as the Cockpit Country, where large communities of maroons lived undetected for decades. The island experienced six major slave revolts between 1673 and 1694, one of which lasted a year (1685–1686). White authorities dealt ruthlessly with rebels, killing any they captured, but many survivors escaped to the maroons. Jamaican slaves demonstrated by force of arms the love for liberty, which their fellows on other English sugar islands could express only by passive resistance.

4.4: Sugar, Slaves, and the Atlantic Order

4.4   Report the shift of slave traffic to the West Indies due to its abundant sugarcane output

By the mid-1650s, the plunge into African slavery had already made Barbados one of the Atlantic World's leading sugar producers. Indeed, the island's output was quickly overtaking that of Brazil, which had dominated world markets in the first half of the century. This development was prompting London officials to think of the Caribbean—indeed, of the New World as a whole—in new ways. The region retained its strategic significance in the clash with Catholic Europe, yet England's Caribbean possessions no longer functioned solely as outposts for raids on Spanish shipping. The islands were beginning to produce a treasure that could rival Spanish American silver, bringing about a fundamental shift in the Atlantic economy. West Indian plantations were providing important new markets for New England farmers. They were attracting a flurry of new London investors. Barbadian sugar was enriching the Dutch merchants whose ships carried it to European markets, even more so than the Chesapeake tobacco trade that Dutch carriers also dominated. Barbadian demand was stimulating a tragic commerce in African slaves. London merchants and policymakers were searching for ways to direct more of the new Caribbean treasure to Bristol and London.

The dim outline of a new Atlantic order was beginning to emerge, thanks in great measure to the growing West Indian traffic in sugar and slaves. It was beginning to transform the international contest for New World dominion as rival powers competed to direct the transatlantic flow of wealth and power. That new impulse was increasingly marking the complex struggle among European and Native American rivals over North America as well.

Chronology

1624	Captain Thomas Warner establishes English colony on St. Christopher
1626	Sir William Courteen establishes sugar planting on Barbados
1628	Anthony Hilton leads colonization of Nevis
1631	English Puritans establish colony on Providence Island
1632	English establish plantations on Antigua, Montserrat
1635	Providence Islanders begin raids on Spanish ports and shipping
1640	African slave population on Barbados reaches 20,000, European 23,000
1641	General Francisco Díaz Pimienta captures Providence Island
1661	Barbadian legislature passes race-based slave code
1667	Irish servants on St. Christopher, Montserrat join French against English masters
1675	African slaves reach 71,000, 75 per cent of Barbados population

Chapter 5
Cities on a Hill
Bible Commonwealths in New England, 1620–1660

 Learning Objectives

5.1 Describe the demographic effects of Anglo-native contact that began in New England

5.2 Recount the plight and the struggles of the refugees aboard the Mayflower

5.3 Review the role played by the Puritans in sparking new thinking about republican government and popular sovereignty

5.4 Evaluate life of the Puritans in New England in the mid-1600s

5.5 Report the continuous process of adaptation that the natives of New England underwent

5.6 Express how New England settlers in the 1630s created a reformed Protestant outpost in the New World

5.7 Summarize how some of the first generation New England Puritans created a growing number of native Indian converts

Governor John Winthrop assured the settlers who traveled with him to Massachusetts Bay that they were on a special mission, sanctioned by God. In the New World, they would emulate the Jews of the Old Testament, creating a "city on a hill" which would stand as a beacon for Protestant reformers throughout Europe. But whatever their mandate, the ordinary men and women who followed Winthrop to America encountered physical conditions that tested their religious resolve.

In March 1631, one man of humble background recounted his initial experiences in a sobering letter to his father in England. The sea voyage had been horrendous. The entire Pond family—a wife and two children—suffered from smallpox that scarred the children and killed fourteen passengers. The land itself was not what the young farmer had expected. It was rocky and hilly, the soil too shallow and littered with stones, better for livestock than for grain. The struggling colonists lacked the equipment needed to go fishing; they found hunting in the dense forests harder than they had imagined. During these first very difficult months, Pond and his neighbors relied on Indian trade and supplies from England. They had crossed the Atlantic Ocean to do God's work, but as Pond confessed to his father, he desperately needed "help with provisions from ould eingland."

Like most families who sailed for Massachusetts Bay during the 1630s, the Ponds discovered how seriously they had underestimated the hardships of settlement. One historian has observed that the vast majority of colonists expressed disappointment at what they found in New England. The New England poet Anne Bradstreet wrote that at first her "heart rose" in rebellion against the "new world and new manners" she encountered in Massachusetts, but "after I was convinced it was the way of God, I submitted to it and joined the church at Boston." The deputy governor Thomas Dudley warned prospective settlers that "if any come hither to plant for worldly ends that can live well at home, he commits an error, of which he will soon repent him." Only those who came for "spiritual" reasons would "find here what may well content" them. Yet despite such reports, an estimated twenty-one thousand settlers embarked for New England during the Great Migration of the 1630s. More than seventeen thousand of those remained to build a stable communal society that contrasted starkly with England's Chesapeake dominions.

5.1: Indigenous Peoples

5.1 **Describe the demographic effects of Anglo-native contact that began in New England**

The English who began settling coastal New England in 1620 encountered scattered bands of native peoples whose numbers had been decimated by "a great and grievous plague" that ravaged the region in 1616. Although demoralized, the survivors possessed extensive knowledge of European ways acquired from almost a century of trade and

interaction. They remained highly resourceful in using that knowledge to pursue their own interests in an ongoing Anglo-Indian exchange.

Anglo-native contact began in New England when obscure fifteenth-century fishermen came ashore to dry their catches before returning home (see Chapter 1). There they encountered bands of largely self-sufficient peoples living in a patchwork of territories defined by the region's bays and river valleys. The Massachusett, for example, lived around Massachusetts Bay and its tributaries, while neighboring Algonquian tribes inhabited Cape Cod, southeastern Massachusetts, and the eastern side of Narragansett Bay. Narragansetts inhabited the western side of that bay, Mohegan-Pequots inhabited the region of what is now eastern Connecticut and Long Island, and Quiripi bands inhabited the Connecticut River valley and central Long Island.

Before the arrival of intensive European trade, southern New England peoples pursued a way of life centered on cycles of farming, hunting, and winter foraging. As much as three-quarters of their diet came from maize, beans, and squash, which women farmers planted together in densely tangled fields that "load[ed] the Ground with as much as it [would] bear." Men supplemented this nutritious diet through hunting and fishing, risky activities that took them away from home for extended periods. Villages celebrated harvest with feasting, dancing, and gambling combined with rituals in which wealthy individuals gave away most of their possessions to seal reciprocal relations of mutual support and obligation among followers or allies. At the end of these festivals, villages moved into fall hunting camps from which the men ranged individually or in groups to track fattened game such as bear and deer. Women hauled the dead animals back to camp where they butchered and processed the meat and hides for later use. December snowfalls drove villagers to sites that offered shelter from the winter elements and provided hunters and fishermen a base of operations for their ongoing expeditions.

Tribal chiefs, usually called *sagamores* from Massachusetts Bay north and *sachems* toward the south, obtained their status through matrilineal inheritance coupled with charismatic leadership. Sagamores further secured their position by generous gift-giving to followers who reciprocated with support and loyalty. Women could also wield authority, as the Pawtucket "Squaw Sachem" of Massachusetts Bay did during the early 1630s. A loose hierarchy of leadership existed similar to that of Chesapeake Algonquians, with sagamores of lesser villages often paying tribute to more powerful leaders in exchange for support and protection. Followers supported their sagamores with tribute in fish, corn, furs, game, or hospitality: "a flower in the prince's crown and a royalty paid him," as the Connecticut minister Jared Elliot observed.

The growth of European trade during the sixteenth century stimulated subtle shifts in native economies. The tribes had previously relied on regional exchange networks to supplement their own supplies of food and obtain scarce items such as highly valued purple wampum shells supplied by the Montauks of Long Island. After the French arrived, their northern Micmac fur-trading partners became more dependent on outside sources of food and supplies as their hunters specialized in procuring commodities for trade rather than game for subsistence. The same process began to draw in the Abenakis of Maine in the late sixteenth and early seventeenth century. Abenakis adapted by entering trading partnerships in which they exchanged goods obtained from the French for surplus Massachusett crops. Micmacs responded to the new state of affairs by raiding both Abenaki competitors and native farmers of southern New England for tribute in agricultural goods, transforming the Abenaki–southern New England partnership into a political and military alliance. Dutch fur traders working from the Hudson River were stimulating similar economic and political adjustments among the tribes of Long Island Sound and western Narragansett Bay. By the early seventeenth century, Indians within both the French and Dutch spheres of trade were slipping into dependence on European commerce.

When English adventurers began exploring the region after 1600, groups such as the Abenaki approached them as potential allies who could help their people achieve a competitive advantage in trade. The English, however, repeatedly antagonized native peoples through hostile actions that included kidnapping and taking captives to England, where schemers such as Sir Ferdinando Gorges hoped to transform them into agents for various colonial enterprises. Squanto, the English-speaking Pawtucket whom schoolchildren remember for assisting the Pilgrims during their first years of settlement, was one such captive. A dozen years of exploration, contact, and occasional trade gained the English extensive knowledge of the region. It also acquainted native inhabitants with prickly English ways, which may explain why no tribe formed a lasting trading partnership with them. In 1614, the indomitable Captain John Smith set out to succeed where his countrymen had hitherto failed, reconnoitering and mapping the region he named New England before returning home to lay plans for a new colony there. Smith planned to use tactics he had practiced on the Powhatans of Virginia to browbeat New England Indians into trading furs and corn, but those plans came to nothing after his expedition fell apart.

Despite the social and economic changes introduced by European trade, New England tribes successfully resisted European domination. They could not, however, resist epidemic disease. From 1616 to 1618, the region's native peoples underwent horrific devastation, succumbing by the tens of thousands to what was probably some strain of plague unwittingly introduced by French traders. Historians estimate that the coastal population dropped as much as 90 percent. Whole tribes, such as that of the famous Pawtucket, Squanto, disappeared completely, their very memory eventually obliterated as other peoples absorbed their tattered remnants. Where John Smith had seen a land "planted with Gardens and Corne fields, and so well inhabited with a goodly, strong, and well-proportioned people," later visitors found abandoned fields choked with underbrush. When the Englishman Thomas Morton arrived in 1622, the unburied skeletons lying about "made such a spectacle . . . it seemed to me a new found Golgatha [sic]."

Thus the English settlers who began arriving in 1620 found only the remnants of once robust bands struggling to regroup in the wake of unimaginable catastrophe. Surviving sagamores labored to consolidate their people into bands that incorporated the remnants of tribes now too few in number to continue as separate peoples. The Reverend Francis Higginson reported in 1629 that "the greatest sagamores about us cannot make above three hundred men, and other less sagamores have not above fifteen subjects and others near about us but two." Higginson observed that so few people could not "make use of one-fourth part of the land." Under such conditions, the sachems were only too willing to welcome English colonists as allies who could help them repel the advances of interior tribes who had escaped the epidemic. Yet even in this weakened condition, the survivors proved adept at using trade and diplomacy to retain a significant degree of self-determination and control over their own affairs.

5.2: Pilgrims and Strangers

5.2 **Recount the plight and the struggles of the refugees aboard the Mayflower**

The Pilgrims enjoy almost mythic status in American history. These brave refugees crossed the cold Atlantic in search of religious liberty, signed a democratic compact aboard the Mayflower, landed at Plymouth Rock, and gave us Thanksgiving Day. As with most legends, this one contains only a core of truth.

The Pilgrims were not crusaders who set out to change the world. Rather, they were humble

English farmers. Their story began in the early 1600s in Scrooby Manor, a small community located approximately 150 miles north of London. Many people living in this area believed the Church of England retained too many traces of its Catholic origin. To support such a corrupt institution was like winking at the devil. Its very rituals compromised God's true believers, and so, in the early years of the reign of James I, the Scrooby congregation formally left the established state church. Like others who followed this logic, they were called Separatists. Since English statute required citizens to attend Anglican services, the Scrooby Separatists moved to Holland in 1608–1609 rather than compromise.

The Netherlands provided the Separatists with a good home—too good. The members of the little church feared they were losing their distinct identity; their children were becoming Dutch. In 1617, therefore, a portion of the original Scrooby congregation vowed to sail to America. Included in this group was William Bradford, a wonderfully literate man who wrote *Of Plymouth Plantation*, one of the first and certainly most poignant accounts of an early American settlement.

Poverty presented the major obstacle to their plans. They petitioned for a land patent from the Virginia Company of London. At the same time, they looked for someone willing to underwrite the staggering costs of colonization. These negotiations went well, or so it seemed. Thirty Pilgrims under the leadership of William Brewster embarked in July 1620, stopping in England long enough to take on supplies and recruit additional voyagers, most of whom were non-Separating "Strangers." In September, 102 Pilgrims and Strangers set off for America aboard the Mayflower, armed with a patent to settle in Virginia and indebted to a group of English investors who were only marginally interested in religious reform.

For reasons not entirely clear, the eight-week voyage brought the Pilgrims to New England instead of Virginia. The patent for which they had worked so diligently had no validity in this region.

In fact, the crown had granted New England to another company. Without a patent, the colonists possessed no authorization to form a civil government, a serious matter since the non-Separatist majority threatened mutiny. To preserve the struggling community from anarchy, forty-one men agreed on November 21 to "covenant and combine our selves together into a civil body politick."

The Mayflower Compact could not ward off disease and hunger. In early December, the settlers selected the abandoned village of Pawtucket as their new home, renaming it Plymouth. It was a poor season to begin any settlement. Supplies had run dangerously low and the nearby Pokanoket kept their distance, thwarting hopes of trading for food. Colonists tried to survive by foraging and occasionally pilfering stores of corn from Indian villages. Despite their efforts, death claimed approximately half of the 102 original passengers.

The spring of 1621 brought new hope for the survivors as the Pokanoket relaxed their wariness to enter a pact with the colony which the sachem Massasoit hoped would enhance his tribe's prestige and empower them to resist their Narragansett rivals to the west. Plymouth gained a crucial trading partner as well as the invaluable aid of the Pawtucket Squanto, who had his own reasons for cooperating with the English. Squanto's services as a guide, interpreter, and diplomat proved at least as valuable to the colonists as his agricultural advice, for Plymouth continued to rely on Indian-produced corn to supplement their own crops during the first three years of settlement.

Early relations between Plymouth colonists and native inhabitants were bedeviled by misunderstandings and conflicting agendas on all sides. The English wanted to extend authority over all tribes in their sphere of influence as subjects "of our Soveraign lord [King James], His Heirs and Successors." They also hoped to gain title to "all the Lands adjacent, to them and their Heirs forever." Massasoit, on the other hand, sought to gain economic and military advantages over his Narragansett rivals. His authority over other Pokanoket sachems, however, rested on prestige and generosity, not coercive force, and any who judged the treaty harmful to their interests could follow a different course. Squanto may have hoped that his favored status with the English would help him reconstitute the Pawtuckets and oust their historic Pokanoket rivals from English favor. In time, Squanto's schemes were exposed and the English came to understand that they could only extend their sphere of influence through separate agreements with each sachem of the region. Under Captain Miles Standish, the colony pursued a militaristic Indian policy to obtain the grudging assistance of their neighbors.

Plymouth colonists extricated themselves from dependence on Pokanoket corn by 1624, cultivating surpluses that not only sustained them through the winters but gave them a valuable commodity to trade for furs. Corn surpluses enabled the colonists to step into the void left by the demise of native New England farmers to establish a profitable fur-trading partnership with the Abenakis to the north. Plymouth gradually expanded its reach west as well, striking additional trading partnerships that eventually included the Dutch as well as Indians. By 1629, the colony was enjoying modest success as a commercial center.

Even with the fur trade, Plymouth colonists found it difficult to escape the burden of debts contracted in England. The company backing the colony dissolved in 1625, cutting off additional financial support and demanding repayment of funds invested. To their credit, the Pilgrims honored their financial obligations, but it took almost twenty years to satisfy the English investors. Without Bradford, whom they elected as governor, the settlers might have allowed adversity to overwhelm them. Through strength of will and self-sacrifice, however, Bradford persuaded frightened men and women that they could survive in America.

In time, the Pilgrims replicated the humble little farm communities they had once known in England. They formed Separatist congregations to their liking; the population slowly increased. The Abenaki fur trade declined rapidly after 1630, and early experiments with commercial fishing never generated substantial income. Most families relied on mixed husbandry, grain, and livestock. Because Plymouth offered limited economic prospects, it attracted only a trickle of new settlers. In 1691, the colony was absorbed into its larger and more prosperous neighbor, Massachusetts Bay.

5.3: A "New" England in America

5.3 Review the role played by the Puritans in sparking new thinking about republican government and popular sovereignty

In the early decades of the seventeenth century, an extraordinary spirit of religious reform burst forth in England. Before it had burned itself out, Puritanism had transformed the face of England and America. Modern historians have difficulty comprehending this powerful force. Some consider the Puritans neurotic individuals who condemned liquor and sex, dressed in drab clothes, and minded their neighbors' business.

The crude caricature is based on a profound misunderstanding of the actual nature of this broad popular movement. Seventeenth-century Puritans were more like today's radical political reformers, men and women committed to far-reaching institutional change, than like naive do-gooders or narrow Victorian fundamentalists. To their enemies, of course, the Puritans were an irritant, always pointing out civil and ecclesiastical imperfections. A great many people, however, shared their vision. Puritans not only founded several American colonies, but also sparked the English Civil Wars, a revolution that generated bold new thinking about republican government and popular sovereignty (see Chapter 5).

The Puritans were products of the Protestant Reformation. They accepted a Calvinist belief that an omnipotent God chose or "elected" some people to receive salvation while leaving the rest of sinful humanity to eternal damnation (see Chapter 1). Instead of waiting passively for Judgment Day, the Puritans examined themselves for signs of grace, for hints that God had in fact placed them among his "elect." A member of this select group, they argued, would try to live according to Scripture, battle sin, and eradicate corruption.

For the Puritans, the logic of everyday life was clear. If the Church of England contained unscriptural elements—clerical vestments, for example—then they must be eliminated. If the pope in Rome was in league with the Antichrist, then Protestant kings had better not form alliances with Catholic states. If God condemned licentiousness and intoxication, then local officials should punish whores and drunks. There was nothing improper about an occasional beer or passionate physical love within marriage, but when sex and drink became ends in themselves, the Puritans thought England's ministers and magistrates should speak out. Persons of this temperament were more combative than the Pilgrims had been. They wanted to purify the Church of England from within, and before the 1630s at least, separatism held little appeal for them.

From the Puritan perspective, the early Stuarts—James I and Charles I—seemed unconcerned about the spiritual state of the nation. James tolerated corruption within his own court, condoning gross public extravagance. His foreign policy appeased European Catholic powers. At one time, James tried to marry his son to a Spanish Catholic princess, and Charles I eventually did marry the fervently Catholic Princess Henrietta Maria of France. Neither king showed interest in purifying the Anglican church. In fact, Charles fanned Puritan suspicions by accommodating his queen's Catholic faith, permitting her to keep a priest at court and to attend private masses. He also assisted the rapid advance of William Laud, a bishop who represented everything the Puritans detested. Laud defended "popish" church ceremonies that they found obnoxious. He persecuted Puritan ministers, forcing them to either conform to his theology or lose their licenses to preach. As long as Parliament met, Puritan voters in the various boroughs and counties throughout England elected men sympathetic to their point of view. These outspoken representatives criticized royal policies and hounded Laud. Because of their defiance, Charles decided in 1629 to rule England without Parliament and four years later named Laud, archbishop of Canterbury, the highest office in the Church of England. The last doors of reform slammed shut. The corruption remained.

John Winthrop, the future governor of Massachusetts Bay, was caught up in these events. Little about his background suggested such an auspicious future. He owned a small manor in Suffolk, one that never produced sufficient income to support his growing family. He dabbled in law. But the core of Winthrop's life was his faith in God, a faith so intense his contemporaries immediately identified him as a Puritan. The Lord, he concluded, was displeased with England. Time for reform was running out. In May 1629, he confided to his wife, "I am verily perswaded God will bringe some heavye Affliction upon this lande, and that speedylye." He was, however, confident that the Lord would "provide a shelter and a hidinge place for us."

Other Puritans, some of them wealthier and politically better connected than Winthrop, reached similar conclusions about England's future. They turned their attention to the possibility of establishing a colony in America, and on March 4, 1629, their Massachusetts Bay Company obtained a charter directly from the king. Charles and his advisers apparently thought the Massachusetts Bay Company was a commercial venture no different from the dozens of other joint-stock companies that had recently sprung into existence.

Winthrop and his associates knew better. On August 26, 1629, twelve of them met secretly and signed the Cambridge Agreement. They pledged to each other to be "ready in our persons and with such of our severall familyes as are to go with us . . . to embark for the said plantation by the first of

Colonists elected John Winthrop to serve a total of 13 years as governor and 10 years as deputy governor of Massachusetts. Winthrop proved very effective at translating Puritan values into practical policy.

March next." There was one loophole. The charters of most joint-stock companies designated a specific location where business meetings were to be held. For reasons not entirely clear—a timely bribe is a good guess—the charter of the Massachusetts Bay Company did not contain this standard clause. It could hold meetings anywhere the stockholders, called "freemen," desired, even America. If they met in America, moreover, the king and his archbishop could not easily interfere in their affairs.

5.3.1: A Covenanted People in America

The Winthrop fleet departed England in March 1630. Within a year, almost two thousand people had arrived in Massachusetts Bay. Throughout the 1630s, thousands more came to carve new

English farms and villages from what they regarded as a "howling" American wilderness.

A great deal is known about the background of these particular settlers. A large percentage of them originated in an area northeast of London called East Anglia, a region in which Puritan ideas had taken deep root. London, Kent, and the West Country also contributed to the stream of emigrants. In some instances, entire villages such as Higham were reestablished across the Atlantic. Many Bay colonists had worked as farmers in England, but a surprisingly large number came from commercial centers, such as Norwich, where cloth was manufactured for the export trade.

Whatever their backgrounds, the Puritans moved to Massachusetts as nuclear families, fathers, mothers, and their dependent children, a form of migration strikingly different from the one that peopled Virginia and Maryland. Moreover, because the settlers had already formed families in England, the colony's sex ratio was more balanced than that found in the Chesapeake colonies. Finally, and perhaps more significantly, once they had arrived in Massachusetts, these men and women survived. Indeed, their life expectancy compares favorably to that of modern Americans. Many factors help explain this phenomenon—clean drinking water and a healthy climate, for example. The Reverend Francis Higginson ascribed it to the "extraordinary clear and dry" New England air "that is of a most healing nature." While the Puritans could not have planned to live longer than did colonists in other parts of the New World, this remarkable accident reduced the emotional shock of long-distance migration.

The first settlers possessed another source of strength and stability. They were bound together by a common sense of purpose. God, they insisted, had formed a special covenant with the people of Massachusetts Bay. On his part, the Lord expected them to live according to Scripture, to reform the church; in other words, to create a biblical "city on a hill" that would stand as a beacon of righteousness for the rest of the Christian world. If they fulfilled their side of the bargain, the settlers could anticipate peace and prosperity. No one, not even the lowliest servant, was excused from this divine covenant, for as Winthrop stated, "Wee must be knitt together in this worke as one man." Even as the first ships departed England, John Cotton, a popular Puritan minister, urged the emigrants to go forth "with a publicke spirit, looking not on your owne things only, but also on the things of others." Many people throughout the ages have espoused such communal rhetoric, but these particular men and women went about the business of forming a new colony as if they truly intended to transform a religious vision into social reality.

In ecclesiastical affairs, the colonists proceeded by what one founder called "experimental footsteps." They arrived in Massachusetts Bay without a precise plan for their church. Although the rituals and ceremonies enforced by Laud had no place in Massachusetts, the American Puritans refused to separate formally from the Church of England. In this matter, they thought the Pilgrims had made a serious mistake. After all, what was the point of reforming an institution if the reformers were no longer part of it?

The Bay colonists gradually came to accept a highly innovative form of church government known as Congregationalism. Under this system, each village church was independent of outside interference. The American Puritans, of course, wanted nothing of bishops. "Elect" women and men (the "saints") together with their baptized children were the church, and as a body, they pledged to uphold God's laws. In the Salem church, for example, the members covenanted "with the Lord and with one another and do bind ourselves in the presence of God to walk together in all his ways."

Simply because a person happened to live in a certain community did not mean he or she automatically belonged to the local church. Unlike the parish institutions they knew in England, the churches of Massachusetts were voluntary institutions. To join one a man or woman had to provide testimony—a personal confession of faith—before neighbors who had already been admitted as full members. It was a demanding process. Whatever the personal strains, however, most men and women in early Massachusetts aspired to full membership. Church membership entitled them to the sacraments—participation in the Lord's supper and baptism for their infants—and gave some of them responsibility for choosing ministers, disciplining backsliders, and determining difficult questions of theology. Although women and blacks could not vote for ministers, they did become members of the Congregational churches. Over the course of the seventeenth century, women made up an increasingly large share of the membership.

Congregational autonomy had limits, to be sure, and civil magistrates sometimes took the lead in ferreting out heretical beliefs. Those who did not become church members were compelled to attend regular religious services. Perhaps because of the homogeneity of the colony's population, however, the loose polity of the Congregational churches held together for the entire colonial period.

In creating a civil government, the Bay colonists faced a particularly difficult challenge. Their charter allowed the investors in a joint-stock company to set up a business organization. When the settlers arrived in America, however, company leaders—men like Winthrop—moved quickly to transform the commercial structure into a colonial government. An early step in this direction took place on May 18, 1631, when the category of "freeman" was extended to all adult males who had become members of a Congregational church. This decision greatly expanded the franchise of Massachusetts Bay, and historians estimate that during the 1630s, at least 40 percent of the colony's adult males could vote in colonywide elections. While this percentage may seem low by modern standards, it was higher than anything the emigrants would have known in England. The

freemen voted annually for a governor, a group of magistrates called the Court of Assistants, and after 1634, deputies who represented the interests of the individual towns. Even military officers were elected in Massachusetts Bay.

Two popular misconceptions about this government should be dispelled. It was neither a democracy nor a theocracy. The magistrates elected in Massachusetts did not believe they represented the voters, much less the whole populace. They ruled in the name of the electorate, but their responsibility as rulers was to God. In 1638, Winthrop warned against overly democratic forms, since "the best part is always the least, and of that best part the wiser is always the lesser." Second, the Congregational ministers possessed no formal political authority in Massachusetts Bay. They could not even hold civil office, and it was not unusual for the voters to ignore the recommendations of a respected minister such as John Cotton.

In New England, the town became the center of public life. In other regions of British America where the county was the focus of local government, people did not experience the same density of social and institutional interaction. In Massachusetts, groups of men and women voluntarily covenanted together to observe common goals. The community constructed a meetinghouse where religious services and town meetings were held. This powerful sense of shared purpose—something that later Americans have greatly admired—should not obscure the fact that the founders of New England towns also had a keen eye for personal profit. Seventeenth-century records reveal that speculators often made a good deal of money from selling "shares" in village lands. But acquisitiveness never got out of control, and recent studies have shown that entrepreneurial practices rarely disturbed the peace of the Puritan communities. Inhabitants generally received land sufficient to build a house and to support a family. Although villagers escaped the kind of feudal dues collected in other parts of America—quitrents, for example—they were expected to contribute to the minister's salary, pay local and colony taxes, establish schools, and serve in the militia.

5.3.2: "Trucking with the Indians"

Puritan leaders hoped that their Christian commonwealth would become an example not only to Europeans but also to the New England Indians among whom they would be settling. Indeed, the Massachusetts Bay Company's seal depicted Indian imploring would-be colonists to "come over and help us." Every Puritan would have recognized this familiar New Testament phrase and understood it as a call to follow St. Paul's missionary example by carrying the Gospel of salvation to seventeenth-century "heathen" who had presumably never heard it. During the colony's first years, leaders paid close attention to whether or not their Massachusett and Pawtucket neighbors spoke "well of our God." Early relations between the two peoples, however, consisted primarily of mundane exchanges associated with establishing a new colony.

The tribes near Massachusetts Bay had only begun recovering from the epidemic of 1616, and Puritans who arrived in 1630 found "but few" native inhabitants. The survivors welcomed the colonists as trading partners and "walls to their bloody enemies," the Micmac of present-day New Brunswick. Indeed, to understand such behavior we must remember that local bands identified themselves as members of specific tribes, not as members of a united racial group. They therefore saw no problem in making alliances with Europeans against other Native Americans.

Although Bay Company officials had instructed colonial leaders to negotiate purchases of any lands settled, the Pawtucket and Massachusett readily granted colonists the right to occupy the land in exchange for protection. They also bartered their labor and services, clearing fields, assisting in building, performing domestic tasks, and killing wolves near the settlements.

Like the Plymouth colonists a decade before, Bay Colony leaders assumed that their legal dealings with native peoples included native acceptance of English sovereignty, and they tried to incorporate native peoples into an English framework of hierarchical authority. For example, early colonial magistrates hauled the Pawtucket "Sagamore John" and the Massachusett sagamore Chicataubut into court when their followers killed English livestock, ordering the sagamores to enforce English judgments against native offenders. Colonial officials tried to replicate this pattern in subsequent negotiations for land and sovereignty as English settlement of the region expanded. Native leaders did not share Puritan conceptions of hierarchy or sovereignty, and they resisted colonial officials' efforts to dominate them whenever they could. Leaders of large groups such as the powerful Narragansetts and Pequots possessed sufficient political and military strength to insist that Bay Colony leaders respect them as equals. Sagamores of small bands could do less but sought to buffer English domination while their followers continued to order their lives as much as possible by tribal custom and tradition.

The rapid expansion of Puritan settlements in the 1630s precipitated a dramatic shift in power relations among the region's Indian nations. The nearby Massachusett and Pawtucket bands suffered yet another epidemic of smallpox in the early 1630s, prompting Governor John Winthrop to declare that "God hath hereby cleared our title to this place." For other tribes, however, the expansive English presence in the region presented an unforeseen opportunity. Narragansett leaders seized the moment to break a Dutch monopoly on trade in Narragansett Bay and to launch a military offensive against their former Pequot allies who dominated Connecticut River commerce. Pequot leaders likewise vied for commercial advantage by playing the English off against the Dutch, eventually inviting the English to settle around the mouth of the Connecticut River. By 1636, new English settlements were pressing rapidly up the Connecticut River into Pequot territory, outstripping the capacity of either Bay Colony officials or leading Pequot sachems to control their expansion.

This complex struggle for land, trade, and dominion came to a head in the Pequot War of 1636–1637. Armed conflict erupted after the murder of an English trader named John Oldham was blamed on Pequot tributaries, the eastern Niantics. For nine months, colonists and Pequots periodically raided each other's villages, and Pequot warriors mounted a siege of Fort Saybrook on the Connecticut River. In late May 1637, Connecticut's Captain John Mason led a combined counterforce from his own colony, Massachusetts Bay, and Plymouth along with Narragansett and Mohegan allies. On the morning of May 26, the force surrounded and set fire to the Pequots' Mystic River stronghold. While the dwellings burned, the English and their allies killed those attempting to flee. Within an hour, all but seven inhabitants lay dead. Appalled Narragansett witnesses protested that the English way of fighting was "too furious, and slays too many men," but Captain Mason exulted that the Lord himself had "judged among the Heathen, filling the Place with Dead Bodies!"

The Pequot War marked the emergence of a pattern of English–Indian relations that persisted until the 1670s. Remaining Pequot villages disappeared as survivors fled or were captured and enslaved, and in 1638, the Treaty of Hartford declared their nation dissolved. Their former allies the Mohegans gained greatly from the war, becoming the major brokers between the English and lesser tribes in the region. For the Narragansetts, however, the victory proved pyrrhic as they found themselves pressed from all sides by increasingly hostile, expansive English settlements in Connecticut, Massachusetts, and Plymouth. Despite this turn in fortune, however, groups such as the Narragansett continued to wield significant power to extract concessions from colonial officials and protect tribal interests.

5.3.3: Dissenting Voices: Diversity and Fragmentation

The 1630s proved as tumultuous for the Massachusetts Bay's internal affairs as it did for diplomatic relations with native neighbors. Colonists managed to resolve most of their disputes within the framework of English law and custom. This was a remarkable achievement considering the chronic instability that plagued other colonies at this time. The Bay colonists disagreed over many issues, sometimes vociferously; whole towns disputed with neighboring villages over common boundaries. But the people inevitably relied on the courts to mediate differences. They believed in a rule of law, and in 1648, the colonial legislature, called the General Court, drew up the *Lawes and Liberties*, the first alphabetized code of law printed in English. This innovative document is of fundamental importance in American constitutional history. In clear prose, it explained to the colonists their rights and responsibilities as citizens of the commonwealth. The code engendered public trust in government and discouraged magistrates from the arbitrary exercise of authority.

Some of the sharpest clashes during the first decade arose from differences in religious belief among Massachusetts Bay colonists. The ordered New England society, which seems in hindsight to have emerged so quickly, was actually a product of intense and creative theological debate among leaders of passionate conviction. Subtle variations in Puritan theology, which had seemed unimportant in the face of persecution by the English government, took on fresh significance as ministers and magistrates began implementing their ideas of a pure church and commonwealth. This ferment of opinion compounded the tensions and uncertainty of life in this New World environment, while creating an opening for some ideas that the leading magistrates and ministers perceived as heretical.

The most serious challenges to Puritan orthodoxy in Massachusetts Bay came from two remarkable individuals. The first, Roger Williams, arrived in 1631 and immediately attracted a body of loyal followers. Indeed, everyone seems to have liked him as a person. Williams's ideas, however, created controversy. He preached extreme separatism. He declared the Bay colonists impure in the sight of the Lord so long as they remained even nominal members of the Church of England. Moreover, he questioned the validity of the colony's charter, since the king had not first purchased the land from the Indians, a view that threatened the integrity of the entire colonial experiment. Williams also insisted that the civil rulers of Massachusetts had no business punishing settlers for their religious beliefs. God, not men, was responsible to monitor people's consciences. The Bay magistrates were prepared neither to tolerate views they considered heresy nor to accede to Williams's other demands. In 1636, after attempts to reach a compromise had failed, they banished him from the colony.

Williams worked out the logic of his ideas in Providence, a village he founded in what would become Rhode Island. The colony became a haven for dissidents from Old and New England alike. Williams himself was one of the most outspoken. His spiritual pilgrimage as a "Puritan Seeker" ultimately led him to conclude that he could enjoy Christian fellowship with none but his wife. He also became a fierce theological opponent of dissenting groups such as the Quakers whom he nevertheless welcomed as full partners in his colonial enterprise. The colony's location within Narragansett territory gave Williams the opportunity to study native culture closely, and the sympathetic observations recorded in his *Key to the Language of America* remain a valuable source of information on seventeenth-century native cultures. Williams's friendship with the Narragansetts also made him an important figure in early Anglo-Indian relations.

While the magistrates of Massachusetts Bay labored to suppress Roger Williams, an even graver threat to the peace of their commonwealth emerged under the leadership of Anne Hutchinson. This extremely intelligent woman, her husband William, and her children followed the learned minister John Cotton to New England in 1634. Even contemporaries found her arcane religious ideas somewhat confusing, but authorities eventually branded them as antinomianism, a heretical position that reputedly held that true believers were completely released from conformity to divine law. Whatever her thoughts, Hutchinson shared them with other Bostonians, many of them women. Her outspoken views scandalized orthodox leaders of church and state. She suggested that all but two ministers in the colony had lost touch with the Holy Spirit and had begun preaching that people must live a righteous life to be saved, an idea she termed a "covenant of works."

When authorities demanded she explain her assertions, Hutchinson announced that the Holy Spirit had given her a special ability to discern the spiritual condition of other people. She hinted that she could exercise this gift independently of either the Bible or the clergy. Authorities recognized that if Hutchinson really believed in direct revelation, her teachings could not be tested by Scripture, a position that seemed dangerously subjective. Indeed, her theology called the very foundation of Massachusetts Bay into question. Without clear, external standards, one person's truth was as valid as that of anyone else. From Winthrop's perspective, Hutchinson's views invited civil and religious anarchy.

When Hutchinson described Congregational ministers—some of them the leading divines of Boston—as unconverted men and false Christians, the General Court intervened. For two very tense days in 1637, the ministers and magistrates of Massachusetts Bay cross-examined Hutchinson. In this intense theological debate, she more than held her own. She knew as much about the

Bible as did her inquisitors, and no doubt her brilliance at that moment provoked the court's misogyny.

Hutchinson challenged ministers and magistrates to demonstrate exactly where she had erred. Just when it appeared that this gifted woman had outmaneuvered—indeed, thoroughly embarrassed—her opponents, she let down her guard. She declared that what she knew of God came "by an immediate revelation. . . . By the voice of his own spirit to my soul." Here was what her accusers had suspected all along but could not prove. She had confessed in open court that the human spirit could commune with God apart from conformity to the external moral teachings of the Bible. This antinomian statement challenged the authority of the Bay rulers, and they were relieved to exile Hutchinson and her followers to Rhode Island.

5.3.4: Breaking Away

Massachusetts Bay spawned four new colonies, three of which survived to the American Revolution. New Hampshire became a separate colony in 1677. Its population grew very slowly, and for much of the colonial period, New Hampshire remained economically dependent on Massachusetts, its neighbor to the south.

Far more people were drawn to the fertile lands of the Connecticut River valley. In 1636, settlers founded the villages of Hartford, Windsor, and Wethersfield. No one forced these men and women to leave Massachusetts, and in their new surroundings, they created a society that looked much like the one they had known in the Bay Colony. Through his writings, Thomas Hooker, Connecticut's most prominent minister, helped all New Englanders define Congregational church polity. Puritans on both sides of the Atlantic read Hooker's beautifully crafted works. In 1639, representatives from the Connecticut towns passed the Fundamental Orders, a blueprint for civil government. In 1662, Charles

II awarded the colony a charter of its own, one that recognized annual elections for all civil offices, including governor.

In 1638, another group, led by Theophilus Eaton and the Reverend John Davenport, settled New Haven and several adjoining towns along Long Island Sound. These emigrants, many of whom had come from London, lived briefly in Massachusetts Bay but then insisted on forming a Puritan commonwealth of their own, one that established a closer relationship between church and state than the Bay colonists had allowed. The New Haven colony never prospered, and in 1662, it was absorbed into Connecticut.

Rhode Island experienced a wholly different history. From the beginning, it was populated by exiles and troublemakers, and according to one Dutch visitor, Rhode Island was "the receptacle of all sorts of riff-raff people. . . . All the cranks of New-England retire thither." This description, of course, was an exaggeration. Roger Williams founded Providence in 1636; two years later, Anne Hutchinson took her followers to Portsmouth. Other groups settled around Narragansett Bay. Not surprisingly, these men and women appreciated the need for toleration. No one was persecuted in Rhode Island for his or her religious beliefs.

One might have thought these separate Rhode Island communities would cooperate for the common good. They did not. Villagers fought over land and schemed with outside speculators to divide the tiny colony into ever-smaller pieces. In 1644, Parliament issued a patent for the "Providence Plantations," and in 1663, the Rhode Islanders obtained a remarkably liberal charter that allowed voters to select their own governors. These successes did not calm political turmoil. For most of the seventeenth century, colonywide government existed in name only. Despite their constant bickering, however, the settlers of Rhode Island—many of whom became Quakers or Baptists—established a profitable commerce in agricultural goods.

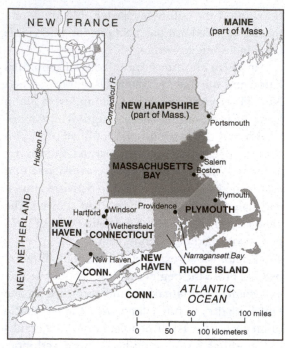

Map 5.1 New England Colonies 1650

5.4: The Puritan Order in New England

5.4 Evaluate life of the Puritans in New England in the mid-1600s

Seventeenth-century New Englanders successfully replicated in America a traditional social order they had known in England. The transfer of a familiar way of life to the New World seemed less difficult for these Puritan migrants than it did for the many English men and women who settled in the Chesapeake colonies. Their contrasting experiences, fundamental to an understanding of the development of both cultures, can be explained, at least in part, by the development of Puritan families.

5.4.1: Longevity, Family, and Society

Early New Englanders believed God ordained the family for human benefit. This biological unit was essential to the maintenance of social order, since outside the family, men and women succumbed to carnal temptation. Such people had no one to sustain them or remind them of Scripture. "Without Family care," declared the Reverend Benjamin Wadsworth, "the labour of Magistrates and Ministers for Reformation and Propagating Religion, is likely to be in great measure unsuccessful."

The godly family, at least in theory, was ruled by a patriarch, father to his children, husband to his wife, the source of authority, and object of unquestioned obedience. The wife shared responsibility for the raising of children, but in decisions of importance, especially those related to property, she was expected to defer to her spouse.

The New Englanders' concern about the character of the godly family is not surprising. This institution played a central role in shaping their society. In contrast to those who migrated to the colonies of Virginia and Maryland, New Englanders crossed the Atlantic within nuclear families. That is, they moved within established units consisting of a father, mother, and their dependent children rather than as single youths and adults. People who migrated to America within families preserved local English customs more fully than did the youths who traveled to other parts of the continent as single men and women. The comforting presence of immediate family members reduced the shock of adjusting to a strange environment 3,000 miles from home. Even in the 1630s, the ratio of men to women in New England was fairly well balanced, about three males for every two females. Persons who had not already married in England before coming to the New World could expect to form nuclear families of their own.

The outbreak of the English Civil Wars in 1642 reduced the flood of people moving to Massachusetts Bay to a trickle. Nevertheless, by the end of the century, the population of New England had grown from less than 20,000 to almost 120,000, an amazing increase considering the small number of original immigrants. Historians have been hard pressed to explain the striking rate of growth. Some have suggested the New Englanders married very young, thus providing couples extra years in which to produce large families. Other scholars have maintained that New England women must have been more fertile than their Old World counterparts.

Neither demographic theory adequately explains how so few migrants produced such a large population. Early New England marriage patterns, for example, did not differ substantially from those recorded in seventeenth-century England. The average age of men at first marriage was the mid-twenties. Wives were slightly younger than their husbands, the average age being about 22. There is no evidence that New Englanders favored child brides. Nor, for that matter, were Puritan families unusually large by European standards of the period.

The explanation for the region's extraordinary growth turned out to be survival rather than fertility. Put simply, people who, under normal conditions, would have died in contemporary Europe lived in New England. Indeed, the life expectancy of seventeenth-century settlers was not very different from twenty-first-century Americans. Males who survived infancy might have expected to see their seventieth birthday. Twenty percent of the men of the first generation reached the age of 80. The figures for women were only slightly lower. Why the early settlers lived so long is not entirely clear. No doubt, pure drinking water, a cool climate that retarded the spread of fatal contagious disease, and a dispersed population promoted general good health.

Longer life altered family relations. New England males lived not only to see their own children reach adulthood but also to witness the birth of grandchildren. One historian has suggested that New Englanders "invented" grandparents. In other words, this society produced real patriarchs. This may have been one of the first societies in recorded history in which a person could reasonably anticipate knowing his or her grandchildren, a demographic surprise

that contributed to social stability. The traditions of particular families and communities literally remained alive in the memories of the colony's oldest citizens.

5.4.2: A Commonwealth of Families

The life cycle of the seventeenth-century New England family began with marriage. Young men and women generally initiated courtships. If parents exercised a voice in such matters, it was to discourage union with a person of unsound moral character. Puritan ministers advised single people to choose godly partners, warning:

> *The Wretch that is alone to Mammon Wed,*
> *May chance to find a Satan in the bed.*

In this highly religious society, young people seldom strayed far from shared community values. The overwhelming majority of the region's population married, for in New England, the single life was not only morally suspect but also physically difficult. A couple without land could not support an independent and growing family in these agrarian communities. While men generally brought inherited farmland to the marriage, prospective brides were expected to provide a dowry worth approximately one-half what the bridegroom offered. Women often contributed money or household goods that parents had set aside for them.

The household was primarily a place of work—very demanding work. One historical geographer estimates that a Pennsylvania family of five needed 75 acres of cleared land just to feed itself. Additional cultivation allowed the farmer to produce a surplus that could then be sold or bartered, and since agrarian families required items that could not be manufactured at home—metal tools, for example—they usually grew more than they consumed. Early American farmers were not economically self-sufficient; the belief that they were is a popular misconception.

During the seventeenth century, men and women generally lived in the communities of their parents and grandparents. New Englanders usually managed to fall in love with a neighbor, and most marriages took place between men and women living less than 13 miles apart. Moving to a more fertile region might have increased their earnings, but such thoughts seldom occurred to early New Englanders. Religious values, a sense of common purpose, and the importance of family reinforced traditional communal ties.

Towns, in fact, were collections of families, not individuals. Over time, these families intermarried, so the community became an elaborate kinship network. Social historians have discovered that in many New England towns, the original founders dominated local politics and economic affairs for several generations. Not surprisingly, newcomers who were not absorbed into the family system tended to move away from the village with greater frequency than did the sons and daughters of the established lineage groups.

Congregational churches were also built on a family foundation. During the earliest years of settlement, the churches accepted persons who could demonstrate they were among God's "elect." Members were drawn from a broad social spectrum. Once the excitement of establishing a new society had passed, however, New Englanders began to focus more attention on the spiritual welfare of their own families. This quite normal parental concern precipitated a major ecclesiastical crisis. The problem was the status of the children within a gathered church. Sons and daughters of full church members regularly received baptism, usually as infants, but as these people grew to adulthood, they often failed to provide testimony of their own "election." Moreover, they wanted their own children to be baptized. A church synod—a gathering of Congregational ministers—responded to this generational crisis by adopting the so-called Half-Way Covenant (1662). The compromise allowed the grandchildren of persons in full communion to be baptized even though their parents could not demonstrate

conversion. Congregational ministers assumed that "God cast the line of election in the loins of godly parents." Because of the New Englanders' growing obsession with family—termed tribalism by some historians—the Congregational churches by the end of the seventeenth century were increasingly turning inward, addressing the spiritual needs of particular lineage groups rather than reaching out to the larger Christian community.

Colonists regarded education as primarily a family responsibility. Parents were supposed to instruct children in the principles of Christianity, and so it was necessary to teach boys and girls how to read. In 1642, the Massachusetts General Court reminded the Bay colonists of their obligation to catechize their families. Five years later, the legislature ordered towns containing at least fifteen families to open an elementary school supported by local taxes. Villages of a hundred or more families had to maintain more advanced grammar schools, which taught a basic Latin curriculum. At least eleven schools were operating in 1647, and despite their expense, new schools were established throughout the century.

This family-based education system worked. A large majority of the region's adult males could read and write, an accomplishment not achieved in the Chesapeake colonies for another century. The literacy rate for women was somewhat lower, but by the standards of the period, it was still impressive. A printing press operated in Cambridge as early as 1639. The *New-England Primer*, first published in 1690 in Boston by Benjamin Harris, taught children the alphabet as well as the Lord's Prayer. This primer announced:

He who ne'er learns his ABC,
forever will a blockhead be.
But he who to his book's inclined,
will soon a golden treasure find.

But the best-seller of seventeenth-century New England was the Reverend Michael Wigglesworth's *The Day of Doom* (1662), a poem of

224 stanzas describing in terrifying detail the fate of sinners on Judgment Day. In words that even young readers could comprehend, Wigglesworth wrote of these unfortunate souls:

> *They cry, no, no: Alas! and wo!*
>
> *Our Courage all is gone:*
>
> *Our hardiness (fool hardiness)*
>
> *Hath us undone, undone.*

Many New Englanders memorized the entire poem.

After 1638, young men could attend Harvard College, the first institution of higher learning founded in England's mainland colonies. The school was originally intended to train ministers, and of the 465 students who graduated during the seventeenth century, over half became Congregational divines. Harvard had a demanding curriculum. The boys read logic, rhetoric, divinity, and several ancient languages, including Hebrew. Yale College followed Harvard's lead, admitting its first students in 1702.

5.4.3: Puritan Women in New England

The role of women in the agrarian societies north of the Chesapeake remains a controversial subject among colonial historians. Some scholars point out that common law as well as English custom treated women as inferior to men. Other historians, however, depict the colonial period as a "golden age" for women. According to this interpretation, wives worked alongside their husbands. They were not divorced from meaningful, productive labor. They certainly were not transformed into the frail, dependent beings much admired by middle-class males of the nineteenth century. Both views provide insights into the lives of early American women, but neither fully recaptures their community experiences.

To be sure, women worked on family farms. They did not, however, necessarily do the same jobs that men performed. Women usually handled separate tasks, including cooking, washing, clothes making, dairying, and gardening. Their production of food was absolutely essential to the survival of most households. Sometimes wives—and the overwhelming majority of adult seventeenth-century women were married—raised poultry, and by selling surplus birds they achieved some economic independence. When people in one New England community chided a man for allowing his wife to peddle her fowl, he responded, "I meddle not with the geese nor turkeys for they are hers." In fact, during this period women were often described as "deputy husbands," a label that drew attention to their dependence on family patriarchs as well as to their roles as decision makers.

Women also joined churches in greater numbers than men. Within a few years of founding, many New England congregations contained two female members for every male, a process historians describe as the "feminization of colonial religion." Contemporaries offered different explanations for this gender shift. Cotton Mather, the leading Congregational minister of Massachusetts Bay, argued that God had created "far more godly Women" than men. Others thought that the life-threatening experience of childbirth gave women a deeper appreciation of religion. The Quakers gave women an even larger role in religious affairs, which may help to explain the popularity of this sect among ordinary women.

In political and legal matters, society sharply curtailed the rights of colonial women. According to English common law, a wife exercised no control over property. She could not, for example, sell land. If her husband decided to dispose of their holdings, he was free to do so without her permission. Divorce was extremely difficult to obtain in any colony before the American Revolution. Indeed, a person married to a cruel or irresponsible spouse had little recourse but to run away or accept the unhappy situation.

Yet most women were neither prosperous entrepreneurs nor abject slaves. Surviving letters indicate that men and women generally accommodated themselves to the gender roles they thought God had ordained. One of early America's most creative poets, Anne Bradstreet, wrote movingly of the fulfillment she had found with her husband. In a piece titled "To my Dear and loving Husband," Bradstreet declared:

> If ever two were one, then surely we.
>
> If ever man were lov'd by wife, then thee;
>
> If ever wife was happy in a man,
>
> Compare with me ye women if you can.

Although Puritan couples worried that the affection they felt for a husband or a wife might turn their thoughts away from God's perfect love, this was a danger they were willing to risk.

5.4.4: Rank and Status in New England Society

During the seventeenth century, the New England colonies attracted neither noblemen nor paupers. The absence of these social groups meant that the American social structure seemed incomplete by contemporary European standards. The settlers were not displeased that the poor remained in the Old World. The lack of very rich persons—and in this period great wealth frequently accompanied noble title—was quite another matter. According to the prevailing hierarchical view of the structure of society, well-placed individuals were natural rulers, people intended by God to exercise political authority over the rank and file. Migration forced the colonists, however, to choose their rulers from men of more modest status. One minister told a Plymouth congregation that since its members were "not furnished with any persons of *special eminency above the rest*, to be chosen by you into office of government," they would have to make do with neighbors, "not beholding in them the ordinariness of their persons."

The colonists gradually sorted themselves out into distinct social groupings. Persons who would never have been "natural rulers" in England became provincial gentry in the various northern colonies. It helped, of course, if an individual possessed wealth and education, but these attributes alone could not guarantee that a newcomer would be accepted into the local ruling elite, at least not during the early decades of settlement. In Massachusetts and Connecticut, Puritan voters expected their leaders to join Congregational churches and defend orthodox religion.

The Winthrops, Dudleys, and Pynchons—just to cite a few of the more prominent families—fulfilled these expectations, and in public affairs they assumed dominant roles. They took their responsibilities quite seriously and certainly did not look kindly on anyone who spoke of their "ordinariness." A colonist who jokingly called a Puritan magistrate a "just ass" found himself in deep trouble with civil authorities.

The problem was that while most New Englanders accepted a hierarchical view of society, they disagreed over their assigned places. Both Massachusetts Bay and Connecticut passed sumptuary laws—statutes that limited the wearing of fine apparel to the wealthy and prominent—to curb the pretensions of those of lower status. Yet such restraints could not prevent some people from rising and others from falling within the social order.

Governor John Winthrop provided a marvelous description of the unplanned social mobility that occurred in early New England. During the 1640s, he recorded in his diary the story of a master who could not afford to pay a servant's wages. To meet this obligation, the master sold a pair of oxen, but the transaction barely covered the cost of keeping the servant. In desperation, the master asked the employee, a man of lower social status, "How shall I do . . . when all my cattle are gone?" The servant replied, "You shall then serve me, so you may have your cattle again." In the margin of his diary next to this account, Winthrop scribbled "insolent."

Most northern colonists were yeomen (independent farmers) who worked their own land. While few became rich in America, even fewer fell hopelessly into debt. Their daily lives, especially for those who settled New England, centered on scattered little communities where they participated in village meetings, church-related matters, and militia training. Possession of land gave agrarian families a sense of independence from external authority. As one man bragged to those who had stayed behind in England, "Here are no hard landlords to rack us with high rents or extorting fines. . . . Here every man may be master of his own labour and land . . . and if he have nothing but his hands he may set up his trade, and by industry grow rich."

During the seventeenth century, this independence was balanced by an equally strong feeling of local identity. Not until the late eighteenth century, when many New Englanders left their familial villages in search of new land, did many northern yeomen place personal material ambition above traditional community bonds.

It was not unusual for northern colonists to work as servants at some point in their lives. This system of labor differed greatly from the pattern of servitude that developed in seventeenth-century Virginia and Maryland. New Englanders seldom recruited servants from the Old World. The forms of agriculture practiced in this region, mixed cereal and dairy farming, made employment of large gangs of dependent workers uneconomic. Rather, New England families placed their adolescent children in nearby homes. These young persons contracted for four or five years and seemed more like apprentices than servants. For such persons, servitude was not simply a means by which one group exploited another. It was a form of vocational training program in which the children of the rich as well as the poor participated.

A small minority of seventeenth-century immigrants did come as servants, however, and slavery was not unheard of in early New England. Ships' manifests often listed servants among the members of first-generation households, persons who performed domestic tasks or worked as field hands until they completed their terms of service. Indian or African slaves performed similar tasks for a few prominent individuals such as the Salem minister Samuel Parris. New England commanders occasionally enslaved native captives during conflicts such as the Pequot War, exporting most to plantation colonies in the Caribbean or Chesapeake. The population of servants and slaves rose slowly in seventeenth-century Boston as the city's growing importance as a colonial port increased the demand for sailors and dockworkers. The Rhode Island community of Newport grew notorious by the end of the century as a haven for privateers and slave traders.

5.5: A Changing Environment

5.5 Report the continuous process of adaptation that the natives of New England underwent

The extraordinary growth of Puritan society radically altered New England's landscape and embroiled its native peoples in a continuous process of adaptation. As the line of English settlement moved rapidly up river valleys and more slowly into the woodland, forests were transformed into open fields, paths became roads, and English livestock displaced American game. The region's forest floors became choked with brush as English settlers discontinued the native habit of burning the undergrowth each year. Where native women had cultivated multiple crops in small clearings, English men plowed large fields and seeded them with a single crop. Where native peoples had framed their dwellings of slim cord-lashed saplings and sided them with rush mats or bark, colonists sawed great trees into lumber for sturdy English-style houses. Timber was so abundant that settlers were soon using it to roof and side their dwellings, practices that would have seemed wasteful in timber-poor England. As New England towns spread further across the countryside, some native groups moved further away while others found themselves increasingly surrounded as they remained on dwindling patches of ancestral lands.

5.5.1: Varieties of Adaptation

New England Indians adapted to this rapidly changing environment in a variety of ways. Those living beyond the settlement line could scarcely ignore the presence of so many Europeans, and they seldom wanted to. Living nearby white settlements entailed huge difficulties but they also brought advantages in the form of manufactured goods, resources, and military alliances. Several large tribes such as the Narragansetts, the Pequots, and the Abenakis took early advantage of these opportunities.

The approach of settlements confronted native inhabitants with a fresh set of challenges and opportunities. Settlers bid for native land but also sought diplomatic aid in dealing with tribes further away. They also employed forest-wise Indians for services such as hunting, trapping, pest control, and production of useful goods such as baskets and brooms. It was a very delicate business to adapt in ways that would preserve native self-determination while accommodating colonial demands. The Pequots had attempted wholesale armed resistance when English settlers challenged their control of land and trade along the Connecticut River. The outcome of that contest convinced neighboring groups to search for alternative ways to adapt. When the Narragansetts found themselves similarly pressed a few years later, they could convince no other tribe in the region to join them in resisting the English. Indeed, no native leader took the Pequot road to resistance again until Metacom, or King Philip, led his large-scale uprising in 1676 (see Chapter 6).

The Pequots' former allies and kinspeople, the Mohegans, found a different way to deal with the challenge of advancing settlement. As English-Pequot tensions rose, the opportunistic and resourceful Mohegan sachem Uncas (d. 1683) sided with the English. The defeat of the Pequots opened the way for the Mohegans to take their place alongside the English and the Narragansetts as the third great power in the region, a position confirmed by the Treaty of Hartford. Uncas conceded overarching jurisdiction in Anglo-Mohegan relations to Connecticut, making sachems liable for Mohegan damage to English property and eventually restricting tribal settlement near land ceded to the English. In exchange, he won virtual autonomy for his people in managing their own affairs. As English settlements slowly grew up around them, Mohegan villagers continued to observe traditional beliefs and customs while structuring their lives around annual cycles of migration from summer fields to fall and winter hunting grounds. Through a combination of intrigue and skillful negotiation, Uncas remained an influential broker between Connecticut officials and surrounding New England tribes for the next forty years, and secured for his people an enduring presence in the region.

5.5.2: "Praying Indians"

Conversion to Puritan Christianity presented New England Indians with yet another way to adapt to their changing environment, survive the trauma of disease and loss, or even strengthen their position within their own societies through conversion to Christianity. Bay colonists made only occasional attempts to evangelize native peoples during the first decade of settlement. Rhode Island's Roger Williams, however, made a serious effort to master "the language of America" and communicate the light of Puritan Christianity to his native neighbors. Thomas Mayhew, Jr., led the way in Massachusetts missionary endeavors when he began conversing on religious matters with the native inhabitants of Martha's Vineyard in 1642. John Eliot, however, emerged as the colony's leading missionary after 1646, when he began preaching to members of the Natick band near his parish in Roxbury, Massachusetts.

Eliot shared the common Puritan habit of identifying Christianity with English culture while dismissing native culture as irreligious, uncivilized, and at times demonic. He argued that true conversion of Indians to Christianity would require them to reject traditional culture in favor of English ways of dress, dwelling, farming, marriage, child-rearing, and cycles of daily life. To accomplish this enormous cultural transformation, Eliot proposed that the colony establish "praying towns" modeled on English villages, where native converts would learn to order their lives in Christian English ways. He negotiated with the Massachusetts government to set aside 6,000 acres for the first praying town, Natick, and in 1650, he persuaded converts from the nearby Natick band to move there permanently. By 1675, nearly a quarter of the native population of southeastern New England lived in fourteen praying towns.

These native conversions have recently become subjects of sharp historical debate. Why did so many native peoples seem willing to turn their backs on their own traditions to adopt an alien culture? Some historians have argued that the massive dislocation brought about by disease and rapid change left them unusually weak and susceptible to the missionaries' efforts. Others have viewed the Indians' choice as a self-conscious recognition of conversion as a necessary means of survival, a way to preserve their core native identity under a veneer of Christianity. Both perspectives no doubt help to explain many conversions. Yet the fact that large numbers of natives remained able to resist conversion has prompted still other historians to conclude that many converts perceived real advantages in the choices they made.

Indian converts to Puritan Christianity seem to have responded selectively to the Englishmen's Gospel and its attendant cultural prescriptions, incorporating features that seemed beneficial while resisting those that seemed harmful. Puritan missionaries scrutinized converts' testimonies for authenticity, and surviving accounts indicate that many praying Indians sincerely believed that Christian faith would save them. Yet conversion held benefits for this life as well. In contests over tribal leadership, for example, conversion could enhance the prestige of one rival by providing access to more power or resources than other contenders. Eliot's first convert, Waban, captured the sachemship of his band by acquiring the missionary's powerful patronage when he accepted the new faith. Eliot's patronage also provided all Natick converts a means of resisting Uncas, who was attempting to bring the band under Mohegan control during the 1640s. Acceptance of the omnipotent God of the English could also enable converts to bypass the influential tribal *powwow* or shaman in their quest for spiritual power.

Life in the praying towns presented inhabitants with even more opportunities for selective appropriation of English culture. Missionaries provided praying Indians a steady supply of English goods such as tools, clothing, cooking utensils, even firearms. Native converts could learn English technologies such as spinning, a craft in which the Natick band expressed particular interest. English literacy enabled native readers and writers to trade and negotiate more effectively with the English. Other aspects of English life held less attraction. Inhabitants of praying towns, for example, often preferred traditional wigwams rather than the English-style houses Eliot had planned. Bands of praying Indians also clung to a variety of traditional lifeways such as hunting and fishing despite English attempts to make sedentary farmers of them.

Praying town life ultimately transformed native converts' culture in spite of their attempts to control the pace and scope of change. The practice of Puritan religious life required converts to order their days much differently, exchanging familiar seasonal patterns of life for weekly cycles of worship and labor. English ideas of gender, marriage, and child-rearing replaced native ones, with mixed consequences for family life and work.

Men initially resisted taking on traditional women's tasks such as cultivation and house building, while women embraced those aspects of gender redefinition that discouraged vices such as alcohol abuse and wife beating. English ideas of modesty prompted many praying Indians to adopt English dress and encouraged a growing number to erect partitions in their wigwams to give married couples privacy from other family members.

5.6: New England in a Wider World

5.6 Express how New England settlers in the 1630s created a reformed Protestant outpost in the New World

The localism that was characteristic of so much of seventeenth-century New England life should not obscure the fact that these colonies' inhabitants remained aware of their place in a larger Atlantic World, and many sought to expand it. The steady stream of migration from Old England to New during the 1630s helped to stimulate the colonial economy as settled colonists produced supplies for newcomers. Returning ships carried a small stream of disappointed colonists back to England along with furs, timber products, ever-growing quantities of fish, and correspondence to families and friends back home. First-generation New England ministers maintained a lively correspondence with colleagues throughout England and Protestant Europe to inform them of religious affairs in the colonies and to keep abreast of new developments in Europe. During the early decades of settlement, commerce between Old England and New quickly expanded into the larger Atlantic World.

5.6.1: New England and the Protestant Atlantic

The establishment of successful Puritan colonies in New England served to add a transatlantic dimension to a robust transnational Calvinist movement. New England ministers such as John Cotton, Thomas Hooker, and John Davenport were figures renown in England and Protestant Europe for their learning in biblical languages and for their effectiveness in interpreting and preaching the Bible. In Old England they had served as key figures to advance the teaching and practice of the Reformed branch of Protestantism that had also taken firm hold in Scotland, the United Provinces of the Netherlands, various German principalities along the Rhine, Switzerland, and parts of France. Although leaders of this greater European Calvinist movement found themselves pressed in many of their homelands, they also saw themselves as nothing less than the hope of the world. They believed themselves champions of true Christianity against the forces of "Popish superstition" in Rome and "heathen darkness" elsewhere in the world.

As such, New England Puritans functioned as the shock troops of the international Calvinist challenge to Catholic Spain's pretentions to the Americas. Though not the first such challenge—Virginia's charter had also tacitly included this as one of its aims—it became one of the most successful. Many of New England's first-generation ministers and magistrates were keenly aware of their position as a Reformed Protestant outpost in the New World. Their efforts to establish a "Gospel Order" in New England were aimed at both securing and consolidating that outpost and developing a model of Protestant church and society that could be adapted to religious life in England and Europe as well. They drew on the thought of leading international Protestant figures such as William Ames and Franciscus Gomarus. They corresponded with Reformed ministers and theologians on the Continent as well as England, giving and receiving advice on pastoral matters, theology, and church affairs. The Boston minister John Cotton, for example, exchanged letters with ministers in Germany and the Netherlands as well as many parts of England as he strove to serve God in Massachusetts Bay. Leading New England ministers also participated in published debates over theological matters in England, composing manuscripts and sending them to printers in London and Holland. Through such activities, they established a place in a transatlantic network of Reformed ministers and theologians that persisted and grew throughout the seventeenth and eighteenth centuries.

5.6.2: New England and Atlantic Commerce

From the English Crown's perspective, the Massachusetts Bay Company was one among many joint-stock commercial ventures just as Jamestown that had preceded it. Indeed, some of its organizers had invested in earlier joint-stock ventures themselves and were well connected with other investors in similar contemporary operations. They hoped to make a profit on the enterprise and saw no inherent conflict between their commercial and religious interests. Accordingly, the leaders of Massachusetts Bay plunged into commercial ventures from the colony's beginning and persisted until they hit upon avenues of trade that could secure New England's economic future and make at least a few of its colonists rich.

Fish and furs formed the primary commodities of the first generation's Atlantic trade. Boston's relative proximity to the Grand Banks fisheries gave some advantages to its coastal fishermen, who worked together with London merchants to develop a trade that benefited both. Rivers such as the Charles, the Mystic, and the Connecticut provided access to an interior trade in furs with native peoples. After the defeat of the Pequots in 1637, New England colonists gained control of the fur trade on the Connecticut River against Dutch rivals from New Amsterdam. The

merchant William Pynchon capitalized on this opportunity from his base at his recently established town of Springfield, the northernmost settlement on the river that ships could reach. There he corralled the bulk of the fur trade in the region and made a fortune shipping furs to Europe.

New England merchants and magistrates experimented with several different means of establishing other viable commodities for export during the first decades. The most significant venture, Governor John Winthrop's effort to establish an iron industry, became its most costly failure. Through persistent effort, New England seafarers eventually hit on a profitable pattern of Atlantic trade. Timber products such as white pine masts for ships and oaken barrel staves for wine production provided export commodities, which could be exchanged in Europe for finished products or commodities desired in America. Ships laden with barrel staves, for example, could sell their cargoes in Spain, use some of the profits to buy wine, then sail to slave ports in Africa to take on slaves for sale in the Caribbean before returning to New England with Spanish wine and Caribbean sugar.

As the English presence in the West Indies grew and more land on the islands was placed into sugar production, a new market emerged for agricultural goods. As early as 1640, Governor John Winthrop drew on his friendship with his former English neighbor Thomas Warner—now governor of the island of St. Christopher in the Lesser Antilles (see Chapter 4)—to establish a trading link between the two colonies. Planters there and in other British West Indian colonies eventually came to rely on grain and salt pork produced by New England farmers to feed their servants and slaves (see Chapter 4). The wealthy sugar colony of Barbados, in particular, came to depend heavily on agricultural goods from New England. By 1660, the Puritan colonists had developed patterns of trade, which would integrate them as leading agents in the growth of the Atlantic World economy throughout the following century.

5.7: The First Generation's Legacy

5.7 Summarize how some of the first generation New England Puritans created a growing number of native Indian converts

By the mid-1660s, a second generation of New England Puritans had begun sketching the outline of a compelling story about their own history in the New World. The founders had been extraordinarily godly men and women, and in a heroic effort to establish a purer form of religion, pious families had passed "over the vast ocean into this vast and howling wilderness." Godly missionaries such as John Eliot and Thomas Mayhew had averted God's wrath for the founders' early neglect by filling praying towns with a growing number of Indian converts. Although the children and grandchildren of the first generation sometimes questioned their own ability to please the Lord, they recognized the mission to the New World had been a success: they were "as Prosperous as ever, there is Peace & Plenty, & the Country flourisheth."

Chronology

1616-18	Native peoples of coastal New England decimated by epidemic disease
1620	Pilgrims sign Mayflower Compact
1625	Charles I ascends English throne
1629	Charles I decides to rule without Parliament
1630	John Winthrop transfers Massachusetts Bay charter to New England
1633	William Laud named Archbishop of Canterbury
1636	Connecticut valley settlements, Rhode Island founded
1636-37	Pequot War
1638	Anne Hutchinson banished to Rhode Island, New Haven founded
1638	Harvard College founded
1639	First printing press operating in Cambridge, Connecticut towns accept Fundamental Orders
1642	Thomas Mayhew establishes mission to native inhabitants of Martha's Vineyard
1646	John Eliot begins preaching to Natick band near Roxbury
1648	Cambridge Platform regularizes Congregational order in New England
1650	Natick, first Indian Praying Town, established

Chapter 6
England's Quest for a Commercial Empire

 Learning Objectives

6.1 Review the power struggle between the English and the Dutch, French, or the Spanish merchants in the Atlantic

6.2 Recognize how policies helped English commerce in the Atlantic

6.3 Indicate the environment of religious tolerance in America in the era of colonization

6.4 Review the impact of George Fox's idea of inner light on the masses

6.5 Compare life in Carolina and in New England during the colonial period

6.6 Evaluate the contradictions in life in the Restoration-era colonies of England

For Arnoldus de la Grange, the narrow road to salvation and prosperity ran along the edge of the Atlantic World between New York City and New Castle in newly established Pennsylvania. By 1686, this former shopkeeper and recent convert to the teachings of the French mystic Jean Labadie had become a leading citizen in New Castle. In England, la Grange's views would have disqualified him for office, since they required him to leave the Church of England and live simply among a strict community of self-denying fellow believers. In Pennsylvania, however, William Penn himself had appointed the Labadist to the important local office of Justice of the Court. In England, thousands of Dissenters from the Church of England had been fined into bankruptcy, jailed, or deprived of their estates for persisting in their religious convictions. But in New Castle, the Labadist and his Quaker neighbors

were enjoying bountiful harvests on fertile land purchased from the Lenni Lenape Indians.

La Grange harvested 1,000 bushels of wheat in 1686. Neighboring farmers also produced far more grain than they needed. The enterprising Labadist processed this surplus grain at a mill he shared with two Swedes. He then sold the flour on the Atlantic market to the West Indies, where sugar planters now depended on imported grain to feed their slaves. The high profits from his share of the business enabled la Grange to help purchase a 3,000-acre estate in neighboring Maryland. His path to heaven eventually led him there to live out his days in simple community with other Labadists, supported in part by profits from Atlantic World commerce.

La Grange's career might have offered excellent support for an argument often repeated by English pamphleteers: in a competitive Atlantic marketplace, religious toleration was good for trade. The Atlantic was an open, experimental world where enterprising individuals such as la Grange could provide an edge in the contest for empire, regardless of their religious convictions. The Dutch seemed to have learned this early. While their empire prospered under a policy of toleration, England endured a bloody civil followed by a decade of instability without a king. Restoration of the monarchy in 1660 brought harsh suppression of religious dissent. Only by the 1680s, as Arnoldus la Grange was shipping Pennsylvania flour to the Caribbean, did English arguments for toleration begin taking hold. In an Atlantic environment so fraught with opportunity and peril, it no longer made sense to drive away the empire's brightest and best for following their own religious path.

6.1: Conflict in England and the Atlantic

6.1 Review the power struggle between the English and the Dutch, French, or the Spanish merchants in the Atlantic

The middle years of the seventeenth century were wracked with political upheaval in England and escalating competition for trade in the Atlantic, particularly with the Dutch. Neglect of English colonies during the English Civil War permitted widespread Dutch incursion into English colonial trade. When the Parliament turned its attention to colonial commerce after 1650, Dutch dominance of Atlantic trade had grown to become an acute problem in the eyes of English merchants and policymakers. Parliament responded by initiating a series of measures that gathered force to propel English commercial expansion over the next several decades.

6.1.1: Civil War, Commonwealth, and Restoration

The accession of Charles I to the English throne in 1625 exacerbated conflict between the Crown and Parliament that had existed since 1603 when Charles's father James became the first Stuart monarch. Many royal policies—the granting of lucrative commercial monopolies to court favorites, for example—fueled popular discontent, but the crown's hostility to far-reaching religious reform sparked the most vocal protest. Throughout the kingdom, demands for change of the English Church became increasingly adamant. Tensions grew so severe that in 1629, Charles attempted to rule the country without Parliament's assistance. The strategy backfired. When Charles was finally forced to recall Parliament in 1640 because he was running out of money, Parliament demanded major constitutional reforms. Militant religious reformers in England and neighboring Scotland persuaded members of Parliament to restructure the church, starting with abolition of the office of bishop. In this angry political atmosphere, Charles took up arms against the supporters of Parliament.

The confrontation between Royalists and Parliamentarians set off a long and bloody series of civil wars. In 1649, the victorious Parliamentarians beheaded Charles. For almost a decade, Oliver Cromwell, a skilled general and committed Puritan, governed England. During the 1650s, Cromwell and Parliament strove to forge policy in an environment of chronic political instability and religious upheaval. Dozens of boisterous new religious movements—groups with names such as "Quaker," "Ranter," and "Leveler"—emerged as a result of Cromwell's policy of religious toleration. Cromwell's commercial advisors also sought to gain greater control of an increasingly lucrative colonial trade. In addition, he sought to advance Protestant interests in the New World through his Western Design, a program that included military campaigns to seize vulnerable territories in the Spanish Caribbean.

In 1658, Oliver Cromwell died. By 1660, discontent with his son Richard's poor leadership and fatigue with England's chronic instability prompted Parliament to restore Charles II (r. 1660–1685) to the English throne. Tens of thousands of people lined the flower-strewn road during his return to London, celebrating the Restoration with shouts of "God save King Charles" while women tossed posies of sweet herbs at the royal carriage.

The political and diplomatic situation that awaited the king the Parliament who restored him was less congenial. The Restoration-era struggle for stability shaped English colonial development and England's place in the Atlantic World. Two decades of conflict had saddled Charles II with chronic political instability, a heavy burden of debt, commercial, and diplomatic tension with the Dutch and a war with Spain that the country could ill afford. It also confronted him with chaotic religious scene that he and his advisors found troubling, offensive, and threatening. Neither Charles nor his brother James II (r. 1685–1688) was able to resolve the political or economic problems of the Restoration period, and harsh Restoration efforts to impose religious order stirred deep discontent. In this environment, England's New World colonies entered a new phase of development. The Crown intensified efforts to expand its control over Atlantic commerce in an effort to direct more of its growing colonial trade to England and to replenish the royal coffers. Restoration-era religious repression simultaneously sparked a significant new wave of religiously motivated migration to the North American mainland.

6.1.2: The Dutch Challenge

The Civil Wars wrenched English attention from the Atlantic World at a crucial moment. The volume and value of colonial commodity production was rising rapidly and new commercial competitors such as the French and the Dutch were muscling their way into territory once dominated by the Spanish and Portuguese. The wars left England's New World colonies to fend largely for themselves. Dutch shippers were only too happy to step into the gap. Their economical, wide, flat-bottomed *fluitschips* gave them a competitive edge against English and French vessels, enabling them to capture an ever-growing share of the Atlantic market. In 1601, high-capacity Dutch ships outnumbered English in the Port of London by 360 to 207. By 1670, the Dutch merchant fleet outnumbered those of England, France, Spain, Portugal, and Germany combined. This whirl of new commercial competition left Spain struggling to maintain its hold on New World territory as its aggressive rivals overtook it by developing the commercial potential of their American outposts.

In welcoming Dutch vessels, English planters in the Chesapeake and Caribbean were merely recognizing how much seventeenth-century Atlantic trade depended on Dutch shipping. By the 1650s, the Dutch had come to concentrate their Atlantic enterprises on shipping rather than colonization. Their settlements were few but strategically located for the carrying trade. The Dutch maintained excellent deepwater harbors in islands of Curaçuao and St. Eustatia, strategic ports located in the heart of the lucrative sugar-producing region. Portuguese planters in Brazil relied on Dutch vessels to get Brazilian sugar to market, even though Portugal defended the Brazilian coast tenaciously against any Dutch effort to establish a colony there. After 1640, most enslaved Africans who labored on seventeenth-century Brazilian and Caribbean sugar plantations arrived on Dutch ships. The Dutch captured the Portuguese fort of Elmina in 1637 and another Portuguese outpost at Axim in 1641 (both located on the coast of modern Ghana). From 1641 to 1649, they also occupied Angola. From these African ports, Dutch ships carried hundreds of thousands of slaves on the transatlantic leg of an efficient trading circuit that linked Europe, Africa, Brazil, the Caribbean, and North America. Dutch investors reaped handsome profits from ships that seldom left an Atlantic port without a cargo in humans or goods.

In mainland North America, the Dutch held the colony of New Amsterdam from the early 1620s through the middle of the seventeenth century. The colony's excellent harbor at the mouth of the Hudson River gave the Dutch ready access to Iroquois fur trade as well as English plantations. In 1655, the Dutch West India Company also gained extensive claims on the Delaware by asserting control over the rival colony of New Sweden. In the early years, the Dutch population of these regions stagnated because the company offered unattractive terms, treating colonists as salaried employees and refusing to grant them land. During the 1640s, however, the company began granting land to attract new settlers from the Netherlands and other European nations. Dutch America soon contained an extraordinary ethnic mix. One visitor to New Amsterdam in 1644 maintained he had heard "eighteen different languages" spoken in the city. Even if this report was exaggerated, there is no doubt the Dutch colony drew English, Finns, Germans, and Swedes.

Further up the Hudson, Fort Orange and the nearby town of Beverwyck (which the English renamed Albany) hosted an equally diverse population of "Flemings, Scandinavians, Frenchmen, Portuguese, Croats, Irishmen, Englishmen, Scotsmen, Germans, Spaniards, blacks from Africa and the West Indies, Indians and people of mixed blood." A core population of Dutch families held this polyglot trading settlement together and fashioned the townscape into a replica of a low-country community. They constructed Dutch-style townhouses on narrow frontages, cramming the buildings tightly together. The families who occupied those houses gained their living by trade, and used their profits to build strong networks of wealth and kinship that enabled people of Dutch descent to dominate the region's politics and social life for generations. Dutch remained the most commonly spoken language, and the Reformed Church dominated the town's religious life.

The "Swedish nation" which had been established on the Delaware in 1638 still existed at the time of English conquest as a cluster of distinct communities under Dutch control. The population consisted of only a few hundred Swedes and Finns who obtained their living by trading for furs, planting tobacco, and farming grain. The Swedes sought to preserve a strong ethnic identity in their insular communities, and nursed for many years the forlorn hope that their king would send a fleet of warships to rescue their colony from foreign domination. In the meantime, they submitted grudgingly to the succession of Dutch and English governors and cooperated with their non-Swedish neighbors in common ventures.

The Dutch West India Company's heavy involvement in the slave trade made New Amsterdam a destination for many African slaves as well. In its early years, the company had sought to compensate for the colony's labor shortage by introducing African slaves. Many remained company property. Slaves took advantage of their uncertain status in seventeenth-century Dutch law to sue for greater rights as well as for outright freedom. By the 1640s, the company had manumitted many of its slaves. These formed the nucleus of a free black community that persisted throughout the colonial period. Many won only "half freedom," a status usually open only to older slaves on an individual basis. Children of the half-free remained enslaved, and those manumitted remained employees of the Dutch West India Company. The company assigned them plots of land on which they could grow their own crops and livestock. Black workers had to pay an annual a percentage of their produce to the company or face reenslavement. Some broke entirely free of the company to pursue independent livelihoods as artisans or farmers. They created stable families and participated in the religious life of the Dutch Reformed Church, taking communion and baptizing their children alongside Dutch families. Others remained slaves, and the company brought more every year to augment its own labor force or sell to free colonists. By 1664, blacks comprised between 20 and 25 percent of the New Amsterdam's population.

New Netherlands' culture was further fragmented by New England Puritans who left Massachusetts and Connecticut to stake out farms on Long Island and along the east bank of the Hudson. The English brought along their strong traditions of local government and legal rights which they sought to assert in relations with their new Dutch rulers, especially when concentrated in predominantly English settlements such as Flushing. English living further east within the Dutch jurisdiction of Long Island acted more as extensions of New England than of New Netherlands, ignoring Dutch rule wherever possible and dealing far more with Boston and New Haven than New Amsterdam. The communities on the island's easternmost end—Easthampton Southold, and Southampton—remained under Connecticut's jurisdiction until 1664.

6.1.3: The Iroquois and the Atlantic Competition for Furs

European planters were not the only American inhabitants whose profits depended on Atlantic trade and access to cheap Dutch shipping. The Iroquois were no mere frontier acquaintances of the Dutch. They, too, had come to wield an enormous stake in transatlantic markets. A trading triangle among the Iroquois, New England, and New Amsterdam also benefited English traders. Dutch merchants bartered imported goods for valuable wampum, rare shells found only along Long Island Sound and Narragansett Bay. They then sailed up the Hudson to trade wampum for beaver pelts. All parties in the

Northeast profited from an exchange in which wampum circulated as currency. The beautifully crafted wampum belts that became a trademark of Iroquois culture emerged as a product of this cross-cultural trade, which brought a wave of unprecedented prosperity to Dutch and Iroquois alike.

Dutch visitors to mid-seventeenth-century Iroquois villages could find ample evidence of the popularity their trade goods enjoyed. Longhouses often sported "interior doors made of split planks furnished with iron hinges." Others contained "iron chains, bolts, harrow teeth, hoops, [and] spikes." Visitors commonly met Iroquois men and women wearing imported linen shirts, which served as excellent rainwear when treated with bear grease. Jewelry of glass, silver, copper, and brass adorned the bodies of women and men alike. Individuals wore in their hair decorative combs carved with intricate new designs made possible by European metal tools. Iroquois women cooked meals in brass and iron kettles instead of ceramic pots. Worn-out kettles furnished metal for arrowheads and jewelry. As European imports displaced traditional items of bone and stone, knowledge of those crafts died out, increasing Iroquois dependence on European goods. Many popular trade items virtually guaranteed a steady market in replacements and supplies. Guns, for example, required an ongoing supply of bullets and powder.

Commerce with the Iroquois opened opportunities for shrewd entrepreneurial persons of varying background whose adaptability empowered them to flourish in this competitive—yet highly personal—environment. The trader Jacob Eelckens, for example, earned an enduring place in Iroquois memory as "the Governor Called Jacques" by trading according to Iroquois standards of generous reciprocity. So trusted was Eelckens that when Dutch West India Company officials ousted him in the mid-1620s, he was able to entice most of his Iroquois friends and customers to trade with the English instead. Observers noted that, during Eelckens's 1633 expedition "the Indians would not trade with the Dutch" as long as he was among them. Later Dutch traders learned to lubricate the wheels of trade by according at least grudging consideration for Iroquois standards of hospitality and exchange.

By the 1650s, Iroquois-Dutch relations began to come unraveled under new political and economic strains. Overproduction of wampum made it much less valuable as currency. Warfare between the Dutch and native peoples on Long Island and Mahicans on the lower Hudson disrupted Dutch-Iroquois trade. Desperate Dutch merchants began hiring *boslopers* or "woods runners" who were little better than thugs, often coercing their Iroquois trading partners to accept low prices or stealing goods outright. The repercussions of these actions rippled throughout Iroquoia, sparking war between Iroquois and surrounding tribes as headmen sought to recoup trading losses with new sources of furs and tribute, as well as to acquire captives whom they could adopt to replace kinsmen lost to warfare or disease. Mohawk warriors wrought havoc as far east as the Connecticut River valley, intensifying strains between the Dutch and the English as well as the Indian allies of each.

6.1.4: French Missions and Merchandise

Divisions among Iroquois factions also deepened as clans alienated by Dutch abuses sought open alliances with the French of the St. Lawrence River valley. Before 1650, Iroquois resistance had frustrated French traders and Jesuit missionaries, who decried the "perfidy which they have shown toward the Preachers of the Gospel." Indeed, during the 1640s, the Iroquois waged war against Quebec's Huron allies, culminating in the destruction of the central Huron villages and the French mission of Ste.-Marie in 1649. Iroquois took hundreds of Huron captives for adoption, martyred three Jesuit

missionaries, and deprived the French of the native commercial and military allies on whom they had hitherto relied to check Iroquois-Dutch ascendancy in the region.

This loss, coupled with the promise of new converts, made the Jesuits eager to exploit mid-century Iroquois-Dutch tensions. They readily accepted the invitation of Seneca, Onondaga, and Mohawk emissaries to establish missions in tribal villages. Iroquois headmen hoped that resident priests would encourage Catholic Huron adoptees more willing to remain in Iroquois villages. They also hoped to establish trade on terms more favorable than those the Dutch *boslopers* had begun offering.

The arrival of French Jesuit missionaries in Iroquois villages often initiated long-term relationships that supplemented spiritual benefits with tangible gains in trade, weapons, and military assistance. From 1639, the Jesuits acted as agents for the Associates of the Company of New France, displacing the traders they regarded as a hindrance to their work. Their dual role gained toeholds for the missionaries in Huron villages. By the 1650s, it was making inroads to Iroquoia, where eagerness for trade overcame hostility to Catholic faith. Jesuit missionary traders gradually began to divert Iroquois furs from the Hudson to the St. Lawrence River.

In addition to cultivating new friendships among the Iroquois, French missionaries and traders labored to expand their contacts throughout the Great Lakes as colonists consolidated settlements on the St. Lawrence River. By mid-century, New France boasted a population of two thousand colonists, three-fourths of whom supported themselves through traditional European farming. Profits from the fur trade expanded steadily as distant tribes tapped into the French commercial network. Crown officials and French merchants became convinced of New France's commercial promise as fur shipments valued as high as 300,000 livres per year began arriving regularly in French ports.

Iroquois factionalism remained an obstacle to French ambitions for their colony, however. Many headmen remained hostile to French missionaries and traders despite Dutch abuses, and Iroquois proximity to French trade routes made it possible for pro-Dutch factions to disrupt the Great Lakes commerce through frequent raids. French colonial officials had to counter Iroquois ascendancy through military action while traders explored alternative ways of bringing Great Lakes furs to market.

6.1.5: Economic Stagnation on the Spanish Frontier

By the mid-seventeenth century, Spanish dominance of the Atlantic was waning amid challenges from imperial rivals and its own internal difficulties. Spanish officials came to regard their colonies in Florida and New Mexico as defensive outposts for nearby shipping and mining operations rather than launch pads for further expansion. Development of Spanish colonies north of the Rio Grande was hindered by restrictive imperial policies and structural weaknesses in the Spanish economy. Ruinous inflation driven by American gold made Spanish manufactures uncompetitive even within Spain itself, producing a massive trade deficit that left the country dependent on foreign goods. Spanish officials discouraged colonial manufacturing and restricted trade largely to Spanish goods carried on Spanish vessels to only a few American ports. Goods bound for Texas and New Mexico, for example, had to pass through the viceroyalty at Vera Cruz on the Mexican coast. Officials refused to open the Texas coast to shipping throughout the colonial period despite its abundance of good harbors. Efforts by New Mexican colonists to link Santa Fe with the Gulf of Mexico also met with bureaucratic resistance.

Within this restrictive environment, Spanish colonists in the North American borderlands found it difficult to thrive or assert a large role in Atlantic commerce. Nevertheless, they did develop the economic opportunities that were available to them, often by cruel exploitation. Frontier officials in Santa Fe, for example, exacted labor from the region's Pueblos to produce items for export to New Spain such as leather goods, salt, and wagons. New Mexican Spaniards also enslaved nearby native peoples—often enemies of the Pueblos such as the Apaches—for export to the mining regions of New Spain. Spanish traders also fanned out into the Florida and New Mexico countryside in search of more legitimate profits in furs and hides. Deerskins came to serve as currency in the Spanish American southeast. Yet the fur trade never became an important element of the Spanish Atlantic economy, as it did for the French and English. The supply of furs in the Spanish-controlled borderlands was not as large as that further north. Where furs or skins were available, the scarcity and expense of Spanish goods made them uncompetitive with the much greater variety and affordability of English and French merchandise.

Spanish Franciscan missionaries continually spoke out against the abuses of the settlers and occasionally managed to persuade Crown authorities to step in. In one instance, the governor of New Mexico, Juan de Eulate (g. 1618–1625), suffered arrest and conviction for slave trading after Franciscans complained about the practice. All too often, however, the Franciscans' complaints masked their own competition for scarce native labor. Spanish policy allowed the missionaries to use native laborers for "things necessary for the church and convenience of the living quarters," a policy the Franciscans interpreted liberally. Colonial governors regularly charged Franciscans with enriching themselves at Indian expense, and competition for native labor sometimes led to open conflict between the missionaries and their secular rivals.

Despite abuses, many Pueblos found ways to accommodate to some aspects of Spanish rule while resisting others so long as harvests remained sufficient and enemy tribes were kept at bay. Pueblos incorporated aspects of Spanish culture into their daily lives. Many spoke Spanish in everyday business. Potters incorporated Spanish motifs into their vessels while farmers planted and tended Spanish-introduced crops and livestock. Pueblos also learned to make woolen textiles, which changed their manner of dress. A significant minority sincerely embraced Catholicism as well.

Spain's borderland colonies stagnated as a result of Spain's seventeenth-century economic problems and imperial policies. While the Anglo-American population rose dramatically, the colonial population of Spanish Florida and New Mexico remained static or declined. While the English, French, and Dutch reaped ever-increasing profits from their North American trade and plantation enterprises, the borderlands became a steady drain on Spanish royal coffers.

6.2: England's Quest for Atlantic Dominion

6.2 Recognize how policies helped English commerce in the Atlantic

As early as the 1640s, the growing commercial success of English plantations in this competitive Atlantic environment prompted English merchants and policymakers to look for ways of capturing a larger share of the trade. London merchants fretted while Dutch shippers grew richer every year from Chesapeake tobacco and Caribbean sugar. The English Civil Wars, however, prevented Parliament from making any serious initiatives in commercial policy until the execution of Charles I in 1649. Thereafter, English policymakers turned their attention to neglected matters of Atlantic commerce. The great London mercantile companies wanted to strengthen their

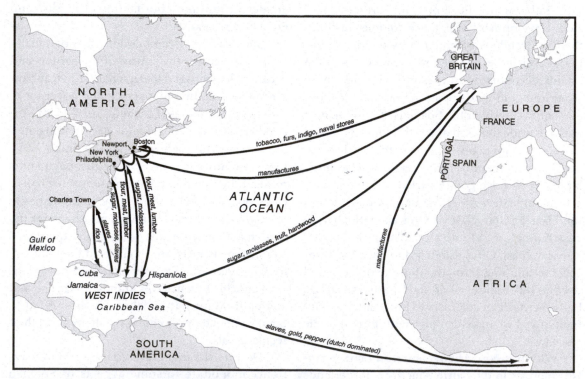

Map 6.1 Major Colonial Trade Routes seventeenth Century

traditional monopolies over trade at the expense of the Dutch. They found the Commonwealth Parliament of the 1650s receptive to their interests. After 1660, the Crown and the Restoration Parliament further intensified efforts to capture for England a growing share of Atlantic wealth.

6.2.1: The First Navigation Act

Commercial tensions between Dutch and English interests reached a breaking point in the early 1650s. For many years, common religious interests and common enemies held the two countries together despite commercial strife. In 1649, however, the Dutch signed a treaty with Denmark that gave Dutch ships preferred access to Baltic ports. Dutch negotiators added damage to insult by rebuffing Parliament's attempts to forge an Anglo-Dutch alliance. The commercial stakes were rising every year as the growth of world trade promised great profits and power to the nations that controlled it. English merchants thought the time had come increase their share of trade by directing English plantation profits to London rather than Amsterdam. In 1651, the Commonwealth Parliament obliged by passing the first navigation act.

The Navigation Act of 1651 was expressly designed to drive Dutch ships out of English colonial markets. It prohibited ships of any nation except England or English plantations from importing colonial commodities of Asia, Africa, or America into any English port. It also prohibited merchants of any nation including England from importing any goods except those loaded in the place where they were actually produced or first shipped, and permitted foreign-owned vessels to import only the commodities of their own people. This threatened to cut deeply into the virtual monopoly which the Dutch exercised over European trade, since after 1651 Dutch merchants could no longer import goods to England indirectly through Holland nor carry goods to England from any other European port.

It was one thing for Parliament to pass the act, but quite another to enforce it. Attempts to do so against Dutch ships in European waters sparked a series of incidents that quickly escalated into the full-blown Anglo-Dutch War of 1652–1654. The English suffered early setbacks, but eventually triumphed under the command of Admiral Robert Blake over what was thought to be an invincible Dutch sea power. Yet after the war's end, the English navy remained too small to police the act effectively, even in European waters. The few ships and soldiers that Cromwell sent to enforce the act in colonial ports succeeded only while they remained. Colonists, left largely to themselves, continued to trade when and where they wished.

6.2.2: The Western Design and Jamaica

Oliver Cromwell made his most enduring contribution to England's American empire almost by accident when he launched a secret, semipiratical expedition to capture a large Spanish island in the Caribbean. Cromwell's "Western Design" arose from a strong religious impulse to strike a crippling blow at the imperial power Puritans regarded as the nation of Antichrist. The "Godly" wanted revenge for all the injuries the Spanish had inflicted on English colonists in the Caribbean. Cromwell and his advisors also hoped to capture a Spanish treasure fleet that could pay the costs of the expedition and supplement sagging revenues at home. The memory of the Elizabethan "Sea Dogs" (see Chapter 2) inspired hope that a Cromwellian force could achieve even greater glory against a foe whose might had now been declining for more than half a century.

Even in decline, Spain proved a tenacious adversary. The force that sailed under the combined command of Admiral William Penn and General Robert Venables failed miserably at their attempt to capture their first target, the island of Hispañola, in the spring of 1655. Tropical heat, poorly disciplined troops, and lack of coordination between the army and naval vessels made them vulnerable to a much smaller Spanish force. Hispañola's defenders slaughtered troops already half-dead from heat and thirst. English losses totaled one thousand men, nearly a fifth of the expedition.

Jamaica proved easier prey and contemporaries soon came to the conclusion that it was "far more proper for their purposes." One observer noted that it had "an excellent harbour and is accounted the most healthful and plentiful" of all Spain's Caribbean possessions. Another gleefully pointed out that it lay "in the very heart of the Spaniard to gall him." The island was poorly defended and its governor, Don Juan Ramirez, surrendered without a fight. Ramirez yielded the island and everything on it—weapons, ships, goods, and estates—to the English. Landowners were allowed to depart with only their clothing, personal effects such as books and writings, and provisions for their voyage. Laborers and artisans who accepted English rule could remain. These terms of surrender echoed those offered English colonists of Providence Island when the Spanish captured it fourteen years earlier (see Chapter 6).

Jamaica ultimately fulfilled the expectations of its early promoters, but not in Cromwell's day. Its good soil and temperate climate supported prosperous sugar plantations and a diversified economy that could survive the vagaries of the sugar market better than islands such as Barbados, whose economy depended almost exclusively on sugar production. In the later seventeenth century, Jamaica proved an ideal staging ground for English raids on Spanish shipping and settlements. One nineteenth-century historian estimated that Jamaica-based raiders netted "a stream of gold and silver flowing into the Bank of England." For Cromwell, however, "this Jamaica business" proved a constant drain. Many of the island's Spanish inhabitants went into hiding in its remote mountain forests, where they organized a stiff guerrilla resistance that terrorized English

settlers and frustrated English troops. Hundreds of soldiers succumbed to tropical diseases such as dysentery and yellow fever during the first year of occupation. Spanish resisters did not give up the fight for the island until restored Charles II proclaimed a cessation of hostilities with Spain in 1660.

6.2.3: The Restoration and Commercial Dominion

The famous eighteenth-century Scottish economist Adam Smith coined the term "mercantilist system" to describe Great Britain's commercial regulations, and ever since, his phrase has appeared in history books. Smith's term, however, is misleading. It suggests that English policymakers during the reign of Charles II had developed a well-integrated set of ideas about the nature of international commerce and a carefully planned set of mercantilist government policies to implement them.

They did nothing of the sort. Administrators responded to particular problems, usually on an individual basis. In 1668, Charles informed his sister, "The thing which is nearest to the heart of the nation is trade and all that belongs to it." National interest alone, however, did not shape public policy. Instead, the needs of several powerful interest groups gave rise to English commercial regulation.

Each group looked to colonial commerce to solve a different problem. For his part, the king wanted money. English merchants remained eager to exclude Dutch rivals from lucrative American markets. The experience of the Interregnum period showed that they needed government assistance to compete successfully with the Dutch, even in Virginia or Massachusetts Bay. Cromwell's success in the Anglo-Dutch War of 1652–1654 had also demonstrated the value of an effective naval force. The landed gentry who sat in Parliament wanted to strengthen the navy and that in turn meant expansion of the domestic shipbuilding industry. Almost everyone agreed that England should establish a more favorable balance of trade, that is, increase exports, decrease imports, and grow richer at the expense of other European states. None of these ideas was particularly innovative, but taken together they provided a blueprint for England's first empire.

6.2.4: An Empire of Trade

The Restoration Parliament took on the Dutch directly, passing a Navigation Act in 1660. This statute, which resembled the earlier act of 1651, became the most important piece of imperial legislation drafted before the American Revolution. Colonists throughout the English Atlantic paid close attention to the statue's details, which stated (1) that no ship could trade in the colonies unless it had been constructs in either England or America and carried a crew that was at least 75 percent English (for these purposes colonists counted as Englishmen) and (2) that certain enumerated goods of great value that were not produced in England—tobacco, sugar, cotton, indigo, dyewoods, and ginger—could be transported from the colonies only to an English or another colonial port. In 1704, Parliament added rice and molasses the enumerated list; in 1705, rosins, tars, and turpentines needed for shipbuilding were included.

The act of 1660 was masterfully conceived. It encouraged the development of domestic shipbuilding and prohibited European rivals from obtaining enumerated goods anywhere except England without restricting English shipping as the act of 1651 had done. Since Americans had to pay import duties in England on enumerated staples such as sugar and tobacco (for this purpose the colonists did not count as Englishmen), the legislation also provided the crown with another source of income.

In 1663, Parliament supplemented this legislation with a second Navigation Act, the Staple Act. It stated that, with a few notable exceptions, nothing could be imported into America unless it had first been transshipped through England, a process that greatly added to the price ultimately paid by colonial consumers.

6.2.5: Eliminating the Dutch

Parliament could not simply legislate the Dutch out of existence, no matter how well-conceived its Navigation Acts. England's principal rival possessed a much larger merchant fleet and an excellent North American port at New Amsterdam, offering ready access to English colonies. In 1664, the crown dispatched a fleet of warships to this Dutch thorn in the side of their budding empire. The commander of this force, Colonel Richard Nicolls, ordered the colonists to surrender. Peter Stuyvesant (g. 1647–1664), the colony's last director-general, rushed wildly about the city urging the settlers to resist the English. But no one obeyed. Even the Dutch remained deaf to Stuyvesant's appeals. They accepted the Articles of Capitulation, a generous agreement that allowed Dutch nationals to remain in the province and to retain their property. New Netherland thus became New York, a chartered English possession that Charles II had already granted his brother James, Duke of York.

The capture of New Netherland in 1664 contributed greatly to the outbreak of the second Anglo-Dutch War later that year. Neither this conflict (1664–1667) nor a third war (1672–1674) achieved decisive results for either side. In 1675, an English observer estimated total Dutch shipping at 900,000 tons to England's 500,000, and English pamphleteers fretted about Dutch competition into the eighteenth century. The wars, however, did help to reduce the Dutch presence in English colonial harbors, creating an opportunity for an unanticipated rival. In their aftermath, New England merchant ships sailed out of Boston, Salem, and Newport to become formidable world competitors in maritime commerce.

6.2.6: Colonial Response and English Adjustment

During the 1660s, the colonists showed little enthusiasm for the new imperial system. Reaction to these regulations varied from region to region. Virginians bitterly protested the Navigation Acts. The collection of English customs on tobacco greatly reduced the colonial planters' profits, which hit the small planters especially hard. Moreover, the exclusion of the Dutch from the trade meant that growers often had to sell their crops at artificially low prices. Even though the governor of Virginia lobbied on the planters' behalf, the crown turned a deaf ear. By 1670, import duties on tobacco accounted for almost £100,000, a sum the king could scarcely do without.

New Englanders at first ignored the regulations. One Massachusetts merchant reported in 1664 that Boston entertained "near one hundred sail of ships, this year, of ours and strangers." The strangers, of course, were the Dutch, who had no intention of obeying the Navigation Acts. Some crafty New England merchants circumvented the Navigation Acts by picking up cargoes of enumerated goods such as sugar or tobacco, sailing to another colonial port (thereby technically fulfilling the letter of the law) and then making directly for Holland or France. Along the way they paid no customs.

Parliament plugged this loophole with the Navigation Act of 1673. This statute established a plantation duty, a sum of money equal to normal English customs duties, to be collected on enumerated goods at all colonial ports. New Englanders could now sail wherever they pleased within the empire, but they could not escape paying customs. Parliament also extended the jurisdiction of the London Customs Commissioners to America. And in 1675, as part of this new imperial firmness, the Privy Council formed a powerful subcommittee, the Lords of Trade, whose members monitored colonial affairs.

It was one thing for Parliament to pass these reforms, but quite another to enforce them. The customs service lacked enough effective agents American ports, and some agents did more harm than good. Edward Randolph, head of the imperial customs service in New England, was such a person. He was dispatched to Boston in 1676 to gather information about the conduct of colonial trade. His behavior was so obnoxious, his reports about New Englanders so condescending, that he became the most hated man in late seventeenth-century Massachusetts. Nevertheless, Randolph's favor with high-ranking London officials enabled him to retain his position. For nearly two decades he conducted a game of imperial cat-and-mouse with New England merchants and magistrates who proved highly adept at finding weaknesses in the new trade regulations. Every new colonial trick for thwarting the Navigation Acts prompted Randolph to fire off another letter to London with a suggestion for closing the loophole. Despite such efforts in New England and other colonial ports, the dream of controlling trade from London proved elusive for much of the century.

6.2.7: Pirates and Privateers

Recalcitrant colonial officials were not the only obstacles to the Navigation Acts' implementation. England's naval force was also too small to enforce the regulations or protect the nation's far-flung commercial interests. All too often, smugglers escaped detection and English merchants lost whole cargoes to the pirates who plied the Caribbean and the North American coast.

The distinction between pirates and patriots remained as obscure in Restoration England as it had been during the days of the Elizabethan Sea Dogs (see Chapter 2). Seventeenth-century buccaneers—so named for Caribbean castaways who provisioned ships with meat smoked on a rack or *boucan*—were considered pirates when preying on English ships but heroes if their victims were Spanish. In wartime, buccaneer captains could obtain "letters of marque" that made them privateers, self-funded agents authorized to seize enemy vessels in the king's name. English officials also issued letters of marque authorizing seizure of smugglers and pirates. They offset the high risks of such expeditions by allowing the owners, captains, and crews of privateer vessels to keep the booty after paying the king his percentage in duties and fees. The promise of riches attracted English investors as well as Atlantic buccaneers, and the uncertainties of international commerce made it relatively easy to claim even legitimate merchant vessels of one's own nation as prizes.

After 1660, Jamaica's Port Royal became a major buccaneer harbor, conferring on the city a reputation as the richest and wickedest of many British colonial ports that offered safe haven to pirates. From there Henry Morgan, the most famous buccaneer captain, staged a series of brash, brutal raids on Spanish colonial shipping and settlements that netted a fortune in gold. A 1670 foray into Panama gained Morgan, his men and his Jamaican investors a total prize worth £70,000. Though that year's signing of the Treaty of Madrid rendered the venture illegal, this technicality neither caused Morgan to forfeit his treasure nor prevented his winning English knighthood and a post as Jamaica's lieutenant governor.

As the volume of Atlantic trade increased, England gradually joined other European trading nations in recognizing that commercial stability was more important than minor pirate victories. Yet piracy and smuggling proved very difficult to stamp out before the 1690s. Port Royal may have been the richest pirate haven, but mainland colonial ports such as Charleston, New York, and Newport often found pirates an important source of scarce goods and specie. Colonial governors frequently winked at the presence of pirate vessels in their harbors, and friendly colonial judges and juries often legitimated captured prizes on flimsy legal grounds.

6.3: A New Wave of Colonization

6.3   **Indicate the environment of religious tolerance in America in the era of colonization**

The Restoration of Charles II ushered in a new era of English colonization. The capture or development of new colonies complemented regulatory efforts to gain control of colonial commerce by helping to expand and diversify production of valuable colonial commodities. The English Crown's efforts to suppress religious dissent also played an important role by prompting founders of some new ventures to offer the religious toleration in America that was being denied in England itself. Such experiments eventually succeeded in attracting new colonists who were being persecuted for their religious beliefs not only in England but in other parts of Europe.

6.3.1: The Duke's Dominions

The capture of New Netherlands from the Dutch in 1664 netted James, Duke of York and brother of King Charles II, a very handsome prize. As lord high admiral of England, York had pressed for action against the Dutch and capture of their North American colony. He believed that New York could become a strategic commercial and military port for England. York's associates John, Lord Berkeley, and Sir George Carteret supported him, knowing that they too could gain from the favors of appointive offices and trade monopolies that a new colony would provide. New Netherlands already boasted a large population and a well-developed fur trade. It exported more tobacco and agricultural crops every year. York's associates assured him that the colony would provide a tidy supplement to his cash-starved income.

Despite these high hopes, the colony's legacy under Dutch rule confronted New York's first English governor, Colonel Richard Nicolls, with a daunting challenge. The fractious population proved resistant to imperial authority, and the vast size of the territory made the job of administration even harder. Charles II had made his brother absolute proprietor over Maine, Martha's Vineyard, Nantucket, Long Island, and the rest of New York all the way to Delaware Bay. Charles perhaps wanted to encircle New England's potentially disloyal Puritan population, but whatever his aims may have been, he created a bureaucratic nightmare.

During the English Civil War, the duke had acquired a thorough aversion to representative assemblies, remembering bitterly that Parliament had executed the duke's father, Charles I, and raised up Oliver Cromwell. The English colonists on Long Island felt betrayed. In part to appease these outspoken critics, Governor Nicolls—one of the few competent administrators to serve in the Middle Colonies—drew up in March 1665 a legal code known as the Duke's Laws. It guaranteed religious toleration and created local governments, but there was no provision for an elected assembly or democratic town meetings. The legal code disappointed the Long Islanders, and when the duke's officers attempted to collect taxes, these people grumbled that they were "inslav'd under an Arbitrary Power."

The Dutch made the transition to English rule with apparent resignation. Governor Nicolls knew that the colony's commercial value depended on securing Dutch cooperation. He moved cautiously in his dealings with them, respecting Dutch property rights, encouraging additional Dutch immigration and allowing Dutch West India Company ships to trade in New York in violation of the Navigation Acts. English authorities did not apply the Duke's Laws to Dutch areas between Manhattan and Albany until Nicolls's successor, Francis Lovelace, implemented them in 1670. Both governors worked to meld Dutch and English legal forms. Early English governors encouraged. Nevertheless, many Dutch officeholders lost their posts to English

aspirants during Nicolls's term as governor. The Dutch population remained keenly sensitive to their status as a conquered people. Prominent Dutch merchants nursed the hope of regaining control of the colony.

Dutch hopes came true for a time in 1672 when a fleet of warships from the Netherlands recaptured the colony during the third Anglo-Dutch War. The Dutch embraced the opportunity to throw off the hated English yoke, seizing English property, rounding up English officials, and shipping them back to England. The invaders restored Dutch names to the colony, Dutch officials to their posts, and Dutch commerce to the merchants. The restoration of Dutch rule proved short-lived. In 1674, the Netherlands gave up all rights to the area in the treaty of Westminster, leaving its former countrymen to fend for themselves against vengeful Englishmen.

The return of New York to the English brought an accelerated effort to Anglicize the government and commerce of the colony. The new governor, Edmund Andros, moved rapidly to dismiss the Dutch from most political offices and to require that all records be kept in English. He also imposed an oath of fidelity and allegiance to the king's government, prohibiting any who refused the oath to engage in any commerce. Eight leading Dutch merchants balked, demanding a guarantee that the oath did not compromise Dutch religious liberties, inheritance customs, freedom from impressment into English military service, or right not to take up arms against their own nation. When Andros remained unmoved, one merchant submitted. The other seven ended up in a court packed with hostile English judges, who convicted them of promoting rebellion and threatened to confiscate their entire estates unless they submitted. The outraged merchants protested so vigorously that one of them, Nicholas Bayard, was thrown into solitary confinement for three days. In the end, the merchants were allowed to keep two-thirds of their estates in exchange for taking the oath, but the trial left deep scars on the Dutch community in New York.

For several decades, the Dutch and English lived side by side in mutual suspicion. Dutch colonists continued to speak their own language, worship in Dutch Reformed Calvinist churches. Dutch merchant families in Manhattan and Albany resisted English intrusion into commerce, especially the fur trade. Even so, the English made inroads. In 1676, fully a third of New York City's wealthiest merchants and artisans were English, and two of the colony's leading English families, the Morrises and the Livingstons, had begun their rise to prominence. Richard Morris, a captain in Cromwell's army, arrived in New York in the 1660s and acquired estates on both sides of the Hudson River. Morris died when his son Lewis was less than a year old, but an uncle, Lewis Morris of Barbados, became the boy's guardian and secured the family's place in New York political and social life. The young Scotsman Robert Livingston arrived in New York in 1674 and soon married into the wealthy Schuyler family of Albany. Even before his marriage Governor Andros appointed him to important offices in Albany. Andros's successor, Governor Thomas Dongan, granted Livingston a princely estate of 160,000 acres on the Hudson, as well as a one-seventh share of another 180,000-acre tract near Saratoga. Livingston Manor on the Hudson became the cornerstone of the family's far-flung commercial enterprises. The Livingstons and the Morrises remained leading families of New York's "landed interest" throughout the colonial period. A few leading Dutch families such as the Schuylers joined them as members of New York's political and commercial elite. Other Dutch families kept their distance, eventually forming an opposition "Dutch party" or faction in New York's political life.

Even with the increasing English numbers, New York remained diverse. Its population included Jews, Scots, Irish, French, and Germans as well as the English and Dutch. By 1700, people of African descent made up 18 percent of the population. Slaves continued to arrive in New York to satisfy a brisk internal demand, and slavery's steady growth undercut the status of free blacks as white masters began viewing them as a threat to security. Nevertheless, slaves themselves continued to enjoy many traditional privileges that set New York apart from the emerging slave societies further south. Slaves could hold their own property and raise their own crops for sale. Slaves could often choose their own masters, which allowed them to move nearer to kin or escape an unsatisfactory situation. The concentration of blacks in New York City permitted them to form strong communal ties centered on distinct cultural forms. Black women and men congregated on Sundays and holidays to celebrate through dance, song, and physical competition. New York blacks developed their own distinctive forms for marriage and funerals and interred their dead in separate graveyards that historian Ira Berlin has called "the first truly African-American institution in the northern colonies."

6.3.2: The English and the Iroquois

The importance of New York's fur trade prompted the first English governor, Richard Nicolls, to secure a treaty with the Iroquois as soon as his agents assumed control of Albany. In it, the English promised to continue trade with the Iroquois on the same terms as the Dutch and to support the Iroquois with English arms and soldiers in case of attack. Factional struggles among the Iroquois themselves as well as the Anglo-Dutch tensions of the 1660s and early 1670s made early Anglo-Iroquois tenuous. Only after the English secured their hold in 1674 were Governors Andros and Dongan able to forge lasting ties in a series of alliances known as the "Covenant Chain." The Covenant Chain positioned New York and the Five Nations to claim roles as principal mediators in Anglo-Indian relations from New England to Virginia.

New York's ongoing dependence on the fur trade helped to keep Anglo-Iroquois relations stable and peaceful well into the eighteenth century. For much of this period the colony's population remained small and clustered along the Hudson and Long Island. New York farmers remained content to farmlands in those regions, reducing the pressure of agricultural expansion that had generated conflict in New England and the Chesapeake. The Five Nations' importance also prompted the Crown to appoint officials directly over Indian affairs rather than entrusting Anglo-Indian relations to governors who might allow their own provincial aims to obscure larger British interests on the continent. The Iroquois shared the desire to keep trade flowing, and their strategic location along the Mohawk and upper Hudson River valleys allowed them to dominate the region's trade. English New York provided an important alternative to commerce with the French as well as a vital military ally against the Five Nations' French and Indian rivals.

6.3.3: Confusion in New Jersey

New Netherlands originally encompassed the region between the Hudson and Delaware Rivers as well as the lands to the north, and Charles II had accordingly included it the charter issued to his brother. Yet only three months after receiving the charter, the Duke of York awarded the land lying between the Hudson and Delaware rivers to John, Lord Berkeley, and Sir George Carteret. This colony was named New Jersey in honor of Carteret's birthplace, the Isle of Jersey in the English Channel. When New York's Governor Nicolls heard what the duke had done, he exploded. In his estimation, this fertile region contained the "most improvable" land in all New York. To give it away so casualty seemed the height of folly.

The duke's impulsive act bred confusion. Soon it was unclear who owned what in New Jersey. Before Governor Nicolls learned of James's decision, he allowed migrants from New England to take up farms west of the Hudson River. He promised them an opportunity to establish an elected assembly, a headright system, and liberty of conscience. In exchange, Nicolls asked only that they pay a small annual quitrent to the duke. The new proprietors, Berkeley and Carteret, recruited colonists on similar terms, codifying them in a document entitled the "Concessions and Agreement." They assumed, of course, that they would receive the rent money.

The result was chaos. The testy New England colonists, who were used to owning their property outright, objected to the quitrents. Colonists argued over whether Nicolls or the new proprietors had authorized their assembly. In fact, neither possessed any legal right to set up a colonial government. James could transfer land to favorite courtiers, but the government remained his personal responsibility. Knowledge of the law failed to quiet the controversy, and Berkeley soon grew tired of a venture which generated headaches rather than quitrents. In 1674, he sold his proprietary rights to a group Quakers, dividing the colony into two separate governments. Neither East nor West Jersey prospered.

Carteret and his heirs tried unsuccessfully to turn a profit in East Jersey. In addition to enticing small farmers with 100- to 200-acre plots of ground, he issued large grants of up to 10,000 acres of land to Barbadian émigrés who would develop tobacco plantations. The planters brought slave labor forces to this area called "New Barbados," to clear fields and plant tobacco and grain for export. Lewis Morris of New York brought a force of nearly seventy African slaves to the "Monmouth grant" near the Atlantic coast where he established the region's first iron plantation, Tinton Manor iron works. Despite these efforts, the East Jersey economy remained focused on family farms, generating little in either quitrents or customs for its proprietor. When Carteret died in 1681, the trustees of his estate sold the disappointing proprietorship to a group of twenty-four investors that included William Penn.

Penn and his partners hoped to secure the entire territory of both Jerseys as well as Pennsylvania for their Quaker coreligionists. The actual management of East Jersey soon fell to the colony's new governor, the Scottish Quaker Robert Barclay. Barclay promoted East Jersey vigorously in his homeland. Nearly five hundred Scots, most of them Presbyterians who were experiencing severe persecution under Charles II, responded to Barclay's enticing advertisements. After 1685, persecution declined, and with it the influx of Scots. Yet most immigrants to Scotland's first American colony remained to exercise influence out of all proportion to their numbers.

The Quaker proprietors of neighboring West Jersey issued in 1677 a remarkable plan of government, the Laws, Concessions, and Agreements. It was never fully implemented. The plan envisioned a unicameral legislature of one hundred elected representatives which would enact all laws and a ten-member "Commission of State" which would manage provincial affairs when the legislature was not in session. The legislature was limited only by the requirement that all laws be consonant with English law and the Concessions themselves. The document provided elaborate safeguards for the people's religious rights, declaring that "no man, nor number of men on earth, hath power or authority to rule over men's consciences in religious matters." Yet this visionary plan floundered as shifting royal policies and internal bickering buffeted the colony for the next two decades. Not even William Penn could bring tranquility to the fractious Quakers' affairs. Penn wisely turned his attention to the unclaimed territory across the Delaware River.

Despite the colony's political instability, the Quaker population did manage to establish a number of prosperous farming communities along a 20-mile-wide strip stretching from Trenton to Delaware Bay. Farmers raised mixed crops of grain, flax, and hemp as well as livestock. On several large operations interspersed among the family farms, African slaves and English indentured servants worked cash crops of tobacco and foodstuffs.

West Jersey soon developed a brisk export trade in agricultural goods to the British West Indies, as well as a trade with England in tobacco, furs, and naval stores such as pitch, tar, resin, and hemp.

The prosperity of individual landholders in East and West Jersey could not save the proprietors of either colony from bankruptcy. In 1702, the proprietors of both surrendered their powers to Queen Anne, who reunited the two Jerseys into a single royal colony. At that time, most of New Jersey's fourteen thousand people lived on scattered family farms. The colony lacked a good deepwater harbor, so never developed a commercial center to rival New York City or Philadelphia. Many large landowners left the bulk of their property undeveloped or sold it off in smaller plots.

Visitors often commented on the diversity of New Jersey's settlers, who came from almost every European nation. The population also included significant numbers of Africans, most of whom were slaves working as field hands on family farms. Some formed a significant labor force for larger farm operations and mining. A few others worked as free laborers or farmed land of their own. The colony's ethnic diversity and religious toleration produced a bewildering range of religious opinion. Congregationalists, Presbyterians, Quakers, Baptists, Anabaptists, Dutch Reformed, and Anglicans managed to live together peacefully in New Jersey.

6.4: Quakers in America

6.4 **Review the impact of George Fox's idea of inner light on the masses**

The founding of Pennsylvania was intertwined with the history of the Quaker movement. This radical sect, a product of English social upheaval during the Civil War, gained its name from the derogatory term that English authorities often used for those who "tremble at the word of the Lord." The name persisted even though Quakers preferred being called Professors of the Light or, more commonly, Friends.

By 1660, the Quakers had developed a strong following throughout England. One person responsible for their success was George Fox (1624–1691), a poor shoemaker whose spiritual anxieties sparked a powerful new message that pushed beyond traditional Protestantism. Fox experienced youthful despair "so that I had nothing outwardly to help me . . . [but] then, I heard a voice which said, 'There is one, even Christ Jesus, that can speak to thy condition.'" Throughout his life, Fox and his growing number

This drawing, The Quakers Unmasked (1691), satirizes the mystical sect and its leaders. William Penn and other Quakers believed that an "Inner Light" of Christ resided within every person, making all men and women equal before the Lord. In meetings such as the one depicted here, members sat in silence until the spirit prompted an individual to speak.

of followers testified to the inner work of the Holy Spirit. They told ordinary men and women that if only they would look, they too would find they possessed an "Inner Light." This was a wonderfully liberating, especially for persons of lower-class origin. The Lord's inward presence would help them attain greater spiritual perfection on earth. Gone were the obstacles of original sin and eternal predestination. Everyone could be saved. Everyone could also preach or prophesy, an activity the Quakers termed "bearing witness to the Truth." They saw no need for a learned ministry. The Inner Light could teach each the true meaning of Scripture.

Quakers practiced humility in their daily lives. They wore simple clothes and employed old-fashioned forms of address that set them apart from their neighbors. They refused to honor worldly position and achievement. They would not doff their hats, bow, curtsey, or use deferential terms of address, even when appearing before royalty. Quakers declined to swear oaths, a refusal that landed many of them in jail for contempt of court. They were also pacifists. To Quakers, all were equal in the Lord's eyes, a belief that generally annoyed people of rank and achievement.

Moreover, the Quakers never kept their thoughts to themselves. They preached conversion constantly, spreading the "Truth" throughout England, Ireland, and America. The Friends exerted influence in early New Jersey, Rhode Island, and North Carolina, as well as Pennsylvania. The "publishers of Truth" wore out their welcome in some places. English authorities harassed the Quakers. Thousands, including Fox himself, were jailed. In Massachusetts Bay between 1659 and 1661, Puritan magistrates ordered several Friends put to death. Such measures proved counterproductive, for persecution only inspired the Quakers to redouble their efforts.

6.4.1: Penn's "Holy Experiment"

William Penn lived according to the Inner Light, a commitment that led eventually to the founding of Pennsylvania. Penn's father had served with some distinction in the English navy. Through luck and skill, he acquired a considerable estate in Ireland, and as a wealthy landowner, he naturally hoped his son would be a favorite at the Stuart court. He befriended the king, the Duke of York, and several other powerful Restoration figures. But William disappointed his father. He was expelled from Oxford University for holding unorthodox religious views. Not even a grand tour through Europe could dissuade him from joining the Society of Friends. His political connections and driving intellect soon propelled him to prominence within the struggling sect. Penn wrote at least forty-two books advocating Quaker principles. Even two years in an English jail could not weaken his faith.

Precisely when Penn's thoughts turned to America is not known. His brief involvement with the West Jersey proprietorship may have suggested the possibility of an even larger enterprise. In 1681, Penn negotiated one of the most impressive land deals in American history, when Charles II awarded him a charter as sole proprietor of a vast area called Pennsylvania (literally, "Penn's woods"). The name embarrassed Penn, but he knew better than to look the royal gift horse in the mouth. Why the king bestowed such generosity on a recent Quaker jailbird remains a mystery. Perhaps Charles wanted to repay an old debt to Penn's father. The king may have seen the colony as a means of ridding England of its troublesome Quaker population. Perhaps he simply liked Penn. In 1682, Penn added to his proprietorship the so-called Three Lower Counties that eventually became Delaware. This astute purchase from the Duke of York guaranteed Pennsylvania access to the Atlantic and ensured even before Philadelphia's establishment that it would become a commercial center.

Penn lost no time in launching his "Holy Experiment." The charter gave Penn the right to create any form of government he desired, and his imagination ran wild. In 1682, he developed a Frame of Government that blended traditional notions about landed aristocracy with daring concepts of personal liberty. Penn guaranteed that colonists would enjoy liberty of conscience, freedom from persecution, no taxation without representation, and due process of law. Penn's ideas drew heavily on the writings of English political philosopher James Harrington (1611–1677), who argued that no government could ever be stable unless it reflected the actual distribution of landed property within society. Both the rich and poor had to have a voice in political affairs. Penn's Frame of Government envisioned a governor appointed by the proprietor, a seventy-two-member Provincial Council responsible for initiating legislation, and a two-hundred-person assembly that could accept or reject the bills presented to it. The frame apparently envisioned a council filled with the colony's richest landholders, "persons of most note for their wisdom, virtue and ability." The governor and council would manage the routine administration of justice. Smaller landowners spoke through the assembly. In America, this clumsy structure crumbled under its own weight.

Penn promoted his colony aggressively throughout England, Ireland, and Germany. He had no choice. His only source of revenue was the sale of land and the collection of quitrents. Penn commissioned pamphlets in several languages extolling the quality of Pennsylvania's rich farmland. The response was overwhelming. People poured into Philadelphia and the surrounding area. In 1685 alone, eight thousand immigrants arrived. Most were Irish, Welsh, and English Quakers who generally moved to America as families. But Penn opened the door to all comers, describing his colony as "a collection of divers nations in Europe, as French, Dutch, Germans, Swedes, Danes, Finns, Scotch, Irish, and English."

The colonists were by no means all Quakers. The founder of Germantown, Francis Daniel Pastorius, called the vessel that brought him to the colony a "Noah's Ark" of religions. His own household included servants who subscribed "to the Roman [Catholic], to the Lutheran, to the Calvinistic, to the Anabaptist, and to the Anglican church, and only one Quaker." Ethnic and religious diversity were crucial in the development of Pennsylvania's politics, which took on a quarrelsome quality absent in more homogeneous colonies such as Virginia and Massachusetts.

Penn himself emigrated to America in 1682 to find his council and assembly reduced to more manageable size but already battling over the right to initiate legislation. Wealthy Quaker merchants, most residents of Philadelphia, dominated the council. By contrast, the assembly included men from rural settlements and the Three Lower Counties who cared little for the Holy Experiment.

In 1684, Penn left his colony and did not return until 1699. During his enforced absence, his religiously tolerant experiment became a booming commercial success. Its agricultural products, especially its excellent wheat, came into demand throughout the Atlantic World. By the time of Penn's return, English West Indian planters were feeding their burgeoning slave populations on Pennsylvania's grain and meat. Yet despite this economic prosperity, the population remained deeply divided. Even the Quakers had briefly split into hostile factions. Penn's handpicked governors failed to win general support for the proprietor's policies. One of them exclaimed that each Quaker "prays for his neighbor on First Days and then preys on him the other six." Few colonists shared the founder's desire to create a godly, paternalistic society.

In 1701, legal challenges in England again forced Penn to depart. Just before sailing, Penn signed a new frame of government, the Charter of Liberties. It created the only unicameral or one-house legislature in colonial America. Representatives now held the right to initiate bills. The assembly could conduct its business without proprietary interference. The charter acquiesced to residents of the Three Lower Counties (Delaware) by separating their government from Pennsylvania. This document served as Pennsylvania's constitution until the American Revolution.

His experience in America must have depressed Penn, now both old and sick. In England, Penn was imprisoned for debts incurred by dishonest colonial agents. In 1718, Pennsylvania's founder died a broken man.

6.4.2: Quakers and Indians

The Friends' principles of equality, brotherhood, and pacifism made the early history of Pennsylvania's Anglo-Indian relations an exception to the usually conflict-ridden story of English colonization. William Penn himself was determined to live in friendship and peace with the Lenni Lenape Indians who had inhabited the Delaware River valley for centuries. Even before coming to the new colony himself, Penn sent a letter to the chief of these people whom the English called Delawares, informing him that "The king of the Countrey where I live, hath given unto me a great Province therein, but I desire to enjoy it with your Love and Consent, that we may always live together as Neighbours and friends." Penn instructed his first deputy governor, William Markham, to "buy land of the true owners" before selling it to prospective settlers. He assured the Delawares that he would put a stop to the injustices they had suffered in previous dealings with Europeans by imposing strict regulations on trade. He also promised to adjudicate any Anglo-Indian disputes through a body composed of "an equal number of honest men on both sides."

The Delawares had heard bland assurances of European friendship before, but a variety of factors disposed them to accept Penn's overtures. Nearly a half century of trade with Swedes, Dutch, and English had taught them the benefits and perils of contact. Like other native nations, the Delawares had suffered devastating epidemics that halved their numbers between 1620 and 1680. Many of their fields lay abandoned. Their one thousand fighting men seemed too few to resist their powerful Iroquois rivals to the north. They saw an opportunity to balance the odds by forging a friendship with this powerful Englishman they called "Brother Onas" (meaning "Quill," a play on Penn's surname). The Delawares were also attracted by the rich variety of goods Penn offered them as "presents and tokens" of his good will. They had never seen such quantities of wampum, cloth, clothing, kettles, firearms, tobacco, and rum, to name only a few of the items Penn offered them in exchange for title to their lands. There was enough to distribute among all members of the band, and Penn's initial generosity promised very favorable terms of trade for the future.

Penn hoped that his overture to the Lenni Lenape would secure not only peace and clear title to the lands, but also a share of the fur trade. The Lenni Lenape had earlier traded with Dutch and Swedish agents and continued to keep Pennsylvania and New Jersey fur traders well-supplied. Penn tried to supplement the Lenni Lenape trade by diverting a percentage of Iroquois trade from New York to Pennsylvania, but New York's governor Dongan moved quickly to thwart this effort.

The dearth of regional native competitors with the Lenni Lenape probably contributed to good relations between them and first-generation Quaker settlers by removing significant sources of frontier conflict. Trade disputes were rare between Indians and Pennsylvania colonists. For most on both sides, Penn's ideal of living together in peace meant living separate lives with only occasional interaction. Rivalry between the Lenni Lenape and other native fur traders remained minimal during the first decades of settlement, enabling Pennsylvanians to avoid the beaver wars that raged periodically between the Iroquois and southern tribes (see Chapter 7). Penn and his deputies succeeded only partially in their efforts to discourage Delaware participation in Iroquois war parties. Even so, they preserved peace sufficiently to make Pennsylvania a refuge for hard-pressed bands of Indians who migrated to the Susquehanna River valley for refuge. The availability of land also enticed western Shawnee and Miami to hunt and plant crops along the Susquehanna.

Pennsylvania seemed to offer plenty of land for everyone—Indian settlers and Europeans alike—during the first generation. William Penn offered the Lenni Lenape generous prices for their ancestral lands as he negotiated his way through the colony between 1682 and 1684. Penn took great pains to make certain the Indians understood that the treaties they signed permanently conveyed the ownership of the land to him. However, he also instructed his Commissioners of Property not to sell the lands to white settlers as long as the original inhabitants continued to live there. When a band did decide to move, they typically settled on abundant land along the banks of the Susquehanna. In two instances, Penn oversaw the resettlement of specific groups of Indian families from their original lands to new reserves, but he did not do so without securing full approval from the families involved.

Penn's efforts to win the Indians' "love and friendship by a kind, just, and peaceable life" earned him great respect among the Lenni Lenape, a respect that he returned. The Quaker leader remarked that he did not know a "Language spoken in Europe that hath words of more sweetness in Accent and Emphasis, than theirs." He also affirmed that "In treaties about land, or traffic [trade], I find them deliberate in council, and as designing as I have ever observed among the politest of our Europeans." Penn himself possessed great skills at negotiation and was determined to enforce his land purchases with severity if he thought it necessary. His insistence on permanently alienating Indians from their ancestral lands suggests that, despite professions of respect, Penn envisioned a future Pennsylvania without Indians. Nevertheless, as long as Brother Onas wielded influence in Pennsylvania's affairs, Anglo-Indian relations remained not only peaceful but relatively equitable.

During the first generation of settlement, Quaker colonists followed Penn's lead in Indian relations, but not all settlers shared the Friends' humane convictions. Quaker family farmers were no less land-hungry than New Englanders, but the Proprietor's policy of land transfers provided them all the acreage they needed. Yet Penn's recruitment among the oppressed religious minorities of Continental Europe and the British Isles eventually brought an influx of other colonists who wished to build new lives and worship freely, and who viewed the Indians as obstacles to their goals. After 1710, the rising influence of such expansionists coincided with a series of debilitating strokes that left the Proprietor unable to direct his colony's Indian affairs, and tensions with the Indians escalated rapidly. The founder's vision of Pennsylvania as an experiment in interracial harmony died with him in 1718.

6.5: Planting the Carolinas

6.5 **Compare life in Carolina and in New England during the colonial period**

"The South"—certainly the fabled solid South of the early nineteenth century—did not exist during the colonial period. From its beginning, Carolina society was marked by substantial differences from the Chesapeake colonies further north. To be sure, planters in both areas forced African slaves to produce staple crops for a world market. But the Carolinas, joined much later by Georgia, stood apart from their northern neighbors. As a historian of colonial Carolina explained, "the southern colonies were never a cohesive section in the same way that New England was. The great diversity of population groups . . . discouraged southern sectionalism."

6.5.1: Proprietors of the Carolinas

Carolina was a product of the Restoration of the Stuarts to the English throne. Court favorites who had followed the Stuarts into exile during the Civil War demanded tangible rewards for their loyalty. New York and New Jersey were obvious plums. So too was Carolina. Sir John Colleton, a successful English planter returned from Barbados, organized a group of eight powerful courtiers who styled themselves the True and Absolute Lords Proprietors of Carolina. On March 24, 1663, the king granted these proprietors a charter to the vast territory between Virginia and Florida and running west as far as the "South Seas."

The failure of similar ventures in the New World taught the Carolina proprietors not to expect instant wealth. Rather, they hoped to obtain a steady source of income from rents. What they needed, of course, were settlers. Recruitment turned out to be no easy task. Improved economic and social conditions in England made people less willing to transfer to America. The cost of transporting settlers across the Atlantic also seemed prohibitive. The proprietors decided instead to save money by enticing men and women from established colonies with incentives such as a generous land policy. Yet even this proved difficult and expensive. American colonists had begun to take their rights and privileges for granted. They wanted a representative assembly, liberty of conscience, and a liberal headright system.

The Carolina proprietors divided their grant into three distinct jurisdictions, anticipating that these areas would become the centers of settlement. The first region, called Albemarle, abutted Virginia. As the earlier ill-fated Roanoke colonists had discovered, the region lacked a good deepwater port. Nevertheless, it attracted a number of dissatisfied Virginians who drifted south in search of fresh land. Farther south, the mouth of the Cape Fear River seemed a second likely site for development. And third, within the present state of South Carolina, the Port Royal region contained a maze of fertile islands and meandering tidal streams.

Colleton and his associates waited for the money to roll in, but to their dismay, no one seemed interested in moving to Carolina. A tiny settlement at Port Royal failed. One group of New Englanders briefly considered the Cape Fear area, but they were so disappointed by what they saw that they departed, leaving behind a sign that "tended not only to the disparagement of the Land . . . but also to the great discouragement of all those that should hereafter come into these parts to settle." By this time, a majority of surviving proprietors had given up on Carolina.

6.5.2: The Barbadian Connection

Anthony Ashley Cooper, later Earl of Shaftesbury, was the exception. In 1669, he persuaded the remaining Carolinian proprietors to invest their own capital in the colony. Once he received sufficient funds, this energetic organizer dispatched three hundred English colonists to Port Royal under the command of Joseph West. The fleet put in briefly at Barbados to pick up additional recruits, and in March 1670, after being punished by Atlantic gales that destroyed one ship, the expedition arrived at Port Royal. Only one hundred people were still alive. The unhappy settlers did not remain long at a place so low-lying and so badly exposed to Spanish attack. They moved northward, locating eventually along the more secure Ashley River. Later the colony's administrative center, Charles Town (it did not become Charleston until 1783) was established at the junction of the Ashley and Cooper rivers.

Ashley also wanted to bring order to the new society. With assistance from the famous English philosopher John Locke (1632–1704), he devised the Fundamental Constitutions of Carolina. Like Penn's Frame of Government, the document bore James Harrington's mark. They created a local aristocracy of proprietors and lesser nobles called landgraves and cassiques, terms as inappropriate to American realities as the idea of creating a hereditary landed elite. Persons who purchased vast tracts of land received a title and the right to sit in the Council of Nobles, a body designed to administer justice, oversee civil affairs, and initiate legislation. Smaller landowners had a voice in a parliament which could accept or reject bills drafted by the council. The very poor were excluded from political life. Ashley thought his scheme maintained the proper "Balance of Government" between aristocracy and democracy, a concept central to Harrington's philosophy. Not surprisingly, the constitutions had little impact on the actual structure of government.

Before 1680, almost half the men and women who settled in the Port Royal area came from Barbados, which had by this time become overpopulated. Wealthy families could not provide their sons and daughters with sufficient land to maintain social status. As the crisis intensified, Barbadians looked to the North American mainland for relief. These colonists, many quite rich, migrated as individuals and in families. Some brought gangs of slaves with them to carve out plantations on the tributaries of the Cooper River. The Barbadians established themselves immediately as the colony's most powerful political faction. Historian Richard Dunn notes that they helped make Carolina a "slave-based plantation society closer in temper to the islands they fled from than to any other mainland English settlement."

Much of the planters' time was taken up with the search for a profitable crop. The early settlers experimented with a number of plants: tobacco, cotton, silk, and grapes. The most successful items turned out to be beef, skins, and naval stores—especially tar used to maintain ocean vessels. Some Carolinians built up great herds of cattle, many of which they slaughtered, salted, and shipped to Barbados to supplement Pennsylvania grain. Traders purchased Indians thousands of deerskins from Indian hunters in the interior,

which they resold for tidy profits to English buyers. They also purchased captive Indians by the score from native trading partners for sale to Caribbean sugar planters. In the 1690s, the planters came to appreciate the high value of rice. It quickly became the colony's main staple.

Proprietary Carolina was in a constant political uproar. Factions vied for privilege. The Barbadian settlers, known locally as the Goose Creek Men, resisted the proprietors' policies at every turn. A large community of French Huguenots in Craven County distrusted the Barbadians. The proprietors appointed a series of utterly incompetent governors who only made things worse. One visitor observed, "the Inhabitants of Carolina should be as free from Oppression as any [people] in the Universe . . . if their own Differences amongst themselves do not occasion the contrary." By 1700, the Commons House of Assembly had assumed the right to initiate legislation. In 1719, the colonists overthrew the last proprietary governor, and in 1729, the king created separate royal governments for North and South Carolina.

6.5.3: Black Carolinians

African slaves were indispensable to the settlement of Carolina. From the earliest years of settlement, one of every three to four newcomers was a black slave. The decision to employ slave labor was not difficult for the Barbadians who brought to the colony long experience in a slave society. The difficulty of recruiting white servants made the decision that much easier. Even the Irish would no longer risk servitude in America. The memory of being shipped to the Caribbean islands "where they were sold as slaves" during Cromwell's rule so terrified them that they would "hardly give credence to any other usage."

The effort to maintain slavery in an early frontier environment presented the Carolinians with unique challenges. Laws and institutions developed for controlling slaves in Barbados required adaptation. There, population density coupled with the boundaries of ocean on every side had made it difficult to run away. By contrast, Carolina rested on the edge of a seemingly boundless frontier filled with Indians who might assist runaway slaves to freedom. Slave owners had to establish good relations with neighboring Indian nations to ensure the return of runaways. Colonists likewise needed appropriate legal codes and practical systems of control to prevent rebellion and keep slaves on task. Carolinians found ways to address each of these issues, but some slaves still managed to escape their chains and disappear into the western forest.

During the earliest years of settlement, most slaves arrived in Carolina from other ports in the western hemisphere, not all of them English. Caribbean pirates raided coastlines for captives. Slavers "salvaged" slaves who had escaped or been marooned in shipwrecks. Traders purchased a few slaves in various ports they visited for resale in Carolina. Some were born in colonial plantations, while others were first-generation slaves with keen memories of life and work in various parts of Africa. The slave population thus comprised a polyglot of European and African languages and a wide array of cultural traditions. Many slaves also brought to Carolina special knowledge and skills that proved very useful in the search for a viable economy.

Africans supplied nearly every type of labor in Carolina. Black craftsmen quickly came to dominate the coopers' trade, supplying barrels for packing export crops and for use around shops and plantations. Many became expert woodsmen, cutting trees to clear fields or scoring pines to collect pitch and turpentine for the colony's trade in naval stores. African cattlemen tended the great herds of their early Carolina masters using methods similar to those employed in the savannahs of their homeland. Skilled African boatmen constructed dugout canoes for use in the early Carolina fishing industry, which they dominated. Anglo-Carolinians relied on their slaves' expert knowledge of canoe travel and river navigation

for transportation as well. African boatmen became indispensable to the fur trade along the Savannah River, which formed "the ordinary thorowfare to the Westward Indians."

African know-how may have been most valuable to Carolinians in the production of rice. Colonists experimented with rice early on, but unfamiliarity with its methods of cultivation led them to discard it. In contrast, slaves from several parts of Africa possessed thorough knowledge of rice cultivation, especially those from West Africa's Gambia River and the Windward Coast, which stretched from modern-day Sierra Leon to Ivory Coast. There, Africans had been growing rice for centuries before European contact. They readily adapted their methods to the new varieties introduced by the Portuguese and French during the 1500s. Not all slaves who came to Carolina understood rice cultivation, but historian Daniel C. Littlefield has shown that, as rice grew in importance as a staple after 1690, Carolinians preferred to purchase slaves from rice-growing regions in Africa. Slaves planted, hoed, and threshed the crop using methods similar to those employed in African rice fields.

Relations between English and Africans were relatively fluid in early Carolina due to its rugged character and its location so close to hostile Spanish Florida. Slaves and masters often worked side-by-side clearing fields, hunted together for the game they shared, and fought together in skirmishes with Spanish or hostile Indians. They also suffered debilitating bouts of disease together in Carolina's humid sub-tropical climate. While never free from the threat of the whip, slaves enjoyed significant latitude to participate in the frontier economy. They often kept their own gardens and hired themselves out after finishing assigned tasks. Many carved out for themselves a degree of economic autonomy. A few slaves saved enough of their earnings to purchase their own freedom. A few others achieved manumission by performing special acts of service or winning unusual favor from their masters.

Africans frequently engaged in sexual relations with both English and Indians in Carolina's early years, sometimes entering unofficial unions that endured for years. White men most commonly took African or Indian female partners, but white women were not punished for joining in sexual relationships with black men until 1717. The offspring of these interracial unions born to slave mothers became slaves themselves unless a white father claimed them, but those whose mother was a white servant or free woman often became free. Some of these free persons of color managed to become members of white society, but most occupied a tenuous status on the lowest rungs of the social ladder and faced a lifelong struggle to retain their freedom.

Black Carolinians interacted constantly with Indians as well as whites. First-generation colonists often put enslaved Indians into the fields to supplement their work force, bringing them into daily contact with Africans. This made possible an ongoing cultural exchange between the two groups. Africans learned much from the Indians concerning their new environment, the geography of the land, the climate, and the use of medicinal plants. A few such as Col. Alexander Mackey's slave Timboe mastered native languages and became highly valued interpreters. Many others took advantage of early Carolina's fluid environment and entered the fur trade as semi-independent agents—so many, in fact, that colonial authorities eventually prohibited slaves from participating except as agents of their masters.

6.5.4: Traders, Raiders, and Indian Slaves on the Carolina Frontier

The first Carolina settlers arrived in an area already transformed by more than a century of ongoing contact with Europeans. The Apalachee, Guale, and Timucua peoples to their south had been incorporated into the Spanish empire and the Roman Catholic Church (see Chapter 2). Many lived in villages transformed and in some cases established by Franciscan missionaries. Their hereditary leaders had become Spanish dons, adopting Spanish dress, receiving Spanish horses, and enjoying the exemptions from corporal punishment, manual labor, and taxation that were due their rank. Each year their loyal service was rewarded by rich gifts of goods from the governor in the name of the King of Spain. In return, they governed the villages, exercising considerable authority even over the Spanish friars and soldiers. They also oversaw the supply of native tribute labor, which the Spanish exacted from the region's inhabitants. The heavy toll this labor exacted in Indian life and health had provoked several rebellions in the two decades before the English settled Carolina, yet the Spanish were still managing to keep their frayed empire intact.

Indians to the west and north of Charles Town had long enjoyed steady commerce with traders from Virginia. Until the 1670s, most English trade to the region passed through Occaneechi middlemen, whose territory straddled the route to the southern Piedmont Indians such as the Cherokees and Creeks. When followers of Nathaniel Bacon decimated the Occaneechis in 1676 (see Chapter 7), they cleared the way for Virginia merchants to trade directly with the southern tribes.

Trade and contact with the Spanish and English had produced its familiar effects on the Indians who engaged in it. The inadvertent introduction of epidemic disease decimated local populations. Villages contracted, moved, or disappeared. The remnants of affected ethnic groups combined to form new nations such as North Carolina's Catawbas. The introduction of useful products such as firearms, metal utensils, and cloth displaced items made with traditional materials and technologies of the forest. As traditional skills were lost, dependency on European trade increased.

Thus Carolina colonists arrived in the 1670s to find a ready market for their goods among the region's native peoples, who already understood the use of these items and were looking only for greater advantages in trade. The Barbadian settlers also quickly recognized that the region's intertribal rivalries presented an opportunity to strengthen their own security and claim to the land by setting the Indians against one another. Captives taken in this intertribal warfare could generate substantial profits when sold as slaves on an Atlantic market. The Proprietors opposed these practices, asserting a monopoly on Indian trade and prohibiting the enslavement of Indians within 400 miles of Charles Town. The colonists, however, did not find it difficult to circumvent regulations imposed from a distance of over 3,000 miles.

Between 1670 and 1700, Charles Town colonists pursued their Indian policy by establishing a series of alliances with Indians who proved useful to their ends, shifting loyalties whenever a given alliance had outlived its purpose. In the early years the Westoes of the Savannah River readily aided their new Charles Town allies in decimating the small coastal groups who stood in the way of English settlement. The Westoes received a rich supply of arms and trade goods for their friendship until 1680, when they found themselves in the way of Carolina's expansion. Ambitious traders then enticed the Lower Creeks and the Savannah band of Shawnees to push eastward, eliminate their Westoe rivals, and enjoy the bounties of English trade.

The Creek and Savannah alliance proved a virtual gold mine for Carolina traders, bringing a steady supply of furs, deerskins, and Indian slaves to Charles Town. The alliance gave traders access deep into the interior. By 1700, the French of Louisiana reported encountering a constant stream of English in search of commodities for trade. Chief among those commodities was the traffic in human laborers, "each person being traded for one gun." Carolina's Lower Creek and

Yamassee trading partners also invaded Florida to enslave Catholic Indians. By 1685, they pushed all the Guale villages to within 50 miles of St. Augustine. Over the next two decades they trained their sights on Apalachee, raiding its villages repeatedly until 1704, when a combined English and Indian force under the leadership of Col. James Moore struck the final blow. Moore's campaign netted over one thousand Christian Indian slaves for sale to Carolina planters, West Indian sugar barons, and mainland colonial customers as far north as New England. St. Augustine was left to preside over a colony in ruins, its villages deserted and its missions destroyed. Florida's governor estimated in 1708 that the Carolina trade in Indian slaves had claimed between ten thousand and twelve thousand of the Spanish crown's Indian subjects.

6.6: An Empire of Contradictions

6.6 **Evaluate the contradictions in life in the Restoration-era colonies of England**

The tragic contrast between the Carolina settlers' actions and the proprietors' ideals was only the most glaring of many ironies that marked the colonies established or seized during the Restoration era. The Long Island towns welcomed York's capture of New Netherlands only to chafe under the Duke's autocratic rule. The Quakers hoped to make Pennsylvania and the Jerseys into models of racial, ethnic, and religious harmony, only to clash with each other over how to govern their "holy experiments." Virtually no Restoration-era colonist detected any conflict between their demand for freedom of conscience and their reliance on African slave labor.

The contradictions of life in England's Restoration-era colonies mirrored the conflict and tensions of later Stuart England itself. Yet overarching all was the determination of English merchants and officials to make their nation pre-eminent in Atlantic trade. By the time of Charles II's death in 1685, the budding success of the newest colonies suggested how far the English had gone toward achieving their goal. Out of this haphazard mixture of colonial ventures was emerging the outline of an English Atlantic commercial system. The legal groundwork for that system had been laid in the Navigation Acts of the 1660s, but the political framework of Anglo-American relations remained strongly contested as Charles's absolutist brother James II ascended the English throne. The coming years would witness a transatlantic constitutional struggle over the shape of England's new empire, one whose outcome would establish the terms of an international rivalry for control of North America.

Chronology

1637	Dutch capture Portuguese slave-trading post at Elmina
1639	French Jesuit trader-missionaries challenge Dutch monopoly on Iroquois trade
1642	English Civil War breaks out
1648	Peace of Westphalia ends Thirty-Years' War in Europe
1649	Charles I beheaded
1651	Commonwealth Parliament passes first Navigation Act
1652	First Anglo-Dutch War breaks out
1653	Oliver Cromwell becomes Lord Protector of England
1655	English forces capture Jamaica
1660	English monarchy restored under Charles
1660	Enumeration Act passed
1663	Staple Act passed
1663	Charles II grants charter to True and Absolute Lords Proprietors of Carolina
1664	Colonel Richard Nicolls captures New Netherlands for Duke of York
1664	Duke of York grants the Jerseys to John, Lord Berkeley, Sir George Carteret
1665	The Duke's Laws establish English Royal government in New York
1670	Barbadian emigrants begin colonizing South Carolina

Chapter 7
Conflict, Transformation, Realignment

 ## Learning Objectives

7.1 Explain how conflict among European neighbors led to conflict in the Atlantic

7.2 Investigate how the colonial governors helped establish the King's authority in America

7.3 Evaluate the struggles within and outside England resulting from Charles II's ascent to power

7.4 Review the European power struggles due to the growth of the English armed forces

7.5 Report the losses suffered by London merchants and their partners due to conflict on the high seas

7.6 Examine how England's attitude towards the American colonies changed over time

A heavy snowstorm brought nightfall to Schenectady, New York, even earlier than usual on February 8, 1690. By 11 p.m. the snow was "above Knee Deep" and the English, Dutch, and Mohawk inhabitants were fast asleep. No one heard as two hundred French and Algonquian raiders silently encircled the frontier outpost on the Mohawk River and slipped past its unguarded gates. At a signal, the entire force rushed at once. So complete was the surprise that few houses made any resistance. Those who awoke in time fired "severall gunns" to raise the alarm to farmers in the surrounding countryside, but the deep snow muffled the shots. No one came to Schenectady's aid. For two hours the Canadian force swarmed

the village, putting "everyone who defended the place to the sword" and setting many houses afire. The raiders made prisoners of twenty-seven surviving inhabitants and spared "some twenty Mohawks" to show them that it was the English and not the Native Americans against whom the grudge was entertained.

Schenectady's inhabitants fell victim that night to a conflict between European powers that quickly engulfed the Atlantic World, transforming even the frontier villages of rival European colonies into prizes for imperial conquest. The great Atlantic contest pitted not only Europeans against one another but embroiled their native allies and trading partners as well, implicating what had once been local rivalries between native factions in a much larger imperial struggle for wealth and power.

Thus the strike on Schenectady, like scores of subsequent frontier clashes, expressed both local and imperial factors. It arose from local rivalry between Iroquois and western Algonquian over trade in furs with rival European powers. England's so-called Glorious Revolution in 1688–1689 transformed that seemingly local conflict into a titanic, Atlantic-wide struggle for dynasty and empire after English leaders ousted the Catholic King James II in favor of James's Protestant daughter Mary and her husband, the Dutch ruler William of Orange. It rekindled an Anglo-French conflict that James had been trying to put to rest in Europe and the colonies, giving the Iroquois new hope for English assistance in their wars against New France's western Algonquian allies.

Colonial politics also expressed this dramatic shift in Atlantic imperial alignments, tragically so for Schenectady's victims. William and Mary's coup in London sparked an uprising in New York that divided the colonists themselves into factions battling over Dutch colonist Jacob Leisler's effort to stage his own Glorious Revolution there. The rivalry for local and imperial legitimacy so consumed Leisler and his foes that they could neither offer effective assistance to their Iroquois allies nor respond to the renewed French threat. News of the "Sack of Schenectady" generated a torrent of finger-pointing between Leislerians and anti-Leislerians. As early as November 1689, both factions had heard of plans by the Canadian governor, Comte Louis de Buade de Frontenac, to capitalize on Anglo-French hostilities by leading a military force to capture New York. Yet colonists failed to respond to this intelligence in time to avert disaster.

From the perspective of imperial politics, Schenectady represented an unforeseen casualty of New York colonists' efforts to take a greater hand in shaping their own place within the English Atlantic. For twenty-five years, crown officials had worked to incorporate New York and other colonies into an orderly commercial empire; to strengthen royal authority throughout English America; and to establish stable, profitable, commercial, and diplomatic relations with the Iroquois and other native allies. William of Orange's dramatic coup disrupted these efforts, providing colonists a chance to rebalance the terms of colonial rule just as Leisler's letters to Schenectady promised. Colonists throughout America seized that chance in various ways, helping to define a new imperial order in which they would hold a greater measure of control over their affairs.

Yet such efforts proved hazardous in an atmosphere of heightened imperial rivalry, as Schenectady's inhabitants learned too late. The Sack of Schenectady reminds us that after 1660, the American colonies—in the Caribbean as well as the mainland—were being drawn into an elaborate world system, where decisions taken in distant places and markets affected warfare on the colonial frontier. We cannot consider European-Indian relations or life along the frontier as somehow removed from this context, for it was in this period that the major European powers—France and England especially—were experiencing military and fiscal changes that transformed the world. The Anglo-American Revolution of 1688–1689 not only made possible a new transatlantic constitutional order; it also plunged French, Algonquian, Iroquois, and English into a seventy-year contest for North American empire.

7.1: Negotiation, Conflict, and Rebellion

7.1 Explain how conflict among European neighbors led to conflict in the Atlantic

Colonial American was not a peaceful region. Long before the outbreak of revolution, settlers clashed with distant British administrators and with each other. Small farmers and Native American families never knew when violence would visit their communities. During the last quarter of the seventeenth century, however, a series of grave crises erupted, prompting officials in London to press for greater control over colonial affairs. Virginia officials were struggling to contain a rising and volatile population of poor yeomen and landless laborers on the colony's hardscrabble fringes, who often clashed with the native population. New England enjoyed more social stability, but steady expansion into traditional native lands along the region's river valleys and beyond was sparking tension and resentment among the indigenous population. New York's governors were struggling to find the best means of ruling a substantial non-English population while cultivating alliance with their powerful Iroquois neighbors. Colonists everywhere perceived their foothold in North America as tenuous. The bounds of settlement remained narrow. They seemed surrounded by hostile indigenous forces and European competitors. In the Caribbean, a wealthy planter elite held a tenacious grip on power everywhere except Jamaica, where planters jockeyed with powerful, wealthy, and unscrupulous buccaneers. Island elites used their power to resist royal intervention.

Royal officials sought to bring order to this chaotic colonial scene not only with new Navigation Acts to control Atlantic trade (see Chapter 6) but also with new efforts in native diplomacy and aggressive reforms in colonial government to strengthen their emerging Atlantic empire. In theory and sometimes in practice, royal governors formed the linchpin in this effort to assert the king's authority in the colonies. The instructions they received at the time of appointment gave the governors great authority. Many of them wielded it in high-handed ways. Such tactics brought the careers of many governors to grief, but others left a lasting mark on the politics of the colonies they strove to control.

7.1.1: Forging the Covenant Chain

One of the most effective of these governors was Edmund Andros (pronounced "Andrews"), a staunch supporter of the Stuart monarchs and a veteran of the Anglo-Dutch wars. Appointed by James, Duke of York, as governor of New York in 1774, Andros moved quickly to consolidate English power after the Dutch finally ceded all claim to the colony that year. Andros understood the role New York had played in the Dutch Atlantic and sought to harness its potential to become a linchpin of English Atlantic power. The governor soon concluded that generous terms of alliance with the colony's powerful Iroquois neighbors would serve England's quest for Atlantic dominion as well. Access to the lucrative Iroquois fur trade had helped to make the colony an attractive prize for capture in 1664. The five-nation Iroquois League also possessed formidable power in the Northeast, and they were using that power to bring neighboring peoples under their influence. Andros recognized that Iroquois aims meshed well with his own desire to simplify Anglo-Indian relations. It would be much easier to deal with a single overarching native authority than a multitude of smaller bands.

The Iroquois perceived advantages in an Anglo-Iroquois alliance that could fend off French aggression and augment the league's power. The French royal minister Jean-Baptiste Colbert began working during the 1660s to transform New France to contribute to the French imperial economy as the English colonies were beginning to do for England. The Five Nations, with their control of furs in the Mohawk and St. Lawrence valleys, constituted an obstacle to these plans. Colbert authorized military action against them. In 1665, the one thousand-man Carignan-Salières regiment launched two campaigns into Mohawk country, destroying villages and food supplies. Iroquois delegates negotiated for peace in the aftermath of the French assault, but its memory continued to rankle.

By early 1675, as Andros began to engage in serious diplomacy with the Five Nations, Iroquois-French tensions were rising further. French explorers in the Great Lakes and Illinois country had begun building a chain of forts that would give their traders a direct link to European markets via the Mississippi. The new route would enable the French to bypass Iroquois middle men in the St. Lawrence trade and would provide a competitive advantage over Seneca traders in western fur markets. While Iroquois leaders may not have grasped the plan's full scope, they experienced its effects in a growing French menace on their western borders and in stiffer competition for western furs.

In this context, alliance with the English promised to ensure continued access to European markets along with military assistance and peace on their eastern, English-controlled boundaries. This in turn would free Iroquois forces to defend their vulnerable northern and western flanks against the French and their native allies. Headmen who had previously sought to blunt French aggression through neutrality or cooperation began to lose influence, while those who had opposed such efforts now coalesced into identifiable Anglophile factions within Iroquois tribes and villages. Several villages expelled French priests along with tribal members who had converted to Catholicism.

During the 1670s, Andros and various Iroquois tribal headmen mediated a series of ad hoc agreements that became the basis for an enduring system of alliances known as the Covenant Chain. One of the chain's central links was an English-brokered end to a long-running Mohawk–Mahican war, which secured safe passage for merchant vessels between Albany and Manhattan. Andros built on this treaty by sponsoring new commercial regulations to prevent abuses that had characterized the earlier Dutch trade. As a result, commerce thrived on the Hudson River. English and Anglo-Dutch merchants prospered, while Anglophile headmen augmented their prestige and influence by acting as brokers between Iroquois villages, Albany merchants, and colonial officials.

Security for the fur trade proved to be only the beginning of what the Covenant Chain alliance could make possible for both the English and the Iroquois. Subsequent events in New England and the Chesapeake demonstrated how well Governor Andros had read the balance of power along the eastern seaboard. The Anglo-Iroquois settlement would soon secure New York's preeminence among England's mainland colonies while strengthening and extending Iroquois influence and political power over native rivals.

7.1.2: Civil War in Virginia: Bacon's Rebellion

As Sir Edmund Andros was negotiating the early provisions of his diplomatic triumph with the Iroquois League, Governor William Berkeley of Virginia was finding himself increasingly enmeshed in a series of intractable problems. For sixteen years, the Virginia economy had steadily declined. Returns from tobacco had not been good for some time, and the Navigation Acts reduced profits even further. Into this unhappy environment came thousands of indentured servants, people drawn to Virginia, as the governor explained, "in hope of bettering their condition in a Growing Country."

The reality bore little relation to their dreams. A hurricane destroyed the entire tobacco crop. In 1667, Dutch warships captured the tobacco fleet as it was departing for England. Indentured servants complained about lack of food and clothing. No wonder that Berkeley despaired of ever ruling "a People where six parts of seven at least are Poor, indebted, Discontented and Armed." In 1670, he and the House of Burgesses disfranchised all landless freemen, persons they regarded as troublemakers, but the threat of social violence remained.

Enter Nathaniel Bacon. This ambitious young man arrived in Virginia in 1674. He came from a respectable English family and set himself up immediately as a substantial planter. But he wanted more. Bacon envied the government patronage monopolized by Berkeley's cronies, a group known locally as the Green Spring faction. He requested a license to engage in the fur trade, a lucrative commerce reserved for the governor's friends. Berkeley rebuffed him. Had Bacon been willing to wait, he might have been accepted into the ruling clique, but Bacon was not a patient man.

Events beyond Bacon's control thrust him suddenly into the center of Virginia politics. In July 1675, a minor clash between a Virginia trader and some of his native partners escalated into a frontier conflict between planters and a loose coalition of Piscataway, Doeg, and Susquehannock warriors. The Susquehannocks had only recently moved into the Potomac region following their defeat by members of the Iroquois League two years before. They had no quarrel with English colonists—indeed, they had settled on the Potomac at the invitation of the Maryland government—until the Virginia militia colonel George Mason mistakenly killed fourteen Susquehannocks during a punitive raid into Maryland. Throughout the autumn of 1675, Susquehannock bands filtered through Virginia's backcountry forests, exacting vengeance on vulnerable outlying plantations.

Terrified Virginians called on the governor to send an army to retaliate. Instead, early in 1676, Berkeley called for the construction of a line of defensive forts, a plan that seemed to the settlers both expensive and ineffective. The strategy raised embarrassing questions. Was Berkeley protecting his own fur monopoly? Was he planning to reward his friends with contracts to build useless forts?

While people speculated about such matters, Bacon stepped forward. He boldly offered to lead a volunteer army against the Indians at no cost to the hard-pressed Virginia taxpayers. All he demanded was an official commission giving him military command and the right to attack other Indians, not just the hostile Susquehannocks. The governor steadfastly refused. With some justification, Berkeley regarded his upstart rival as a fanatic on the subject of Indians. The governor saw no reason to exterminate peaceful tribes simply to avenge the death of a few white settlers.

What followed would have been comic had not so many people died. Bacon thundered against the governor's treachery; Berkeley labeled Bacon a traitor. Both men appealed to the populace for support. Bacon several times marched his followers to the frontier but failed to find the enemy or worse, massacred friendly Indians. At one point, Bacon burned Jamestown to the ground, forcing the governor to flee to the colony's Eastern Shore. Bacon's bumbling lieutenants chased Berkeley across Chesapeake Bay only to be captured themselves. Thereupon, the governor mounted a new campaign.

As the civil war dragged on, it became increasingly apparent that Bacon and his gentry supporters had only the vaguest notion of what they were trying to achieve. The members of the planter elite never seemed fully to appreciate that the rank-and-file soldiers, often black slaves and poor white servants, had serious, legitimate grievances against Berkeley's corrupt government and were demanding substantial reforms, not just a share in the governor's fur monopoly.

Although women had not been allowed to vote in colony elections, they made their political views clear enough during the rebellion. Some were apparently more violent than others. Sarah Glendon, for example, agitated so aggressively in support of Bacon that Berkeley later refused to grant her a pardon. Another outspoken rebel, Lydia Chiesman, defended her husband before Governor Berkeley, noting that the man would not have joined Bacon's forces had she not persuaded him to do so. "Therefore," Chiesman pleaded, ". . . since what her husband had done, was by her meanes, and so, by consequence, she most guilty, that she might be hanged and he pardoned."

When Charles II learned of the fighting in Virginia, he dispatched a thousand regular soldiers to Jamestown. By the time they arrived, Berkeley had regained full control over the colony's government. In October 1676, Bacon died after a brief illness, and, within a few months, his band of rebel followers had dispersed. In 1677, the king recalled an old and embittered Berkeley to England.

Virginia's Indian allies suffered as much as their enemies at the hands of Bacon's militia forces. The Pamunkey, whose late werowance Opechancanough had once ruled the entire Powhatan chiefdom, fell victim to an assault by Bacon's forces, although "it was well known to the whole country that the Queen of Pamunkey and her People had neere at any time betray'd or injuryed the English." Militiamen chased the unresisting Pamunkey into hiding, killing, or capturing those they found and plundering their village.

The aftermath of Bacon's Rebellion brought additional prestige and power to both New York's Edmund Andros and his Iroquois allies, who took a hand in negotiating Anglo-Indian relations in the Chesapeake. The conflict destroyed the already-weakened polity of the Susquehannocks, permitting Andros to persuade them to relocate north. Some returned to their original Susquehanna location, where they became known as Conestogas. Others settled among the Delawares and still others among the Onondaga and Cayuga nations of the Iroquois. Seneca headmen gave assurances for the Susquehannocks' good behavior in a 1677 agreement among Maryland, Virginia, and the Iroquois. In subsequent years, Iroquois bands who had not joined in the 1677 "silver chain" continued to raid Maryland and Virginia frontiers for furs and captives, prompting Andros to broker additional negotiations among Chesapeake and Iroquois leaders. Though the resulting covenants, which the Iroquois termed "handclasps of friendship," were distinct from those with New York, Andros's crucial role nevertheless strengthened his reputation as a man of rare administrative ability.

7.1.3: King Philip's War

From the perspective of London, a crisis like Bacon's Rebellion was sufficient in itself to raise questions about the effectiveness of colonial government. Five hundred miles to the north, however, storms of war were also building on the New England frontier that exposed structural weaknesses and disunity of five English colonies there. Unlike Bacon's Rebellion, the conflict consisted of a series of well-coordinated campaigns by a Wampanoag–Narragansett alliance against land-hungry colonial farmers.

For decades, the Wampanoags and Narragansetts had found themselves pressed into ever-smaller boundaries as officials in Rhode Island, Plymouth, Connecticut, and Massachusetts scrambled to expand their settlements by purchasing native land. The purchases fueled intercolonial tensions and aroused resentment among the Indians, who were often forced into land sales to satisfy debts incurred to the English. Thve gradual depletion of their most valuable resource served as a painful reminder of how dangerously dependent on European trade the Indians had become. The Wampanoag sachem Philip, a son of the Pilgrims' old ally Massasoit (see Chapter 5), observed that the English had impoverished his people so that "but a small part of the dominion of my ancestors remains." Early in 1675, he declared to an intercolonial assembly of leaders that he was "determined not to live until I have no country."

Philip, originally named Metacom, had for several years been laboring to forge alliances of resistance among southern New England tribes.

Rumors that he planned to lead an armed assault on English settlements kept nervous colonial officials busy negotiating, cajoling, and attempting to coerce Philip to come to peaceful terms with the English. Whether Philip intended to strike or merely to gain more diplomatic leverage remains unclear. In late June 1675, however, a band of Wampanoag warriors apparently confirmed the rumors by sacking the Plymouth town of Swansea.

King Philip's War had begun. The powerful Narragansetts joined the Wampanoags. In little more than a year of fighting, the Indians destroyed scores of frontier villages, killed hundreds of colonists, and disrupted the entire regional economy. The speed and scope of King Philip's offensive caught settlers off balance. He seemed to be everywhere at once. Historic rivalries impeded the colonies' efforts to mount a coordinated defense. The absence of a clear structure of command or rules of engagement gave colonists too much leeway to act, which they sometimes exercised through indiscriminate vengeance against Indian neutrals or allies as well as enemies.

For several months, Philip's forces held the upper hand, yet they did not prevail. The tide began to turn during the winter of 1675–1676 as Mohawk forces entered the English side of the conflict and New England troops found effective ways to cooperate. By August 1676, when Philip's death in battle brought an end to the conflict, more than one thousand Indians and New Englanders had perished. The cessation of hostilities left New England colonists deeply in debt and more than ever uncertain of their future.

Frontier conflict continued to rage further north as King Philip's campaign inspired a sympathetic uprising among the Wabenakis of Maine. Although Wabenakis and New Englanders had enjoyed a long history of trade in furs and maize, tensions similar to those in southern New England had been building as settlers in Maine and New Hampshire pushed further into traditional native lands. Massachusetts militia, already wearied and weakened by war on their western flank, found themselves unable to quell the conflict on their northeastern Maine frontier. Only the intervention of New York's Edmund Andros brought cessation of hostilities with the Peace of Casco in 1678.

7.1.4: Counterpoint: Pueblo Revolt in the Spanish Borderlands

In the borderlands 2,000 miles southwest of Boston, a revolt of Pueblo Indians took place against Spanish colonists within four years of King Philip's War that invites comparison with English mainland North America. The Pueblo Revolt suggests that, by thinking of North American colonization in broad, Atlantic terms, patterns, and possible connections can become visible between apparently dissimilar events. If nothing else, it suggests that Indians of the Southwest were experiencing similar threats to their cultural autonomy as were the Wampanoags of New England and the western Indians of Virginia.

By the time of Bacon's Rebellion and King Philip's War, the Spanish had governed New Mexico for more than eighty years. Periodic local revolts that punctuated Spanish rule served mainly to confirm official confidence in the strength of the regime over a fragmented and demoralized native population. In 1660, however, a succession of events plunged the Pueblo peoples into depths of misery that ultimately brought them together against their resented Spanish overlords. It began with a series of droughts that devastated Pueblo villages, sometimes leaving starving inhabitants to die "along the roads, in the ravines, and in their huts." Navajo and

Apache nomads added damage to insult by staging repeated raids on scarce Pueblo maize and livestock. Two decades of starvation, disease, and depredation seemed to expose the impotence of the Franciscans' God, prompting Pueblos to return to traditional religious observance. Spanish attempts to suppress Pueblo ceremonies, often through brutal measures, only served to galvanize Pueblo opposition under the charismatic religious leader Popé.

Throughout the summer of 1680, Popé worked from headquarters in Taos to organize a massive revolt of seventeen thousand Pueblos across hundreds of miles of territory. Runners carried calendars to participating Pueblos in the form of knotted ropes that marked off the days until the planned uprising on August 11. Spanish officials discovered the plot two days early, yet Popé had laid his plans so well that he was able to coordinate his forces to strike a day earlier than planned.

The massive uprising overwhelmed Spanish settlements along the Rio Grande and its tributaries. Popé's forces destroyed ranches and villages, plundering Spanish weapons as they went to increase their firepower. They reserved special treatment for captured Franciscan missionaries, humiliating and torturing them before taking their lives. They targeted churches as well, burning or gutting them and desecrating sacred objects. Many survivors of the initial attack fled to Santa Fe, where they soon found themselves surrounded by well-armed rebels. On September 21, the city fell, and its survivors fled to join the remnants of New Mexico's Spanish and Christian Pueblo exiles in El Paso. Pueblos prevented the Spanish from returning to New Mexico for thirteen years.

The Pueblo revolt sparked a series of uprisings throughout northern New Spain now remembered as the Great Northern Revolt. Unlike the situation in the English colonies, Spanish officials in the region could not turn to powerful native allies such as the Mohawks or to neighboring, well-connected colonial governors such as New York's Edmund Andros. They found themselves hard pressed to suppress native outbreaks against missions and settlements or to find and punish bands who fled from Spanish oppression. Sporadic unrest continued for decades on New Spain's northern frontier.

7.2: Royal Absolutism in America and the Caribbean

7.2 Investigate how the colonial governors helped establish the King's authority in America

King Charles II and his royal brother James, Duke of York shared the belief that kings ruled by the will of God and should have no constitutional limits upon their prerogative to rule as they thought best. Charles (r. 1660–1685) was the more pragmatic of the two, a master of court intrigue whose abilities often enabled him to effect his will without raw displays of power. Nevertheless, he was not afraid to exercise royal might when needed, and he was determined to extend royal authority throughout his dominions by appointing men who shared his absolutist views. Colonial governors in particular represented the king's authority in America, and several appointed under Charles II and James II sought to establish policies that matched their sovereigns' absolutist views.

7.2.1: Edmund Andros and the Dominion of New England

King Philip's War convinced London officials that the time had come to reorganize New England's governments under greater royal authority. The war had exposed the difficulties of coordinating defense among five self-interested governments, and colonists could not hide the fact that a jealous intercolonial scramble for land had antagonized their Indian neighbors in the first place. At the same time, ironically, New England courts seemed to be coordinating efforts to thwart implementation of the Navigation Acts. Massachusetts' Surveyor of Customs, Edward Randolph, waged a relentless letter-writing campaign with London to revoke the colony's charter of 1630. He believed this move would permit reorganization of colonial courts that were refusing to convict shippers who violated the laws. Randolph also joined with merchants newly arrived to Boston, men who like him were Anglicans rather than Congregationalists, in loud complaints against Puritan intolerance. The Anglican faction was never large, but its presence divided Bay leaders. Some Puritan ministers and magistrates resisted compromise with England, while others, recognizing the changing political realities within the empire, urged a more moderate course.

New York's governor Edmund Andros made his first, ill-timed attempt to extend royal control over New England at the outbreak of King Philip's War in 1675. That summer, he sailed with a small military force to Saybrook on the mouth of the Connecticut River, where he planned to claim half the colony for New York. There he found a fort occupied with Connecticut militia and flying the English flag. Andros went ashore, conversed briefly with the commander, and then returned prudently to New York.

Andros spent the next several years giving aid to some of the embattled New England colonies and pursuing Covenant Chain diplomacy with the Iroquois, although he refused military assistance to Connecticut in retaliation for their treatment of him at Saybrook. Andros also labored to consolidate his authority over fractious New York and to assert authority over commerce in the Jerseys, while his colleague Edmund Randolph battled recalcitrant

Massachusetts courts. Andros's imperious manner and high-handed actions earned him the enmity of powerful merchants in New York, and they levied charges of corruption against him. In 1681, the Duke of York recalled him to London to explain himself. Andros remained there for the next five years and witnessed the celebrations when his royal patron was crowned James II of England in 1685.

In 1686, Andros returned from London to New England with the authority he had not possessed on his visit to Saybrook eleven years before. His instructions authorized the new governor to establish a consolidated royal government over all colonies from Connecticut to Maine. They also authorized him to appoint and rule through a new council without an elected assembly. The new royal governor possessed full authority "by and with the advise and consent of our said Councill, or the major part of them," to tax, to appoint all judges and officers of the peace, and to muster and command the militia "for the resisting and withstanding all enemies pyrats and rebells."

Andros moved quickly to extend royal authority over the new Dominion. An experienced military commander, the governor expected his handpicked council to carry out his orders with the same alacrity he demanded of his military subordinates. The day after his arrival in Boston, he ordered that he and other communicants in the Established Church be given space in the Old South meetinghouse to observe Anglican services. Three months later, he converted the building to an Anglican church. Andros also imposed new taxes on the colonists. When the Reverend John Wise of Ipswich led the town meeting in resisting the new rates, Andros ordered him arrested, tried, and fined £10. He dealt similarly with other such attempts to defy his authority and eventually moved to minimize further obstruction by restricting town meetings to one annually.

None of Andros's actions galled colonists so sharply as his declaration that the revocation of

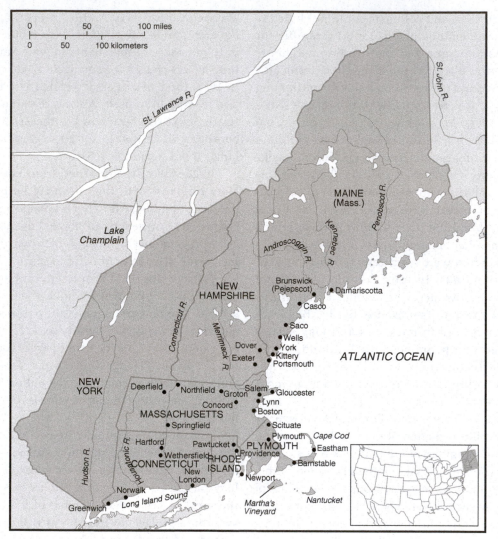

Map 7.1 Dominion of New England

the original Massachusetts charter had voided all their land titles. The governor warned that families who had inherited and farmed their land for the past sixty years were now considered intruders on the king's possessions. Landholders would have to petition the Crown for new royal patents that would legitimate their ownership but make them liable to the Crown for new fees and quitrents. Andros added damage to insult by issuing choice grants of common land and land not yet granted to his friends, including the Bay colonists' old nemesis Edward Randolph.

Without their elected assemblies, and with the Dominion courts now packed against them by Andros's appointments, New England colonists possessed few legal means to resist the Dominion government. Connecticut and Rhode Island enjoyed a brief reprieve because the Crown had temporarily left their charters intact, but by November 1687, both colonies submitted to Andros's rule. By then Massachusetts colonists had concluded that they could gain relief only by petitioning James II himself. In April 1688, Harvard College's president, the Reverend Increase Mather, slipped aboard a ship for London to carry the colonists' grievances against Andros to the king.

7.2.2: The Middle Colonies and the Dominion

Edmund Andros's quest to extend his authority did not pass unchallenged, even by his fellow royal governors. Colonel Thomas Dongan, appointed governor of New Jersey by James II, competed with Andros for rule over Connecticut. Instead, James issued Andros a new commission in the spring of 1688 that extended the Dominion to New York and the Jerseys as well as Connecticut and Rhode Island. The commission may have relieved Dongan of his authority, but it also relieved him of the administrative headache of trying to govern a colony chronically short on funds.

As proprietary colonies, East and West Jersey presented the king and Andros with a more complicated problem. The people of West New Jersey submitted to Andros quickly, but those in the eastern colony remembered earlier conflict with the imperious governor when he had tried to impose customs and meddle in their affairs from his seat in New York. The colony's mostly Scottish proprietors also insisted on submitting only the government of East New Jersey while retaining full ownership and rights to the land. In the end, both the proprietors and Andros got most of what they wanted.

As a favorite of the Stuarts, William Penn managed to remain proprietor of his Holy Experiment throughout James II's reign. Penn was residing in England at the time of James's succession and became closely involved in the monarch's efforts to extend religious indulgence to all non-Anglican Christian Englishmen, Catholics included. Penn served James not only out of gratitude that "the King was always his Friend, & his Father's Friend" but also because James was "a Friend to those of his Persuasion." He hoped by his service to secure permanent liberty of conscience not only for Quakers in America but for those in England as well.

7.2.3: The Dominion and the Covenant Chain

James II's governors attempted to apply their sovereign's absolutist policies to Anglo-Iroquois relations, but their presumption crashed against the Five Nations' power to assert their independence as a "free people" who could make war and peace as they chose. As Sir Edmund Andros arrived in Boston in December 1686, the Iroquois were facing renewed hostilities from the French and their Algonquian allies. In London, however, royal instructions were being dispatched to Andros and New York's governor Dongan to observe a new Treaty of American Neutrality with France, which had been signed only in November. The treaty angered even some of James's closest supporters in England because it settled none of the ongoing territorial disputes between England and France over North America. The treaty's ink had scarcely dried when word reached English officials of new French aggression in America, suggesting that the French had no intention of honoring the terms of neutrality. James's English subjects could only fume as their sovereign insisted on implementing the treaty.

The Five Nations, however, refused to act as English subjects or parties to a treaty made 3,000 miles away. Open war erupted in Iroquois lands the next summer when Jacques-René de Brisay de Denonville led an invasion of French and Algonquian forces into the Seneca country. Denonville captured and enslaved a party of Iroquois diplomats on the way to sacking and burning a broad swath of Seneca countryside. Denonville's treachery toward the diplomats alienated even those Iroquois families and leaders who had earlier favored the French.

New York's governor Dongan recognized that his Covenant Chain obligations to the Five Nations demanded more action than his sovereign would permit. The governor could not "ingage the French" himself and pled ineffectually for his Iroquois "Brethren" to "have a little patience." Nevertheless, American realities prompted Dongan to "put off" his native allies "by giving them Powder, Lead, Arms, and other things fitting and necessary for them," turning a blind eye to how they would be used.

Throughout the winter and spring of 1687–1688, Iroquois warriors used Dongan's presents to wage war against French settlements along the St. Lawrence River. By summer, the experience of having "women and children . . . daily carried off" persuaded Denonville to sue for peace. Governor Dongan employed whatever meager means he possessed to keep his Iroquois "children" from engaging in independent negotiations without English participation. The Five Nations only ignored him. Negotiations continued throughout the summer, only to break down when Wyandot allies of New France ambushed an Iroquois delegation and falsely blamed their action on orders from Denonville.

The Wyandots' treachery united the Five Nations to renew their campaign against the French and Algonquians. By autumn of 1688, when Andros arrived in Albany to proclaim the incorporation of New York under his authority, Iroquois warriors had forced the French to abandon western strongholds including Forts Frontenac and Niagara. They had captured the Jesuit priest Pierre Millet as revenge for Denonville's earlier capture of the Iroquois diplomats. One war party had penetrated as far north as Lachine on Montreal Island, where they killed twenty-four French and took between seventy and ninety prisoners. Andros could only bluster at his Five Nations "Children" to cease their hostilities and abide by the Treaty of American Neutrality.

By the time Andros addressed the Iroquois in Albany, the failure of the Anglo-French treaty had become clear to all. In the fall and winter of 1688–1689, Andros levied a militia force of 709 Massachusetts militia and led them to Maine, where he hoped to secure the province against Wabenaki and French Acadian foes. Andros spent the winter employing a combination of paternalism and military discipline to contain his resentful New England force while he negotiated for peace with the Wabenaki through exchanges of words and gifts. Thus Anglo-Indian diplomacy, in which the governor possessed significant skill, occupied him far from Boston in March 1689 when word reached the capital that James had fled for France.

7.2.4: James II and the Plantation Colonies

Beyond the Dominion's boundaries James II was also acting to bring the plantation colonies under the royal thumb. In Maryland, a long-running power struggle between the Catholic proprietor Cecilius Calvert, the second Lord Baltimore, and aggressive Protestant planters gave James a pretext to begin action against Baltimore's charter. Maryland planters had been agitating for such measures since the 1660s under the leadership of the fiery Anglican assemblyman John Coode. They believed that the proprietor's determination to exercise his prerogative prevented Marylanders from enjoying the full "rights of Englishmen." They hoped that dissolution of the Calvert family's charter and imposition of direct royal government would usher in a more stable government secured by English law and Parliamentary precedent, one in which their own assembly would play a more reliable role in protecting English rights.

James's well-known antipathy to elective assemblies should have made the Maryland planters wary, as should his efforts to consolidate governments and enlarge the governors' prerogatives elsewhere. So opposed were they to proprietary rule, however, that one of Coode's cronies, Nehemiah Blackiston, accepted appointment as His Majesty's collector of customs. In that post he could further undermine Baltimore's precarious position with the Crown by filing damaging official reports that exposed the proprietor's attempts to evade the Navigation Acts. Yet even as opponents in Maryland and London chipped away at Baltimore's charter, Virginia's royal governor, Francis, Lord Howard of Effingham, campaigned for the Crown to consolidate Maryland within his own government. Doing so, Effingham argued, would increase Crown revenues on tobacco as well as augmenting the Virginia governor's own perquisites.

In the British West Indies, James made a series of appointments designed to bring to heel each island's overmighty planter class. As chief stockholder and president of the Royal Africa Company, James instructed his island governors and customs agents to protect the company's monopoly on the slave trade by suppressing all interlopers.

James II's governors in all the sugar islands allied themselves with discontented small planters to overthrow the sugar barons. In the Leewards, Sir Nathaniel Johnson raised taxes and challenged all titles. He made landholders petition for new patents requiring payment of a quit-rent to the king, just as Sir Edmund Andros was doing in New England. In Barbados, Edwin Stede vigorously suppressed interlopers to the slave trade, packed the ruling council with appointments drawn from outside the great planter class,

and rigorously enforced a newly doubled tax on sugar.

Jamaica's new royal governor Christopher Monck, the second duke of Albemarle, sided with the island's buccaneers as well as its small planters to wrest control from the planter class. A profligate, drunken wastrel who had squandered the family fortune in England, Albemarle was only too ready to escape to the Caribbean where he hoped to prey on Spanish treasure. In 1684, he had sponsored the successful expedition of Boston's Sir William Phips to recover 26 tons of Spanish silver treasure from the wreck of the *Almiranta*. The operation had netted Albemarle £50,000, whetting his appetite for even more booty. The buccaneers and small planters helped Albemarle turn the great planters out of most offices and cheerfully supported his treasure hunting efforts. Many big planters, meanwhile, followed their Barbadian and Leeward counterparts to England. There some joined the opposition to James's colonial policy while others retired to enjoy their wealth.

7.3: The Glorious Revolution in England and America

7.3 Evaluate the struggles within and outside England resulting from Charles II's ascent to power

The anger James II aroused through absolutist policies in the colonies echoed growing concern in England itself. Indeed, James had ascended the English throne in 1685 amid grave domestic unrest and diplomatic uncertainty. English Protestants feared that their first Catholic monarch in more than 130 years would eventually renew the anti-Protestant persecution of his ancestor "Bloody Mary" Tudor. Supporters of Parliament feared that he would intensify his late brother's efforts to strengthen and to centralize royal authority at the expense of Lords, Commons, and the localities. Dutch authorities feared he would betray them in their ongoing conflict with France. Shortly after his accession, these acute misgivings sparked a revolt led by Charles II's illegitimate son, James Scott, Duke of Monmouth, and supported by many influential gentry and nobility as well as the famed philosopher John Locke. The newly crowned James commanded enough loyalty to suppress the uprising, but his Catholicizing and authoritarian policies in church and state increased English and Dutch apprehensions about the new monarch's rule.

At home and throughout England's Atlantic empire, loyalty to the king eroded as he and his councilors strengthened royal authority at the expense of Parliament and local government. James's opponents everywhere saw his policies through anti-Catholic and anti-French lenses. Members of the English ruling elite watched with growing alarm as James turned Protestants out of office to install his Catholic favorites. Alarm turned to widespread popular unrest when the king imprisoned seven Anglican bishops for refusing to read from the pulpits his Declaration of Indulgence, which extended toleration to Catholics and dissenting Protestants alike. Against James's expectations, leading Dissenters stood with the bishops against "letting Papists into the Government."

American colonists thought they detected similar patterns in the policies of James's governors. New Englanders rapidly convinced themselves that Andros's negotiations with the Iroquois, Wabenaki, and French Canadians, along with enforcement of the Treaty of American Neutrality, cloaked a "Popish Plot" to "serve the French Interest" and "Ruine New England." In New York, Dutch Calvinists joined English Protestants in worrying that the Catholic Governor Dongan was hatching a similar plot.

7.3.1: The "Second Protestant Wind"

By autumn of 1688, support for James's rule in England was rapidly melting away. Even some of his closest advisors joined a plot to support a Protestant invasion of England led by James's nephew, the Dutch ruler William of Orange, husband of the king's Protestant daughter Mary. In November 1688, William crossed the English Channel with an invasion force of over fifteen thousand men in 250 ships. A "Protestant Wind" swept the Dutch flotilla around the English Channel Fleet to Torbay in southern England. There William landed his troops and began a march toward London, gathering strength as he went. James soon lost his nerve and fled to France with his wife, Mary of Modena, and their new baby son. With the help of a newly elected "Convention Parliament" (so called because it was summoned without an official order from the king), William and Mary quickly consolidated their power and were crowned joint rulers in February 1689.

This "Glorious Revolution" altered the course of English political history, transformed the diplomatic landscape of Europe, and reshaped American colonial affairs. As a part of the settlement of 1689, William and Mary accepted a Bill of Rights, a document stipulating the rights of all Englishmen. In doing so, they surrendered some of the prerogative powers that had destabilized English politics for almost a century. The crown remained a potent force in the political life of the nation, but never again would an English king or queen attempt to govern without Parliament.

The Bill of Rights also aligned England with the Protestant forces of Europe by securing Protestantism firmly within the English Church and state. Catholic heirs of the royal family were excluded "forever" from inheriting "the crown and government of this realm." Monarchs had to swear at their coronation that they would not appoint known Papists to office. The Toleration Act of 1689 rounded out these Protestant safeguards by extending religious toleration to dissenting Protestants while denying it to Catholics.

7.3.2: The Glorious Revolution in New England

In America, the Glorious Revolution commenced a process of political re-Anglicization. Colonies, which had begun as separate, experimental enterprises, became more integrated into an English imperial system. Colonists came to think of themselves as inhabitants of provinces, self-conscious extensions of English culture in America.

In March 1689, rumors of the Glorious Revolution in England stirred the colonists of Boston into action. Sir Edmund Andros hastened to the capital from the outpost in Maine where he had been attempting to secure peace with the Wabenakis. Within weeks after he left, the provincial troops he had brought with him revolted and began making their own way back to Boston. On April 18, Boston townspeople turned out in the streets, with many of the Maine deserters joining in. They quickly formed themselves into companies, arrested Andros's military officers and royal officials, including the colonists' old nemesis, Edward Randolph, and bottled up the governor in the town fort along with a company of regular troops. Sometime during the day, leaders assembled the companies before the Boston Town House to hear a declaration justifying the rebellion in secular terms of the rights of English subjects. Colonists knew that such a declaration would win far more sympathy in England than one that appealed to traditional Puritan ideas of a divine covenant. That afternoon, the local gentry persuaded Andros to leave the fort and meet them in the Town House, where the sheriff arrested him. The next day their previous governor ordered the evacuation of the town's fort and the castle in Boston harbor. New England's version of the Glorious Revolution was complete.

The coup in Boston was so popular that no one came to Andros's defense. The governor was jailed without a single shot having been fired. According to Cotton Mather, a leading Congregational minister, the colonists were united by the "most Unanimous Resolution perhaps that was ever known to have Inspir'd any people."

However united they may have been, the Bay colonists could not take the Crown's support for granted. William III believed that a strong colonial administration would help him achieve his strategic aims. Governor Andros had fully expected the new king to confirm Dominion policies, which enjoyed substantial support among colonial policymakers in England. William could have declared the New Englanders rebels and summarily reinstated Andros, as some of the king's councilors hoped he would do.

Thanks largely to the tireless efforts of Reverend Increase Mather, William instead abandoned the Dominion of New England. Mather had gone to London to petition James II for relief from Andros's abuses, but by the time he arrived events were rapidly moving toward William's invasion. Mather received several audiences with James during the summer of 1688 but spent most days cultivating the influential connections that could help him gain a favorable settlement for Massachusetts. After William and Mary came to the throne, Mather spent two years laboring to thread a middle course between the demands of colonial leaders for a full reinstatement of the 1629 charter and the determination of London officials to strengthen royal power over the colony.

Finally in 1691, Massachusetts received a new royal charter. Reinstatement of the company patent of 1629 had proved politically impossible. It had simply conceded too much autonomy to the colonists. The charter of 1691 no longer allowed freemen to elect their governor. That choice now belonged to the king. The membership in the General Court was determined by annual election. These representatives from the various towns in turn chose the men who sat in the council or upper house, subject always to the governor's veto. Moreover, the franchise, restricted here as in other colonies to adult males, was determined on the basis of personal property rather than church membership, a change that brought Massachusetts into conformity with general English practice. On the local level, town government remained much as it had been in Winthrop's time.

The Glorious Revolution and the charter of 1691 produced a change in the political culture of Massachusetts Bay. The colonists recovered a significant amount of self-determination, but at the price of shifting the theoretical basis of their government from an explicitly religious to a more secular foundation. Ministers and many magistrates still spoke as if the colony was in covenant with God. Yet most argued that government ruled primarily to uphold the rights of Englishmen, especially the property rights that Andros had challenged. Any Protestant could perform that function. This was just as well, for the new charter required that Massachusetts government remain open to non-Puritans. England's Toleration Act of 1689 reinforced this, requiring magistrates to permit the Church of England's *Common Prayer* books and "unwarrantable *Ceremonies*" as well as the worship of other dissenting groups such as Baptists and Quakers.

In granting Massachusetts a new charter, William also reversed much of the Dominion's consolidation of New England territory. Connecticut resumed government under its charter of 1662, which had never been formally annulled. William III eventually restored Rhode Island's charter of 1663. Freemen in both colonies continued to elect their own governors until the American Revolution. New Hampshire received its own royal governor and elected assembly. Tiny Plymouth Colony, however, was absorbed into Massachusetts's jurisdiction, as were the settlements of Maine.

7.3.3: Contagion of Witchcraft

The Salem witchcraft crisis of 1692 has overshadowed Massachusetts's Glorious Revolution in American memory. Few remember that the political upheaval allowed what under normal political conditions would have been an isolated, though ugly, local incident to become a major colonial crisis. Hysterical men and women living in small, struggling Salem Village nearly overwhelmed the colony's new government. Accusations of witchcraft were not uncommon in seventeenth-century New England. Puritans believed that an individual might make a compact with the devil, but during the first decades of settlement, authorities executed only about fifteen alleged witches. Sometimes villagers simply left suspected witches alone. Never before had fears of witchcraft plunged an entire community into panic.

The terror in Salem Village began in late 1691, when several adolescent girls began to behave in strange ways. They cried out for no apparent reason; they twitched on the ground. When concerned neighbors asked what caused their suffering, the girls announced they were victims of witches, seemingly innocent persons who lived in the community. The arrest of several alleged witches did not relieve the girls' "fits," nor did prayer solve the problem. Additional accusations were made, and at least one person confessed, providing a frightening description of the devil as "a thing all over hairy, all the face hairy, and a long nose." In June 1692, a special court convened and began to send men and women to the gallows. By the end of the summer, the court had hanged nineteen people; another was pressed to death. Many more suspects awaited trial.

Then suddenly, the storm was over. Led by Increase Mather, a group of prominent Congregational ministers belatedly urged leniency and restraint. Especially troubling to the clergymen was the court's decision to accept "spectral evidence," that is, reports of dreams and visions in which the accused appeared as the devil's agent. Worried about convicting people on such dubious testimony, Mather declared, "It were better that ten suspected witches should escape, than that one innocent person should be condemned." The colonial government accepted the ministers' advice and convened a new court, which promptly acquitted, pardoned, or released the remaining suspects. After the Salem nightmare, witchcraft ceased to be a capital offense.

No one knows exactly what sparked the terror in Salem Village. The community had a history of religious discord. During the 1680s, the people split into angry factions over the choice of a minister. Economic tensions also played a part as poor subsistence farmers accused members of prosperous, commercially oriented families. The culture's underlying misogyny meant victims were more often women than men. Some historians have suggested that the symptoms of torment resemble the hallucinations, nausea, and prickling sensations characteristic of poisoning from ergot, a mold sometimes found in rye that the colonists cultivated. Others have noted that many of the accused had ties with the war-torn Maine frontier, and it is possible that fear of Indian attack fueled the panic.

Whatever the ultimate sources of this event, jealousy and bitterness apparently festered to the point that adolescent girls who normally would have been disciplined were allowed to incite judicial murder. As so often happens in such incidents—the McCarthy hearings of the 1950s, for example—the accusers later came to their senses and apologized to the survivors for the needless suffering they had inflicted.

7.3.4: Leisler's Rebellion in New York

The Glorious Revolution in New York was more violent than in Massachusetts Bay. Divisions within the ruling class ran deep, involving ethnic as well as religious differences. English newcomers and powerful Anglo-Dutch families who had risen to commercial prominence in New York City and Albany opposed the older Dutch elite.

The leader of New York's uprising, Jacob Leisler, was a man entangled in events beyond his control. The son of a German minister, Leisler emigrated to New York in 1660 and through marriage aligned himself with the Dutch elite. While he achieved moderate prosperity as a merchant, Leisler resented the success of rising Anglo-Dutch families such as the Schuylers, the Van Cortlandts, and the Livingstons.

When news of the Glorious Revolution reached New York City in May 1689, Leisler raised a group of militiamen and seized the local fort in the name of William and Mary. Leisler maintained a tenuous hold over the fort and the city until he managed to organize the election of a Committee of Safety. The committee affirmed his leadership early in June. This action prompted Andros's lieutenant governor in New York, Captain Francis Nicholson, to give up the struggle for control of the colony and sail for England.

Leisler expected an outpouring of popular support, but it never materialized. His rivals waited while "the hott brain'd Capt Leisler" tried desperately to legitimize his rule. Through bluff and badgering, Leisler managed to hold the colony together, especially after French forces burned Schenectady in February 1690. The French threat prodded Leislerians and anti-Leislerians into grudging cooperation for the colony's defense throughout the following year, but Leisler never established a secure political base.

In March 1691, a new royal governor, Henry Sloughter, reached New York and ordered Leisler to surrender his authority. Leisler demanded proof that Sloughter was sent by William rather than the deposed James. When Sloughter refused, Leisler fatally hesitated. Sloughter declared Leisler a rebel. In a hasty trial, a court sentenced him and his chief lieutenant, Jacob Milbourne, to be hanged "by the Neck and being Alive their bodyes be Cutt downe to Earth and Their Bowells to be taken out and they being Alive, burnt before their faces." In 1695, Parliament officially pardoned Leisler, but he not being "Alive," the decision arrived a bit late.

Unlike the New England colonies, New York never received a charter as part of its settlement. Instead, Governor Sloughter convened a council and assembly to pass a declaratory law to ensure New Yorkers a measure of self-determination for which many had been struggling since the 1660s. In a preamble, the act thanked William and Mary for restoring the rights of Englishmen to New Yorkers. It then moved to secure those rights by placing the colony's supreme legislative power in the hands of a royally appointed governor, a council, and the "people" through an assembly of representatives elected annually by male heads of households who possessed "fourty shillings per Annum in freehold." The governor could veto colonial legislation, as could the Crown, but all laws remained effective until the king disapproved them. William's official approval of this law the next year made New York's framework of government permanent.

The settlement of New York's government in 1691 did not bring an end to the colony's fractious political life. Long after Leisler's death, factions calling themselves Leislerians and Anti-Leislerians struggled to dominate New York government. Indeed, in no other eighteenth-century colony was the level of bitter political rivalry so high.

7.3.5: The Glorious Revolution in Maryland

When the first rumors of James's overthrow reached Maryland early in 1689, pent-up antiproprietary and anti-Catholic sentiment exploded. During the spring and early summer wild rumors flew about the countryside that the Catholics had hired the Senecas to butcher the Protestants, that Protestants awaited a fleet of reinforcements to aid them in butchering Catholics, that the English had captured

and beheaded James II. The scarcity of reliable news from England only compounded the problem. Especially troubling was the proprietary government's delay in proclaiming the new monarchs.

When the government of neighboring Virginia proclaimed William and Mary in late April, John Coode's patience ran out. The leader of Maryland's antiproprietary faction formed a group called the Protestant Association. Coode waited more than two months before leading the association's members in a march against the capital at St. Mary's. No one would fight for the proprietor's side. Proprietary officials fled to Mattapany, Baltimore's estate, where Governor William Joseph lay sick. Coode's forces borrowed several cannons from a London vessel in St. Mary's harbor and laid siege to the mansion, whereupon its inhabitants capitulated "to prevent Effusion of blood."

Coode avoided Leisler's fatal mistakes. The Protestant Association, citing many wrongs suffered at the hands of local Catholics, petitioned the crown to make Maryland a royal colony. After reviewing the case, William III accepted Coode's explanation. In 1691, the king dispatched a royal governor to Maryland. A new assembly dominated by Protestants declared Anglicanism the established religion. Catholics were excluded from public office on the grounds that they might be in league with French Catholics in Canada. Lord Baltimore lost control of the colony's government, but he and his family did retain title to Maryland's undistributed lands. In 1715, the crown restored to full proprietorship the fourth Lord Baltimore, who had been raised a member of the Church of England, and Maryland remained in the hands of the Calvert family until 1776.

7.3.6: A Framework for Political Order

England's Glorious Revolution established a framework for imperial politics that remained in place until 1763. In most colonies,

Crown-appointed governors and imperial officials looked after London's interests, usually aided by a council that colonists eventually came to view as a functional equivalent of England's House of Lords.

Crown officials also engaged in a decade-long struggle to eliminate all proprietary charters and bring those governments under direct royal control. The New Jersey proprietors capitulated in 1701, and the two colonies became united under a single royal government. William Penn, however, survived the cloud of suspicion that hung about him in the early years of William and Mary's reign to become the leading defender of proprietary charters. Penn briefly lost his charter rights over Pennsylvania in 1692 when he and his Quaker assembly refused on pacifist principles to support English war efforts. Yet William III restored them in 1694 after Penn promised to support Crown policies, including the laws on trade. During the next decade, he sought to enforce imperial policy in Pennsylvania while defending charter rights before the Board of Trade and in Parliament. Penn lost a battle over the three Lower Counties of Delaware, which became a Crown colony in 1701. He ultimately won the war for Pennsylvania, however, which remained in the Penn family until the Revolution.

In every colony, elected houses of assembly exerted potent checks on Crown or proprietary appointees. The assemblies retained the power of initiating money bills, levying taxes, and even paying the governor's salary. Widespread ownership of land meant that a majority of free male inhabitants in every colony possessed the forty-shilling freehold required to vote, lending the lower houses a degree of popular representation unheard of in England and insulating them from manipulation by royal officials. Though London officials still wielded great power in colonial affairs, the various colonial settlements of the 1690s prevented them from dictating policy as James II's administration had attempted to do. Colonists regained significant power to shape colonial policy in ways favorable to their own interests.

In the following decades, the lower houses worked tirelessly to expand their powers still further. The colonial assemblies increasingly came to see themselves as little Parliaments. The irony is that, as colonial assemblymen made their representative bodies more English in form, they began to defend more fervently against the home government their political rights as Englishmen.

7.4: An Age of Atlantic Wars

7.4 Review the European power struggles due to the growth of the English armed forces

William's invasion of England not only transformed English and colonial politics, but produced a major shift in the balance of power in Europe. Charles II had pursued a pro-French policy throughout his reign while waging intermittent warfare on the Dutch. James II had not followed his brother's active pro-French policies, but he attempted to secure English neutrality in Continental affairs while concentrating on his absolutist and Catholicizing policies at home. William had watched these developments with increasing alarm as his troops fought to defend Dutch territory and commerce against Louis's ambitions. Indeed, the Dutch need for English military support in the face of imminent war with France helped drive William's decision to make a bid for James's crown. It also persuaded Dutch leaders to support their prince's risky enterprise.

The Glorious Revolution thus thrust England into an almost unprecedented role in Continental affairs after 1689. William's invasion sparked a series of hot and cold wars between England and France that would not finally subside until Wellington's defeat of Napoleon in 1815. The conflict began with Louis XIV's declaration of war against the United Provinces of the Netherlands almost immediately after William set foot on English soil. In March 1689, the Sun King sent aid to James II's supporters in Ireland, an act which permitted William III to cast his own English declaration of war against France as a measure "not so properly an act of choice as an inevitable necessity in our own defence." The fevered religious atmosphere in England prompted William's apologists to cast the conflict in stark apocalyptic terms that pitted the forces of an English Protestant constitutional monarchy against Popish French tyranny. The theme played well in America, where the Anglo-French contest spread within a matter of months.

This new role in large-scale European military conflict stimulated the development of what one historian has called England's "fiscal-military state." As the English army and navy grew steadily larger under William III, Parliament increased taxes while the Crown streamlined revenue collection. Heavy borrowing to supplement taxes contributed to a national debt whose growth helped to prompt establishment of the Bank of England in 1694. The debt rose steadily over the next century, eventually making the government the chief force in the English economy. Yet after 1696, the determination of many in the ruling class to preserve their hard-won limits on royal authority led them to obstruct royal adventurism on the Continent. Instead, opposition leaders in Parliament managed to steer the fiscal-military state toward developing a great naval power that could extend England's commercial and colonial interests throughout the world.

7.4.1: Anglo-French Conflict in the West Indies

News of William's invasion and the subsequent French declaration of war sent shock waves throughout England's Caribbean sugar islands. Sir Nathaniel Johnson, governor of the Leewards, wrote William in May 1689 that he could not accept the revolution even as the French on neighboring islands prepared for war. Within a month, 130 Irish servants sacked English plantations on St. Christopher. An invasion force from the French half of the island soon followed to oust the

English completely. English planters on Nevis, Antigua, and Montserrat feared a similar fate when a letter, intercepted in transit from Johnson to the French Governor Blenac, appeared to indicate that Johnson would betray all the Leewards to France. The planters persuaded Johnson to resign and appoint the wealthy West Indian planter Christopher Codrington in his place.

Codrington led English planters in a contest with the French for control of the Lesser Antilles, a costly string of assaults and reprisals that continued with only brief respite for the next fifteen years. Codrington's huge estates on both Barbados and Antigua generated profits, which the governor used to subsidize his military ventures. The investment seemed to pay off in 1690, when Codrington led the English in a successful campaign to retake all of St. Christopher. The governor carved himself yet another vast plantation from some of the island's best French holdings and staffed it with a workforce of plundered slaves. Codrington eventually lost his St. Christopher estate, however, when the Treaty of Ryswick restored the French half of the island to its former owners in 1697.

The insecurity of captured West Indian estates prevented neither the French nor the English from attempting to seize each other's lands and slaves. Neither side could deal a knockout blow to the other. The conflict eventually settled into mutual looting and plundering, resulting in enormous property damage. When the French commander, Comte de Chavagnac, led yet another invasion of St. Christopher in 1706, for instance, the English holed up in Fort Charles to watch as the French seized their slaves and burned their plantations. Chavagnac did not bother laying siege to the fort, nor did the English trouble to put up a fight except to fire cannon on the few French companies that strayed within range. When supplies ran low, Chavagnac abruptly departed, leaving the English to petition the home government for compensation of a staggering £145,000 in losses.

Jamaica endured similar conflict throughout the 1690s but became more stable after 1700.

William's governor of the colony, Sir William Beeston, led islanders in resisting a string of French raids as well as a major invasion of the colony in 1694. The Treaty of Ryswick brought a peace to the island that continued throughout the next decade, thanks to a large garrison of English troops there who discouraged French attack.

Equally significant for Jamaica's future was the final defeat of the buccaneering interest under William and Mary. Spurred by Albemarle's abuses of power there, the great planters formed a lobby in London to argue that their own interest in profits and the Crown's interest in customs revenues were united. The king, persuaded by arguments and falling revenues, restored to planters the offices Albemarle had taken away. The defeated buccaneers moved to new bases on St. Domingue and the Bahamas.

Distance insulated Barbados from the depredations that stalked the Leewards during the reigns of William III and his successor, Queen Anne. Nevertheless, the era's Anglo-French conflict helped transform the dynamics of island life by establishing an enduring pattern of absentee ownership. Warfare discouraged the return of the great Barbadian planters who had departed after James II's appointment of Edwin Stede. Ongoing instability persuaded them to remain in England permanently, where they found they could guard their interests more effectively than by occupying seats in a distant Barbadian assembly. Barbados's leading planter families became a powerful interest group that quickly learned how to obtain favorable policies by lobbying the Crown and Parliament. Great planters in the Leewards and Jamaica formed similar lobbies, making the sugar interests a potent force in the development of imperial commercial policy.

7.4.2: Native Americans and European Wars

English-leaning leaders within the Five Nations welcomed the news of war between France and England when it arrived in June 1689. Mohawk headmen swore on behalf of the Iroquois that, "as they are one hand and Soul with the English, they will take Up the Ax with pleasure against the French." Over the next decade, involvement in the Anglo-French conflict transformed a complex of internal alliances among autonomous Iroquois village leaders into a coherent confederacy. The new Confederacy paralleled the older League, whose sachems continued to preserve Iroquois culture and traditions above the fray of Confederacy factionalism. The political confederacy incorporated old tensions among its Anglophile and Francophile leaders without resolving them. Indeed, tensions only increased as English reluctance to hold up their end of the Covenant Chain exposed the Iroquois to repeated defeats by the French and the western Algonquians.

The conflict of the 1690s pitted the Iroquois allies of England against not only the French but also their Canadian Iroquois cousins and a strengthening alliance of western Algonquians. Earlier in the century, the Iroquois had pressed these groups hard by battling west and north to expand access to beaver pelts. Western Indians such as the Wyandots, Ojibwas, Potawatomis, and Ottawas responded by forging ties with the French through trade, intermarriage, and military alliance. Efforts by La Salle and other French explorers to link the Great Lakes–St. Lawrence and the Mississippi trades began paying off in the 1690s. A painfully won complex of reciprocal friendships, trade, and kinship among French colonists and members of these Algonquian groups—one that historian Richard White has termed the "middle ground"—permitted them to coalesce against their common Iroquois enemy.

Aided by the aggressive military leadership of Governor Louis de Buade de Frontenac and commander Antoine Laumet de La Mothe, Sieur de Cadillac, the western Algonquians hit the Iroquois hard. At the same time, Frontenac made diplomatic overtures to woo the Five Nations away from the English, thereby monopolizing the fur trade and forging an alliance that could ultimately push the English out of North America. This carrot-and-stick approach confirmed to many Iroquois their assessment of the French as treacherous double-dealers. Yet persistent losses prompted them to engage in two years of peace talks with the French after 1694.

New York's governor Benjamin Fletcher, who replaced the deceased Sloughter in 1691, took a dim view of Iroquois peace efforts. Negotiation with the French smacked of an independence inappropriate for a people Fletcher saw as subjects of the English Crown. At worst, the governor feared that such talks could swing the Iroquois to the French. In 1694, a delegation of Five Nations leaders presented Fletcher with a carefully negotiated plan that included concessions from Frontenac and proposed a peace "not only between all the Indians but between all their relations," including the governors of Canada and New York. Fletcher was not authorized to "treat of Peace with the Governour of Canada" and refused. This refusal and an accompanying denunciation of the Five Nations' "shame and dishonour" left the Iroquois peace plans in tatters.

Iroquois leaders also conducted separate peace talks with Wyandots and Ottawas during the mid-1690s. The two sides discovered mutual mistrust of the French, whom the western Indians suspected of attempting to forge a secret deal that would elevate Iroquois interests above those of the west. By summer's end in 1695, the Wyandots and Ottawas had convinced their western neighbors to join a truce with the Iroquois, which both sides hoped would lead to full peace. Yet new French plans for an invasion of Iroquois country ultimately thwarted these efforts as well.

The failure of Iroquois peace efforts spelled suffering in the years ahead. In the summer of 1696, Frontenac himself led a force of two thousand French and native allies into the heart of Iroquoia. The force destroyed the main Onondaga town, burned a neighboring Oneida village to the ground, and wiped out the region's ripening crops. Meanwhile, Cadillac persuaded the western Algonquians to break the hard-won truce of 1695 and step up their raids against the Five Nations. Even the 1697 Peace of Ryswick between England and France brought no relief to the Iroquois. The French governors of Canada vowed to continue war until the Confederacy negotiated a separate peace that would strengthen French pretensions to Iroquois lands.

Thus, hostilities ground on through the turn of the century between the weakened Five Nations and a strengthening alliance of French and western Algonquians. By 1700, the Indians of the Ohio and the western Great Lakes controlled the region's peltries and exchanged them for trade goods, which bound them ever more tightly with their French partners. These ties enabled them not only to threaten the Iroquois but also to augment their strength by extending French influence to groups even further west.

Finally, in 1701, the exhausted Five Nations managed to conclude a peace in the "Grand Settlement" of that year. The Confederacy agreed to remain neutral between the French and English in exchange for French cessation of hostilities and an English commitment to protect their western hunting grounds. The English, probably contrary to Iroquois intentions, understood their part of the bargain as securing a Crown title to western Iroquois territory. In fact, the Grand Settlement of 1701 represented a reassertion of the Five Nations' status as an equal party in mutual covenant with the English. In so doing, it altered the Covenant Chain forged in the 1670s that had formally allied the Five Nations under English sovereignty.

The Grand Settlement also gave various Iroquois factions the flexibility to negotiate semi-independent agreements that would advance their own interests. One faction of neutralists led by Teganissorens forged a covenant chain with western nations that siphoned more furs to Albany. Later groups negotiated similar arrangements with Indian nations and even rival English colonial governments.

The settlement of 1701 forced the Iroquois to recognize the western limits of their power. Losses from the wars of the 1690s soon prompted them to replenish their diminished numbers by renewing the tradition of mourning war to the south, where they had earlier cowed native peoples with their superior military might (Losses from the wars of the 1690s soon prompted them to replenish their diminished numbers by renewing their tradition of "mourning war." Iroquois war parties began raiding weaker native groups to the south for captives that could replace tribal members who had been killed in battle.) After 1700, however, they began encountering stiffer resistance from nations to the west of Virginia and the Carolinas. A flood of European traders and goods into the Piedmont and backcountry had enabled groups such as the Catawbas and Cherokees to even the odds by purchasing firearms, which they used effectively to repel Iroquois raiders and their native allies. At times, Catawba parties retaliated by carrying the fight into Iroquois territory.

The Grand Settlement of 1701 complemented the great European realignments of the 1690s by establishing a new North American framework of commerce, diplomacy, and warfare. Although the Anglo-French contest for empire imposed limits on Iroquois autonomy, the settlement nevertheless demonstrated the Five Nations' resilience and skill in adapting to changing circumstances to achieve their own ends. Though severely pressed and divided by the conflicts of the 1690s, the Iroquois managed to gain a new flexibility in affairs of trade and diplomacy. The ambiguity of the Grand Settlement made them something less than the third imperial force some older historians have made them. Yet the Iroquois Confederacy emerged from the first round of Anglo-French conflict with substantial power to guard their interests against French and English pretensions.

7.5: A Commercial Empire Takes Shape

7.5 **Report the losses suffered by London merchants and their partners due to conflict on the high seas**

Iroquoia and the Caribbean bore the brunt of King William's War in America, but trade throughout the colonies also suffered. During the war's early years, the French conducted a successful campaign to interdict English shipping throughout the Atlantic. In Europe, French naval vessels lay in wait for English merchant vessels entering the English Channel, and the French Crown issued letters of marque to hundreds of French privateers who fanned out into American, Caribbean, African, and East Indian waters in search of lucrative prey. English commerce remained chronically underprotected through the war because the navy could never spare enough "ships of the line"—battle vessels large enough to sail in a line exchanging broadsides with enemy ships. William's commanders periodically disrupted trade even further by hiring private vessels away from merchant shipping to supplement the royal navy in large operations.

London merchants and their colonial trading partners suffered enormous losses. In 1695 and 1696 alone, the Royal Africa Company lost over £57,000 while the Barbados merchants lost a princely £387,000. The trade between the Anglo-American mainland and the Caribbean suffered nearly as much, with New England, Jamaican, and Leeward Island merchants losing £320,000. "The losses from the plantations are double for the nation," the Barbadian planters lamented to Parliament. Without taxes from the re-export of sugar and tobacco to Europe, many English troops would go unpaid and "foreigners will have our silver to be sure, for the exchange is governed by the balance of trade."

The huge financial losses measured only a part of the total cost of conflict on the high seas. Privateers usually tried to capture rather than sink merchant vessels with their valuable cargoes. Nevertheless, many merchant sailors lost their lives attempting to defend their vessels, and many others drowned as their battle-damaged ships sank. Harassment by privateers often prevented Caribbean vessels from leaving port until the height of the hurricane season, resulting in additional loss of life when the ships went down in storms. Warfare at sea made the Middle Passage even more miserable for slaves, who often found themselves caught in the crossfire between their captors and enemy privateers who attempted to seize them for profit.

Warfare did not bring unmitigated disaster to colonial producers, merchants, and shippers, however. The need to provision the English army and navy increased demand for colonial agricultural products. French disruption of Anglo-Swedish trade—a crucial source of naval stores such as pitch, tar, masts, and rope—prompted shipbuilders to look to America for alternate supplies. Crown bounties on naval stores prompted South Carolina planters to head for the woods with their slaves where they collected pine resin for rendering into pitch and tar. New England further bolstered its reputation as a source of valuable white pine masts, and vessels from New England shipyards replaced many losses in the Anglo-American mercantile fleet.

Colonists and London merchants alike exploited the disruptions of King William's War as well. War only exacerbated colonial evasion of the Navigation Acts by forcing the Crown to relax enforcement. Even more vexing were English privateers who abused their commissions to prey on legitimate English shipping. After 1695, Parliament set out to put a stop to these practices by plugging the loopholes in English maritime law. In doing so, Parliament extended London's effective reach ever further, drawing the American colonies into a global commercial system.

7.5.1: Enforcing the Marketplace: 1696

Parliament passed its last major piece of imperial commercial legislation in 1696. Among other things, the statute tightened enforcement procedures, putting pressure specifically on the colonial governors to keep England's competitors out of American ports. The act of 1696 also expanded the American customs service and for the first time set up vice-admiralty courts in the colonies. This decision eventually rankled the colonists. Established to settle disputes that occurred at sea, vice-admiralty courts required neither juries nor oral cross-examination, both traditional elements of the common law. Nevertheless, they were effective and sometimes even popular for resolving maritime questions quickly enough to send the ships to sea again with little delay.

The year 1696 witnessed one other significant change in the imperial system. William III replaced the ineffective Lords of Trade with a body that came to be known as the Board of Trade. This group was expected to monitor colonial affairs closely and to provide government officials with the best available advice on commercial and other problems. For several decades, at least, it energetically carried out its responsibilities.

The members of Parliament believed these reforms would belatedly compel the colonists to accept the Navigation Acts, and in large measure they were correct. By 1700, American goods transshipped through the mother country accounted for a quarter of all English exports, an indication that the colonists found it profitable to obey the commercial regulations. In fact, during the eighteenth century, smuggling from Europe to America dried up almost completely.

7.5.2: Policing Commerce: The War on Piracy

The 1696 Navigation Act's new enforcement procedures also represented Parliament's fresh determination to stamp out piracy. For decades, lax English laws had made it easy to using letters of marque—issued by the Crown to authorize private seizure of a hostile nation's ships—as a cover for preying indiscriminately on commercial shipping. The relative ease of legitimating seized cargoes had often returned handsome profits for privateers and their merchant backers, even when the vessels they seized belonged to fellow English subjects. By the 1690s, however, the steady growth of English shipping had made colonial commerce too valuable to tolerate buccaneers.

Royal officials in London began pressing their counterparts throughout the colonies to round up pirates or drive them out of colonial ports. Jamaica planters were actually ahead of the game, having driven buccaneers off the island in the early 1690s. Royal officials in Pennsylvania sent damaging reports to London that Philadelphia merchants were harboring crew members of the notorious buccaneer, Henry Avery. This blot on his reputation prompted William Penn to launch a vigorous campaign to suppress piracy when he returned to govern the colony in 1699.

The most notorious pirate of the era, Captain William Kidd, inadvertently intensified the campaign against piracy by blundering into a hornets' nest of East Indian and English commercial interests. Had Kidd not chosen this period to embark on his most enterprising voyage, he would probably have ended his days as another of colonial New York's many obscure privateers. But, in 1695, the lure of East Indian gold led this buccaneer to London, where he acquired the backing of the Earl of Bellomont, an ambitious politician who had just been appointed royal governor of New York. In 1696, Kidd and his crew set sail in the thirty-four-gun *Adventure Galley*, armed with a royal commission to capture pirate booty for the profit of himself, his crew, and his investors.

Once in the Indian Ocean, however, Kidd assured the Madagascar pirates that "he was as bad as they," and hoisted the blood-red pirate flag in pursuit of merchant vessels. He invoked the British flag to gain his one valuable prize, the Indian-owned *Quedah Merchant*, after tricking her captain into presenting French papers. Kidd then began a circuitous return voyage to New York in hope that his patron Bellomont, now governor of the colony, would declare the seizure a legal prize of war.

In Kidd's absence, the new Navigation Act of 1696 had made such seizures much more difficult to legitimate, while a diplomatic uproar over the *Quedah Merchant's* seizure made Kidd himself too hot to handle. Circumstances in New York had forced Bellomont to side with the colony's Leislerian faction and to shore up his reputation in England by suppressing pirates sponsored by his anti-Leislerian enemies. In this position, the governor could scarcely afford exposure as a patron of pirates himself, especially one as notorious as Kidd had become. News of the *Quedah Merchant's* capture had circulated from Madagascar throughout the Atlantic ports and into the court of William III. It had also provoked the members of the Indian ruling class to suspend trade with the British East India Company until London took firmer measures to suppress piracy. When Kidd finally returned to Long Island Sound in the fall of 1698, Bellomont had him arrested.

Ultimately, Captain Kidd's crimes hastened the passage of Parliament's first meaningful antipiracy law, the "Act for the More Effectual Suppression of Piracy" of 1700. Word of Kidd's capture arrived in Parliament during a committee report on the bill, prompting members to order Kidd's trial delayed until they could pass the act. The Piracy Act imposed the death penalty on anyone convicted of piracy as well as those found guilty of aiding and abetting pirates. On May 13, 1701, William Kidd and three accomplices died on a gallows by the Thames as the Piracy Act's first victims.

The criminalization of piracy after 1700 contributed to imperial stability while driving a wedge between pirates and the merchants and officials who had once sponsored them. The threat of prosecution prompted colonial officials to uphold order, refusing any longer to harbor pirates in exchange for a share of the booty. The rising value of colonial united the Anglo-American merchant community to secure the sea-lanes and profits against buccaneers who exploits had once injected cash into local economies.

Pirates themselves reflected this alienation through hostility to "base Merchants, and cruel commanders of ships." They spurned family, society, and religion to join ostensibly egalitarian crews governed by written ship's agreements, although they often suffered treachery and capricious violence from their fellows. The "bloody flag" of earlier piracy gave way to grim standards such as the skull and crossbones. The choice to engage in piracy increasingly expressed not a quest for instant wealth, but a desperate attempt to escape low wages, unemployment, or a captain's brutal treatment.

7.6: Common Experiences, Separate Cultures

7.6 Examine how England's attitude towards the American colonies changed over time

"It is no little Blessing of God," Cotton Mather announced proudly in 1700, "that we are part of the English nation." A half-century earlier, John Winthrop would not have spoken these words, at least not with such enthusiasm. The two men were, of course, products of different political cultures. It was not so much that the character of Massachusetts society had changed. In fact, the Puritan families of 1700 were much like those of the founding generation. Rather, the difference was in England's attitude toward the colonies. Rulers living more than 3,000 miles away now made political and economic demands that Mather's contemporaries could not ignore.

Yet the various settlements of 1688–1689 had given the inhabitants of English America significant power to determine how they would meet royal demands. Colonial legislatures protected property rights and guarded the interests of local merchants and producers. Crown officials steadily drew back from the overweening authoritarianism of James II's appointees to concern themselves primarily with regulating imperial commerce. The Iroquois and other native leaders managed to preserve their status as free peoples, staving off royal governors' efforts to extend authority over their persons and lands. Even the strengthening of the imperial commercial system worked to the ultimate advantage of Indians and colonists as well as English merchants, providing an increasingly secure framework in which transatlantic trade could flourish.

The creation of a new imperial system did not erase profound sectional differences. By 1700, for example, the Chesapeake colonies were more, not less, committed to the cultivation of tobacco and slave labor. Although the separate regions were being pulled slowly into England's commercial orbit, they did not have much to do with each other. The elements that sparked a powerful sense of nationalism among colonists dispersed over a huge territory would not be evident for a very long time.

Chronology

1674	Sir Edmund Andros Anglicizes New York government and commerce
1675	King Philip's War breaks out in New England
1676	Bacon's Rebellion breaks out in Virginia

1677	Anglo-Iroquois alliance secured with "Covenant Chain" agreements
1677	New Hampshire becomes a Royal colony
1680	Pueblo Revolt against the Spanish
1681	William Penn receives charter for Pennsylvania
1682	Robert Barclay promotes Scottish emigration to East Jersey
1684	Charter of the Massachusetts Bay Company revoked
1685	Duke of York becomes James II
1686	Dominion of New England established
1688	James II driven into exile during Glorious Revolution
1689	William and Mary crowned joint monarchs in England; Rebellions break out in Massachusetts, New York, and Maryland; War of the League of Augsburg (King William's War) commences
1692	Salem Village wracked by witch trials
1694	Bank of England established
1696	Parliament establishes board of Trade; passes Navigation Act of 1696, Piracy Act
1697	Treaty of Ryswick ends War of the League of Augsburg
1701	"Grand Settlement" among Iroquois, French, and English
1702	East and West Jerseys unite to become single colony under Royal authority

Part III
Provinces in a Contested Empire
The Eighteenth Century

In April 1710, four warriors, billed by their promoters as "kings" of the Iroquois League, rode to Queen Anne's Court of St. James in two royal coaches. Only one was truly a sachem, but that did not matter to the English royal officials who hoped this display of strategic transatlantic alliance would bolster their own influence with the Queen. Her Royal Highness received the emissaries graciously and heard their petition for a new English assault on Canada that would bring an end to "our long and tedious War . . . against her enemies the *French*." The warriors reminded the Queen that as allies they had provided a "strong Wall" for English colonial security, "even to the loss of our best Men." They also promised "a most hearty Welcome" for any Anglican missionaries she might send to counter the "Insinuations" of French priests.

The voyage of the "Indian kings" to England revealed how much had changed over the past hundred years. The arduous process of establishing colonies in America was paying off for England and France alike. The two now boasted extensive empires and vied primarily with each other for control of North American trade and resources. Spain, which had dominated the Western Hemisphere a century before, had seen its southeastern chain of Apalachee missions decimated by English raiders. On the North American Atlantic coast, Spain now retained only St. Augustine, along with a contested presence on the northern Gulf Coast that included Pensacola in Florida and a few forts along the Texas shoreline. Queen Anne's willingness not only to entertain the Iroquois emissaries at court, but to "make a shew" of them on a month-long circuit of official appearances, demonstrated the importance of its North American empire to England's strategic and commercial goals.

The visit of the "Indian kings" also reveals to historians a glimpse of native peoples' shifting fortunes in this European contest for empire. Three of the warriors represented only one faction of a League torn by pro-English, pro-French, and Neutralist advocates. One was not Iroquois at all. Colonization and trade had drawn their people into growing dependence on European goods and exposed them to the ravages of European conflict over land and commerce. American Indians retained control over the North American interior, and their strength in arms forced imperial strategists to seek wartime alliances and deterred most settlers from venturing too far from colonial defenses. Nevertheless, native peoples found themselves increasingly pressed by advancing colonization, forced to react to European initiatives rather than setting the terms of contact and exchange themselves.

Over the next fifty years, the contest between Great Britain and France for North Atlantic empire would intensify along commercial as well as military lines. The success of England's seventeenth-century ventures would breed eighteenth-century growth. The promise of cheap western land attracted second- and third-generation settlers from the coast and drew fresh waves of immigrants from northern Ireland, Scotland, and Germany. Transatlantic commerce also fueled the growth of African slave labor—indeed, the trade in human cargo was becoming one of the most lucrative of the era. The growth in Anglo-American population and commerce was laying a foundation for British dominion, but it would come only through a long and costly struggle.

Chapter 8
Empires of Guns and Goods
North America at the Opening of the Eighteenth Century

 ## Learning Objectives

8.1 Recount how French explorers attempted to set up New France in America

8.2 Recount the Spanish struggles to secure its northern borders in America

8.3 Report the growth of Anglo-America

8.4 Review the conflict for power in the Carolinas among the European imperial powers

8.5 Recall how Queen Anne's war changed the fortunes of North American Indians

8.6 Summarize the continuity of the power struggle for the control of North America

In the summer of 1698, the Spanish officer Francisco Romo de Uriza of St. Augustine visited the port of Charleston, South Carolina, as both a customer of the English and an agent of a rival imperial power. Captain Romo had come to pay for African slaves recently acquired from English traders, but he also hoped to pick up information about English commercial activities near Florida and the Gulf of Mexico. The Gulf, rich with resources and populated by many Indian nations eager for European trade, had already become a coveted target of French imperial expansion.

St. Augustine was now rife with rumors that the English were also reconnoitering the Gulf Coast for trade and settlement. Reported sightings of English vessels alarmed Spanish officials, who were waging a futile struggle to dislodge French interlopers from toeholds they had gained in Louisiana and at Biloxi in present-day Mississippi. French traders were fanning out from those posts to entice southeastern Indians with a wider range of cheaper goods than the Spanish could offer. English intrusion into the area made commercial competition even fiercer by offering better-made goods at prices even cheaper than those of the French. Spanish officials felt their grip on the Gulf Coast slipping despite Spain's historical New World claims.

Romo's suspicions of the English intensified when he spied a group of Indians at the governor's residence. He asked the governor where they came from. The governor walked over to a large map on the wall and pointed out their home near a place marked "Espíritu Santo," which the Spanish had recently renamed "Pensacola Bay" in their effort to assert possession of the Gulf Coast against French interlopers. Romo protested that the king of Spain owned the region. These Indians had no right to trade with the English. The Carolina governor only shook his head and declared that, according to his calculations, Pensacola lay within the king of England's domain. In any case, he told Romo, the governor had read in a gazette that the kings of France and England had agreed to concede ownership of the bay to whomever settled it first. The governor planned to enter the race for settlement the next spring.

When Romo reported back to St. Augustine, the Spanish governor did not pause to wonder about the plausibility of a gentleman's agreement over territory between two such ambitious empire-builders as William III and Louis XIV. He knew already that the French were especially well positioned to expand their presence in the Gulf if he did not act quickly. He hastily assembled an expedition and dispatched it to Pensacola Bay. By mid-November 1698, the Spanish flag was flying over the construction site of a new *presidio* at the bay's entrance.

Romo's visit to Charleston provides a glimpse into the contradictions of turn-of-the-century life in the borderlands of three great European imperial powers and dozens of Indian nations. The Spanish army officer and the English governor represented rival interests in an often bitter contest for New World trade and resources. Yet they also found advantages in their proximity to each other, with the Carolinians supplying a desperate

Spanish need for labor in exchange for hard currency that could lubricate the wheels of Anglo-American commerce. The Treaty of Ryswick had brought peace among the three powers in 1697, making Anglo-Spanish trade easier. Yet eighteenth-century colonists seldom allowed even the fiercest imperial conflict to stand in the way of opportunities for mutual profit.

The Indians at the governor's residence, probably Creeks, knew well how to play these European rivals against one another to gain the greatest advantage in trade. Charleston represented a special danger for Indian nations not allied with this colony of brutal slave catchers, but it also extended the opportunity to acquire an abundance of cheap manufactured goods for those willing to take the risk.

By 1700, cartographers could map out North American centers of colonial territory such as Charleston, St. Augustine, and Louisiana, but their charts captured a woefully incomplete picture of realities on the ground. Mapmakers could even draw on knowledge from colonial officials and backcountry interpreters to identify the approximate territorial range and identity of many native groups such as the Creeks. Yet their maps could not begin to capture the extraordinary dynamics of eighteenth-century America. Like the Carolina governor, rival imperial officials read on the maps opportunities to expand their territories. Cartographers for competing nations gave rival names to contested sites and drew rival boundaries around coveted territory. Sometimes they mapped out deliberate falsehoods, omitting or obscuring the locations of especially sensitive or prized possessions.

Colonists on all sides sensed the insecurity of rival imperial claims to American lands. This uncertainty opened opportunities for inhabitants on the ground to ignore imperial designers in their quest for land, commerce, and power. Native peoples often found themselves caught in the crossfire. But just as often, they found chances to exploit the fierce contest among European rivals to achieve a variety of Indian goals. The blank spaces separating rival imperial possessions on a map obscured highly charged zones of opportunity for those willing to risk their dangers.

8.1: French America after 1700

8.1 Recount how French explorers attempted to set up New France in America

During the last quarter of the seventeenth century, French colonists labored relentlessly to enlarge their sovereign's claims to North American empire along the great interior waterways so crucial to trade and missions. Intrepid explorers such as René-Robert Cavelier, Sieur de La Salle, and Father Jacques Marquette led the way west and south into the Great Lakes basin and the Mississippi River valley (see Chapter 6). At the same time, aggressive governors and military leaders such as Louis de Buade de Frontenac and Antoin Laumet de Lamothe Cadillac sought to secure and extend the Canadian possessions of Louis XIV (see Chapter 7). Colonial traders, some officially licensed and others illicit *coureurs de bois*, carried French goods and influence into Great Lakes forests and along the great interior rivers. By 1701, the French claimed an enormous ring of territory that split Spain's North American possessions in two and threatened to confine Anglo-America to the Atlantic seaboard.

As explorers and governors extended France's North American territorial claims, Louis XIV's ambitious minister Jean-Baptiste Colbert tried to encourage emigration to New France and to strengthen the colony's economic viability. Colbert sent soldiers to secure the colony and provided incentives for them to remain as colonists. He continued to encourage the dispensing of seigneuries, or grants of land, to landholders and helped them recruit the *engagés* or hired men needed to work the grants. These *engagés*

typically contracted for three-year terms to work on the seigneuries. They received pay during that time as well as free passage back to France should they wish to return. Colbert's policy predictably resulted in an overbalance of males, so between 1663 and 1673 the minister recruited and sent to New France over seven hundred *filles du roi*, female orphans without other prospects. The marriages and families that resulted from Colbert's policies brought stability to French American society and contributed to a steady growth in the population.

Despite these enterprising efforts, only around fifteen thousand colonists populated New France in 1700, less than one-sixth the combined population of neighboring New York and New England. Growing opportunities in France itself kept most people at home, and more than half the *engagés* and soldiers returned to prospects in France once their contracts or terms of enlistment had expired. Those who remained exerted a transformative impact that belied their comparatively small numbers.

8.1.1: Whalers, Traders, and Farmers in the Gulf of St. Lawrence

The opening to France's great North American empire lay within the Gulf of St. Lawrence, which hosted significant economic activity in its own right in addition to serving as avenue to the northern interior. Visitors to eighteenth-century New France might receive their first introduction to the colony at one of the four royal trading posts at the mouth of the St. Lawrence River or Baye Phélypeaux at the Strait of Belle Isle. These harsh Atlantic outposts remained largely transient throughout the French colonial period. Traders and fishermen at the four King's Posts worked as employees of the Crown or its agents who reserved most of the profits from trade and fishing for themselves. South of the King's Posts lay Anicosti Island, where French and Basque whalers rendered oil from their yearly catches. The rugged coast of Labrador north of Belle Isle hosted over a thousand French fishermen annually to dry cod netted off the Grand Banks for sale in Europe. A commandant oversaw these operations, enforcing royal regulations and collecting a generous share of valuable fish, fur, and oil.

To the south lay Acadia, the territory encompassing much of present-day Canada's Maritime Provinces. In 1701, Acadia supported just over 1,100 settlers clustered in a few small farming and trading communities near Port Royal, now Annapolis Royal in Nova Scotia. The Acadians forged a tightly knit, homogenous family and community life much like that of France's Poitou region, where many of them originated. They carved out small family farms from marshland in the valley of the Rivière Dauphin (now the Annapolis River), building broad dikes of sod reinforced with branches and logs.

The Acadians' Micmac neighbors cared little for the marshlands and welcomed the manufactured goods the French brought to the region. They quickly incorporated the Acadians into their extensive hunting and trading network. To maintain the flow of trade goods, the Acadians sold furs obtained through the Micmac network and produced small crop surpluses for clandestine sale in New England. After 1718, when Fort Louisbourg was built on Île Royale (now Cape Breton Island), the Acadians carried on a brisk trade supplying the fort with grain and meat.

8.1.2: "A Village Beginning at Montreal and Ending at Quebec"

Canada, the heart of New France, stretched along three main centers of trade and administration on the St. Lawrence: Quebec, Trois-Rivières, and Montreal. A 1699 engraving of Quebec, the seat of government, reveals a small city with several impressive government buildings, a formidable citadel, and at least five beautiful spires arising from the churches, nunneries, hospice, and the city's hospital, the Hôtel Dieu. All three towns boasted planned streets, although the terrain on which they stood thwarted any effort to lay them out on the rectangular grid structure so popular in late seventeenth- and eighteenth-century planning. High stone walls encircled each town, protecting the dwellings within and offering refuge to outlying residents in case of attack. Trade in furs and lumber underpinned the economy of all three towns, providing the flow of cash needed to sustain trades and services characteristic of city life.

Most Canadian *habitants* lived on farms rather than in the cities. Each family wanted river access, and colonial officials obliged by laying out lots or *rotures* perpendicular to the river in long narrow strips around 165 yards wide. In 1700, a single strip of farms lay along each bank of the St. Lawrence except near the cities. There greater demand for land prompted officials to build roads behind the original fields, laying out a second and eventually third and fourth tiers of lots for settlement and cultivation. This pattern persisted throughout the colonial period, presenting the Swedish traveler Peter Kalm in 1749 with the "exceedingly beautiful" prospect of houses lining the river for 180 miles. "It could really be called a village," Kalm remarked, "beginning at Montreal and ending at Quebec."

Although the shape and arrangement of these French colonial plots differed significantly from those of English America, the *habitants* lived on them in a manner similar to the yeoman farming families of English America. They cultivated wheat for their own consumption and other cereal crops such as oats and corn for their sheep, hogs, cattle, and horses. Men cleared timber, drained marshes, and tilled the fields while women kept vegetable gardens, tended poultry and swine, reared children, and managed the household. Women often carded wool, spun thread, knit, and wove. Most families produced modest surpluses of grain, meat, and wool for sale in the towns or trade with neighboring Indians.

Canada's pattern of settlement proved a mixed blessing. The long strips of farms made it difficult for *habitants* to muster for defense in case of attack and provided much less protection than the clustered houses of a village. The layout also rendered more difficult the official tasks of policing and regulating as well as the priests' tasks of caring for souls. People adapted, organizing the *habitants* by parishes and creating a series of riverfront communities called *côtes* to deal with common problems and meet local needs for trades such as blacksmithing and carpentry.

For Canadians, the advantages of riverfront settlement far outweighed its drawbacks. The river gave *habitants* access to vital hunting and fishing. It provided easy transportation to the towns. The difficulties of policing made it easy for young men to slip into boats or canoes and head upstream to the *pays d'en haut*, the high country of the Great Lakes. There they evaded French licensing laws to trade among the Indians as *coureurs de bois*, illegal "forest runners" who turned tidy profits exchanging French manufactured goods for beaver pelts.

8.1.3: Forest Life in the *Pays d'en Haut*

By 1701, New France's governors had forged a series of firm alliances with Great Lakes native peoples that effectively sealed the colony's hold on the vast fur-trading territory beyond Montreal. They had secured key trade routes against Iroquois and English incursions by building Fort Frontenac on Lake Ontario and Fort Detroit on the St. Clair River. They had also won an Iroquois commitment to neutrality in the Grand Settlement of 1701.

Though the French officially claimed the Great Lakes in the great European imperial contest, they actually occupied very little of the region. Soldiers garrisoned at Frontenac and Detroit

formed the nucleus of these small communities. Traders, craftsmen, and a few farming *habitants* also clustered at these posts, accompanied by a priest and often a missionary. From there, French *coureurs de bois*, also called *voyageurs*, fanned across the countryside, establishing other minor trading posts or living among the Indians exchanging goods. By 1700, these traders had overtaken the Jesuit missionaries, who struggled to maintain a dwindling number of missions along Great Lakes shores.

A *voyageur* labored hard for his profits in furs. Many set out from Montreal in early spring, paddling up rivers and along the lakeshores in long canoes laden with European goods. Others wintered at various trading posts or among their native partners, accumulating furs in exchange for goods obtained the previous summer. In late spring or early summer, these too set out to rendezvous at Detroit or Michilimackinac with traders from Montreal. Indian hunters and trappers also joined the rendezvous, which became annual cross-cultural occasions of feasting, conviviality, brawling, and wantonness. There, traders exchanged the pelts they had brought for fresh stocks of goods needed to carry on the next year's trade. Those who had come from Montreal loaded their canoes with pelts and headed downstream on their thousand-mile return trip.

Voyageurs forged ties with native trading partners that extended far beyond a mere commercial relationship. Although the Great Lakes Algonquians desired trade goods, they did not see themselves as mere dependents of the French. Indeed, the Frenchman Nicolas Perrot complained of their "arrogant notion that the French cannot get along without… the assistance they give us." Western Indians saw the transaction of furs for goods itself as an exchange of gifts that imposed mutual obligations of fair dealing, peace, friendship, and political or military alliance. French traders thus found their commerce embedded within systems of implicit cultural understandings, which they ignored at great peril. A Frenchman who made the mistake of bargaining with an enemy of his previous trading partners risked hostile capture or death as a traitor. On the other hand, a trader could confirm and strengthen ties that an exchange of goods had already established by marrying a native woman. Many Frenchmen in the *pays d'en haut* did so not only to benefit from a woman's companionship but also to gain access to her labor and to cement relations with his wife's kin and community.

By the early eighteenth century, hundreds of marriages or more temporary unions between French *coureurs de bois* and native women—far more than was common in English America—had produced a significant population of mixed-blood offspring or *métis*. Many *métis* participated as full members of their own kinship groups and bands, but many others formed separate communities. The *métis* of these communities came to regard themselves as French, but they could also draw on native kinship ties to become important mediators, interpreters, and brokers between the French and various native groups. By contrast, no such communities emerged in English America, though some Anglo-native individuals did become important brokers between English and Indian communities.

Colonial officials and European visitors believed that the *voyageurs'* experience transformed them into a breed apart both from French at home and from other colonial Europeans. The late-seventeenth-century governor, the Marquis de Denonville, complained of the "attraction that this Indian way of life has for all these youths." They freely associated with Indians, ate and dressed like them, slept with native women, and lived in the forest for months or even years at a time, far beyond the effective reach of French law and Roman Catholic sacraments. Nevertheless, observers and others praised the Canadians' strength and prowess. Denonville observed they were "big, well-built, and firmly planted on their legs,

accustomed when necessary to live on very little, robust and vigorous . . . witty and vivacious." The Swedish traveler Peter Kalm remarked that he met "scarcely one of them who was not a clever marksman and who did not own a rifle." Kalm believed that their experience in the forest made them formidable in warfare: "they become such brave soldiers, and so inured to fatigue that none of them fears danger or hardships." One French officer boasted that his Canadian troops "almost always" enjoyed success in battle with the English, "who are not as vigorous nor as adroit in the use of fire arms as they, nor as practices in forest warfare."

Regardless of whether their experience made French colonists better warriors than their Anglo-American neighbors, their access to the Great Lakes, mastery of the forest, and extensive alliances with native peoples enabled the French to press far into the North American west. Indeed, by the early 1730s, Pierre Gaultier de Varennes et de La Vérendrye was pressing westward from Lake Superior's Thunder Bay to extend New France's reach to the foothills of the Rocky Mountains. Vérendrye carved out a new region, the *Mer de l'Ouest* (Western Sea), centered on posts in the basin of Lakes Winnipeg and Manitoba. From there *hommes du nord* carried French manufactured goods up the Assiniboine, Saskatchewan, and Souris Rivers to native partners. Peoples such as the Mandan and Hidatsa, who lived on the Big Bend of the Missouri River in what is now west-central North Dakota, maintained far-flung networks of exchange that carried French manufactured goods to many Plains Indian groups. The *hommes du nord* lived most of their lives among native peoples just as had Frenchmen in the Great Lakes, marrying native women and adopting native ways of life.

Indigenous peoples from the far West also became tragic commodities of exchange as French traders tapped into an existing system of bondage among their native allies to obtain unfree laborers for colonial centers in Canada and beyond. Native peoples throughout North America traditionally enslaved captives in their wars of revenge, often exchanging them with allies and subjecting them to humiliating service before eventually incorporating them into local communities. The French accepted this practice, using Indian slaves for domestic tasks in Detroit or Quebec and incorporating them into their own, very different system of slavery as they sold native captives to traders who shipped them to labor or French sugar plantations in the Caribbean. In this way the French in Canada, like the English in South Carolina, supplemented African slaves in the sugar islands with a stream of indigenous captives from North America.

8.1.4: France on the Mississippi

France entered the eighteenth century with yet another North American treasure on its imperial map: the mouth of the Mississippi River. Early in 1699, Pierre Le Moyne, Sieur d'Iberville, led an expedition of three French naval vessels along the Gulf Coast to the Mississippi Delta. He had set out to establish a fort at Pensacola Bay, but moved on after finding a newly built Spanish stockade there. Iberville became the first European to enter the Mississippi from the sea after stumbling upon its channel when a storm drove him to shore. To secure his prize, Iberville established Fort Maurepas on the shores of Biloxi Bay, leaving behind his brother Jean-Baptiste Le Moyne de Bienville with a small garrison. Only a few months later, Bienville encountered an English ship which had also managed to find its way up the Mississippi and was scouting a suitable site for a proposed colony under the proprietorship of the London physician Daniel Coxe. Bienville warned the English off and reported the incident when his brother returned. Iberville quickly established Fort Mississippi approximately 30 miles south of present-day New Orleans to prevent any further incursions by foreign vessels. By 1700, the new French colony of Louisiana had become a reality.

The French had established a claim with tremendous economic and military potential. The founding of Louisiana broke Spain's hold on the Gulf of Mexico and gave the French access to a vast natural transportation system stretching from the western slopes of the Appalachians to the high plains and the Rockies. Within months of Fort Mississippi's founding, Iberville established trade agreements with nearby native groups of Chickasaws, Choctaws, Mobilians, Alibamons, and Tohomés. During the following decades, French traders made their way up the Mississippi River and its tributaries to establish trading partnerships with native groups along the Arkansas, Missouri, and Ohio River systems. Traders found ready markets for manufactured goods, especially guns, which enabled southeastern groups beleaguered by English-supplied rivals to hold their own and gave Plains Indians such as the Comanches a great advantage over rivals in hunting and warfare.

Louisiana, however, never lived up to its promise. Policymakers and merchants in France invested little in the colony during its early years. After 1713, owners of a succession of monopoly ventures attempted to people the region with immigrants and African slaves who could provide labor for various enterprises. By 1731, two thousand French colonists and four thousand slaves inhabited the colony, many on narrow strips of property fronting the river as in Canada. Company agents sought to extract profits from the inhabitants by imposing rigid trade restrictions and pricing schemes that had demonstrably failed elsewhere in French America.

French mercantilist policies fared poorly in Louisiana as well. *Habitants* simply skirted the regulations to carry on an illegal trade aimed not to fill company coffers, but, as one official complained, to gain "what they need day by day like the Indians who find their happiness in an idle and lazy life." In fact, settlers and slaves

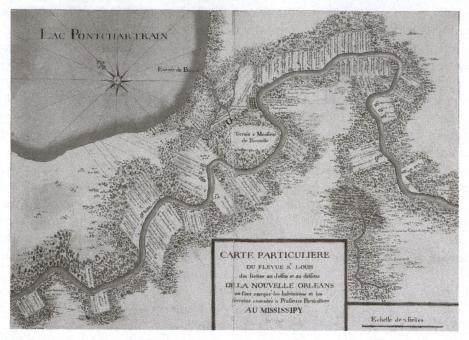

This map of New Orleans parish in 1723 shows long, narrow plots of land fronting the Mississippi River, a pattern of settlement common to French colonies throughout North America.

were no lazier than the Indians. All worked hard to obtain their livelihoods through a mixture of farming, herding, fishing, hunting, and trade. These activities brought the region's inhabitants into frequent contact, giving rise to an intercultural system that historian Daniel Usner has called a "frontier exchange economy." Slaves, settlers, and Indians "pieced subsistence and commercial endeavors together" by participating flexibly in exchange. Members of each group took on a variety of economic roles as circumstances demanded. Slaves, for instance, not only hoed tobacco fields but also worked as boatmen, soldiers, and peddlers. Indian farmers and herdsmen supplied French settlers with daily food and profitable pelts in exchange for manufactured goods. This intercultural economic system made few French investors rich, yet it came to support the region's inhabitants fairly well while supplying modest surpluses in furs, agricultural products, and slaves for French sugar plantations.

The founding of Louisiana stimulated the practically autonomous development of yet another French colony hundreds of miles up the Mississippi: the *pays des Illinois*. This cluster of six small farming villages along the river in what is now Illinois formed almost accidentally. French officials prompted its formation not by planning, but by temporarily closing the French fur trade after its sudden collapse in the 1690s. Stranded *coureurs de bois* from Canada carved out small farms and began cultivating crops for their own consumption. When the French gained control of the Mississippi's mouth a few years later, farmers from the *pays des Illinois* began cultivating small surpluses of grain for sale to the French sugar islands. The opportunity to set up as independent farming families on good prairie land attracted a small stream of migrants from Canada and France during the eighteenth century. The *pays des Illinois* never grew large, however; by 1750, the population reached only around three thousand, one-third of which were slaves.

8.2: Spanish Borderlands of the Eighteenth Century

8.2 Recount the Spanish struggles to secure its northern borders in America

The southernmost regions of North America remained home to the oldest European empire of the hemisphere. Centered in highly developed urban centers such as Vera Cruz, Puebla, and Mexico City, New Spain remained a powerful, if waning, military and commercial power. Its great silver mines continued to supply much of the hard currency that served as the medium of exchange for Atlantic commerce. Its beautiful urban architecture, formidable coastal fortresses, and ordered mission convents anchored a great part of the curious and unstable mosaic of the Atlantic World.

By 1700, however, Spanish authorities were feeling increasing pressure on their vast northern frontier from resistant native peoples and determined European competitors. Spain had only recently reasserted control over the Pueblos of New Mexico after a thirteen-year interruption precipitated by Popé's revolt of 1680 (see Chapter 7). Colonial officials had begun strengthening settlements along the Texas coast to prevent the French from gaining a foothold there. The Spanish governor of St. Augustine hoped that a new fort at Pensacola would dampen English and French competition in the region, but control of such a colonial backwater scarcely compensated for severe losses to neighboring South Carolina and the French occupation of the Mississippi.

Yet Spain continued to hold an unsteady grasp on far-flung communities from Santa Fe to St. Augustine. In these borderland communities, European colonists mixed with peoples of other races and backgrounds, forming multicultural societies. According to historian Ramón A.

Gutiérrez, the Spanish provinces present a story of "the complex web of interactions between men and women, young and old, rich and poor, slave and free, Spaniard and Indian, all of whom fundamentally depended on the other for their own self-definition."

8.2.1: Securing the Northern Frontier

Spain's position in Florida had become very precarious by 1700 in the face of aggressive competition from both French and English rivals. Despite the existence of an impressive fort at St. Augustine, the colony had never managed to attract many Spanish migrants. "It is hard to get anyone to go to St. Augustine because of the horror with which Florida is painted," the governor of Cuba complained in 1673. "Only hoodlums and the mischievous go there from Cuba." In the absence of sufficient colonists, Spain had attempted to consolidate control over the region through the missions and trade. Yet since 1680, Carolina raiders and their Indian allies had devastated the Spanish missions and client Apalachee communities (see Chapter 6). Indeed, by 1706, officials in St. Augustine were writing that in all of Florida's "extensive dominions and provinces, the law of God and the preaching of the Holy Gospel have now ceased."

The missions never recovered. Throughout the eighteenth century, Spain's presence in Florida remained confined to three coastal outposts: St. Augustine, Fort San Marcos de Apalachee on the Gulf Coast some 30 miles south of present-day Tallahassee, and the *presidio* of San Carlos de Austria at the mouth of Pensacola Bay. Ongoing imperial competition with the French and the English prevented Spain from abandoning its Florida posts, but officials came to regard them as money-losing garrisons useful mainly for securing Spanish interests farther south and west.

Spanish officials continued to view Texas and New Mexico as strategically important despite hostility they encountered from the region's native peoples and the failure to find precious metal there. French intrusions into the region during the last two decades of the seventeenth century kept the Spanish sharply aware that their presence in Texas and New Mexico formed a vital line of defense for the silver mines of Zacatecas, some of the richest in the world. In 1686, rumors reached Mexico that the French explorer, René-Robert Cavelier, Sieur de La Salle, had established a secret fort on the Texas coast. Authorities there sent out several expeditions to find and destroy the settlement. They feared that such a toehold would enable the French to "settles as far as New Mexico and make themselves Lords of many Kingdoms and Provinces." After three years of searching, the veteran frontier soldier and explorer Sargento Mayor Alonso de León found an abandoned Fort St. Louis on the shore of Matagorda Bay. Most of La Salle's men lay dead, but some had murdered the commander himself and fled to live among the neighboring Indians.

The new French forts at the mouth of the Mississippi only intensified the threat to Spain's northern frontier. Soon aggressive French traders were making their way westward along the Gulf Coast enticing native peoples with comparatively inexpensive manufactured goods. León had urged Spanish authorities to respond to these incursions by establishing a line of forts, but the strapped colonial government opted instead to encourage Franciscan missions. Although the missions cost the government almost nothing to operate, they depended on the cooperation of their Indian hosts to remain in existence. Franciscan missionaries had not established a good record of maintaining such cooperation for long, and their attempts to win converts in Texas were no exception. The prosperous Caddo farmers of what is now east Texas initially welcomed one such missionary, Father Damián Mazanet. Yet within a few years the friars wore out their welcome among the Caddos or Hasinai, who called themselves "Tejas" or "friends." When a smallpox epidemic ravaged the Caddo, Mazanet only declared it was "God's holy will." The Caddo warned him to leave or die and refused baptism for decades afterward in the belief that it would kill them. The Caddo turned instead to French traders, who were far more willing than the Spanish to tolerate their cultural differences and to engage them as equals.

Texas proved frustrating to Spanish attempts to control and rife with danger for Spanish missionaries and agents. Spanish officials eventually concluded that Franciscan missions could neither subdue the native population nor secure the region against French interlopers. Instead, they spent money on garrisons. In 1718, the Texas governor Martín de Alarcón founded a *villa* and mission at San Antonio and strengthened other missions and garrisons in east Texas. Three years later another governor, the Marqués de San Miguel de Aguayo, established Los Adaes only 12 miles from French Natchitoches. It remained the capital of Texas until 1763.

Farther west, concern over French ambitions prompted the Spanish nobleman Diego de Vargas to attempt the reconquest of New Mexico in 1693. Vargas worried that French access to the Mississippi River system might eventually yield a path to the Pueblos and that a Franco–Pueblo alliance would in turn open the way to French intrusion into New Spain's silver mining region. A preliminary campaign the year before from his base at El Paso had won token submission of twenty-three Pueblo communities. Vargas found it far more difficult to reassert full Spanish rule. He stormed Santa Fe with the aid of Indian allies and appeals to *Nuestra Señora de la Conquista*, a wooden image of the Virgin Mary which surviving Spanish had carried away after Popé's revolt in 1680. From his headquarters in Santa Fe, Vargas campaigned throughout 1694 to subdue the remaining Pueblos. The Franciscans followed up with an attempt to rebuild their missions, encountering stiff Pueblo resistance that exploded into a second revolt in 1696.

The second Pueblo rebellion did not achieve independence. It did, however, force the Spanish to reach some accommodation with the surviving Indians in order to secure New Spain's hold on the region. Vargas suppressed the revolt with a costly war of attrition, destroying food supplies and striking hard at rebel positions. Yet after regaining influence over all but the Hopi community farthest to the west, Spanish officials took greater care to avoid provoking further rebellions. Eighteenth-century friars, too, learned to wink at persistent Pueblo religious practices that their predecessors had tried to stamp out. The image popularly called *La Conquistadora* became the ethnic symbol of a New Mexico marked by peaceful coexistence between Spanish and Pueblos.

California never figured prominently in Spain's plans for the New World. Early explorers had reported finding only impoverished Indians living along the Pacific coast. Adventurers saw no natural resources worth mentioning, and since the area proved extremely difficult to reach from Mexico City—the overland trip could take months—California received little attention. Fear that the Russians might seize the entire region belatedly sparked Spanish activity, however, and after 1769, two indomitable servants of the empire, Fra Junipero Serra and Don Gaspar de Portolá, organized permanent missions and *presidios* (forts) at San Diego, Monterey, San Francisco, and Santa Barbara.

The threat of French competition for empire—along with the steady westward push of English rivals as well—kept the Spanish active in North American borderland regions that contributed very little to the wealth of their empire. On the contrary, the cost of military operations in New Mexico, Texas, and Florida proved a constant drain on Spanish imperial resources. Nevertheless, Spanish officials saw no choice but to pour money, arms, and missions into the borderlands to secure vital interests farther south. Spain's persistence marked the region with a distinctive cultural character. Their competition with the French for native alliance shaped Indian life west of the Mississippi, permitting groups such as the Comanches to draw on Spanish resources to prosecute their own campaigns for territorial expansion and to control the terms of exchange with all comers—Spanish, French, English, and native alike.

8.2.2: Peoples of the Spanish Borderlands

Viewed from the perspective of the eighteenth-century contest for North American empire, the ongoing Spanish presence in the borderlands held significance despite the small size of the Spanish population. Greatly outnumbered by the native population—in sharp contrast to the English frontier settlements—the Spanish had to adapt both their ways of life and their patterns of exchange in ways that acknowledged American Indians as independent actors in the imperial chess game. A few Catholic priests and imperial administrators traveled to the northern provinces, but the danger of Indian attack as well as a harsh physical environment discouraged ordinary colonists. The European migrants were overwhelmingly male, most of them soldiers in the pay of the empire. Although some colonists came directly from Spain, most had been born in other Spanish colonies such as Minorca, the Canaries, or New Spain. Because European women rarely appeared on the frontier, Spanish males formed relationships with Indian women, fathering large numbers of *mestizos*, children of mixed race.

As in other European frontiers of the eighteenth century, encounters with Spanish soldiers, priests, and traders altered Native American cultures. The experience here was quite different from that of the whites and Indians on the British frontier. In centers of power such as El Paso and Santa Fe, the Spanish exploited native labor, reducing entire Indian villages to servitude. Many Indians moved to the Spanish towns, and although they lived in close proximity to the

Europeans—something rare in British America—they were consigned to the lowest social class, objects of European contempt. No matter how much their material conditions changed, the Indians of the Southwest resisted strenuous efforts to convert them to Catholicism. The Pueblos maintained their own religious forms—often at great personal risk—and they sometimes murdered priests who became too intrusive. Angry Pueblos at Taos reportedly fed the hated Spanish friars corn tortillas containing urine and mouse meat.

The Spanish empire never had the resources necessary to dominate the northern frontier. The small military posts were intended primarily to discourage other European powers such as France, Great Britain, and Russia from taking possession of territory claimed by Spain. It would be misleading, however, to stress the fragility of Spanish colonization. The urban design and public architecture of many southwestern cities still reflect the vision of the early Spanish settlers, and to a large extent, the old borderlands remain Spanish speaking to this day.

8.3: Anglo-America on the Move

8.3 Report the growth of Anglo-America

In 1700, England seemed the upstart power in the great quest for North American empire. Yet, although France and Spain each claimed control over territories far more vast than England's colonial possessions, both were coming to regard English America as their gravest threat. Indeed, as war loomed over Europe in 1701, the French minister Louis Phélypeaux, Comte de Pontchartrain, did his best to persuade Spanish officials that the new French forts on the Mississippi would actually protect New Spain from English encroachment. With a population estimated at "more than 60,000 families," Pontchartrain warned, the English might soon overrun the continent. Only

by uniting with France against Anglo-American expansion could the Spanish crown—recently inherited by Louis XIV's grandson, the Duc d'Anjou—ensure protection of its Mexican silver mines.

Pontchartrain and Iberville may have exaggerated for effect, but England's North American colonies were indeed expanding in 1700. Most Anglo-American settlement remained concentrated along rivers and inlets of the Atlantic coastal plain. Inhabitants of each colonial region often maintained stronger ties with London than with people in neighboring colonies. Yet the Anglo-American population was growing rapidly and colonists were moving west, some of them quite far. Carolinians were regularly trading and raiding for pelts and slaves as far west as the Mississippi. English traders farther north were also pressing westward into the great Appalachian Mountains in search of furs and skins. Anglo-American farmers and planters were following the trails to take possession of fresh land, pressing the line of settlement gradually closer to the Appalachians and the French claims beyond. At over 260,000 people, the population of English America dwarfed that of New France, with only 15,000, and the Spanish borderlands, with just over 4,000.

8.3.1: Families and Farms in New England

By 1700, the third generation of New Englanders had shaped an agricultural landscape that contrasted sharply with the riverfront farmstrips of New France and the *presidios* of New Spain's borderlands. Like European settlements everywhere in North America, New England's farming communities were shaped by a complex interaction of local environment, relations with indigenous peoples, and the cultural motives and values of the colonists who came. Once cleared, the land permitted development of farms and communities that resembled those of the English countryside from which the colonists had come. Driven by a rate of increase that doubled the population every twenty-seven years, these heirs of the great Puritan migration of the 1630s had extended the line of settlement 50 miles inland from the coast and more than 100 miles up the Connecticut River. The towns and farms they carved out of the forest bore strong resemblance to their communities of origin further east (see Chapter 5). Town councils governed local affairs from a meetinghouse that often also housed Sunday worship. Dissent from the established Congregational order was rare, though visitors to some communities might find a few Quaker or Baptist families living on the outskirts of town. Ties of kinship, friendship, and faith knit the people of the frontier settlements together with those along the coast, further strengthening the homogeneity of New England society while setting it apart from both England and more diverse English colonies to the south.

Early-eighteenth-century New England was becoming a thriving Anglo-American province, but it had fallen short of its Puritan founders' hopes. The Boston minister Cotton Mather admitted to his chagrin that European visitors "will not find *New-England* a New Jerusalem." The region's culture had come to revolve around local cycles of farm, family, and community life, punctuated by seasons of planting, harvest, birth, marriage, and death. Yet, parochial though it had become, New England culture remained highly literate. Most adults could follow in their own Bibles as the minister read Scripture from the pulpit, and they were not afraid to challenge their pastor's interpretation of a passage based on their own judgment of its meaning. Many farmers consulted almanacs for advice on planting and tending their crops, sometimes jotting crabbed notes on the weather or local matters into the margins of a page. They also read almanacs for astrological insights into life and love, for pithy wisdom, and for knowledge of distant or exotic events and places.

Third-generation Puritans neither neglected their lofty past nor severed their transatlantic ties.

On the Connecticut valley frontier, the Northampton, Massachusetts, minister Solomon Stoddard sparked successions of local revival with fiery sermons that called his parishioners to the repentance and conversion that had formed the core of their grandparents' religious experience. Similar revivals became a regular feature of religious life elsewhere in New England. A literate elite of ministers and magistrates sustained links between past and present, New England and Old, by various means. Cotton Mather wrote massive tomes expounding the wonders of the invisible world and tracing God's providential guidance in New England's history. He published literally hundreds of works in England as well as America and contributed well-received letters to London's Royal Society on popular scientific topics of his day, including astronomy, botany, zoology, geology, and meteorology. Mather also maintained a voluminous correspondence with friends in England, Scotland, Germany, Holland, India, France, and the West Indies. Royal administrators strengthened these transatlantic ties even further by serving as visible representatives of England's government and by enforcing colonial compliance with English commercial regulations. Boston merchants imported British manufactured goods on a modest scale for sale to colonial customers.

As New England settlers pushed the frontier line further inland, native inhabitants of coastal regions such as the Narragansetts and Mohegans found themselves occupying increasingly marginal positions in their ancestral land. As postcolonial peoples, they eked out a living in praying towns or on small fractions of their former territories. They exchanged goods and services with their Anglo-American neighbors, selectively adopting whatever European practices and beliefs they found useful for preserving their own identity. They also participated with white neighbors in military expeditions against hostile Indians and French beyond the line of English settlement. There the Abenaki, whose villages and hunting grounds occupied the gradually narrowing territory between New England and New France, constituted a daunting obstacle to Anglo-American expansion. Many Abenakis had allied with the French and adopted Roman Catholicism. Their resentment of English colonization generated tension even in times of peace and made the New England frontier deadly in times of war.

8.3.2: Trade and Diversity in the Middle Colonies

The ethnically diverse Middle Colonies, especially New York, held far more strategic significance for England's imperial ambitions than did homogenous New England. New York's powerful English and Anglo-Dutch merchant families controlled the commerce of the Hudson River valley, a highway not only for the lucrative fur trade with the Iroquois but also for recurring military conflicts with French Canada. The colony hosted Anglo-America's only permanent garrison of British regular troops to protect the crucial Hudson River-Lake Champlain corridor. A relatively small but diverse population of Dutch, English, Huguenot, and German farmers cultivated land as tenants on princely Hudson River estates owned by families such as the Livingstons and the Rensselaers or maintained their own small farms near the river or on Long Island. The port city of five thousand on Manhattan Island boasted even greater ethnic and religious diversity. Along with the Dutch, Germans, English, and French, New York City supported a small Jewish community. In addition, enslaved Africans comprised as much as 15 percent of the population.

New Jersey, Pennsylvania, and Delaware boasted a similar diversity. The Delaware and Susquehanna Rivers gave some inhabitants of this region access to trade with the Iroquois as well, but most obtained their living by farming the fertile lands of the Delaware Valley. Philadelphia's Quaker merchants cultivated connections throughout the Atlantic, finding ready markets for the region's furs, iron, and agricultural products in exchange for European manufactures and West Indian sugar. The Delaware Valley's cheap, plentiful land attracted English, German, Welsh, Scottish, Irish, and French Huguenot colonists to settle among the remaining Dutch and Swedes. By 1700, over twenty-one thousand settlers had arrived in Pennsylvania alone, making it the fastest growing colony in North America.

In the Middle Colonies, members of churches that were officially sanctioned in Europe lived at peace with sectarian neighbors who had fled persecution by those very religious establishments. In England, the Quakers remained a small minority whose persecution had only recently ceased, but Pennsylvania Quakers outnumbered all other groups and controlled the colony's government. Quakers also formed a large minority of New Jersey's population. Sundays dawned in New York upon Anglicans making their way to churches in one part of the city as Dutch Reformed worshipers met in another. German Lutheran and Reformed groups remained suspicious of one another in New York as they had in Europe, but many cooperated to share a building for worship, meeting at different times of day. German Anabaptists seized on William Penn's promise of religious freedom to settle on fertile land in southeastern Pennsylvania, where their Mennonite and Amish descendants remain to this day. So also did more exotic groups such as the learned mystic Johannes Kelpius, founder in 1694 of The Woman in the Wilderness, a community of forty ascetics who lived in tiny cells contemplating magic numbers, esoteric symbols, and alchemical formulas.

The Lenni-Lenape of the Delaware Valley did not fare so well. Although William Penn insisted on paying for Lenni-Lenape lands before deeding them to European colonists, he understood the transaction as permanently alienating the soil from the Indians, a pattern of land use not shared by native peoples (Chapter 6).

As Pennsylvania settlers flooded west, the Lenni-Lenape, whom colonists called the Delaware, withdrew. By 1700, many Delaware were vying for space along the Susquehanna River along with migrating Shawnee, Conoy, Susquehannock, and Iroquois groups. To protect the Delaware from Euro-American squatters, the Pennsylvania government set aside "manors" where the Indians could pursue their traditional way of life. Yet the white settlements that soon surrounded these manors restricted native access to hunting and fishing, prompting the Lenni-Lenape to withdraw once more westward to the Alleghenies and beyond.

8.3.3: "Venturing Backward" in Virginia

In the Chesapeake, a momentous transformation from indentured servitude to slave labor was well under way even as the majority of Virginia and Maryland inhabitants eked out a precarious living on small western tracts. Since the 1680s, the supply of English indentured servants had been declining by about 3 percent annually while the demand rose about the same amount. The resulting turn to African slaves had by 1700 boosted the black population to around 20 percent of Virginia's sixty thousand inhabitants. Most African slaves labored singly alongside their masters or with one or two other slaves or indentured servants. The relative wealth of those few masters who could afford ten or more slaves was making families such as the Wormeleys, Carters, Byrds, Beverleys, and Lees the core of a rising Chesapeake gentry.

Few of the great brick houses that now adorn the banks of the Potomac, Rappahannock, York, and James Rivers were standing in 1700. Residents themselves reported that the colony "looks all like a wild desart; the high-lands overgrown with trees, and the low-lands sunk with water, marsh, and swamp." Yet wealthy Virginians aspired for their children a place among a transatlantic elite, graced by a liberal education and supported by the patronage of powerful and well-connected "friends" in England. Such men plowed their surpluses into more slaves and more land, gradually squeezing the smaller planters away from the Tidewater region onto less desirable western soil. In sharp contrast to the settled town life of New England, most Chesapeake planters lived in small wooden houses a mile or more apart, "dribbled over the landscape without apparent design," as one wry observer reported.

By 1700, the rising Virginia gentry were also busily pressing their own land claims westward along the rivers into the Piedmont, pushing out white squatters and incorporating the remnants of Virginia's once-great Powhatan Chiefdom into a postcolonial order. Virginia's Indian population had fallen a disastrous 87 percent to only 1,900, most of whom lived well to the west of their ancestral homes on land increasingly claimed by white elites. They paid meager tribute or rent from crops raised on marginal lands and found themselves subjected to English laws and customs. They exchanged furs and deerskins for European goods, often serving as brokers as well as buffers between Virginia traders and more robust western nations such as the Shawnees, Tuscaroras, and Cherokees. The skins they sold helped make the fortunes of traders such as William Byrd I, who operated a lucrative fur-trading network from a base at the frontier post of Fort Charles near the site of present-day Richmond. In 1710, a newly arrived lieutenant governor, Alexander Spotswood, initiated a flurry of negotiations with western Indians to strengthen the fur trade and ensure security for migrating colonists. Spotswood also encouraged colonists to "venture backwards" to the west. In 1716, he personally led an expedition beyond the Blue Ridge Mountains into the Shenandoah Valley. By 1720, settlements were springing up along the Shenandoah River and its tributaries.

8.3.4: Carolina Planters and Traders

Less than 30 miles south of Virginia, a scattering of meager farms and villages along Albemarle and Pamlico Sounds formed the core of what was becoming the colony of North Carolina. Still a formal part of the vast territory that Charles II had granted to the Carolina proprietors in 1665, Albemarle lagged far behind Charles Town in population and commerce. In the first decade of the eighteenth century, however, the region was beginning to attract Huguenot and Palatine immigrants despite a ring of coastal sand reefs that impeded access to the ocean and Atlantic trade. Religious and ethnic strife dogged Albemarle's inhabitants as they scratched out a living by raising tobacco, cereal crops, and cattle on the sandy soil. The coves along the Outer Banks and the inlets of the sounds provided excellent hideouts for smugglers and pirates such as Edward Teach, the notorious Blackbeard. Local settlers and the deputy governor himself often sheltered these freebooters, who sold goods more cheaply than established merchants and who injected scarce cash into the economy by purchasing provisions and spending in the taverns.

To the south, Charles Town was becoming the center of a thriving, if brutal, colony of planters, traders, and bondspeople. White indentured servants and African and Indian slaves comprised nearly half of its seven thousand inhabitants in 1703. These unfree laborers worked side by side with masters to clear fields, herd cattle, plant experimental crops, and extract naval stores from the pine forests. Yet the sharing of common tasks hardly put slaves on an equal footing with their masters. One colonist observed that anyone who could "get a few slaves and… beat them well to make them work hard" might make a good living in South Carolina. The colony's Barbadian immigrant elite enforced their dominion with a harsh slave code modeled on that of their sugar island home.

While early South Carolina planters experimented their way toward the cultivation of rice and indigo that would eventually become the colony's eighteenth-century staples, rapacious Carolina traders ranged west as far as the Mississippi in search of deerskins and Indian captives (see Chapter 8). By 1700, they were shipping to London an average of fifty-four thousand deerskins per year, a figure that would rise rapidly in the following decades. Indian slaves were harder to obtain but far more profitable to Carolinians and their native allies. In 1708, a Chickasaw hunter could collect "a Gun, ammunition, horse, hatchet, and a suit of Cloathes" for each slave sold to Carolina traders, a deal whose worth the historian James Axtell has estimated at "a whole year's worth of deerskins."

The South Carolinian lust for Indian slaves cost their northern neighbors dearly when hostilities broke out between Tuscaroras and North Carolinians in 1711. Appalled by reports of Tuscarora atrocities, the South Carolina legislature dispatched Colonel John Barnwell with a force of over a thousand English, Yamasee, Wateree, Congaree, Waxhaw, and Pee Dee troops. Carolina law permitted Barnwell and his army to sell Tuscarora captives as slaves, but circumstances initially thwarted their quest for profit. When Tuscarora defenses proved more formidable than anticipated, nearly half of Barnwell's force deserted. The colonel salvaged his campaign by capturing a Tuscarora fort and forcing its inhabitants to flee, a victory that persuaded the Tuscaroras to come to terms with the North Carolinians. Yet only on the return trip to South Carolina did the remnants of Barnwell's army manage to score a profit by inviting an unsuspecting company of Tuscaroras to parlay and then capturing them for sale on the slave market. Barnwell and his allies claimed that they had acted before the conclusion of peace, but news of his treachery nevertheless sparked a new round of brutal frontier warfare that lasted more than a year. The conflict ended with most Tuscarora survivors migrating north

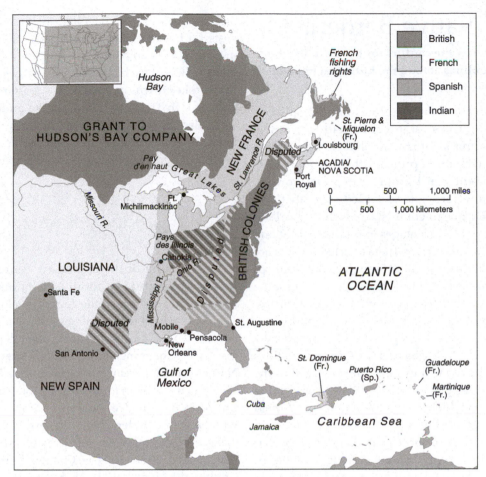

Map 8.1 Conflicting Claims in eighteenth Century North America

to settle as "little brothers" of the Iroquois. In the meantime, Virginia's lieutenant governor Alexander Spotswood declared that Barnwell's greed had left North Carolina "in a worse condition than he found" it.

Only three years after the Tuscarora War, South Carolina experienced its own frontier conflict when the Yamassee broke their alliance and attacked, killing ninety of the colony's hundred traders and attacking border settlements. Other Indian nations—including Choctaws, Cherokees, Apalachees, Shawnees, and Santees—joined the Yamassees to settle old scores with the Carolinians or seize portions of their trading system. This powerful Indian alliance drove Carolina colonists back toward Charles Town, closing off the western routes by which the colony's traders had devastated the Southeast in vicious trade wars with Indian, Spanish, and French competitors. Warfare subsided only after Carolina diplomats managed to pry the Cherokees away from other Indian nations. Besides the loss of life and property, the war cost South Carolina much of its western commerce as Virginia traders moved in. Carolina proprietors also lost their charter for South Carolina, which was made a royal colony in the aftermath of the Yamassee War.

8.4: Native Borderlands

8.4 Review the conflict for power in the Carolinas among the European imperial powers

The conflicts in the Carolinas formed only one theater of a vast eighteenth-century contest for trade and territory, one that engaged native peoples who often pursued their own interests independently of European imperial powers. Indigenous participants exploited competition among European colonists as well as rival native groups for advantages in trade, territory, and military alliance. The settlers affected Indians not only by disease but also through commercial opportunities that in turn forced new, perhaps more deadly, competition among Native Americans. Everyone had to accommodate to unforeseen conditions, sometimes giving rise to whole new peoples. The Catawba and the Cherokee nations were just two such groups who emerged in the first decades of the eighteenth century, as disparate survivors of wars and epidemics forged new identities from the remnants of cultural traditions or were absorbed into larger groups that had escaped the devastation. Stronger nations or leagues such as the Iroquois incorporated weaker ones such as the Tuscarora as tributaries or lesser members. Skillful Indian diplomats often managed to wrest advantages not only by playing one European power against another but also by negotiating tacit cooperation among rival European groups, even in wartime. Indeed, Indians could often pit representatives of rival English colonies against one another, as traders and government officials jockeyed for control of trade in skins and furs.

The impact of this contest reached far beyond the direct reach of Europeans themselves. Indians who had never seen a European traded avidly with native middlemen for European knives, hatchets, mirrors, and guns. Some goods made their way along native trade routes to places thousands of miles from the place where they were originally traded. Archaeological evidence suggests, for instance, that Spanish goods first traded in central Mexico could pass overland through many different exchanges among native peoples to Cherokee towns in what is now western North Carolina. By the early 1700s, native middlemen were also carrying French goods from western Lake Superior or newly founded settlements on the Mississippi Delta to peoples of the plains.

8.4.1: Covenant Chains and Middle Grounds: From the Hudson to the Great Lakes

At the opening of the eighteenth century, the Iroquois constituted a formidable military and commercial presence in the American Northeast. The League held sway over a great swath of territory from Lake Ontario south, often deploying war parties that ranged into western Virginia and North Carolina in search of captives for adoption. The Covenant Chain forged during the 1680s continued to link the Iroquois in trading alliances with New Englanders, New Yorkers, Pennsylvanians, and Virginians as well as with various Indian nations to the west (see Chapter 7). Yet in the Grand Settlement of 1701, an Iroquois Confederacy exhausted by more than a decade of war had gained respite by negotiating a position of formal neutrality in conflicts between their French and English neighbors (see Chapter 9). The historian Daniel Richter has called the settlement more a "precarious framework for an elusive new system of intercultural relationships," yet it did provide the Iroquois time to rebuild their population and gave them new commercial opportunities to exploit. French and English, equally eager to court Iroquois favor and gain influence in tribal councils, sent missionaries and interpreters as well as resident blacksmiths and gunsmiths who supplied village residents with cheap iron tools and kept their guns in good repair. Peace with New France also gave the Iroquois a chance to cultivate commercial relations with Mississaugas, Ottawas,

Wyandots, and Miamis, diverting their supplies of peltry from the St. Lawrence to the Hudson in exchange for cheaper, more plentiful English goods.

The Algonquian peoples to the west of Iroquoia remained allied to the French through a complex set of formal and informal arrangements, often involving intermarriage as well as exchange of gifts and military aid. The historian Richard White has termed this system of Franco-Indian relations a "middle ground," a conceptual as well as geographical space where Indians and French could "adjust their differences through... creative, often expedient misunderstandings," producing new meanings and practices that enabled both sides to work together for overlapping goals. The Algonquians no more intended to isolate themselves from European contact than did any other native group. They relied on French traders to provide essential metal goods and weapons. The goal of nations such the Ojibwa, Ottawa, Potawatomi, and the Miami was rather to maintain a strong independent voice in these commercial exchanges. So long as they had sufficient military strength—that is, large numbers of healthy armed warriors—they compelled everyone who came to negotiate in the "middle ground" to give them proper respect. Western Algonquians took advantage of French, Iroquois, and English rivals when possible; they compromised when necessary. It is best to imagine the middle ground as an open, dynamic process of creative interaction.

8.4.2: Between Empires: Indians of the Southeast

Around 1700, the Southeast was emerging as a new site of intense and creative contact among Europeans and Indians. This territory bounded by the Mississippi River, the Gulf Coast, and the Carolina coast was home to many large Indian nations with complex societies that stretched back in many cases to Mississippian origins (see Chapter 1). Many were refugees, the remnants of

Native American groups who had lost so many people to warfare and epidemic disease that they could no longer sustain an independent cultural identity. These survivors joined with other Indians to establish new multiethnic communities. In this respect, Native American villages may not have seemed all that different from the mixed European settlements of the backcountry.

Stronger groups of Indians generally welcomed the refugees. Strangers were formally adopted to take the places of family members killed in battle or overcome by sickness, and we should appreciate that many seemingly traditional Indian villages of the eighteenth century actually represented innovative responses to rapidly shifting external conditions. As historian Peter Wood explains, "Physically and linguistically diverse groups moved to form loosely organized confederacies, unions of mutual convenience, that effectively restrained interethnic hostilities."

Like their native neighbors to the north and east, native peoples of the Southeast pursued diplomacy and trade with Europeans when they could, yet these dealings often unfolded in a climate of conflict and danger that differed from the middle-ground experience of the Great Lakes Algonquians. Their relatively large numbers and control of strategic territory gave many southeastern Indians considerable leverage in their dealings with Europeans. Yet the Indian nations themselves were too divided and the competition among rival European trading partners too intense for Great Lakes–style "creative misunderstandings" to foster widespread intercultural cooperation.

Instead, each nation exercised its bargaining power pragmatically in pursuit of its own ends. The diverse peoples of the Catawba River valley in the Carolina Piedmont shrewdly played rival Virginia and South Carolina traders against each other to get the best price for their deerskins. The Chickasaws on the eastern banks of the Mississippi allied with Carolinians against their Choctaw rivals, using English firearms to capture

Choctaws for sale on the slave market. Choctaws responded by seeking arms from the French and using them to disrupt Chickasaw-Carolinian trade caravans. The Creek towns of what is now southeastern Alabama and southwestern Georgia divided their loyalties between English, Spanish, and French. The trading preferences of the eastern allies of the English enriched Creeks of the Lower Towns but eventually embroiled them in a devastating civil war with the western Upper Town allies of France. The Cherokee capitalized on their position at the southern Appalachian crossroads of early-eighteenth-century leather-trading routes to act as powerful middlemen between English and western nations in the deerskin trade.

Yet southeastern Indians understood all too well when their own uses of exchange to augment their spiritual power and cultural well-being clashed with French or English desires for profit in skins, land, or slaves. When such conflicts came to light, natives resisted as specific circumstances demanded. Individual Indian trappers and hunters might make an unscrupulous trader pay for his duplicity by capturing his goods or taking his life, a warning for other traders to follow more honorable codes of conduct. European demands sometimes pushed rival Indian nations into alliance against the aggressors, and the resulting wars produced sudden shifts in Euro-Indian relations. Cherokees and Choctaws joined Yamassees in arms against South Carolinians in 1715, killing the traders and driving the colonists back toward Charleston.

Just as often, conflicting aims among different Indian nations led one nation to ally with a European power against another. Southeastern Westoes, Shawnees, and Yamassees forged a succession of alliances with South Carolinians against Apalachee neighbors that eventually forcing Apalachee survivors to forsake their traditional homelands for refuge towns near St. Augustine and Pensacola. In the Yamassee War of 1715, the Cherokees eventually forsook their native allies and came to occupy the Yamassees' former place in the Carolina leather trade. Differing political and religious aims prevented some nations such as the Natchez from ever establishing stable relations with Europeans. Franco-Natchez relations eventually degenerated into a war of conquest that wiped out the Natchez as a distinct nation. Like an environmental ecotone or zone of transition between two different habitats, the Indians' new south represented a constantly shifting borderland of opportunity and danger.

8.5: The Border Conflicts of Queen Anne's War

8.5 Recall how Queen Anne's war changed the fortunes of North American Indians

By the first decade of the eighteenth century, a complex tangle of interethnic and imperial conflict and cooperation laced across eastern North America, linking some rivals into unlikely partnerships while setting natural allies against one another. Nowhere was this dynamic more evident than in the imperial contest English colonists called Queen Anne's War, known in Europe as the War of the Spanish Succession (1702–1713). The conflict pitted Spain and France against England, Holland, and Austria after Spain's last Hapsburg monarch, Charles II, designated as his heir Philippe d'Anjou, grandson of France's Louis XIV. A little more than a year after war broke out in Europe, a Canadian force of French soldiers and their Indian allies opened a North American front by attacking English frontier settlements in Maine. Queen Anne's War plunged North American Indians and colonists into a ten-year welter of border conflicts and informal, often illegal alliances that brought windfall profits to some participants and devastation to many others.

Table 8.1 A Century of Conflict : Major Wars, 1689–1763

Dates	European Name	American Name	Major Allies
1689–1697	War of the League of Augsburg	King William's War	Britain, Holland, Spain, their colonies, and Native American allies against France, its colonies, and Native American allies
1702–1713	War of the Spanish Succession	Queen Anne's War	Britain, Holland, their colonies, and Native American allies against France, Spain, their colonies, and Native American allies
1743–1748	War of the Austrian Succession (War of Jenkins's Ear)	King George's War	Britain, its colonies, and Native American allies, and Austria against France, Spain, their Native American allies, and Prussia
1756–1763	Seven Years War	French and Indian War	Britain, its colonies, and Native American allies against France, its colonies, and Native American allies

8.5.1: New England Captives and Iroquois Neutrals

Queen Anne's War inflicted a decade of imperial conflict that ravaged farms and communities all along the New England frontier. On March 1, 1704, only a few months after the French attack on Maine, a detachment of Abenaki warriors left their French allies in camp and crossed the frozen Connecticut River to strike the frontier town of Deerfield, Massachusetts, the most famous raid of the war. Nearly fifty settlers—many of them women and young children deemed unable to survive a long winter's march—lost their lives in the "Sack of Deerfield." The Abenaki rounded up 112 survivors and marched them through the deep snow to Canada. Once arrived, the surviving captives were adopted into Abenaki bands or redeemed by the French for prisoner exchanges. The chief prize of the raid, Deerfield's minister John Williams, spent three years negotiating for his captive congregation's return to New England. Canadian authorities eventually agreed to exchange Williams and other English captives for French captives being held in Boston. Williams memorialized his peoples' ordeal in a popular narrative, *The Redeemed Captive, Returning to Zion* (1707). Yet William's own daughter Eunice remained unredeemed in New France, where she converted to Roman Catholicism and married an Abenaki man with whom she spent the rest of her life.

Throughout Queen Anne's War, many other New England settlers lost their lives or were taken captive to Canada in similar raids. Massachusetts authorities responded by granting tax relief to frontier communities and reinforcing the towns with small garrisons of militia. Many colonists, especially those in Maine and New Hampshire, retreated to more densely populated areas near the coast. The English retaliated against the French from the sea by raiding settlements along the Acadian coast and the mouth of the St. Lawrence.

Not all inhabitants of the Northeast suffered equally. While New England frontier settlements and French coastal communities bore the brunt of imperial conflict, the Five Nations struggled to preserve their hard-won neutrality between England and France for the first several years of the war. Neutrality served not only Iroquois interests but also the interests of New France, New York, and the Great Lakes Algonquians, all of whom profited from wartime commerce. Quebec merchants carried on a lucrative clandestine trade with their counterparts in Albany, exchanging beaver pelts for the English woolen cloth, duffel, and stroud preferred by Abenaki trading partners for their superior quality at a lower price. Meanwhile, the Iroquois capitalized on their peace with New France by diverting the Great Lakes fur trade from Canada to Albany. Neutrality allowed the Five Nations to negotiate peace with France's Algonquian allies and then guide them on safe passage through Iroquoia to the Hudson. Iroquois guides gained from employment by western Algonquians, Iroquois villages collected from each party appropriate ceremonial gifts, yet the Algonquians still netted higher profits in Albany than they could earn from Quebec.

These lucrative but illicit arrangements could not last forever. In 1709, New York authorities persuaded Mohawk warriors to join a major military expedition against Canada. The expedition fizzled out on the shores of Lake Champlain, but in 1711, the English tried again to launch a combined land and naval assault against Quebec. This campaign likewise ended in disaster when the English naval commander, Sir Hovenden Walker, ran part of the fleet aground on an island in the St. Lawrence with a loss of over seven hundred lives.

The 1711 campaign against Quebec was not a total loss, however. On its way up the coast to the St. Lawrence, the English fleet had captured the Acadian town of Port Royal. Their ability to hold the port for the remainder of the war gave British diplomats leverage to claim Acadia during peace negotiations. In 1713, France ceded the region to Great Britain in the Treaty of Utrecht, and Acadia became Nova Scotia.

8.5.2: War and Exchange in the Southeast

In the Southeast, the presence of a Bourbon on the Spanish throne prompted French and Spanish colonists to suppress their historic rivalries against their common English enemy. The English, however, struck the first blow of the war when South Carolina's governor James Moore personally led a force of 50 colonists and 1500 Yamassees to attack Spanish Florida by sea. Moore's army devastated the Spanish district of Guale en route to St. Augustine and burned the town to the ground once he arrived. He lacked the mortars or scaling ladders needed to take the fort, however, so after an eight-week siege he gave up the fight and retreated overland to Charleston. Two years later, Moore led another force on a path of death and destruction across northern Florida, laying waste to all remaining Apalachee missions and forcing the Spanish to abandon the district. In 1707, Carolinians burned the town of Pensacola but failed to take the fort. The Spanish managed to fend off a second English assault on Pensacola in 1711. By then, however, the remaining Indians of northern Florida had allied firmly with the English, reducing Spanish influence to tattered refugee settlements near St. Augustine and Pensacola Bay.

Spanish officials in Florida did not leave English aggression wholly unanswered. French allies from Louisiana had provided vital aid in the defense of Pensacola, and the Spanish turned again to them for help in launching an offensive against South Carolina. In 1706, a combined force of French and Spanish privateers sailed from Havana, Cuba, to attack Charles Town but failed to take the city.

While Queen Anne's War put Spanish Florida on the defensive, Franco-Spanish cooperation gave Louisiana colonists and traders breathing room to establish their presence firmly in the Southeast. Spanish officials permitted French traders to extend their influence among Gulf Coast Indians as far eastward as Pensacola. Other French traders made their way west up the Red River to cultivate contacts with the Caddo Indians, whose friendship and trade the Spanish had earlier worked so hard to keep for themselves. Louisiana traders could not capitalize fully on these new contacts, however. The war diverted resources away from colonial development and made trade goods scarce and expensive. The ability of English traders to offer greater variety and quantity for better rates enabled them to win more Indian allies and slowed French expansion into the interior.

8.6: The Stakes of Conflict

8.6 Summarize the continuity of the power struggle for the control of North America

The second colonial war ended in 1713 when Great Britain and France signed the Treaty of Utrecht. English diplomats scored significant territorial gains on the peripheries of North America as Nova Scotia, Newfoundland, and Hudson's Bay all passed to Great Britain. The negotiators showed much less interest in the New World's military situation. Their major concern was preserving a balance of power among the European states. A decade of intense fighting had taken a heavy toll in North America, but neither French nor English colonists had much to show for their sacrifice.

After George I replaced Anne on the throne in 1714, parliamentary leaders were determined to preserve peace—mainly because of the rising cost of war. Yet on the American frontier, the hostilities continued with raids and reprisals. As people on both sides of this conflict now realized, the stakes of the war were very high; they were fighting for control over the entire West, including the Mississippi Valley.

Both sides viewed this great contest in conspiratorial terms. From South Carolina to Massachusetts Bay, colonists believed the French planned to "encircle" the English settlements and to confine the English to a narrow strip of land along the Atlantic coast. The English noted that in 1682, La Salle had claimed for the king of France a territory—Louisiana—that included all the people and resources located on "streams and Rivers" flowing into the Mississippi River. To make good on their claim, the French constructed forts on the Chicago and Illinois rivers. In 1717, they established a military post 200 miles up the Alabama River, well within striking distance of the Carolina frontier, and in 1718, they settled New Orleans. One New Yorker declared in 1715 that "it is impossible that we and the French can both inhabit this Continent in peace but that one nation must at last give way to the other."

On their part, the French suspected their rivals intended to seize all of North America. Land speculators and frontier traders pushed aggressively into territory claimed by the French and owned by the Native Americans. In 1716, one Frenchman urged his government to hasten the development of Louisiana, since "it is not difficult to guess that their [the British] purpose is to drive us entirely out… of North America."

To their great sorrow and eventual destruction, the original inhabitants of the frontier, the Native Americans, became swept up in this undeclared war. The Indians maneuvered to hold their own in the steadily shrinking zone between the European colonial powers. In the Northeast, the Iroquois favored the British; the Algonquian peoples generally supported the French. Indians of the Southeast played English against French and rival English for advantage in trade and warfare. But regardless of the groups to which they belonged, Indian warriors—acting independently and for their own strategic reasons—found themselves enmeshed in imperial policies set by distant European kings.

Chronology

1694	Vargas initiates campaign to reconquer Pueblos
1700	Iberville founds Fort Mississippi, first settlement of French Louisiana
1701	Cadillac founds Detroit
1702	War of the Spanish Succession (Queen Anne's War) begins
1704	French and Indians sack Deerfield, Massachusetts
1706	Spanish and French assault Charles Town
1707	Carolinians sack Pensacola
1711	English capture Port Royal, Acadia; Tuscararora War breaks out in North Carolina
1713	Peace of Utrecht ends War of the Spanish Succession
1714	Yamasee War in South Carolina
1716	Spottswood opens Shenandoah Valley to settlement
1718	San Antonio founded by Spanish; New Orleans founded by French
1769	California missions founded at San Diego, Monterey, San Francisco, Santa Barbara

Chapter 9
Shifting Borderlands
Migrations in Eighteenth-Century America

 ## Learning Objectives

9.1 Relate the spread of the coastal population into the American heartland to the influx of immigrants

9.2 Recount the events leading to the creation of the state of Georgia

9.3 Report the increase in ethnic diversity of Britain's North American's colonies

9.4 Summarize how the native Indians adapted to the westward advance of the Europeans

9.5 Examine effects of the expansion of the European territory into the American west in the eighteenth century

On August 1, 1740, a delegation of western Indians arrived in Philadelphia to discuss with Pennsylvania's leaders disturbing new frontier conflicts that were arising from the colony's rapid expansion. The delegation of Delaware and Mingo—or western Iroquois—from the border region between French and English America attracted a crowd of curious Philadelphians as they passed. The travelers had trekked more than three weeks across the mountains from Kittanning on the banks of the Allegheny River, carrying to Pennsylvania proprietor Thomas Penn 160 buckskins "to make you Gloves." When they arrived at the city's Quaker Meetinghouse, Penn welcomed them inside to join a council meeting with himself and a delegation of colonial officials. The townspeople followed, packing the seats with "as many of the Inhabitants of Philada[delphia] as the House could conveniently hold."

The Delaware spokesman Sassoonan opened the meeting by laying a woven belt of wampum shell beads upon the council table, reminding his hosts as he did so that his people had not "forgot[ten] this place." Sassoonan, also known as Alumapees, had led his band of Delawares sixteen years earlier from the banks of the Schuylkill River near Philadelphia to "Allegheny a Long way off" after selling much of their eastern lands to English newcomers. His people "loved to

203

hunt" at Allegheny, Sassoonan declared, "because we there meet with some of our Brethren your Indian Traders who furnish us with Powder and Shot and other things." This commerce, he said, had helped sustain his people's affection for the English despite the distance between Kittanning and Philadelphia. The Delaware leader assured Pennsylvania officials that "we do not listen to any Idle Tales or Lies which we may have heard" from hostile natives or French who constantly attempted to draw his people away from alliance with the English. "We know where our Brethren dwell."

Yet the road between Allegheny and Philadelphia had recently begun bringing not only the traders whose commerce secured the bonds of loyalty, but also unwelcome English hunters who competed directly with the Delawares and western Iroquois for game. "Your young Men have killed so many Deer, Beavers, Bears, and Game of all sorts," Sassoonan complained, "that we can hardly find any for our selves." He therefore asked Thomas Penn to prevent further European hunting in Allegheny. "God has made us Hunters," Sassoonan declared, but the "white people have other Ways of living without that."

The 1740 meeting between Sassoonan and Thomas Penn provides a revealing glimpse at a central dynamic of eighteenth-century colonial development. Fifteen years earlier, the pressure of incoming European settlers had pushed Sassoonan's band off their ancestors' land. Now an advance guard of English hunters and trappers were knocking on the Delaware door in faraway Allegheny. Indeed, the European demand for North American land was rising exponentially as the coastal population burgeoned and unprecedented numbers of immigrants poured in from across the Atlantic.

But the backcountry coveted by European settlers was not a vast empty territory awaiting their arrival, as historical maps often suggest. West of Atlantic coastal cities, towns, farms, and plantations lay much more than a huge blank area with no mark of civilization. Indeed, Sassoonan and his people would not have understood such maps. They had made some of the empty space on the maps their home. The Allegheny Delawares experienced it as a populous, contested, rapidly shifting border zone stretching far beyond the horizon of the Delawares' experience—from New England and New France to the Spanish borderlands of the far Southwest.

The pace of change in those borderlands accelerated dramatically after the Treaty of Utrecht in 1713, which ended the War of the Spanish Succession, known to English colonists as Queen Anne's War. The period of peace that followed made the Atlantic relatively safe for passenger vessels and slave ships, while the older coastal settlements provided a staging ground for colonization of the interior of North America. No longer did colonists have to look to European investors and suppliers for crucial aid in occupying and settling the land. The hold of colonial governments often seemed tenuous, given their limited reach and the recurring tension among European and Indian rivals that could leave frontier settlers vulnerable to attack. Even so, Europeans were in North America to stay. Furthermore, they had put in place a framework of military, diplomatic, economic, and legal structures to provide at least a measure of support for those eager to colonize the western lands between empires.

Faced with the consequent intrusion of Europeans into the interior, native peoples adapted in a variety of ways to seize new opportunities while maintaining their independence. Most eagerly tapped into expanding trade networks. Many pushed further west to avoid being surrounded by foreigners. Others played rival European powers against one another to gain concessions that preserved and even augmented native power. When all else failed, Native Americans fought. Cooperation, exchange, and conflict in the borderlands produced ripples of change far beyond the direct influence of Europeans, across the Great Plains and to the Rocky Mountains.

Eighteenth-century North America had become a new, alternately exciting, and dangerous place for all its inhabitants. Colonial governments founded variously by Puritans, planters, and entrepreneurs had passed through a century of experimentation. They were entering a new period in which they sought self-consciously to shape their polities after an English model. Colonists cooperated eagerly with London officials to reincorporate their communities into an imperial order, where trade links were more secure, military might were more effective, and waves of settlers were pouring in as they had not done before. German and Irish migrants were joining English colonists under an imperial umbrella but with plans of their own. As the empires became stronger in military terms, the swelling population ironically became increasingly ungovernable as people on the ground scattered far and wide in diverse ethnic communities. In the end, the Indians could not be protected from relentless encroachment no matter how many treaties they signed.

9.1: "An Increase Without Parallel": Growth and Migration

9.1 Relate the spread of the coastal population into the American heartland to the influx of immigrants

The phenomenal growth of British America during the eighteenth century amazed Benjamin Franklin, one of the first persons to bring scientific rigor to the study of demography. The population of the English colonies doubled approximately every twenty-five years. Franklin calculated in 1751 that, if the expansion continued at such an

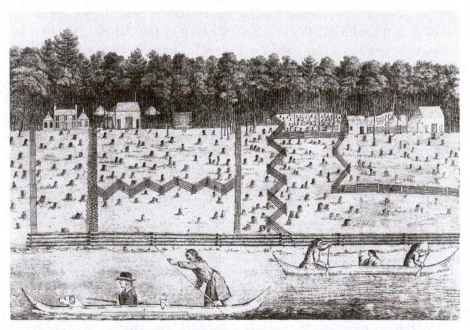

This engraving from the mid-eighteenth century depicts a vast clearing of trees whose stumps would either be pulled out or cultivated around. Rivers formed the colonists' and Indians' best means of travel and communication.

extraordinary rate for another century or so, "the greatest Number of Englishmen will be on this Side [of] the water." Not only was the total population increasing rapidly; it also was becoming more dispersed and heterogeneous. Each year witnessed the arrival of thousands of non-English Europeans. Most soon moved to the rugged western frontiers of Pennsylvania and the southern colonies.

Accurate population data from the colonial period are extremely difficult to find. The first national census did not occur until 1790. Still, various sources surviving from pre-Revolutionary times indicate quite clearly that the total white population of Britain's thirteen mainland colonies rose from about 250,000 in 1700 to 2,150,000 in 1770, an annual growth rate of 3 percent.

Few societies in recorded history have expanded so rapidly, and if the growth rate had not dropped substantially during the nineteenth and twentieth centuries, the current population of the United States would stand at well over one billion people. Natural reproduction was responsible for most of the growth. More families bore children who in turn lived long enough to have children of their own. Because of this sudden expansion, the population of the late colonial period was strikingly young; approximately one-half of the populace at any given time was under age 16.

In New England and the Chesapeake, the regions of oldest English settlement, natural increase contributed heavily to frontier expansion. Heirs of the first settlers employed established institutions and forms to extend familiar patterns of life and labor into new territory. This made for a great deal of homogeneity among the population of New England. In colonies further south, settlers from families long established in America shared territory with newcomers from the British Isles and the Continent of Europe. By contrast, chronic instability and repeated waves of epidemic disease inhibited the growth of Indian populations during this period.

9.1.1: Families, Land, and Movement in New England

In New England, the generous parcels of land granted to first-generation townspeople made it possible for most children and grandchildren to marry and raise families in the same communities as their parents. As many as three generations of fathers in towns such as Andover, Massachusetts, could divide family lands equally among sons while remaining confident that each would have enough to support his own family. Young people in New England often moved soon after marriage, but only a short distance away. They might remain within the same town, supporting their families on parcels that had earlier been set aside for future use, or move to a neighboring town where a father had managed to purchase additional lands. Ties of kinship and friendship kept most of these yeomen farming families close to their ancestral homes. So did the expectation of hardship in frontier settlements, where recurring outbreaks of warfare reminded colonists how dangerous the "howling wilderness" remained (see Chapters 7 and 8).

These patterns gradually changed during the eighteenth century as family parcels became too small to subdivide further and successive generations came to occupy the towns' reserve lands. A growing minority of young men found it necessary to move north to frontier lands along the Connecticut River or east to the forests of Maine. These frontier settlers usually carried with them a cash inheritance sufficient to purchase cheap frontier tracts large enough to sustain their own families in the same kind of landed independence that their parents had enjoyed. The governments of Massachusetts, Connecticut, and New Hampshire continued to regulate frontier settlement much as they had in the seventeenth century. By law, settlers had to cluster on home lots of 3 to 4 acres near twenty to thirty other families, forming communities for mutual support and protection. Once established, these communities could attract additional migrants as inhabitants wrote home to inform relatives about the progress of settlement and the availability of land. Such patterns of chain migration made many frontier towns virtual colonies of older communities near the coast.

Eighteenth-century expansion produced another kind of mobility in New England as a growing number of laboring poor began traveling the countryside in search of work. These mostly young people lacked the funds needed to obtain and cultivate frontier lands. They relied for support on temporary agricultural employment during planting and harvest, or on unskilled jobs in nearby towns. Some made their way to port towns such as Boston, Massachusetts; New London, Connecticut; or Newport, Rhode Island, where they found work on the docks or in warehouses and workshops. Some became sailors. Others with a farming background found themselves recruited by the proprietors of great estates along the Hudson River, who sought to develop their holdings by renting parcels to capable New England farmers on favorable terms.

9.1.2: Diversity and Growth in the Middle Colonies

The multiethnic population that had settled the Hudson and Delaware Valleys during the seventeenth century was multiplying rapidly in the early decades of the eighteenth century. In 1700, New York's nineteen thousand people remained the most ethnically diverse in British America, yet the colony's numbers were soon surpassed by more recently settled Pennsylvania, the fastest-growing English colony of the century.

The mid-colonial population was also extraordinarily mobile. In the first decades of the eighteenth century, modest Dutch farmers began migrating from the Hudson River valley to New Jersey. Many had supported Jacob Leisler in the upheavals of the early 1690s (see Chapter 7) and were now fleeing what they saw

as the corrupting influence of the increasingly Anglicized Dutch merchants of Albany and New York City. They were also responding to demographic pressures similar to those in coastal New England. The Dutch practice of dividing land inheritances equally among all children of the deceased gradually reduced average land parcels to sizes that could not sustain all heirs. Cheap New Jersey lands enabled Dutch migrants to re-create the rural, highly separatist communities that had evolved in New York during the seventeenth century.

The Dutch farming families of the Hackensack River valley in New Jersey established what one historian has described as a "domestically oriented hybrid adaptation to North American conditions." They built gambrel-roofed barns and houses influenced more by Friesian and Danish rather than Dutch traditions. Unlike English custom, a Dutch widow retained control of property when her husband died and inherited half the family estate, while Dutch daughters received inheritance portions equal to the sons. Dutch American children put wooden shoes outside their doors at Christmastime for Sinter Claes (now known as Santa Claus) to fill with presents. Dutch mothers taught their children to speak the Dutch language, read the Dutch Bible, sing Dutch hymns, and listen to Dutch Reformed sermons preached in the language of their homeland. New Jersey Dutch women and men soon drifted toward a radical brand of pietism that emphasized informal worship, simple singing of psalms, spontaneous prayer, and fiery preaching from charismatic ministers such as the Dutch immigrant Theodore Frelinghuysen.

Pennsylvania Quakers also developed a distinctive, child-centered pattern of domestic life on what one historian has described as "the most economically successful" family farms in colonial North America. Profits gleaned from the cultivation and sale of wheat on the Atlantic market enabled Quaker mothers and fathers to raise large families, rearing each child in an affectionate atmosphere of "holy conversation." By the early 1730s, the Quaker practice of bequeathing equal shares to each heir was reducing farm sizes, and this combined with rising property values was prompting a few third-generation Quaker sons and daughters to migrate south and west in search of cheaper, more abundant land. Others followed to escape the growing eighteenth-century consumer economy (see Chapter 10) whose temptations they feared would entice their children from lives of holy conversation.

Quaker migrants moved farther from their place of origin than migrants in New England. In the late 1720s, a small stream of Pennsylvania Quakers began exiting eastern Pennsylvania to establish new communities in North Carolina's Cape Fear region. One of those migrants was young Benjamin Franklin's first partner, Hugh Meredith, who left Philadelphia and the printing business in 1730 to return to farming in Cape Fear, "where land is cheap." The next year Franklin published in the *Pennsylvania Gazette* two letters written by Meredith to entice even more Quaker farmers to join the Cape Fear settlement. Similar unpublished correspondence from migrant Quaker communities in the Virginia Piedmont attracted single people and young families to leave Pennsylvania via the Great Wagon Road, which ran west and south along the Blue Ridge Mountains. Quaker migrants who arrived at these frontier destinations recreated the landed domesticity they had known in Pennsylvania.

This frenzy for land produced a degree of land ownership unmatched by the northern European countries from which the settlers had come, and which also contrasted with the much more urban societies of Spanish America. Rather than settle as artisans in the port cities or seek the types of farm leases many had held in Europe, new arrivals to British America aspired to own farms. This culture of ownership promised a level of economic security not easily found in their homelands. It also shaped patterns of settlement, exchange, and conflict with the land's original inhabitants. British officials pursued imperial agendas for fostering trade, exploiting resources, and conquering territory, but on the ground, ordinary families sought land above all else. This often set the colonists at odds with their own political and military leaders, who frequently pursued trade and military alliance with the very native groups on whose lands Anglo-American colonists were steadily encroaching. American Indians lost the frontier battle not because of Anglo-American armies, but because thousands of aggressive individuals pushed their way west to take possession of farmsteads. They often did so in outright defiance of the imperial officials who tried to prevent them.

9.1.3: From Tidewater to Piedmont: Expansion of the Chesapeake Colonies

The tobacco colonies of Virginia and Maryland expanded rapidly in the eighteenth century as the population grew and demand for tobacco rose. The skewed sex ratio of the seventeenth century had evened out considerably among Anglo-Americans, increasing the rate of marriages and births to a level comparable with that of New England. Eighteenth-century Virginia already boasted a total population greater than that of New England, and its rapid birthrate ensured that it would remain the most populous colony in British North America until well after the American Revolution. The children and grandchildren of small landholders, most of whom had come to the Chesapeake as servants, attempted like their New England counterparts to establish households near the place of their birth. By the early 1700s, however, the price of Tidewater land was prompting small landholders to sell out and move west toward the mountains or south toward the Carolinas, leaving the bulk of coastal plantations in the hands of some of the wealthiest Virginians.

Virginia's gentry also established the pattern for settlement of the Piedmont. Small planters who attempted to settle this region between the coast and the Blue Ridge Mountains often found that leading planters had beaten them to the choicest soil. During the late seventeenth century, families such as the Byrds and the Randolphs carved out vast western estates beyond the falls of the James River. They developed the best tracts into tobacco plantations; the rest they set aside for future development or sold to newcomers at a profit. Some great planters such as William Byrd II managed their western lands from Tidewater mansions, while others such as Thomas and Isham Randolph built imposing Piedmont estates. Other gentry families moved into the upper James River valley and intermarried with the Randolph clan, establishing in the process a powerful kinship network that maintained an unbreakable hold on the region.

The Randolph clan's grip on the upper James River was so tight that even royal officials had to look elsewhere for land. Lieutenant Governor Alexander Spotswood, one of eighteenth-century Virginia's most enterprising crown appointees, sought his landholding fortune in the more remote Rappahannock River valley. As the impecunious heir of an ancient but declining British family, Spotswood had to rely on his wits and the favor of well-placed English patrons to amass wealth commensurate with his aspirations. He exercised actual power in Virginia for twenty-seven years, thanks to the absentee governorship of George Hamilton, Earl of Orkney, who never visited the colony. Spotswood used his position as acting governor to acquire more than 83,000 acres—nearly 130 square miles—of land in the Piedmont and Shenandoah Valley, which he organized as Spotsylvania County in 1720. He also worked with allies in the Virginia government to secure passage of a law exempting settlers in new counties from taxes for ten years, while requiring all property holders to cultivate 3 acres out of every 50 in their possession or forfeit their claim.

Thanks to Spotswood, Virginia law promoted rapid settlement of the Piedmont while discouraging absentee speculators from buying up vast tracts but leaving them untouched for long periods. Those who acquired large patents of land either settled on them or parceled them out and sold them to small planters willing to move west for cheap lands. Even before 1730, some gentry families were establishing tobacco plantations of 1,000 to 15,000 acres near the Blue Ridge Mountains. Small planters also moved onto less desirable parcels of 100 to 500 acres, which they gradually cleared and planted in tobacco and grain. Lieutenant Governor Spotswood himself took a leading role in settling the region. He recruited miners to establish the fortified community of Germanna in the Shenandoah Valley, where they developed mines and ironworks for the governor. During his tenure, Spotswood also carved fifty-seven plantations out of his Piedmont and Shenandoah lands.

9.1.4: Slavery and Settlement

The larger Piedmont plantations could not have operated without the labor of African slaves. Planters brought many of the slaves on their western plantations from the Tidewater. They supplemented domestic slaves from time to time with "outlandish" slaves brought directly from Africa and a smaller percentage purchased from intercolonial trade with the British West Indies. The planters sought to maintain a roughly equal ratio of male to female slaves and usually permitted them to supplement their diet by cultivating their own garden plots. The favorable sex ratio and relatively good nutrition helped to promote slave marriages and child rearing, contributing to a steady growth in the African American population.

The population growth among African Americans on the Piedmont mirrored development in the Tidewater itself, where since as early as 1710 a relative parity between male and female slaves had made it possible for Chesapeake planters to meet at least some of their need for labor through the natural increase of the existing slave population. Early in the century, planters nevertheless imported large numbers of African slaves—almost thirty-five thousand between 1700 and 1740. Yet already in 1724, the Virginia clergyman Hugh Jones could comment that "the Negroes are not only encreased by fresh supplies from Africa and the West Indian Islands but also are very prolific among themselves." Although the planters continued to prefer purchasing male slaves from the Atlantic trade, the women who arrived survived in greater numbers than in the Caribbean. The proportion of women among the slave population grew steadily, enabling even more growth. By 1750, the number of African slaves had grown to about 40 percent of Virginia and Maryland's total population. Four-fifths of them were creoles born in the colony. Another 26,700 Africans arrived between 1740 and 1775, but after that date, Virginia planters relied almost entirely on the natural increase to supply their need for slave labor. The highest concentration of slaves remained in the Tidewater, with smaller percentages in the Piedmont.

Important though the slaves were to the development of a distinctive Virginian slaveholding society, the majority of eighteenth-century freeholding inhabitants of the Piedmont did not own slaves. Indeed, even the great majority of slaveholders owned no more than one or two slaves who helped to cultivate staple crops, tend livestock, clear land, and perform domestic chores. The largest landholders tended to distribute their slave workforce among several plantations, so that few estates held more than thirty-five slaves (see also Chapter 11).

9.1.5: The Lower South's Black Majority

The population of South Carolina lagged well behind that of the Chesapeake and northern colonies during the first third of the eighteenth century. It also constituted the only colony in mainland British North America where the majority population was of African rather than European descent. Indeed, in 1721, one year after South Carolina became a royal colony, census figures pegged the black population at nearly 12,000, 84 percent more than the 6,500 whites who inhabited the colony. Nearly a third of the slaves counted in that census were born in South Carolina. Epidemic disease and warfare stunted the growth of the white population until the 1720s, but during the following two decades the proportion of white colonists in the population gradually rose to about 40 percent of the total. Nevertheless, Africans remained in the majority throughout the colonial period.

South Carolina's black majority grew mainly by the forced immigration of slaves from Africa and the Caribbean. For a short time between 1690 and 1710, the population sustained itself through natural increase. As rice became the colony's staple, however, imports of African slaves rose dramatically. Between 1700 and 1740, nearly thirty-five thousand slaves arrived in the colony. More than half of that number—17,700—arrived in the 1730s alone. Slave imports dropped off dramatically in the next decade to only 1,580, but shot up again after 1750. Between 1750 and 1775, slave ships brought to South Carolina almost forty-five thousand black men and women in chains.

The predominance of African and creole slaves in the population impressed a permanent mark on all aspects of South Carolina's growth, including its westward expansion. One observer noted in the 1730s that "if one wishes to plant anything" on newly distributed western lands, "especially in the beginning when it must be cleared, it requires strong hand-work." Slaves and masters labored side by side in South Carolina forests, clearing fields, digging irrigation ditches, planting rice, tending livestock, cutting pine masts for ships, and rendering pine tar, pitch, rosin, and turpentine for naval stores.

White settlers relied on slave boatmen to transport goods and passengers from inland settlements to the coasts and to guide migrants to new plantations on the frontier. Slave militiamen also served as comrades in arms with their white masters during the frontier wars of the early eighteenth century, but rising concern about internal security eventually prompted masters to disarm their slaves (see Chapters 8 and 11).

9.1.6: Bondage and Death in the British West Indies

When considered in its proper Atlantic context, the self-sustaining nature of British North America's slave population was remarkable. Neither in the British West Indies nor in any other plantation colony in the Americas did the slave population begin growing through natural increase until the first third of the nineteenth century. To be sure, West Indian slave women and men formed temporary or enduring unions and produced offspring. But the fertility rate was low, and poor nutrition and tropical diseases took a heavy toll in infant mortality. Hard labor in often hazardous working conditions killed many slaves within seven years of their arrival on the islands. Consequently, the Caribbean slave population experienced not an increase, but a *depletion* rate of 2 to 4 percent annually.

Nevertheless, the British West Indian slave population grew dramatically during the eighteenth century, even as Euro-Caribbean numbers declined. Between 1700 and 1748, the total white population of all British Caribbean possessions rose from 31,000 to 43,900. At the same time, the total black population rose from 114,300 to 258,500. The distribution of the population throughout the British West Indies, already uneven at the beginning of the century, became even more skewed by 1750. While Barbados maintained a fairly steady ratio of one white to every three black slaves, the ratio in the Leeward Islands rose from one white to three blacks in 1700 to nearly one white to eight

blacks by 1748. In Jamaica, the shift in the ratio of whites to blacks was evident to Lieutenant Governor Thomas Handasyd as early as 1703. "Our number of Slaves Augments dayly," he wrote to the Board of Trade, "but to my great grief the Number of white men dayly decrease." Indeed, by 1748, the proportion of whites in Jamaica's population had decreased to less than one for every eleven blacks.

Of all the British sugar islands, Jamaica grew most dramatically during the eighteenth century. Barbados reached the practical limits of its growth during the first third of the century. The Leeward Islands took several years to recover from the depredations of the turn-of-the-century wars for empire (see Chapter 7), but by the 1750s, they too were approaching the limits of their growth. Jamaica's much larger size enabled more planters to build sugar estates, enlarge them, and staff them with more slaves every year throughout the eighteenth century. By 1748, Jamaica hosted a total population of 128,000—almost 42 percent of the entire British West Indian population—and produced 17,399 tons of sugar, about 42 percent of the sugar islands' total output. By the end of the century, Jamaica boasted a population of 402,700, well over twice that of Barbados and the Leewards combined, and produced 73,849 tons of sugar, almost 58 percent more than the other historic sugar islands.

The dramatic rise in the eighteenth-century slave population masked the terrible human cost of British West Indian slavery, since planters boosted their slave labor forces only by importing massive numbers to replace those who died. In Barbados between 1712 and 1734, for instance, only one slave baby was born for every six adult slaves who died. Other West Indian islands repeated the pattern to some degree. By century's end, British sugar planters had imported 1.6 million slaves to the Caribbean, yet the slave population of the sugar islands remained less than 600,000 (see also Chapter 11).

9.2: Convicts, Debtors, and Buffer Colony

9.2 Recount the events leading to the creation of the state of Georgia

The African slaves were not the only large group of people brought to the New World in bonds. During the eighteenth century, thousands of British convicts were transported to America. Still others signed contracts of indenture, choosing a term of servitude in the colonies to escape debtors' prison in England. By the early 1730s, the problem of indebtedness and bankruptcy was inspiring various proposals for reform. George Oglethorpe, an enterprising general and member of Parliament, managed to join this reforming impulse to an ambitious plan for grabbing additional territory from Spain. Parliament embraced Oglethorpe's scheme, and the colony of Georgia was born.

9.2.1: Convicts for America

In 1718, Parliament passed the Transportation Act, allowing judges in England, Scotland, and Ireland to send convicted felons to the American colonies. Between 1718 and 1775, the courts shipped approximately fifty thousand convicts across the Atlantic. Some of these men and women may actually have been dangerous criminals, but the majority seem to have committed minor crimes against property. Although transported convicts—almost 75 percent of whom were young males—escaped the hangman, they found life difficult in the colonies. Eighty percent of them were sold in the Chesapeake colonies as indentured servants. At best they faced an uncertain future, and it is probably not surprising that few former convicts prospered in America.

British authorities lavished praise on this system. According to one writer, transportation drained "the Nation of its offensive Rubbish, without taking away their Lives." Although Americans purchased the convict servants, they expressed fear that these men and women would create a dangerous criminal class. In one irate essay, Benjamin Franklin asked his readers to consider just how the colonists might repay the leaders of Great Britain for shipping so many felons to America. He suggested that rattlesnakes might be the appropriate gift. "I would propose to have them carefully distributed," Franklin wrote, "in the Gardens of all the Nobility and Gentry throughout the Nation; but particularly in the Gardens of the Prime Ministers, the Lords of Trade and Members of Parliament." The Revolution forced the British courts to redirect the flow of convicts to another part of the world; an indirect result of American independence was the founding of Australia by transported felons.

9.2.2: Fledgling Colony— The Founding of Georgia

The early history of Georgia was strikingly different from that of Britain's other mainland colonies. Its settlement was really an act of aggression against Spain, a country that had as good a claim to this area as did the English. During the eighteenth century, the two nations were often at war (see Chapters 8 and 12), and South Carolinians worried that the Spaniards moving up from bases in Florida would occupy the disputed territory between Florida and the Carolina grant.

The colony owed its existence primarily to James Oglethorpe, a British general and member of Parliament who believed that he could thwart Spanish designs on the area south of Charles Town while at the same time providing a fresh start for London's worthy poor, saving them from debtors' prison. Although Oglethorpe envisioned Georgia as an asylum as well as a garrison, the military aspects of his proposal were especially appealing to the leaders of the British government. In 1732, the king granted Oglethorpe and a board of trustees a charter for a new colony to be located between the Savannah and Altamaha

Rivers and from "sea to sea." The trustees living in the mother country were given complete control over Georgia politics, a condition the settlers soon found intolerable.

During the first years of colonization, Georgia fared no better than had earlier utopian experiments. The poor people of England showed little desire to move to an inclement frontier, and the trustees, in their turn, provided little incentive for emigration. Each colonist received only 50 acres. Another 50 acres could be added for each servant transported to Georgia, but in no case could a settler amass more than 500 acres. Moreover, land could be passed only to an eldest son, and if a planter had no sons at the time of his death, the holding reverted to the trustees. Slavery was prohibited. So too was rum.

Almost as soon as they arrived in Georgia, the settlers complained. The colonists demanded slaves, pointing out to the trustees that unless the new planters possessed an unfree labor force, they could not compete economically with their South Carolina neighbors. The settlers also wanted a voice in local government. In 1738, 121 people living in Savannah petitioned for fundamental reforms in the colony's constitution. Oglethorpe responded angrily, "The idle ones are indeed for Negroes. If the petition is countenanced, the province is ruined." The settlers did not give up. In 1741, they again petitioned Oglethorpe, this time addressing him as "our Perpetual Dictator."

While the colonists grumbled about various restrictions, Oglethorpe tried and failed to capture the Spanish fortress at Saint Augustine (1740). This personal disappointment coupled with the growing popular unrest destroyed his interest in Georgia. The trustees were forced to compromise their principles. In 1738, they eliminated all restrictions on the amount of land a man could own and allowed women to inherit land. In 1750, they permitted the settlers to import slaves. Soon Georgians could drink rum. In 1751, the trustees returned Georgia to the king, undoubtedly relieved to be free of what had become a hard-drinking, slave-owning plantation society much like that in South Carolina. The king authorized an assembly in 1751, but even with these social and political changes, Georgia attracted very few new settlers.

9.3: "Bettering Their Condition": Eighteenth-Century Immigration

9.3 Report the increase in ethnic diversity of Britain's North American's colonies

Between 1700 and 1775, more than 250,000 immigrants arrived from the European Continent and the British Isles. The flow of immigrants ebbed and surged periodically as events prompted people to look beyond the localities of their birth for opportunities to improve their prospects. All over western Europe and the British Isles, warfare and economic change were prompting people to move from the countryside to growing coastal cities as well as to farming and grazing lands in central and eastern Europe. Those who crossed the Atlantic represented only a fraction of this vast movement of people. Yet their decision to embark for British America prompted important shifts in the character of Atlantic shipping and increased the ethnic diversity of Great Britain's North American colonies.

9.3.1: The North Atlantic Passage

A person or family considering a voyage to the New World had to confront legal, financial, and psychological obstacles. A decision to embark for America carried migrants and their families across thousands of miles of ocean, far from familiar networks of kinship and community.

Migrants from continental Europe had to transfer their loyalty to a new sovereign. Those from the Continent and Ireland alike often faced opposition at home from local rulers and landlords whose wealth depended heavily on their ability to retain people who would work the land and pay the required dues, taxes, or rents. The high price of passage posed yet another obstacle. Fares to North America ranged from £5 to £8—a sum well beyond the means of many who wanted to go. Merchants and shippers extended credit to those who could not pay in advance, but on terms that required payment soon after arrival at their destinations. Such people often became redemptioners, indentured servants whose American masters paid their passage in exchange for four to seven years' labor. Many redemptioners initially took passage on credit in hopes that friends or relatives in America would help them pay but were sold when their American contacts failed to come through for them.

Prospective immigrants braved these daunting obstacles for a variety of reasons. Some were refugees of war or famine. In 1709–1710, for instance, thousands of "Palatines" from the region of the upper Rhine River migrated down the river to escape wartime devastation and crop failures. English officials eventually sent 2,500 of them on to New York and the Carolinas. Twenty years later, a severe famine in Ireland prompted more than five thousand Scotch-Irish to flee to British North America. Similar outbreaks of war and famine sent additional surges to America in every decade after 1730.

Dim economic prospects in Europe or the British Isles, coupled with reports of cheap land and generous wages in America, prompted many others to take the trip. Promotional literature often exaggerated North America's promise, but migrants could often verify the reports for themselves against firsthand accounts from relatives who had gone before. German farmers and artisans who labored under heavy taxes and hidebound local regulations took hope in letters from family members painting America as a place where they could "buy, settle and borrow without restrictions" and "all trades and professions are free." Scotch-Irish tenant weavers, though not as strapped as many Germans, found appealing the prospect of becoming freeholders themselves. All immigrants took cheer in reports of Anglo-American religious toleration.

The volume of European migrants seeking passage to America prompted eighteenth-century merchants and shippers to adapt to the demand. They refitted vessels to accommodate more passengers and provisions, hoping to reap profits greater than they could expect by shipping trade goods alone. Many shipowners employed agents—often successful migrants or "newlanders" who received free return passage from America in exchange for their service—to travel the countryside recruiting migrants to sail for America on their employers' vessels. Owners' preoccupation with the bottom line often prompted them to crowd on too many passengers and to stock the ship with provisions of poor quality or insufficient quantity for the voyage.

Cramped quarters and spoiled provisions often made the voyage to America difficult to endure, especially when compounded with rough weather conditions. Passengers crowded into tiny compartments whose bunks or hammocks measured no larger than 6 feet by 18 inches, piling all their chests and baggage around them to prevent theft. Those located between decks had to stoop constantly to avoid hitting their heads on the low ceilings. Parents squeezed together in the small bunks with any children under the age of 5, while older children shared half a bunk with a sibling or another passenger close in age. Single passengers were assigned berths with no consistent effort to segregate them by sex. In good weather, passengers could go up to the main deck and exercise, socialize, and take their meals. During a storm, however, all had to remain below with the hatches and portholes battened down.

Cramped quarters remained a constant feature of transatlantic voyages, but other conditions on board vessels could vary widely. A harsh captain or a rough voyage could make life miserable even on a well-fitted and provisioned vessel, while a smooth, quick passage could at least mitigate the misery on a poorly fitted one. The dyspeptic German observer Gottfried Mittelberger complained that his ship to America was "full of pitiful signs of distress—smells, fumes, horrors, vomiting, various kinds of sea sickness, fever, dysentery" and worse, all caused by the "age and highly salted state of the food" and the "very bad and filthy water." A Huguenot immigrant remembered a much happier voyage during which "the women, the young girls, and the young children gathered on deck almost every day for diversion."

Arrival in an American port brought relief to the passengers and excitement onshore. Crowds of prospective masters gathered to bid for immigrants "exposed for redemption sale." Fellow countryfolk already settled in America came on board to refresh expected relatives and friends with bread, fruit, and beer or to glean news and collect letters from home. Paying passengers settled accounts and gathered belongings, while those sailing on credit tried to arrange for payment or prepared themselves for terms of servitude. Customs collectors checked the cargo for smuggled goods, while health officials inspected the passengers for signs of infectious disease or scurvy. Non-British passengers then made their way to the courthouse, where English officials required them to take the oath of allegiance to the king and his successors, renounce any allegiance to the Pope, and abide by the laws of the colony where they were settling. Afterward, immigrants could complete whatever arrangements they needed to begin a new life in America.

9.3.2: Ethnic Diversity in the Backcountry

Newly arrived immigrants had come to America in the hope of obtaining their own property and setting up as independent farmers. They found land abundantly available in the backcountry, a region stretching approximately 800 miles from western Pennsylvania to Georgia. Although they planned to follow customs they had known in Europe, they found the challenge of surviving on the British frontier far more demanding than they had anticipated. They plunged into a complex, fluid, often violent society that included large numbers of Native Americans and African Americans as well as other Europeans.

The largest group of newcomers consisted of Scotch-Irish. The experiences of these people in Great Britain influenced not only their decision to move to the New World but also their behavior once they arrived. During the seventeenth century, English rulers thought they could thoroughly dominate Catholic Ireland by transporting thousands of lowland Scottish Presbyterians to the northern region of that war-torn country. The plan failed. English officials who were members of the Anglican church discriminated against the Presbyterians. They passed laws that placed the Scotch-Irish at a severe disadvantage when they traded in England; they taxed them at exorbitant rates. After several poor harvests, many of the Scotch-Irish elected to emigrate to America, where they hoped to find the freedom and prosperity that had been denied in Ireland. "I have seen some of their letters to their friends here [Ireland]," one British agent reported in 1729, ". . . in which after they set forth and recommend the fruitfulness and commodities of the country [America], they tell them, that if they will but carry over a little money with them, they may for a small sum purchase considerable tracts of land." It is estimated that 150,000 Scotch-Irish migrated to the colonies before the Revolution.

Most Scotch-Irish immigrants landed initially in Philadelphia, but instead of remaining in that city, they carved out farms on Pennsylvania's western frontier. The colony's proprietors welcomed the influx of new settlers, for it seemed that they would form an ideal barrier between the Indians and the older, coastal communities.

The Penn family soon had second thoughts, however. The Scotch-Irish squatted on whatever land looked best, and when colony officials pointed out that large tracts had already been reserved, the immigrants retorted that "it was against the laws of God and nature that so much land should be idle when so many Christians wanted it to labour on and to raise their bread." Wherever they located, the Scotch-Irish challenged established authority.

A second large body of non-English settlers, more than 100,000 people, came from the upper Rhine Valley, the German Palatinate. Some of the migrants, especially those who relocated to America around the turn of the century, belonged to small pietistic Protestant sects whose religious views were somewhat similar to those of the Quakers. These Germans moved to the New World primarily in the hope of finding religious toleration. Under the guidance of Francis Daniel Pastorius (1651–1720), a group of Mennonites established in Pennsylvania a prosperous community known as Germantown.

By mid-century, however, the characteristics of the German migration had begun to change. Large numbers of Lutherans transferred to the Middle Colonies. Unlike members of the pietistic sects, these men and women were not in search of religious freedom. Rather, they traveled to the New World looking to better their material lives. The Lutheran church in Germany initially tried to maintain control over the distant congregations, but even though the migrants themselves fiercely preserved many aspects of traditional German culture, they were eventually forced to accommodate to new social conditions. Henry Melchior Mühlenberg (1711–1787), a tireless leader, helped German Lutherans through a difficult cultural adjustment. In 1748, Mühlenberg organized a meeting of local pastors and lay delegates that ordained ministers of their own choosing, an act of spiritual independence that has been called "the most important single event in American Lutheran history."

The German migrants—mistakenly called Pennsylvania Dutch because the English confused deutsch (meaning "German") with Dutch ("a person from Holland")—began reaching Philadelphia in large numbers after 1717. By 1766, persons of German stock accounted for more than one-third of Pennsylvania's total population. Even their most vocal detractors admitted the Germans were the best farmers in the colony.

Ethnic differences in Pennsylvania bred disputes. The Scotch-Irish as well as the Germans preferred to live with people of their own background, and they sometimes fought to keep members of the other nationality out of their neighborhoods. The English were suspicious of both groups. They could not comprehend why the Germans insisted on speaking German in America. In 1753, for example, Franklin described these settlers as "the most stupid of their nation." He warned that "unless the stream of [German] importation could be turned from this to other colonies … they will soon outnumber us…. [and] all the advantages we have, will in my opinion, be not able to preserve our language, and even our government will become precarious."

Such prejudice may have persuaded members of both groups to search for new homes. After 1730, Germans and Scotch-Irish pushed south from western Pennsylvania into the Shenandoah Valley, thousands of them settling in the backcountry of Virginia and the Carolinas. The Germans usually remained wherever they found unclaimed fertile land. By contrast, the Scotch-Irish often moved two or three times, acquiring a reputation as a rootless people.

Wherever the newcomers settled, they often found themselves living beyond the effective authority of the various colonial governments. To be sure, backcountry residents petitioned for assistance during wars against the Indians, but most of the time they preferred to be left alone. These conditions heightened the importance of religious institutions within the small ethnic communities.

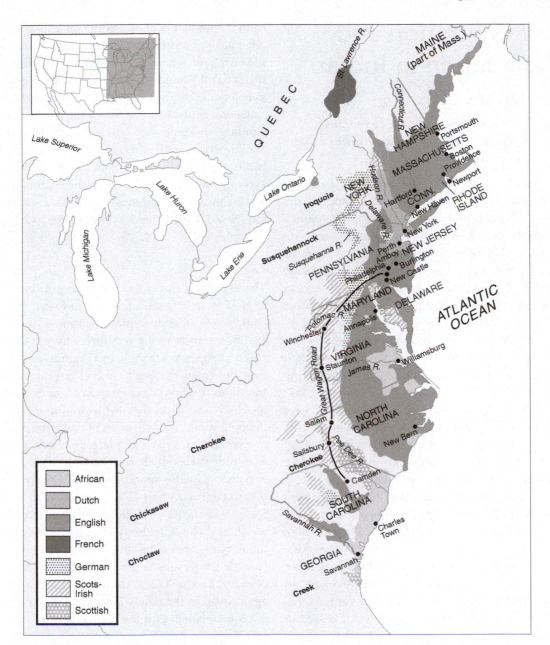

Map 9.1 Ethnic Groups in America

Although the original stimulus for coming to America may have been a desire for economic independence and prosperity, backcountry families—especially the Scotch-Irish—flocked to evangelical Protestant preachers, to Presbyterian, Baptist, and, later, Methodist ministers who not only fulfilled the settlers' spiritual needs but also gave these scattered backcountry communities a pronounced moral character that survived long after the colonial period.

9.4: Migration and Adaptation in Indian Country

9.4 Summarize how the native Indians adapted to the westward advance of the Europeans

The rapid westward movement of Europeans after Queen Anne's War brought dramatic changes to eighteenth-century native peoples. The permanent presence of conflicting, expansive European empires shaped the terms of encounter far more decisively than they had done in the seventeenth century. Native Americans had to adapt flexibly and quickly to a constantly shifting situation. They had to develop new strategies of trade, diplomacy, and warfare to cope with an expanding European population, to stem the decline of their own numbers, and to maintain their self-determination. Some accomplished this demanding task superbly, not only recovering from earlier losses but even strengthening their position in the contest for land and influence. Those who failed became absorbed into stronger groups or wound up on tiny reservations in a now-alien land.

During the 1720s and 1730s, the site of the most intense and creative contact between Europeans and Indians shifted to the cis-Mississippian west, that is, to the huge territory between the Appalachian Mountains and the Mississippi River, where several hundred thousand Native Americans made their homes. As in the previous century, contact brought unintended consequences. Contagious disease, for instance, continued to take a fearful toll. In the southern backcountry between 1685 and 1790, the Indian population dropped an astounding 72 percent. In the Ohio Valley, the numbers suggest similar rates of decline. Intermittent conflict between natives and Europeans only exacerbated the losses.

Yet Indians experienced more than dispossession and decline. Many formed new communities from the remnants of old. Some relocated to take advantage of more abundant game and more fertile farmland. Their location between competing British and French empires gave many groups new leverage in negotiating favorable terms for trade and protection. As the century progressed, similar experiences of European encroachment and imperial conflict prompted leaders of various bands and nations to overcome ancient divisions and forge new kinds of unities, the beginnings of a self-conscious awareness of a shared set of interests and identity across traditional ethnic lines.

9.4.1: Indian Pioneers

The experience of migration was nothing new to Native Americans. Members of many nations could recite legends of mass relocation from distant homelands to the territories they occupied when Europeans arrived, and linguistic analysis has confirmed the essential truth of many such traditions. De Soto's exploration of the Southeast in the sixteenth century set in motion cycles of depopulation, reconstitution of new groups, and movement from place to place that only intensified after the English arrived in 1607. Iroquois expansion in the seventeenth and early eighteenth centuries had cleared areas such as the Susquehanna River valley, the Carolina Piedmont, and the Allegheny Plateau of long-time inhabitants. Shawnees and Delawares moved in to settle the Susquehanna in the late seventeenth century. By the 1720s, they were on the move again, even as the newly formed Catawba nation of western North Carolina took possession of former Tuscarora land.

The first substantial Delaware trek beyond the Appalachians took place in 1724, when the headman Sassoonan led his people to found Kittanning on the banks of the Allegheny River in what is now western Pennsylvania. Sassoonan's people took this momentous step to escape European encroachments that were thinning out their game and chipping away at their lands on the

Schuylkill River near Philadelphia. Sassoonan's band finally sold their remaining eastern lands to the Pennsylvania agent James Logan and settled permanently on the Allegheny Plateau. Shawnees from the Susquehanna Valley soon followed, while crop failures and shortages of game pushed Senecas southwest into the region from their homelands near western Lake Ontario.

The rapid influx of European settlers into Pennsylvania pressed additional Delaware bands to sell out and move west. Since the Delawares possessed no centralized leadership or confederacy, each headman conducted independent negotiations with Pennsylvania agents. Agents often took advantage of individual headmen's greed, styling them "kings of the Delaware" and enticing them to trade their people's farming and hunting grounds for goods, rum, and status. Shawnee and Iroquois observers soon complained that Delaware leaders were allowing their land to "pass through their guts" in the form of rum.

Agents also capitalized on ambiguities in the terms of exchange. In the infamous "Walking Purchase" of 1737, for instance, James Logan gained title to a huge tract of Delaware territory in the Lehigh Valley through a clause that specified one boundary as extending as far north from a point near Trenton as a man could walk in a day and a half. To the Delawares, the expression denoted a journey of that length at a normal traveling pace, perhaps 15 miles on foot. Logan, however, cleared a path through the woods and hired three tall and specially trained walkers to pace off a 60-mile northward boundary. A second line from the termination point eastward to the Delaware River, fully 65 miles away, completed a triangle that encompassed all Delaware villages in the area. Logan set aside a paltry 10 square miles of the land for a Delaware reservation and began selling the rest to incoming English and German settlers. The original inhabitants protested the landgrab repeatedly until 1762, when they finally relinquished all claims in exchange for additional concessions from Pennsylvania.

Although the Delawares and Shawnees possessed insufficient strength or unity to resist European encroachment onto their eastern lands, they did manage to carry familiar forms of social organization and cultural practice to their new homes in the Ohio Country. They quickly established patterns of community life as familiar to them as were the barns, fences, and crops to the Europeans who built and farmed on former native land. Delaware towns such as Kittanning consisted of multiple clustered settlements, each identified with a prominent headman, an arrangement much like that of eastern Delaware communities. Shawnee settlements such as Sewikaley's Town and Seneca communities such as Aliquippa's Town similarly reflected traditional forms of organization. Town inhabitants plied traditional farming and hunting practices, trading skins and furs for European goods, which they incorporated into traditional patterns of use.

During the next several decades, the towns of the Allegheny Plateau attracted additional migrants who shared connections of kinship and ethnicity. Other Indian refugees also drifted to the region, often joining multiethnic communities of farmers, hunters, and traders such as Shamokin and Logg's Town. The various groups forged webs of formal and informal relations among one another and nearby Indian nations that contributed to a common regional identity. The resources controlled by these Ohio Indians made them coveted trading partners of English from Pennsylvania as well as French from Quebec. As long as they remained united, the Ohio Indians could play the two European powers against each other to maintain their own independence.

9.4.2: Persisting Indian Power

The native peoples of the Ohio Country managed to gain by migration a degree of power similar to that enjoyed by their Indian neighbors to the north and south. Increasingly during the eighteenth century, the key to maintaining influence and self-determination lay in native groups' access to French as well as English resources and their ability to play the interests of one against the other. The possibility that a powerful Indian nation could join the French to drive back British settlement made officials in London and the colonies more solicitous of Indian interests. "The prosperity of our Colonies on the Continent," the British official Edmund Atkin observed in 1755, "will stand or fall with our Interest and favour among [the Indians]. While they are our Friends, they are the Cheapest and strongest Barrier for the Protection of our Settlements; when Enemies, they are capable ... to render those Possessions almost useless."

The Iroquois capitalized on this dynamic to replenish numbers lost in the devastating imperial wars of the 1690s as well as to compensate for loss of influence in the west (see Chapters 7 and 8). The Iroquois Confederacy turned south, where the presence of weaker nations presented an opportunity for them to capture adoptees through a fresh round of mourning wars. Even if they had been inclined to do so, British colonial officials could seldom have intervened in these wars. The Iroquois wielded substantial military might, and the English could not afford to risk action that might drive them into the arms of the French governor at Quebec. Furthermore, the extension of Iroquois authority over other frontier Indians served British interests by reducing the number of native political entities with which they had to negotiate.

Eighteenth-century Iroquois expansion often proceeded with the nervous blessing of British officials. One of the century's earliest examples was the incorporation of the Tuscaroras after 1713 (see Chapter 8), a move that enlarged the Iroquois Confederacy to Six Nations and augmented Iroquois fighting strength with warriors who possessed detailed knowledge of the southern terrain. Other acts of expansion soon followed. Pennsylvania officials made the Iroquois overlords of all other native peoples within the colony's boundaries by a peculiar interpretation of the Anglo-Iroquois Albany Treaty of 1722. "The Five Nations ... have included you" in the treaty, James Logan declared to Pennsylvania's Delaware and Conoy people, "and have obligded you to observe it as well as themselves." The Iroquois did not hesitate to exert this newfound influence over additional tributary peoples when it suited their interests. They also took advantage of access to markets in Philadelphia to negotiate more favorable terms of trade with competing merchants in New York and Quebec.

British colonial competition for Iroquois trade proved advantageous to the Five Nations as well, because it gave them leverage to negotiate better terms for their goods. Iroquois spokespersons made it their business to know the relative value of trade items in various markets, and cited prices offered by a rival colony's traders in an effort to obtain the same price nearby. Other nations within the Five Nations' orbit followed suit. "Our Brethren the Mingoes [western Iroquois] got so great a price for their Skins" at Albany "that I am ashamed to tell them how small a price the Delawares get from you," the headman Sassoonan declared to a Pennsylvania council in 1740. "We hope you will Allow Us something of a better price for the future."

The Iroquois reach extended further south during the eighteenth century than ever before, but they reached their limit at the edge of Catawba territory in the Carolina Piedmont. This powerful, warlike nation had emerged in the first decades of the eighteenth century as a disparate core of remnant peoples absorbed other refugees of the period's vicious warfare (see Chapter 8). By the early 1730s, the Catawbas had even managed to absorb whole bands of neighboring weaker peoples through cajoling and veiled threats. In the process they acquired a reputation as fearsome fighters among the English and other Indian nations alike. The Catawbas earned implacable hatred from the

Iroquois as "disorderly … Irregular … false … and deceitful People" so treacherous they had even murdered Iroquois peace envoys in cold blood.

South Carolinians anxiously courted Catawba cooperation to serve as a "Bulwark at our Backs" as well as a barrier to slave escape. Indeed, one South Carolina official argued that without the Catawbas, runaway slaves might well "get to a head in the Woods and prove as mischevious a thorn in our sides as the fugitive Slaves in Jamaica did in theirs." Catawbas could not stop the flow of runaways completely, and reports of runaway "maroon communities" in the Carolina forests persisted throughout the eighteenth century. Nevertheless, South Carolinians' need for native allies ensured a constant stream of diplomatic traffic between Catawba towns and Charleston to maintain good relations. Catawbas held their own in these exchanges, extracting important concessions from South Carolina officials that enabled them to preserve their independence into the 1760s.

9.4.3: The "Five Civilized Tribes" Take Shape

Native peoples to the south and west of the Catawbas were also struggling during the eighteenth century to cope with loss of population and encroachment of European settlers. Like the Iroquois, these groups occupied a territory between competing European imperial powers and were able to use that position to some advantage in their quest for continuing self-determination. In contrast to the Six Nations, however, native peoples of the Southeast began to coalesce into multiple confederacies that often clashed with one another as well as with French and English colonists. In the decades after Queen Anne's War, the largest and most influential of these groups began a process of economic, social, and political adaptation to their new situation. These adaptations gradually gave shape to powerful native nations that, by the early nineteenth century, European Americans were calling the "Five Civilized Tribes."

In the 1730s and 1740s, the balance of power in the southeastern backcountry shifted increasingly to the towns of the Cherokees as Catawba strength began to ebb while the French pressed north and east from the Gulf of Mexico and the Mississippi River valley. Cherokees themselves struggled to maintain their strength in the face of intermittent warfare and epidemic disease. A smallpox epidemic in 1739 caused "a most depopulating shock" among the Cherokee villages, and their numbers continued to decline until the Revolution. The changing demographics, combined with pressure from the competing Creek Confederacy, prompted some Cherokee bands to relocate northward into areas where Europeans were also settling. The intersection of Cherokee and European migration gave rise to intercultural environments such as the Long Cane settlement of western South Carolina, where European settlers farmed and raised cattle while Cherokees continued to hunt in nearby forests. Yet the Cherokees' grip on the strategic Upper Towns of the western Carolinas and Georgia—a territory South Carolina's governor James Glen (g. 1743–1756) regarded as "the Key of Carolina"—gave them the power to inflict costly casualties in times of war and to extract generous concessions in exchange for peace.

Increasing contact with Europeans prompted Cherokee people to adapt in a variety of ways. The power Cherokee women enjoyed within their villages enabled them to play a decisive role in the process of adaption. Native women often decided whether or not to go to war and usually determined the fate of wartime captives. As warfare and disease reduced Cherokee numbers, village matrons increasingly chose to adopt the newcomers. This contributed greater ethnic diversity as villages incorporated fugitive groups of Natchez and Creeks as well as European and African captives. Women's control of village trade sometimes prompted them to marry French or English traders to strengthen their competitive advantage in the market for European goods. These marriages introduced conflict between European patriarchy and Cherokee matriarchy. Over time, women's influence gradually eroded in some aspects of domestic and social life, but Cherokee women continued to exercise political authority throughout the colonial period. The *métis* offspring of Cherokee-white unions often possessed intense loyalty to their Cherokee clans and villages as well as an intimate knowledge of European ways. Some *métis* took advantage of their dual identity to become powerful brokers in Anglo-Cherokee trade and diplomacy, whereas others repudiated their European identity and took leading roles in resisting further colonization.

To the west of the Cherokee towns the Chickasaws still thrived in a region they had occupied since well before de Soto's expedition in the 1540s (see Chapter 1). This powerful group's position near the Mississippi River, within easy striking distance of both New Orleans and the Illinois country, made them critical allies of the English. One English observer called them the "Spartans" of southeastern Indian peoples because they made "martial virtue, and not riches" their "only standard of preferment." The Chickasaws proved their military prowess by dealing repeated, often humiliating losses to French forces and their Indian allies between 1720 and 1763. South Carolina governors labored to keep these powerful allies well supplied with cheap British arms and trade goods. English horses supplemented stock acquired from trans-Mississippi Indian tribes to give the Chickasaws a mounted force of raiders who could strike French and Indian targets from north of the Ohio to the Gulf Coast. English-supplied African slaves became dependent laborers for Chickasaw patrons, bearing burdens and working fields. Over time, enslaved African laborers became a permanent element of Chickasaw society.

The Chickasaws' enemies to the south, the Choctaws, also depended on horses to wage warfare, carry trade goods, and herd the cattle that by the 1730s had become a part of the Choctaw economy. Like the Chickasaw, the Choctaw received some of their first horses from trans-Mississippi Indian traders who had captured or traded them from the Spanish or had domesticated them from wild herds descended from Spanish stock. Choctaw cattle also derived from Spanish stock that since de Soto's expeditions had roamed rich southeastern river bottoms along with deer and buffalo. Both animals took on increasing importance in Choctaw life during the eighteenth century. Indeed, Choctaws imparted a sacred significance to horses in funeral rituals by sacrificing and feasting on the horses of a deceased village member.

The French relied on this ancient and numerous people—at twenty thousand members the largest unified group in the region—to counter English influence in the Southeast. French officials kept Choctaw warriors well supplied with arms and encouraged them to raid Chickasaw villages. Yet the enticement of cheap English goods drew an increasing number of Choctaw bands into an Anglo-Chickasaw orbit toward the middle of the eighteenth century despite the unscrupulous practices of many English traders. Only by preserving a reputation for "good faith in trading" were the French able to keep most of their Choctaw allies "attach[ed] to our side."

East of the Choctaws, the powerful Creek Confederacy was taking shape, but its position between empires was proving a mixed blessing. In contrast to other southeastern groups, the Confederacy actually grew in numbers during the eighteenth century by uniting several surrounding bands into a loose, consensual coalition, adopting native refugees, and incorporating runaway slaves from South Carolina and Georgia. This confederacy embraced the Creek name, which the English had habitually applied to all the tribes of the Deep South. The common name, however, belied deep internal divisions. English-leaning factions enjoyed access to better trade goods at cheaper prices than did factions favoring the French. The only exception was in firearms, whose weight made them more difficult for English traders to transport. French control of the waterways enabled them to transport firearms to Creek and other native trading partners. As a result, French weapons helped fuel a conflict among Creek factions until the 1750s, when native leaders finally secured peace.

Like other groups, the Creeks had to adjust to rapid westward migration of Europeans. By the 1750s, Georgia ranchers had begun moving into Creek hunting grounds with domestic cattle that drove off the bear and displaced the deer. Creeks initially protested, but soon began adjusting both their approach to property and their way of life. Some Creeks began acquiring and herding cattle themselves, a practice which prompted them to begin incorporating European ideas of property. Leading Creek cattlemen were often children of a mixed European and Creek marriage such as the famous Revolutionary-era headman Alexander McGillivray, who understood both worlds but remained loyal to his native kin. These and other Creek ranchers incorporated progressively more European ways of life, soon building plantations and acquiring slaves.

Successive groups of Creeks also migrated south during the eighteenth century into the depopulated lands of Florida, where they herded wild cattle introduced by Spanish missionaries of the previous century. Over time, these bands of people whom the Spanish called *cimmarónes*, or wild men, developed a distinct identity as Seminoles. The Seminoles obtained their living as cattlemen, fishermen, and hunters. They also developed a significant trade with Cuba, lading large cypress canoes with deerskins, dried fish, and honey and then crossing the Gulf of Mexico to trade in Havana for Spanish consumer goods.

9.4.4: Horses, Raiders, and Traders: Native Mobility on the Great Plains

The dramatic changes overtaking the world between the Appalachians and the Mississippi were not confined to the great river's eastern banks. The peoples who occupied the hills and plains beyond were also experiencing a transformation in their ways of life. Native pioneers were pushing west across the river into plains hunting grounds as eastern game became scarce and European settlers occupied traditional lands. Mounted native raiders from the Rocky Mountains were sweeping east and south into what is now Kansas, Oklahoma, and Texas in search of captives and game.

Even in the Great Lakes region, where pressure from European colonists was remote, overhunting of deer and fur-bearing animals prompted groups like the Ojibwas and Crees to range further west into the Cheyenne and Lakota Sioux hunting grounds of what is now Minnesota. French weapons gave the Ojibwa sufficient military advantage to drive their enemies west, where the Sioux began hunting buffalo in what is now the Dakotas and Nebraska. The Cheyenne followed buffalo herds even further west to present-day eastern Wyoming and Colorado. Mounted Comanche raiders rode out from traditional homelands in the foothills of the Colorado Rockies to harass not only Cheyenne hunters but also groups as far south as Texas. Shoshones also moved east on horseback from traditional homelands in the Great Basin, but moved back to the Rockies later in the eighteenth century as more eastern groups arrived on the plains. A large group of Hidatsas migrated westward from the Big Bend of the Missouri River to form a new life as the Crow people of what is now northern Montana.

In the Southwest, competition between the French and the Spanish for native trade intensified as outposts established in the aftermath of

Queen Anne's War began to thrive. In Texas, San Antonio began drawing Apache farmers to settle nearby where they could gain access to Spanish goods and military defense against Comanche raiders. El Paso, Santa Fe, and Taos provided similar havens for Pueblo farmers, many of whom, ironically, were seeking defense against mounted Apache raiders who celebrated the horses on which they rode as gifts of Apache gods. French Louisiana's Red River trading village of Natchitoches attracted native migrants such as the Caddoes and the Wichitas from plains homelands hundreds of miles to the west. Other French outposts along the Arkansas and Missouri Rivers enticed similar migrant communities to gain advantages in European trade against native competitors.

The peoples of the trans-Mississippi West were experiencing a burst of migratory activity almost unprecedented in its speed and scope, one that transformed the landscape and settlement patterns of the entire Great Plains in less than one hundred years. The world Lewis and Clark encountered in their famous expedition of 1804 was not the pristine result of thousands of years of natural development, as people continued to believe until well into the twentieth century. Rather, it was a product of the very recent past, an environment shaped by creative human adaptations to often wrenching eighteenth-century events and conditions.

9.5: Worlds of Motion

9.5 Examine effects of the expansion of the European territory into the American west in the eighteenth century

In 1761, the Quaker itinerant John Woolman paid a visit to a Delaware band who lived "on the east branch of the river Susquehanna." As he journeyed, Woolman meditated on the change in circumstances native peoples had experienced since the coming of Europeans.

In some places natives had sold fertile, well-watered lands with easy river access "for trifling considerations," Woolman mused, whereas in other places they had been "driven back by superior force." Many now lived so far away that they had to "pass over mountains, swamps, and barren deserts, where travelling is very troublesome in bringing their furs and skins to trade with us." The expansion of European settlements and hunting had also produced drastic ecological change, reducing the numbers of "wild beasts which the natives chiefly depend on for subsistence." Indeed, Woolman lamented, "people too often, for the sake of gain," induced the natives to "waste their skins and furs in purchasing a liquor which tends to the ruin of them and their families."

Woolman observed only a portion of the many far-reaching effects of eighteenth-century expansion. Not all Indians allowed their lands to "pass through their guts" in the form of liquor. Intense imperial conflict enabled many native groups to consolidate their hold on territory and power. But Europeans did keep pressing westward across the Atlantic to North America's eastern shores and from those shores into the Appalachian Mountains, transforming the continent into a world of swirling motion stirred by interrelated currents of growth and migration.

The variety of eighteenth-century North American experience defies easy generalization. The striking differences that had developed among Anglo-American colonies during the seventeenth century were now complemented by increasing ethnic and racial diversity within. Yet as European observers surveyed North America's rapid growth, they could not help recognizing its commercial and political significance. Its diverse population could secure crucial territory in the great contest for empire. It also offered European merchants and manufacturers a market for consumer goods that had become too big to ignore.

Chronology

1700	British colonial mainland population at 250,000
1710	Palatines arrive in New York
1718	Passage of Transportation Act authorizing transport of convicts to America
1720	Pennsylvania Quaker migrants establish settlements in Cape Fear region of North Carolina; Spottswood County organized in Shenandoah Valley
1721	South Carolina's black population at 12,000, whites at 6,500
1724	Sassoonan founds Kittanning on Allegheny River
1728	Famine pushes Scotch-Irish immigrants to America
1732	James Oglethorpe founds Georgia
1737	"Walking Purchase" sparks tension between Pennsylvania English and Delawares
1750	Slavery permitted in Georgia
1748	American Lutheran ministers ordained in Philadelphia
1770	British colonial mainland population at 2,150,000

Chapter 10
The Anglicization of Provincial America

 ## Learning Objectives

10.1 Report the wave of fashion and sophistication that defined class and status in the Atlantic

10.2 Compare American Enlightenment with European Enlightenment

10.3 Evaluate how the Awakening altered the future course of American history

10.4 Examine how the American Awakening, way of life, and beliefs influenced the native Indians

In the summer of 1744, the physician Alexander Hamilton—no relation to the more famous first Secretary of the Treasury—set out Annapolis, Maryland, to tour the colonies for his "health and recreation." This successful Scottish immigrant valued "polite conversation" as well as the finest English luxuries. In a burgeoning consumer-oriented world, which measured class and status by how a person dressed or spoke, Hamilton judged those he met on the road by a new set of cosmopolitan tastes that was then sweeping through the Atlantic World. Few colonists fared well against such exacting standards. Most of those Hamilton met on his 1,600-mile journey dressed poorly, smelled badly, ate barbarously, sprinkled their English with regional colloquialisms, or spoke with heavy accents.

Hamilton ridiculed Americans for failing to emulate the British manners in which he had himself been groomed. They just did not understand the rules of polite society. Customers in every tavern he visited proved eager to discuss

news from the latest weekly journals. They kept abreast of English politics, fashionable London gossip, and the imminent "French war," yet their manners fell consistently short. One "rough-spun, forward, clownish blade" who traveled a short distance with Hamilton attempted to establish his credentials as a cosmopolitan American gentleman by "damning" the recently deceased British leader Sir Robert Walpole "for a rascal." When Hamilton challenged the man's impertinence in cursing the famous former prime minister, the would-be gentleman offered additional evidence that he was much more than the "plain, homely fellow" he seemed. He declared that his bags contained "good linen . . . a pair of silver buckles, silver clasps, and gold sleeve buttons, two Holland shirts and some neat nightcaps." Furthermore, "his little woman at home drank tea twice a day."

Most colonists Hamilton encountered—even the poorest—displayed similar aspirations to British fashion and sophistication. Even those who had no knowledge of science discussed the findings of the great physicist Sir Isaac Newton. Rustic country doctors claimed knowledge of the latest European medical theories. Nearly everyone possessed some British imported goods. These ordinary Americans seemed determined to become more English; they just did it on their own terms. The colonial dilemma became apparent to Hamilton when he happened to visit the house of a family so poor that fresh-picked blackberries provided the only present they could offer the Scottish visitor. Even so, they "showed an inclination to finery," displaying a "looking-glass with a painted frame, half a dozen pewter spoons, and as many plates" as well as a "set of stone tea dishes and a teapot." In Rhode Island, the physician visited an "Indian King named George"—the Niantic leader Ninigret—who ironically managed to live "after the English mode" more successfully than many colonists. Ninigret lived in a great house surrounded by over 20,000 acres of prime land on which he kept "a good stock of horses and other cattle." The king's wife, Hamilton recorded, "goes in a high modish dress in her silks, hoops, stays, and dresses," and his children learned "the *belles lettres*." This "very complaisant, mannerly man" treated Hamilton and his traveling companions with a "glass of good wine" before they took their leave.

Hamilton's journal reveals a mid-eighteenth-century Anglo-American world where the growth of population, communication, and commerce had brought colonists much closer to one another than had been the case even thirty years before. Although the physician encountered a great deal of mutual suspicion among inhabitants of different colonies, his entries also reveal that colonists everywhere were scrambling to become part of a larger Anglo-American world. The change was striking. Colonists whose parents or grandparents had come to the New World to confront a "howling wilderness" now purchased imported European manufactures, read English journals, participated in imperial wars, and sought favors from a growing number of resident royal officials.

No one—not even the inhabitants of the distant frontiers—could escape the influence of Britain. The cultural, economic, and political links connecting the colonists to the imperial center in London grew stronger as the eighteenth century progressed. In other words, Americans were becoming more, not less, English with the passing of time.

This surprising development raises a difficult question. If the eighteenth-century colonists were so powerfully attracted to Great Britain, then why did they ever declare independence? The answer may well be that as the colonists became more British, they inexorably became more American as well. This was a development of major significance, for it helps to explain the appearance after mid-century of genuine nationalist sentiment. Colonists sought to fulfill their aspirations in ways adapted to the particular social and physical environments that they and their forebears had built over the previous century. In doing so, the commercial and cultural links that brought them into more frequent contact with Great Britain also made them more aware of other colonists. It was within an expanding, prosperous empire that they first began seriously to consider what it meant to be American. And, of course, it was greatly annoying to be told by the likes of an arrogant Scottish traveler that no matter how many goods they purchased from Britain, they were still second-class subjects in the empire.

10.1: Bonds of Empire

10.1 **Report the wave of fashion and sophistication that defined class and status in the Atlantic**

The rapid growth of transatlantic commerce excited many eighteenth-century colonial observers. In 1741, an essayist writing in Philadelphia's gentleman's periodical, the *American Magazine*, celebrated commercial policies "unknown to the ancient *Romans*," which were enabling England to surpass that renowned empire in its quest for greatness. Year by year, the American colonies were contributing to British greatness by channeling their own trade "like rivulets . . . into the great *British* Stream, which will swell and rise in the same Proportion as those Rivulets do." The growing market for American staples also brought an expanding range of British imported goods to colonial shopkeepers' shelves. Communication became more frequent as a growing number of ships crossed the Atlantic and plied American coastal waters. The influx of vessels into colonial ports gradually made cities such as Boston more cosmopolitan, more sinful, and, in Alexander Hamilton's words, "more civilized."

10.1.1: Economic Transformation

The British American economy kept pace with the colonial population's rapid growth. During the first three-quarters of the eighteenth century, the population increased at least tenfold (see Chapter 9). Yet even with so many additional people to feed and clothe, the per capita income did not decline. Indeed, with the exception of poor urban dwellers, such as sailors whose employment varied with the season, white Americans did quite well. An abundance of land and the extensive growth of agriculture accounted for their economic success. New farmers were able not only to provide for their families' well-being but also to sell their crops in European and West Indian markets. Each year, more Americans produced more tobacco, wheat, or rice—to cite just the major export crops—and by this means, they maintained a high level of individual prosperity without developing an industrial base.

At mid-century, colonial exports flowed along well-established routes. More than half of American goods produced for export went to Great Britain. The Navigation Acts (see Chapter 7) were still in effect, and "enumerated" items such as tobacco had to be landed first at a British port.

Furs were added to the restricted list in 1722. The White Pines Acts passed in 1711, 1722, and 1729 forbade Americans from cutting white pine trees without a license. The purpose of this legislation was to reserve the best trees for the use of the Royal Navy. The Molasses Act of 1733—also called the Sugar Act—placed a heavy duty on molasses imported from foreign ports; the Hat and Felt Act of 1732 and the Iron Act of 1750 attempted to limit the production of colonial goods that competed with British exports.

These statutes might have created tensions between the colonists and the mother country had they been rigorously enforced. Crown officials, however, generally ignored the new laws. New England merchants imported molasses from French Caribbean islands without paying the full customs; ironmasters in the Middle Colonies continued to produce iron. Even without the Navigation Acts, however, a majority of colonial exports would have been sold on the English market. The emerging consumer society in Great Britain was beginning to create a new generation of buyers who possessed enough income to purchase American goods, especially sugar and tobacco. There had always been elite consumers, of course—European aristocrats who purchased porcelain and spices from Asia—but this was the first broad marketplace that catered to ordinary men and women. For the first time in history, people of modest means could participate in the pleasures of self-fashioning. The transformation radically altered the character of the entire Atlantic World.

The transatlantic demand not only stimulated production of colonial staples but also sparked the growth of a significant colonial shipping industry. Shipyards had existed in Massachusetts since the early 1630s. During the seventeenth century others were established in Connecticut, Rhode Island, New York, Pennsylvania, the Chesapeake, and South Carolina. Most concentrated on building modest vessels for the coastal and West Indian trade until the early decades of the eighteenth century, when they began building larger ships for the ocean trade. By the 1760s, colonial shipyards were selling as many as half their annual total of new vessels to overseas buyers, usually sending them on their maiden voyages packed with cargoes of colonial staples for sale in the same European port as the ship itself. In 1784, American-built ships constituted as much as 30 percent of the total British merchant fleet.

Most vessels remaining in the colonies entered the fleets of great colonial merchant families such as the Hancocks of Boston, the Browns of Newport, the Livingstons of New York, or the Whartons of Philadelphia. Colonial merchants cultivated far-flung trading connections, and the goods they imported kept great numbers of small shopkeepers and craftsmen in business from year to year.

10.1.2: The West Indian Connection

Colonial merchants operating out of Boston, Newport, and Philadelphia also carried substantial tonnage to the West Indies. Indeed, no account of the eighteenth-century Atlantic World could ignore the central role of the Caribbean in reshaping the imperial economy. In 1768, this market accounted for 27 percent of all American exports. The West Indies played a vital role in preserving American credit in Europe. Without this source of income, colonists would not have been able to pay for the manufactured items they purchased from the mother country. To be sure, they exported American products in great quantity to Great Britain, but the value of the exports seldom equaled the cost of British goods shipped back to the colonists. To cover this small but recurrent deficit, colonial merchants relied on profits made in the West Indies.

The West Indian planters' efforts to maximize sugar production ensured that mainland colonists in places such as Pennsylvania and Connecticut would find a ready market for their agricultural staples. By the mid-eighteenth century, planters on Barbados and the Leeward Islands had cleared the vast majority of productive land and placed it into sugar cultivation. To feed their large slave labor force, these planters relied almost entirely on imports of corn, salted pork, beef, and fish produced in mainland colonies from Virginia north to New England. Indeed, a few of the wealthiest Caribbean planters even attempted to reduce their expenses by purchasing grain plantations on the mainland, staffing them with slaves, and shipping the yearly harvests at cost to their island holdings. Eighteenth-century West Indian planters also imported lumber, iron, tar, and building materials from the mainland, since their own forests had disappeared long before. Among Britain's sugar colonies, only Jamaica retained enough land and forests to supply local demand for lumber and foodstuffs.

In return for agricultural goods from the mainland, the West Indian planters exported sugar and molasses in growing quantities. Sugar rose in popularity as a sweetener for three other tropical goods—tea, coffee, and chocolate—and consumption of all four commodities rose as their prices fell steadily within reach of more colonial buyers. Colonists quickly learned to bake sugar and molasses into a growing range of custards, cakes, pastries, sweetbreads, and creams. Molasses also supplied New England distillers with the raw material for making a very high-proof rum, which sold more cheaply than West Indian varieties and became an important regional commodity for export.

Historians once thought this so-called triangular trade with West Africa defined British American transatlantic trade, but further investigation has revealed other, more significant patterns. Indeed, most colonial ships sailed directly for the Caribbean with agricultural and forestry goods and then returned immediately to the mainland colonies with their cargoes of sugar products. Recent research indicates, contrary to the beliefs of earlier generations of historians, that eighteenth-century trade with Africa involved less than 1 percent of all American exports. In fact, many slaves landed first on one of the Caribbean islands and then were reshipped to various mainland colonies.

10.1.3: Birth of a Consumer Society

Even with the West Indian connection, the balance of trade turned dramatically against the colonists after mid-century. The reasons for this change were complex, but, in simplest terms, Americans began buying more English goods than had their parents or grandparents. Between 1740 and 1770, English exports to the American colonies increased by an astounding 360 percent.

In part, this shift reflected a fundamental transformation in the British economy. Although the Industrial Revolution was still far in the future, the pace of the British economy picked up dramatically after 1690. Small work sites produced certain goods more efficiently and more cheaply than the colonists could. The availability of these products altered the lives of most Americans, even those with modest incomes. Staffordshire china replaced crude earthenware; imported cloth replaced homespun. Benjamin Franklin noted in his *Autobiography* how changing consumer habits affected his life. For years, he had eaten his breakfast in an earthenware bowl with a pewter spoon, but one morning it was served "in a china bowl, with a spoon of silver." Franklin observed that "this was the first appearance of plate and china in our house which afterwards in the course of years, as our wealth increased, augmented gradually to several hundred pounds in value." In this manner, British industrialization undercut American handicraft and folk art.

To help Americans purchase manufactured goods, British merchants offered generous credit. Colonists deferred settlement by agreeing to pay interest on their debts. The temptation to acquire English finery blinded many people to hard economic realities. They gambled on the future, hoping bumper farm crops would reduce their dependence on the large merchant houses of London and Glasgow. Obviously, some persons lived within their means, but the aggregate American debt continued to grow. Colonial leaders tried various expedients to remain solvent—issuing paper money, for example—and while these efforts delayed a crisis, the balance-of-payments problem was clearly very serious.

The eighteenth-century American mainland also saw a substantial increase in intercoastal trade. Southern planters sent tobacco and rice to New England and the Middle Colonies, where these staples were exchanged for meat and wheat as well as goods imported from Great Britain. By 1760, approximately 30 percent of the colonists' total tonnage capacity was involved in this extensive "coastwise" commerce. In addition, backcountry farmers in western Pennsylvania and the Shenandoah Valley carried their grain to market along an old Iroquois trail that became known as the Great Wagon Road, a rough, hilly highway that by the time of the Revolution stretched 735 miles along the Blue Ridge Mountains to Camden, South Carolina. Most of their produce was carried in long, gracefully designed Conestoga wagons. These vehicles—sometimes called the "wagons of empire"—had been invented by German immigrants living in the Conestoga River valley in Lancaster County, Pennsylvania.

The shifting patterns of trade had immense effects on the development of an American culture. First, the flood of British imports eroded local and regional identities. The first English colonies such as Massachusetts and Virginia had been experiments—places founded to promote purer religious practices or to satisfy the desire for quick profits. But during the eighteenth century, commerce helped to "Anglicize" American culture by exposing colonial consumers to a common range of British manufactured goods. Deep sectional differences remained, of course, but Americans from New Hampshire to Georgia were increasingly drawn into a sophisticated economic network centered in London. Second, the expanding coastal and overland trade brought colonists of different backgrounds into more frequent contact. Ships that sailed between New England and South Carolina, and between Virginia and Pennsylvania, provided dispersed Americans with a means to exchange ideas and experiences on a more regular basis.

10.1.4: Communication and the "Public Prints"

Correspondence and print enhanced the exchange of ideas even further throughout the Atlantic World. An increasing number of colonists had commercial dealings or ties of kinship and friendship with people across the Atlantic, in neighboring colonies, or along the colonial frontier. Migrants linked old localities with new by emotional and familial bonds, maintained by correspondence and occasional visits (see Chapter 9). News from one community could spread throughout an entire region through the agency of family visitors or traveling peddlers.

Letters among distant family members augmented an existing network of intercolonial and transatlantic correspondence and spurred the organization of an empirewide postal system. The increase of commercial shipping aided the growth of this correspondence network and the speed of communication during the eighteenth century. An increase in the number and range of travelers, who often carried letters from one place to another, supplemented the postal system. As the century progressed, these two means of corresponding drew formerly isolated communities steadily closer to one another.

The most important development in communication, however, came with the extension of what one historian has termed "print capitalism" across the Atlantic and into an increasing number of locales. The production of books, sermons, pamphlets, broadsides, chapbooks, and almanacs for sale to the empire's literate populace became a means for colonists to learn about and adopt a common way of speaking and thinking about issues that affected their everyday lives.

The rise of weekly newspapers multiplied this effect a thousandfold. Under the Licensing Act of 1662, the Crown had restricted publication to only one newspaper, the *London Gazette*. When Boston printers attempted to produce newssheets during the 1680s, Crown officials moved swiftly to enforce the law in America as well. In 1695, however, the Crown and Parliament allowed the act to expire. Presses responded quickly, pouring forth a flood of competing periodicals in London, the English provinces, and the colonies.

The first American newspaper with a sustained circulation, the *Boston Weekly News-Letter*, made its debut in 1704. By 1740, Boston had four newspapers, New York two, Philadelphia two, Williamsburg one, and Charleston one. In these and a number of lesser colonial journals, colonists could read reports from correspondents in other colonies, London, the various English provinces, and the Continent. In addition, colonial publishers regularly reprinted news items, essays, and poetry from other colonial journals, London newspapers, and gentlemen's magazines. This vast increase in the volume and relative currency of information began to give people in the various locales of the British Atlantic a greater sense of kinship with distant, anonymous people who were now sharing common news and forming similar opinions about it.

Newspapers constituted a special type of consumer good. Colonists who could afford subscriptions bought them not only for information of important events but also for learning about the availability of other types of goods. Even those who could not purchase or read the paper for themselves could often browse a copy or hear it read at the local tavern. Merchants quickly learned to use newspapers in sophisticated ways to hawk the "latest English fashions" to inhabitants of the British Atlantic. The popularity of newspapers and imported English goods complemented each other in transforming colonial tastes and fostering greater awareness of colonial commonalities.

10.1.5: Provincial Cities

The colonial port cities provided crucial links between colonial Americans and the eighteenth-century British Atlantic, despite the small percentage of colonists who lived there. Boston, Newport, New York, Philadelphia, and Charles Town (later Charleston)—the five largest cities—contained only about 5 percent of the colonial population. In 1775, none had more than forty thousand persons. Their highly specialized commercial character explains both the relatively slow development of colonial American cities and the extent of their influence. Colonial port towns served as entrepôts, intermediary trade and shipping centers where bulk cargoes were broken up for inland distribution and where agricultural products were gathered for export. They did not support large-scale manufacturing. Indeed, the pool of free urban laborers was quite small, since the type of person who was forced to work for wages in Europe usually became a farmer in America.

Yet despite the limited urban population, cities profoundly influenced colonial culture. It was in the cities that Americans were exposed to and welcomed the latest European ideas. Wealthy colonists—merchants and lawyers—tried to emulate the culture of the mother country. They sponsored concerts and plays. They learned to dance. They rehearsed the posture, manners, pronunciation, and conversational habits of the English gentry. Women as well as men picked up the new fashions quickly, and even though most of them had never been outside the colony of their birth, they sometimes appeared to be the products of London's best families.

It was in the cities, also, that wealthy merchants transformed commercial profits into architectural splendor. In their desire to outdo one another, they built grand homes of enduring beauty. Most of these buildings are described as Georgian because they were constructed during the reign of Britain's early Hanoverian kings, who all happened to be named George. Actually these homes were provincial copies of grand country houses of Great Britain. They drew their inspiration from the great Italian Renaissance architect Andrea Palladio (1508–1580), who had incorporated classical themes into a rigidly symmetrical form. Palladio's ideas were popularized in the colonies by James Gibbs, an Englishman whose *Book of Architecture* (1728) provided blueprints for the most spectacular homes of mid-eighteenth-century America.

Their owners filled the houses with fine furniture. Each city patronized certain skilled craftsmen, but the artisans of Philadelphia were known for producing magnificent copies of the works of Thomas Chippendale, Great Britain's most famous furniture designer. These developments gave American cities an elegance they had not possessed in the previous century. One foreign visitor noted of Philadelphia in 1748 that "its natural advantages, trade, riches and power, are by no means inferior to any, even of the most ancient towns of Europe." As this traveler understood, the cultural impact of the cities went far beyond the number of people who actually lived there.

10.1.6: Families and Farms in the Colonial Countryside

Life outside the major port centers varied significantly according to the density of the regional population and the distance from the coast and major port cities. Most free white families farmed for a living, forming rural communities where they could buy and sell goods, labor, and specialized services such as carpentry and metalworking in regional exchange economies. Most aspired to what one historian has termed "competency" in their standard of living—a modest prosperity that ensured adequate housing, apparel, food, possessions sufficient to maintain a community standard of comfort and decency, and an inheritance that could assist children to achieve a competency in the next generation. Ownership of land unencumbered by too much debt secured the independence needed to achieve this goal.

Historians continue to debate the extent to which eighteenth-century farming families sought to enter the growing market economy. Some argue that families resisted the influx of the market, with its pressure to compete and to compromise independence by staking too much on a single cash crop. And indeed, studies of colonial farming habits do show that families often diversified production in ways consistent with a regional exchange economy.

Nevertheless, recent research also suggests that the standard of competency was gradually shifting in eighteenth-century America. The increasing quantity and affordability of British imported goods attracted more rural buyers, growing cities increased demand and opened new opportunities for farmers to enter the market, and transportation steadily improved to connect more rural communities with coastal cities and the Atlantic market beyond. Examinations of estate inventories in eighteenth-century New England reveal that families there were filling their homes with an increasing quantity and variety of British imported goods. By the 1740s, ordinary farmers in New England and the Middle Colonies were demanding new issues of paper money so that they could participate in the burgeoning market economy. And in southeastern Pennsylvania, German and Quaker farmers plunged into the grain export market with both feet, fueling a rapid rise to a standard of living they could scarcely have imagined in Europe. Indeed, even though many urban Quakers insisted on wearing simple garments, they often made them from the very best imported cloth available, thus joining the consumer world in subtle ways.

The entry of rural families into the Atlantic market stimulated a gradual shift in the pattern of household production, transforming the experience of colonial women. During the eighteenth century, a growing number of wives and daughters began working in nonfarm occupations to

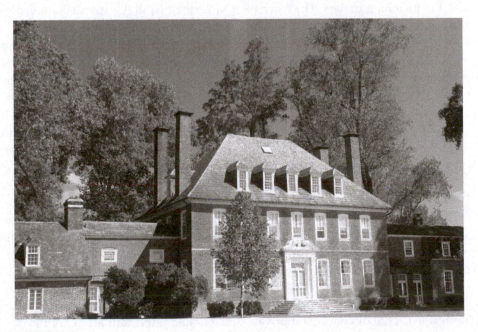

WESTOVER

gain the extra income needed to participate in the consumer economy. Women followed a variety of pursuits, including midwifery and shopkeeping, but the most common nonfarm occupation for women was in textile production. Many families purchased carding equipment, spinning wheels, and looms so that the women of the household could produce yarn, thread, and cloth for sale on a regional market. Textile work was tedious and repetitive, but it gave a growing number of rural women the opportunity to earn money and conduct business at the local shop. One historian has observed that this experience, coupled with evidence that more "country girls were attending school and learning how to write" suggests that eighteenth-century women were beginning to gain "greater control over their own lives."

The market and its attendant changes extended only gradually into inland settlements. Visitors to the backcountry commented frequently on the poverty they observed among the settlers. Yet even on the frontier, British imported goods found a market among recent white arrivals, who competed with native hunters for hides and furs to sell to incoming traders. The reach of the Atlantic markets was very long, and nowhere did colonists offer much resistance to its allure so long as they could find some way to pay for the "baubles of Britain."

10.2: A Transatlantic Community of Letters

10.2 Compare American Enlightenment with European Enlightenment

The expansion of trade, the rising consumption of British manufactured goods, the proliferation of print and correspondence, the growth of small but influential urban centers—all contributed to an emerging culture of what one literary historian has termed "civil discourse and private society" in eighteenth-century America. In every colonial city, literate colonists who aspired to polite standards of learning and civility converged in settings where they could engage and challenge one another through witty conversation on various fashionable topics. In doing so, participants shaped the rules of entry into local circles of power and influence while enforcing polite standards of fashion and conduct upon members of those circles. They also transmitted new European ideas to America and stimulated gifted colonists to contribute theories and inventions of their own to the intellectual revolution that was sweeping across eighteenth-century Europe.

10.2.1: Taverns, Salons, and "Private Societies"

Eighteenth-century colonists who aspired to European standards of fashion and civility sought to transform the culture of some traditional gathering places, while at the same time introducing new forms already fashionable in Europe. Taverns, for instance, were traditionally considered places of drunkenness, loitering, and brawling. Nevertheless, they provided convenient public places for men of "substance and parts" to gather and conduct business, discuss important political matters, and exchange ideas on topics ranging from agriculture to philosophy and religion. Not every tavern-keeper was willing to discourage the patronage of paying customers whose conduct fell short of genteel. By mid-century, however, every colonial city boasted taverns such as Philadelphia's Indian King, which catered to a polished clientele of leading merchants and professionals.

Similar sites for civil exchange formed around popular imported beverages such as coffee and tea. Coffeehouses provided aspiring gentlemen with an alternative to the taverns. There they could meet to sip sweetened coffee or chocolate and share pipefuls of tobacco while discussing important affairs of the day or reading to each other from manuscript literature. Tea tables provided women with similar settings for exchanging local news and commenting on fashion, topics of conversation whose influence extended beyond the parlor or drawing room to shape social conduct and expectations in the larger community. Over time, prominent women in many communities transformed the ladies' tea tables into mixed-gender salons where women could exert more direct influence in public affairs by challenging men to cultivate "sense" concerning important issues of the day. The colonial poet Elizabeth Graeme, for instance, expressed the belief that a sensible woman (represented in the following passage by "Rossela") could exercise a civilizing effect on a man:

> His Passions should be guided
> By Reason's ruling Hand;
> And with Good Sense provided,
> *Rossela* to Command.

Rising Anglo-American gentlemen also established social clubs where they could engage in table games and free conversation on topics of the day. Clubs often met in semiprivate rooms set aside for the purpose in taverns and coffeehouses. There the local gentry would enjoy dinners together, often capped with toasts to various persons of affairs in state and society. These toasts, which ranged from sincere to boldly satirical and irreverent, served as a vehicle for displaying wit as well as perception about matters of economy, governmental policy, international affairs, religious life, or scientific investigation. Conversation often centered on manuscript literature produced by one of the club's own number or circulated from club to club along an expanding intercolonial gentleman's network. These literary performances honed the skills of writer and critic alike in the rhetorical strategies most prized for debating, selecting, and expressing the powerful ideas that could shape official public action taken by members of the ruling class.

10.2.2: American Enlightenment

The various forms of private society provided fertile ground for the spread in British America of new ideas from Europe. European historians often refer to the eighteenth century as an Age of Reason. During this period, a body of new, often radical, ideas swept through the salons and universities, altering the way that educated Europeans thought about God, nature, and society. This intellectual revolution, called the Enlightenment, involved the work of Europe's greatest minds—men like Newton, Locke, Voltaire, and Hume. The writings of these thinkers eventually reached the colonies, where they gained a cautious reception. Americans welcomed experimental science, but most balked at attacks on Scripture and traditional Christian belief. On the whole, the American Enlightenment was a rather tame affair compared to its European counterpart.

Enlightenment thinkers shared basic assumptions. Philosophers of the Enlightenment replaced the concept of original sin with a much more optimistic view of human nature. A benevolent God, having set the universe in motion, gave human beings the power of reason to enable them to comprehend the orderly workings of his creation. Everything, even human society, operated according to these mechanical rules. The responsibility of right-thinking men and women, therefore, was to make certain that institutions such as church and state conformed to self-evident natural laws. It was possible—or so some of the *philosophes* claimed—to achieve perfection in this world. In fact, human suffering had come about only because people had lost touch with the fundamental insights of reason.

For many Americans, the appeal of the Enlightenment was its focus on a search for useful knowledge, ideas, and inventions that would improve the quality of human life. What mattered was practical experimentation. A speech delivered in 1767 before the members of the American

Society in Philadelphia reflected the new utilitarian spirit: "Knowledge is of little Use when confined to mere Speculation," the colonist explained, "But when speculative Truths are reduced to Practice, when Theories grounded upon Experiments . . . and the Arts of Living made more easy and comfortable . . . Knowledge then becomes really useful." The Enlightenment spawned scores of earnest scientific tinkerers, people who dutifully recorded changes in temperature, the appearance of strange plants and animals, and the details of astronomic phenomena. While these eighteenth-century Americans made few earth-shattering discoveries, they did encourage their countrymen, especially those who attended college, to apply reason to the solution of social and political problems.

10.2.3: Benjamin Franklin

Benjamin Franklin (1706–1790) absorbed the new cosmopolitan culture. European thinkers regarded him as a genuine *philosophe*, a person of reason and science, a role that he self-consciously cultivated when he visited England and France in later life. Franklin had little formal education, but as a young man working in his brother's print shop, he managed to keep up with the latest intellectual currents. In his *Autobiography*, Franklin described the excitement of discovering a new British journal. It was like a breath of fresh air to a boy growing up in Puritan New England. "I met with an odd volume of *The Spectator*," Franklin recounted; ". . . I had never before seen any of them. I bought it, read it over and over, and was much delighted with it. I thought the writing excellent, and wished if possible to imitate it."

Franklin's opportunity came in August 1721 when he and his brother founded the *New England Courant*, a weekly newspaper that satirized Boston's political and religious leaders in the manner of the contemporary British press. Writing under the name Silence Dogood, young Franklin asked his readers "Whether a Commonwealth suffers more by hypocritical Pretenders to Religion, or by the openly Profane?" Proper Bostonians were not prepared for a journal that one minister described as "full freighted with Nonesense, Unmannerliness, Railery, Prophaneness, Immorality, Arrogance, Calumnies, Lyes, Contradictions, and what not, all tending to Quarrels and Divisions and to Debauch and Corrupt the Minds and Manners of New England." Franklin got the point; he left Massachusetts in 1723 in search of a less hostile intellectual environment.

After he had moved to Philadelphia, leaving behind an irritable brother as well as New England Puritanism, Franklin devoted himself to the pursuit of useful knowledge, ideas that would increase the happiness of his fellow Americans. Franklin never denied the existence of God. Rather, he pushed the Lord aside, making room for the free exercise of human reason. Franklin tinkered, experimented, and reformed. Almost everything he encountered in his daily life aroused his curiosity. His investigation of electricity brought him world fame, but Franklin was never satisfied with his work in this field until it yielded practical application. In 1756, he invented the lightning rod. He also designed a marvelously efficient stove that is still used. In modern America, Franklin has become exactly what he would have wanted to be, a symbol of material progress through human ingenuity.

Franklin energetically promoted the spread of reason. In Philadelphia, he organized groups that discussed the latest European literature, philosophy, and science. In 1727, for example, he "form'd most of my ingenious Acquaintances into a Club for mutual Improvement, which we call'd the Junto." Four years later Franklin took a leading part in the formation of the Library Company, a voluntary association that for the first time allowed people like him to pursue "useful knowledge." The members of these societies communicated with Americans living in other colonies, providing them not only with new information but also with models for their own clubs and associations.

10.3: Religious Revivals in Provincial Societies

10.3 **Evaluate how the Awakening altered the future course of American history**

In contrast to many European societies, American colonists had no trouble accepting the new practical or experimental science of Newton while promoting popular Protestantism. Religion and science were compatible. There was no reason for American Christianity to take on an anti-intellectual or anti-Enlightenment character. While clubs like Franklin's Junto occupied the interest of a small, largely urban Anglo-American elite, most colonists continued to pursue their daily lives in a spiritual environment shaped by the Protestant beliefs in which they had been raised. In the 1730s, the contours of their social world began shifting rapidly under the impact of a spontaneous series of Protestant revivals known as the Great Awakening. This unprecedented evangelical outpouring altered the course of American history. In our own time, of course, the force of religious revivals has been witnessed in different regions throughout the world. It is no exaggeration to claim that a similar populist movement took place in mid-eighteenth-century America, and the highly personal appeal to a "new birth" in Christ caused men and women of all backgrounds to rethink basic assumptions about church and state, institutions, and society. What made the eighteenth-century Atlantic World so challenging—and so exciting—was that ordinary men and women were simultaneously purchasing the goods of empire while also bringing forth a form of religion that was radically new. Neither development alone explains the

coming of the American Revolution. But the two strands of change together—religion and the marketplace—created a powerful force for shaping a distinct American identity.

10.3.1: The Great Awakening

Only with hindsight does the Great Awakening seem a unified religious movement. Revivals occurred in different places at different times; the intensity of the events varied from region to region. The first signs of a spiritual awakening appeared in New England during the 1730s, but within a decade the revivals in this area had burned themselves out. It was not until the 1750s and 1760s that the Great Awakening made more than a superficial impact on the people of Virginia. The revivals were most important in Massachusetts, Connecticut, Rhode Island, Pennsylvania, New Jersey, and Virginia. Their effect on religion in New York, Delaware, and the Carolinas was marginal. No single religious denomination or sect monopolized the Great Awakening. In New England, revivals shattered Congregational churches, and in the South, especially in Virginia, they had an impact on Presbyterians, Methodists, and Baptists. Moreover, there was nothing peculiarly American about the Great Awakening. Mid-eighteenth-century Europe experienced a similar burst of religious emotionalism.

Whatever their origins, the seeds of revival were generally sown on fertile ground. In the early decades of the century, many Americans—but especially New Englanders—complained that organized religion had lost vitality. They looked back at Winthrop's founding generation of Puritans with nostalgia, assuming that common people at that time must have possessed greater piety than did later, more worldly colonists. Congregational ministers seemed obsessed with dull, scholastic matters; their preaching no longer touched the heart. And in the southern colonies, there were simply not enough ordained ministers to tend to the religious needs of the population.

The Great Awakening arrived unexpectedly in Northampton, a small farm community in western Massachusetts, sparked by Jonathan Edwards, the local Congregational minister. Edwards accepted the traditional teachings of Calvinism (see Chapter 5), reminding his parishioners that their eternal fate had been determined by an omnipotent God, there was nothing they could do to save themselves, and they were totally dependent on the Lord's will. He thought his fellow ministers had grown soft. They left men and women with the mistaken impression that sinners might somehow avoid eternal damnation simply by performing good works. "How dismal will it be," Edwards told his complacent congregation, "when you are under these racking torments, to know assuredly that you never, never shall be delivered from them." Edwards was not exaggerating his message in an attempt to be dramatic. He spoke of God's omnipotence with such self-assurance that even people who had not thought deeply about religious matters were shaken by his words.

Why this uncompromising message set off several religious revivals during the mid-1730s is not known. Whatever the explanation for the popular response to Edwards's preaching, young people began flocking to the church. They experienced a searing conversion, a sense of "new birth" and utter dependence on God. "Surely," Edwards pronounced, "this is the Lord's doing, and it is marvelous in our eyes." The excitement spread, and evangelical ministers concluded that God must be preparing Americans, his chosen people, for the millennium. "What is now seen in America and especially in New England," Edwards explained, "may prove the dawn of that glorious day."

10.3.2: The Voice of Popular Religion

News of the Northampton revivals under Edwards spread throughout New England and traveled across the Atlantic to London and Scotland through a correspondence network of Calvinistic ministers. The reports sparked outbreaks of revival in other New England towns, and the famous Dissenting minister and hymn writer Isaac Watts saw to it that Edwards's *Faithful Narrative of the Surprising Work of God in Northampton* was printed in England. Yet Edwards, brilliant theologian though he was, he did not possess the dynamic personality required to sustain the revival. That responsibility fell to a gifted young Anglican preacher named George Whitefield—a man as important in American history as was Benjamin Franklin.

Whitefield made his first great preaching tour of the Anglo-American mainland in 1739 and 1740. A young associate of the great Methodist leaders John and Charles Wesley, he had already achieved fame in England for his stirring messages. While Whitefield was not an original thinker, he was an extraordinarily effective public speaker as well as an innovative promoter. Like his friend Benjamin Franklin, Whitefield came to symbolize the powerful cultural forces that were transforming the Atlantic world. According to Edwards's wife, Sarah, it was wonderful to witness what a spell Whitefield "casts over an audience . . . I have seen upwards of a thousand people hang on his words with breathless silence, broken only by an occasional half-suppressed sob."

Whitefield's audiences came from all groups of American society: rich and poor, young and old, rural and urban. While Whitefield described himself as a Calvinist, he welcomed all Protestants. He spoke from any pulpit that was available. "Don't tell me you are a Baptist, an Independent, a Presbyterian, a dissenter," he thundered, "tell me you are a Christian, that is all I want."

Whitefield was a brilliant entrepreneur. Like Franklin, with whom he published many popular volumes, the itinerant minister possessed an almost intuitive sense of how this burgeoning consumer society could be turned to his own

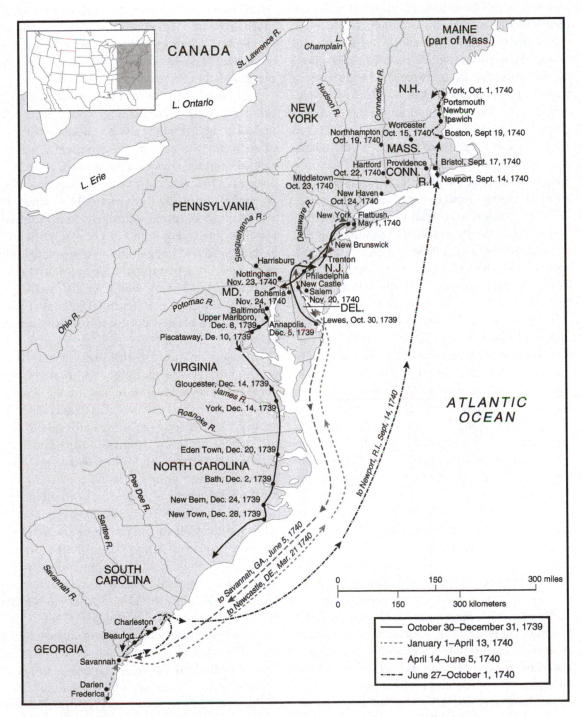

Map 10.1 George Whitefield in America

advantage, and he embraced the latest merchandising techniques. He appreciated, for example, the power of the press in selling the revival, and he regularly promoted his own work in advertisements placed in British and American newspapers. The crowds flocked to hear Whitefield, while his critics grumbled about the commercialization of religion. One anonymous writer in Massachusetts noted that there was "a very wholesome law of the province to discourage Pedlars in Trade" and it seemed high time "to enact something for the discouragement of Pedlars in Divinity also."

Other, American-born itinerant preachers followed Whitefield's example. The most famous was Gilbert Tennent, a Presbyterian of Scots-Irish background who had been educated in the Middle Colonies. His sermon "On the Danger of an Unconverted Ministry," printed in 1741, set off a storm of protest from established ministers who were understandably insulted. Lesser-known revivalists traveled from town to town, colony to colony, challenging local clergymen who seemed hostile to evangelical religion. Men and women who thronged to hear the itinerants were called "New Lights," and during the 1740s and 1750s, many congregations split between defenders of the new emotional preaching and those who regarded the entire movement as dangerous nonsense.

Despite Whitefield's successes, many ministers remained suspicious of the itinerants and their methods. Some complaints may have amounted to little more than sour grapes. One "Old Light" spokesman labeled Tennent "a monster! impudent and noisy." He claimed Tennent told anxious Christians that "they were damned! damned! damned! This charmed them; and, in the most dreadful winter I ever saw, people wallowed in snow, night and day, for the benefit of his beastly brayings; and many ended their days under these fatigues." Charles Chauncy, minister of the prestigious First Church of Boston, raised much more troubling issues. How could the revivalists be certain God had sparked the Great Awakening? Perhaps the itinerants had relied too much on emotion? "Let us esteem those as friends of religion," Chauncy advised, ". . . who warn us of the danger of enthusiasm, and would put us on our guard, that we may not be led aside by it."

Although Tennent did not condone the excesses of the Great Awakening, his attacks on formal learning invited the crude anti-intellectualism of such fanatics as James Davenport. This deranged revivalist traveled along the Connecticut coast in 1742 playing upon popular emotion. At night, under the light of smoky torches, he danced and stripped, shrieked, and laughed. He also urged people to burn books written by authors who had not experienced the New Light as defined by Davenport. Like so many fanatics throughout history who have claimed a special knowledge of the "truth," Davenport later recanted and begged pardon for his disruptive behavior.

To concentrate on the bizarre activities of Davenport—as many critics of the Great Awakening have done—is to obscure the positive ways in which this vast revival changed American society. First, despite occasional anti-intellectual outbursts, the New Lights founded several important centers of higher learning. They wanted to train young men who would carry on the good works of Edwards, Whitefield, and Tennent. In 1746, New Light Presbyterians established the College of New Jersey, which later became Princeton University. Just before his death, Jonathan Edwards was appointed its president. The evangelical minister Eleazar Wheelock launched Dartmouth (1769); other revivalists founded Brown (1764) and Rutgers (1766).

The Great Awakening also encouraged men and women who had been taught to remain silent before traditional figures of authority to speak up, to take an active role in their salvation. They could no longer rely on ministers or institutions. The individual alone stood before God. Knowing this, New Lights made religious choices that shattered the old harmony among Protestant sects, and in its place, they introduced a noisy, often bitterly fought competition. As one New Jersey Presbyterian explained, "There are so many particular sects and Parties among professed Christians . . . that we know not . . . in which of these different paths, to steer our course for Heaven."

The itinerancy introduced by Whitefield also provided an extraordinarily effective means for his followers to carry Whitefield's message of the New Birth to parts of Anglo-America where few churches yet existed. The new evangelical style of preaching found substantial support among New England's Congregational clergy and the Middle Colonies' Presbyterian and Pietistic Dutch Reformed groups. Yet its most explosive growth occurred outside these older traditions, where it could flourish unhindered by clerical attempts to control it. New Light Baptist and Methodist preachers honed their message and methods to resonate powerfully with the experiences of ordinary people. These itinerants were usually simple lay preachers whose only claim to the ministry was an overpowering sense that God had called them. Unencumbered by the requirements of long, formal preparation in ministry, they spread a simple, Bible-centered form of Protestant Christianity among the mobile backcountry population. By the 1760s, the influence of such people was prompting the Anglican missionary Charles Woodmason to complain that his mission field in the backcountry of South Carolina was "eaten up by Itinerant Teachers, Preachers, and Impostors from New England and Pennsylvania—Baptists, New Lights, Presbyterians, Independents, and an hundred other Sects."

The Great Awakening also opened opportunities in many communities for women to express themselves and assert leadership in the religious sphere. Women were at the forefront of many praying societies that sprang up during the Awakening. A number of women joined men in exhorting and took leadership in local revivals. A few even preached from colonial pulpits. Opponents attacked such practices as evidence of the revivalists' mad "enthusiasm," and many "friends of revival" attempted to suppress women's activities. Other New Lights defended female leadership, searching the Bible for evidence that the Lord would bless the gracious words of women who spoke out in "publick assembly." During their earliest years, revivalist Separate Baptists permitted women to vote on matters of policy and discipline. The radical practices of female exhortation, preaching, and voting disappeared as the revival fires subsided. Even so, evangelical religion gave women a new sense of their own worth in the eyes of God and of their importance in sustaining the spiritual fervor of their congregations and homes through prayer and pious example.

Expressive evangelicalism struck a particularly responsive chord among African Americans (see Chapter 11). Itinerant ministers frequently preached to large sympathetic audiences of slaves. Richard Allen (1760–1831), founder of the African Methodist Episcopal Church, reported that he owed his freedom in part to a traveling Methodist minister who persuaded Allen's master of the sinfulness of slavery. Allen himself was converted, as were thousands of other black colonists. According to one historian, evangelical preaching "shared enough with traditional African styles and beliefs such as spirit possession and ecstatic expression . . . to allow for an interpenetration of African and Christian religious beliefs."

With religious contention came an awareness of a larger community, a union of fellow believers that extended beyond the boundaries of town and colony. In fact, evangelical religion was one of several forces at work during the mid-eighteenth century that brought scattered colonists into contact with one another for the first time. In this sense, the Great Awakening was a "national" event long before a nation actually existed.

People who had been touched by the Great Awakening shared an optimism about the future of America. With God's help, social and political progress was possible, and from this perspective, of course, the New Lights did not sound much different than the mildly rationalist American spokesmen of the Enlightenment. Both groups prepared the way for the development of a revolutionary mentality in colonial America.

10.4: Indian Awakenings in Eighteenth-Century America

10.4 Examine how the American Awakening, way of life, and beliefs influenced the native Indians

North America's native peoples also felt the impact of eighteenth-century colonial cultural and economic developments. To be sure, American Indians had been experiencing the transforming effects of a "consumer revolution" in European manufactured goods for well over a hundred years. They had also been contending with massive influxes of epidemic disease, increasing dislocation, dramatic reductions in game, and chronic warfare. Even so, a growing number of native leaders discerned new features in the situation confronting them by the early 1740s. Those who remained as postcolonial minorities behind the line of European settlement experienced directly the same forces of change as their white neighbors, but they responded to those changes in their own way and for their own purposes. Native leaders in the borderlands of the Ohio Country and the Southeast discerned new challenges and opportunities in the accelerating expansion of the Anglo-American population, the pace of change in native communities themselves, the extension of native networks of travel, communication, and exchange across a widening territorial expanse.

10.4.1: Living Like "Our Christian English Neighbors"

Alexander Hamilton's encounter with the Niantic leader Ninigret reveals how some native peoples responded to the growing availability of British consumer goods in ways that, superficially at least, resembled the responses of Anglo-Americans themselves. Indians had always selectively incorporated some European goods and methods into the way they lived. By the mid-eighteenth century, however, a growing number were beginning to appear less distinct from their English neighbors than they had fifty years earlier.

Ninigret's adoption of large-scale ranching to support his heavily Anglicized way of life was reproduced among many native communities, even those far from the coast such as the Creeks of the colonial Southeast. The overhunting of deer and the loss of habitat for wildlife made herding of cattle increasingly necessary for those who wished to retain access to meat and skins. The value of horses for transportation and farming made them a natural choice to add to the livestock on the farm or ranch. To be sure, native ranching could increase occasions for conflicts with neighboring Euro-Americans, who were prone to accuse Indian ranchers of stealing livestock. As long as the disputants remained calm enough to undertake a legal investigation, however, native ranchers could often prove their ownership of the horses or cattle in question.

The poverty of most eighteenth-century Indians prevented the bulk of native dwellings from attaining the relative grandeur of Ninigret's great house. Nevertheless, by the mid-eighteenth century a growing number of native peoples were adopting European house styles. Iroquois families, for instance, gradually moved out of the communal, clan-based longhouses their ancestors had known into single-family log homes. Eighteenth-century Iroquois villages were more often composed of scattered single-family dwellings than of the compact, palisaded communities that seventeenth-century visitors had observed. The Swedish visitor Peter Kalm recorded that mid-eighteenth-century Hurons of Quebec had abandoned their bark dwellings for houses built "after the French fashion." Houses in the Indian Praying Towns of New England tended to look like the clapboard-sided saltboxes of white colonists nearby, though eighteenth-century visitors often commented on the number of bark dwellings still visible in towns such as those of the Narragansetts and Mohegans. Creeks, Choctaws, and Cherokees of the Southeast adopted the log home styles introduced by nearby Scots-Irish, German, or French settlers. The move to single-family dwellings often weakened traditional clan ties. One historian has observed that many native children "grew up in what, in the context of their societies, constituted 'broken homes.' "

Like Ninigret's wife who dressed in English-style "silks, hoops and stays," a growing number of Indians also dressed in English fashions at least some of the time. The clothing made from European cloth often proved more comfortable and convenient than that made from hides. To be sure, Indians often wore their clothing in non-European ways—leaving shirttails hanging, cutting off pants to make leggings, wearing shirts but no "breeches"—often to the ridicule or chagrin of European observers. Yet many Indians wore complete outfits of English clothing, shoes, and hats, frequently causing Anglo-American observers to "mistake them for English." Moreover, Ninigret's taste for English fashion was far from exceptional. English observers at eighteenth-century diplomatic or treaty councils frequently noted that Indian participants wore laced hats, laced matchcoats, and ruffled shirts.

The donning of European clothing served a variety of Indian purposes. English clothes could often smooth the way for various dealings with European neighbors. Indian interpreters and brokers often signified their status and skills by the mixing of English and Indian articles of dress. The most observant and successful English brokers, people such as the eighteenth-century Indian agent Sir William Johnson, recognized the value of cultural cross-dressing and followed suit themselves. Johnson knew how to cut a very grand figure indeed among his Mohawk allies by dressing and painting himself "after the manner of an *Indian* War Captain."

Ninigret's determination to give his children an education in the *belles lettres* was also becoming more common among eighteenth-century Indians. Colonists attempted to accommodate this desire on their own terms, establishing boarding schools and seats at colonial colleges where Indian children could be educated away from the "pernicious influence of their Parents' Example," as the New England minister Eleazar Wheelock put it. Such efforts often met with resistance from Indians who, like the Onondaga leader Canasatego, observed that Indian alumni who returned home from English schools often proved worthless, unable to find their way around in the woods or to string a bow and shoot an arrow. They also objected to the harsh treatment Indian pupils received from English teachers, who were notorious for speaking roughly, flogging their charges "for every little mistake," and working their students at household and farm chores more than at their academic subjects.

Despite these obstacles, some Indian leaders did send their children to English schools. Those who survived the experience often acquired skills that proved valuable in achieving native objectives. Proficiency in speaking, reading, and writing English gave those who wielded it significant advantages in trade and diplomatic negotiations. An understanding of Anglo-American politics, history, and international affairs enhanced those advantages further still. The Mohawk Joseph Brant, a graduate of Eleazar Wheelock's school, returned to his home in New York to translate the four Gospels of the New Testament into his native language. During the American Revolution he put his considerable talents to use in diplomacy and military service, leading many of the Mohawks into alliance with Great Britain.

10.4.2: The Great Awakening in Indian Country

Joseph Brant exemplifies a small but growing number of eighteenth-century American Indians who not only embraced Protestant Christianity themselves, but sought to foster its spread in their communities. The religious revivals of the 1740s contributed to this growth in part by stimulating a fresh surge of missionary zeal among colonists. The Moravians, a German-speaking sect associated with the Wesleys, introduced a variety of Protestantism that appealed to native groups in the Appalachians and Ohio Country. The Moravians arose out of European Pietism, a brand of Protestantism that cultivated sincere spirituality among ordinary believers, often reinforced by inward visions and sensations of divine rapture. The lay-oriented style of the Moravians and other evangelicals appears to have been especially attractive to native converts, since it allowed Indians to take greater initiative in adapting Christianity to their own interests, aims, and religious sensibilities.

Indians in New England frequently participated in the Great Awakening, and some took an active role in spreading it to new communities. In Westerly, Rhode Island, for instance, the Congregational minister Joseph Park wrote that the "Power of GOD . . . began to be most remarkable among *the Body of the Indians*" in his parish only when a group of New Light Indians brought the message of New Birth from neighboring Stonington, Connecticut. Park himself could make only a small contribution to the local Awakening, a prayer that God's "Kingdom might be seen coming with Power." When he attempted to preach or do anything more, the *"Outcry"* of native souls in distress became so loud he had to "give it up." The Indians from Stonington took over, leading a "wonderful Time of God's Power" which continued for two days. *"From that Time,"* Park declared, "the *Indians* were generally stirred up to seek after eternal Life."

Anglo-American missionaries who felt the Spirit's call to carry the Awakening to native peoples did not often enjoy such a fervent response. David Brainerd, the most famous eighteenth-century missionary to the Indians, encountered varying degrees of resistance as he preached among the Delaware or Lenape of Pennsylvania. The scattered, demoralized bands who remained living near European communities behind the line of settlement proved more receptive to Brainerd's message of New Birth than those beyond, who preferred to "live as their fathers lived and go where their fathers were when they died." The emotionally fragile evangelist slipped into despair when the Lenape bands at the Forks of the Delaware River repeatedly "refused to believe the truth" of what Brainerd taught them. He regained hope, however, when his ministry among "Settlement Indians" in well-colonized New Jersey sparked a modest number of conversions. Yet even there, Brainerd discovered that he had to adapt his message to native tastes if he hoped to win a sympathetic hearing. His Delaware converts responded poorly to "harangues of [Hell's] terror," preferring instead "the free offers of divine Grace to needy and distressed Sinners."

Many native groups preferred Moravian Pietism—newly imported in the 1740s from German-speaking Saxony—to the Calvinism of Brainerd and other New Light missionaries. Where evangelical Calvinists held native converts to stringent doctrinal standards for baptism, Moravians simply required that they express a "love and Desire" to believe in Jesus. The Moravians' mystical approach to dreams and visions resembled natives' own belief that these phenomena could provide access to the spiritual world. By helping their converts interpret dreams, Moravian missionaries stepped into roles similar to those of traditional shamans. Moravians also supplemented their preaching with visual images of the wounded, bleeding Jesus enduring the tortures of the Cross, a practice

Calvinists regarded as idolatrous. One historian has suggested that the strong emphasis on the blood of Christ in Moravian art, hymns, and preaching transformed Jesus into the ultimate warrior captive, making Christianity powerfully attractive to young Delaware and Shawnee males who aspired to a similar stoicism. As a result, Moravian missionaries won several hundred converts among the Delaware, Shawnee, and Mingo people of western Pennsylvania and the Ohio Country. The Moravians' peaceful ways also earned them friendship with many non-Christian Indians who distrusted other white settlers.

The Great Awakening also inspired native converts such as the Mohegan Samson Occom to become ordained ministers and missionaries themselves. Occom became the most famous of these Indian preachers by partnering with the revivalist minister Eleazar Wheelock to promote what eventually became Dartmouth College. Wheelock initially billed the college as an extension of Moore's Indian Charity School, which he had been operating for several years. Occom was a natural publicist for the new college, having put his own learning under Wheelock to effective use as an ordained minister and missionary to the Montauk Indians of Long Island. In 1765, Occom agreed to undertake a two-year preaching tour in England on behalf of Wheelock's new venture, anticipating that it would benefit mostly young native men. The tour, which Occom and his companions modeled on Whitefield's market-savvy methods, made the Mohegan itinerant a celebrity in England and raised an enormous sum of £12,000 for the New Hampshire college. Dartmouth, however, trained few native youth, becoming instead another center of higher learning for aspiring Anglo-American gentry and clergy. Deeply disillusioned, Occom broke with Wheelock to found the Brothertown community, a haven for New England's Christian Indians in the Oneida country of central New York.

Samson Occom's bitter experience demonstrates that even the most sincere native converts to evangelical Christianity saw no inconsistency in using their newfound faith to pursue advantages for their own people. The new religious ways could help families and communities survive dislocation and social strain. Christian faith could give young men access to an education that could make them more effective in protecting native legal and commercial interests. Conversion to Christianity could give new force to native demands for equal treatment under the law. Even if such demands did not often succeed, they could provide temporary respite while Anglo-American officials scrambled to find new justifications for discriminatory policies. Similarities between certain strands of Protestant and native belief also allowed Indian Christians to preserve important cultural practices such as seeking spiritual guidance through dreams and visions. Even those Indians who refused conversion incorporated select elements of Christianity into traditional belief systems, sometimes producing compelling new forms of challenge and resistance to Anglo-American advance.

10.4.3: Prophets of Resistance in the Borderlands

The sweeping cultural changes that made evangelical Christianity attractive to some native groups prompted others to call for total repudiation of all things European. By the 1740s, it had become evident to all perceptive observers that the balance of power in Anglo-Indian relations had shifted drastically in favor of the English. Multiethnic Indian towns such as Logstown and Sonioto on the Ohio River were choked with refugees who had been displaced by English migrants or had seen their home villages decimated by European disease (see Chapter 9). Native dependence on European imported goods had taken a heavy toll in the loss of traditional crafts and the overhunting of game. Rum, one of the most abundantly traded eighteenth-century commodities, was wreaking havoc among native families and clans through addiction and abuse. Indeed, native leaders commonly blamed the rapid loss of tribal lands on the weakness for rum among individual Indians and lesser chiefs.

The experience of dislocation and distress made many borderlands Indians especially receptive to the message of a new group of prophets who began appearing in the late 1730s among Indian towns from Pennsylvania's Wyoming Valley to the French Illinois country. The earliest of these visionaries preached simple separation from white society. The Pennsylvania agent Conrad Weiser reported in 1737 that one such seer had warned starving Shawnee and Delaware inhabitants of the Susquehanna valley to stop trading skins for English rum. God had "driven all the wild animals out of the country" as a punishment for this practice, he declared, and if they refused to listen he would wipe them "from the earth." A decade later, a Naticoke appeared in the same region to warn that God "was not at peace" with either whites or Indians. If Indians did not stop associating with whites, he warned, "the white people would devour all of them." In the Wyoming Valley, a Delaware woman preached that God had originally made "three men and three women, the indians, the negro, and the white man." He intended each group to live and worship separately, with whites alone following the Bible.

Prophets sought to restore Indian spiritual power by revitalizing traditional religious practices through ritual, dance, and song, but these forms could also include new elements borrowed from Christianity. In the early1760s, for instance, the Delaware prophet Neolin traveled the Ohio Country teaching followers to dance, sing, kneel, and pray to a "little God" whose function of carrying "petitions & present[ing] them to a Great Being" resembled certain Christian teachings about Jesus. Neolin also urged Indians to "learn to live without any Trade or Connections with the White people, Clothing & Supporting themselves as their forefathers did." Like most prophets, Neolin preached against the use of rum, substituting an herbal emetic known as the "black drink," whose repeated use over a seven-year period would purge his followers of the "White people's Ways and Nature." Ritual drinking and vomiting of the tea spread throughout the Ohio valley, becoming so common in the Shawnee town of Wakatomica that English traders began calling it "vomit town."

Like the itinerancy of George Whitefield among Anglo-American settlements, the circulation of prophets like Neolin served to make Indians of the Ohio and southeastern borderlands aware of each other and of the common challenges they faced. Their Indian hearers shared the experience of cultural change through participation in Atlantic trade, one parallel in some ways to the experience of English colonists. Yet English manufactured goods often failed to raise native standards of living. For most, they had done quite the reverse, reducing Indian consumers to chronic dependency, addiction, dislocation, and death.

Prophets of revitalization offered a cure for the common Indian affliction of dependency on European trade. They reached intentionally across ancient divisions of geography and ethnicity, inviting their listeners to unite in a nativist movement that could restore Indian power to resist the advance of European trade and settlement.

The nativist message exerted an especially powerful appeal as Franco-British imperial conflict over North America intensified between 1745 and 1763. Yet the prophets of those decades could not overcome the competing alliances, conflicts of interest, and ongoing reliance on trade that would set native peoples and their French or English allies against one another in the looming war for North American empire.

Chronology

1704	*Boston News-letter* begins publication
1706	Birth of Benjamin Franklin
1714	George I of Hanover becomes monarch of Great Britain
1721	*New England Courant* begins publication
1728	James Gibbs' *Book of Architecture* published
1732	Birth of George Washington; *Poor Richard's Almanac* begins publication
1737	Jonathan Edwards' *Narrative of Surprising Conversions* published; nativist prophet warns Shawnee and Delaware to stop trading skins for rum
1739	George Whitefield begins his first American tour
1741	David Brainerd becomes missionary to the Lenape
1746	College of New Jersey (Princeton University) founded
1764	Rhode Island College (Brown University) founded
1760	Birth of African Methodist Episcopal founder Richard Allen
1765	Mohegan minister Samson Occom embarks on preaching tour of England
1766	Queens College (Rutgers) founded
1769	Dartmouth College founded

Chapter 11
Slavery and Empire
African American Cultures in the Colonial British Atlantic

 ## Learning Objectives

11.1 Review how the slave economy fuelled the prosperity of colonial America

11.2 Recognize the ethnic diversity of the African slaves

11.3 Identify the difference in the socio-demographic conditions of the slaves across the American geography

11.4 Recognize that slaves in the eighteenth-century colonial world were valued only by their ability to work

The story of the British empire in North America was inseparably intertwined with the enslavement of Africans. Profits in the New World required a supply of cheap labor. As the founders of Georgia discovered, no one could escape the exploitative logic of early modern capitalism. In December 1738, a group of "settlers, freeholders, and inhabitants of the province of Georgia" petitioned the colony's trustees to lift their ban on the importation and use of African slave labor. The petitioners complained that well-intentioned efforts to found a colony without slaves had only doomed Georgia to economic failure. Neighboring South Carolina planters could use slaves to prepare and ship timber, Georgia's most promising export, for "one half of the price we can do." The petitioners expressed confidence that "in time, silk and wine may be produced here," but not at competitive prices so long as the ban on slaves remained. Neighboring Carolinians could "raise every thing this colony can," the colonists reminded the trustees, "and they having their labor so much cheaper will always ruin our market." Permitting the "use of negroes," they concluded, would "both occasion great numbers of white people to come here, and also render us capable to subsist ourselves . . . until we could make some produce fit for export."

Although not all Georgians supported the Remonstrance of 1738, the petition helps illuminate eighteenth-century slavery's central role in the economics of empire. By 1740, slave-based plantations had become the engines that drove the British Atlantic economy. The most lucrative colonial staples—tobacco, dyes, rice, and above all, sugar products—were cultivated overwhelmingly by slave labor at relatively low cost for handsome profits to planters and merchants alike. Ownership of slaves had become the key to success throughout much of British America. Planters such as Virginia's William Byrd II derived their fortunes— complete with great, elegantly furnished country houses, luxury goods, fashionable clothing, and English educations—from the backbreaking labor of slaves who cultivated their fields.

It is easy to overlook how much slavery influenced the lives of Europeans who did not themselves own slaves. Many free farmers in places such as Pennsylvania and Rhode Island supported themselves by selling crops to distant plantations. This commerce allowed slave masters to concentrate on making sugar or rice. And, of course, as with so many empires, the people living in England—the heart of empire—enjoyed their sugar without giving too much thought about the human suffering that went into its production. Out of sight, out of mind. Not a few great mansions in the English countryside owed their existence to the unfree labor of the New World.

In such an environment, the Georgia petitioners could legitimately ask "what should induce persons to bring ships here" to purchase commodities when they could obtain the same goods at "one half the expense" in a nearby slave colony. Georgia's founder, Governor James Oglethorpe, might retort that a few wealthy landowners stood to gain most by slavery's introduction to Georgia, but the fact remained that the colonial slave economy elsewhere was making it increasingly difficult for the fledgling colony to prosper as many inhabitants desired without the competitive advantage that slavery would bring.

The demand for cheap labor excused practices so cruel that English people living in London would never have condoned them—that is, if they had witnessed them in England. Thus, Georgia's sagging fortunes over the next twelve years made proslavery arguments increasingly difficult to resist, and in 1750 the trustees finally lifted the ban. Within a decade, the colony became as dependent on slave labor as neighboring South Carolina.

Georgia planters, like Anglo-Americans elsewhere, came to enjoy the growth of the eighteenth-century consumer economy at exorbitant human cost. The Atlantic slave trade coincided with the eighteenth-century "consumer revolution," reaching a peak of 5.1 million souls between 1700 and 1800. Most enslaved Africans ended up on sugar plantations in Brazil or the Caribbean. Around 4 percent of the total number—some 200,000 persons—found themselves in North America.

As eighteenth-century European immigrants struggled to improve Anglo-American holdings— for many the first real property they had ever owned—African newcomers faced the wrenching challenge of adjusting to colonial life as an article of human property. Indeed, slaves constituted one of the most important commodities of British Atlantic trade, valuable chattel acquired and distributed throughout the empire on the basis of supply and demand. Yet slaves never forgot that they were far more than mere chattel, nor did they let their masters forget.

We should not forget that there was another side to the story of unfreedom in America. Wherever they found themselves, slaves strenuously resisted European efforts to reduce them to mere property as "human tools." Each New World destination confronted Africans newcomers with a different environment, a different set of demands, and a different range of resources that they could employ to influence the conditions of life in slavery. During the eighteenth century, African slaves and their descendants—the African Diaspora of the Atlantic World—created a rich range of cultures as they struggled daily with specific local processes of adaptation to unfamiliar persons, novel surroundings, and unaccustomed tasks.

11.1: European Markets; American Slavery

11.1 Review how the slave economy fuelled the prosperity of colonial America

Eighteenth-century Atlantic commerce rested squarely on a foundation of trade in plantation staples produced by slaves transported to America from many different parts of Africa. Like the automobile industry in twentieth-century America, the colonial-era plantation system generated a range of high-demand goods as well as many more enterprises that were linked in some way to the primary staple market. By the 1690s, British observers could plainly see the plantation system's importance to the English Atlantic economy. The Bristol merchant John Cary celebrated the circuit of Atlantic trade which carried from Africa the workers "whereby our Plantations are improved, and 'tis by their Labours such great Quantities of *Sugar, Tobacco, Cotton, Ginger*, and *Indigo* are raised." These "bulky Commodities" in turn required "great Numbers of our Ships for their transporting hither." The increase of ships on Atlantic trade routes stimulated in its own turn "the greater number of Handecraft Trades at home," carried more British goods to Atlantic markets, and generated a demand for "more Saylors, who are maintained by the separate Imploy." By 1700, the labor demands of large-scale plantation production had prompted Anglo-American planters to follow the lead of their West Indian counterparts in relying on African slaves rather than English or Irish indentured servants (see Chapters 4 and 7). Consumption of the goods produced by these slaves fueled eighteenth-century commercial growth.

11.1.1: An Empire of Sugar and Slaves

In the mid-eighteenth century, West Indian sugar constituted Great Britain's most important colonial staple. The value of sugar imported to the British Isles rose from £630,000 between 1699 and 1701 to over £2,362,000 between 1772 and 1774, enormous sums that would be measured in billions of dollars today. By the latter period, North American colonists imported £2,168,000 worth of sugar, almost as much as the mother country itself. The breathtaking growth of sugar production reflects the commodity's transformation from a luxury item consumed mainly by the wealthy to a common good consumed by all but the poorest members of eighteenth-century British society. By 1750, sugar's incorporation into the daily diet of ordinary people assured its dominance over all other plantation staples. The volume of capital at stake in the sugar trade gave West Indian planters access to the highest levels of power and prestige in London. The price of the sugar barons' power was borne by their African slaves, most of whom were doomed to comparatively short lives of cultivating and processing this most grueling of plantation crops.

The end of the War of the Spanish Succession in 1714 (see Chapter 8) established the conditions for a shift in the balance of production on the British sugar islands, with a consequent shift in the number of slaves destined for each. In 1714, Barbados still outstripped Jamaica and the Leeward Islands—St. Christopher, Nevis, Antigua, and Montserrat—in total output, producing nearly 50 percent of all sugar exported from the British West Indies. Over the next few decades, however, production in the Leewards and Jamaica both surpassed that of Britain's oldest sugar island, which slipped to less than one-fifth of the total by 1750. During the same period, the number of slave laborers on Barbados increased from 50,000 to 69,000, while those on the Leewards nearly tripled to just under 63,000 and those on

Jamaica almost quadrupled to 118,000. Only the massive importation of new slaves could have supported such phenomenal population growth. Indeed, because death rates on the sugar islands remained higher than rates of birth until well after 1750, the numbers of slaves actually transported from Africa greatly exceeded the number of those who survived to be counted at mid-century.

This rapidly expanding circuit of sugar, slaves, and capital placed the British West Indies at the vortex of the empire's economic growth. The rising demand for labor employed more than a hundred slaving vessels each year in bringing thousands of men and women from West Africa to the islands. Between 1720 and 1729, for instance, slavers brought over 72,000 slaves to Jamaica alone, an annual average of 7,200 persons. The West Indian demand for fish, livestock, agricultural products, building materials, and barrel staves attracted a steady stream of ships each year from North America. By the end of the colonial period, the annual value of Anglo-American goods shipped to the British West Indies was approaching £850,000, nearly three-fifths of the value of North American goods shipped to the England and Scotland themselves. This is a familiar tale of how market desire transformed a human and physical landscape many thousands of miles away from where consumers actually celebrated the pleasures of a new product.

11.1.2: Chesapeake Tobacco and Carolina Rice

As West Indian sugar plantations dominated the British Atlantic economy, so the tobacco and rice plantations of the Chesapeake and the low-country South dominated the Anglo-American export market. Indeed, Chesapeake tobacco ranked second in importance only to sugar until the 1760s, when it was surpassed by tea, an equally exploitative product harvested in South Asia. Exports to Europe from the eighteenth-century South—mainly Maryland, Virginia, and South Carolina—outstripped those from the North by almost two to one. By far the largest percentage of these products came from slaves laboring on tobacco and rice plantations. Chesapeake and South Carolina slaves also produced much of the wheat, corn, boards, and barrel staves shipped from southern ports to the Caribbean.

Tobacco planters' dependence on slavery grew rapidly after 1700. The crop was labor intensive but required little initial investment beyond land, a tobacco shed, and a few hand tools. Thus, yeomen farmers could continue to grow the crop on small, single-family plots of less than 200 acres even as larger planters began amassing land and slaves. Indeed, most plantations employed fewer than eleven slaves until mid-century, and the majority of bondpeople lived on plantations of less than twenty slaves throughout the colonial period. By the 1730s, however, the great Tidewater planters living along the James, York, and Rappahannock estuaries had begun building large estates staffed with twenty or more slaves. Many wealthy planters also established plantations for their children in the Virginia Piedmont and staffing each with eleven or more slaves, even as ordinary freeholders began purchasing additional land along with one or two slaves to increase their own production.

The corresponding demand for slave laborers prompted white Virginians to import more than sixty-two thousand Africans between 1700 and 1775. Unlike the slave population in the British West Indies, however, the existing slave population in Virginia and Maryland always contributed to overall population growth. In the West Indies, harsh labor conditions suppressed slave women's fertility and killed more workers than the birthrate could replace. Even in the first decade of the century, when imports nearly doubled the number of slaves in Virginia, births contributed 0.2 percent to the total black population growth. Natural increase peaked at 4.7 percent between 1740 and 1750, and averaged 2.6 percent over the entire period.

Old Plantation, a watercolor by an unknown artist (about 1800) shows that African customs survived plantation slavery. The man and women in the center dance to the music of drum and banjo, possibly to celebrate a wedding. Instruments, turbans, and scarves reflect a distinctive African American culture in the New World.

In contrast to Virginia tobacco, the production of South Carolina rice depended on slave labor from the very beginning. Planters who began cultivating the crop after 1695 quickly came to believe that a rice plantation had to start out as a large-scale operation to achieve profitability. The planter Thomas Nairne estimated an initial outlay of at least £1,000 to purchase equipment and the minimum thirty slaves needed for clearing, draining, damming, and ditching the land as well as planting and tending the crop. Despite the daunting expense, Carolina rice plantations multiplied, and imports to England surged from a negligible amount in 1700 to a value of over £340,000 between 1772 and 1774. The rapid growth in rice production stimulated a demand for slaves that made Africans the majority population in South Carolina as early as 1708. Between 1700 and 1770, the number of slaves increased from 2,400 to 82,000, with most growth coming by importation from Africa.

The development of new crops and slave-based plantation enterprises brought about a dramatic shift in the distribution of blacks throughout Britain's eighteenth-century Atlantic empire. In 1700, most of the empire's blacks—nearly 200,000—resided in the Caribbean, more than a quarter of them on Barbados. Less than 20,000 lived in North America. By 1750, however, the combination of importations and natural increase had boosted the proportion of blacks living on the mainland to four in ten. In the Caribbean, Jamaica's black population had far outstripped that of Barbados, and a much greater proportion of West Indian blacks labored on sugar plantations in the Leewards. The harsh conditions of sugar production on the islands—and in Brazil as well—simply prevented the births that would have enabled the slave population to grow by natural increase. By 1774, mainland blacks constituted a majority of the empire's population, outnumbering the islands' black population by more than thirty thousand souls. The processes of migration, adaptation, birth, growth, and death took place within a wide variety of Atlantic World environments. The empire's black diaspora encountered an extraordinary range of experience that nevertheless remained unified by a number of common elements.

11.2: Common Threads of African Experience

11.2 Recognize the ethnic diversity of the African slaves

Contrary to what some people today claim, there was no single African background that defined the slave experience in the new world. Just as we would not argue that all European migrants shared a common culture—think of German, Irish, and Dutch colonists, for example—we cannot posit a monolithic African past. The men and women doomed to slavery came from different regions of the continent; they spoke many different languages. From this perspective, we can say that the eighteenth-century Atlantic slave trade wrenched millions of sub-Saharan Africans from exceedingly diverse cultural settings and thrust them into a wrenching process of bondage, forced migration, and resettlement an ocean away from their homes. The cramped, reeking vessels that carried these slaves to various Atlantic destinations also confronted them with one of the earliest of several common threads, which ran through the divergent experiences of bondage (see Chapter 3). No matter where they ended up, new arrivals faced other common challenges. The effort to communicate with one another, to learn the ropes of work and survival, and to forge new patterns of community and family life from the remembered fragments of disparate languages and traditions—these together posed a series of difficulties that engaged the highest creative energies of the Africans who survived the Middle Passage.

11.2.1: Coercion, Resistance, Negotiation

No matter where slavery took root or what justifications its practitioners offered, the institution remained violent at its very core. There were some masters, of course, who claimed that bondage was a blessing—that it exposed Africans to true religion, for example. But such rationalizations were entirely self-serving. For Africans, slavery began in violence through war or capture and was sustained in violence through the process of sale and transatlantic transport. In the Caribbean islands and the American mainland, violence continued to lurk just beneath the surface of the slave-master relationship. Slaves and masters always worked at crossed purposes: the masters relentlessly seeking to extract the maximum labor possible from their slave property, the slaves constantly snatching up opportunities for even a moment's freedom from forced toil. Masters used all incentives at their disposal—rewards as well as punishments—to gain their objectives. Yet the final resort always remained close to hand: the whip, maiming, torture, even death. And indeed, many slaves chose resistance to the death over a lifetime of unrelieved bondage.

Eighteenth-century mainland slaves faced much harsher regimes of discipline and punishment than had their seventeenth-century predecessors. Smaller numbers of slaves in the seventeenth-century mainland colonies, coupled with the frequent need for masters and slaves to live and work side by side, had required different patterns of accommodation. But as the slave numbers boomed after 1700, harsh measures that had already become common in British West Indian slave societies took hold in the Chesapeake and the low country as well. Planters lived in constant fear of slave uprisings and used brutal measures to nip any resistance in the bud. Slaves endured vicious lashings for infractions such as working too slowly or balking at orders. Masters made humiliating examples of recalcitrant slaves who failed their expectations or resisted their orders. The Virginia planter William Byrd punished his house-slave Eugene for bed-wetting by forcing him to "drink a pint of piss." Byrd and South Carolina planter Joseph Ball fitted metal bits into the mouths of slaves who persistently ran away.

The Virginia planter Robert "King" Carter preferred to chop off the toes of "Incorrigible" runaways. Masters throughout colonial America bound offending slaves to pillories, lashed them mercilessly at whipping posts, subjected some to torture, and hung others on the gallows.

To be sure, masters did not rely on violence alone to bring their slaves into line. They recognized the usefulness of leniency and reward, and most defined their own role within an ideology which made them a *pater familias*, the benevolent, if sometimes necessarily strict, head of a household that extended beyond his wife and children to all the slaves residing on his plantation. William Byrd compared himself to one of the biblical patriarchs with a "large family" that included "my flocks and my herds, my bond-men and bond-women." Planters expressed their benevolence through such practices as granting midday breaks, setting aside Sundays as days of rest, allowing slaves to visit spouses or gather for merrymaking off the plantation, and granting occasional holidays—usually Christmas, Easter, and Whitsuntide, a church holiday falling in late May or early June. Many delegated the harshest duties of daily discipline to the plantation overseer. They positioned themselves as stern but fair authorities who might occasionally intervene to adjudicate disputes between slaves and overseers, reducing or suspending punishments where such an act could burnish their reputation for benevolence without undermining labor discipline.

Slaves resisted the plantation regime of work and discipline through a variety of measures ranging from feigning illness or stupidity to outright rebellion. Newly arrived slaves pretended ignorance of the language to avoid work. As one visitor to Maryland observed, "Let an hundred Men shew" a new slave "how to hoe, or drive a Wheelbarrow, he'll still take one by the bottom, and the Other by the Wheel." Slaves on rice plantations often absconded into the surrounding swamps during harvest season to escape the punishing task of threshing and processing the crop. Slaves on tobacco or sugar plantations might break hoes or feign illness to get out of work. Running away was a constant problem, and planters salted the advertising sections of colonial newspapers with notices detailing missing slaves' appearance, attire, habits, and manners of speech or behavior. Where terrain such as Jamaica's Cockpit Country or South Carolina's swamps permitted, runaways formed maroon communities where members could evaded capture for months or years. Indeed, Jamaican maroons became a permanent presence on the island, feared for their fierce, well-organized raids and a tenacious defense of territory that eventually forced planters to recognize their independence.

Occasionally, slaves in Britain's mainland colonies protested their debasement through organized revolt. The most serious slave rebellion on the colonial mainland was the Stono Uprising, which took place in September 1739. One hundred fifty South Carolina blacks rose up and, seizing guns and ammunition, murdered several white planters. "With Colours displayed, and two Drums beating," they marched toward Spanish Florida, where they had been promised freedom. The local militia soon overtook the rebellious slaves and killed most of them. Jamaican slaves mounted many such rebellions throughout the eighteenth century. In 1760, for instance, Tacky's Rebellion embroiled several parishes around Kingston in a conflict that lasted for several weeks and took an alliance of regular British troops and local militia to suppress. Although no slave revolt succeeded in overthrowing the plantation regime until the 1790s, recurrent outbreaks of rebellion persuaded whites everywhere that their own blacks might secretly be planning bloody revolt. Fear bred paranoia. When an unstable white servant woman in New York City announced in 1741 that blacks intended to burn the town, frightened authorities executed 32 suspected arsonists and dispatched 175 others to the West Indies. Although interracial violence remained sporadic and comparatively low, everyone recognized that the blacks—in the words of one Virginia governor—longed "to Shake off the fetters of Slavery."

Most slaves recognized the improbability of successful revolt and chose instead to extract concessions from the planters that could ameliorate the conditions of slavery. The eighteenth-century master-slave relationship thus involved an incessant, if often clandestine, struggle that pitted the planter's demand for labor against the slave's desire for liberty. The balance of power and coercion remained with the masters, who did not hesitate to employ whatever method seemed most effective. Yet the slaves possessed their own means of prosecuting the struggle, and their resources increased with new knowledge and new skill. Experienced field hands on tobacco plantations knew how to ruin the crop by hoeing in the wrong places or cutting the leaves at the wrong time. Slaves on a sugar estate could sabotage the mill during the critical harvest season, decimating production as the cane dried in the fields while the equipment was being repaired. A strategic swipe of a hoe in an irrigation ditch might flood a rice field prematurely or drain it to let the plants bake dry in the midsummer sun. A toxin extracted from a local herb and slipped into a hated planter's food might leave the victim doubled over with abdominal pains or put him into an early grave. As the slaves' ability to undertake such actions grew, so did their masters' willingness to extend them limited concessions—longer breaks, additional time off, monetary compensation for overwork, and the right to sell produce from provision plots—in order to avoid costly mishaps or the trouble and expense of tracking down runaways.

11.2.2: Race and Freedom

Africans who disembarked from eighteenth-century slave ships stepped into a world in which their place had become more sharply bounded by evolving European notions of immutable racial difference. In this respect their situation differed markedly from that of the seventeenth century, when blacks had lived in a comparatively fluid social environment governed more by categories of status and ethnicity than race. To be sure, Caribbean and Anglo-American masters of that period had often justified the practice of slavery in racist terms. English writers had frequently associated blacks in Africa with heathen religion, barbarous behavior, and sexual promiscuity—in fact, with evil itself. From such a perspective, the enslavement of Africans had seemed unobjectionable. The planters maintained that if black slaves converted to Christianity, shedding their supposedly savage ways, they would benefit from their loss of freedom. Yet practice had not yet fully conformed with this rhetoric of race. Not all unfree blacks were enslaved for life, and those who gained their freedom after a time of servitude could gain entry into colonial society as property holders and owners of slaves themselves.

By the first decade of the eighteenth century, the legal status of the empire's unfree black people was no longer in doubt. Nearly every plantation colony had on its law books a set of black codes that, among many other things, designated unfree persons of African descent as slaves for life, along with their children after them. This transformation reached British North America somewhat later than the West Indies because of the lag in African American population growth on the mainland. Yet as the black population expanded, lawmakers in colonies from the Carolinas to New England drew up increasingly strict slave statues that codified the racism always latent in New World societies. Slavery came to be based unequivocally on the color of a person's skin. Blacks fell into this status simply because they were black.

A vicious pattern of discrimination had been set in motion. Even conversion to Christianity could not free an African from bondage. Associations between blacks and poor whites diminished as African slaves displaced white servants. Increasingly discriminatory laws made it difficult for free blacks to remain in plantation colonies. Similar statutes pushed free blacks to the margins of life in New England and the Middle Colonies. The new racial code permitted white planters to deal with their black property as they alone saw fit. One Virginia statute excused a master who had killed a slave on the grounds that no rational person would purposely "destroy his own estate." Children born to a slave woman became slaves regardless of the father's race. Unlike the Spanish colonies, where persons of lighter color enjoyed greater legal privileges in society, the English colonies tolerated no mixing of the races. Mulattoes and those of pure African descent fell under the same legal designation as slaves for life.

11.2.3: African, Creole, Mulatto

The enactment of black codes prevented neither whites nor blacks from recognizing and acting upon a wide range of differences among the members of the slave population. One of the primary tensions confronting slaves throughout the eighteenth-century British empire was that between newly arrived "outlandish" Africans and those who had been born and reared within a slave society. The ongoing large-scale importation of Africans made this a constant dynamic within slave communities everywhere, one that altered as the balance shifted from African to creole predominance. Where Africans formed the majority population—as they did in the Caribbean for much of the century and in the Carolina for many years—creoles often suffered derision, mockery, and exclusion from community life. Newly arrived men and women from Africa were far more likely to run away, assault their masters, and organize rebellion than were the creole slaves. The people described in colonial newspaper advertisements as "New Negroes" tried desperately to regain control over their lives. In 1770—just to cite one moving example—two young Africans, both recently sold in Virginia, "went off with several others, being persuaded that they could find their way back to their own Country."

As creoles became the majority, they often began looking down on Africans as "Guineabirds" or "Salt-water Negroes" and sometimes took advantage of the newcomers' lack of experience. Caribbean creoles might take a new arrival into their household and force him to work their garden plots. The creole community could make life very difficult for Africans who held themselves aloof or who resisted adaptation to local custom. Yet creoles could also be very helpful, assisting new arrivals to perfect the language, teaching them how to master their tasks, showing them how to evade punishment, and helping them survive the hardships of slave life.

As slaves adapted to their environment and began rearing children, a second tension emerged between those of fully African descent and those mixed race. Colonial law may have distinguished between black and white, and various colonial legislatures attempted to enforce the separation by prohibiting miscegenation, or the fathering of mixed-race children. Nevertheless, interracial sexual liaisons frequently occurred, producing mulatto offspring who inherited their mother's legal status. Caribbean planters thought of mulattoes as a distinct group of "coloureds" between blacks and whites. Mainland planters seldom made such distinctions in speech or writing, but they often followed their island counterparts in extending relatively privileged treatment to mulatto slaves. Caribbean planters never assigned mulattoes to field work, as often happened in the Chesapeake and the low country. Yet in all regions, lighter-skinned mulattoes tended receive preference for places of domestic service and for training in crafts such as carpentry, masonry, and blacksmithing. These distinctions alone created divisions of rank within local African American communities, often fostering a sense of superiority among the lighter-skinned domestics and skilled laborers and resentment among the common field hands.

Mulattoes were also more likely to receive their freedom than other slaves, a fact that further complicated their place within the empire's larger African American communities. To be sure, manumission remained rare throughout the eighteenth century. In 1770, freedmen constituted a mere 2 percent of the black population in Jamaica and Virginia, and less than 1 percent in South Carolina and Barbados. Yet when masters did consent to free a slave, the favor most often went to lighter-skinned mulattoes. Because of their preferment in crafts, mulattoes also frequently enjoyed additional trade skills needed to meet conditions of manumission, which often included the earning and payment of their value on the slave market.

Once they gained liberty, however, mulatto freedmen occupied a tenuous place in plantation society. Their practical situation often differed little from the legal status they had so recently escaped. Freedmen usually continued to associate most closely with slaves. Ties of kinship or financial need often kept them working at the same tasks for the same employers they had formerly served in bondage.

11.2.4: Family and Community

Eighteenth-century slaves had to overcome formidable obstacles in order to marry and raise families. British American slave codes recognized only the mother-child tie, primarily to determine the legal status of the child. The law offered no recognition or protection of slave marriages. The preponderance of males among new arrivals—more than two-thirds throughout the eighteenth century—made it impossible for many men to find wives. Ethnic differences and linguistic barriers among new arrivals also deterred slaves from marrying. Masters often housed new arrivals from Africa into sex-segregated barracks as a means of controlling their labor force. Slave women, married or not, remained vulnerable to the unwanted sexual attention and assault of their masters. Masters intervened constantly in the parent–child relationship, conferring names of their own choice on children as they did on

African parents, sending mothers back into field work while consigning care of their children to others, determining the age at which children could be assigned tasks, and overruling parental discipline and protection to impose the master's own regime of punishment and reward. Slave sales could separate children, parents, and spouses from each other at any time.

Yet historians now recognize that many slaves exercised extraordinary resourcefulness in overcoming these barriers to establish resilient networks of family and kin. Even where families proved most difficult to form and maintain—places such as the mainland North and the rapidly expanding Leeward sugar islands of the 1720s and 1730s—slaves practiced "fictive kinship" in which they faithfully cared for each other's children as their own. First-generation Africans who married tended to establish nuclear family units, and married couples lived together wherever possible in a dwelling that also housed the woman's children.

Despite the absence of legal sanctions, marriage among slaves became commonplace as the population became established in a region. Slaves wedded "after their own way" in rites that took various forms throughout the British mainland and Caribbean colonies. Most remained simple ceremonies in which the proposing groom offered a gift—a "*Brass Ring* or some other *Toy*" in the tobacco country, roasted peanuts in South Carolina—whose acceptance by the prospective bride sealed the marriage. European observers considered such unions remarkably casual, believing that a wife could dissolve a marriage simply by returning the husband's gift. Europeans also commented frequently on the persistence of the African custom of polygyny—the union between a man and more than one woman—which the Anglican minister Francis Le Jau described as "a General Sin" among South Carolina slaves. Although such comments reflected a great deal of misunderstanding about the cultural significance of marriage among Africans, they do demonstrate the slaves' resourcefulness in reconstructing one of the central institutions of their social life.

As marriages became more common, slaves developed kinship networks that spanned several plantations. Slave couples frequently lived on different estates. Guy, a slave carpenter who lived on the Sabine Hall estate of Virginia planter Landon Carter, left frequently to spend the night with his wife on a neighboring plantation. Like many other planters throughout the British Atlantic, Carter usually granted permission for Guy to visit, but the carpenter harbored no scruples about leaving even without his master's permission. Like other planters, Carter usually conceded what he could not prevent. Planters living on adjoining estates might allow slave couples multiple visits each week, whereas those living more than 10 miles apart might allow visits only once per month or less. Such circumstances strained the nuclear family arrangement of husband, wife, and children which creole slaves attempted to reconstruct, demanding the creation of larger networks of kin, both real and fictive. Through these networks, the center of family life shifted from households and couples to more extensive units involving one or more grandparents, uncles, aunts, and cousins as well as spouses.

The extension of kinship networks across several plantations also facilitated the growth of slave communities over time. As with the development of family life, slaves had to confront various legal and practical barriers to the formation of community. Black codes typically prohibited unauthorized travel or gathering of slaves or the observance of secret rituals. They also proscribed certain activities such as the beating of drums and the blowing of horns, items that slaves might use to signal a revolt. In addition to these legal restrictions, new arrivals confronted barriers of language and custom, and often of distance as well. Yet slaves managed to overcome these barriers to community life, sometimes with their masters' permission of their masters and other times behind the masters' backs.

Visitors to the southern mainland colonies and the Caribbean alike commented frequently on the community life they observed among the slaves. The arrangements of slave houses themselves afforded the first evidence of community formation. Where slaves were given the latitude to build housing after their own design, they arranged dwellings in patterns that supported communal living. Quarters constructed by West African slaves frequently resembled the clustered compounds of small shelters they had known in Africa. Even when European-style construction and layout was used, archaeological evidence reveals that slaves conducted most daily activities such as cooking, eating, and washing in the common outdoor space around the quarters. This practice fostered frequent opportunities to socialize and forge community. Aspects of building construction and layout changed in various ways over time depending on local circumstances, but the communal features of life in the slave quarters persisted into the nineteenth century.

Slaves throughout the British Atlantic took many other opportunities to socialize. Field laborers in Virginia and the Carolinas frequently followed back paths between the plantations to open meadows or forest clearings where they would meet to socialize and dance at the end of the day. The evangelist George Whitefield encountered one such group "dancing round the fire" as he traveled through rural South Carolina in the winter of 1739. Thomas Jefferson marveled at the stamina his own slaves displayed as they congregated in back meadows to dance and sing until midnight after completing a full day's work in his tobacco fields. In South Carolina and the Caribbean islands, slaves also developed thriving internal markets for the sale and exchange of produce they grew on their provision plots. The Scottish traveler Janet Schaw observed during her visit to Antigua in the mid-1770s that slaves were "the only market people. Nobody else dreams of selling provisions." In colonial New York, where their employment as domestics and farm hands impeded the communal life that emerged on the plantations, blacks found other ways to come together. New York slaves, for instance, transformed the traditional Dutch Pinkster festival into an opportunity for celebration, dance, and song that reflected strong African influences.

Marriages and funerals also became occasions for communal celebration. Though the marriage rites were simple and private, the news of a slave marriage brought celebrants together from surrounding plantations for dancing and feasting. Masters permitted the celebrations at night after the day's work had been completed, and sometimes contributed a hog to the festivities. Funerals drew slaves together to mourn the loss of a friend or kin. Visitors to the British West Indies remarked upon slaves' highly structured funerals. Rites on Montserrat, according to the 1760s traveler John Singleton, included long processions attended with mourning dances, chants sung in "full chorus," and graveside rituals performed by a religious leader to "compose the spirit of the dead."

11.2.5: Slave Religion

Slave funerals and burial customs reveal the persistence of African religious beliefs and practices that imparted deep spiritual significance to the lives of eighteenth-century slaves. Salt water slaves clung to their religious traditions with a tenacity that frustrated Christian missionaries and prompted frequent comment from masters and visitors to the plantations. To these Europeans, slaves seemed determined to remain "as much under the influence of Pagan darkness, idolatry, and superstition, as they were at their first arrival from Africa." Such comments provide a record of African beliefs too fragmentary for historians to reconstruct into a coherent system, although they do suggest that African religion remained a powerful element in the slaves' lives.

The religious beliefs that Africans brought to the New World varied according to the region from which they came. Some, especially those shipped from the region of Gambia, were Muslims or familiar with Islam, and a select few were literate in Arabic. Another smaller group came from regions such as the Kingdom of Kongo where Christianity was practiced. The vast majority, however, observed neither Christianity nor Islam, but belonged to various "overlapping networks of religious relationship," in the words of one historian of Africa in this period. Many venerated their ancestors and believed in various benevolent and malevolent spirits whose power they might harness for good or ill. Others had likely belonged to hunters' guilds or were initiates into spirit possession cults. Some brought sufficient knowledge to act as conjurors or healers, and at least a few of these may have served as herbalists, witch doctors, or diviners in their African homelands.

Africans called on whatever spiritual resources they had brought with them to help them survive in the New World. Caribbean slaves fused together certain religious practices and offices into religious form which European visitors referred to as "Obeah," an Anglicized term combining two different West African words: *ubio*, a charm that caused sickness or death, and *o-bayifo*, a sorcerer. Practitioners of Obeah reputedly possessed the power to diagnose and treat diseases, to detect witches and cure the bewitched, and to predict the future. Though mainland observers never mentioned Obeah directly, similar practices of conjuring were everywhere known and feared. Conjurers brought with them a fund of herbal lore and quickly found or discovered New World plants from which they could extract a variety of poisons and remedies. Planters throughout the empire took precautions to protect themselves against poisoning by their slaves. Slaves likewise feared being poisoned by a vengeful conjuror. Indeed, the historian Philip D. Morgan has asserted that slavery brought about a decisive shift away from "benevolent lesser spirits" to "those spirits deemed useful in injuring other people." Still, slaves and masters alike could benefit from herbal remedies concocted by experienced conjurors. Over time, European planters and physicians learned to respect and ask—or force—African conjurors to divulge the secret properties of various medicinal herbs.

Blacks expressed persistent African beliefs through customs ranging from dance and music to the way they buried their dead. European observers were convinced that the "great activity and strength of Body" exerted in dance, coupled with its apparent eroticism and the wearing of adornments such as masks and animal skins or tails, possessed religious significance. Archaeological evidence from Maryland to Barbados reveals that slaves buried their dead with talismans, beads, and pots of food and drink which Europeans thought were intended to assist the departed on their journey to the place of the dead.

Most first-generation Africans took refuge in their traditional beliefs and strenuously resisted the religion of their masters, but by the mid-eighteenth century the empire's emerging creole population began turning to Christianity. Their manner of adopting the new faith suggests that converts sought in it an alternative set of spiritual resources that could help them adapt to their circumstances, even though many of their kin continued to find African religion sufficient for this purpose. A comparative few submitted to Anglican baptism and presented their infants for baptism as well. Most, however, were repelled by eighteenth-century Anglicanism's stiff, creedal forms, the racial condescension of its clergy, and the blatant racism of Anglo-American church members. Black converts found much more congenial the greater spontaneity and egalitarianism of the evangelical Christianity popularized by the first Great Awakening.

Early evangelical leaders demonstrated much greater sympathy for the slaves and a far greater readiness to present the message of Christian conversion in terms they could readily embrace. Indeed, John Wesley, the founder of the Methodist movement and an Anglican missionary to Georgia during the 1730s, was highly critical of slavery and of planter opposition to converting the slaves. Wesley's concern struck a powerful chord among many slaves who heard him, as did the preaching of his successor, George Whitefield. During Whitefield's first great tour of the mainland colonies in 1739 and 1740 (see Chapter 10), the Grand Itinerant criticized slavery frequently and invited blacks to respond to his message of New Birth on terms no different than those he extended to white hearers. His South Carolina followers Hugh and Jonathan Bryan encouraged their slaves to convert to evangelical Christianity. Later evangelists such as the Presbyterian Samuel Davies also devoted special attention to making black converts. Davies himself held meetings especially for "poor Negroes" at his home in Hanover County, Virginia. To be sure, few of these early evangelical leaders opposed slavery completely, and Whitefield eventually joined in lobbying the Georgia trustees to lift their ban on slavery. Nevertheless, the evangelicals' open, sympathetic preaching of the New Birth resonated with black listeners.

Blacks embraced evangelical Christianity for its emphasis on experience, its potent themes of salvation and deliverance, and the opportunity it offered for converts to take the initiative in participation and leadership. The historian Mechal Sobel has suggested that evangelicalism—especially in its Baptist form—shared with West African religion a similar emphasis on sudden conversion accompanied by a ritual bath signifying death and rebirth. Evangelical Baptists and Methodists expressed their devotion in boisterous meetings accompanied by exuberant singing, dancing, skipping, and falling, physical demonstrations of faith that invited black participation on familiar terms. Early evangelicals also welcomed black converts into church membership on an equal basis with whites. In so doing, they gave concrete expression to hopes for Christ's return to deliver his oppressed people and establish a millennial kingdom of righteousness, justice, liberty, and peace. Evangelicals also stressed the Holy Spirit's readiness to empower blacks as well as whites to preach and exhort, opening the way for many black laypersons to assume places of leadership in evangelical circles. Black lay preachers soon began establishing their own congregations on southern plantations, and many hit the road to preach in neighboring locales. Runaway slave ads of the period reveal that some black preachers used their itinerancy as a path to freedom.

Because evangelicalism emerged only late in the colonial period, the number of black converts in British America remained small before the 1770s. Evangelicalism proved more popular among the creole population of the Chesapeake and the colonial North than in the African-dominated low country and West Indies. South Carolina slaves did not turn to Christianity in large numbers until after the American Revolution. Evangelical Methodism began attracting a few converts on Antigua and Jamaica in the 1760s. Obeah, however, remained popular in the Caribbean well into the nineteenth century. In Jamaica the new African-derived Myalism, with its initiation ceremony of public burial and resurrection, also appeared in the 1760s to offer a compelling alternative to evangelicalism.

The efforts to reconstruct viable family, community, and religious lives engaged African and creole slaves in an imaginative reshaping of African and European customs. As first-generation Africans married spouses from different ethnic groups, the partners worked to learn a new language and to meld remembered traditions into new cultural forms that could facilitate life together. Fictive kinships and communal living arrangements required similar adjustments, as did the development of larger networks of kin and community. Blacks transformed Christianity into an expression of religious feeling with vibrant African ingredients. In music and folk art, they gave voice to a cultural identity that even the most degrading conditions could not eradicate. Out of these daily patterns of interaction and experience, blacks forged a series of truly African American cultures.

11.3: Constructing African American Identities

11.3 Identify the difference in the socio-demographic conditions of the slaves across the American geography

Despite the common strands that ran through eighteenth-century African experience, no single colonial African American culture emerged. The circumstances of black slavery and freedom simply varied too much, making daily life quite different for a black person in South Carolina or Jamaica than for an African American who happened to live in Pennsylvania or Massachusetts Bay.

A variety of factors shaped the development of particular black cultures. The proportion of slaves in the local population, the climate of the region, the crops most often cultivated, the differences between rural and urban settings—all influenced profoundly how blacks experienced and adapted to life in the New World. The single greatest factor was the rate of natural increase among the empire's slaves. Where deaths exceeded births, as they did throughout the British West Indies until well after mid-century, high import rates impeded the development of stable family and community life. Where birthrates exceeded death rates, as occurred on the colonial mainland by 1720, slave communities began gaining greater stability and coherence.

11.3.1: West Indian Slaves

The centrality of sugar production to the British Atlantic economy meant that great majority of slaves transported from Africa to the British colonies ended up laboring and dying on a Caribbean sugar plantation. Sugar was a brutal taskmaster that kept nearly 90 percent of the plantation's slaves at hard labor in the cane fields from sunup to sundown while the crop was maturing. Harvest season kept them busy round the clock (see Chapter 4). Planters exempted from field work only children under the age of 6 and the few who managed to outlive their effective laboring years. The rigors of field work coupled with inadequate diet suppressed the fertility of slave women, who bore far fewer children than their counterparts on the mainland. The sugar barons took few measures to ameliorate working conditions or encourage childbearing until after mid-century, when rising prices prompted them to reassess the widely held notion that it cost less to buy a new laborer than to raise one.

The resulting predominance of salt water slaves in this harsh West Indian environment ensured both the stronger survival of African cultural forms and a chronic instability of family and community life. The sex ratio in the Caribbean remained unbalanced throughout much of the eighteenth century. More than half the new arrivals lived with friends rather than spouses or relatives. Caribbean planters were much less reluctant than those on the mainland to cohabit with slave women, and their habit of keeping concubines further reduced opportunities to establish black families. The tendency to associate by ethnic groups divided slaves into separate and sometimes conflicting communities such as

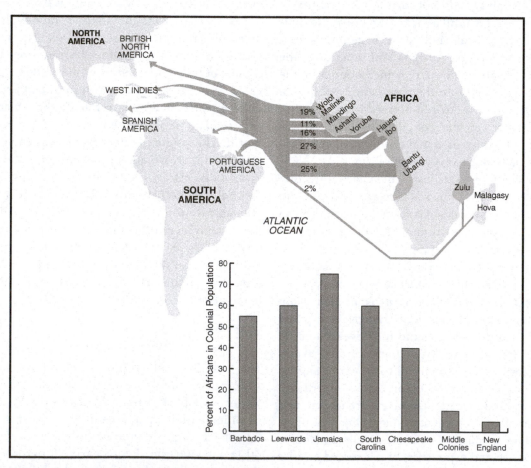

Map 11.1 Africans in America

Ashanti, Yoruba, and Igbo while dividing all from the creole minority.

On the other hand, the existence of black majorities on all the sugar islands, coupled with high rates of absentee ownership among the planters, permitted slaves to re-create African cultural forms with far fewer European influences. The creole languages that emerged on various sugar islands incorporated English vocabularies into African grammatical forms. Music and dance on the islands combined elements from various African sources into rich new forms that owed little to European structures of tonality and rhythm. Religion, too, remained strongly African in content and form. Slaves carved out time to grow produce on their provision grounds and sold it in African-style markets on Sundays. The markets provided settings where slaves could not only engage in commerce but also socialize, make music and dance, and share food and drink.

Although sugar production devoured the lives and labor of most Caribbean slaves, blacks also served in many other roles. A growing minority worked on coffee plantations after 1750 as the beverage's increasing popularity stimulated demand. Cocoa, cotton, and spice production occupied other Caribbean slaves. The work on such plantations was less arduous than that on sugar estates, as was labor in trades, domestic service, fishing, and ranching. Slaves who worked in areas other than sugar production could squeeze more personal time out of their daily schedules. In some settings, such as coffee plantations, that gain was somewhat offset by the smaller size and relative isolation of holdings, which constricted opportunities for social interaction and family life. Slave artisans gradually won concessions from their masters such as limited hours, the right to work for pay on their own time, the right to trade on their own account, and a limited right to property. Some gained permission to set up separate households for themselves.

Jamaica also hosted the British empire's largest enduring maroon society. During the eighteenth century, the Maroons grew from a few hundred runaways to a large, self-sustaining population with its own coherent structures of leadership and cultural life. English planters tried repeatedly to suppress them, but the tenacity of Maroon warriors and the inaccessibility of their Cockpit Country homeland defeated such efforts. The planters finally settled for peace on terms that bound the Maroons to return future runaways and to assist the English in maintaining order on the island. Maroons agreed to these terms, in part to prevent their own numbers from rising too rapidly to sustain and to keep out potential troublemakers. By 1760, relations had become so stable that when the Jamaican slave Tacky led large uprising, Maroons readily allied with planters to suppress it. A Maroon bullet ended Tacky's life.

11.3.2: Rice and Slaves

Of all the eighteenth-century mainland colonies, South Carolina most resembled the Caribbean in the structure of its plantation society. Rice proved nearly as punishing to produce as sugar, and disease and malnutrition killed low-country slaves almost as rapidly as those in the West Indies. Like Caribbean sugar barons, low-country planters had to rely on the Atlantic slave trade to meet their labor demands. The colony's black majority, like its Caribbean counterpart, did not begin reproducing itself until the 1760s.

African men and women who arrived in eighteenth-century South Carolina found themselves on large, isolated rice plantations, where their contact with whites was nearly as limited as that of slaves on Caribbean sugar plantations. Most planters spent the summer months in Charleston to escape the sultry low-country heat and malarial mosquitos. They left overseers and trusted black drivers to supervise the slaves in the heavy work of weeding rice, clearing and draining swamps, and digging mazes of irrigation ditches through the sticky clay soil. During harvest the slaves worked late into the nights gathering the crop and beating the rice kernels in large mortars. The Anglo-American painter Benjamin West regarded this "excessive hard labor" fatal to many slaves, "carrying off great numbers every winter." Desperately overtaxed, slaves sometimes burned down the threshing barns to escape the hated mortars. The cycle of rice production occupied the entire year, and slaves often found themselves planting a new crop while still threshing the previous year's harvest.

Other low-country slaves produced indigo, a weed that yielded a brilliant blue dye used in Britain's textile industry. The crop required less field work, but the process of rendering the harvested plants kept slaves sweating for weeks over steaming vats of fermenting vegetation. The putrid reek drew hordes of flies that tormented the slaves as they worked. They had to stir the mixture constantly while pouring it through a series of containers, setting its color with lime at the critical moment, and then draining and drying the blue sediment into blocks for shipping. Dye making demanded great skill, and the slaves who endured the process to learn its secrets gained power to bargain concessions from masters whose profits depended on the dye-makers' expertise.

These circumstances of low-country plantation work—a majority black population, limited contact with whites, and some slave control over production—permitted slaves to preserve many African elements within their culture. The process of creating a culture remained slow and uneven, however, hindered by factors similar to those in the Caribbean. Although planters desired to create a relatively homogenous labor force from the rice-producing regions of Gambia and Senegal, limited supply forced them to accept less-desirable slaves from regions such as Angola. The resulting divisions among new arrivals, as well as between slaves and creoles, took time to overcome. So too did the sexual imbalance which slowed the development of slave families.

The size of plantations—averaging well over 500 acres with a resident labor force of thirty or more slaves—made contact among groups from different plantations more difficult and tended to foster insular plantation communities.

Over time, however, a distinctive low-country culture did emerge among South Carolina blacks. Creole languages mixed the basic vocabulary of English with words borrowed from various African tongues. Until the end of the nineteenth century, one creole language, Gullah, was spoken on some of the Sea Islands along the Georgia–South Carolina coast. Slaves also established elaborate and enduring kinship networks. They created an extensive internal market in provisions and crafted goods such as ceramic pots. The practice of using black slaves as drivers created opportunities to negotiate concessions, the most important of which was the task system of labor management. By persuading planters to agree to a specified quota of work per slave per day, drivers and field slaves managed to limit the number of hours spent working on the master's crop and preserved some time for cultivating provisions, raising families, and socializing. An eighteenth-century field slave's life remained difficult, but such developments may have helped reduce the more dehumanizing aspects of bondage on South Carolina's rice and indigo plantations.

The hardening of racial lines that attended rice and indigo cultivation propelled divergent changes on the Carolina frontier and in Charleston. Slaves, free blacks, and mulattoes who had experienced a more fluid environment on the seventeenth-century frontier responded to shifts in race relations by fleeing to Indian country or to Spanish Florida. Groups of runaway slaves also found hiding places in the swamps where they could form mobile maroon communities and evade capture for long periods. Blacks who reached Cherokee, Chickasaw, or Choctaw villages were often able to exchange an African for an Indian identity through adoption into the local community (see Chapter 10). Those who reached St. Augustine could join a growing black community whose freedom was guaranteed by the Spanish crown and defended by the guns of the San Marcos *castillo*. The governor of Florida continued extending sanctuary to runaway slaves until 1748 as a means of destabilizing South Carolina and Georgia.

In Charleston, African American women and men created a distinctive urban culture. Mulattoes who had gained their freedom by the early eighteenth century sought to protect their hard-won status by avoiding contact with slaves and passing wherever possible into white society. By the 1750s, Charleston's slaves managed to accumulate a range of concessions that gave them significant, though still limited, autonomy. The demand for skilled labor permitted male slave artisans to earn money for themselves after satisfying their daily obligations to the master. As in the Caribbean, some artisans gained permission to set up their own households, and a tiny minority earned enough to purchase their freedom.

Many of Charleston's slave women also found opportunities for employment and profit outside their masters' households. Some made tidy sums as cooks, seamstresses, or weavers. Many others became prosperous hawkers of consumer goods, which they marketed from street carts. Still others opened shops and taverns that catered to an African American clientele. Groups of younger slave women developed thriving clandestine markets in prostitution, organizing balls for entertaining sailors, merchants, and planters alike. This choice of profession registered the terrible constraints that confronted African women in Charleston. Even so, slave prostitutes often shared with hawkers, cooks, and seamstresses the ability to dress fashionably, adorn themselves with watches or jewelry, and gain a measure of control over their lives. The visitor Benjamin West nevertheless observed that these "genteelly dressed" slaves had to endure "their full share of floggings."

White South Carolinians found unsettling the relative liberty and prosperity of the city's slaves. Critics decried the Charleston slaves' appetite for luxury in the *South Carolina Gazette*. Legislators tried to curtail slave spending through sumptuary laws that prohibited slaves from wearing finery considered appropriate only for free white gentry. Yet white buyers continued to generate profits for African American consumers by hiring slave tradesmen and patronizing slave-run enterprises. Slaves simply ignored the sumptuary laws and continued to adorn themselves with the scraps of self-assertion they had managed to wrest from the masters' grudging grasp.

11.3.3: Slave Life on the Tobacco Plantations

A significantly different pattern emerged in the tobacco-producing regions of the Chesapeake and Virginia Piedmont. There the black population, though large, never reached more than 40 percent of the total. Most slaves lived in groups of twenty or fewer on moderately sized plantations with a resident white master or overseer, his wife, and children. Several great planter families held well over a hundred slaves, and the largest held over three hundred. But even these planters tended to divide their work force into smaller units, which they scattered throughout the Chesapeake and Piedmont onto multiple holdings of a few hundred acres each. These factors established an environment of frequent contact among Europeans and Africans and regular communication among white and black residents on neighboring plantations.

Tobacco cultivation was not so onerous as labor in a rice field, but it kept slaves busy throughout the year at tedious, time-consuming tasks. The season began with sowing seed into small, protected seedbeds "as early after Christmas as the weather will permit." As the seedlings grew during the next few months, slaves hoed the main fields into rows of small tobacco hills in preparation for transplanting. During the anxious months of April, May, and early June, the entire work force, children included, awaited downpours that would loosen the soil and permit the wet labor of transplanting the seedlings without damage. The summer occupied the slaves in daily tasks of weeding, "topping"—removing the flowering portion—and pruning each plant of suckers to encourage maximum growth in the leaves. September brought the cutting season, a critical time when the ripe plants were gathered and hung in barns for curing. Once plants had dried to exactly the right point—a condition known as "case"—slaves began to "prize" them into hogsheads for shipping. Planters who received the highest returns also put skilled slaves to work before packing in "stemming" or removing all stem fibers from the leaves, a delicate and boring process that kept those involved working deep into the nights. If everything went perfectly, the heavy hogsheads were ready for shipping by Christmas, leaving just a few days to celebrate the holiday before the next cycle began.

This work regimen, along with other factors, hindered Chesapeake slaves from creating the African patterns of economy and agricultural life that emerged in the rice country. Masters organized their laborers into gangs which worked long days in the fields, leaving less time for discretionary activities. Slaves cultivated small gardens and raised a few barnyard fowl, but rarely produced enough for sale on a larger market. Masters rationed out staples of corn and meat while providing their slaves specified allotments of fabric or clothing each year. The predominance of creole over African slaves in the Chesapeake tended to inhibit the survival of African customs. Creole blacks learned to cope with whites on a daily basis and looked with contempt on slaves who had just arrived from Africa. "Outlandish" Negroes were forced by blacks as well as whites to accept elements of English culture. It was especially important for newcomers to speak English. Consider, for example, the pain of 12-year-old

Olaudah Equiano, an African sold in Virginia in 1757. "I was now exceedingly miserable," later Equiano recalled, "and thought myself worse off than any . . . of my companions; for they could talk to each other [in English], but I had no person to speak to that I could understand. In this state I was constantly grieving and pining, and wishing for death."

If the presence of a large percentage of creoles made life difficult for salt-water slaves, it also facilitated the growth of family life. Masters took an active interest in promoting slave families as well, if only to encourage the growth of a self-reproducing labor force. Chesapeake slaves parlayed this interest into a series of concessions that achieved some security for family life. In addition to granting visitation privileges to spouses living on separate plantations, masters sometimes agreed to purchase spouses so that couples could live together. Women demanded a period of respite from field work to breast-feed their infants. Husbands saw to it that their pregnant wives and young families received food beyond the daily ration. A new area of negotiation and resistance emerged as parents strove with planters for greater control over their children's upbringing and work patterns. Masters who refused to grant such concessions often found themselves paying for their reluctance as aggrieved slaves ran away, refused to work, or sabotaged tools or crops. Eventually, most masters chose to endure the inconvenience of concessions.

By the 1750s, the maturation of Chesapeake tobacco culture had brought a measure of stability to plantation life, while previous years' prosperity combined with the decline of tobacco production motivated planters to diversify. Many planters sought to create relatively self-sufficient estates where skilled slaves provided most essential trades and produced most of the food consumed on the plantation. Some planters began producing wheat and other small grains for export as well. Grain required much less attention than tobacco, and slaves who cultivated it gained time for other economic activities. Some began tending draft animals and livestock; others moved into related trades as wagoners, tanners, and leather workers. The growth of modest urban centers such as Williamsburg and Baltimore opened opportunities for more slaves to move into domestic service and trades in the towns. Like those in other urban areas, Chesapeake slave artisans often hired themselves out on their own time to gain a modest source of independent income. Some planters "rented" slaves as tobacco economy decreased. A few slave artisans in the Chesapeake as in South Carolina managed to save enough to purchase their freedom.

These developments broadened the range of African American experience and opened new fields of struggle between slaves and masters for control of time, labor, and resources. Yet masters always commanded by far the greatest share of power in this contest. All aspects of slave life—family, customary privileges, discretionary time, and earnings—remained fragile, their continuation always subject to the master's pleasure.

11.3.4: Slaves and Free Blacks in the North

In the New England and Middle Colonies, African Americans made up a far smaller percentage of the population. A combination of natural increase and significant importation boosted the mid-eighteenth-century slave population to 8 percent of the Pennsylvania total, 10 percent in New Jersey, 16 percent in the five southernmost counties of New York, and 3 percent in Massachusetts. In such environments, contact between blacks and whites became even more frequent than in the Chesapeake. Slaves worked at a far greater variety of tasks, often side by side with white servants, laborers, or masters. Those working outside of the cities most often served as field hands on a family farm, though Pennsylvania's nascent iron industry brought groups of slaves together to labor in mines and foundries.

In northern cities, most slaves worked as domestics or artisans and lived in the houses of their masters. Urban slaves saw other blacks more frequently than did those living on family farms, but they had far less opportunity than southern blacks to develop creole languages or reaffirm a common African past.

Family life among northern slaves proved very hard to sustain. Few masters maintained more than one or two domestics or artisans, which meant that most slave couples lived in separate households. Masters discouraged childbearing among their female slaves because of the expense and loss of labor it entailed, and many sold slave women at the first sign of pregnancy. Masters frequently failed or refused to provide enough food for slave families, producing high infant mortality rates among northern blacks. Nevertheless, many slaves defied the odds, marrying and doing their best to sustain the relationship despite living in households several miles apart.

Northern slaves had to adopt more European cultural forms in order to survive. First-generation Africans arriving in the North soon learned to speak English proficiently, and those working for Dutch masters learned that language as well. An increasing number learned to read and write. Literacy enabled black slaves to participate in a greater range of activities as well as to bid for freedom by forging passes and documents. A few eventually applied their writing skills to poetry and prose. Colonial African American poets Phillis Wheately and Jupiter Hammond gained enduring fame through such literary efforts. Black musicians learned to play the fiddle, combining African and European elements into ballads and dance tunes that became popular throughout the north. Many northern blacks embraced Christianity during the Great Awakening of the 1740s and became sought-after lay preachers who followed their calling in itinerant ministries. Blacks in New York and New Jersey embraced Pinkster, the Dutch celebration of Pentecost or Whitsuntide, and made it their own.

In New England, Negro Election Day filled a similar role. Both holidays offered one of the few times during the year in which slaves could share remembered traditions using African musical instruments, dance, and song. Both also provided slaves an opportunity to assert a separate identity in ritual role reversals that mocked white society.

The northern colonies also hosted a small population of free blacks, but it began to dwindle in the eighteenth century as slavery took greater hold. Many who remained free were descendants of black slaves who had been brought to a northern colony in the seventeenth century and later gained freedom there. Others were descendants of free blacks who migrated north as hardening racial lines closed opportunities for them in the Chesapeake. An unknown percentage were fugitive slaves who escaped detection to build new lives for themselves as free people, and small number were slaves manumitted by northern masters, often through a will after the owner's death. Such candidates for manumission often continued languishing in slavery for years while the estate was being settled.

Free blacks found themselves occupying an increasingly marginal status in the eighteenth-century North. They pursued many of the same occupations as did slaves. A small number owned farms. Augustine and Rachel Van Donck, for instance, operated a small cattle farm near Tappan, New Jersey, from the late 1720s until the 1770s, when they parceled it out to their three children. Yet the prosperity and status of free blacks slipped as northern colonial law strengthened the structural links between race and slavery. Free blacks were often barred from voting and serving on juries. Some colonies or localities required them to carry a pass when traveling and to obtain special licenses to trade or carry a firearm. Colonies such as Pennsylvania established special courts for trying free blacks as well as slaves, and made some offenses committed by free blacks punishable by enslavement.

11.3.5: Coastal Blacks— Boatmen, Fishermen, Sailors

Recent scholarship has discovered that during the eighteenth century many black men throughout the empire gained a degree of personal freedom by working as boatmen, fishermen, or mariners. Many first-generation slaves brought considerable skills from their homelands along African rivers and coasts. Masters were quick to put these skills to use in an expanding commercial environment that relied heavily on water transport. South Carolina slaves constructed large dugout canoes known as "pettiaugers" and painted them in bright colors reminiscent of styles familiar in their homeland. They poled, paddled, or rowed these canoes through the labyrinth of low-country waterways, becoming intimately familiar with them. North Carolina boatmen became similarly familiar with the numerous inlets and waterways along that coast. The largest of the pettiaugers frequently sported a mast and sail that could carry its navigator and cargo out into open water.

Slaves became proficient fishermen as well, another skill they brought from Africa and adapted to North American conditions. Africans slaves knew how to obtain large catches by drugging the fish in a stream or using special seines and weirs to capture them. They also possessed considerable skill in coastal fishing, which masters often exploited to supplement provisions for their labor force. Slaves and free blacks exploited the skill as well, plying an independent trade that gained them considerable profit.

Many eighteenth-century blacks also set out to sea. It is now estimated that by 1803, African Americans held at least 18 percent of all jobs open to American seamen, and although the number of positions may have been fewer before the Revolution, black colonial sailors—many of them slaves—sought work on sailing vessels to escape the drudgery of life on rice or tobacco plantations. Knowledge of sailing could provide runaways an avenue to freedom, and many notices cautioned "all masters of vessels" not to carry runaway sailors out of a colony. These African American seamen connected black communities scattered throughout the Caribbean and along the mainland coast, bringing news about distant rebellions and spreading radical political ideologies to slaves who might otherwise not have known much about the transforming events of the eighteenth century.

11.4: A World within a World

11.4 Recognize that slaves in the eighteenth-century colonial world were valued only by their ability to work

Eighteenth-century masters and slaves alike lived amid a swirl of expanding horizons, burgeoning growth, and rapid change. Planters had to remain constantly attentive and diligent in managing their affairs if they hoped to thrive in this unforgiving environment, where so many factors lay beyond anyone's control. The South Carolina overseer Josiah Smith, Jr., reminded his absentee employer George Austin that to turn a profit, a rice planter had to keep a steady eye on the fluctuations of the market, seizing opportunities to sell on favorable terms without fixating too rigidly on the exact price he would consider acceptable. He had to remain attentive to seasonal shipping patterns, the price of storage, and the effects of long-term storage on the quality of his crop. He had to remain abreast of transatlantic events in politics and international relations, both of which could affect trade. In short, an "able Planter" must remain "ever employ'd in the contriving every thing that can make for their Advantage, save every Expence that can possibly be avoided, & often by hard-driving, save a Crop from Destruction." "Such persons," Smith declared, "have enrich'd themselves very much, especially of late years by the hard Labour & Sweat of wretched Slaves."

Smith's observations remind us that, from the masters' perspective, the slaves' primary place in this colonial commercial world was to provide the "hard Labour & Sweat" that produced their profits. All other contributions they made to that world—the thriving Sunday markets, the colorful pettiaugers, the production of "country cloth," the lively music, the herbal remedies, the nursing and tending of the masters' children—remained subordinate their role as laborers in the staples that maintained the circulation of people and goods in the British Atlantic.

By choosing to fill that role with enslaved Africans, Europeans had created a world that by the first third of the eighteenth century was explicitly divided by race and power. The master-slave relationship was permeated with calculation. No other relationship in eighteenth-century America matched it. Every conversation between master and slave, every show of affection, every outburst of anger, every stroke of the whip, marked an exchange between owner and owned. Very few transactions remained free of the calculus of exploitation, negotiation, resistance, and concession between profoundly unequal parties. Masters took all they could and rarely conceded anything to their slaves without a fight. Slaves gave what the balance of power prevented them from keeping—their labor, their bodies, often their very lives.

This contradiction of owning a person as property rested at the heart of the eighteenth-century British empire. Its dynamic framed the conditions for the emergence of an African American world at once an indispensable element of that the larger British Atlantic World and inaccessibly other. Slaves like the Virginia runaway Peter Deadfoot exhibited intelligence and resourcefulness that their masters could not help admiring. Deadfoot became "an indifferent shoemaker, a good butcher, ploughman, and carter; an excellent sawyer, and waterman, understands breaking oxen well, and is one of the best scythemen, either with or without a cradle, in *America*: in short, he is so ingenious a fellow, that he can turn his hand to any thing."

The African Diaspora in the British Atlantic was replete with men and women who employed their collective ingenuity in adapting to the harsh economic and social environments into which they found themselves so violently thrust. They contributed their labor to the products others consumed, to the prosperity others enjoyed, to the fashions others displayed, and to the houses in which others lived. They built their own worlds from resources others considered stolen—fragments of time, material, and human relationships that others grudgingly conceded because of the slaves' desperate persistence. Out of this patchwork of suffering and pain, of worn remnants, broken tools, broken bodies, broken families, broken lives, they created cultures of enduring beauty and sustaining power.

Chronology

1696	South Carolina passes colony's first slave code
1700	Black population of British Caribbean and mainland at 200,000; less than 20,000 on the mainland
1701	Annual imports of West Indian sugar to Great Britain £210,000; of Chesapeake tobacco to Great Britain £83,000 of South Carolina rice to Great Britain £0
1705	Virginia slave code passed
1729	Average slave imports to Jamaica reaches 7,200
1739	Stono Uprising breaks out in South Carolina
1741	Rumored slave plot to burn New York prompts execution of 32 suspected arsonists
1750	Black population of British Caribbean and mainland at 542,000; 247,000 on the mainland
1760	Tacky's Rebellion breaks out in Jamaica
1774	Annual value of West Indian sugar to Great Britain £787,000; to British colonial mainland £723,000; Annual value of Chesapeake tobacco £173,000; of Carolina rice to Great Britain £340,000

Chapter 12

Imperial Competition for the American Market

Learning Objectives

12.1 Report replication of the English constitution in British America

12.2 Compare the governance of New England with that of New France

12.3 Evaluate the causes of the fresh transatlantic wars between England, Spain, and France

12.4 Describe the effects of the Seven Years' War on American society

12.5 Recognize the political and cultural influence of Great Britain on colonial Americans of British background

During the summer of 1749, Captain Pierre-Joseph Céloron de Blainville led an armed flotilla of canoes down Allegheny and Ohio Rivers—now western Pennsylvania—to reassert France's formal claims to the region. The French envoy well knew he was entering lands controlled by native peoples determined to preserve their sovereignty and to trade wherever they could obtain the best European imports. Along his route, Céloron found discouraging evidence that the British colonists were winning the contest for Ohio country markets. The drive for imperial domination turned on access to the latest manufactured goods, rather than on naked coercion.

Céloron tried to counter the English competitors. At one village where he found a newly constructed trading post, the captain made the inhabitants promise to turn away the British traders and leave the unfinished building "only . . . to amuse the youth." At several Indian communities, Céloron confronted even more British traders. He sent them packing, carrying letters warning British colonists to stay away from the "Belle Rivière."

Céloron faced an impossible challenge. With many of the Ohio country Indians "drawn into a very bad disposition" toward the French, he had to act with extreme caution. Indeed, at two important river towns, Logstown and Sonioto, the native inhabitants signaled their defiance by firing British-supplied musket balls into the air over the heads of Céloron's soldiers. Despite such moments of tension, the captain managed to avoid bloodshed in his quest to "reassure the

271

natives of these countries" and "treat with them of good things." In councils with local leaders Céloron expressed surprise at their disloyalty to "their father Onontio," the French governor of Canada. He warned that the British harbored intentions for their "entire ruin." "They will make themselves masters of this whole country and drive you away if I would let them do so," the French envoy cautioned. To make his point that the Ohio was in fact French territory, Céloron's men buried several lead plates at various points in the riverbank, each accompanied by a French royal coat of arms nailed to a nearby tree. The French captain apparently hoped that these curious markers would dissuade the Indians from buying cheaper and better-made British goods.

Céloron's mission to the Ohio offers a glimpse of how the contest for North American empire intensified at mid-century. Although competition for trade occupied the captain's immediate attention, his speeches to native leaders reveal the French conviction that they were actors in a great contest between two empires for the control of the continent. By 1749, the pattern had become clear. While commercial exchange remained the focus of Franco-Indian relations, the trails blazed by British and colonial American traders soon became avenues that brought to the Ohio country a swarming population intent on transforming the entire landscape, clearing the countryside of trees and game to make room for European crops and livestock.

Yet even though the Ohio country Indians themselves recognized the truth of Céloron's warnings, the appeal of cheap British goods proved hard to resist. In this great contest for North American empire, the advantage was shifting to the British. Military force could not easily reclaim Indian loyalty to the French, for the villagers had "a grand refuge in the flat plains from which they are not far." Moreover, the French traders could "never give our merchandise at the price the English do." Indeed, Céloron mused,

Canadian traders earned most of their own profits through clandestine trade with their British rivals, exchanging beaver pelts for other "peltry, cats, otters, and skins" which fetched higher prices on the French market. This experienced military man could see only one solution: to "make a strong defense," fortifying strategic locations in the Ohio country.

If Céloron found Ohio expedition discouraging, British American colonists responded to his activities with alarm. Indeed, the imperial rivalry that brought the French captain to their western frontier framed British thinking about nearly every aspect of trade, settlement, government, and defense. The French threat to their north and west—along with an ongoing rivalry with Spanish America to the South—pushed British American colonists to adapt political and military institutions that could raise the increasing amounts of funds and troops needed to secure their frontiers. In the process, a distinctive imperial order emerged between colonial governments and the administration in London, one defined by a mutual need for accommodation and compromise to maintain the bonds of empire. As Anglo-French conflict intensified toward mid-century from the high seas to the Ohio frontier, leaders of various British colonies also began seeking ways to overcome mutual suspicions and devise unprecedented measures for intercolonial military and political cooperation.

Native Americans remained crucial participants in these efforts, situated as they were between these great imperial rivals who competed for native trade and military alliance. Indeed, native peoples found it difficult to avoid entanglement in the intensifying contest for empire. They responded by adapting their own institutions of leadership and interethnic cooperation to preserve native independence against European encroachment. As the century progressed, however, their efforts increasingly took on the character of rearguard actions, responses to imperial policies set by distant European kings.

12.1: Commerce, Politics, and Empire

12.1 Report replication of the English constitution in British America

Eighteenth-century American politics were forged in the crucible of a vast Atlantic imperial conflict in which commercial wealth formed the grand prize. Authorities in British, French, and Spanish America all did their best to model their institutions of government and administration on patterns they had known in the mother countries. By doing so, each imperial power hoped to secure and expand the trade, territory, and labor that had come to form the basis of their wealth and power. Yet varying economic conditions, local circumstances, and imperial pressures produced differences that set the colonial political cultures apart, particularly in the British mainland colonies.

In every mainland colony, British Americans repeatedly stated their desire to replicate the mother country's political institutions. Parliament, they claimed, provided a model for the American assemblies. They revered the English constitution—that unwritten political and legal order that had emerged over time out of a complex mix of custom, legal precedent, royal proclamation, and parliamentary legislation. However, the more the colonists studied British political theory and practice—in other words, the more they attempted to become British—the more aware they became of major differences. By trying to copy Great Britain, they unwittingly discovered something about being American.

Eighteenth-century French and Spanish colonial government possessed a more sharply military cast. Colonial governors were always experienced officers who exercised supreme authority over both military and civil affairs, frequently combining the two. Indeed, the entire government of New France reflected a military chain of command under the governor general, who oversaw all colonial administration, and the intendants, who oversaw military supply as well as civil matters. Yet to visitors, the *habitants* of New France seemed remarkably unburdened by taxes or regulations, proud, and independent.

12.1.1: The English Constitution

During the eighteenth century, Anglo-Americans—those colonists of English descent born and raised in Britain's American colonies—took the British constitution as their starting point for nearly all political discussion. It was the object of universal admiration among leaders of Europe's Enlightenment. Unlike the U.S. Constitution of 1788, the British constitution was not a formal written document. It was something much more elusive. The English constitution found expression in a growing body of law, court decisions, and statutes, a sense of traditional political arrangements that people of all classes believed had evolved from the past, preserving life, liberty, and property. Eighteenth-century political commentators reluctantly admitted that the constitution had in fact changed. Historic confrontations between king and Parliament had generated new understandings about what the constitution did or did not allow. Nevertheless, almost everyone regarded change as dangerous and destabilizing, a threat to the political tradition that seemed to explain Britain's greatness.

In theory, the English constitution contained three distinct parts. The monarch was at the top, advised by handpicked court favorites. Next came the House of Lords, a body of 180 aristocrats who served with 26 Anglican bishops as the upper house of Parliament. Third was the House of Commons, composed of 558 members elected by various constituencies scattered throughout the realm.

Political theorists waxed eloquent on workings of the British constitution. Each of the three parts of England's "mixed government," it seemed, represented a separate socioeconomic interest: king, nobility, and common people. Acting alone, each body would run to excess, even tyranny, but operating within a mixed system, they automatically checked each other's ambitions for the common good. "Herein consists the excellence of the English government," explained the famed eighteenth-century jurist Sir William Blackstone, "that all parts of it form a mutual check upon each other." Unlike the delegates who wrote the Constitution of the United States, eighteenth-century Englishmen did not perceive their constitution as a balance of executive, legislative, and judicial branches.

12.1.2: The Reality of British Politics

The reality of daily political life in Great Britain, however, bore little relation to theory. The three elements of the constitution did not, in fact, represent distinct socioeconomic groups. Men elected to the House of Commons often came from the same social background as those who served in the House of Lords. All represented the interests of Britain's landed elite. Moreover, there was no attempt to maintain strict constitutional separation. The king, for example, organized parliamentary associations, loose groups of political followers who sat in the House of Commons and who openly supported the monarch's policies in exchange for patronage or pension.

The claim that the members of the House of Commons represented all the people of England also seemed far-fetched. As of 1715, no more than 20 percent of Britain's adult males had the right to vote. Property qualifications or other restrictions often greatly reduced the number of eligible voters. In addition, the size of the electoral districts varied throughout the kingdom. In some boroughs—towns that could elect a member of Parliament—representatives were chosen by several thousand voters. In many districts, however, a handful of electors controlled the result. These tiny, or "rotten," boroughs were an embarrassment. The Methodist leader John Wesley complained that Old Sarum, an almost uninhabited borough, "in spite of common sense, without house or inhabitant, still sends two members to the parliament." Because these districts were so small, a wealthy lord or ambitious politician could easily bribe or otherwise "influence" the entire constituency, something done regularly throughout the century.

Before 1760, few people spoke out against these constitutional abuses. The main exception was a group of radical publicists whom historians have labeled the Commonwealthmen. These writers decried the corruption of political life, noting that a nation that compromised civic virtue, that failed to stand vigilant against fawning courtiers and would-be despots, deserved to lose its liberty and property. The most famous Commonwealthmen were John Trenchard and Thomas Gordon, who penned a series of essays titled *Cato's Letters* between 1720 and 1723. If England's rulers were corrupt, they warned and then the people could not expect the balanced constitution to save them from tyranny. In one typical article, Trenchard and Gordon observed, "The Appitites . . . of Men, especially of Great Men, are carefully to be observed and stayed, or else they will never stay themselves. The Experience of every Age convinces us, that we must not judge of Men by what they ought to do, but by what they will do."

But however shrilly these writers protested, they won little support for political reforms. Most eighteenth-century Englishmen admitted there was more than a grain of truth in the commonwealth critique, but they were not willing to tamper with a system of government that had so recently survived a civil war and a Glorious Revolution. Americans, however, took Trenchard and Gordon to heart.

12.1.3: Governing England's Colonies: The North American Experience

The mainland colonists assumed—perhaps naively—that their own various colonial governments were modeled on the balanced constitution of Great Britain. They argued that within their political systems, the governor corresponded to the king and the governor's council to the House of Lords. Anglo-Americans perceived their colonial assemblies as American reproductions of the House of Commons and expected them to preserve the interests of the people against those of the monarch and aristocracy. As the colonists discovered, however, general theories about a mixed constitution reflected American political reality even less than British.

By mid-century a majority of the mainland colonies had royal governors appointed by the king. Many were career army officers who through luck, charm, or family connection had gained the ear of someone close to the king. These patronage posts did not generate income sufficient to interest the most powerful or talented English personalities of the period, but they did draw middle-level bureaucrats who were ambitious, desperate, or both. It is perhaps not surprising that most governors decided simply not to "consider any Thing further than how to sit easy."

George Clinton, who served as New York's governor from 1743 to 1753, was probably representative of the men who hoped to "sit easy." Before coming to the colonies, Clinton had compiled an extraordinary record of ineptitude as a naval officer. He gained the governorship more as a means to get him out of England than as a sign of respect. When he arrived in New York City, Clinton ignored the colonists. "In a province given to hospitality" wrote one critic, "[Clinton] erred by immuring himself in the fort, or retiring to a grotto in the country, where his time was spent with his bottle and a little trifling circle."

Whatever their demerits, royal governors in America possessed enormous powers. In fact, royal governors could do certain things in America that a king could not do in eighteenth-century Britain. Among these were the rights to veto legislation and to dismiss judges. The governors also served as military commanders in each province.

Political practice in America differed from the British model in another crucial respect. Royal governors were advised by a council, a body usually consisting of about twelve wealthy colonists. These had to be recommended by the governor for approval to the Board of Trade in London, which set policy and exercised oversight of colonial administration. During the seventeenth century, governors' councils had played an important role in colonial governments, but their ability to exercise independent authority declined steadily over the course of the eighteenth century as the power of colonial legislatures increased. Its members certainly did not represent a distinct landed and titled aristocracy of lords and ladies within American society.

If royal governors did not look like kings, nor American councils like the House of Lords, colonial assemblies bore little resemblance to the eighteenth-century House of Commons. The major difference was the size of the American franchise. In most colonies, adult white males who owned a small amount of land could vote in colonywide elections. One historian estimates that 95 percent of this group in Massachusetts was eligible to participate in elections. The number in Virginia was about 85 percent. These figures—much higher than those in contemporary England—have led some scholars to view the colonies as "middle-class democracies," societies run by moderately prosperous yeomen farmers who—in politics at least—exercised independent judgment. There were too many of them to bribe, no "rotten" boroughs, and when these people moved west, colonial assemblies usually created new electoral districts.

Colonial governments were not democracies in the modern sense of that term. Possessing the right to vote was one thing, exercising it quite another. Americans participated in elections when major issues were at stake—the formation of banks in mid-eighteenth-century Massachusetts, for example—but most of the time they were content to let members of the rural and urban gentry represent them in the assemblies. To be sure, unlike modern democracies, these colonial politics excluded women and nonwhites from voting.

The point to remember, however, is that the power to expel legislative rascals was always present in America, and it was this political reality that kept autocratic gentlemen from straying too far from the will of the people.

12.1.4: British American Assemblies

Elected members of the colonial assemblies believed that they had a sacred obligation to preserve colonial liberties. They perceived any attack on the legislature as an assault on the rights of British Americans. The elected representatives brooked no criticism, and several colonial printers landed in jail because they criticized actions taken by a lower house.

So aggressive were these bodies in seizing privileges, determining procedures, and controlling money bills that some historians have described the political development of eighteenth-century America as "the rise of the assemblies." No doubt this is exaggerated, but the long series of imperial wars against the French, which demanded large public expenditures, transformed the small, amateurish assemblies of the seventeenth century into the more professional, activist legislatures of the eighteenth century.

This political system seemed designed to generate hostility between governors and assemblies. There was simply little incentive for the colonial legislators to cooperate with officials appointed from London. Alexander Spotswood, Virginia's acting governor from 1710 to 1722, for example, attempted to institute a bold new land program backed by the crown. Wealthy Virginia planters saw the plan as a threat to their own ambitions to acquire huge acreage at virtually no cost. He tried persuasion and gifts and, when these failed, chicanery. But the members of the House of Burgesses refused to support a plan that did not suit their own interests. Before leaving office, Spotswood gave up trying to carry out royal policy in America. Instead, he allied himself with the local Virginia gentry who controlled the House as well as the Council, and because they rewarded the compliant governor with large tracts of land, he became a wealthy man.

A few governors managed briefly to re-create in America the political culture of patronage, the system that eighteenth-century Englishmen took for granted. Most successful in this endeavor was William Shirley, who held office in Massachusetts from 1741 to 1757. The secret to his political successes in America was his connection to people who held high office in Great Britain. But Shirley's practices—and those of men like him—clashed with the colonists' perception of politics. They really believed in the purity of the balanced constitution. They insisted on complete separation of executive and legislative authority. Therefore, when Americans suspected a governor, or even some of their own representatives, of employing patronage to influence government decisions, their protests seem to have been lifted directly from the pages of *Cato's Letters*.

The weekly newspapers offered a major source of shared political information as well as a forum for vigorous public debate on issues of the day (see Chapter 10). In New York and Massachusetts especially, weekly newspapers urged readers to preserve civic virtue, to exercise extreme vigilance against the spread of privileged power. In the first issue of the *Independent Reflector*, published in New York (November 30, 1752), the editor announced defiantly that no discouragement shall "deter me from vindicating the civil and religious RIGHTS of my Fellow-Creatures: From exposing the peculiar Deformity of publick Vice, and Corruption; and displaying the amiable Charms of Liberty, with the detestable Nature of Slavery and Oppression." This pattern of highly charged political rhetoric gained only marginal respectability in Britain during the eighteenth century. In America, however, it became America's normal form of political discourse, especially after 1765.

The rise of the assemblies shaped American culture in other, subtler ways. Over the course of the century, the language of the law became increasingly Anglicized, taking on the structure and vocabulary of legal custom and practice in England. The Board of Trade, the Privy Council, and Parliament scrutinized court decisions and legislative actions from all thirteen mainland colonies. As a result, varying local legal practices that had been widespread during the seventeenth century became standardized. Indeed, according to one historian, the colonial legal system by 1750 "was substantially that of the mother country." Not surprisingly, many men who served in colonial assemblies were either lawyers or persons who had received legal training. When Americans from different regions met—as they frequently did in the years before the Revolution—they discovered that they shared a commitment to the preservation of what they had come to see as the English common law.

As eighteenth-century political developments drew the colonists closer to the mother country, they also brought Americans a greater awareness of each other. As their horizons widened, they learned they operated within the same general imperial system, and the problems confronting the Massachusetts House of Representatives were not too different from those facing Virginia's House of Burgesses or South Carolina's Commons House. Like the revivalists and merchants—people who crossed old boundaries—colonial legislators laid the foundation for a larger cultural identity. Colonists increasingly came to understand themselves as sharing common institutions, a common identity as British Americans, similar procedures for relating to the government in London, and similar challenges in making the imperial structure work in the interests of both the colonists and the mother country.

Despite colonists' growing awareness of their common political experience, no real intercolonial political unity emerged prior to the 1760s. Colonial assemblies remained intensely focused on internal provincial concerns. Political life in nearly every colony was severely divided. Popular coalitions representing various agricultural and commercial interests thought of themselves in good English fashion as virtuous, independent "Country" representatives. They vied strenuously against politicians aligned with royal appointees or proprietors, whom they considered members of corrupt "Court" factions. Members of the Country faction in particular saw themselves as replicating their own American version of a great struggle against corruption that British pamphleteers had been waging since before 1700.

Some divisions, such the one between as New York's DeLancey and Livingston factions, pitted powerful merchant and landowning families against each other for influence and control of patronage. Competition for western land and Indian trade also sparked intercolonial rivalries that only intensified as the century wore on. By the early 1750s, for example, Pennsylvania was locked in a fierce struggle with Virginia over Ohio country lands while simultaneously laboring to fend off a bid by Connecticut agents for rights to the Wyoming Valley. Disputes over land and trade also pitted Virginia officials against South Carolina counterparts and New York agents against rivals from New Hampshire. Colonial agents in London lobbied for the interests of the colony or faction that employed them while working to undermine the influence of opponents. Such practices drew colonies closer to London even as they perpetuated intercolonial divisions.

12.1.5: Sugar and Politics in the British West Indies

The political history of the British West Indies mirrored that of the mainland British colonies in many respects. The legislatures of these wealthy plantation colonies proved if anything even more truculent in defending their rights against what they perceived as royal encroachment. Indeed, as early as 1651 the Barbados assembly had taken a stand which mainland assemblies would not dare to do until 1774 by denying parliamentary authority to legislate for them (see Chapter 4). Well into the 1750s, the Jamaican assembly remained unique among Anglo-American colonies in its refusal to insert into any law a clause allowing the Board of Trade to suspend its implementation until the law could be reviewed. West Indian colonists shared with their mainland counterparts the constitutional ideals of eighteenth-century Commonwealthmen such as Trenchard and Gordon.

Yet important differences marked the West Indian political experience. The transience of the British population on most islands, coupled with the presence of black slave majorities on all, produced at least two distinctive features of politics in the British sugar islands. The first was the white minority's reliance on British Regular Army forces to control the volatile slave population. The British minority simply lacked the numbers to police their slaves. Absentee plantation owners and a large proportion of first-generation Africans only made the problem worse. British West Indians lived in constant fear of resistance, escape, and rebellion. Indeed, before the British abolition of slavery in 1837, the sugar islands experienced seventy-five incidents of slave revolt (see Chapter 11). As a result, all British West Indian legislatures except Barbados voted large annual subsidies to maintain garrisons of British Redcoats on the islands. The assemblies jealously guarded their exclusive rights to levy the local taxes from which these subsidies were paid. Nevertheless, their willing reliance on the British army and navy for security contrasted sharply with mainland colonial opposition to a standing army.

West Indian planters possessed much stronger ties of patronage and political influence in England than mainland colonists, simply because more of them resided in England or Scotland as absentee proprietors of their vast plantations. West Indian planter elites commonly viewed their residence on the islands as temporary. Most planned to return to the mother country with fortunes sufficient to retire on a magnificent country estate. Planters built few schools and colleges, instead sending their sons to England or Scotland for their education. There the scions of wealthy sugar planters—called "nabobs" by their contemporaries—could establish friendships and connections with members of the English ruling and mercantile elites, strengthening networks of credit and influence that could benefit them if they returned to the islands. They could also hire others to manage their island plantations and remain in England, joining the growing community of West Indian returnees who formed highly influential segments of local society in London, Bath, and Bristol.

Members of the absentee West Indian planter community formed an important element of the most powerful colonial lobby in London. They helped shape English colonial policy in effective collaboration with the islands' official agents, powerful English merchants in the West Indies trade, and members of Parliament with West Indian connections. Mainland colonial agents resented the influence of the West Indian lobby, which often favored measures prejudicial to North American interests. The value of sugar was so great and the trade so important to the British economy that it proved hard for British politicians to deny the interests of the great planters. While serving as agent for Pennsylvania in the 1760s, Benjamin Franklin complained that "the West Indies vastly outweigh us of the Northern Colonies" in parliamentary influence.

The West Indian political experience functioned to draw the British inhabitants of the sugar islands far closer to England than to the mainland North American colonies. While commercial ties did stimulate increasing interaction between the islands and the mainland, London exerted a far greater cultural and political pull. Few West Indian absentee families settled in British North America, and West Indian planters spurned colonial colleges, preferring to send their children to British universities which boasted "the ablest Teachers in every Branch." Many returning sugar nabobs found entry into the British ruling elite for themselves or their children through marriage, patronage, and reception of minor titles such as baronetcies. The frequent clash of mainland and West Indian interests in matters of policy also drove a wedge between the two parts of Britain's American empire.

12.2: Rival Atlantic Empires

12.2 Compare the governance of New England with that of New France

In the decades after the War of the Spanish Succession ended in 1713 (see Chapter 9), British views concerning their imperial rivals underwent a gradual transformation as Spain's hold on North America slipped while France's seemed to grow stronger. Until the 1740s, officials in South Carolina and Georgia worried as much about the threat of Spanish Florida as did northern officials about the French in Canada. By the later 1740s, however, concerns about the Spanish waned as British officials everywhere became increasingly convinced of French designs to seize control of all North America.

12.2.1: Spanish Garrisons in the Northern Borderlands

Contrasting patterns of rule between French and Spanish North America help to account for this shift in British American anxieties. After 1713,

Spanish colonial officials found themselves increasingly occupied with rearguard actions designed to preserve their tenuous hold on a few remaining northern outposts of its tottering empire. The Spanish presence in the Southeast consisted almost exclusively of three military garrisons, the Atlantic fortress of St. Augustine, the small Gulf Coast Fort San Marcos de Apalachee near present-day Tallahassee, and the presidio of San Carlos de Austria on Pensacola Bay (see Chapter 10). St. Augustine remained a formidable bastion protecting the northernmost edge of Spain's Caribbean empire, one never conquered despite repeated attacks by the English. Yet its military governors lacked the resources to preserve order more than 50 miles beyond the fortress walls. Spanish officials chose to invest a greater proportion of their meager resources to securing Texas against French encroachment, but chronic lack of security and insufficient numbers of colonists hampered their efforts.

New France's river empire, on the other hand, drew grudging admiration from English observers who marveled at its leaders' ability to influence "an extent of country larger perhaps than all Europe . . . only with a few woods-men and Indians." English analysts credited this achievement to the combined effects of French colonial administration and shrewd Franco-native diplomacy. French rule in North America appeared highly centralized, with most colonial authority concentrated in the hands of the governor-general and the intendant. As principal representative of the Crown, the Canadian governor-general maintained obedience to the monarchy and possessed exclusive jurisdiction over military affairs and diplomacy. Always a professional soldier, the governor-general exercised authority through a clear chain of command that included two lieutenant governors, one at Montreal and another at Trois Rivières, as well as a militia captain in each parish who could muster all able-bodied men from 16 to 60 years old.

The colonial intendant, though second to the governor-general in authority, wielded almost independent control over taxes, economic policy, and judicial matters. A Superior Council aided him in meting out justice over New France by serving as a court of appeal from lower courts. The captains of parish militia also served the intendant by acting as local agents of civil administration and law enforcement. In practice, militia captains exercised this authority loosely. As *habitants*, they shared the peasant status of most of their neighbors, a factor which made them much more sympathetic in the administration of local justice than a member of the colonial nobility might have been. The absence of taxation, coupled with modest prosperity and a low crime rate, also made their jobs much easier. Indeed, visitors to New France frequently commented on how lightly the Canadians were governed. As Colonel Louise-Antoine de Bougainville remarked in 1757, "The ordinary habitants . . . pay no taxes . . . have the right to hunt and fish, and . . . live in a sort of independence."

However lightly it rested on the *habitants*, New France's government remained military in form. Indeed, the governor-general's authority extended beyond the militia to include a permanent army of *troupes de la marine*, whose officers by the eighteenth century had come to form a significant element of a true colonial aristocracy. Leading Canadian families avidly lobbied the governor and intendant to recommend their sons for commissions in the *troupes de la marine*. The governor's role in securing these commissions prompted the colonial aristocracy to curry his favor. The King's minister in France retained the exclusive right to grant these commissions, a policy that bound the loyalties of aspiring Canadians closely to the French crown. English advocates of colonial reform admired this method of fostering a loyal Canadian aristocracy. Some urged the English administration to adapt a similar system to Anglo-American colonies as a means of weaning the gentry from their annoying attachment to provincial charters and assemblies.

Canadians complemented the military organization of their settlements with an extensive network of alliances that usually treated native peoples as equal partners in trade and warfare. English official Thomas Pownall perceptively described the Franco-native treaties as founded and maintained "according to the true Spirit of the Indian Laws of Nations." Although French officials may have desired to exercise full dominion over North American territory and its native inhabitants, they recognized that French numbers remained far too small for any such attempt. Indeed, their dependence on native partners required Canadians to continue accommodating native interests as they had since the early seventeenth century (see Chapters 7 and 8). By 1757, this policy of accommodation, in Pownall's estimation, had won the French full access to the North American interior, where they could acquire a strategic "Knowledge of all the Waters, Passes, Portages, and Posts that may hold Command" of the continental waterways. French officials had used that knowledge to place a system of forts at strategic locations along the great interior waterways. Pownall rightly recognized that without the cooperation of native allies, "all the Power of France" could not support such an extensive military presence. "<'Tis> the Indian Interest alone," he observed, "that does maintain these Forts."

12.2.2: Power, Leadership, and Empire in Indian America

The constant flux of eighteenth-century diplomatic relations among French, Indians, and English reflected shifting balances of power within Native American communities themselves. Since the close of the seventeenth century, native peoples had found it necessary to adjust their patterns of leadership, diplomacy, trade, and warfare to the permanent presence of competing European imperial powers. Some groups managed to respond more effectively than others.

Groups who remained loosely structured in semiautonomous bands under a multiplicity of local leaders often found themselves unable to hold on to power or land in the face of European encroachments. Delaware bands in Pennsylvania, for instance, steadily lost ground as English agents and settlers cut separate deals with various local headmen for rights to land and trade. Such headmen constantly resisted European efforts to make them subjects, guarding as best they could their power to act on their own initiative and manage their own affairs. Yet as Indians grew more dependent on imported goods, headmen often found themselves caught in a bind between a desire for autonomy and a need to hold on to prestige and power by maintaining the flow of trade. The dilemma proved almost impossible to escape, and many groups found themselves having to choose between abandoning tribal homelands for new hunting grounds further west or remaining in a condition of chronic poverty and dependence among a dominant English population. The Delawares, like several other eighteenth-century tribes within the Iroquois sphere of influence, faced third alternative. They could escape subjugation to the English Crown by becoming clients of the Six Nations (see Chapter 11). Yet such groups resented client status and looked for opportunities to reassert their autonomy, often under new leaders who criticized the older headmen and called on native people to renounce European ways.

The Iroquois' strategic position between two great European imperial rivals continued to provide important advantages in trade and diplomacy during the first half of the eighteenth century. Iroquois leaders used their leverage well to preserve their status as the dominant native power in the Northeast. The creation of an Iroquois Confederacy in the 1690s to complement the older Iroquois League proved a very effective political adjustment to new economic and diplomatic realities, one that coincided with the emergence of new Anglo-American political practices in the aftermath of the Glorious Revolution (see Chapter 9). The Confederacy's flexible system of alliances enabled Iroquois headmen to respond to new opportunities and challenges in a comparatively unified manner. Its framework enabled them to incorporate the Tuscaroras as the sixth nation of the Iroquois in 1712 (see Chapter 10), as well as augment their strength by making clients of neighboring groups.

The inner workings of the Confederacy also enabled individual Iroquois leaders to use intercolonial rivalries to their own advantage as well as that of the Six Nations as a whole. Iroquois participation in Pennsylvania's infamous Walking Purchase of 1737 illuminates this dynamic. While the transaction constituted a tragedy for the Delawares defrauded of their lands (see Chapter 12), it increased the regional influence of the Oneida leader Shikellamy and the Seneca Hetaquantagechty by enabling them to assert authority over new Delaware clients. The prestige of the two rose even further when the larger Confederacy confirmed the Walking Purchase and Delaware clientage, terms that Shikellamy, Hetaquantagechty, and three other leaders had at first negotiated on their own initiative. Other Iroquois headmen did not object to such independent action when its benefits to the Six Nations were so readily apparent. The Walking Purchase presented a golden opportunity not only to gain important new clients but also to stir up rivalries among Pennsylvania, New York, and Maryland. In playing the three colonial governments against each other, the Confederacy shrewdly undercut their ability to act in concert against Iroquois interests.

Despite the Confederacy's flexibility and its leaders' formidable diplomatic skill, Iroquois power gradually eroded. By the late 1740s, the steady westward advance of traders from

By the Honorable Sir William Johnson Bar.t His Majesty's sole Agent and Super-Intendant of Indian Affairs for the Northern Department of North America. Colonel of the Six United Nations their Allies and Dependants &c. &c.

To

Whereas I have received repeated proofs of your Attachment to his Britanic Majesty's Interests, and Zeal for his Service upon Sundry occasions, more particularly

I do therefore give you this public Testimonial thereof as a proof of his Majesty's Esteem & Approbation. Declaring you the said   to be a   of Your   and recommending it to all his Majesty's Subjects and faithfull Indian Allies to Treat and Consider you upon all occasions agreable to your Character, Station, and Services._____

Given under my Hand and Seal at Arms at Johnson hall the   day of   17

By Command of Sir W.m Johnson.

This certificate issued by William Johnson, superintendent of Indian affairs, signifies an alliance between the English settlers and the Native Americans in the "middle ground." Calumets (ceremonial pipes), wampum belts, and medals were other tokens used to mark alliances.

Pennsylvania and Virginia undercut Iroquois control over commerce in trans-Appalachian hunting grounds (see Chapters 10 and 12). It also enabled clients like the western Delawares and Shawnees, who had always resented Iroquois interference, to make fresh bids for self-determination in trade and communal affairs. Renewed French interest in the Ohio country after 1749 opened further opportunities for the western Indians to assert their independence by taking a page from Iroquois diplomacy itself, playing French, Six Nations', and rival Anglo-American colonial interests against one another.

The Ohio Indians' bid for power entailed enormous risk in the heightened imperial tensions of the mid-eighteenth century. The advancing line of English settlement, the renewed French effort to control commerce along the continent's great interior waterways, and the Indians' own chronic dependence on European imported goods, all worked together increasingly to constrain the political and diplomatic options of all native groups east of the Mississippi River. The time was rapidly approaching when the options of most would be reduced to one question: whether to side with England or France in a great war for North American empire.

12.3: The Struggle for North Atlantic Supremacy

12.3 Evaluate the causes of the fresh transatlantic wars between England, Spain, and France

For nearly three decades after the close of Queen Anne's War in 1714, the great European rivals for North American Empire—Great Britain, France, and Spain—remained officially at peace. Even so, British colonists frequently clashed with their French and Spanish counterparts over trade, territory, and shipping rights. Everyone involved recognized that a transatlantic contest for empire lay behind even the most seemingly minor intercultural dispute. Yet only gradually would the latent threat to security force people in different British colonies to overcome their mutual suspicion and begin devising measures for military and political cooperation.

On paper, at least, the British colonies enjoyed military superiority over its imperial rivals for North America. The small, demoralized border outposts of New Spain posed only a minor threat to the southernmost colonies, though St. Augustine's harbor did shelter Spanish privateers who could harass British vessels engaged in transatlantic or Caribbean trade. New France possessed a more extensive American empire, yet its population remained tiny in comparison to British America. In 1754, New France contained only 75,000 inhabitants as compared to 1.2 million people living in Britain's mainland colonies. Despite its military organization and the permanent presence of French *troupes de la marine*, the challenge of defending Canada's far-flung river empire seemed almost impossible for such small numbers.

For most of the century, the theoretical advantages enjoyed by the English colonists did them little good. While the British settlements possessed a larger and more prosperous population, they were divided into separate governments that sometimes seemed more suspicious of each other than of the French. When war came, French officers and Indian allies exploited these jealousies with considerable skill. Moreover, although the population of New France was comparatively small, it was concentrated along the St. Lawrence River, so that although the French found it difficult to mount effective offensive operations against the English, they could easily mass the forces needed to defend Montreal and Quebec. Smaller outposts on the Mississippi at New Orleans and in Illinois were protected by their sheer remoteness from the English colonies.

Most importantly, the French colonists constantly cultivated the support of Native American allies in the regions they claimed. Indeed, they often functioned as valued clients of their more populous and powerful native neighbors, especially those along the Mississippi and its tributaries. The propensity to overlook this factor led officials in eighteenth-century London—as well as many historians since—to underestimate the actual strength of France's American empire. Canadian military officers from the governor on down understood and accommodated to native ways of warfare. Canadian militiamen adopted native ways of fighting. They also accepted the right of native allies to engage in military action on their own terms, including the taking of captives for ritual torture or adoption and the taking of scalps as trophies of valor in battle. Such practices led not only the English, but also visiting French officers themselves, to view Canadian warriors as barbaric. Yet it gave the Canadians an advantage in terror and tactics in backcountry campaigns, and helped secure the loyalty of native allies so long as the Indians could participate on their own terms.

During the 1720s and 1730s, the decades following the close of Queen Anne's War (see Chapter 9), the full strength of the three European rivals for empire remained untested. To be sure, an eighteenth-century version of cold war generated a string of skirmishes on the frontier and high seas. Even so, parliamentary leaders in England were determined to preserve official peace, mainly so that they could hold the line on military expenditures. Yet the tensions could not remain suppressed forever either in America or in Europe. In the late 1730s, a running feud between Anglo-American smugglers and Spanish privateers widened into open conflict between Spain and England. Once begun, the war took on a life of its own.

12.3.1: Jenkins' Ear and War

The fresh outbreak of transatlantic war originated in British and Spanish disputes over trade and shipping rights. Throughout the first third of the eighteenth century, British and Anglo-American smugglers had been tapping into lucrative Spanish American markets. The clandestine trade brought manufactured goods to New Spain's ports in quantities far larger and at prices far lower than overregulated Spanish merchants could supply them. Smugglers returned with plantation goods and the Spanish "pieces of eight" that supplemented colonists' scarce supply of hard currency. To suppress this illicit trade, Spanish officials deployed often privately owned patrol vessels known as *guardacostas*, which possessed authority to stop and search suspected smugglers. The *guardacostas* became notorious for the harsh treatment they meted out to captured English sailors as well as for the questionable practice of seizing rival nations' ships in international waters.

The seamen's cause became a rallying point for English nationalism, and leaders of the parliamentary opposition to Sir Robert Walpole's administration—termed the "ministry" among eighteenth-century English politicians—seized the moment to call for war on Spain to secure the "Freedom of the seas." The opposition's posterboy for Spanish depredations was an obscure one-eared mariner named Robert Jenkins, who testified before Parliament in 1738 that Spanish *guardacostas* had cut off his ear without provocation after waylaying and plundering his ship. Captain Jenkins punctuated his testimony by displaying the severed ear as tangible evidence of Spanish brutality. The captain's testimony helped pressure Walpole's ministry into issuing a declaration of war against Spain in 1739 that became known as the War of Jenkins' Ear.

In America, the war against Spain recapitulated exploits of the famed sixteenth-century Sea Dogs and the seventeenth-century English buccaneers (see Chapters 2 and 4). British Vice Admiral Edward Vernon led a small fleet to Jamaica, where he planned to stage a series of raids on Spanish targets. His first victory came at Portobello on the coast of Panama, which Sir Henry Morgan had also raided in 1670. Vernon's booty of 10,000 Spanish dollars fell disappointingly short of Morgan's earlier £70,000 prize, but the admiral managed to disable a notorious haven for *guardacostas* and capture three of the hated vessels. Vernon's success encouraged an even more ambitious effort to capture the Spanish port of Cartagena, starting point of the fabled treasure convoys of the *Carrera de Indias*. This campaign, which involved approximately 3,600 Anglo-American recruits, ended in miserable failure. The troops died like flies in the fever-ridden lowlands outside the fortress, and the tragic remnant who returned to their colonial homes became heroes merely for surviving the ordeal of Cartagena. One Virginia survivor, Lawrence Washington, commemorated the event by naming his family estate Mount Vernon after the commander of the Cartagena campaign.

In North America itself, the war initially pitted James Oglethorpe's Georgia against the Spanish fortress of San Marcos at St. Augustine. In 1740, Oglethorpe invaded with a combined force of two thousand English, Creeks, Cherokees, and Chickasaws. The allies captured several outlying posts and laid siege to San Marcos for thirty-eight days before a Spanish relief force from

Cuba forced Oglethorpe's force to withdraw. The Spanish attempted to retaliate against Frederica, Georgia in 1742, but withdrew after suffering defeat at the Battle of Bloody Marsh. The hostilities dragged on until 1748 in a series of inconclusive raids along the Georgia-Florida frontier, but the war soon widened and its main theater shifted north.

In 1743, France and England declared war on one another, dragging the Americans into a much wider imperial conflict. During King George's War (1743–1748), known in Europe as the War of the Austrian Succession, the colonists scored a magnificent victory over the French. Louisbourg, a gigantic fortress on Cape Breton Island, the easternmost promontory of Canada, guarded the approaches to the Gulf of St. Lawrence and Quebec. It was described as the Gibraltar of the New World. An army of New England troops under the command of William Pepperrell captured Louisbourg in June 1745, a feat that demonstrated the British colonists were able to fight and to mount effective joint operations.

The Americans, however, were in for a shock. When the war ended with the signing of the Treaty of Aix-la-Chapelle in 1748, the British government handed Louisbourg back to the French as the treaty required. Such decisions exposed the deep and continuing ambivalence the colonists felt about participation in imperial wars. They were proud to support Great Britain, of course, but the Americans seldom fully understood why the wars were being fought, why certain tactics had been adopted, and why the British accepted treaty terms that so blatantly ignored colonial interests.

12.3.2: Unstable Interlude

Officials of the exhausted Spanish empire welcomed the return of peace, and Anglo-Spanish relations improved after 1748. The French, on the other hand, were not prepared to surrender an inch of their vast American empire to the English. But as they recognized, time was running against them. Not only were the English colonies growing more populous, but they also possessed a seemingly inexhaustible supply of manufactured goods to trade with the Indians. The French decided in the early 1750s, therefore, to seize the Ohio Valley before the Virginians could do so. They established forts throughout the region, the most formidable being Fort Duquesne, located at the strategic fork in the Ohio River and later renamed Pittsburgh.

The French entertained no illusions about their ability to maintain their new line of forts without the cooperation of nearby native peoples. Officials in Quebec sent large quantities of gifts and trade goods, which the forts' commanders could use to forge alliances. The agreements, they hoped, would yield new bundles of pelts and food supplies for the garrisons as well as assistance in arms against the English. The French found many Ohio Delawares and Shawnees eager to cooperate. An alliance with the French would give them a chance to throw off the Iroquois yoke and push back the tide of English settlement.

Although France and Great Britain had not officially declared war, British officials advised the governor of Virginia to "repell force by force." The Virginians needed little encouragement. They were eager to make good their claim to the Ohio Valley, and in 1754, militia companies under the command of an ambitious young officer, George Washington, constructed Fort Necessity not far from Fort Duquesne. The plan failed. A joint force of French and Indians—including many newly allied Delaware and Shawnee warriors—overran the badly exposed outpost (July 3, 1754). Among other things, the humiliating setback revealed that a single colony could not defeat the French.

In addition to this setback in the Ohio country, colonial officials also confronted a serious rift in Anglo-Iroquois relations in 1754. The Mohawk leader Hendrick, exasperated with the corruption and fraudulent dealing of Albany merchants and traders, declared broken the Covenant Chain system of alliances that had sustained peace and trade since the previous century (see Chapter 8). "Brother," he declared to New York's Governor Clinton, "you are not to expect to hear of me any more, and Brother we desire to hear no more of you."

12.3.3: Albany Congress and Braddock's Defeat

The twin crises of renewed French aggression and Anglo-Iroquois tension prompted British colonial leaders to advance an unprecedented proposal for intercolonial cooperation in the summer of 1754. Representatives from the northern colonies met at Albany that June to discuss how to mend relations with the Iroquois. Benjamin Franklin, who traveled to the Albany Congress as Pennsylvania's representative, used the occasion to present a bold blueprint for colonial union. His so-called Albany Plan envisioned the formation of a Grand Council, made up of elected delegates from the various colonies, to oversee matters of common defense, western expansion, and Indian affairs. A President General appointed by the king would preside. Franklin's most daring suggestion involved taxation. He insisted the council be authorized to collect taxes to cover military expenditures.

Many colonial leaders reacted enthusiastically to the Albany Plan. To take effect, however, it required the support of the separate colonial assemblies as well as Parliament. It received neither. The assemblies were jealous of their fiscal authority, and the British thought the scheme undermined the Crown's power over American affairs. Despite Benjamin Franklin's strenuous persuasive efforts—including his famous "Join or Die" political cartoon in which a poor severed rattlesnake illustrated the predicament of the disunited colonies—the Albany Plan of Union failed.

In 1755, the Ohio Valley again became the scene of fierce fighting. Even though there was still no formal declaration of war, the British resolved to destroy Fort Duquesne, and to that end, they dispatched units of the regular army to America. In command was Major General Edward Braddock, an obese, humorless veteran who inspired neither fear nor respect. One colonist described Braddock as "very indolent, Slave to his passions, women & wine, as great an Epicure as could be in his eating, tho a brave man."

That summer, Braddock led a joint force of 2,500 British Redcoats and colonists to humiliating defeat. For more than a month, Indian scouts had tracked the British as they cut noisily through "an hundred and ten Miles [of] . . . uninhabited Wilderness" toward the new French post. On July 9, a force of French and Indians opened fire as Braddock's army waded across the Monongahela River, about 8 miles from Fort Duquesne. Along a freshly cut road already congested with heavy wagons and confused men, Braddock ordered a counterattack, described by one of his officers as "without any form or order but that of a parcell of school boys coming out of s[c]hool." Nearly 70 percent of Braddock's troops were killed or wounded in western Pennsylvania. The general himself died in battle. The attackers, including many Delaware and Shawnee warriors, suffered only light casualties. The French remained in firm control of the Ohio Valley.

The entire affair profoundly angered Washington, who fumed, "We have been most scandalously beaten by a trifling body of men." The British thought their Iroquois allies might desert them after the embarrassing defeat. The Indians, however, took the news in stride, observing that "they were not at all surprised to hear it, as [Braddock's redcoats] were men who had crossed the Great Water and were unacquainted with the arts of war among the Americans."

12.3.4: The First World War for American Empire

Braddock's defeat shocked British officials on both sides of the Atlantic, yet for the next two years no one in England or America seemed to possess the leadership necessary to respond effectively. French and Indian war parties raided the Pennsylvania and Virginia backcountry at will, devastating frontier communities and pushing back the line of Anglo-American settlement more than 100 miles to the east.

Braddock's successor in the supreme command, Massachusetts governor William Shirley, prepared for open war with New France by sending two New England battalions and a detachment of regulars to secure the strategic province of Nova Scotia. After capturing the French post of Beauséjour, New Englanders began rounding up and deporting the French-speaking Acadians who had been living their under British rule since 1714 (see Chapter 10). In doing so, Anglo-Americans hoped to defuse a threat to their northern borders as well as to take over rich Acadian farmsteads for resettlement by New Englanders. The "Great Upheaval" proceeded with a brutal efficiency that eventually left Nova Scotia virtually depopulated. Most Acadians found themselves refugees, dispersed to England or the mainland British colonies. Some escaped to the Canadian mainland or Îsle-St.-Jean (now Prince Edward Island), where they joined forces with Abenakis and Micmacs in an attempt to recapture their homeland. The deportees faced terrible hardship among a hostile Anglo-American population. Many eventually emigrated once again to New Orleans, where they formed the core of Louisiana's Cajun people.

French officials responded to unfolding events in America by sending a detachment of several hundred regular troops under the capable command of Louis-Joseph, Marquis de Montcalm-Gozon de Saint-Véran, early in 1756. The cabinet of George II (r. 1727–1760) moved more slowly, its members lacking the will to organize and finance a sustained military campaign in the New World. Governor William Shirley fell victim to cabinet intrigues and intercolonial rivalry and was recalled to London in the summer of 1756. Shirley's replacement, John Campbell, earl of Loudon, quickly learned that even a formal declaration of war (May 18, 1756) was not sufficient to secure colonial cooperation. Indeed, Loudon's high-handed demands for men and money only alienated colonial assemblies, impeding his efforts to prosecute the conflict.

Imperial lack of direction coupled with increasing colonial disunity cost Anglo-Americans dearly in the early phase of the Seven Years' War— known to colonists as the French and Indian War. In 1756, the French commander Montcalm led a combined force of French regulars, Canadian militiamen and *troupes de la marine*, and allied Indians to his first American victory with the capture of Fort Oswego near Lake Ontario.

The magnitude of the French victory over Oswego persuaded an army of two thousand western Algonquians—representing more than thirty nations from as far away as Lake Superior— to join Montcalm's force of six thousand French and Canadians for the 1757 campaign against New York. Montcalm led the bulk of this force in a siege of Fort William Henry, which guarded the upper Hudson River valley from its location at the south end of Lake George. On August 9, the fort's commander completed negotiations with Montcalm for a surrender of the fort with the "honors of war." Defenders would receive safe passage to another British fort, carrying with them their possessions, arms, and colors. The French would care for the wounded until they could be transported home.

Montcalm, however, had made a fatal mistake for the future of Franco-Indian cooperation. His own disdain for allies whom he regarded as barbarians had prompted the French commander to break with historic Canadian policy, excluding Indian leaders from the negotiations over the terms of the fort's surrender. When the victorious Montcalm issued a peremptory order not to take captives, plunder, or trophy scalps, the Algonquians simply ignored this ally who had presumed to act as their overlord. As the British began departing the next day, Algonquian warriors surrounded the provincials near the rear of the retreating column. They seized captives, plundered food, clothing, and weapons, and took scalps from the wounded as battle trophies. The killing and plunder ended within minutes, and the Algonquians departed abruptly for home with what they regarded as just compensation for their part in the campaign.

The "massacre of Fort William Henry" incensed the British, who resolved never again to give the French the honors of war in any future terms of surrender. The incident also confirmed Montcalm in his opinion of Indians as bloodthirsty barbarians, and left him determined to avoid further joint campaigns with them. He need not have worried. After experiencing what they regarded as Montcalm's betrayal of their interests, many Algonquians refused to cooperate any further in the war effort. The campaign of 1757 marked the high point of Franco-Indian alliance. From then on, Indian numbers dwindled steadily leaving the French ever more alone to defend their river empire.

12.3.5: Pitt and Victory

Had it not been for William Pitt, the most powerful minister in George's cabinet, the Anglo-French contest for empire might have ground down to a stalemate. This supremely self-confident Englishman believed he was the only person capable of saving the British Empire, an opinion he publicly expressed. When he became effective head of the ministry in December 1756, Pitt had an opportunity to demonstrate his talents.

In the past, warfare on the European continent had worked mainly to France's advantage. Pitt saw no point in continuing to concentrate on Europe. Even as Fort William Henry fell in 1757, Pitt was advancing a bold new imperial policy based on commercial assumptions. In Pitt's judgment, the critical confrontation would take place in North America, where Britain and France were struggling to control colonial markets and raw materials. Indeed, according to Pitt,

America was "where England and Europe are to be fought for." He was determined, therefore, to expel the French from the continent, however great the cost.

To effect this ambitious scheme, Pitt took personal command of the army and navy. He mapped strategy. He even promoted young promising officers over the heads of their superiors. He also recognized that the success of the war effort could not depend on the generosity of the colonial assemblies. Great Britain would have to foot most of the bill. Pitt's military expenditures, of course, created an enormous national debt that would soon haunt both Britain and its colonies, but at the time, no one foresaw the fiscal consequences of victory in America.

To implement his grand campaign, Pitt moved late in 1757 to replace the imperious Lord Loudon with two relatively obscure officers, Jeffrey Amherst and James Wolfe. It was a masterful choice, one that a less self-assured man than Pitt would never have risked. Both officers were young, talented, and ambitious. On July 26, 1758, forces under their direction captured Louisbourg, the same fortress the colonists had taken a decade earlier!

This victory helped cut the Canadians' main supply line with France. The small population of New France could no longer meet the military demands placed on it. As the situation became increasingly desperate, the French forts of the Ohio Valley and the Great Lakes began to fall. Duquesne was simply abandoned late in 1758 as French and Indian troops under the Marquis de Montcalm retreated toward Quebec and Montreal. During the summer of 1759, the French surrendered key forts at Ticonderoga, Crown Point, and Niagara. Their remaining native allies quietly abandoned them to return to Great Lakes homes or to make peace with the English who now held a permanent presence in the Ohio country.

The climax to a century of war came dramatically in September 1759. Wolfe, now a major general, assaulted Quebec with nine thousand men. But it was not simply force of arms that brought victory. Wolfe proceeded as if he were preparing to attack the city directly, but under cover of darkness, his troops scaled a cliff to dominate a less well defended position. At dawn on September 13, 1759, they took the French from the rear by surprise. The decisive action occurred on the Plains of Abraham, atop a bluff high above the St. Lawrence River. Both Wolfe and Montcalm were mortally wounded. When an aide informed Wolfe the French had been routed, he sighed, "Now, God be praised, I will die in peace."

Bereft of their Indian allies, prevented from reinforcement and supply by the destruction of the French fleet in Europe, New France tottered and fell. An effort to retake Quebec failed in May 1760. During the summer, Amherst sailed up the St. Lawrence with a fleet of troop transports, encountering little effective resistance along the way. On September 8, 1760, Amherst accepted the final surrender of the French army at Montreal.

12.4: Troubled Triumph

12.4 Describe the effects of the Seven Years' War on American society

Even as Amherst and Wolf were converging on Quebec in the summer of 1759, British naval and amphibious forces had captured two jewels of France's Caribbean empire, the rich sugar islands of Guadeloupe and Marie-Galante. Another campaign in 1761 secured the island of Martinique. And in 1762, Spain belatedly entered the war as an ally of France only to lose Havana, the key of its Caribbean possessions. The immediate extension of liberal terms to French and Spanish West Indian planters increased British Atlantic commerce by literally millions of pounds sterling during the early 1760s. Yet even as these new

Caribbean acquisitions began generating profits and payments on Britain's burgeoning war debt, fresh challenges emerged in the trans-Appalachian West that would reveal the high cost of managing a vast New World empire.

12.4.1: The Cherokee War

The first indication of future trouble in Anglo-Indian relations emerged in the Southeast as Geoffrey Amherst was savoring the fall of Quebec and preparing his final campaign to Montreal. Late in 1759, border strife between Carolina settlers and the Cherokees, up to this point one of South Carolina's most reliable allies, escalated into a full-scale war. Western Carolina settlers had been encroaching on Cherokee hunting grounds and corn fields for several years. In the fall of 1758, however, thirty Cherokee warriors lost their lives to colonial militia as they traveled home from a joint campaign with British forces. Warriors from the Cherokee Lower Towns arrived home to find that colonists from the nearby Long Canes settlement had invaded their hunting grounds. The poaching had cut deeply into supplies of game that the Cherokees needed to survive the winter.

Throughout the summer of 1759, the Cherokees debated what to do as border incidents continued. Finally that fall, nativist warriors conducted retaliatory raids that claimed the lives of thirty backcountry settlers, a number roughly equivalent to the Cherokees killed the year before. South Carolina governor William Henry Lyttelton responded with an embargo on all gunpowder shipments. The Cherokees, who desperately needed the gunpowder for winter hunts, sent a delegation of chiefs to negotiate with Lyttelton. The governor promptly imprisoned them as hostages until their kinsmen surrendered the warriors who had participated in the raids.

Lyttelton accomplished precisely the opposite of his intention. Rather than cowing the Cherokees into submission, he had managed to remove the moderate chiefs from Cherokee councils. The remaining nativist leaders launched an offensive that by October 1760 pushed the line of colonial settlement back eastward more than 100 miles. It took a combined force of 2,800 British regulars, colonial rangers, and Catawba and Chickasaw warriors to "chastise the Cherokees" during the summer of 1761. Only after months of fighting in the rugged Carolina mountains did the Cherokees submit, compelled by the prospect of a winter without corn to eat, gunpowder for the hunt, or shelter sufficient for a population largely burned out of house and home.

12.4.2: Pontiac's War

Scarcely had the Cherokee War subsided when a fresh threat to British rule appeared in the Ohio country. In 1762, Delaware prophet Neolin called for a pan-Indian movement dedicated to renouncing European goods and returning to ancient ways of worship, hunting, and cultivation. The prophet's message found a growing audience among western Indians of the Ohio country and the Great Lakes, who had observed the establishment of permanent British garrisons in the region with increasing alarm. They knew from experience that permanent garrisons meant an eventual influx of settlers. Indeed, the new military road to Fort Pitt was bringing more settlers to western Pennsylvania every year, filling up the region with European competitors for land and game. General Geoffrey Amherst's recent reforms in Indian policy fueled discontent even further. Amherst had known that he would provoke some unrest by instituting new trade regulations and sharply curtailing gifts to native allies but had persuaded himself that the British could no longer afford the expense of lubricating Anglo-Indian relations by the tradition of gift-giving. In any case, Amherst reasoned, the defeat of the French would leave the Indians no choice but to accept the new policy. The British commander-in-chief therefore dismissed as "Meer Bugbears" the

rumors of Indian war that filtered toward him in the fall of 1762.

The pan-Indian uprising of 1763 thus took the British high command almost completely by surprise. It began on May 9, when the Ottawa leader Pontiac led a combined force of Ottawa, Potawatomi, Wyandotte, and Chippewa warriors to besiege the small British garrison at Fort Detroit. Pontiac had invoked Neolin's teachings in his call for war against the English. Within a month, a vast alliance of Great Lakes peoples had seized thinly manned British garrisons throughout the region—Fort Michilimackinac on the Lake Michigan–Lake Huron straits, Fort St. Joseph near present-day Niles Michigan, Fort Miami (now Fort Wayne, Indiana), Fort Ouiatenon near present-day Lafayette, Indiana, and Fort Sandusky on the west end of Lake Erie. The garrison commander of the remote Fort Edward Augustus on Green Bay handed over the post to the local Sioux and began an overland trek to British-controlled territory, only to be captured by Ottawa and Chippewa warriors who carried them to Montreal for ransom.

Pontiac kept the British bottled up in Fort Detroit throughout the summer of 1763. Meanwhile, an alliance of Ottawa, Chippewa, and Seneca warriors captured all posts between Fort Niagara and Fort Pitt, while Shawnee, Delaware, and Mingo warriors severed communications between Fort Pitt and eastern Pennsylvania. While the British fumbled to respond, Indians raided almost at will throughout the Pennsylvania and Virginia backcountry. Finally in mid-July, Captain James Dalyell led a 260-man relief convoy to Fort Detroit while Colonel Henry Bouquet marched with 460 troops to relieve Fort Pitt and "extirpate" the native "vermin." Both commanders discovered, however, that their Indian foes would not be pushovers. On July 31, Dalyell lost his life at the Battle of Bloody Run when he led a sortie from Fort Detroit straight into Pontiac's ambush. Bouquet's force narrowly escaped being extirpated itself in a similar ambush at Bushy Run

Creek. Only brilliant, desperate maneuvering saved his force.

Pontiac finally lifted the siege of Detroit on October 15, after the French commandant in Illinois refused to support the campaign. Realization that the French had relinquished their North American claims prompted some Indian nations to advocate accommodating the English. As divisions among their leaders grew, many Indians slipped homeward to begin the winter hunt. The Ottawa leader's inability to maintain or force the English to terms damaged his credibility irreparably. He faded into obscurity and was eventually murdered by a Peoria warrior in April 1769.

The lifting of Pontiac's siege saved Fort Detroit, but Anglo-Indian hostilities dragged on into 1765 before finally coming to an end in a practical victory for the Indians. The British mistook several lightly opposed operations in 1764 and 1765 as military victories, but the treaties they forged conceded to the Indians all the major issues of the war. Anglo-American officials resumed diplomatic gift-giving, ended limitations on trade in arms and ammunition, and reopened the rum trade. The British also established the Proclamation Line of 1763 along the Appalachian fall line to keep white settlers from encroaching further on Indian lands. As normal trade resumed, both sides chose to ignore for the time being the renewed rush of European settlers into the Ohio country.

12.4.3: Peace

The Peace of Paris signed on February 10, 1763, almost fulfilled William Pitt's grandiose dreams. Great Britain took possession of an empire that stretched around the globe. Only Guadeloupe and Martinique, the Caribbean sugar islands, were given back to the French. After a century-long struggle, the French had been driven from the mainland of North America. Even Louisiana passed out of France's control into Spanish hands. The treaty gave Britain title to Canada, Florida, and all the land east of the Mississippi River. Moreover,

with the stroke of a diplomat's pen, eighty-thousand French-speaking Canadians, most of them Catholics, became the subjects of George III.

The Americans were overjoyed. It was a time of good feelings and national pride. Together, the English and their colonial allies had thwarted the "Gallic peril." Samuel Davies, a Presbyterian who had brought the Great Awakening to Virginia, announced confidently that the long-awaited victory would inaugurate "a new heaven and a new earth."

12.4.4: Perceptions of War

The Seven Years' War made a deep impression on American society. Even though Franklin's Albany Plan had failed, the military struggle had forced the colonists to cooperate on an unprecedented scale. It also drew them into closer contact with Britain. They became aware of being part of a great empire, military and commercial, but in the very process of waging war, they acquired a more intimate sense of an America that lay beyond the plantation and the village. Conflict had carried thousands of young men across colonial boundaries, exposing them to a vast territory full of opportunities for a booming population. Moreover, the war trained a corps of American officers, people like George Washington, who learned from firsthand experience that the British were not invincible.

British officials later accused the Americans of ingratitude. England, they claimed, had sent troops and provided funds to liberate the colonists from the threat of French attack. The Americans, appreciative of the aid from England, cheered on the British but dragged their feet at every stage, refusing to pay the bills. These charges were later incorporated into a general argument justifying parliamentary taxation in America.

The British had a point. The colonists were, in fact, slow in providing the men and materials needed to fight the French. Nevertheless, they did make a significant contribution to the war effort, and it was perfectly reasonable for Americans to

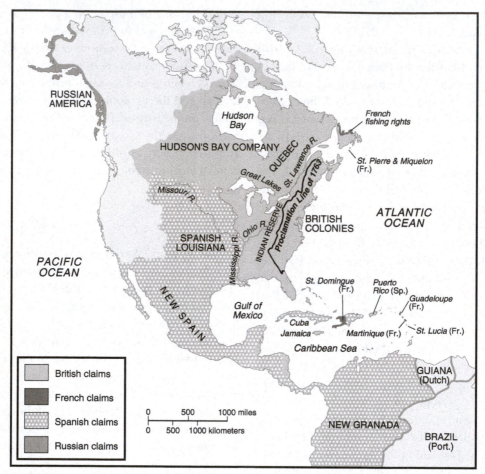

Map 12.1 North America after 1763

regard themselves at the very least as junior partners in the empire. After all, they had supplied almost twenty thousand soldiers and spent well over £2 million. In a single year, in fact, Massachusetts enlisted five thousand men out of an adult male population of about fifty thousand, a commitment that, in the words of one military historian, meant "the war was being waged on a scale comparable to the great wars of modern times." After making such a sacrifice—indeed, after demonstrating their loyalty to the mother country—the colonists would surely have been disturbed to learn that General James Wolfe, the hero of Quebec, had stated, "The Americans are in general the dirtiest, the most contemptible, cowardly dogs that you can conceive. There is no depending upon them in action. They fall down in their own dirt and desert in battalions, officers and all."

12.5: Rule Britannia?

12.5 Recognize the political and cultural influence of Great Britain on colonial Americans of British background

James Thomson, an Englishman, understood the hold of empire on the popular imagination of the eighteenth century. In 1740, he composed words that British patriots have proudly sung for more than two centuries:

> Rule Britannia, rule the waves,
>
> Britons never will be slaves.

Colonial Americans—at least, those of British background—joined the chorus. By mid-century they took their political and cultural cues from Great Britain. They fought its wars, purchased its consumer goods, flocked to hear its evangelical preachers, and read its many publications. Without question, the empire provided the colonists with a compelling source of identity.

An editor justified the establishment of New Hampshire's first newspaper in precisely these terms. "By this Means," the publisher observed, "the spirited Englishman, the mountainous Welshman, the brave Scotchman, and Irishman, and the loyal American, may be firmly united and mutually RESOLVED to guard the glorious Throne of BRITANNIA . . . as British Brothers, in defending the Common Cause." Even new immigrants, the Germans, Scots-Irish, and Africans, who felt no political loyalty to Great Britain and no affinity to English culture, had to assimilate to some degree to the dominant English culture of the colonies.

Americans hailed Britannia. In 1763, they were the victors, the conquerors of the backcountry. In their moment of glory, the colonists assumed that Britain's rulers saw the Americans as "Brothers," as equal partners in the business of empire. Only slowly would they learn the British had a different perception. For them, "American" was a way of saying "not quite English."

Chronology

1739	War of Jenkins' Ear begins
1741	British-led Siege of Cartagena fails
1742	Battle of Bloody Marsh halts Spanish campaign against Frederica, Georgia
1743	War of the Austrian Succession (King George's War) begins
1745	Colonial troops capture Louisbourg
1748	Treaty of Aix-la-Chapelle concludes King George's War
1754	Albany Congress meets; Virginians under George Washington defeated at Fort Necessity in Pennsylvania
1755	Braddock is defeated by the French and Indians in western Pennsylvania
1756	Seven Years' War is formally declared
1757	Fall of Fort William Henry
1759	British victorious at Quebec, Wolfe and Montcalm killed in battle; Cherokee War breaks out in the Carolinas
1760	George III becomes king of Great Britain
1762	British forces capture Havana
1763	Peace of Paris ending French and Indian War is signed; Pontiac's Uprising in Great Lakes, cis-Mississippi West

Part IV

An Independent America in the Atlantic World

"We have it in our power to begin the world over again," Thomas Paine declared to his fellow Americans in 1776. The famous pamphleteer's defense of this audacious claim demonstrated that both he and his readers were thinking of their chances of success as independent actors in an Atlantic context. Paine pointed to American resources developed within a British imperial framework: a capacity to produce great volumes of commodities valued highly in European ports, a growing ability to manufacture not only weapons of war but also finished goods for trade, a vast wealth of natural resources that could supply everything from timber for ships to iron for guns and horseshoes. "Europe, and not England, is the parent country of America," Paine declared, and he boasted that the colonists who had found refuge on British American shores had multiplied so rapidly that "our present numbers are sufficient to repel all the force in the world."

Paine also exhibited a keen awareness that America's intensifying conflict with Great Britain was unfolding within an Atlantic context. The British navy remained the most powerful in the world, despite Paine's dubious claim that "not one tenth" of His Majesty's ships were "at any one time fit for service." The proposal he laid out in *Common Sense* to build a rival American fleet was quixotic, as he and every patriot leader knew. To succeed, the War for Independence would need more than simple neutrality from Great Britain's rival Atlantic powers. It would need the support of French and Spanish navies. Patriot smugglers would also need access to the Atlantic ports of France, Spain, and the Netherlands where they could trade for arms, ammunition, and military supplies.

Engaging with such potential allies was fraught with hazards, since both France and Spain remained absolutist monarchies and were hardly sympathetic to the idea of the kind of representative republican governments that the United Colonies were already beginning to formulate. The Netherlands was nominally republican, but its highly aristocratic rulers were intermarried with the royal dynasties of Europe and were no more sympathetic to leadership by men they viewed as upstart commoners and amateurs at the business of governing. France, still smarting from the loss of its North American river empire thirteen years earlier, hoped to exploit the conflict to regain a toehold on the continent. Meanwhile, Spanish reformists were reorganizing imperial rule, strengthening government in their existing colonies, and appointing aggressive officials in New Orleans who sought to make Louisiana the base for Spanish expansion into the Southeast and the Mississippi valley. Only with shrewd, clandestine negotiation were the American Peace Commissioners eventually able to gain the cession of the trans-Appalachian West against such treacherous imperial allies in the Treaty of 1783.

Assuming a "separate and equal station" among the "powers of the earth," as the Declaration of Independence put it in 1776, meant that the new United States had of necessity to become an Atlantic power capable of holding its own against mighty imperial rivals. Victory in the War for Independence marked only the first stage of a long and precarious struggle to achieve that goal. As the British Empire before it, the development of the United States remained a human story of creative adaptation playing out among its varied peoples in thousands of specific local conflicts, unexpected alliances, bold ventures, tragic failures, and triumphs large and small.

Chapter 13

Colonial Alienation within the British Empire

 ## Learning Objectives

13.1 Evaluate effects of the Stamp Act on the breakdown of bonds between the colonists and their mother country

13.2 Review the collapse of the mutual trust between the parliament and the King of England

13.3 Recount the budgetary crisis faced by Great Britain

13.4 Examine effects of the mistrust between policy makers in London and the colonists

13.5 Identify events leading to the pickup of the American economy

13.6 Interpret effects of the erosion of the colonial goodwill in America

On February 13, 1766, colonial agent Benjamin Franklin testified before angry members of the British House of Commons to explain why American colonists had reacted so violently to the Stamp Act, an extensive tax on colonists they had enacted the previous year. Since then, correspondence from America had been filled with accounts of colonial behavior that most British officials regarded as rebellious. Colonial newspapers had published open challenges to parliamentary authority. Ordinary Americans had sworn to boycott British goods rather than paying the tax. Crowds of agitators calling themselves Sons of Liberty had intimidated Stamp Tax agents. In Boston, a mob had burned down a warehouse full of paper bearing the hated stamp and dismantled the house of Lieutenant Governor Thomas Hutchinson, who had sworn to enforce the tax. Colonial lawmakers, instead of throwing the ringleaders in jail, had used such occasions to pass resolutions that not only rejected the tax but also denied Parliament's authority to impose it.

By the time Franklin appeared before Parliament, it had become obvious to everyone that the bonds of affection between colonists and the mother country had become badly frayed and were in danger of breaking completely. Why, the members of Parliament wondered, had the "temper of America towards Great Britain" and

297

their "respect for Parliament" soured so suddenly? Franklin responded that a "concurrence of causes" had produced the unexpected turn. "Restraints lately laid on their trade" had prevented the circulation of hard currency back to the colonies from England. Parliamentary prohibition of colonial paper currency had only exacerbated the problem. But there was more, an emotional element that energized resistance. The Stamp Act had treated the Americans like second-class subjects in the empire—as not quite proper Englishmen—an insult made all the worse by the fact that Parliament had assigned enforcement of the act to admiralty courts, which did not include juries. Only a repeal of the Stamp Act would satisfy the Americans. Without that, Franklin warned, Great Britain would suffer "a total loss of the respect and affection the people of America bear to this country, and of all the commerce that depends on that respect and affection."

Franklin's testimony before Parliament placed colonial protest of the Stamp Act within a context of Atlantic empire and global commerce. The Peace of Paris in 1763 had resolved a century-long contest over control of North America in favor of Great Britain, but victory over the French had introduced a whole new set of problems. Over the next decade, Parliament and British officials wrestled with practical problems such as how to pay for the crushing debt incurred during the Seven Year's War, how to organize the administration of their newly won empire, how to incorporate the Catholic, French-speaking population of Quebec and Louisiana into a Protestant, mostly English-speaking dominion, and how to manage diplomacy and trade with the native peoples who inhabited the vast North American interior. From the perspective of London, the old system of British-colonial reciprocity, which had held the empire together against the threat of an encircling French river empire (see Chapters 8 and 12), now seemed woefully inadequate. The new empire stood in desperate need of innovative forms of territorial

organization, new methods of administration and diplomacy, and new sources of revenue to fund the enterprise.

As Benjamin Franklin explained to Parliament, however, the colonists had come to see themselves as active subjects, partners in winning and ruling the empire. They expected that they would continue to share in their own government, taxation, and economic policy. This expectation had become embedded in their institutions and political culture over the previous century and a half of colonial development. They could never accept Parliament's assertion, in the Declaratory Act of 1766, that it "had, hath, and of right ought to have, full power and authority to make laws and statutes of sufficient force and validity to bind the colonies and people of America, subjects of the Crown of Great Britain, in all cases whatsoever." This phrase—in all cases whatsoever—seemed a needless insult. The Americans were not plotting for independence. This goal was far from anyone's expectations. But they did want assurance that Parliament would respect local political traditions, which sometimes differed from those found in England. This sense of alienation—a failure of mutual respect—became the focal point of a contest that brought the mainland colonies to the brink of civil war with the mother country by 1774.

13.1: Colonial Society Following the Seven Years' War

13.1 Evaluate effects of the Stamp Act on the breakdown of bonds between the colonists and their mother country

The Americans celebrated the victory over the French in Canada. They believed that they had more than demonstrated their loyalty to the British.

They regarded themselves as full partners in the empire. From their perspective, the years after 1763 were a "postwar" period, a time of heightened economic and political expectation following the successful conclusion of the Seven Years' War.

For many Americans, the period generated great optimism. The population continued to grow, a sign that young couples anticipated rising prosperity. Indeed, by 1776, approximately 2.5 million people, black and white, were living in the thirteen mainland colonies. The striking ethnic and racial diversity of these men and women amazed European visitors who apparently rated homogeneity more highly than did the Americans. In 1775, for example, a traveler corrected the impression in London that the "colonists are the offspring of Englishmen." To be sure, many families traced their roots to Great Britain, but one also encountered "French, Dutch, Germans innumerable, Indians, Africans, and a multitude of felons." He then asked rhetorically, "Is it possible to tell which are the most turbulent amongst such a mixture of people?"

During the 1760s, the population of mainland British America was also extraordinarily young, a fact of great importance in understanding the development of effective political resistance. Nearly 60 percent of the colonists of European descent were under age 21. That number held steady during the entire revolutionary period. At any given time, most people in this society were small children, and many of the young men who fought the British during the Revolution either had not been born or had been infants when their parents' generation had protested the Stamp Act. Grievances were learned within families and communities rather than directly experienced. Any explanation for the developing strains within the empire, therefore, must take into account the continuing process of political socialization of so many young people.

Postwar Americans also experienced a high level of prosperity. To be sure, some major port cities went through a difficult period as colonists who had been employed during the fighting were thrown out of work. Sailors and ship workers, for example, were especially vulnerable to layoffs of this sort. Yet in general, the material lives of the colonists were not substantially lower than those of the English, or for that matter, the Dutch. In 1774, the per capita wealth of the Americans, blacks and whites included, was £37.4. This sum exceeds the per capita wealth of many developing countries today, adjusted for inflation. On the eve of revolution, £37.4 would have purchased about 310 bushels of wheat, 1,600 pounds of rice, 11 cows, or 6 horses. A typical white family of five—a father, mother, and three dependent children—not only would have been able to afford decent food, clothing, and housing but also would have had money left over with which to purchase consumer goods. Even the poorest colonists seem to have benefited from a rising standard of living, and although they may not have done as well as their wealthier neighbors, they too wanted to preserve gains they had made. Economic explanations in themselves are not sufficient to explain the revolution.

Wealth, however, was not evenly distributed throughout this society. Regional variations were striking. The southern colonies enjoyed the highest levels of personal wealth in America, which can be explained in part by the ownership of slaves. More than 90 percent of America's unfree workers lived in the South, and they represented a huge capital investment. Even without including the slaves in these wealth estimates, the South did quite well. In terms of aggregate wealth, the Middle Colonies also scored impressively. In fact, only New England lagged noticeably behind, a reflection of its relative inability to produce large amounts of exports for a growing world market.

13.1.1: Greater North America

The extraordinary diversity of Britain's post-1763 empire was strikingly enhanced by the inclusion for the first time of the former French claims in Canada and those of Spain in Florida, a huge expansion of British control over all of North America east of the Mississippi River. The Treaty of Peace of Paris in 1763 confirmed Great Britain's possession of the whole of what is now Nova Scotia, whose deepwater port at Halifax made it an excellent administrative center. Many New England colonists migrated to the island to establish farms in the 1760s. Over seventy thousand French-speaking colonists remained under British rule in Canada. They continued to ply traditional occupations and trade, including ongoing participation of ordinary voyageurs in the fur trade, which was now channeled through British merchants. French Canadians also retained their devotion to Roman Catholicism, despite the fact that Catholic adherence was formally illegal under the Act of Toleration of 1689.

Florida remained a marginal enterprise for the British just as it had been for the Spanish, despite efforts of British governors there to encourage settlement and development. Few English families moved to the area during the twenty years of British rule from 1763 to 1783. The tiny Spanish population vacated the garrison communities of St. Augustine and Pensacola for Cuba after the British took possession. The emerging Seminole peoples of Florida, however, continued to coalesce and develop during this period. British officials termed nearly all Indians of Florida "Seminole," despite the fact that many of them were Creeks who had migrated south from Georgia. Distance from other Creek bands, absorption of the remnants of other people groups from the region, and intermarriage with slaves all contributed to the emergence of a distinct Seminole identity. Seminole groups often became cattle herders as well as traders in skins and meat for the Caribbean trade, which pulled them more firmly into British Atlantic commerce.

Elsewhere in American Indian country, commerce and colonization continued to transform native societies at an accelerating pace. By the 1760s, many native peoples lived as neighbors of European colonists, greeting them in the streets of colonial towns, often dressing like them, living in similar houses, drinking tea from imported ceramics, and eating from pewter plates. Indeed, the historian Colin Calloway has observed that archaeological evidence from this period often reveals very little difference between the material conditions of colonists and Indians. Even further from established towns, American Indians depended significantly on British trade for such basic items as clothing, knives, axes, cookware, and guns for hunting. Under these circumstances, any disturbance in commerce between Great Britain and the colonies was bound to affect the livelihoods of native peoples as well.

British colonial administrators had learned from Pontiac's War that they had both to accommodate the traditional terms of native exchange and diplomacy as well as assuming a new position as protectors from white encroachment on Indian land (see Chapter 12). Part of the solution they developed was to attempt to centralize imperial diplomacy with native peoples in the West, channeling it through two recently created superintendencies for Indian affairs. Sir William Johnson of New York was appointed superintendent for the northern district (1756), which included the powerful Iroquois League, whereas John Stuart of South Carolina became superintendent for the southern district, which included the Cherokees, Chickasaws, Choctaws, and Creeks. British officials also established the Proclamation Line of 1763 (see Chapter 12), to protect Indian hunting grounds from Anglo-American encroachment.

Neither measure proved effective. Colonial governments whose charters included large western claims refused to recognize the authority of the imperial superintendents, continuing to conduct their own diplomacy and employ their own Indian agents. Land-hungry young settlers pushed west across the Proclamation Line even before the ink on the map was dry, antagonizing the Indians who resided in the Ohio Country by carving farmsteads out of the hunting grounds.

The two Indian superintendents managed to antagonize colonists and Indians alike by presiding over a trio of treaties in the late 1760s— the Treaty of Fort Stanwix in the north and Fort Augusta and Hard Labor in the south—that ceded large new western territories for surveying, sale, and European settlement. Officials and land speculators in Virginia rejected the treaties as encroachments on their rights and prejudicial to their interests, whereas native nations such as the Shawnee rejected Iroquois leaders' rights to sign away lands the Shawnee saw as theirs. Such actions produced increasing resentment that broke out periodically into violent conflict between native inhabitants and Anglo-American colonists on the frontier. Contempt for greedy American settlers would drive many Native Americans to support the British during the Revolution, a tragic decision that spelled disaster for them after the colonists won independence.

13.1.2: The Sugar Islands in the 1760s

The British West Indies remained much the same after 1763 as before, though the terms of the peace did net them undisputed claim to the four new islands of Grenada, Saint Vincent, Dominica, and Tobago. The sugar plantations of the West Indies remained major drivers of the British Atlantic economy, which held profound implications for the shape of society and politics there. The West Indies hosted a population of well over 300,000 at this time, over 67 percent of which were slaves. The great planters of the region followed the long-established pattern of living in the most fashionable areas of England and managing their plantations from afar through resident stewards and overseers.

Government and politics on West Indian islands such as Jamaica and Barbados formally resembled those of the mainland colonies, yet two factors hindered the kind of cooperation that emerged among mainland colonial leaders. The

first was the sheer distance separating the islands, complicated by the difficulties of navigating between them for local purposes. One thousand miles separated Jamaica from Barbados, for example, and the colonists on all West Indian islands saw more reason to communicate with their merchant partners and absentee landlords in London than with each other. The residence in England of a large, wealthy, and powerful West Indian planter community also made for political dynamics very different from that of the mainland colonies, whose voices were muted by distance and who had to rely on a handful of colonial agents to lobby for their interests in London.

13.2: Breakdown of Political Trust

13.2 Review the collapse of the mutual trust between the parliament and the King of England

Although Parliament exercised almost complete sovereignty within the British constitution, many people—especially in colonial America—looked to the monarch to preserve the empire during hard times. One could challenge the decisions of parliament while at the same time professing loyalty to the king. The man who held the crown was not prepared for the challenge. When George III became king of England in 1760, he was only 22 years of age, inexperienced in political affairs, uncomfortable in social situations, and stubborn in his opinions. However unprepared he was for the job, he declared his intention to play an aggressive role in government. No one had expected this move. The decision frightened England's parliamentary leaders, who assumed that they alone determined imperial policy. For decades, a powerful, though loosely associated, group of men known as Whigs—wealthy members of the aristocracy and landed gentry—had controlled the nation's finances and as a reward, liberally distributed contacts and patronage to friends and family. George II, the new king's grandfather, had accepted this self-serving situation, and so long as the Whigs in Parliament did not meddle with his beloved army, the king had let them rule the nation.

In one stroke, George III destroyed this cozy relationship. He selected as his chief minister the Earl of Bute, a Scot whose chief qualification for office appeared to be his friendship with the young king. The Whigs who dominated Parliament were outraged. Bute had no ties with the members of the House of Commons; he owed them no favors. It seemed to the Whigs that with the appointment of Bute, George was trying to turn back the clock to the time before the Glorious Revolution (see Chapter 7), in other words, attempting to reestablish a personal absolutist monarchy free from traditional constitutional restraints. However corrupt their own practices may have been, the Whigs blamed Bute for every wrong, real or imagined. As it turned out, George did not, in fact, harbor plans radically to restructure political practices, but many parliamentary leaders thought he did. And in politics perceptions count for as much as reality.

By 1763 Bute, who lacked diplomatic skills, left office. But the damage had been done. His departure neither restored the traditional Whigs to preeminence nor dampened the king's constant meddling in domestic politics. Everyone agreed George had the right to select whomever he desired for major cabinet posts such as the chancellor of the exchequer, but until 1770, no one seemed able to please the monarch. Ministers came and went, often for no other reason than George felt uncomfortable in their presence. Because of this chronic instability in everyday government, the minor officials who directed routine affairs did not know what was expected of them. In the absence of clear long-range policy, some officials made narrowly based decisions; others did nothing. Most devoted their energies to finding a political patron capable of satisfying the fickle

king. Talent played little part in the scramble for office, and incompetent hacks were advanced as frequently as were men of vision. With such turbulence surrounding him, the king showed little interest in the American colonies. Instead of addressing the major issues of the day, the empire drifted without direction.

The king, however, does not bear the sole responsibility for England's loss of empire. The members of Parliament who actually drafted the legislation that gradually drove a wedge between the colonies and Britain must share the blame, for they failed to provide innovative answers to the explosive constitutional issues. The problem was not stupidity or even obstinacy, qualities found in equal measure among all peoples. But like so many elected representatives over the centuries, they focused on personal rewards and ignored the issues that cried out for attention.

In part, the impasse resulted from ignorance. Few Englishmen active in government had ever visited America. For those who attempted to follow colonial affairs, accurate information proved extremely difficult to obtain. Packet boats carrying passengers and mail sailed regularly between London and the various colonial ports, but the voyage across the Atlantic required at least four weeks. Furthermore, all correspondence was laboriously copied in longhand by overworked clerks serving in understaffed offices. One could not expect to receive from America an answer to a specific question in less than three months. As a result of the lag in communication between England and America, rumors sometimes passed for true accounts, and misunderstanding influenced the formulation of colonial policy.

Even when reasonably accurate information was available, the two sides were often unable to understand each other's positions. They gave the words of a shared language very different meanings. The central element in this Anglo-American debate was a concept known as "parliamentary sovereignty." The English ruling classes viewed the role of Parliament from a historical perspective that most colonists never shared. They insisted that Parliament was the dominant element within the constitution. Indeed, this elective body protected rights and property from an arbitrary monarch. During the reign of the Stuarts, especially under Charles I (r. 1625–1649), the authority of Parliament had been challenged, and it was not until the Glorious Revolution of 1688 that the English Crown formally recognized Parliament's supreme authority in matters such as taxation (see Chapter 8). Almost no one, including George III, would have dissented from a speech made in 1766 before the House of Commons, in which a representative declared, "The parliament hath, and must have, from the nature and essence of the constitution, has had, and ever will have a sovereign supreme power and jurisdiction over every part of the dominions of the state, *to make laws in all cases whatsoever.*"

The logic of this argument seemed self-evident to the British. In fact, parliamentary leaders could never quite understand why the colonists were so difficult to persuade. In frustration, Lord Hillsborough, the British secretary of state, admonished the colonial agent for Connecticut, "It is essential to the constitution to preserve the supremacy of Parliament inviolate; and tell your friends in America . . . that it is as much their interest to support the constitution and preserve the supremacy of Parliament as it is ours."

13.2.1: The American Perspective

Americans most emphatically did not see it in their "interest" to maintain the "supremacy of Parliament." The crisis in imperial relations forced the colonists first to define and then to defend principles deeply rooted in their own political culture. For more than a century, their ideas about the colonies' role within the British Empire had remained a vague, untested bundle of assumptions about personal liberties, property rights, and representative institutions.

By 1763, however, certain fundamental American beliefs had become clear. From Massachusetts to Georgia, colonists aggressively defended the powers of their own provincial assemblies. They drew on rich legislative histories that often went back to the beginning of the seventeenth century. Over time, the American assemblies had steadily expanded their authority over taxation and expenditure, over appointments and Indian affairs. Since no one in Britain bothered to clip their legislative wings, these provincial bodies assumed a major role in policymaking and routine administration. In other words, by mid-century the assemblies looked like American copies of Parliament. It seemed unreasonable, therefore, for the British suddenly to insist on the supremacy of Parliament, for as the legislators of Massachusetts observed in 1770, "This house has the same inherent rights in this province as the house of commons in Great Britain."

The constitutional crisis turned ultimately on the meaning of representation itself. In 1764, a British official informed the colonists that even though they had not elected members to Parliament—indeed, even though they had had no direct contact with the current members—they were nevertheless "virtually" represented by that august body. The members of Parliament, he declared, represented the political interests of all subjects who lived in the British empire. It did not really matter whether everyone had cast a vote.

The colonists ridiculed the notion of virtual representation. The only representatives the Americans recognized as legitimate were those actually chosen by the people for whom they spoke. On this crucial point they would not compromise. As John Adams insisted, a representative assembly should actually mirror its constituents: "It should think, feel, reason, and act like them." Because the members of Parliament could not possibly think like Americans, it followed logically they could not represent them. And if they were not genuine representatives, the members of Parliament—pretensions to sovereignty notwithstanding—had no business taxing the American people. Thus, in 1764, the Connecticut Assembly declared in bold letters, "NO LAW CAN BE MADE OR ABROGATED WITHOUT THE CONSENT OF THE PEOPLE BY THEIR REPRESENTATIVES."

13.2.2: Ideas about Power and Virtue

Americans expressed their political beliefs in a language they had borrowed from English POLITICAL THEORISTS. The person most frequently cited was John Locke, the influential LATE seventeenth-century philosopher whose *Two Treatises of Government* (first published in 1690) seemed, to colonial readers at least, a brilliant description of what was in fact American political practice. Locke claimed that all people possessed natural and inalienable rights. To preserve these God-given rights of life, liberty, and property, for example, free men (the status of women in Locke's work was less clear) formed contracts. These agreements were the foundation of human society as well as civil government, and they required the consent of the people who were actually governed. There could be no coercion. Locke justified rebellion against arbitrary forms of government that were by their very nature unreasonable. Americans delighted in Locke's ability to unite traditional religious values with a spirited defense of popular government, and even when they did not fully understand his technical writings, they seldom missed a chance to quote from the works of "the Great Mr. Locke."

Colonial Americans also enthusiastically subscribed to the so-called Commonwealthman tradition, a body of political assumptions generally identified with two eighteenth-century English publicists, John Trenchard and Thomas Gordon (see Chapter 10). The writings of such figures—most of whom spent their lives in political opposition—helped persuade the colonists that power was extremely dangerous, a force that would surely destroy liberty unless it was countered by virtue. Persons who shared this highly charged moral outlook regarded bad policy as not simply the result of human error. Rather, it was an indication of sin and corruption.

Insistence on public virtue—the sacrifice of self-interest to the public good—became the dominant theme of revolutionary political writing. American pamphleteers seldom took a dispassionate, legalistic approach to their analysis of power and liberty. More commonly, they exposed plots hatched by corrupt courtiers such as the Earl of Bute. None of them—or their readers—had any doubt that Americans were more virtuous than were the people of England.

13.3: A Constitutional Crisis Provoked

13.3 Recount the budgetary crisis faced by Great Britain

The Seven Years' War saddled Great Britain with a national debt so huge that more than half of the annual national budget went just to pay the interest on it. Almost everyone in government assumed that with the cessation of hostilities, the troops would be disbanded, thus saving a lot of money. George III had other plans. He insisted on keeping the largest peacetime army in British history on active duty, supposedly to protect Indians from predatory frontiersmen and to preserve order in the newly conquered territories of Florida and Quebec.

Maintaining such a force so far distant from the mother country fueled the budgetary crisis. The growing financial burden weighed heavily on restive English taxpayers and sent government leaders scurrying in search of new sources of revenue.

For their part, colonists doubted the value of this expensive army. Britain did not leave enough troops in America to maintain peace on the frontier effectively. Pontiac's War in 1763 had dramatically demonstrated the army's weakness (see Chapter 12). Even after the return of formal peace, the presence of Redcoat garrisons proved unable to prevent the periodic outbreak of frontier violence. In addition, colonists viewed the Proclamation Line of 1763, along which the garrisons were located, as an obstruction to legitimate economic development.

13.3.1: Paying Off the National Debt

The task of reducing England's debt fell to George Grenville, the rigid, somewhat unimaginative chancellor of the exchequer who replaced Bute in 1763 as the king's first minister. After carefully reviewing the state of Britain's finances, Grenville concluded that the colonists would have to contribute to the maintenance of the army. The first bill he steered through Parliament was the Revenue Act of 1764, known as the Sugar Act.

This legislation placed a new burden on the Navigation Acts that had governed the flow of colonial commerce for almost a century (see Chapter 6). Those acts had forced Americans to trade almost exclusively with Britain. The statutes were not, however, primarily intended as a means to raise money for the British government. The Sugar Act—and the acts that soon followed—redefined the relationship between America and Great Britain. Parliament now expected the colonies to generate revenue for the British government's coffers. The preamble of the Sugar Act proclaimed explicitly: "It is just and necessary a revenue be raised . . . in America for defraying the expenses of defending, protecting, and securing the same." The purpose of the Sugar Act was to discourage smuggling, bribery, and other illegalities that prevented the Navigation Acts from being profitable. Parliament reduced the duty on molasses (set originally by the Molasses Act of 1733) from 6 to 3 pence per gallon. At so low a rate, Grenville reasoned, colonial

merchants would have little incentive to bribe customs collectors. Much needed revenue would be diverted from the pockets of corrupt officials into the treasury so that it might be used to maintain the army.

Grenville had been too clever by half. The Americans immediately saw through what they regarded as his flagrantly unconstitutional scheme. According to the members of the Rhode Island Assembly, the Sugar Act taxed the colonists in a manner "inconsistent with their rights and privileges as British subjects." James Otis, a fiery orator from Massachusetts, exclaimed the legislation deprived Americans of "the right of assessing their own taxes."

The act generated no violence. In fact, ordinary men and women were only marginally involved in the drafting of formal petitions. The protest was still confined to the members of the colonial assemblies, to the merchants, and to the well-to-do Americans who had personal interests in commerce.

13.3.2: Popular Protest

Passage of the Stamp Act of 1765 transformed a debate among gentlemen into a more formidable political movement. The imperial crisis might have been avoided. Colonial agents had presented Grenville with alternative schemes for raising money in America. But Grenville was a stubborn man, and he had little fear of parliamentary opposition. The majority of the House of Commons assumed that Parliament possessed the right to tax the colonists, and when the chancellor of the exchequer announced a plan to squeeze £60,000 annually out of the Americans by requiring them to purchase special seals or stamps to validate legal documents, the members responded with enthusiasm. The Stamp Act was scheduled to go into effect on November 1, 1765. In anticipation of brisk sales, Grenville appointed stamp distributors for every colony.

During discussion in Parliament, several members warned that the act would raise a

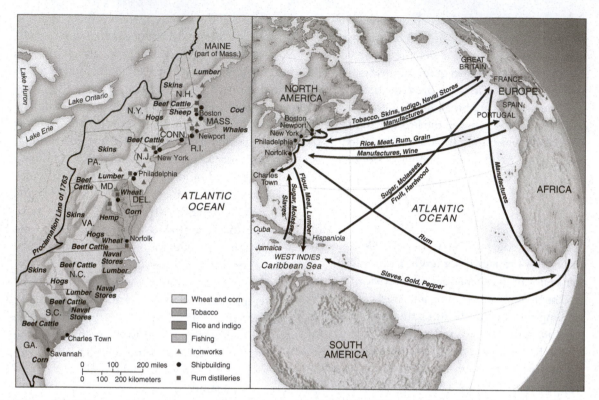

Map 13.1 Colonial Products and Trade

storm of protest in the colonies. Colonel Isaac Barre, a veteran of the Seven Years' War, reminded his colleagues that the Americans were "sons of liberty" and would not surrender their rights without a fight. But Barre's appeal fell on deaf ears.

Word of the Stamp Act reached America in May, and it was soon clear that Barre had gauged the colonists' response correctly. The most dramatic incident occurred in Virginia's House of Burgesses. Patrick Henry, young and eloquent, whom contemporaries compared in fervor to evangelical preachers, introduced five resolutions protesting the Stamp Act on the floor of the assembly. He timed his move carefully. It was late in the session; many of the more conservative burgesses had already departed for their plantations. Even then, Henry's resolves declaring that Virginians had the right to tax

themselves as they alone saw fit passed by narrow margins. The fifth resolution, stricken almost immediately from the legislative records, announced that any attempt to collect stamp revenues in America was "illegal, unconstitutional, and unjust, and has a manifest tendency to destroy British as well as American liberty." Henry was carried away by the force of his own rhetoric. He reminded his fellow Virginians that Caesar had had his Brutus, Charles I his Cromwell, and he hoped that "some good American would stand up for his country"—but an astonished speaker of the house cut Henry off in mid-sentence, accusing him of treason.

The Virginia Resolves might have remained a local matter had it not been for the colonial press. Newspapers throughout America printed Henry's resolutions, but perhaps because editors did not really know what had happened in

Williamsburg, they reported that all five resolutions had received the burgesses' full support. Several journals even carried two resolves that Henry had not dared to introduce. A result of this misunderstanding, of course, was that the Virginians appeared to have taken an extremely radical position on the issue of the supremacy of Parliament, one that other Americans now trumpeted before their own assemblies. No wonder Francis Bernard, royal governor of Massachusetts, called the Virginia Resolves an "alarm bell."

Not to be outdone by Virginia, Massachusetts called a general meeting to protest Grenville's policy. Nine colonies sent representatives to the Stamp Act Congress that convened in New York City in October 1765. It was the first intercolonial gathering held since the abortive Albany Congress of 1754. If nothing else, the new congress provided leaders from different regions with an opportunity to discuss common problems. The delegates drafted petitions to the king and Parliament that restated the colonists' belief "that no taxes should be imposed on them, but with their own consent, given personally, or by their representatives." The tone of the meeting was restrained, even conciliatory. The congress studiously avoided any mention of independence or disloyalty to the crown.

Resistance to the Stamp Act soon spread from the assemblies to the streets. By taxing deeds, marriage licenses, and playing cards, the Stamp Act touched the lives of ordinary women and men. Anonymous artisans and seamen, angered by Parliament's apparent insensitivity and fearful that the statute would increase unemployment and poverty, organized mass protests in the major colonial ports.

Imperial politics played out on the streets of American cities as traditional rivalries between neighborhood youths and anti-Catholic sentiment suddenly was redirected against alleged parliamentary oppression. In Boston, the "Sons of Liberty" burned in effigy the local stamp distributor, Andrew Oliver, and when that action failed to bring about his resignation, they tore down one of his office buildings. Even after he resigned, the mob nearly demolished the elegant home of Oliver's close associate, Lieutenant Governor Thomas Hutchinson. The violence frightened colonial leaders, yet evidence suggests that they encouraged the lower classes to intimidate royal officials. Popular participation in these protests was an exciting experience for people who had traditionally deferred to their social betters. After 1765, it was impossible for either royal governors or patriot leaders to take for granted the support of ordinary men and women.

By November 1, 1765, stamp distributors in almost every American port had publicly resigned, and without distributors, the hated revenue stamps could not be sold. The courts soon reopened; most newspapers were published.

Daily life in the colonies was undisturbed with one exception: the Sons of Liberty persuaded—some said coerced—colonial merchants to boycott British goods until Parliament repealed the Stamp Act. The merchants showed little enthusiasm for such tactics, but the threat of tar and feathers stimulated cooperation.

The boycott movement was in itself a masterful political innovation. Never before had a resistance movement organized itself so centrally around the market decisions of ordinary consumers. The colonists depended on British imports—cloth, metal goods, and ceramics—and each year, they imported more consumer goods than they could possibly afford. In this highly charged moral atmosphere, one in which ordinary people talked constantly of conspiracy and corruption, it is not surprising that Americans of different classes and backgrounds advocated a radical change in buying habits. Private acts suddenly became part of the public sphere. Personal excess threatened to contaminate the entire political community. This logic explains the power of an appeal made in a Boston newspaper: "Save your money and you can save your country."

The boycotts mobilized colonial women. They were excluded from voting and civil office, but such legal discrimination did not mean that women were not part of the broader political culture. Since wives and mothers spent their days involved with household chores, they assumed special responsibility to reform consumption, to root out luxury, and to promote frugality. Indeed, in this realm they possessed real power; they monitored the ideological commitment of the entire family. Throughout the colonies, women altered styles of dress, made homespun cloth, and shunned imported items on which Parliament had placed a tax.

13.3.3: West Indian Counterpoint

The Stamp Act applied not only to the mainland colonies but also to those in the West Indies. Indeed, the Act taxed West Indian estates of more than £20 at double the rate of the mainland for "any probate of will, letters of administration, or of guardianship," a highly burdensome provision for any island family managing an inheritance. West Indian leaders shared many of the assumptions of their mainland counterparts concerning the "rights of Englishmen" and the nature of their legislatures' place in the English constitution, including assumptions about representation. Absentee planter families living in England circulated petitions opposing the Act and used their influence to pressure members of Parliament wherever possible. Legislatures on all of the islands debated how best to respond to the Act, and all but one eventually passed memorials expressing opposition to it on a variety of grounds. Yet overall, the West Indian response differed markedly from that of the mainland colonies.

Officials in London estimated that the islands would generate far more revenues than the mainland because of their greater volume of commerce and allocated more stamps for the Caribbean than the mainland. The two largest islands, Jamaica and Barbados, did not disappoint expectations

in the four and a half months the act remained in force, even though leaders in both colonies and their representatives in London voiced opposition to it. The stamp commissioners appointed in both islands retained their positions until the Act was repealed without suffering any serious challenge. Colonists paid the tax even though they could have easily resisted. The historian Andrew Jackson O'Shaughnessy noted that in Jamaica, the commissioner entrusted the stamps to two slaves "whose master ordered them to run off if attacked," but no such attack materialized. Jamaica ultimately forwarded more stamp duties than the rest of the empire to London while the Act remained in effect.

The Leeward Islands—Antigua, Nevis, St. Kitts, and Montserrat—offered greater resistance. On St. Kitts, a well-organized riot forced the deputy stamp commissioner to resign his office and marched the commissioner himself, William Tuckett, to the public market in the island capital of Basseterre, where he promised to publish his resignation in the local paper "to avoid being suspended" on a gibbet. The crowd also seized and burned as many stamps as they could find. Tuckett soon fled to Nevis where he began to distribute stamps there, but prompt pursuit by the Nevis Sons of Liberty quickly forced him to flee that island as well. On Nevis, the protestors burned two houses and a navy longboat filled with stamps. In Antigua, where the governor resided backed by the Sixty-Eighth Regiment of regular British troops, the islanders managed to obstruct payment of the duties after initially paying "sorely against their wills." Word of William Tuckett's fate in St. Kitts and Nevis apparently persuaded the appointed commissioners to resign quickly, and by the end of December no colonist could be found who would risk accepting the hated job of stamp tax collector.

Whether paying the stamp duty or resisting, official West Indian protests tended to remain much more modest and conciliatory than those on the mainland. The island legislatures did not form a general congress to respond to the Act as did the mainland colonies. Most responded individually, and two—those of Antigua and Barbados—made no official response at all. Each also avoided the language of natural rights upon which the mainland colonies so quickly seized, preferring instead to stress the practical hardships of enforcement such as the burden on trade and the lack of sufficient hard currency to pay the tax in sterling as the Act required. The West Indian press was largely silent throughout the Stamp Act crisis.

The West Indian response outraged mainland colonists, who denounced "the *SLAVISH* islands of *Barbados* and *Antigua*" for paying the duty even though the latter had done so only briefly. The Pennsylvania lawyer John Dickinson penned a hostile *Address to the Committee of Correspondence in Barbados* (1766) chastising the colony's leaders for their cowardice in complying with the Act. Mainland colonists organized boycotts of trade with the West Indies both to punish them for their timidity and from fear that American ships carrying unstamped papers would be seized in West Indian ports. By the spring of 1766, the boycotts had begun causing shortages on several islands, making calls for repeal all the more urgent, when the news of repeal brought with it a resumption of normal trade.

13.4: Failed Attempts to Save the Empire

13.4 Examine effects of the mistrust between policy makers in London and the colonists

What most Americans did not yet know—after all, communication with Britain required months—was that in July of 1765, Grenville had fallen from power. This unexpected shift came about not because the king thought Grenville's policies inept, but rather because George did not like the man. Whatever the reason, a growing coalition of London merchants, colonial agents, members of Parliament, and royal administrators cheered the decision. Months of unrest and disruption of trade had convinced them that a shift in policy was needed.

Unfortunately for both sides, the cool, patient, shrewd leadership needed to meet the crisis was not to be found. For the next several years, prime ministers came and went while Parliament tried to patch together policies and legislation that would restore stability to imperial administration. The ineptitude of leadership in London was more than matched by that of colonial administrative officials, who blundered their way from one crisis to another. Lagging communication between the colonies and London, coupled with the mainland colonists' growing disposition to interpret all decisions taken in London as evidence of a conspiracy against their liberties, further exacerbated the tensions. In this atmosphere of mistrust, even the best-intended efforts could easily backfire.

13.4.1: Stamp Act Repeal

Grenville's replacement as first lord of the treasury, Lord Rockingham, was young, inexperienced, and terrified of public speaking; a serious handicap to launching a brilliant parliamentary career. The Rockinghamites—as his followers were called—envisioned a prosperous empire founded on an expanding commerce and local government under the gentle guidance of Parliament. Rockingham wanted to repeal the Stamp Act, but because of the shakiness of his own political coalition, he could not announce such a decision until it enjoyed broad national support. He, therefore, urged merchants and manufacturers throughout England to petition Parliament for repeal of the act, claiming that the American boycott would soon drive them into bankruptcy and spark urban riots.

On March 18, 1766, the House of Commons voted 275 to 167 to rescind the Stamp Act. Lest its retreat on the Stamp Act be interpreted as weakness, the House of Commons passed that same day the Declaratory Act, a shrill defense of parliamentary supremacy over the Americans "in all cases whatsoever." The colonists' insistence on no taxation without representation failed to impress British rulers. England's merchants, supposedly America's allies, claimed sole responsibility for the Stamp Act repeal. The colonists had only complicated the task, the merchants lectured, and if the Americans knew what was good for them, they would keep quiet. West Indian pamphleteers joined the chorus, denying American accusations of cowardice for their approach and defending their response as appropriately moderate and effective. They noted wryly that, while repealing the Act, Parliament had after all pointedly rebuffed the mainland colonies' claims concerning representation and rights.

To George Mason, a leading political figure in Virginia, such advice sounded patronizing. The British merchants seemed to be saying, "We have with infinite difficulty and fatigue got you excused this one time; pray be a good boy for the future, do what your papa and mama bid you, and hasten to return them your most grateful acknowledgements for condescending to let you keep what is your *own*." This, Mason snapped, was "ridiculous!"

The Stamp Act crisis also eroded the colonists' respect for imperial officeholders in America. Suddenly, these men—royal governors, customs collectors, and military personnel—appeared alien, as if their interests were not those of the people over whom they exercised authority. One person who had been forced to resign the post of stamp distributor for South Carolina noted several years later, "The Stamp Act had introduc'd so much Party Rage, Faction, and Debate that the ancient Harmony, Generosity, and Urbanity for which these People were celebrated is destroyed, and at an End." Similar reports came from other colonies, and it is testimony to the Americans' lingering loyalty to the British Crown and constitution that rebellion did not occur in 1765.

13.4.2: Fueling the Crisis

Rockingham's ministry soon gave way to a government headed once again by William Pitt, the prime minister who had led Britain to victory in the Seven Year's War. The aging Pitt, now titled the Earl of Chatham, suffered horribly from gout. During his long absences from London, Charles Townshend, his chancellor of the exchequer, made important policy decisions. Townshend was an impetuous man whose mouth often outran his mind. During a parliamentary debate in January 1767, he surprised everyone by blithely announcing that he knew a way to obtain revenue from the Americans. The members of the House of Commons were so pleased with the news that they promptly voted to lower English land taxes, an action that threatened fiscal chaos.

The ensuing budgetary crisis forced Townshend to make good on his extraordinary boast. His scheme turned out to be a grab bag of duties on American imports of paper, glass, paint, lead, and tea, which collectively were known as the Townshend Revenue Acts (June–July 1767). He hoped to generate sufficient funds to pay the salaries of royal governors and other imperial officers, thus freeing them from dependence on the colonial assemblies.

The chancellor recognized that without tough instruments of enforcement, his duties would not produce the promised revenues. Therefore, he created an American Board of Customs Commissioners, a body based in Boston and supported by reorganized vice-admiralty courts located in Boston, Philadelphia, and Charles Town. And for good measure, Townshend induced Parliament to order the governor of New York to veto all bills passed by that colony's assembly until it supplied resident British troops in accordance with the Quartering Act (May 1765) that required the colonies to house soldiers in barracks, taverns, and vacant buildings and to provide the army with firewood, candles, and beer, among other items. Many Americans regarded this as more taxation without representation, and in New York, at least, colonists refused to pay.

Mainland colonists showed no more willingness to pay Townshend's duties than they had to buy Grenville's stamps. No congress was called; none was necessary. Recent events had taught people how to coordinate protest, and they moved to resist the unconstitutional revenue acts. In major ports, the Sons of Liberty organized boycotts of British goods. Protest often involved what one historian has termed "rituals of nonconsumption." In some large towns, these were moments of public moral reaffirmation. Men and women took oaths before neighbors promising not to purchase certain goods until Parliament repealed unconstitutional taxation. In Boston, ordinary people were encouraged to sign "subscription rolls." "The Selectmen strongly recommend this Measure to Persons of *all ranks*," announced the *Boston Gazette*, "as the most honorable and effectual way of giving public Testimony of their Love to their Country, and of endeavouring to save it from ruin."

On February 11, 1768, the Massachusetts House of Representatives drafted a circular letter, a provocative appeal which it sent directly to the other colonial assemblies. The letter requested suggestions on how best to thwart the Townshend Acts. Not surprisingly, legislators in other parts of America, busy with local matters, simply ignored this general appeal, but not Lord Hillsborough, England's secretary for American affairs. This rather mild attempt to create a united colonial front struck him as gross treason, and he ordered the Massachusetts representatives to rescind their "seditious paper." After considering Hillsborough's demand, the legislators voted 92 to 17 to defy him.

Suddenly, the circular letter became a cause célèbre. The royal governor of Massachusetts hastily dissolved the House of Representatives. That decision compelled the other colonies to demonstrate their support for Massachusetts. Assembly after assembly now felt obligated to take up the circular letter, an action Hillsborough had specifically forbidden. Assemblies in other colonies were dissolved, creating a much broader crisis of representative government. Throughout America, the number 92 (the number of legislators who voted against Hillsborough) immediately became a symbol of patriotism. In fact, Parliament's challenge had brought about the very results it most wanted to avoid: a foundation for intercolonial communication and a strengthening of conviction among the colonists of the righteousness of their position.

13.4.3: Fatal Confrontation

In October 1768, British rulers made another mistake, one that raised tensions almost to the pitch they had reached during the Stamp Act riots. The issue at the heart of the trouble was the army. In part to save money and in part to intimidate colonial troublemakers, the ministry transferred four thousand regular troops from Nova Scotia and Ireland to Boston. Most of the army had already been withdrawn from the frontier to the seacoast to save revenue, thereby raising more acutely than ever the issue of why troops were in America at all. The armed strangers camped on the Boston Common, and when citizens passed the site, Redcoats shouted obscenities. Sometimes, in accordance with martial law, an errant soldier was whipped within an inch of his life, a bloody sight that sickened Boston civilians. To make relations worse, Redcoats—men who were ill-treated and underpaid—competed in their spare time for jobs with local dockworkers and artisans. Work was already in short supply, and the streets crackled with tension.

Colonial pamphleteers had a ready answer to the widespread question of why the army had been sent to a peaceful city. The Redcoats were there to further a conspiracy originally conceived by George III's first prime minister, Lord Bute, to oppress Americans, to take away their liberties, and to collect illegal revenues.

Grenville, Hillsborough, Townshend—they were all, supposedly, part of the plot. Today such rhetoric may sound excessive, but to Americans who had absorbed the political theories of the Commonwealthmen, a pattern of tyranny seemed obvious.

Colonists had no difficulty interpreting the violence that erupted in Boston on March 5, 1770. In the gathering dusk of that afternoon, young boys and street toughs threw rocks and snowballs at soldiers in a small, isolated patrol outside the offices of the hated customs commissioners in King Street. The details of this incident are obscure, but it appears that as the mob grew and became more threatening, the soldiers panicked. In the confusion, the troops fired, leaving five Americans dead.

Pamphleteers promptly labeled the incident a massacre. The victims of this "Boston Massacre" were seen as martyrs and were memorialized in extravagant terms. In one eulogy, Joseph Warren addressed the dead men's widows and children, dramatically re-creating the gruesome scene in King Street. "Behold thy murdered husband gasping on the ground," Warren cried, ". . . take heed, ye orphan babes, lest, whilst your streaming eyes are fixed upon the ghastly corpse, your feet slide on the stones bespattered with your father's brains." Apparently, to propagandists like Warren, it mattered little that the five civilians had been bachelors! Paul Revere's engraving of the massacre, appropriately splattered with blood, became an instant bestseller. Confronted with such intense reaction and with the possibility of massive armed resistance, Crown officials wisely moved the army to an island in Boston Harbor.

At this critical moment, the king's new first minister restored a measure of tranquility. Lord North, congenial, well-meaning, but not very talented, became chancellor of the exchequer

BOSTON MASSACRE

following Townshend's death in 1767. North was appointed the first minister in 1770, and for the next twelve years—indeed, throughout most of the American crisis—he managed to retain his office. His secret formula seems to have been an ability to get along with George III and to build an effective majority in Parliament.

One of North's first recommendations to Parliament was the repeal of the Townshend Duties. Not only had these ill-conceived duties unnecessarily angered the colonists, but they also hurt English manufacturers. By taxing British exports such as glass and paint, Parliament had only encouraged the Americans to develop their own industries; thus, without much prodding, the House of Commons dropped all the Townshend Duties—with the notable exception of tea. The tax on tea was retained not for revenue purposes, North insisted, but as a reminder that England's rulers still subscribed to the principles of the Declaratory Act. They would not compromise the supremacy of Parliament. In mid-1770, however, the matter of tea seemed trivial to most Americans. The colonists had drawn back from the precipice, a little frightened by the events of the past two years, and desperately hoped to head off future confrontation with the British.

13.5: Troubled Reprieve for Imperial Rule, 1770–1773

13.5 Identify events leading to the pickup of the American economy

For a short while, American colonists and British officials put aside their recent animosities. Like England's rulers, some colonial gentry were beginning to pull back from protest, especially violent confrontation with established authority, in fear that the lower orders were becoming too assertive. It was probably in this period that

Loyalist Americans emerged as an identifiable group. Colonial merchants returned to familiar patterns of trade, pleased no doubt to end the local boycotts that had depressed the American economy. British goods flooded into colonial ports, quickly exceeding the annual rate of imports that had obtained before the Townshend Duties went into effect. The appetite for British imported goods appeared to be stronger than ever, and the level of American indebtedness soared to new highs.

Even so, much remained unsettled throughout The British Empire. The repeal of the Townshend Duties had left Parliament without a clear alternative means of shoring up its inadequate revenues. The myriad challenges of adapting English forms of government and administration to the ethnically French population of Quebec were only slowly being addressed, complicated as they were by infighting among the minority population of British merchants and administrators who had taken control of the captured colony. Anglo-native relations were increasingly fraught with tensions as colonists ignored the Proclamation Line of 1763 to stake out farms on Shawnee and Delaware hunting grounds. Any one of these issues entailed in itself a host of vexing problems. Taken together, and as interconnected as they were, a misstep in any given arena could easily bring the whole structure of imperial administration crashing down.

13.5.1: The Quest for a Postwar British Government in Quebec

The conquest of Quebec in 1759 had given the British control of a vast new swath of territory reaching from the mouth of the St. Lawrence River to far inland beyond the Great Lakes, populated by over sixty-five thousand French inhabitants and tens of thousands of native peoples. The initial efforts of military commanders to impose unilateral terms of trade and diplomacy had sparked Pontiac's War (see Chapter 12), and abrupt efforts to shift to British law and administration had provoked widespread discontent among the French Canadians as well. The first British governor appointed to Quebec, James Murray, soon decided to take a more gradual approach, analyzing French laws, customs, and governmental forms to develop recommendations for an administrative system in Canada best suited to the local needs and expectations of a French Catholic population. His efforts quickly ran afoul of the British merchant community who had moved into Quebec to take control of commerce there. The merchants wanted him to implement the British commercial regulations that they understood and could readily exploit to their advantage. They complained to London that Murray was sacrificing their interests to the old French colonists, resulting in his recall in 1766 to give account of his actions.

Murray's interim replacement as governor, Sir Guy Carlton, continued his predecessor's policies in the face of continued English opposition. Carlton was a respected and accomplished military officer, but as yet had little experience at governing. He learned quickly, however, taking advantage of the extensive authority given him under the terms of his appointment to purge the existing Governor's Council and appoint capable officials loyal to him. The Council assisted him in developing and implementing a set of provisional reforms that eventually became the basis of Canada's government under the provisions of the Quebec Act of 1774.

Carlton's friends and associates characterized his rule as a benevolent despotism. He ruled through his Council without ever instituting a representative assembly, despite the agitation of the English merchant community who clamored for one that they hoped would move more quickly to institute English laws and regulations. The French Canadians, however, had never experienced government under such a body, nor had they experienced other features of government, judicial, and civic life that English people had come to regard as rights. They viewed representative bodies and even jury trials with suspicion not only from lack of familiarity, but also because they feared such institutions could be used to advance English interests at their own expense. They also regarded representative rule as the source of much of the unrest that was embroiling the older English colonies to their south during the 1760s. Old French Canadian elites, therefore, cooperated with Carlton in instituting his policies. Some of them obtained government appointments at the colonywide and local levels, securing positions that their families managed to retain for generations. Carleton further secured French Canadian loyalty by permitting them free exercise of their traditional Catholic faith, even though this was formally prohibited under the English Act of Toleration of 1689.

During Carleton's initial years in Quebec, he busied himself analyzing the old colonial government and judicial system of the colony to develop a massive report containing recommendations for adapting a permanent British government to the existing situation. In August 1770, only a few months after repeal of the Townshend Duties, he sailed for London to advocate adoption of his report into a bill that would frame the permanent government of Quebec. He spent his next four years there cultivating his political connections and making the social circuits while waiting for the creeping wheels of parliamentary procedure to take up debate on his recommendations.

13.5.2: Louisiana Becomes a Spanish Colony

The southern end of France's former North American river empire was placed under Spanish rule in the Treaty of 1763. The early transition there went little better than did British attempts to impose new terms of trade on its native trading partners. The first governor, Antonio de Ulloa, arrived with too few forces to impose Spanish authority and too much ambition to impose immediate, wholesale change. The former French soldiers who had been ordered to assist the transition to

Spanish rule offered only sullen cooperation. He plunged the colony into an economic depression by attempting to restrict trade only to official, licensed Spanish merchants and vessels carrying goods exclusively to Spanish ports. Such efforts far outweighed the improvements in military installations and Indian diplomacy. On October 27, 1768, residents of New Orleans disabled the cannons defending the city and captured the city while Ulloa's Commandant of New Orleans, the Frenchman Charles Philippe Aubry, stood passively by. Ulloa fled to a Spanish frigate anchored in the river, where he soon conferred with Aubry concerning his next steps. Aubry advised him to leave the colony and Ulloa did so, never to return.

Ulloa's successor, General Alejandro O'Reilly, returned the following year with two thousand troops to reestablish Spanish rule over Louisiana. O'Reilly met no resistance as he paraded into the city of New Orleans with great pomp at the head of his column. He granted amnesty to all those involved in the previous year's rebellion except thirteen ringleaders, whom he placed on trial. He presided over their trial as judge and jury, according to the provisions of Spanish law. He acquitted a printer who had published news and propaganda concerning the insurrection, but sentenced six to long prison terms and the other six to death by firing squad, a verdict which earned him the nickname "Bloody O'Reilly."

Despite this harsh beginning to his administration, O'Reilly proved effective at transforming Louisiana's government into a Spanish system. He abolished the old French Superior Council, replacing it with the Cabildo, a form of city council for New Orleans that also advised the governor on colonial policy. He also instituted a set of Spanish colonial laws adapted to Louisiana and known there as the "Code O'Reilly." By March 1770, he had completed these reforms and formally transferred power to the new governor, Luis de Unzaga.

Unzaga proved perceptive and flexible regarding the realities of government and economic life in Louisiana. Although he instituted Spanish forms of government, he also took a relaxed approach to regulating trade in recognition of its importance for this colony of fourteen thousand souls. The Treaty of 1763 allowed British vessels free access to navigation on the Mississippi, and captains routinely anchored conveniently close to Louisiana villages where they carried on a brisk illegal trade. Unzaga ignored this practice as well as the Louisiana merchants' practice of sailing to French and British ports. He also accepted the overland exchange with British American traders and their native allies that brought cheap British-made goods to Louisiana consumers. These practices laid the foundation of a prosperity during the following decades that made Louisiana an important source of trade for all inhabitants of the Ohio Country and the Southeast. It also provided rebellious colonists with a crucial source of military supplies carried by flatboat from New Orleans up the Mississippi and Ohio Rivers to Fort Pitt, from where they could be distributed overland to Washington's army.

13.5.3: Nativism and Conflict in the West

The growing importance of the Ohio River as an avenue of commerce held great strategic importance both for native peoples who inhabited and hunted in the Ohio Country and for Anglo-American migrants who were moving into the region at an ever-increasing rate. The ability to ship agricultural products to New Orleans for sale on an Atlantic market increased the potential value of the Ohio lands in which speculators had sunk large investments. The Delawares, Mingoes, Miamis, and Shawnees who occupied those lands objected strenuously to Anglo-American encroachment there. The Proclamation Line's main role in this dynamic, the historian Daniel Richter has argued, was to stimulate the formation of new racial identities on either side. Colonists east of the line who had formerly seen themselves in such ethnic terms as Germans or Scotch-Irish now saw themselves as whites united against an Indian foe. For their part, many native groups continued to embrace the message of the Delaware prophet Neolin, whose vision of a pan-Indian alliance had united western peoples under Pontiac in 1763 (see Chapter 12).

Shawnee spokesmen took the lead in actively seeking to build a pan-Indian alliance. Nativist prophets among them called upon native peoples everywhere to follow the teachings of the "Master of Life," a spiritual figure who had appeared in Neolin's compelling vision several years earlier. Followers promised to renounce consumption of alcohol, break their dependence on British trade goods, and join in resisting white encroachment. Not all followed the message. Cherokees, for instance, rejected it, preferring to seek their own interests in trade and diplomacy with colonial neighbors. Many Delaware villages had become Christian under the influence of Moravian missionaries such as John Heckwelder and David Zeisburger, and these too refused to renounce their Christian beliefs to follow the Master of Life. The Shawnees, on the other hand, viewed the Moravians and other Christian missionaries with great suspicion as agents of white encroachment. They often denied missionaries admission to their villages and rejected their message out of hand.

In 1769, Shawnee leaders convened a conference of western Indians at their new council house near the confluence of the Scioto and Ohio Rivers. There they hoped to forge an alliance along the western frontier that would reaching as far south as the Cherokees in the western Carolinas and Georgia and as far north as the Ottawas in what is now Michigan. The Cherokees, currently benefiting from British trade, rejected their offer, as did many Christian Indians in the Ohio Country and western Pennsylvania. Nevertheless, the Shawnees made enough headway to concern the British officials who monitored these events from a distance.

The drumbeat of frontier violence steadily increased in the early 1770s as Pennsylvanians and Virginians vied to promote rival white settlements in the Ohio Country in flagrant disregard of the Proclamation Line, the treaties negotiated by the two superintendents for Indian affairs, and the rights of the Shawnees, Mingoes, and Delawares who lived there. Bands of Shawnee raiders conducted lightning strikes against encroaching white farmsteads, killing or capturing white settlers and driving the survivors back to the safety of towns and villages further east. Colonists retaliated or initiated their own deadly raids, killing Indians, burning their crops, and seeking to drive them off the land. Many whites made no distinction between peaceful Christian Indians and native rivals, killing indiscriminately with impunity. Whites often refused to give evidence against each other when such killings took place, and the commander in charge of British regular forces, General Thomas Gage, ruefully observed that "all people of the frontiers, from Pennsylvania to Virginia inclusive, openly avow, that they will never find a man guilty of murder, for killing an Indian."

13.5.4: Diverging West Indian Experience

Inhabitants of the British West Indies, most of whom offered a notably milder response to the Stamp Act than had mainland colonists, took an increasingly divergent course in subsequent imperial disputes. The Townshend Duties, which galvanized mainland colonists into active opposition, did not affect as greatly islands where the population was more than 60 percent slave and many of whose wealthiest landowners lived and spent in the mother country. One of the chief constitutional issues on the mainland, the use of Townshend revenues to pay the governor and free him from dependence on the legislature, did not resonate in islands where governors had always enjoyed such independence. Indeed, several

West Indian legislatures followed that of Barbados in actually welcoming this move because they had long been lobbying for Parliament to shoulder their governor's salary.

West Indian planters had for many decades held much greater influence in London than mainland colonists ever enjoyed, and they employed it to full effect after 1766. While members of some influential West Indian families in London voiced opposition to the Townshend Duties and other aspects of colonial policy in Parliament, they also worked behind the scenes to obtain preferential treatment for the islands. Such efforts often won the support of members of Parliament who wished to reward the West Indies for their comparative moderation during the Stamp Act crisis. Effective lobbying, for example, won the West Indies an exemption from jurisdiction of the American Board of Commissioners of Customs and the four vice-admiralty courts set up to enforce the Townshend Duties in 1767. This averted the sorts of ugly clashes with stringent and corrupt customs officials whose actions aroused such universal hatred on the mainland.

Divergent experiences with imperial policy produced divergent responses. No West Indian legislature passed resolutions against the Townshend Duties. No West Indian legislature petitioned Parliament. Only one, the Barbadian, registered any official expression of sympathy for mainland colonists' constitutional concerns and buried the statement in a few lines of an address to the governor. No nonimportation movement sprang up in the West Indies. No protests of the Quartering Act emerged in the islands, where regular troops already had adequate barracks and their presence was welcomed to control the slave population. The Stamp Act crisis proved the high point of West Indian protest. Afterward, as the Barbadian legislature boasted, "Good order and Tranquility" became the order of the day as the islands bore patiently "the pressure of those burthens which have thrown our more numerous Brethren upon the northern Continent into a flame."

13.5.5: Ongoing Agitation in the Thirteen Colonies

The great majority of colonists on the mainland welcomed the apparent reconciliation that came with the Townshend Duties' repeal in 1770. The appointment in Massachusetts of Thomas Hutchinson as governor seemed to offer a measure of how far the colonies had come toward the restoration of amicable relations with the mother country. In 1765, a mob had demolished Hutchinson's home while his family and friends kept him hidden to protect him from personal assault. Yet when Hutchinson's commission as governor arrived in March 1771, the people of Massachusetts—even of Boston—decided they could accept him. After all, he was one of their own, an American.

Appearances were deceiving. The bonds of imperial loyalty remained fragile, and even as Lord North attempted to win the colonists' trust, Crown officials in America created new strains. Customs commissioners whom Townshend had appointed to collect his duties remained in the colonies long after his Revenue Acts had been repealed. If they had been honest, unobtrusive administrators, perhaps no one would have taken notice of their behavior. But the customs commissioners routinely abused their powers of search and seizure, and the process lined their own pockets. In Massachusetts, Rhode Island, and South Carolina—to cite the most notorious cases—these officials drove local citizens to distraction by enforcing the Navigation Acts with such rigor that a small boat could not cross Narragansett Bay with a load of firewood without first obtaining a sheaf of legal documents. One mistake, no matter how miniscule, could bring confiscation of ship and cargo.

The commissioners were not only corrupt; they were shortsighted. If they had restricted their extortion to the common folk, they might have avoided becoming a major American grievance.

But they could not control their greed. Some customs officers harassed the wealthiest, most powerful men around, men such John Hancock of Boston and Henry Laurens of Charles Town. The commissioners' actions drove some members of the colonial ruling class into opposition to the king's government. When in the summer of 1772, a group of disguised Rhode Islanders burned a customs vessel, the *Gaspee*, Americans cheered. A special royal commission sent to arrest the culprits discovered that not a single Rhode Islander had the slightest idea how the ship could have come to such an end.

Samuel Adams (1722–1803) refused to accept the notion that the repeal of the Townshend Duties had secured American liberty. During the early 1770s, while colonial leaders turned to other matters, Adams kept the cause alive with a drumfire of publicity. He reminded the people of Boston that the tax on tea remained in force. He organized public anniversaries commemorating the repeal of the Stamp Act and the Boston Massacre. Adams was a genuine revolutionary, an ideologue filled with a burning sense indignation at the real and alleged wrongs suffered by his countrymen. To his contemporaries, this man resembled a figure o of New England's Puritan past. He seemed obsessed with the preservation of public virtue. The American goal, he declared, was the creation of a "Christian Sparta," an ideal commonwealth in which vigilant citizens would constantly guard against the spread of corruption, degeneracy, and luxury.

With each new attempt by Parliament to assert its supremacy over the colonists, more and more Bostonians listened to what Adams had to say. He observed ominously that the British intended to use the tea revenue to pay judicial salaries, thus freeing the judges from dependence on the assembly. When in November 1772 Adams suggested the formation of a "committee of correspondence" to communicate grievances to villages throughout Massachusetts, he received broad support. Americans living in

other colonies soon copied his idea. It was a brilliant stroke. Adams developed a structure of political cooperation completely independent of royal government.

13.6: An Empire on the Brink

13.6 Interpret effects of the erosion of the colonial goodwill in America

By early 1773, imperial tensions had relaxed considerably despite the ongoing agitation of Samuel Adams and his radical associates. Many colonists were persuaded that outstanding grievances, such as differences over constitutional issues and the abuses of customs officials, could be addressed over time through existing channels of authority. However much colonial legislatures may have united in their response to the Stamp Act and Townshend Duties, their interests clashed on local matters such as Indian diplomacy and ownership of western lands. The West Indian legislatures had taken their own course, drawing away from the moderate support they had displayed during the Stamp Act crisis. The predominantly French inhabitants of Quebec had never offered a show of support of the Anglo-American struggle for rights and liberties. Viewed from the distance of London, the remaining unrest could easily be seen as the work of a fringe group of rabble-rousers.

Yet the fissures in the imperial system ran much deeper than London officials could appreciate. The virtual state of war that existed on the trans-Appalachian frontier signaled a drastic failure of imperial policy there. By refusing to curb the corruption of its customs agents, Parliament left in place a powerful corrosive that quickly eroded colonial good will. The central constitutional dispute between Parliament and mainland colonial leaders remained unaddressed and deeply misunderstood in London.

Indeed, both Parliament and the imperial administration continued to aggravate matters through efforts to strengthen the independence of colonial governors and meddle with the procedures of colonial legislatures. The thirteen mainland colonies had become a powder keg. A single spark could detonate it and blow the fractured empire apart.

Chronology

1763	Peace of Paris ends the Seven Year's War
1764	Parliament passes Sugar Act to collect American revenue
1765	Stamp Act receives support of House of Commons (March)
1765	Stamp Act Congress meets in New York City (October)
1766	Stamp Act repealed the same day that the Declaratory Act becomes law (March 18)
1767	Townshend Revenue Acts stir American anger (June)
1767	First Scioto conference of Shawnee nation for organizing pan-Indian alliance (summer)
1768	Massachusetts assembly refuses to rescind their circular letter (February)
1768	Sir Guy Carleton becomes governor of Quebec (April)
1769	General Alejandro O'Reilly occupies New Orleans with 2,000 Spanish troops
1770	Parliament repeals all Townshend Duties except that on tea (March)
1770	British troops fire on American civilians in Boston, the "Boston Massacre" (March)
1772	Samuel Adams forms committee of correspondence

Chapter 14
Crucible of Liberty
Varieties of Independence in the Revolutionary War

Learning Objectives

14.1 Review the Boston Tea Party's role as the turning point that led to the American War of Independence

14.2 Analyze the effects of 'unconstitutional' government acts on the colonists

14.3 Identify the main elements that neutralized the position of the British army in America

14.4 Analyze the Treaty of Paris of 1783

14.5 Evaluate the challenges of nation building faced by Americans

Those who believe the American Revolution was not very revolutionary should consider the case of David George, a slave who lived on the frontier of Georgia. A Scottish trader George Galphin bought him from his Native American master and took him to Silver Bluff, an isolated settlement on the banks of Georgia's Ogeechee River. While working at Galphin's large trading post, George learned the business of buying and selling. Here he met and married Phillis, a woman of mixed Indian and African ancestry who bore him several children. It was also here that David George encountered George Liele, a black preacher whose powerful message of salvation persuaded him to repent and be baptized into the Christian faith. In time, George learned to read the Bible and become an influential preacher in his own right. When Galphin fled

Silver Bluff to escape an advancing British army, David George defected to the British and soon came under the protection of Lieutenant Colonel Thomas Brown.

Over the next several years under Brown's patronage, George developed a prosperous livelihood, first as a vendor of provisions to various garrisons of British troops and then as a butcher in Savannah. For a time, George partnered with his old mentor George Liele in the provisions trade while teaming with Liele to preach on various occasions. Together, the two men established what was probably the first black Baptist church in America near George's longtime home in Silver Bluff. Near the end of the war in 1782, George took his family to a more secure location in Charles Town, South Carolina. From there he was eventually evacuated to Nova Scotia, where he established Baptist churches in Shelburn and Preston before moving to nearby St. John, New Brunswick, where he established yet another church. After nine years of ministry in the Canada's emerging maritime communities, George took nearly the whole of his congregation from St. John to Sierra Leon, where he died in 1810 as a leader of the pro-British faction in Sierra Leon and a missionary to the indigenous Koya Temne of the region.

David George's career reminds us of the many forms the struggle for freedom could take during the American War for Independence. The majority of Anglo-American colonists took up arms to defend a conception of liberty grounded in independent ownership of family property and representation by a local or provincial body of elected officials. Most did not link their own quest for independence from Great Britain with a movement to end slavery. Indeed, many southern planters defended and sought to strengthen the institution. For the slaves within those same communities, however, personal freedom was paramount. They would trade their labor or their military service to whichever side offered it, and some who made this bargain gained access to unprecedented freedom of movement and choice throughout the Atlantic World.

The dislocations of war spelled dramatic change for others as well. A significant minority of colonists remained committed to the belief that the British constitution best preserved their rights and liberties, often at great sacrifice to themselves and their families. American Indians chose sides as their interests dictated, and their experience varied widely throughout the war years. News of the disruptions on the mainland traveled throughout the Atlantic World and far beyond, arousing great interest among Britain's rivals in Europe, among colonial peoples throughout the Americas, and within slave communities everywhere.

Most patriots—from gentry leaders to the ordinary farmers and craftsmen that made up the revolutionary rank and file—stopped well short of the most radical implications that could be read into the rhetoric of liberty. Some historians have argued from this fact that what transpired in 1776 fell far short of a true revolution. Yet both the patriots and their European observers shared a deep sense that the American cause was striking at the very root of the traditional order of government and society. They saw themselves, and were seen by observers, as "setting the world ablaze" and "beginning the world over again." They were well aware that such an enterprise entailed the great risk of setting loose rhetoric and shaping examples of action that could spin off into such unintended consequences as slave revolt and radical social leveling. Yet they remained convinced that their cause was just and worth the risk. Revolutionary leaders also shared George Washington's keen awareness that their war for independence was unfolding on a global stage, that "if we now shamefully fail, we shall become infamous before the whole world."

14.1: The Boston Tea Party and the Final Rupture

14.1 Review the Boston Tea Party's role as the turning point that led to the American War of Independence

In May 1773, Parliament passed the Tea Act, legislation many members supposed that Americans would welcome. After all, it lowered the price for their favorite beverage. Parliament hoped to save one of Britain's largest businesses, the East India Company, from possible bankruptcy. This commercial giant imported Asian tea in England, where it was resold to wholesalers. The tea was subject to heavy duties. The company tried to pass these charges on to the consumers, but American tea drinkers preferred the cheaper leaves that were smuggled in from Holland.

BOSTON TEA PARTY

The Tea Act changed the rules. Parliament not only allowed the company to sell directly to American retailers, thus cutting out intermediaries, but also eliminated the duties paid in England. If all had gone according to plan, the agents of the East India Company in America would have undersold their competitors, including the Dutch smugglers, and with the new profits would have saved the business.

But Parliament's logic was flawed. First, since the tax on tea, collected in American ports, remained in effect, this new act seemed a devious scheme to win popular support for Parliament's right to tax the colonists without representation. Second, the act threatened to undercut powerful colonial merchants who did a good business trading in smuggled Dutch tea. Considering the American reaction, the British government might have been well advised to devise another plan to rescue the ailing company. At Philadelphia, and then at New York City, colonists turned back the tea ships before they could unload. Third, by taxing a general consumer item, the British managed to touch the daily lives of ordinary Americans, a move that helped turn a protest among elite leaders into a widespread popular movement.

In Boston, a major colonial port, the issue was not easily resolved. Governor Hutchinson, a strong-willed man whose sons were major tea importers, would not permit the vessels to return to England. Local patriots would not let them unload. And so, crammed with the East India Company's tea, the ships sat in Boston Harbor waiting for the colonists to make up their minds. On the night of December 16, 1773, they did so in dramatic style. A group of men disguised as Mohawk Indians boarded the ships and pitched 340 chests of tea worth the enormous sum of £10,000 over the side. Whether Samuel Adams organized the famed Boston Tea Party is not known. No doubt he and his allies were not taken by surprise. Even at the time, John Adams, Samuel's distant cousin, sensed the event would have far-reaching significance. "This Destruction of the Tea," he scribbled in his diary, "is so bold, so daring, so firm, intrepid, and inflexible, and it must have so important consequences, and so lasting, that I can't but consider it as an *epocha* in history."

14.1.1: Parliamentary Response: The Coercive Acts

When news of the Tea Party reached London in January 1774, the ministry of Lord North was stunned. The people of Boston had treated parliamentary supremacy with utter contempt, and British rulers saw no humor whatsoever in the destruction of private property by subjects of the Crown dressed in costume. To quell such rebelliousness, Parliament passed in early 1774 a series of laws called the Coercive Acts (in America, they were referred to as the Intolerable Acts). The legislation consisted of four acts. The Boston Port Bill (March 31) closed the port of Boston until the city fully compensated the East India Company for the lost tea. The Administration of Justice Act (May 20) allowed the royal governor to transfer British officials arrested for offenses committed in the line of duty to be tried in Halifax, Nova Scotia, or in Britain itself, where there was little likelihood they would be convicted. The Massachusetts Government Act (May 20) restructured the Massachusetts government by transforming the upper house from an elective to an appointed body and restricting the number of legal town meetings to one a year. The Quartering Act (June 2) authorized the army to quarter troops wherever they were needed, even if this required the compulsory requisition of uninhabited private buildings. George III enthusiastically supported this tough policy. To enforce it, he appointed General Thomas Gage, who apparently won the king's favor by announcing that in America, "Nothing can be done but by forcible means." Occupation and coercion invited organized resistance.

The sweeping denial of constitutional liberties confirmed the colonists' worst fears. To men like Samuel Adams, it seemed as if Britain really intended to enslave the American people. Colonial leaders who had counseled moderation found their position shaken by the vindictiveness of the Coercive Acts. Using military force to win the hearts and minds of almost always fails. It did so in 1774. Edmund Burke, one of America's last friends in Parliament, noted sadly on the floor of Commons, "This is the day, then, that you wish to go to war with all America, in order to conciliate that country to *this*."

14.1.2: The Quebec Act Confirms Colonial Fears

While Parliament was debating and passing the various components of the Coercive Acts, it also took up Canadian governor Sir Guy Carleton's recommendations for a permanent government in Quebec (see Chapter 13). Carleton's report, which had been languishing for more than three years, called for a highly centralized government consistent with what most inhabitants had known under French rule. Legislation was to be vested in a crown-appointed council, whose acts were subject to the royal veto. All taxation apart from that levied by local communities would be strictly reserved to Parliament. As with the French judicial system, there would be no provision for jury trials. Roman Catholics would receive toleration and full civil rights. Even Carleton's friends in London acknowledged that the recommendations proposed a "benevolent despotism." Yet the Quebec Act, passed on the same day as the Administration of Justice and Massachusetts Government Acts, adopted Carleton's recommendations with little change. The Act also extended the boundaries of Quebec to the Ohio River, incorporating territory north of the river that was already claimed and contested by Virginia, Massachusetts, Connecticut, Pennsylvania, and New York.

Colonists found all aspects of the Quebec Act alarming. The coincidence of its passage with the Coercive Acts smacked to them of a conspiracy to eliminate all colonial legislatures, to strip colonists of major civil rights, and to invest Parliament with vast new unrepresentative powers over taxation and all legislation in the colonies. The extension of toleration to Roman Catholics tapped into deep-seated fears that the traditional faith of the French Canadians posed grave threats to religious and civil liberty. The extension of Quebec's boundary to the Ohio seemed to be a massive landgrab, threatening the titles of the speculators who had invested large sums in surveying and claiming large tracts of excellent farmland for development and sale.

14.1.3: The Other Colonies Respond

If in 1774 the House of Commons thought it could isolate Boston from the rest of America, it was in for a rude surprise. Colonists living in other parts of the continent recognized immediately that the principles at stake in Boston affected all Americans. As one Virginian explained, "There were no Heats and Troubles in Virginia till the Blockade of Boston." Few persons advocated independence, but they could not remain passive while Boston was destroyed. They sent food and money and, during the fall of 1774, reflected more deeply than ever on what it meant to be an American subject in the British empire.

The sticking point for the mainland colonies remained—as it had been in 1765—the sovereignty of Parliament. No one in Britain could think of a way around this constitutional impasse. An extreme claim for authority invited no negotiation. In 1773, Benjamin Franklin had offered a suggestion. "The Parliament," he observed, "has no right to make any law whatever, binding on the colonies . . . the king, and not the king, lords, and commons collectively, is their sovereign." But so long as it still seemed possible to coerce the Americans into obedience, to punish these disobedient children, Britain's rulers rejected compromise in favor of force, a strategy of might that almost never works.

14.2: Steps toward Independence

14.2 Analyze the effects of "unconstitutional" government acts on the colonists

During the summer of 1774, committees of correspondence analyzed the perilous situation in which the colonists found themselves. Something, of course, had to be done, but what? Would the southern colonies support resistance in New England? Would Pennsylvanians stand up to Parliament? Not surprisingly, the committees endorsed a call for a Continental Congress, a gathering of fifty-five elected delegates from twelve colonies (Georgia sent none but agreed to support the action taken). This First Continental Congress convened in Philadelphia on September 5. It included some of America's most articulate, respected leaders; among them were John Adams, Samuel Adams, Patrick Henry, Richard Henry Lee, Christopher Gadsden, and George Washington.

The delegates were strangers to one another. They knew little about the customs and values, the geography and economy of Britain's other provinces. As John Adams explained on September 18, "It has taken Us much Time to get acquainted with the Tempers, Views, Characters, and Designs of Persons and to let them into the Circumstances of our Province." During the early sessions of the Congress, the delegates eyed each other closely, trying to gain a sense of the strength and integrity of the men with whom they might commit treason.

Differences of opinion soon surfaced. Delegates from the Middle Colonies—Joseph Galloway of Pennsylvania, for example—wanted to proceed with caution, but Samuel Adams and other more radical members pushed the moderates toward confrontation. Boston's master politician engineered congressional commendation of the Suffolk Resolves, a bold statement drawn up in Suffolk County, Massachusetts, that encouraged forcible resistance of the Coercive Acts. The colonists declared that they were not obliged to obey government acts that they deemed unconstitutional.

After this decision, the tone of the meeting was established. Moderate spokesmen introduced conciliatory measures, which received polite discussion but failed to win a majority vote. Just before returning to their homes (September 1774), the delegates created the "Association," an intercolonial agreement to halt all commerce with Britain until Parliament repealed the Intolerable Acts. This was a totally revolutionary decision. Ordinary people were placed in charge of enforcing revolutionary goals. The Association authorized a vast network of local committees to enforce nonimportation. Violators were exposed, shamed, and forced either to apologize publicly for their actions or to be shunned by all their patriot neighbors. In many of the communities, the committees were the government, distinguishing, in the words of James Madison, "Friends from Foes."

In many colonial communities, the committees also went beyond mere enforcement of the Association's efforts to halt commerce. The Suffolk Resolves had also called on the people to arm and form their own militias, and many complied. Local militias of "minutemen"—volunteers who pledged themselves ready to arm and fight at a moment's notice—began training on town commons across the colonies. Local committees of correspondence organized their members to collect and cache arms and ammunition in secret hiding places such as cellars and compartments under floorboards. Youths socialized with one another while packing powder and musket balls into paper wrappings known as "cartridges," which could be kept in leather pouches at a soldier's waist for quick retrieval to load a musket under fire.

George III, who did not understand the sources of popular mobilization, sneered at such activities. "I am not sorry," he confided, "that

the line of conduct seems now chalked out . . . the New England Governments are in a state of Rebellion, blows must decide whether they are to be subject to this country or independent."

14.2.1: Resistance and the Blood of American Martyrs

The king was correct. Before Congress reconvened, "blows" fell at Lexington and Concord, two small farm communities in eastern Massachusetts. On the evening of April 18, 1775, General Gage dispatched troops from Boston to seize rebel supplies he had learned were being stored there. Paul Revere, a renowned silversmith and dedicated insurgent, warned the colonists that the redcoats were coming. The militia of Lexington, a collection of ill-trained farmers, boys as well as old men, decided to stand on the village green on the following morning, April 19, as the British soldiers passed on the road to Concord. No one planned to fight, but in a moment of confusion, someone (probably a colonist) fired; the redcoats discharged a volley, and eight Americans lay dead.

Word of the incident spread rapidly. By the time the British force reached its destination, the countryside swarmed with to respond instantly to military emergencies. The redcoats found nothing of significance in Concord and so returned. The long march back to Boston turned into a rout. Lord Percy, a British officer who brought up reinforcements, remarked more in surprise than bitterness that "whoever looks upon [the American soldiers] as an irregular mob, will find himself much mistaken." On June 17, colonial militiamen again held their own against seasoned troops at the battle of Bunker Hill (actually Breed's Hill). The British finally took the hill, but after this costly "victory" in which he suffered 40 percent casualties, Gage complained that the Americans had displayed "a conduct and spirit against us, they never showed against the French" during the Seven Years' War.

14.2.2: Halting Steps toward Solidarity

Members of the Second Continental Congress gathered in Philadelphia in May 1775. They faced an awesome responsibility. British government in the mainland colonies had almost ceased to function, and with Americans fighting redcoats, the country desperately needed strong central leadership. Slowly, often reluctantly, Congress took control of the war. The delegates formed a Continental Army and appointed George Washington its commander, in part because he seemed to have greater military experience than anyone else available and in part because he looked like he should be commander in chief. The delegates were also eager to select someone who did not come from Massachusetts, a colony that seemed already to possess too much power in national councils. The members of Congress purchased military supplies and, to pay for them, issued paper money. But while they were assuming the powers of a sovereign government, the congressmen refused to declare independence. They debated and fretted, listened to the appeals of moderates who played on the colonists' remaining loyalty to Britain, and then did nothing.

14.2.3: The Disastrous Canada Campaign: The Northern Limit of Union

Washington moved in the early months of his command to secure the siege of Boston that had coalesced in the aftermath of Lexington and Concord. He recognized, however, that his makeshift army was untrained and vulnerable, and he consulted with his commanders on the best avenues for strengthening his military position. Quebec and Montreal represented a great potential threat—bases to which the British could transport troops up the St. Lawrence and stage a major offensive from the north—but an immediate opportunity, if he could make a quick, decisive strike. In 1775, the garrisons remained small. In fact, on May 10, well before Washington reached Boston, the commander Benedict Arnold had joined his own small force to that of Ethan Allen to capture Fort Ticonderoga on the southern end of Lake Champlain, gaining a rich prize of artillery, arms, and ammunition to support the siege of Boston. The forty-three redcoats manning Ticonderoga had yielded without a fight. The patriots knew that garrisons at Montreal and Quebec were also relatively small and believed that a sufficient force could dislodge them fairly easily. A successful campaign would halt the efforts of Canada's governor Sir Guy Carleton, who had returned from London and was rumored to be recruiting a Canadian force to invade New York. Patriot commanders also hoped that French and British inhabitants of Quebec would be sympathetic and form common cause with them against Parliament.

The patriot leaders misjudged both the sympathy of Quebec's inhabitants and the effectiveness of its fighting force under Carleton. Congress initially authorized General Philip Schuyler of New York to raise a force and seize strategic points along the border with Quebec. Brigadier General Richard Montgomery soon replaced the ailing Schuyler and led American forces in capturing the garrison of St. John's near Montreal and occupying the city itself by mid-November. Meanwhile, Benedict Arnold led a force of 1,100 volunteers overland from the coast of Maine to Quebec City, where Montgomery joined him in December. On the 31st, the combined force launched an early-morning assault that ended in disaster. Montgomery perished in battle and Arnold was wounded. Carleton's Canadian and British forces killed or wounded one hundred patriot volunteers and captured over three hundred. Arnold maintained a weak cordon around the city for the rest of the winter, but the army retreated the following spring when redcoat reinforcements reached Carleton.

The hope of incorporating Canada into the American resistance died with the failure of Montgomery's and Arnold's assault. Canadians had made their choice clear, and the St. Lawrence remained a major strategic threat in the early years of the war. The lands north of the border also became a safe haven for pro-British Iroquois factions as well as for Loyalists from New England and New York who were forced into exile by the conflict.

14.2.4: West Indians Close Ranks with Britain

As the mainland colonies moved toward open rebellion against the mother country, colonists in the British West Indies took steps to disassociate themselves from the protest. The West Indian colonists had never shared their mainland counterparts' insistence on defining the scope of parliamentary sovereignty or asserting the equality of their own legislatures' authority with that of Parliament. Most West Indian leaders in the islands, along with agents of the West Indian interest in London, recoiled at news of the Boston Tea Party. One Member of Parliament from a West Indian family, Rose Fuller, proposed that Parliament impose on Boston a levy of £20,000—twice the value of the tea thrown overboard—to compensate the East India Company for its losses. Others simply "did not chuse to step forth in opposition" to the Coercive Acts as issues "not immediately affecting them." West Indian planters increasingly resolved not to follow the path of taken by the "Boston firebrands" but to pursue their own course of preserving as much autonomy as possible in the government of their own internal affairs while participating in the benefits of the mightiest, most prosperous empire on earth.

Once the fighting broke out on the mainland, West Indian planters and their agents in London shifted their support to Parliament. They feared that an outbreak of civil war in the British Atlantic would introduce disruptions and create opportunities for their slaves to revolt. Indeed, the new rhetoric of freedom from parliamentary "slavery" was already circulating among actual slaves throughout the Atlantic, inspiring scattered attempts to break their very real bonds. Tobago witnessed two small slave uprisings in March and April 1774. That same year in August, a plot was uncovered in Westmoreland, Jamaica, only a few months after an uprising among maroons in the southern part of the island. The following March, a band of maroons staged a series of raids on white targets in St. Vincent.

In an Atlantic context of unrest and budding revolt, such outbreaks appeared to West Indian authorities to be no accident. While mainland Americans worked themselves into a frenzy over imagined parliamentary conspiracies to deprive them of their rights, British West Indian planters from Jamaica to Barbados spent sleepless nights worrying that their slaves, fired with the rhetoric of liberty, would murder them in their beds.

West Indian whites accordingly moved quickly to suppress dissent and shore up support for the mother country. Local authorities arrested visitors from the mainland who expressed support for the patriot cause, throwing them into prison on suspicion of sedition and treason. Island legislatures voted petitions expressing loyalty to Crown and Parliament. In Antigua, one of the two colonies that had staged protests against the Stamp Act in 1765, over six hundred "friends of government" gathered at a tavern in 1776 to toast "success to his Majesty's Arms in America" and "confusion to Congress." Planters throughout Britain's Caribbean colonies offered their slaves for military service in His Majesty's cause in America. Rum producers contributed casks of their product to the army as a show of support. West Indian ports welcomed British commerce, British naval vessels, and soon, Loyalist refugees from the mainland.

14.2.5: Beginning "The World Over Again"

In December 1775, as Montgomery and Arnold were advancing on Quebec City, Parliament declared war on American commerce by passing the Prohibitory Act. Until the colonists begged for pardon, they could not trade with the rest of the world. The British navy blockaded their ports and seized American ships on the high seas. Lord North also hired German mercenaries (the Russians drove too hard a bargain) to put down the rebellion. And in America, Virginia's royal governor Lord Dunmore further undermined the possibility of reconciliation by urging the colony's slaves to take up arms against their masters. Few did so, but the effort to stir up black rebellion infuriated the Virginia planters.

Thomas Paine (1737–1809) pushed the colonists even closer to independence. Nothing in this man's background suggested he would write the most important pamphlet in American history. In England, Paine had tried and failed in a number of jobs, and exactly why he elected to move to America in 1774 is not clear. While still in England, Paine had the good fortune to meet Benjamin Franklin, who presented him with letters of introduction to the leading patriots of Pennsylvania. At the urging of his new American friends, Paine produced *Common Sense*, an essay that became an instant bestseller. In only three months, it sold more than 120,000 copies.

Common Sense systematically stripped kingship of historical and theological justification. For centuries, the English had maintained the fiction that the monarch could do no wrong. When the government oppressed the people, the royal counselors received the blame. The Crown was above suspicion. To this, Paine cried nonsense, Monarchs ruled by force. George III was simply a "royal brute," who by his arbitrary behavior had surrendered his claim to the colonists' obedience. The pamphlet also attacked the whole idea of a mixed and balanced constitution.

Indeed, *Common Sense* was a powerful democratic manifesto.

Paine's greatest contribution to the revolutionary cause was persuading ordinary folk to sever their ties with Great Britain. It was not reasonable, he argued, to regard England as the mother country. "Europe, and not England," he explained, "is the parent country of America. This new world hath been the asylum for the persecuted lovers of civil and religious liberty from every part of Europe." No doubt that message made a deep impression on Pennsylvania's German population. The time had come for the colonists to form an independent republic. "We have it in our power," Paine wrote in one of his most moving statements, "to begin the world over again . . . the birthday of a new world is at hand."

14.2.6: Defining the Cause of Independence

More than a year of fighting transpired before the Second Continental Congress took clear steps to define exactly what they were fighting for. Some members such as John Adams had been convinced that war was inevitable and were ready to cut ties immediately in 1775. Others such as the Pennsylvania delegate John Dickinson urged reconciliation. Most initially followed Dickinson's lead. On July 8, 1775, three weeks after the Battle of Bunker Hill had made martyrs of many New England patriots, members of Congress signed what became known as the Olive Branch Petition. Drafted by Dickinson, it disavowed any intent to seek independence and requested that the king negotiate taxation and trade regulations with the colonists. On August 21, 1775, however, George III refused audience to Richard Penn and Arthur Lee, the Congressional emissaries who carried the petition to London. Two days later, the king issued a Proclamation for Suppressing Rebellion and Sedition.

The king's rebuff pushed more members toward the cause of independence. Over the following several months, Congress sought to coordinate and finance the growing military resistance while intermittently debating the exact form that a formal declaration of independence should take. In April 1776, focused debate began in earnest, and on June 7, Virginia's Richard Henry Lee proposed a resolution to declare independence. Three days later, Congress appointed a Committee of Five to draft a formal statement of the reasons for taking the United Colonies out of the British empire. Thomas Jefferson, whom John Adams had urged Congress to place on the committee, crafted the initial draft of the document. The committee reviewed it and recommended several revisions, most of which were incorporated into the document.

On July 2, 1776, Congress voted as a committee of the whole in favor of independence on a 9–2 vote with two abstentions. Over the next two days, its members reviewed the draft declaration and made final revisions, striking a critical reference to the English people and, most significantly, a clause against the slave trade and slavery itself. On July 4, Congress formally voted for independence and the adoption of the final document. Like the skilled lawyer he was, Jefferson presented the evidence for independence in a list of grievances against the king, but the document did not become famous for that list. Long after the establishment of the new republic, the Declaration challenged Americans to make good on its powerful statement of political principles based upon fundamental human rights, which included the principle that "all men are created equal." John Adams nicely expressed the patriots' fervor when he wrote on July 3, "Yesterday the greatest question was decided, which ever was debated in America, and a greater perhaps, never was or will be decided among men."

Many revolutionary leaders throughout the Atlantic World and beyond—in Europe and Latin America as in Africa and Asia—have echoed Adams's assessment. Of all the documents written during this period, including the Constitution, the Declaration remains the most powerful and radical invitation to Americans of all backgrounds to demand their equality and full rights as human beings.

14.3: Fighting for Independence

14.3 Identify the main elements that neutralized the position of the British army in America

Only fools and visionaries expressed optimism about America's prospects of winning independence in 1776. The Americans had taken on a formidable military power. The population of Britain was perhaps four times that of its former colonies. England also possessed a strong manufacturing base, a well-trained regular army supplemented by thousands of hired German troops (Hessians), and a navy that dominated the world's oceans. Many British officers had battlefield experience. They already knew what the Americans would slowly learn: waging war would require discipline, money, and sacrifice.

As later events demonstrated, however, Britain had become involved in an impossible military situation, in some ways analogous to that in which the United States would find itself in Vietnam some two hundred years later. Three separate elements neutralized advantages held by the larger power over its adversary. First, the British had to transport men and supplies across the Atlantic, a logistic challenge of unprecedented complexity. Unreliable lines of communication broke down under the strain of war.

Second, America was too vast to be conquered by conventional military methods. Redcoats might gain control over the major port cities, but as long as the Continental Army remained intact, the rebellion continued. As Washington explained, "the possession of our

Towns, while we have an Army in the field, will avail them little. . . . It is our Arms, not defenceless Towns, they have to subdue." Even if England had recruited enough soldiers to occupy the entire country, it would still have lost the war. As one Loyalist instructed the king, "if all America becomes a garrison, she is not worth your attention." Britain could only win by crushing the American will to resist.

And the third, British strategists never appreciated the depth of the Americans' commitment to a political ideology. In the wars of eighteenth-century Europe, such beliefs had seldom mattered. European troops before the French Revolution served because they were paid or because the military was a vocation, but most certainly not because they hoped to advance a set of constitutional principles. Americans were different. To be sure, some young men were drawn to the military by bounty money or by the desire to escape unhappy families. A few were drafted. But taking such people into account, one still encounters among the American troops a remarkable commitment to republican ideals. One French officer reported from the United States, "It is incredible that soldiers composed of men of every age, even of children of fifteen, of whites and blacks, almost naked, unpaid, and rather poorly fed, can march so well and withstand fire so steadfastly."

14.3.1: Building a Professional Army

During the earliest months of rebellion, American soldiers—especially those of New England—suffered no lack of confidence. Indeed, they interpreted their courageous stands at Concord and Bunker Hill as evidence that brave yeomen farmers could lick British regulars on any battlefield. George Washington spent the first years of the war disabusing the colonists of this foolishness, for as he had learned during the French and Indian War, military success depended on endless drill, careful planning, and tough discipline—rigorous preparation that did not characterize the minutemen's methods.

Washington insisted on organizing a regular well-trained field army. Some advisers urged the commander in chief to wage a guerrilla war, one in which small partisan bands would sap Britain's will to rule Americans. But Washington rejected that course. He recognized that the Continental Army served not only as a fighting force but also as a symbol of the republican cause. Its very existence would sustain American hopes, and so long as the army survived, American agents could plausibly solicit foreign aid. This thinking shaped Washington's wartime strategy; he studiously avoided "general actions" in which the Continental Army might be destroyed. Critics complained about Washington's caution, but as they soon discovered, he understood better than they what independence required.

If the commander in chief was correct about the army, however, he failed to comprehend the political importance of the militia. These scattered, almost amateur, military units seldom altered the outcome of battle, but they did maintain control over large areas of the country not directly affected by the British army. Throughout the war, they compelled men and women who would rather have remained neutral to actively support the American effort. In 1777, for example, the militia of Farmington, Connecticut, visited a group of suspected Tories, as Loyalists (people who sided with the king and Parliament during the Revolution) were called, and after "educating" these people in the fundamentals of republican ideology, a militia spokesman announced, "They were indeed grossly ignorant of the true grounds of the present war with Great Britain . . . [but] They appeared to be penitent of their former conduct, [and] professed themselves convinced . . . that there was no such thing as remaining neuters." Without local political coercion, Washington's task would have been considerably more difficult.

14.3.2: Assault on New York

After the embarrassing defeats in Massachusetts, the king appointed General Sir William Howe to replace Gage. British rulers now understood that a simple police action would not be sufficient to crush the American rebellion. Parliament authorized sending more than fifty thousand troops to the mainland colonies, and after evacuating Boston—an untenable strategic position—the British forces stormed ashore at Staten Island in New York Harbor on July 3, 1776. From this more central location, Howe believed he could cut the New Englanders off from the rest of America. He enjoyed the powerful support of the British navy under the command of his brother, Admiral Lord Richard Howe.

When Washington learned the British were planning to occupy New York City, he transferred many of his inexperienced soldiers to Long Island, where they suffered a major defeat (August 27, 1776). In a series of engagements disastrous for the Americans, Howe drove the Continental Army across the Hudson River into New Jersey. Because of his failure to take full advantage of the situation, however, General Howe lost what seemed in retrospect an excellent opportunity to annihilate Washington's entire army. Nevertheless, the Americans were on the run, and in the fall of 1776, contemporaries predicted the rebels would soon capitulate.

14.3.3: "Times That Try Men's Souls"

Swift victories in New York and New Jersey persuaded General Howe that few Americans enthusiastically supported independence. He issued a general pardon, therefore, to anyone who would swear allegiance to George III. The results were encouraging. More than three thousand men and women who lived in areas occupied by the British army took the oath. This group included one intimidated signer of the Declaration of Independence. Howe perceived that a lasting peace in America would require his troops "to treat our enemies as if they might one day become our friends." A member of Lord North's cabinet grumbled that this was "a sentimental manner of making *war*": a shortsighted view considering England's experience in attempting to pacify the Irish. The pardon plan eventually failed not because Howe lacked toughness but because his soldiers and officers regarded loyal Americans as inferior provincials, an attitude that did little to promote good relations. In any case, as soon as the redcoats left a pardoned region, the rebel militia retaliated against those who had deserted the patriot cause.

In December 1776, Washington's bedraggled army retreated across the Delaware River into Pennsylvania. American prospects appeared bleaker than at any other time during the war, The Continental Army lacked basic supplies, and many men who had signed up for short-term enlistments prepared to go home. "These are the times that try men's souls," Paine wrote in a pamphlet titled *American Crisis*. "The summer soldier and the sunshine patriot will, in this crisis, shrink from the service of their country, but he that stands it *now* deserves . . . love and thanks. . . ." Before winter, Washington determined to attempt one last desperate stroke.

Howe played into Washington's hands. The British forces were dispersed in small garrisons across the state of New Jersey, and although the Americans could not possibly have defeated the combined British army, they did possess the capacity—with luck—to capture an exposed post. On the night of December 25, Continental soldiers slipped over the ice-filled Delaware River and at Trenton took nine hundred sleeping Hessian mercenaries by complete surprise.

Cheered by success, Washington returned a second time to Trenton, but on this occasion the Continental Army was not so fortunate. A large British force under Lord Cornwallis trapped the

Americans. Instead of standing and fighting—really an impossible challenge—Washington secretly, by night, marched his little army around Cornwallis's left flank. On January 3, 1777, the Americans surprised a British garrison at Princeton. Washington then took the American army into winter quarters. The British, fearful of losing more outposts, consolidated their troops, thus leaving much of the state in the hands of the patriot militia.

14.3.4: Saratoga Stuns the British

In 1777, England's chief military strategist, Lord George Germain, still perceived the war in conventional European terms. Like many imperial planners, he never fully understood the conditions on the ground. A large field army, he reasoned, would somehow maneuver Washington's Continental troops into a decisive battle in which the British would enjoy a clear advantage. Complete victory over the Americans certainly seemed within England's grasp. Unfortunately for the men who advocated this plan, the Continental forces proved extremely elusive, and while one British army vainly tried to corner Washington in Pennsylvania, another was forced to surrender in the forests of upstate New York.

In the summer of 1777, it seemed as if the British strategy might just work. General John Burgoyne, a dashing though overbearing officer, descended from Quebec with a force of more than seven thousand troops. They intended to clear the Hudson Valley of rebel resistance, join Howe's army—which was to come up to Albany—and thereby cut New England off from the other states. Burgoyne commanded in a grand style. Accompanied by a German band, thirty carts filled with the general's liquor and belongings, and two thousand dependents and camp followers, the British set out to thrash the Americans. The campaign was a disaster. Military units, mostly from New England, cut the enemy force apart in the deep woods north of Albany. At the battle of Bennington (August 16), the New Hampshire militia under Brigadier General John Stark overwhelmed a thousand German mercenaries. After this setback, Burgoyne's forces struggled forward, desperately hoping that Howe would rush to their rescue, but when it became clear that their situation at Saratoga was hopeless, the haughty Burgoyne was forced to surrender 5,800 men to the American General Horatio Gates (October 17).

Soon after Burgoyne left Canada, General Howe unexpectedly decided to move his main army from New York City to Philadelphia. Exactly what he hoped to achieve was not clear, even to Britain's rulers, and of course, when Burgoyne called for assistance, Howe was sitting in the new nation's capital still trying to devise a way to destroy the Continental Army. Howe's campaign began in late July. The British forces sailed to the head of the Chesapeake Bay and then marched north to Philadelphia. Washington's troops obstructed the enemy's progress, first at Brandywine Creek (September 11) and then at Paoli (September 20), but the outnumbered Americans could not stop the British from entering Philadelphia.

Anxious lest these defeats discourage Congress and the American people, Washington attempted one last battle before the onset of winter. In an engagement at Germantown (October 4), the Americans launched a major counterattack on a fog-covered battlefield, but just at the moment when success seemed assured, they broke off the fight. "When every thing gave the most flattering hopes of victory," Washington complained, "the troops began suddenly to retreat." Bad luck, confusion, and incompetence contributed to the failure. A discouraged Continental Army dug in at Valley Forge, 20 miles outside of Philadelphia, where camp diseases took 2,500 American lives. In their misery, few American soldiers realized their overall military situation was not nearly so desperate as it had been in 1776.

14.3.5: The French Alliance

Even before the Americans declared their independence, agents of the government of Louis XVI began to explore ways to aid the colonists. The French monarchy was no lover of the republican cause, but the American rebellion represented an irresistible opportunity to embarrass the English. The French deeply resented the defeat they had sustained during the Seven Years' War. They offered secret support to the Revolution from the conflict's earliest days. But when American representatives, Benjamin Franklin for one, pleaded for official recognition of American independence or for outright military alliance, the French advised patience. The international stakes were too great for the king to openly back a cause that had little chance of success.

The American victory at Saratoga convinced the French that the rebels had formidable forces and were serious in their resolve. Indeed, Lord North drew the same conclusion. When news of Saratoga reached London, North muttered, "This damned war." In private conversation, he expressed doubts about England's ability to win the contest, knowing the French would soon enter the fray. In Paris, Franklin performed brilliantly. In meetings with French officials, he hinted that the Americans might accept a British peace initiative. If the French wanted the war to continue—if they really wanted to embarrass their old rival—then they had to do what the English refused: formally recognize the independence of the United States.

The stratagem paid off handsomely. On February 6, 1778, the French presented American representatives with two separate treaties. The first, called the Treaty of Amity and Commerce, established commercial relations between France and the United States. It tacitly accepted the existence of a new, independent republic. The Treaty of Alliance was even more generous, considering America's obvious military and economic weaknesses. In the event that France and England went to war (they did so on June 14, as everyone expected), the French agreed to reject "either Truce or Peace with Great Britain . . . until the independence of the United States shall have been formally or tacitly assured by the Treaty or Treaties that shall terminate the War." Even more amazing, France surrendered its claim to all territories formerly owned by Great Britain east of the Mississippi River. The Americans pledged they would not sign a separate peace with Britain without first informing their new ally. And in return, France made no claim to Canada, asking only for the right to take possession of certain British islands in the Caribbean.

Never had Franklin worked his magic to greater effect. French intervention instantly transformed British military strategy. What had been a colonial rebellion suddenly became a world conflict, a continuation of the great wars for empire of the late seventeenth century (see Chapters 7, 8, and 12). Scarce military resources, especially newer fighting ships, had to be diverted from the American theater to guard the English Channel. In fact, there was talk in London of a possible French invasion. Although the threat of such an assault was not very great until 1779, the British did have cause for concern. The French navy posed a serious challenge to the overextended British fleet. By concentrating their warships in a specific area, the French could hold off or even defeat British squadrons, an advantage that would figure significantly in the American victory at Yorktown.

14.3.6: An Atlantic Conflict

The French Alliance expanded what had been from the war's earliest days an Atlantic conflict. Previous French aid alone had made it so, since the French quietly opened their ports both in France and the Caribbean to American privateers in violation of treaties promising not to give harbor to Great Britain's enemies. Intrepid captains, the most famous of whom was John Paul Jones, docked there to outfit and repair their ships.

From French ports they sailed into the English Channel and Irish Sea to harass British shipping and capture merchant vessels laden with supplies or valuable cargo that could be traded for badly needed weapons and powder. French ports in the Caribbean offered similar haven for privateers as well as docks for the blockade-runners to lade their vessels with essential military supplies. The negotiations for these arms involved secret agents and fictitious transatlantic trading companies, the type of clandestine operation more typical of modern times than of the eighteenth century.

Dutch officials also frequently looked the other way when American patriot privateers entered their ports, despite the fact that the Dutch remained officially neutral in the conflict until 1782, when they finally signed a treaty of amity and commerce modeled on that with France. In the Dutch Caribbean island of St. Eustatius, Governor Johannes de Graaf ordered what was probably the first official foreign salute of a U.S. flag from the guns of the island's fort, answering Captain Isaiah Robinson's salute of the Dutch colors as he entered port in the Continental warship *Andrew Doria* on November 16, 1776. St. Eustatius provided a major source of arms, ammunition, and supply throughout most of the war. British cruisers patrolled off the island's coast, demanding ingenuity of American skippers to evade capture. The British could not stem the flow of arms from St. Eustatius until after 1780, when the discovery of a draft treaty with the Dutch among the belongings of captured American diplomat Henry Laurens gave Great Britain a pretext to declare war on Holland. This freed Admiral Sir George Rodney to attack and capture the formerly neutral island in February 1781, by which time many other sources of war material had opened to the United States.

The real naval war of the Revolutionary period was largely a European affair. John Paul Jones's battle with the British warship *Serapis* was an exception to the more common use of the small Continental navy to harass commercial shipping and launch occasional clandestine attacks on British naval vessels, often from open whaleboats under cover of darkness. The French navy, by contrast, possessed some of the fastest ships in the world and could take the war to Great Britain on the high seas. French warships fanned out across the globe to attack strategic British possessions and cripple British commerce. The Caribbean became a major theater of naval operations, with the French sugar islands such as Saint-Domingue, Guadaloupe, and Martinique providing bases along with several American ports.

14.3.7: Spain Enters the War

The Atlantic scope of the conflict widened still further when Spain declared war on Great Britain on June 21, 1779. Spain did not join France in formal alliance with the United States, and the subsequent diplomatic efforts of John Jay to win formal recognition from the Spanish crown failed. Nevertheless, the declaration of war enabled Spain to cooperate openly with the United States as a cobelligerent, greatly expanding the covert assistance they had provided all along. In 1776, Spain and France together loaned Congress over one million French francs to prosecute their struggle for independence. Spanish agents formed covert trade agreements with American patriot merchants and set up one of the covert trading companies, the Paris-based Roderique Hortalez et Cie. War material purchased through that front made its way on Spanish, French, and Dutch ships to St. Eustatius, where it could was transferred to vessels bound for New Orleans and again to flatboats for transport up the Mississippi and Ohio Rivers, supplying the western campaign as well as the main Continental forces via Fort Pitt.

Spain's declaration of war permitted the governor of Louisiana, Bernardo de Gálvez (for whom Galveston, Texas, is named), to move against British forts on the Mississippi in the late summer of 1779, further securing trade with

Americans along the great river system. It also permitted him to mount campaigns against two strategically crucial British posts on the Gulf of Mexico. Fort Charlotte in Mobile Bay fell in March 1780, clearing the way for a siege of the much larger and better-guarded Fort George at Pensacola. The redcoat defense of Fort George diverted men and material from other British operations in America. The fort's fall to Gálvez in May 1781 further shifted the balance toward Continental forces in the Southeast, depriving southern Loyalists a base while opening a shorter line of supply to the Gulf Coast than New Orleans could offer.

14.3.8: The Last Campaign

British General Henry Clinton replaced Howe, who resigned after the battle of Saratoga. Clinton was a strangely complex individual. As a subordinate officer, he had impressed his superiors as imaginative but easily provoked to anger. When he took command of the British army, his resolute self-confidence suddenly dissolved. Perhaps he feared failure. Whatever the explanation for his vacillation, Clinton's record in America was little better than Howe's or Gage's.

Military strategists calculated that Britain's last chance of winning the war lay in the southern colonies, a region largely untouched in the early years of fighting. Intelligence reports reaching London indicated that Georgia and South Carolina contained a sizable body of Loyalists, men who would take up arms for the crown if only they received support and encouragement from the regular army. The southern strategy devised by Germain and Clinton in 1779 turned the war into a bitter guerrilla conflict, and during the last months of battle, British officers worried that their search for an easy victory had inadvertently opened a Pandora's box of uncontrollable partisan furies.

The southern campaign opened in the spring of 1780. Savannah had already fallen, and Clinton reckoned that if the British could take Charles Town, they would be able to control the entire South. A large fleet carrying nearly eight thousand redcoats reached South Carolina in February. Complacent Americans had allowed the city's fortifications to decay, and in a desperate, last-minute effort to preserve Charles Town, General Benjamin Lincoln's forces dug trenches and reinforced walls, but to no avail. Clinton and his second in command, General Cornwallis, gradually encircled the city; and on May 12, Lincoln surrendered an American army of almost six thousand men.

The defeat took Congress by surprise, and without making proper preparations, it dispatched a second army to South Carolina under Horatio Gates, the hero of Saratoga. He too failed. At Camden, Cornwallis outmaneuvered the raw American recruits, capturing or killing 750 during the course of battle (August 16). Poor Gates galloped from the scene and did not stop until he reached Hillsboro, North Carolina, 200 miles away.

Even at this early stage of the southern campaign, the dangers of partisan warfare had become evident. Tory raiders showed little interest in serving as regular soldiers in Cornwallis's army. They preferred night riding, indiscriminate plundering, or murdering of neighbors against whom they harbored ancient grudges. The British had unleashed a horde of banditti across South Carolina. Men who genuinely supported independence or who had merely fallen victim to Loyalist guerrillas bided their time. They retreated westward, waiting for their enemies to make a mistake. Their chance came on October 7 at King's Mountain, North Carolina. In the most vicious fighting of the Revolution, the backwoodsmen decimated a force of British regulars and Tory raiders who had strayed too far from base. One witness reported that when a British officer tried to surrender, he was summarily shot down by at least seven American soldiers.

Cornwallis, badly confused and poorly supplied, squandered his strength chasing American forces across the Carolinas. Congress sent General Nathanael Greene to the South with a new army. This young Rhode Islander was the most capable general on Washington's staff. Greene joined Daniel Morgan, leader of the famed Virginia Riflemen, and in a series of tactically brilliant engagements, they sapped the strength of Cornwallis's army, first at Cowpens, South Carolina (January 17, 1781), and later at Guilford Courthouse, North Carolina (March 15). In both engagements, Green's army appeared to have suffered defeat as it retreated from the field, but it remained an intact and nimble fighting force despite the losses of men. Clinton fumed in New York City. In his estimation, the inept Cornwallis had left "two valuable colonies behind him to be overrun and conquered by the very army which he boasts to have completely routed but a week or two before."

Cornwallis pushed north into Virginia, planning apparently to establish a base of operations on the coast. He selected Yorktown, a sleepy tobacco market located on a peninsula bounded by the York and James Rivers. Washington watched these maneuvers closely. The canny Virginia planter knew this territory intimately, and he sensed that Cornwallis had made a serious blunder. When Washington learned the French fleet could gain temporary dominance in the Chesapeake Bay, he rushed south from New Jersey with two thousand Continental soldiers. With him marched thousands of well-trained French troops under the Comte de Rochambeau. Within a month, his combined force covered nearly 400 miles to join the army already well established in siege works surrounding Yorktown. All the pieces fell into place. The French admiral, the Comte de Grasse, cut Cornwallis off from the sea, while Washington and his lieutenants encircled the British on land. On October 19, 1781, Cornwallis surrendered his entire army of six thousand men. When Lord North heard of the defeat at Yorktown, he moaned, "Oh God! It is all over." The British still controlled New York City and Charles Town, but except for a few skirmishes, the fighting ended. The task of securing the independence of the United States was now in the hands of the diplomats.

14.3.9: The Indians' Revolution

The American Revolution affected Indians differently according to their particular local circumstances. Delegates to Congress were keenly aware of the importance of securing alliances wherever possible and neutrality at the very least. Congress, however, had only limited influence in Indian diplomacy at the outset of the war, leaving most negotiations to the various states and, where circumstances demanded, to military commanders leading campaigns that impinged upon the territory or interests of particular native nations. In practical terms, this meant that the pattern of local relations that had been under development prior to the war exerted the dominant influence on how warfare, neutrality, and alliance after the fighting broke out.

East of the frontier, patterns of Indian participation resembled that of their white neighbors. Some supported the patriot cause, others remained at least closet Loyalists, whereas many remained neutral in a fight they did not see as theirs.

The Iroquois, who had engaged in the system of Covenant Chain alliances with Great Britain for over a century (see Chapter 6), divided into factions as they had always done. Although the full Iroquois council pledged neutrality to Congress in 1775, the member nations remained divided. Many Mohawks remained loyal to their old allies, bound now by family ties to the British imperial agent Sir William Johnson, whose common-law Mohawk wife Mary Brant bore him nine children. After Johnson's death in 1774, Mary became an influential intermediary

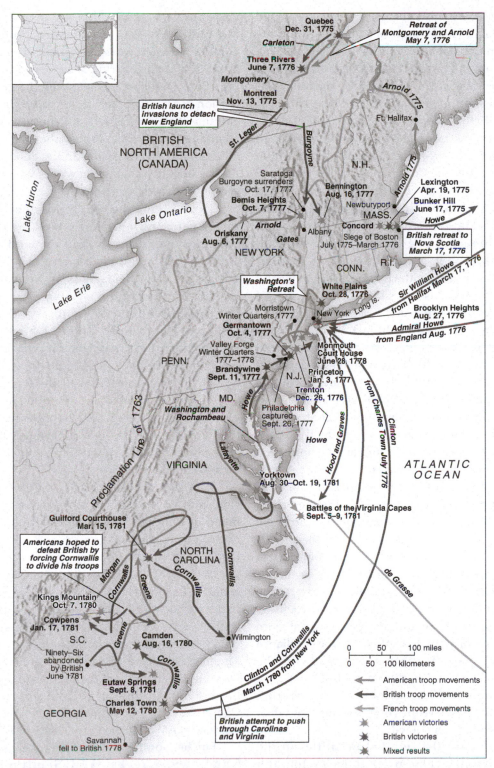

Map 14.1 The American Revolution

between the British and the Iroquois as well as white Loyalists, whom she supported from her home in Canajoharie, New York early in the war. Her brother Thayendanegea or Joseph Brandt held the rank of war chief among the Mohawks and was appointed Captain of Mohawk forces by the British superintendent in 1775. Brant commanded Loyalist various Mohawk and white militia forces through the early years of the war. After the Continental Army's victory at Saratoga, many more Iroquois decided that an alliance with Great Britain was a losing bet, but Brant kept up the fight, leading or sharing leadership in raids along the New York and Pennsylvania frontier. He was branded as "Monster Brant" for his role in the infamous Wyoming and Cherry Valley massacres that routed the Patriot militia and resulted in scores of brutal deaths among noncombatants. In fact, Brant had tried to restrain Seneca warriors who perpetrated most of the atrocities in retaliation for depredations they had suffered at the hands of white frontiersmen. In 1779, Brant received a regular army commission as Captain and continued to command the Northern Confederated Indians in military operations throughout the northwest for the remainder of the war.

Shawnee and Mingo peoples throughout the Ohio Country experienced the American Revolution as a continuation of their struggle to push white settlement back from their hunting grounds. Many Delaware bands joined them in alliance along with other Indians in the regions such as the Miami and the Wyandot, while Christian Delawares attempted to remain neutral. The outbreak of war gave this pan-Indian alliance a fresh opportunity to exploit the type of alliance and diplomacy that they had enjoyed with the French prior to 1763, pitting the British against their now-rebellious colonists while treating locally for peace with white frontiersmen when circumstances demanded.

The spark that ignited hostilities in the Ohio Country came prior to Lexington and Concord, when Virginia's Governor John Murray, fourth Earl of Dunmore, provoked a conflict between white Virginians living near Fort Pitt and neighboring Shawnees. The resulting "Lord Dunmore's War" secured a grudging cession of Shawnee land rights to Virginia, preempting the efforts of a rival Pennsylvania land company to gain title. It also alienated former allies among the Delaware and engendered enduring hostility among Shawnees who did not accept the cession's terms.

Throughout the war years, conflict in the Ohio Country primarily took the form of struggles over possession of the land. Trans-Appalachian Virginians, many of whom increasingly saw themselves as Kentuckians, battled to preserve the farming communities they had carved out of the forests along the Ohio and Cumberland Rivers. Ohio Country Indians battled to drive them off. Vicious fighting characterized all sides in the West, though one of the worst atrocities of the Revolutionary era was committed at the Moravian village of Gnadenhutten in 1782, where Pennsylvania militiamen under David Williamson systematically murdered over ninety Christian Delaware men, women, and children.

To be sure, the war had its quasi-conventional side, with Virginia militia forces under the command of George Rogers Clark battling for the capture of strategic forts such as Kaskaskia on the Ohio in Illinois country and Vincennes on the Wabash in what is now Indiana. The British commanders in the region saw alliance with the Indians as their best chance of recovering strategic control of the Ohio and Mississippi waterways, thus preserving their claim to the region. The Virginians' ability to hold key forts throughout the war, and the inability of the Indians to drive out the settlers, played a role in the American Peace Commission's ability to negotiate for the trans-Appalachian West in the Peace Treaty of 1783.

Further south, the Cherokees, Chickasaws, Choctaws, Creeks, and Seminoles all experienced a mix of conflict, loss, and unexpected opportunity when the war broke out. Cherokees experienced pressure from expanding white settlement similar to that of the Shawnee and had prosecuted their own war to preserve their lands in the early 1760s. The Cherokee war chief Dragging Canoe, encouraged and supplied by the southern British superintendent John Stuart from Pensacola, initiated a campaign against white settlers from the Carolinas and Georgia in 1776. Yet his inability to gain alliance with the Creeks, who had made a separate pact of neutrality with the patriots, ultimately doomed his efforts. Militia forces from the three colonies and Virginia ripped through Cherokee country during the summer and fall of that year, prompting the older Cherokee chiefs to sue for peace. Sporadic outbreaks of conflict continued to wrack the region until after 1780, when Spanish campaigns against key posts at Mobile and Pensacola first disrupted supply lines and then closed them with the successive capture of those posts.

Creeks, Chickasaws, and Choctaws were each divided by internal factions as well, but the location of all three groups nearer British and Spanish forts and harbors enabled them to the principle belligerents against each other for tribal advantage and continued independence. The British superintendent John Stuart offered incentives to members of all three groups to guard the Mississippi and Gulf Coast against intrusion by rebellious merchants and raiders. Louisiana's Governor Gálvez complained periodically that Chickasaw raiders were firing on Spanish vessels as they navigated the Mississippi. Yet the British could not rely consistently on any of the three groups to provide consistent military support. All three placed the interests of their own communities first and refused to become mere auxiliaries to British military operations. When Gálvez captured Mobile and Pensacola, pro-British factions among the Chickasaws, Creeks, and Choctaws virtually melted into the southern forest as Spain became the dominant European force in the region.

Further east in Florida near St. Augustine, the fortunes of war pushed a large collection of southern Creek communities further along their development into a separate identity as Seminoles. "Seminole Creeks," as British agents often called them, remained some of Great Britain's most reliable native allies. Their economy prospered thanks to the steady British market for Seminole beef and deerskins. East Florida never developed into a theater of war, but when the Georgia patriot militia periodically threatened raids into Florida territory, the war chiefs responded readily to British calls for military assistance. Seminoles and other southern Creek bands incorporated runaway slaves from the war-torn South into their families, often by re-enslaving them into a somewhat milder form of servitude. Separate black maroon communities also formed in east Florida near Seminole villages. Over time the two groups learned to cooperate toward common goals of trade and defense, practices encouraged by both British and succeeding Spanish government officials. When the Peace Treaty of 1783 ceded all of Florida to Spanish rule, the Seminole economy remained tied to the British through Scottish traders that continued to control most of the trade.

14.3.10: The Loyalist Dilemma

No one knows for certain how many Americans actually supported the Crown during the Revolution. Some Loyalists undoubtedly kept silent and avoided making a public commitment that might have led banishment or loss of property. But for many persons, neutrality proved impossible. Some wealthy colonists, such as the wealthy West Indian planter John Vassal who resided in Cambridge, Massachusetts, left their homes early in the fighting expecting to return after the British army quelled the radicals. Most of these, like Vassal, forfeited their property in

America and never returned. Some served as spies and informers. Others, like the former Massachusetts governor Thomas Hutchinson, served as imperial office holders. Yet in the main, however, they came from all ranks and backgrounds.

Many ordinary Loyalists served the British cause as militiamen and partisans. During Burgoyne's campaign of 1777, for example, thousands of farmers joined redcoat and Loyalist Iroquois troops under Brigadier General Barrimore St. Leger on a supporting campaign down the New York's Mohawk River in an attempt to join forces with the hapless Burgoyne at Albany. After the defeat of Saratoga, many of these farmers retreated into Upper Canada for safety. By the war's end, the English-speaking population of former New Englanders and New Yorkers in Upper Canada had reached nearly 30,000, forming the base of what eventually became the province of Ontario.

In total, nearly 100,000 men and women permanently left America. In addition to those who resettled to Upper Canada, many moved to the maritime region that included Nova Scotia, New Brunswick, Prince Edward Island, and Labrador. Others relocated to England, the West Indies, or Africa.

The political ideology of the Loyalists did not differ substantially from that of their opponents. Like other Americans, they believed that men and women were entitled to life, liberty, and the pursuit of happiness. The Loyalists were convinced, however, that independence would destroy these values by promoting disorder. By turning their backs on Britain, a source of tradition and stability, the rebels seemed to have encouraged licentiousness, even anarchy, in the streets. The "Sons of Liberty . . . did not deserve the name, for it was evident all they wanted was liberty from oppression that they might have liberty to oppress!"

The Loyalists were caught in a difficult squeeze. The British never quite trusted them. After all, they were Americans. During the early stages of the war, Loyalists organized militia companies and hoped to pacify large areas of the countryside with the support of the regular army. The British generals were unreliable partners, however, for no sooner had they called on loyal Americans to come forward than the redcoats marched away, leaving the Tories exposed to rebel retaliation. And in England, the exiles found themselves treated as second-class citizens. Although many of them received monetary compensation for their sacrifice, they were never regarded as the equals of native-born English citizens. Not surprisingly, the Loyalist community in London was gradually transformed into a collection of bitter men and women who felt unwelcome on both sides of the Atlantic.

Americans who actively supported independence saw these people as traitors who deserved their fate of constant, often violent, harassment. In many states—but especially in New York—revolutionary governments confiscated Loyalist property. Other friends of the king received beatings, or as the rebels called them, "grand Toory [sic] rides." A few were even executed as traitors, informers, or spies. According to one patriot, "A Tory is a thing whose head is in England, and its body in America, and its neck ought to be stretched."

Long after the victorious Americans turned their attentions to the business of building a new republic, Loyalists remembered a receding colonial past, a comfortable, ordered world that had been lost forever at Yorktown. Although many Loyalists eventually returned to their homes, a sizable number could not do so. For them, the sense of loss remained a heavy emotional burden. Perhaps the most poignant testimony came from a young mother living in exile in Nova Scotia. "I climbed to the top of Chipman's Hill and watched the sails disappear in the distance," she recounted, "and such a feeling of loneliness came over me that though I had not shed a tear through all the war I sat down on the damp moss with my baby on my lap and cried bitterly."

14.3.11: African Americans in the War

For the half million African American colonists, most of them slaves, the fight for independence took on special poignancy. After all, they wanted to achieve personal as well as political freedom, and many African Americans supported those who seemed most likely to deliver them from bondage. As one historian explained, "The black soldier was likely to join the side that made him the quickest and best offer in terms of those 'unalienable rights' of which Mr. Jefferson had spoken." Virginia governor Lord Dunmore was one of the first to recognize this when, in November 1775, he issued a proclamation declaring "all indentured Servants, Negroes, or others free that are able and willing to bear arms, they joining his Majesty's troops as soon as may be." Nearly eight hundred slaves ran away to Dunmore's lines in response to the offer. Virginians responded quickly, publishing a warning in the *Virginia Gazette* that slaves should not be tempted by Dunmore's proclamation to "ruin themselves." The patriot Virginia Convention soon offered a pardon to runaway slaves who would return to their masters. Even so, when Dunmore left Virginia in August 1776, he took three hundred runaways with him.

Other British commanders made similar offers to slaves throughout the war: General William Howe in 1777 when he invaded the Chesapeake and again shortly before Saratoga, General Henry Clinton when he invaded the south in 1778, and Lord Cornwallis when he captured Charles Town in 1780. News of approaching British forces regularly prompted slaves to escape their bonds and make a run for British lines. Some fled further to frontier regions, where they were adopted into native communities or formed maroon communities of their own. Others headed for occupied cities such as New York and Charlestown, where they pursued livelihoods in the local economy.

A large number also found service with the British army. In the South, especially in Georgia and South Carolina, more than ten thousand African Americans supported the British during the war. A few served in special combat units such as Dunmore's Ethiopian Regiment or the Black Carolina Corps, but most served as support troops. The Pioneer Corps was the primary such unit. Recruits there constructed military roads, bridges, and earthworks. They also engaged in demolition of strategic facilities such as bridges, stockades, and docks that the Continental army might use for attack or supply.

To be sure, the British were selective in their liberation of slaves, limiting this privilege only to those who ran from plantations owned by rebellious colonists. They sought to keep the slaves of Loyalists in bondage. Where possible, British ships carried cargos of slaves from Loyalist plantations to the West Indies where they could be more securely held. Thousands of southern slaves were transported from Savannah and Charles Town to Jamaica and Florida by their Loyalist masters between 1782 and 1784.

On the patriot side of the line, it is estimated that some five thousand African Americans took up arms to fight against the British. The Continental Army included two all-black units, one from Massachusetts and the other from Rhode Island. The law governing conscriptions allowed potential conscripts to offer substitutes in their place and many slaves filled this role, usually with a promise of freedom thrown into the bargain. In 1777, the constitution of the new Republic of Vermont cleared the way to recruit African Americans directly into local militias when it banned slavery, freeing males over the age of 21 and women 18 and older. In 1778, the legislature of Rhode Island voted to free any slave who volunteered to serve, because, according to the lawmakers, history taught that "the wisest, the freest, and bravest nations . . . liberated their slaves, and enlisted them as soldiers to fight in defence of their country." Other states followed suit.

Opportunities for slave uprisings were not limited to the rebellious mainland colonies. In the British West Indies, too, repercussions of the American Revolution affected many aspects of life. West Indian planters had come to rely on the mainland to supply food for their slave labor force (see Chapter 11), so the disruption of food shipments in the early war years precipitated shortages that generated widespread unrest. A great slave rebellion broke out in Jamaica in 1776 because, as one slave explained, "they were angry too much with the white people, because they had taken from them their bread." White planters worried that careless talk in favor of the American Revolution would be overheard by slaves, who would form their own ideas of what a war for freedom could mean. The need for regular troops to prosecute war on the mainland reduced the size of garrisons on the islands, spreading the forces thin and creating security vulnerabilities that slaves could sometimes exploit. Such opportunities grew more frequent as the war progressed, especially after the French Alliance engulfed the Caribbean in a more general war. British planters feared that French agents would foment rebellion among their slaves, and on occasion, both French agents and American privateers actually did so. The approach of the French also emboldened maroon communities in the islands to raid plantations.

The disruption of security made it possible for more runaways to join maroon communities.

The British West Indians responded to the shortage of troops able to serve just as their revolutionary counterparts on the mainland did: they recruited black troops slave and free into wartime military service. The need was acute, both because regular recruits were so desperately needed on the mainland and because of the catastrophic incidence of disease and death among British regulars sent to the Caribbean. Many black recruits from the islands were assigned to British units on the mainland, where they served as soldiers, sailors, and laborers in supporting roles.

The governor of Jamaica created a British army regiment of free blacks and free coloreds in 1778 that was reputedly the best on the island, "except the regulars." When the French threatened to invade Barbados in 1779, the legislature voted to arm the slaves with cutlasses and to ensure that free blacks were equipped with firearms. The need for sailors prompted the royal navy to accept black recruits, and captains cared little whether they had the permission of their masters or were runaways.

The War for Independence proved truly revolutionary for many African Americans on a personal level at the very least by opening a path to

Table 14.1 Major Battles of the Revolution

Battle	Date	Victor
Lexington	Apr. 19, 1775	British
Concord	Apr. 19, 1775	Americans
Bunker Hill	Jun. 17, 1775	Mixed Results
Montreal	Nov. 13, 1775	Americans
Quebec	Dec. 31, 1775	British
Brooklyn Heights	Aug. 27, 1776	British
White Plains	Oct. 28, 1776	British
Trenton	Dec. 26, 1776	Americans
Princeton	Jan. 3, 1777	Americans
Bennington	Aug. 16, 1777	Americans
Brandywine	Sept. 11, 1777	British
Saratoga, First Battle: Freeman's Farm	Sept. 19, 1777	Mixed Results
Philadelphia Captured	Sept. 26, 1777	British
Germantown	Oct. 4, 1777	British
Saratoga, Second Battle: Bemis Heights	Oct. 7, 1777	Americans
Charles Town	May 12, 1780	British
Camden	Aug. 16, 1780	British
Kings Mountain	Oct. 7, 1780	Americans
Cowpens	Jan. 17, 1781	Americans
Guilford Courthouse	Mar. 15, 1781	British
Yorktown	Aug. 30 to Oct. 18, 1781	Americans and French

freedom for themselves and their families. After the patriots had won the war, many who had obtained their freedom preserved it by leaving the United States, relocating to Nova Scotia, Upper Canada, and the British Isles, with some eventually resettling in Africa. Wartime exigencies prompted new state legislatures and courts to extend freedoms on at least a temporary basis that they might never have contemplated in peacetime. In some cases, these initial steps quickly led to more comprehensive legislation abolishing slavery.

14.4: Winning the Peace

14.4 Analyze the Treaty of Paris of 1783

Congress appointed a skilled delegation to negotiate a peace treaty: Benjamin Franklin, John Adams, and John Jay. According to their official instructions, they were to insist only on the recognition of the independence of the United States. On other issues, Congress ordered its delegates to defer to the counsel of the French government.

But the political environment in Paris was much different from what the diplomats had been led to expect. The French had formed a military alliance with Spain, and French officials announced that they could not consider the details of an American settlement until after the Spanish had recaptured Gibraltar from the British. The prospects for a Spanish victory were not good, and in any case, it was well known that Spain coveted the lands lying between the Appalachian Mountains and the Mississippi River. Indeed, there were even rumors afloat in Paris that the great European powers might intrigue to deny the United States its independence.

While the three American delegates publicly paid their respects to French officials, they secretly entered into negotiations with an English agent. The peacemakers drove a remarkable bargain, a much better one than Congress could have expected. The preliminary agreement, the Treaty of Paris of 1783, signed on September 3, not only guaranteed the independence of the United States; it also transferred all the territory east of the Mississippi River, except Spanish Florida, to the new republic. The treaty established generous boundaries on the north and south and gave the Americans important fishing rights in the North Atlantic. In exchange, Congress promised to help British merchants collect debts contracted before the Revolution and compensate Loyalists whose lands had been confiscated by the various state governments. Even though the Americans negotiated separately with the British, they did not sign a separate peace. The preliminary treaty did not become effective until France reached its own agreement with Great Britain. Thus did the Americans honor the French alliance. It is difficult to imagine how Franklin, Adams, and Jay could have negotiated a more favorable conclusion to the war. In the fall of 1783, the last redcoats sailed from New York City, ending 176 years of colonial rule.

14.5: Conclusion: Preserving Independence

14.5 Evaluate the challenges of nation building faced by Americans

The American people had waged war against the most powerful nation in Europe and emerged victorious. They had not done so alone, as most were well aware. The transatlantic alliances and cobelligerencies they had formed during the war had proven indispensable to the outcome. So had the crucial lines of clandestine supply that crossed the Atlantic from European ports to the Caribbean, along the eastern and Gulf coastlines, and up the great interior river systems to Washington's army and patriot militias.

The treaty marked the conclusion of a colonial rebellion, but it remained for the men and women who had resisted taxation without representation to work out the full implications of republicanism. What would be the shape of the new government? What powers would be delegated to the people, the states, and the federal authorities? How far would the wealthy, well-born leaders of the rebellion be willing to extend political, social, and economic rights?

For many Americans the challenge of nation building appeared even more formidable than waging war against Great Britain. As Philadelphia physician Dr. Benjamin Rush explained, "There is nothing more common than to confound the terms of American Revolution with those of the late American war. The American war is over, but this is far from being the case with the American Revolution. On the contrary, nothing but the first act of the great drama is closed."

Chronology

1773	Lord North's Government passes Tea Act (May)
1773	Bostonians hold Tea Party (December)
1774	Parliament punishes Boston with Coercive Acts (March-June)
1774	Parliament passes Quebec Act (May)
1774	First Continental Congress convenes (September)
1775	Battle of Lexington and Concord (April)
1775	Second Continental Congress (May)
1775	Battle of Bunker Hill (June)
1776	Declaration of Independence is signed (July)
1776	Washington defeated on Long Island (August)
1776	Battle of Trenton and Princeton (December)
1777	General Burgoyne surrenders at Saratoga (October)
1778	Congress ratifies Treaty of Amity and Commerce and Treaty of Alliance with France (May)
1779	Spain enters the conflict as a co-belligerent
1780	British take Charles Town (May)
1781	Cornwallis surrenders to Washington at Yorktown (October)
1783	Peace treaty signed in Paris

Chapter 15

Independence in an Atlantic World

Learning Objectives

15.1 Recognize how independence provided renewed confidence to America

15.2 Relate changes to American society with respect to liberty, equality, and republican virtues

15.3 Examine the effects of the Continental Congress's invitation for the states to adopt constitutions in May, 1776

15.4 Analyze the struggles of the government in the mid-1780s

15.5 Report the Constitutional reforms adopted in America in the late 1800s

15.6 Describe the campaign for ratification that began in America

15.7 Recognize the effects of Enlightenment-era thinking and British constitutional heritage on the federal constitution

In late August 1789, the ambassador from the United States to France, Thomas Jefferson, wrote to his friend James Madison about the revolution he was witnessing firsthand in Paris. He was excited. These events seemed to overthrow a very long tradition of monarchs and aristocratic privilege. Six weeks before, the people of the city had stormed the royal Bastille fortress. Its fall was more than a symbolic victory: it secured an enormous store of arms and ammunition that could be used to defend the National Constituent Assembly against royal forces, while radical legislators enacted sweeping changes in French government.

Jefferson had been anxious to receive official leave from Congress so he could return to Virginia to take care of pressing business, but at this moment he reconsidered, "this scene is too interesting to be left at present." French political leaders were laying plans to draft a new constitution with a separation of powers that included a limited executive branch, a bicameral legislature, and an independent judiciary. Though the details of this scheme remained sketchy, Jefferson was gratified to report that the new U.S. Constitution "has been professedly their model." Americans could not have "desired better dispositions toward us," he wrote, "than prevail in this assembly. Our proceedings have been viewed as a model for them on every occasion," and recent American writing on government and political theory "has been treated like that of the bible, open to explanation but not to question." As in the days of John Winthrop, America served as a beacon of reform for the nations of Europe.

The early months of the French Revolution proved heady times indeed for this erstwhile colonist from the far marches frontiers of the British empire, whose ideas and role in the modern world's first successful republican revolution had catapulted him to the center of world historical change. Jefferson departed Paris for home in the autumn of 1789, before the French disenchantment with new American political forms set in and their revolution took an even more radical and bloody turn. Yet from his perspective he had witnessed his ideals of liberty and natural rights spread throughout the Atlantic World and beyond, inspiring demands for independence and equality that soon struck even to the heart of slavery itself, an issue of some embarrassment for the founders of the American republic.

As Jefferson sailed back to Virginia that fall, he looked to the future of the United States with hope. Over the previous year, he had monitored the proceedings of the Constitutional Convention at Philadelphia. He filled his letters from France to James Madison with advice for about framing the new government. He searched the bookshops of Paris for the latest European treatises on political theory and shipped packages of books for his friend who was the chief architect of the new American system. Like many of the founding fathers, Jefferson harbored reservations about the outcome of the Constitutional Convention, but he expressed satisfaction that the new government had "ushered itself to the world as honest, masculine, and dignified." He also expressed his deep confidence in "his countrymen's" ability to resist any attempt at undermining the spirit of democracy. Contrary to the views of some historians who focus on the Constitution's conservative elements—the Electoral College and the indirect election of senators, for example—Jefferson continued to believe that the document preserved the liberty the people had fought for during the Revolution.

15.1: Independence in an Atlantic Context

15.1 Recognize how independence provided renewed confidence to America

Neither Jefferson nor any other American had been so confident in their radical experiment even a few years earlier. The Treaty of Paris of 1783 gained the new United States a far greater territory than anyone had expected, along with a range of commercial rights and concessions that awarded its merchants, planters, fishermen, and budding manufacturers a chance to develop a robust national economy. Independence also gave Americans renewed confidence in the rightness of their quest for liberty and the significance of their victory over Great Britain upon a world historical stage.

American leaders such as Thomas Jefferson, John Adams, and George Washington worried, however, that they might not successfully meet the challenge of securing a lasting republic of virtue and liberty, or develop a government capable of maintaining the unity of thirteen fractious republics. They understood that most revolutions end badly. Unity breaks down. Former allies turn their weapons on each other. Certainly, deep flaws in the structure of the national government were becoming ever more apparent as state legislatures dragged their feet at responding to appeals from Congress for funds to perform the basic responsibilities of government. The members of state legislatures—worried about their own sovereignty—seemed unable to lift their gaze above the petty concerns of their own constituencies. Potential fragmentation was not the only challenge. The territory won from Britain seemed too vast to govern effectively. Lack of ready access to domestic or international markets restricted the development of large-scale economic activity in the trans-Appalachian West. The new nation possessed a large merchant marine, but no navy capable of defending its commercial vessels from pirate attack or seizure by hostile nations. Its predatory imperial neighbors to the north and south were rumored to be plotting to ignore the treaties they had just signed and to carve up the bulk of the western lands between them.

15.1.1: Steps toward International Trade

Even though the United States experienced an economic depression that lasted much of the 1780s, the long-term prospects for trade seemed bright. Commerce figured centrally in the recovery. In 1785, British authorities gave the new nation most favored trade status with Great Britain, and all French and Dutch ports remained open as well. Such staples of pre-Revolutionary American trade as furs, tobacco, rice, indigo, and grain remained valuable commodities on the Atlantic market. American exports proved attractive beyond the Atlantic as well, as the 1784 voyage of the *Empress of China* demonstrated. That year, the financier Robert Morris partnered with a group of investors to provide financial backing for the ship's voyage from New York to Canton, China with a cargo of American goods. The enterprise represented a bold and innovative step for the United States. The vessel returned from Asia in May 1785 laden with Chinese products such as tea, silk, and porcelain, opening a lucrative trade link with Canton. American fisheries remained profitable as well, despite British restrictions on waters off Newfoundland and Nova Scotia.

Yet obstacles remained. One historian has observed that, as Great Britain sought to reorder its Atlantic empire after the loss of the thirteen mainland colonies, it often behaved as if it could get along entirely without its former North American possessions. This was nowhere more evident than in its ongoing closure of British West Indian ports to American commodities. The West Indian planters turned to other suppliers to feed its slaves, prolonging America's postwar

depression as farmers and merchants searched for new markets for their agricultural goods. British merchants were prohibited from owning a vessel built or repaired in a United States shipyard, depressing the shipbuilding industry. During the 1780s, American diplomats in London discovered that the British were in no hurry to treat the United States as anything other than a minor league player in world affairs.

The British navy also took a hands-off approach to the American merchant vessels it had once protected, leaving them vulnerable to capture by pirates and hostile nations. The Barbary States of Algiers, Tunis, and Tripoli took particular advantage of the newly independent nation's weakness at sea, demanding enormous sums in tribute for the right to trade on the Mediterranean Sea. Without naval protection, American vessels were vulnerable to seizure by Barbary corsairs and their captured crews condemned to languish for years in harsh servitude while the sultans demanded exorbitant ransoms for their release. In 1787, the sultan of Morocco agreed to forego such seizures in exchange for a gift from Congress of the princely sum of $10,000, but the other Barbary states demanded sums that Congress simply could not raise.

Trade even among the confederated states themselves could sometimes take the form of foreign transactions. Most states imposed individual protective tariff duties on Great Britain in retaliation for closing the West Indian ports to American shipping, but sometimes they charged fees on each other's coastal shipping as well. In 1787, New York imposed entrance and clearance fees on vessels from Connecticut and New Jersey, prompting each state to retaliate by boycotting New York products. Such interstate conflict contributed to growing disillusionment with the government of the new nation.

15.1.2: Challenges in the West

The extension of the new nation's boundaries to the Great Lakes and the Mississippi River was one of the great prizes of negotiation in the Treaty of 1783, yet the trans-Mississippi West remained a coveted object of powerful Atlantic rivals. Indeed, trans-Appalachian West had been a major point of contention among the thirteen states themselves. The vast tracts of western land represented the single greatest source of wealth for the new nation, not only in their value for agriculture but also in the lumber and mineral resources they contained.

Conflict over ownership of the West delayed ratification of the nation's first constitution, the Articles of Confederation, until 1781. Some states claimed land all the way from the Atlantic Ocean to the elusive "South Seas," in effect extending their boundaries to the Pacific coast by virtue of royal charters. State legislators—their appetites whetted by aggressive land speculators—anticipated generating large revenues through land sales. Virginia, Connecticut, New York, Pennsylvania, and North Carolina laid rival and overlapping claims to the Northwest Territory (the land west of Pennsylvania and north of the Ohio River) as well as to a large area south of the Ohio, beyond the Cumberland Gap, known as Kentucky. The western boundaries of other states, including Maryland, Delaware, and New Jersey, had been established many years earlier. Leaders from these states, worried that their people would be permanently cut off from the anticipated bounty, stubbornly refused to ratify the Articles of Confederation. Since all the states had made sacrifices for the common good during the Revolution, it seemed only fair that all states should profit from the fruits of victory, including the sale of western lands. Maryland's leaders in particular feared that if Congress did not void neighboring Virginia's excessive claims, then Marylanders would desert their home state in search of cheap Virginia farms, leaving Maryland an underpopulated wasteland.

Virginians scoffed at the pleas for equity. They suspected that behind the Marylanders' statements of high purpose lay the greed of speculators. Private land companies had sprung up before the Revolution and purchased large tracts from the Indians in areas claimed by Virginia (see Chapters 12 and 13). Earlier efforts to win recognition of these claims by Parliament had failed, but after the Declaration of Independence, the companies shifted the focus of their lobbying to Congress. By liberally distributing shares of stock, officials of the Indiana, Illinois, and Wabash companies gained powerful supporters such as Benjamin Franklin, Robert Morris, and Thomas Johnson, governor of Maryland. Such efforts to buy ratification by sharing the wealth eventually induced some of the states to join the Confederation, but Maryland held out until 1781, when the Virginians finally resigned their western claims. Like many others in the state, Jefferson worried about expanding Virginia beyond the mountains; with poor transportation links, it seemed impossible to govern such a large territory effectively from Richmond. And worse, the western settlers might even come to regard Virginia as a colonial power insensitive to their needs.

Maryland finally ratified the Articles on March 1, 1781, after Virginia agreed to cede its holdings north of the Ohio River to the Confederation on condition that Congress nullify the land companies' earlier purchases from the Indians. Congress required another three years to work out the details of the Virginia cession. Other landed states followed Virginia's example. These transfers established an important principle, for after 1781, it was agreed that the West belonged not to the separate states but to the federal government, which to this day exercises full sovereignty over ungranted acreage.

15.1.3: Conflict with Native Inhabitants

At the commencement of peace in 1783, the rapidly expanding settlements west of the Appalachians confronted the Confederation Congress with a problem of territorial administration similar to that Great Britain itself had encountered when it had gained dominion over this territory from France in the Treaty of 1763 (see Chapters 12 and 13). Congress claimed the whole territory by right of cession and conquest, and thousands of white settlers acted on this claim by staking out farms on Ohio Country soil. Western Indians such as the Shawnee, Wyandot, and Miami, however, regarded the land as their own. They did not consider themselves either vanquished peoples or parties to white men's treaties negotiated 3,000 miles away. Fearful of losing their own independence, they continued to fight against white encroachment onto their Ohio Country lands.

Congress initially responded to the growing tensions in the West much as Parliament had done twenty years earlier. In 1785, it authorized the formation of a seven-hundred-man army that established garrisons at Fort Harmar in Ohio near the confluence of the Muskingum and Ohio Rivers, Fort Knox at Vincennes on the Wabash in what is now Indiana, and Fort Finney between the two at the falls of the Ohio near present-day Clarksville, Indiana. The army's mission was threefold: to secure voluntary withdrawal of Indians progressively from the Ohio Country, with the ultimate goal of negotiating cession of all native lands in the Northwest Territory; to protect white settlements on lands already ceded and purchased; and to drive white squatters off both Indian land and tracts owned by Congress or land companies.

All three aims proved difficult to achieve with so small a force. Squatters forced off the land soon returned. At Fort Stanwix near present-day Rome, New York, the Iroquois disclaimed any right to the Ohio Country in a treaty signed on October 22, 1784. The next July, leading chiefs of the Wyandot, Delaware, Ottawa, and Chippewa nations agreed to cede lands southeast of a diagonal line stretching from the Cuyahoga River near present-day Cleveland to Vincennes. A contingent of Shawnee chiefs joined the cession at the Treaty of Fort Finney on January 31, 1786, but the Shawnee quickly repudiated the treaty and continued to mount raids on white settlements in Ohio.

15.1.4: British Troops in the Northwest

The Treaty of Paris provided for the withdrawal of British troops from garrisons in the newly ceded territories of the Northwest. Parliament, however, ordered its soldiers to remain on U.S. soil because Congress proved unable to enforce repayment of legitimate prewar debts, as the treaty also required. Many states simply refused to honor that provision. The Continental forces stationed in the Ohio Country were too few to force the British out.

As a consequence of the ongoing British presence, the Shawnee and their neighbors found themselves in a position similar to that of the western Indians who had played the French against the British before the Seven Years' War. British garrisons at Niagara, Detroit, and Mackinac Island served as refuge as well as trading posts where the Indians could obtain valuable manufactured goods, including guns and ammunition. Armed with British muskets, the western Indians maintained fierce resistance against white encroachment, usually through lightning raids on white settlements. The constant threat of attack kept settlers on their guard and resulted white reprisals in which militiamen destroyed native villages and burned crops.

Amid the frontier turmoil, Shawnee prophets and chiefs continued to labor for a pan-Indian union that could halt the expansion of white settlement in the trans-Appalachian West. The future Shawnee leader Tecumseh and his brother Lalawethika, later known as Tenskwatawa the Shawnee Prophet, were teenagers at this time. The two watched and learned from older pan-Indian visionaries among their people who reached out to nations throughout the West to appeal for union. Shawnee leaders communicated extensively with both Cherokees and Creeks in the Southeast in an effort to coax them into alliance against settlers and troops from the United States.

15.1.5: Spain and Indian Country in the Southeast

Native peoples of the Southeast enjoyed a similar position to those in the Ohio Country, thanks to the robust Spanish presence in Louisiana and Florida. Spain had entered the war in 1779, not as an ally of the United States but as a cobelligerent, fighting against a common British foe in pursuit of its own effort to strengthen and extend its own Atlantic empire. A separate peace with Great Britain gave Florida back to Spain, including the entire Gulf Coast to Louisiana, without specifying a northern boundary. The Spanish exploited this omission to press into lands claimed by the United States, forging trading alliances with Creeks, Choctaws, Chickasaws, and Cherokees that offered a powerful counterbalance to white American influence.

Spain soon closed the Mississippi River to navigators from the United States, cutting the access to Atlantic markets for western farmers and planters and diminishing the value of western lands. As a result, many of those living in Kentucky and along the Cumberland River in what became Tennessee began to debate the possibility of transferring their allegiance to Spain in order to gain access to the commerce that would enable them to prosper. Diplomatic efforts to reopen the Mississippi River foundered, and the Continental Army, already too weak to force the redcoats out of the Northwest, could do little.

As diplomatic and commercial challenges multiplied during the 1780s, it became increasingly clear that winning the peace of 1783 was only the beginning of the struggle to "assume the separate and equal station" with other "powers of the earth." Neither the words of the Declaration of Independence nor the ink on the Treaty of Paris could equal the economic and military might of the United States' two great Atlantic rivals. The authority of Congress under the Articles of Confederation likewise seemed powerless to marshal the states to unify against its foreign competitors for trade and sovereignty.

15.2: Liberty, Equality, and Republican Virtue

15.2 Relate changes to American society with respect to liberty, equality, and republican virtues

The challenges encountered in the Atlantic and the West after 1783 seemed to mirror flaws within the fabric of the new republic itself. Many Americans who read deeply in ancient and renaissance history knew that most republics had failed, often within a few years, only to be replaced by tyrants who cared not at all what ordinary people thought about the public good. Revolutionary figures such as Samuel Adams worried that the signs of such failure were appearing in the new nation all too soon. Too many Americans seemed to be substituting "luxury, prodigality, and profligacy" for "prudence, virtue, and economy." Too many leaders seemed to be intent on pursuing narrow self-interest at the expense of the public good. The language of liberty and equality itself had taken on a life of its own, producing disturbing changes in the new republican society that no one had fully anticipated.

Viewed from the opposing perspective, however, these developments so feared by classical republicans such as Adams may have been—at least in part—the expression of a liberated people taking advantage of their freedom to construct better lives. The older republican tradition contained an elitist element, a sense that a "better sort" of educated, genteel patriarchs knew what was best for their poorer, simpler neighbors and bore an obligation to protect them from their baser inclinations. Ordinary farmers and crafts-men, who had begun to take their equality and liberty for granted, took umbrage at such notions. The Revolution had inspired them to seize upon their natural right to pursue their own happi-ness in the economic sphere as well as in social and spiritual matters, and they rejected elitist ef-forts to tell them what they should buy, what they should wear, or what kinds of entertainment they should seek. The Revolutionary experience of freedom among white Americans had opened a fundamental debate about the meaning of equal-ity in American society, some of which remain as pressing today as during the 1780s.

15.2.1: Commerce and Corruption

Even before England signed a treaty with America, its merchants flooded American ports with consumer items and offered easy credit. Families that had postponed purchases of imported goods—either because of British blockade or personal hardship—now rushed to buy European finery. This sudden renewal of trade with Great Britain on such a large scale strained the American economy. Gold and silver flowed back across the Atlantic, leaving the United States desperately short of hard currency. When large merchant houses called in their debts, ordinary American consumers often found themselves on the brink of bankruptcy. "The disagreeable state of our commerce," observed James Wilson, an advocate of strong national government, has been the result "of extravagant and injudicious importation. . . . We seemed to have forgot that to pay was as necessary in trade as to purchase."

To many Americans—especially those leaders from propertied families—the purchase of British imports on credit signified a wild, destructive scramble for material wealth that would plunge

the nation back into the very "slavery" from which it had just emerged. Surely a republic could not long survive unless its citizens showed greater self-control. The drive for personal gain appeared to be spreading from the market to po-litical life as well. Far too many popularly elected representatives seemed to lack what men of prop-erty defined as real civic virtue: an ability to work for the common good rather than their private interests. Many ordinary Americans, however, suspected that such concerns on the part of the "propertied class" masked jealousy to maintain their own status at their countrymen's expense. As one Pennsylvania legislative leader put it: "No man has a greater claim of special privilege for his $100,000 than I have for my $5."

15.2.2: Equality and Reform

To many later historians, the postwar quest for equality has seemed relatively moderate in com-parison to what happened in the wake of later events such as the French or Haitian Revolutions. In the 1780s, however, the changes seemed pro-found. Even so committed a republican as George Washington had to be reminded that the slight-est hint of aristocratic pretention was contrary to republican principles. In 1783, he and the officers who had served during the Revolution formed the Society of the Cincinnati, a hereditary or-ganization of former officers of the Continental Army in which membership passed from father to eldest son. The soldiers meant no harm; they simply wanted to maintain old friendships. But anxious republicans throughout America let out a howl of protest, and one South Carolina legis-lator, Aedanus Burke, warned that the Society intended to create "an hereditary peerage . . . [which would] undermine the Constitution and destroy civil liberty." After an embarrassed Wash-ington called for appropriate reforms of the So-ciety's bylaws, the Cincinnati crisis receded. The fear of privilege remained, however, and wealthy

Americans dropped honorific titles such as "esquire." Lawyers of republican persuasion chided judges who had adopted the English custom of wearing great flowing wigs to court.

The appearance of equality was as important as its actual achievement. In fact, the distribution of wealth in postwar America was more uneven than it had been in the mid-eighteenth century. The sudden accumulation of large fortunes by new families made other Americans particularly sensitive to aristocratic display, for it seemed intolerable that a revolution waged against a monarchy should produce a class of persons legally, or even visibly, distinguished from their fellow citizens.

Republican ferment—particularly the belief that all adult white males were at least in theory equal—also encouraged many states to lower property requirements for voting. After the break with Great Britain, such a step seemed logical. As one group of farmers declared, no man can be "free & independent" unless he possesses "a voice . . . in the choice of the most important Officers in the Legislature." Pennsylvania and Georgia allowed all white male taxpayers to participate in elections. Other states were less democratic, but with the exception of Massachusetts, they reduced property qualifications. The reforms, however, did not significantly expand the American electorate. Long before the Revolution, an overwhelming percentage of free white males had owned enough land to vote. In any case, during the 1780s, republican lawmakers were not prepared to experiment with universal manhood suffrage; John Adams observed that if the states pushed the reforms too far, "New claims will arise, women will demand a vote . . . and every man who has not a farthing, will demand an equal vote with any other."

The most important changes in voting patterns were the result of western migration. As Americans moved to the frontier, they received full political representation in their state legislatures, and because new districts tended to be poorer than established coastal settlements, their representatives seemed less cultured, less well trained than those sent by eastern voters. Moreover, western delegates resented traveling so far to attend legislative meetings, and they lobbied successfully to transfer state capitals to more convenient locations. During this period, Georgia moved the seat of its government from Savannah to Augusta, South Carolina from Charles Town to Columbia, North Carolina from New Bern to Raleigh, Virginia from Williamsburg to Richmond, New York from New York City to Albany, and New Hampshire from Portsmouth to Concord.

Many Revolutionary Americans regarded the postwar persistence of established churches as a vestige of aristocratic privilege, which they labored to destroy. In New England, the Baptist minister Isaac Backus preached and agitated against the privileged legal status of the Congregational churches in Massachusetts and Connecticut, arguing that rulers had no right to interfere with the free expression of an individual's religious beliefs. As governor of Virginia, Thomas Jefferson strenuously advocated the disestablishment—the removal of state support—of the Anglican Church, an institution that had received tax monies and other benefits during the colonial period. Jefferson and his allies regarded the church's receipt of tax money as an aristocratic special privilege as well as a denial of religious freedom.

In 1786, Virginia cut the last ties between church and state with the passage of the Virginia Statute for Religious Freedom, authored by Thomas Jefferson. Other southern states disestablished the Anglican Church, but in Massachusetts and New Hampshire Congregational churches continued to enjoy special status. Moreover, while Americans championed toleration, they seldom favored philosophies that radically challenged Christian values. And they remained deeply suspicious of Catholics.

15.2.3: African Americans and the Republican Experiment

Revolutionary fervor forced some Americans to confront the most appalling contradiction to republican principles—slavery. The Quaker leader John Woolman (1720–1772) probably did more than any other white person of the era to remind people of the evils of this institution. A trip he took through the southern colonies as a young man forever impressed upon Woolman "the dark gloominess" of slavery. In a sermon, the outspoken humanitarian declared that "though we made Slaves of the Negroes, and the Turks made Slaves of the Christians, I believed that Liberty was the natural Right of all Men equally."

During the revolutionary period, abolitionist sentiment spread. Both in private and in public, people began to criticize slavery in other than religious language. No doubt, the double standard of their own political rhetoric embarrassed many white Americans. They hotly demanded liberation from parliamentary enslavement at the same time that they held several hundred thousand blacks in permanent bondage. Many enlightened Virginia and Maryland planters found this position painfully embarrassing. To be sure, they were also made more receptive to the idea of manumitting their slaves by the fact that the tobacco economy was in decline at this time. This had prompted many to shift to wheat production, which did not require large bodies of field workers other than at harvest time. They could make do with fewer unfree laborers. All this changed when cotton production in the lower South seemed to make slavery profitable once again.

By keeping the issue of slavery before the public through writing and petitioning, African American leaders demanded freedom. They reminded white lawmakers that their own people possessed the same natural right to liberty as did other Americans. In 1779, for example, a group of African Americans living in Connecticut pointedly asked the members of the state assembly "whether it is consistent with the present Claims, of the United States, to hold so many Thousands, of the Race of Adam, our Common Father, in perpetual Slavery."

The scientific accomplishments of Benjamin Banneker (1731–1806), Maryland's African American astronomer and mathematician, and the international fame of Phillis Wheatley (1753–1784), Boston's celebrated "African muse," made it increasingly difficult for white Americans to maintain credibly that African Americans could not hold their own in a free society. Wheatley's poems went through many editions, and after reading her work, the great French philosopher Voltaire rebuked a friend who had claimed "there never would be Negro poets." As Voltaire discovered, Wheatley "writes excellent verse in English." Banneker, like Wheatley, enjoyed a well-deserved reputation, in his case for contributions as a scientist. After receiving a copy of an almanac that Banneker had published in Philadelphia, Thomas Jefferson concluded "that nature has given to our black brethren, talents equal to those of the other colors of *men*."

In the northern states, there was no real economic justification for slavery, and white laborers, often recent European immigrants, resented having to compete in the workplace against slaves. This economic situation, combined with the acknowledgment of the double standard represented by slavery, contributed to the establishment of antislavery societies. In 1775, Franklin helped organize a group in Philadelphia called the Society for the Relief of Free Negroes. Unlawfully Held. John Jay, Alexander Hamilton, and other prominent New Yorkers founded a Manumission Society in 1785. By 1792, antislavery societies were meeting from Virginia to Massachusetts, and in the northern states at least, these groups, working for the same ends as various Christian evangelicals, put slaveholders on the intellectual defensive for the first time in American history.

In several states north of Virginia, the abolition of slavery took a number of different forms. Even before achieving statehood, Vermont drafted a constitution (1777) that specifically prohibited slavery for adult African Americans. In 1780, the Pennsylvania legislature passed a law effecting the gradual emancipation of slaves. Although the Massachusetts assembly refused to address the issue directly, the state courts took up the challenge and liberated the African Americans. By 1800, although New York was slow to reform the labor market, slavery was well on the road to extinction in the northern states.

These developments did not mean that white people accepted blacks as equals. In fact, in the very states that outlawed slavery, African Americans faced systematic discrimination. Free blacks were generally denied rights and responsibilities usually associated with full citizenship, such as voting, juries, and militia duty. They rarely enjoyed access to education, and in cities such as Philadelphia and New York, where African Americans went to look for work, they ended up living in segregated wards or neighborhoods. Even in the churches—institutions that had often spoken out against slavery—free African Americans were denied equal standing with white worshipers. Humiliations of this sort persuaded African Americans to form their own churches. In Philadelphia, Richard Allen, a former slave, founded the Bethel Church for Negro Methodists (1793) and later organized the African Methodist Episcopal Church (1816), an institution of great cultural as well as religious significance for nineteenth-century American blacks.

Even in the South, where African Americans made up a large percentage of the population, slavery disturbed thoughtful white republicans. Some planters simply freed their slaves, and, by 1790, the number of free blacks living in Virginia was 12,766. By 1800, the figure had reached 30,750. There is no question that this trend reflected the uneasiness among white masters. Richard Randolph, one of Virginia's wealthier planters, explained that he freed his slaves "to make restitution, as far as I am able, to an unfortunate race of bond-men, over whom my ancestors have usurped and exercised the most lawless and monstrous tyranny." George Washington also manumitted his slaves. To be sure, most southern slaveholders, especially those living in South Carolina and Georgia, rejected this course of action. Perhaps more significant, however, is the fact that no southern leader during the era of republican experimentation defended slavery as a positive good. Such overtly racist rhetoric did not become part of the public discourse until the nineteenth century.

The abolitionist impulse of the American Revolution reached beyond the boundaries of the United States. Former American slaves who managed to escape at the end of the war on evacuating British vessels frequently contributed to the growing abolitionist movement in Great Britain, telling their stories in organizational meetings and contributing narratives for publication. American sailors carried their new enthusiasm for liberty and equality to ports throughout the Atlantic World, and the slaves who conversed with them quickly connected republican rhetoric their own condition. British officials at Cape Coast Castle in what is now Ghana, for example, reported that visiting American seamen were spreading a "spirit of republican freedom and independence" along with the rum they had brought to trade.

African American seamen, both slave and free, spread the gospel of liberty and equality throughout the Atlantic with even greater fervor. Coastal planters often contracted their slaves to captains for service, and merchant vessels provided many other slaves with an opportunity to escape their bondage. Free blacks also found ready employment on oceangoing vessels. All enjoyed ample contact with slaves in the plantation ports from the Caribbean to the African coast. This strengthened and further extended an underground communication network that had been developing among the African Diaspora since the seventeenth century (see Chapters 4 and 11). The language of liberty spread throughout this network, sparking hope that a new day was coming when the bonds of slavery would be shattered forever.

Yet during the 1780s, the day of jubilee still lay beyond the horizon for most slaves in Atlantic World. In the American South, the economic incentives to maintain a servile labor force, especially after the invention of the cotton gin in 1793 and the opening up of the Alabama and Mississippi frontier, overwhelmed the initial abolitionist impulse. An opportunity to translate the principles of the American Revolution into social practice had been lost, at least temporarily.

15.2.4: "Remember the Ladies"

The revolutionary experience accelerated changes in the way ordinary people viewed the family. At the beginning of the eighteenth century, fathers claimed authority over other members of their families simply on the grounds that they were fathers. As patriarchs, they demanded obedience. If they behaved like brutal despots, so be it; fathers could treat wives and children however they pleased.

The English philosopher John Locke (1632–1704) powerfully undermined arguments of this sort, and at the time of the American Revolution, few seriously accepted the notion that fathers—be they tyrannical kings or heads of ordinary families—enjoyed unlimited powers over women and children. Indeed, people in England as well as America increasingly described the family in terms of love and companionship. Instead of duties, they spoke of affection. This transformation in the way men and women

viewed relations of power within the family was most evident in the popular novels of the period. Americans devoured *Pamela* and *Clarissa*, stories by the English writer Samuel Richardson about women who were the innocent victims of unreformed males, usually deceitful lovers and unforgiving fathers.

In this changing intellectual environment, American women began making new demands not only on their husbands but also on republican institutions. Abigail Adams, one of the generation's most articulate women, instructed her husband, John, as he set off for the opening of the Continental Congress: "I desire you would Remember the Ladies, and be more generous and favourable to them than your ancestors. Do not put such unlimited power into the hands of the Husbands." John responded in a condescending manner. The "Ladies" would have to wait until the country achieved independence. In 1777, Lucy Knox took an even stronger line with her husband, General Henry Knox. When he was about to return home from the army, she warned him, "I hope you will not consider yourself as commander in chief in your own house-but be convinced . . . that there is such a thing as equal command."

If Knox accepted Lucy's argument, he did so because she was a good republican wife and mother. In fact, women justified their assertiveness largely on the basis of political ideology. If survival of republics really depended on the virtue of their citizens, they argued, then it was the special responsibility of women as mothers to nurture the right values in their children and as wives to instruct their husbands in proper behavior.

Ill-educated women could not possibly fulfill these high expectations. They required education that was at least comparable to what men received. Scores of female academies were established during this period to meet what

ABIGAIL ADAMS

many Americans, men as well as women, now regarded as a pressing social need. The schools may have received widespread encouragement precisely because they did not radically alter traditional gender roles. After all, the educated republican woman of the late eighteenth century did not pursue a career; she returned to the home, where she followed a familiar routine as wife and mother.

During this period, women began to petition for divorce on new grounds. One case is particularly instructive concerning changing attitudes toward women and the family. In 1784, John Backus, an undistinguished Massachusetts silversmith, was brought before a local court and asked why he beat his wife. He responded that "it was Partly owing to his Education for his father treated his mother in the same manner." The difference between Backus's case and his father's was that Backus's wife refused to tolerate such abuse, and she sued successfully for divorce. Studies of divorce patterns in Connecticut and Pennsylvania show that after 1773 women divorced on about the same terms as men.

The war itself presented some women with fresh opportunities. In 1780, Esther De Berdt Reed founded a large volunteer women's organization in Philadelphia—the first of its kind in the United States—that raised more than $300,000 for Washington's army. Other women ran family farms and businesses while their husbands fought the British. And in 1790, the New Jersey legislature explicitly allowed women who owned property to vote.

Despite these scattered gains, republican society still defined women's roles exclusively in terms of mother, wife, and homemaker. Other pursuits seemed unnatural, even threatening, and it is perhaps not surprising, therefore, that in 1807 New Jersey lawmakers—angry over a close election in which women voters apparently determined the result—repealed female suffrage in the interests of "safety, quiet, and good order and dignity of the state."

15.3: Excess of Democracy?

15.3 **Examine the effects of the Continental Congress's invitation for the states to adopt constitutions in May, 1776**

When the Second Continental Congress convened in 1775, the delegates found themselves waging war in the name of a country that did not yet exist. As the military crisis deepened, Congress gradually—often reluctantly—assumed greater authority over national affairs, but everyone agreed such narrowly conceived measures were a poor substitute for a legally constituted government. The separate states could not possibly deal with the range of issues that now confronted the American people. Indeed, if independence meant anything in a world of sovereign nations, it implied the creation of a central authority capable of conducting war, borrowing money, regulating trade, and negotiating treaties. They began to draw up a plan for confederation, but it was soon overshadowed by similar efforts in each state to form new republican constitutions to replace the old colonial charter governments.

The Second Continental Congress's invitation to the states to adopt constitutions in May 1776 stimulated some of the Revolutionary period's boldest and most innovative experimentation in the forms and structure of governments and legal systems. Some of the best patriot minds poured their efforts into creating new republics out of the old colonies where they lived. Rhode Island and Connecticut already enjoyed republican government by virtue of their unique seventeenth-century charters that allowed the voters to select both governors and legislators. Eleven other states plus Vermont created new political structures, and their deliberations reveal how Americans living in different regions and reacting to different social pressures defined fundamental republican principles. Several constitutions were boldly experimental, and some states later rewrote documents that had been drafted in the first flush of independence.

A combination of enthusiasm for state constitution making and fear of centralized authority resulted in a balance of authority that strongly favored local governments over the national Congress. Indeed, while most state constitutions were ratified and in place by 1777, the Articles of Confederation languished unratified until 1781. Even after ratification, the states held sole authority for raising revenue and a virtual veto over much of the Confederation Congress's power. Even before peace was finalized, many national leaders were grumbling that shortsighted legislators elected by rural constituencies were holding the future of the nation hostage to narrow local interests. "The evils we experience flow from an excess of democracy," Elbridge Gerry of Massachusetts complained in 1787. "The people do not want virtue, but are the dupes of pretended patriots."

15.3.1: The Novelty of Written Constitutions

Despite disagreements over details, Americans who wrote the various state constitutions shared certain political assumptions that drew both from their study of the latest European theories of government and local insights drawn from more than a century of practical experience in colonial governance. First, they insisted on preparing written documents. For many, this seemed a natural development from the royal charters under which they had lived as colonists. Documents such as the Connecticut charter of 1662, for example (see Chapter 5), guaranteed that the colonists would enjoy the rights of Englishmen even after they had moved to the New World. Framers of the new state constitutions simply adapted written documents of the type on which they had always based fundamental jurisprudence to the new task of founding independent republican governments.

However logical the decision to produce written documents may have seemed to the Americans, it represented a major break with English practice. Political philosophers in the mother country had long boasted of Britain's unwritten constitution, a collection of judicial reports and parliamentary statutes. But this highly vaunted system had not protected the colonists from oppression; hence, after declaring independence, Americans demanded that their state constitutions explicitly define the rights of the people as well as the power of their rulers, an act of creative adaptation which has survived to shape deep present-day assumptions about how to ensure and preserve good government.

The authors of the state constitutions believed men and women possessed certain natural rights over which government exercised no control whatsoever. So that future rulers—potential tyrants—would know the exact limits of authority, these fundamental rights were carefully spelled out in eight of the original thirteen state constitutions. The length and character of these lists varied, but in general, they affirmed three fundamental freedoms: religion, speech, and press. They protected citizens from unlawful searches and seizures; they upheld trial by jury. George Mason, a shrewd political thinker who had written important revolutionary pamphlets, penned the most influential declaration of rights. It was appended to the Virginia Constitution of 1776, and the words were incorporated into other state constitutions as well as the famed Bill of Rights of the federal Constitution.

In almost every state, delegates to constitutional conventions drastically reduced the power of the governor, an office that had embodied royal authority under British rule (see Chapter 11) and regarded as a vestige of monarchy. The constitutions of Pennsylvania and Georgia abolished the governor's office. In four other states, terms such as "president" were substituted for "governor." Even those constitutions that retained the title of governor severely circumscribed the office's authority. Governors could make almost no political appointments. State legislators closely monitored the executive, but no governor other than that of Massachusetts possessed a veto over legislative decisions. Most early constitutions lodged nearly all effective power in the legislature. This decision expressed Americans' resolve to preserve the republican character of their new governments by keeping a tight reign on the executive. Indeed, state constitution-makers so feared the concentration of power in the hands of one person that they failed to appreciate that elected governors—like the representatives themselves—were now the servants of a free people.

The legislature dominated early state government. Most states authorized the creation of two houses, but even as they did so, some of the more demanding republicans wondered why America needed a senate or upper house at all. What social and economic interests, they asked, did that body represent that could not be more fully and directly voiced in the lower house? After all, America had just freed itself from an aristocracy.

Constitution-makers in Pennsylvania and Georgia acted on these observations by providing for a unicameral, or one-house, system. Since any male taxpayer could cast a ballot in these states, their legislatures became the nation's most democratic. Some leaders in those states soon began to suspect that their constitutions had gone too far. Certain checks on the popular will, however arbitrary they might have appeared, were necessary to preserve minority rights. In the end, such considerations helped the familiar two-house form to survive the Revolution.

15.3.2: "The Democratical Element"

Massachusetts did not adopt a constitution until 1780, after two earlier efforts drafted by the legislature failed to win ratification. The former Bay Colony finally succeeded through yet another creative adaptation: the remarkable political innovation of a specially elected convention of delegates whose sole purpose was the "formation of a new Constitution." Such an extraordinary body, convened outside the ordinary channels of election and legislation, seemed designed to approximate the theoretical process for forming government outlined by the philosopher John Locke. It also provided an eminently practical way of bypassing the long-recognized hazards of interest politics that dominated the Massachusetts political process and had derailed the previous constitutional efforts.

At the Massachusetts constitutional convention, John Adams took a leading role as the chief architect of the document. The framework of government included a house and senate, a popularly elected governor with a veto over legislative bills, and property qualifications for officeholders as well as voters. The constitution's most striking aspect, however, was the wording of its opening sentence: "We . . . the people of Massachusetts . . . agree upon, ordain, and establish," a powerful statement later echoed in the federal Constitution.

The Massachusetts experiment modeled what appeared to be a safer way to define fundamental rights. Rather than entrusting so important a task to ordinary legislators, the job required a convention of delegates who could legitimately claim to speak for the people.

The state constitutions attracted avid attention abroad. As soon as the documents were printed, they entered a transatlantic network of correspondence and publication to spread throughout Great Britain, the Continent, and the Atlantic littoral. Indeed, the historian Linda Colley has argued that the comparative speed of ocean and overland travel meant that "some Britons learned about the details of the new texts faster than some Americans." As another historian, David Armitage, has argued, "conjuring states out of colonies was the single most radical act of the American Revolution." Foreign observers eagerly pored over the contents of the new state constitutions to learn how their authors had adapted well-known theories of republican government into actual practice.

In 1780, however, no one knew whether the state experiments would succeed. A different type of person had begun to appear in public office who seemed, to the local gentry at least, a little poorer and less polished than they would have liked. One Virginian observed that the newly elected House of Burgesses in 1776 was "composed of men not quite so well dressed, nor so politely educated, nor so highly born as some Assemblies I have formerly *seen*." The observer approved of such change, for he believed that "the People's men," however plain they might appear, possessed honesty and sincerity. They were, in fact, representative republicans, people who insisted they were anyone's equal in this burgeoning society.

Other Americans were less optimistic about the nation's immediate prospects. The health of a small republic depended entirely on the virtue of its people. If they or their elected officials succumbed to material temptation, if they failed to comprehend the moral dimensions of political power, or if personal liberty threatened the rights of property, then the state constitutions were no more than worthless pieces of paper. The risk of excess seemed great. In 1778, a group of New Englanders, fearful that unbridled freedom would create political anarchy, observed, "The idea of liberty has been held up in so dazzling colours that some of us may not be willing to submit to that subordination necessary in the freest states."

15.3.3: Failed Adaptation: The Articles of Confederation

Concerns about excesses of liberty and overweening state power seemed increasingly justified as Americans turned to developing and conducting government on the national level. Too often, the very state governments into which leaders had poured so much energy and creativity seemed to lack the capacity to "submit to the subordination necessary." At the outset of independence in 1776, most delegates to Congress gave their first allegiance to the states they represented. They recognized some form of national confederation that could govern such matters as the prosecution of the war effort, and the conduct of diplomacy, but most assumed any such constitution would authorize only a loose federation of states. When a Congressional committee appointed to write the document recommended forming a strong central government, they were shocked. John Dickinson, who had written an important revolutionary pamphlet titled *Letters from a Farmer in Pennsylvania*, led the committee in drafting a document that called for equal representation from the states, taxing authority based on the population of each state, and congressional control of the western territories claimed by the separate states.

The Articles of Confederation that Congress finally approved in November 1777 bore little resemblance to Dickinson's original plan. The Articles jealously guarded the sovereignty of the states out of the republican conviction that power—especially power so far removed from the people—was inherently dangerous.

To preserve liberty, the drafters placed so many constraints on federal authority that many regarded the new government as powerless. The Articles provided for a single legislative body consisting of representatives selected annually by the state legislatures. Each state possessed a single vote in Congress. It could send as many as seven delegates, as few as two, but if they divided evenly on a certain issue, the state lost its vote. There was no independent executive and no veto over legislative decisions. The Articles also denied Congress the power of taxation, a serious oversight in time of war. The national government could obtain funds only by asking the states for contributions, called "requisitions," but if a state failed to cooperate—and many did—Congress limped along without financial support. When a British army marched through a state, creating a need for immediate military aid, people spoke positively about central government and urged support for requisitions, but as soon as the threat had passed, they sang a different tune. Amendments to this constitution required assent by all thirteen states. The authors of the new system expected the weak national government to handle foreign relations, military matters, Indian affairs, and interstate disputes.

Few greeted ratification of the Articles in March 1781 with much enthusiasm. Indeed, the small bureaucracy that soon took shape provoked further controversy. While Departments of War and Diplomacy were clearly necessary to win the peace, the new superintendent of the Department of Finance, Robert Morris (1734–1806), aroused suspicion. Although a brilliant manager, this freewheeling Philadelphia merchant hardly seemed a model republican. Morris mixed public funds under his control with personal accounts, and he never lost an opportunity to make a profit. While such practices were not illegal, his apparent improprieties undermined his own political agenda. He desperately wanted to strengthen the central government, but highly vocal critics resisted, labeling Morris a "pecuniary dictator."

15.3.4: Creating the Northwest Ordinance

Whatever the weaknesses of Congress may have been, it did score one impressive triumph. Congressional action brought order to western settlement, especially in the Northwest Territory, and incorporated frontier Americans into an expanding federal system. In 1781, the prospects for success did not seem promising. Thousands of men and women, most of them squatters, were pouring across the Appalachian Mountains. They built willy-nilly on parcels already owned by land companies, refused to pay, and drove the investors into bankruptcy. Millions of acres reverted to federal ownership, leaving the problem of surveying, registering, and selling the lands in the lap of a strapped Congress. Many viewed the frontier emigrants as "the least worthy subjects in the United States," in the words of New Englander Timothy Pickering. "They are little less savage than the Indians; and when possessed of the most fertile spots, for want of industry, live miserably." Such people might well exchange loyalty to the United States for access to Atlantic markets through Spanish New Orleans. Violence was endemic in the region. Congress could not provide sufficient federal troops to maintain order and had no administrative apparatus in place. It needed to act quickly to impose order.

Thomas Jefferson, then serving as a member of Congress, led the way in crafting an ingenious series of ordinances based on republican ideals. In effect, they maximized local initiative, inviting the people of a given western region to organize their own lands and governments within a federal framework. Jefferson's initial ordinance recommended carving ten new states out of the western lands located north of the Ohio River and recently ceded to the United States by Virginia. He specified that each new state establishes a republican form of government. When the population of a territory equaled that of the smallest state already in the Confederation, the region could apply for full statehood. In the meantime, free white males could participate in local government, a democratic guarantee that frightened some of Jefferson's more conservative colleagues. A second ordinance, passed in 1785 and called the Land Ordinance, established an orderly process for laying out new townships and marketing public lands.

The Northwest Ordinance of 1787, one of the final acts passed under the Confederation, capped these efforts by providing a new structure for government of the Northwest Territory. The plan authorized the creation of between three and five territories, each to be ruled by a governor, a secretary, and three judges appointed by Congress. When the population reached five thousand, voters who owned property could elect an assembly, but its decisions were subject to the governor's absolute veto. Once sixty thousand persons resided in a territory, they could write a constitution and petition for full statehood. While these procedures represented a retreat from the most democratic elements of Jefferson's original proposal, the Northwest Ordinance of 1787 guaranteed the settlers the right to trial by jury, freedom of religion, and due process of law. In addition, the act outlawed slavery, a prohibition that freed the future states of Ohio, Indiana, Illinois, Michigan, and Wisconsin from the curse of human bondage.

By contrast, settlement south of the Ohio River received far less attention from Congress. Long before the end of the war, thousands of Americans streamed through the Cumberland Gap into a part of Virginia known as Kentucky.

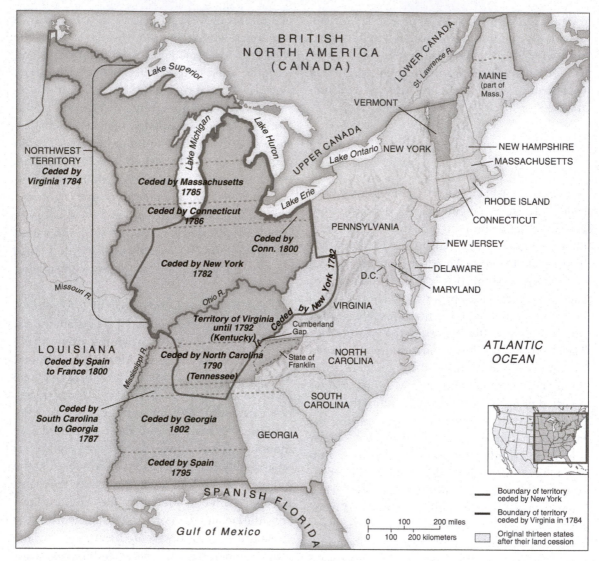

Map 15.1 Western Land Claims

The most famous of these was Daniel Boone. In 1775, the population of Kentucky was approximately one hundred; by 1784, it had jumped to thirty thousand. Speculators purchased large tracts from the Indians, planning to resell this acreage to settlers at handsome profits. In 1776, one land company asked Congress to reorganize the company's holdings into a new state called Transylvania. Nothing came of this request, but in 1784, an even more aggressive group of speculators carved the State of Franklin out of a section of present-day Tennessee, then claimed by North Carolina. Rival speculators prevented formal recognition of Franklin's government. By 1790, the entire region south of the Ohio River had been transformed into a crazy quilt of claims and counterclaims that generated lawsuits for many years to come.

15.4: "The Situation in Congress Is Truly Deplorable"

15.4 Analyze the struggles of the government in the mid-1780s

By the mid-1780s, the Confederation could claim several notable achievements. It brought order out of the chaos of conflicting western land claims. It also designed an administrative system through its various departments that ultimately survived the Articles.

Still, as anyone could see, the government was struggling. It lacked crucial powers. Its inability to regulate trade contributed to the slowness of the recovery from the postwar depression. So too did its lack of powers to tax, which hampered its ability to pay off the war debt and brought the Confederacy to the brink of default. The lack of fiscal stability made Continental currency worthless. Congress met irregularly. Some states did not even bother to send delegates, and pressing issues often had to be postponed for lack of a quorum. Postwar delegates regularly bemoaned the "deplorable state" of Congress. The nation even lacked a permanent capital, and Congress drifted from Philadelphia to Princeton to Annapolis to New York City, prompting one humorist to suggest that the government purchase an air balloon. This newly invented device, he explained, would allow the members of Congress to "float along from one end of the continent to the other" and "suddenly pop down into any of the states they please."

In response, an aggressive group of men announced that they knew how to save the Confederation. The nationalists—persons such as Alexander Hamilton, James Madison, and Robert Morris—called for major constitutional reforms. One of their earliest efforts was the Impost of 1781, an amendment allowing Congress to collect a 5 percent tax on imported goods sold in the states. Revenues would reduce the national debt. Twelve states accepted the amendment, but Rhode Island—where local interests argued that the tax would make Congress "independent of their constituents"—refused. One negative vote on this proposed constitutional change, and the taxing scheme was dead.

State leaders frankly thought the nationalists were up to no good. The "localists" especially distrusted Robert Morris. His profiteering as superintendent of finance appeared a threat to the moral fiber of the young republic. One person declared that, should a Congressional impost pass, Morris "will have all [the money] in his Pocket." When Morris proposed to create a national bank, Richard Henry Lee and Samuel Adams, men of impeccable patriotic credentials, decried the scheme. Such an institution would attract a flock of social parasites, the kind of people that Americans associated with corrupt monarchical government.

The nationalists regarded their opponents as economically naive. A country with the potential of the United States required a complex, centralized fiscal system. But for all their pretensions to realism, the nationalists of the early 1780s were politically inept. They underestimated the depth of republican fears, and in their rush to strengthen the Articles, they overplayed their hand.

A group of extreme nationalists even appealed to the army for support. To this day, no one knows the full story of the Newburgh Conspiracy of 1783. Officers of the Continental Army stationed at Newburgh, New York, worried that Congress would disband them without funding their pensions, lobbied intensively for relief. In March, they scheduled general meetings to protest the weakness and duplicity of Congress. The officers' initial efforts were harmless enough, but frustrated nationalists such as Morris and Hamilton hoped that if the army exerted sufficient pressure on the government, perhaps even threatened a military takeover, then stubborn Americans might be compelled to amend the Articles.

The conspirators failed to take George Washington's integrity into account. No matter how much he wanted a strong central government, he would not tolerate insubordination by the military. Washington confronted the officers directly at Newburgh, intending to read a prepared statement. Fumbling with his glasses before his men, he commented, "Gentlemen, you must pardon me. I have grown gray in your service and now find myself growing blind." The unexpected vulnerability of this great soldier reduced the troops to tears, and in an instant, the rebellion was broken. Washington deserves credit for preserving civilian rule in this country.

By 1785, the country seemed to have lost direction. The buoyant optimism that sustained revolutionary patriots had dissolved into pessimism and doubt. Many Americans, especially those who had provided leadership during the Revolution, agreed something had to be done. In 1786, Washington bitterly observed, "What astonishing changes a few years are capable of producing. Have we fought for this? Was it with these expectations that we launched into a sea of trouble, and have bravely struggled through the most threatening dangers?"

15.5: Constitutional Reform

15.5 Report the Constitutional reforms adopted in America in the late 1800s

The conviction of people such as Washington that the nation was in a state of crisis reflected broad tensions within republican thought. To be sure, they open elections and the right of individuals to advance their own economic well-being. Yet when these elements seemed to undermine social and political order, they expressed the fear that perhaps liberty had been carried too far. They began to doubt the wisdom of actions they had taken as recently as the 1770s, when they had transformed state governors into mere figureheads and weakened the Confederation in the name of popular liberties. By the mid-1780s, however, persons of property and standing saw the problem in a different light. Recent experience suggested to them that ordinary citizens did not in fact possess sufficient virtue to sustain a republic. The states had been plagued not by executive tyranny but by an excess of democracy, by a failure of the majority to preserve the property rights of the minority, by an unrestrained individualism that promoted anarchy rather than good order.

But how, they wondered, could men of republican principles strengthen central authority over so large a nation without opening the door to tyranny? According to the most widely accepted political wisdom of the age, they could not. Baron de Montesquieu (1689–1755), a French political philosopher of immense international reputation and author of *The Spirit of the Laws* (1748), declared flatly that a republican government could not flourish in a large territory. The reasons were clear. If the people lost direct control over their representatives, they would fall prey to tyrants. Large distances allowed rulers to hide their corruption; physical separation presented aristocrats with opportunities to seize power.

In the United States, Montesquieu's theories were received as self-evident truths. His writings seemed to demonstrate the importance of preserving the sovereignty of the states, for however much these small republics abused the rights of property and ignored minority interests, it was plainly unscientific to maintain that a republic consisting of thirteen states, several million people, and thousands of acres of territory could long survive.

15.5.1: The Adaptive Genius of James Madison

James Madison rejected Montesquieu's argument, and in so doing, he helped Americans to think of republican government in radical new ways. This soft-spoken, rather unprepossessing Virginian was the most brilliant American political thinker of his generation. Madison delved into the writings of a group of Scottish philosophers, the most prominent being David Hume (1711–1776), and from their works he concluded that Americans need not fear a greatly expanded republic. Yet as state constitution-makers had done before him, Madison also combined these theoretical insights with practical lessons drawn from American experience. He perceived that it was in small states such as Rhode Island that legislative majorities tyrannized the propertied minority. In a large territory, he explained, "the Society becomes broken into a greater variety of interest, of pursuits, of passions, which check each other, whilst those who feel a common sentiment have less opportunity of communication and contact."

Madison did not, however, advocate a modern "interest group" model of political behavior. The contending parties were incapable of working for the common good. They were too mired in their own local, selfish concerns. Rather, Madison thought competing factions would neutralize each other, leaving the business of running the central government to the ablest, most virtuous persons the nation could produce. In other words, Madison's federal system was not a small state writ large; it was something entirely different, a government based on the will of the people and yet detached from their narrowly based demands. This thinking formed the foundation of Madison's most famous political essay, *The Federalist* No. 10.

15.5.2: Overhauling the Articles

A concerted movement to overhaul the Articles of Confederation began in 1786, when Madison and his friends persuaded the Virginia assembly to recommend a convention to explore the creation of a unified system of "commercial regulations." Congress supported the idea. In September, delegates from five states arrived in Annapolis, Maryland, to discuss issues that extended far beyond commerce. The occasion provided strong nationalists with an opportunity to hatch an even bolder plan. The Annapolis delegates advised Congress to hold a second meeting in Philadelphia "to take into consideration the situation of the United States, to devise such further provisions as shall appear to them necessary to render the constitution of the Federal Government adequate to the exigencies of the Union." Whether staunch states' rights advocates in Congress knew what was afoot is not clear. In any case, Congress authorized a grand convention to gather in May 1787.

Events played into Madison's hands. Soon after the Annapolis meeting, an uprising known as Shays's Rebellion, involving several thousand impoverished farmers, shattered the peace of western Massachusetts. No matter how hard these men worked the soil, they always found themselves in debt to eastern creditors. They complained of high taxes, of high interest rates, and, most of all, of a state government insensitive to their problems. In 1786, Daniel Shays, a veteran of the Battle of Bunker Hill, and his armed neighbors closed a county courthouse where creditors were suing to foreclose farm mortgages. At one point, the rural insurgents threatened to seize the federal arsenal located at Springfield. Congress did not have funds sufficient to support an army, and the arsenal might have fallen had not a group of wealthy Bostonians raised an army of four thousand troops to put down the insurrection.

For the Nationalists throughout the United States, Shays's Rebellion symbolized the breakdown of law and order that they had long predicted. "Great commotions are prevailing in Massachusetts," Madison wrote. "An appeal to the sword is exceedingly dreaded." The time had come for sensible people to speak up for a strong national government. The unrest in Massachusetts persuaded persons who might otherwise have ignored the Philadelphia meeting to participate in drafting a new constitution.

15.5.3: The Philadelphia Convention

The Philadelphia Convention, like that of Massachusetts in 1780, represented a creative, practical response to the impasse that had prevented earlier efforts to reform the Articles of Confederation. In the spring of 1787, fifty-five men representing twelve states traveled to Philadelphia. Rhode Island refused to take part in the proceedings, a decision that Madison attributed to its "wickedness and folly." The delegates were practical people—lawyers, merchants, and planters—many of whom had fought in the Revolution and served in the Congress of the Confederation. The majority were in their 30s or 40s. The gathering included such prominent participants as George Washington, James Madison, George Mason, Robert Morris, James Wilson, John Dickinson, Benjamin Franklin, and Alexander Hamilton. John Adams and Thomas Jefferson were away conducting diplomacy in Europe; Patrick Henry, a localist suspicious of strong central government, remained in Virginia, announcing he "smelled a rat."

As soon as the Constitutional Convention opened on May 25, the delegates made several procedural decisions of the utmost importance. First, they voted "that nothing spoken in the House be printed, or communicated without leave." The rule was stringently enforced. Sentries guarded the doorways to keep out uninvited visitors, windows stayed shut in the sweltering heat to prevent sound from either entering or leaving the chamber, and members were forbidden to copy the daily journal without official permission. As Madison explained, the secrecy rule saved "both the convention and the community from a thousand erroneous and perhaps mischievous reports." It also has made it extremely difficult for modern lawyers and judges to determine exactly what the delegates had in mind when they wrote the Constitution.

In a second procedural move, the delegates decided to vote by state, but in order to avoid the kinds of problems that had plagued the Confederation, they ruled that key proposals needed the support of only a majority instead of the nine states required under the Articles.

15.5.4: Structuring a National Government

Even before all the delegates had arrived, Madison drew up a framework for a new federal system known as the Virginia Plan. Madison wisely persuaded Edmund Randolph, Virginia's popular governor, to present this scheme to the convention on May 29. Randolph claimed that the Virginia Plan merely revised sections of the Articles, but everyone, including Madison, knew better. "My ideas," Madison confessed, "strike . . . deeply at the old Confederation." He was determined to restrain the state assemblies, and in the original Virginia Plan, Madison gave the federal government power to veto state laws.

The Virginia Plan set the agenda for the Convention. It envisioned a national legislature consisting of two houses, one elected *directly* by the people and the other chosen by the first house from nominations made by the state assemblies. Representation in both houses was proportional to the state's population. The Virginia Plan also provided for an executive elected by Congress. Since most delegates at the Philadelphia convention sympathized with the nationalist position, Madison's blueprint for a strong federal government initially received broad support, and the Virginia Plan was referred to further study and debate.

The Virginia Plan had been pushed through the convention so fast that opponents hardly had an opportunity to present their objections. On June 15, they spoke up. William Paterson, a New Jersey lawyer, advanced the so-called New Jersey Plan, a scheme that retained the unicameral legislature in which each state possessed one vote and that at the same time gave Congress extensive new powers to tax and regulate trade. Paterson argued that these revisions, while more modest than Madison's plan, would have greater appeal for the American people. The delegates listened politely and then soundly rejected the New Jersey Plan on June 19. Indeed, only New Jersey, New York, and Delaware voted in favor of Paterson's scheme.

Rejection of this framework did not resolve the most controversial issue before the convention. Paterson and others feared that under the Virginia Plan, small states would lose their separate identities. These delegates maintained that unless each state possessed an equal vote in Congress, the small states would find themselves at the mercy of their larger neighbors.

This argument outraged the delegates who favored a strong federal government. It awarded too much power to the states. "For whom [are we] forming a Government?" Wilson cried. "Is it for men, or for the imaginary beings called States?" It seemed absurd to claim that the 68,000 people of Rhode Island should have the same voice in Congress as Virginia's 747,000 inhabitants.

15.5.5: The "Grand Committee" Saves the Convention

Mediation clearly offered the only way to overcome what Roger Sherman, a Connecticut delegate, called "a full stop." On July 2, a "grand committee" of one person from each state was elected by the convention to resolve persistent differences between the large and small states. Benjamin Franklin, at age 81 the oldest delegate, served as chair of the committee, while the two fiercest supporters of proportional representation based on population, Madison and Wilson, were left off. The committee recommended that the states be equally represented in the upper house of Congress, whereas representation was to be proportionate in the lower house. Only the lower house could initiate money bills. Franklin's committee also decided that one member of the lower house should be selected for every thirty

thousand inhabitants of a state. Southern delegates insisted that this number include slaves. In the so-called three-fifths rule, the committee agreed that for the purpose of determining representation in the lower house, slaves would be counted, but not as much as free persons. For every five slaves, a congressional district received credit for three free voters, a deal which gave the South much greater power in the new government than it would have otherwise received. As with most compromise solutions, this one fully satisfied no one. It did, however, overcome a major impasse, and after the small states gained an assured voice in the upper house, the Senate, they cooperated enthusiastically in creating a strong central government.

15.5.6: Tragic Compromise

During the final days of August, a deeply disturbing issue came before the convention. It was a harbinger of the great sectional crisis of the nineteenth century. Many northern representatives detested the slave trade and wanted it to end immediately. They despised the three-fifths ruling that seemed to award slaveholders extra power in government simply because they owned slaves. "It seemed now to be pretty well understood," Madison jotted in his private notes, "that the real difference of interest lay, not between the large and small but between the Northern and Southern States. The institution of slavery and its consequences formed a line of discrimination."

Whenever northern delegates—and on this point they were by no means united—pushed too aggressively, Southerners threatened to bolt the convention, thereby destroying any hope of establishing a strong national government. Curiously, even recalcitrant Southerners avoided using the word "slavery." They seemed embarrassed to call the institution by its true name, and in the Constitution itself, slaves were described as "other persons," "such persons," and "persons held to Service or Labour," in other words, as everything but slaves.

Largely ignoring northern attacks, the delegates reached an uneasy compromise on the continuation of the slave trade. Southerners feared that the new Congress would pass commercial regulations adversely affecting the planters—taxes on the export of rice and tobacco, for example. They demanded, therefore, that no trade laws be passed without a two-thirds majority of the federal legislature. They backed down on this point, however, in exchange for guarantees that Congress would not interfere with the slave trade until 1808. The South even came away with a clause assuring the return of fugitive slaves. "We have obtained," Charles Cotesworth Pinckney told the planters of South Carolina, "a right to recover our slaves in whatever part of America they may take refuge, which is a right we had not before."

Although these deals disappointed many Northerners, they conceded that establishing a strong national government was of more immediate importance than ending the slave trade. "Great as the evil is," Madison wrote, "a dismemberment of the union would be worse."

15.5.7: The Final Draft

On July 26, the convention formed a Committee of Detail, a group who prepared a rough draft of the Constitution. After the committee completed its work—writing a document that still, after so many hours of debate, preserved the fundamental points of the Virginia Plan—the delegates reconsidered each article. The task required the better part of a month.

During these sessions, the members of the convention concluded that the president, as they now called the executive, should be selected by an electoral college, a body of prominent men in each state chosen by local voters. The number of "electoral" votes held by each state equaled its number of representatives and senators. This awkward device guaranteed that the president would not be indebted to the Congress for his office. Whoever received the second largest number of votes in the Electoral College automatically became vice president. In the event that no person received a majority of the votes, the election would be decided by the lower house—the House of Representatives—with each state casting a single vote. Delegates also armed the chief executive with veto power over legislation as well as the right to nominate judges. Both privileges, of course, would have been unthinkable a decade earlier, but the state experiments revealed the importance of having an independent executive to maintain a balanced system of republican government.

As the meeting was concluding, some delegates expressed concern about the absence in the Constitution of a bill of rights. Such declarations had been included in most state constitutions, and Virginians such as George Mason insisted that the states and their citizens needed explicit protection from possible excesses by the federal government. While many delegates sympathized with Mason's appeal, they noted that the hour was late and, in any case, that the proposed Constitution provided sufficient security for individual rights. During the hard battles over ratification, the delegates to the convention may have regretted passing over the issue so lightly.

15.5.8: We, the People

The delegates adopted an ingenious procedure for ratification, yet another creative application of theory to the practical realities of local interest-based politics which could very well have undone the Convention's work. Instead of submitting the Constitution to the various state legislatures, all of which had a vested interest in maintaining the status quo and most of which had two houses, either of which could block approval, they called for the election of thirteen state conventions especially chosen to review the new federal government. The delegates may have picked up this idea from the Massachusetts experiment of 1780. Moreover, the Constitution would take effect after the assent of only nine states. There was no danger, therefore, that the proposed system would fail simply because a single state like Rhode Island withheld approval. Gouverneur Morris of Pennsylvania, devised the brilliant phrase "We the People of the United States" to accommodate both the innovation of state ratifying conventions and the reduced number of states required for ratification. The new nation was a republic of the people, not of the states.

On September 17, thirty-nine men signed the Constitution. A few members of the convention, like Mason, could not support the document. Others had already gone home. For more than three months, Madison had served as the convention's driving intellectual force. He now generously summarized the experience: "There never was an assembly of men, charged with a great and arduous trust, who were more pure in their motives, or more exclusively or anxiously devoted to the object committed to them."

15.6: The Campaign for Ratification

15.6 Describe the campaign for ratification that began in America

Supporters of the Constitution recognized that ratification would not be easy. After all, the convention had been authorized only to revise the Articles. Instead it produced a new plan that fundamentally altered relations between the states and the central government. The delegates dutifully dispatched copies of the Constitution to the Congress of Confederation, then meeting in New York City, and that powerless body referred the document to the separate states without any specific recommendation. The fight for ratification had begun.

15.6.1: Federalists and Anti-Federalists

Proponents of the Constitution enjoyed great advantages over the unorganized opposition. In the contest for ratification, they took no chances. Their most astute move was the adoption of the label Federalist. The term cleverly suggested that they stood for a confederation of states rather than for the creation of a supreme national authority. Critics of the Constitution, who tended to be somewhat poorer, less urban, and less well educated than their opponents, cried foul, but they were stuck with the name Anti-Federalist. The misleading term made their cause seem a rejection of the very notion of a federation of the states.

The Federalists recruited the most prominent public figures of the day. In every state convention, speakers favoring the Constitution were more polished and more fully prepared than were their opponents. In New York, the campaign to win ratification sparked publication of *The Federalist*, a brilliant series of essays written by Madison, Hamilton, and Jay during the fall and winter of 1787 and 1788. The nation's newspapers threw themselves overwhelmingly behind the new government. In some states, the Federalists adopted tactics of questionable propriety in order to gain ratification. In Pennsylvania, for example, they achieved a legal quorum for a crucial vote by dragging several opposition delegates into the meeting from the streets. In New York, Hamilton intimidated upstate Anti-Federalists with threats that New York City would secede from the state unless the state ratified the Constitution.

In these battles, the Anti-Federalists articulated a political philosophy that had broad popular appeal. Like the extreme republicans who drafted the first state constitutions, the Anti-Federalists were deeply suspicious of political power. During the debates over ratification, they warned that public officials, however selected, would be constantly scheming to expand their authority. The preservation of individual liberty required constant vigilance. It seemed obvious that the larger the republic, the greater the opportunity for political corruption. Local voters could not possibly know what their representatives in a distant national capital were doing.

Anti-Federalists demanded direct, personal contact with their representatives. They argued that elected officials should reflect the character of their constituents as closely as possible. It seemed unlikely that in large congressional districts, the people would be able to preserve such close ties with their representatives. According to the Anti-Federalists, the Constitution favored persons wealthy enough to have forged a reputation that extended beyond a single community. Samuel Chase told the members of the Maryland ratifying convention that under the new system, "the distance between the people and their representatives will be so great that there is no probability of a farmer or planter being chosen . . . only the *gentry*, the *rich*, and the well-born will be elected."

Federalist speakers mocked their opponents' localist perspective. The Constitution deserved general support precisely because it ensured that future Americans would be represented by "natural aristocrats," individuals possessing greater insights, skills, and training than did the ordinary citizen. These talented leaders, the Federalists insisted, could discern the interests of the entire population.

It would be a mistake, however, to see the Anti-Federalists as "losers" or as persons who could not comprehend social and economic change. Although their rhetoric echoed an older moral view of political culture, they accepted more easily than did many Federalists a liberal marketplace in which ordinary citizens competed as equals with the rich and well born. They believed the public good was best served by allowing individuals like themselves to pursue their own private interests. That is what they had been doing on the local level during the 1780s, and they resented the imposition of elite controls over their affairs.

The Constitution drew support from many different types of people. In general, Federalists lived in more commercialized areas than did their opponents. In the cities, artisans as well as merchants called for ratification, while those farmers who were only marginally involved in commercial agriculture frequently voted Anti-Federalist.

Despite passionate pleas from Patrick Henry and other Anti-Federalists, most state conventions quickly adopted the Constitution. Delaware acted first (December 7, 1787), and within eight months of the Philadelphia meeting, eight of the nine states required to launch the government had ratified the document. The contests in Virginia (June 1788) and New York (July 1788) generated bitter debate, but they too joined the union, leaving only North Carolina and Rhode Island outside the United States. Eventually (November 21, 1789, and May 29, 1790), even these states ratified the Constitution. Still, the vote had been very close. The Constitution was ratified in New York by a tally of 30 to 27, in Massachusetts by 187 to 168, and in Virginia by 89 to 79. A swing of a few votes in several key states could have defeated the new government.

While the state conventions sparked angry rhetoric, Americans soon closed ranks behind the Constitution. An Anti-Federalist who represented one Massachusetts village explained that "he had opposed the adoption of this Constitution; but that he had been overruled . . . by a majority of wise and understanding men [and that now] he should endeavor to sow the seeds of union and peace among the people he represented."

15.6.2: The Bill of Rights

The first ten amendments to the Constitution are the major legacy of the Anti-Federalist argument. In almost every state convention, opponents of the Constitution pointed to the need for greater protection of individual liberties, rights that people presumably had possessed in a state of nature. "It is necessary," wrote one Anti-Federalist, "that the sober and industrious part of the community should be defended from the rapacity and violence of the vicious and idle. A bill of rights, therefore, ought to set forth the purposes for which the compact is made, and serves to secure the minority against the usurpation and tyranny of the majority." The list of fundamental rights varied from state to state, but most Anti-Federalists demanded specific guarantees for jury trial and freedom of religion. They wanted prohibitions against cruel and unusual punishments. There was also considerable, though not universal, support for freedom of speech and freedom of the press.

During the ratification debates, Madison and others regarded the proposals with little enthusiasm. In *The Federalist* No. 84, Hamilton bluntly reminded the American people that "the constitution is itself . . . a BILL OF *RIGHTS*." But after the adoption of the Constitution had been assured, Madison moderated his stand. If nothing else, passage of a bill of rights would appease able men such as George Mason and Edmund Randolph, who might otherwise remain alienated from the new federal system.

The crucial consideration was caution. A number of people throughout the nation advocated calling a second constitutional convention, one that would take Anti-Federalist criticism into account. Madison wanted to avoid such a meeting, and he feared that some members of the first Congress might use a bill of rights as an excuse to revise the entire Constitution or to promote a second convention.

Madison carefully reviewed these recommendations as well as the various declarations of rights that had appeared in the early state constitutions, and on June 8, 1789, he placed before the House of Representatives a set of amendments designed to protect individual rights from government interference. Madison told the members of Congress that the greatest dangers to popular liberties came from "the majority [operating] against the minority." A committee compressed and revised his original ideas into ten amendments that were ratified and became known collectively as the Bill of Rights. For many modern Americans these amendments are the most important section of the Constitution.

The Bill of Rights protected the freedoms of assembly, speech, religion, and the press; guaranteed speedy trial by an impartial jury; preserved the people's right to bear arms; and prohibited unreasonable searches. Other amendments dealt with legal procedure. Some opponents of the Constitution urged Congress to provide greater safeguards for states' rights, but Madison had no intention of backing away from a strong central government. Only the Tenth Amendment addressed the states' relation to the federal system. This crucial article, designed to calm Anti-Federalist fears, specified that those "powers not delegated to the United States by the Constitution nor prohibited by it to the States, are reserved to the States respectively, or to the people."

On September 25, 1789, the Bill of Rights passed both houses of Congress and by December 15, 1791, the amendments had been ratified by three-fourths of the states. Madison was justly proud of his achievement. He had effectively secured individual rights without undermining the Constitution. When he asked his friend Thomas Jefferson for his opinion of the Bill of Rights, Jefferson responded with typical republican candor: "I like [it] . . . as far as it goes; but I should have been for going further."

15.7: A New Order for the Ages

15.7 Recognize the effects of Enlightenment-era thinking and British constitutional heritage on the federal constitution

By 1789, one phase of American political experimentation had come to an end. Leaders at both the state and national levels had labored to build their new governmental institutions for a promising future by drawing on the best Enlightenment-era thinking and the best from their British constitutional heritage. Bemused British observers noted that the resulting federal Constitution "preserved a republican government" that remained "yet in some measure similar to our own." The Parliamentary leader Charles James Fox was even more explicit in noting that the Constitution's authors "preserved as much as they possibly could of the old form of their governments . . . monarchy, aristocracy, and democracy blended, though under a different name."

British leaders of the period, still smarting from the loss of their mainland American empire, expressed skepticism that a written frame of government would prove either as enduring or as adaptable as their unwritten Constitution. Nevertheless, they perused the document with great interest as British printers all over the empire churned out copies for an avid reading public. French printers quickly followed suit, and within a few years, a vast, interconnected network of printing and distribution was circulating copies of the Constitution throughout the Continent, the British Isles, and the Atlantic World. Many theorists remained uncertain for decades to come that governments based upon written constitutions would succeed, and

indeed, the United States itself faced a number of grave Constitutional crises. Only after its survival through the great Civil War of 1861–1865 did the question seem resolved.

In his first inaugural address on April 30, 1789, George Washington reminded those he pointedly called his "fellow citizens" that they were conducting this experiment in republicanism before a global audience. The stakes could not be higher. The world's respect for the new nation, and the global cause of freedom itself, hung upon the Constitution's success. "The preservation of the sacred fire of liberty, and the destiny of the Republican model of Government," he warned, "are justly considered as deeply, perhaps as finally staked, on the experiment entrusted to the hands of the American people." To win the world's respect would take decades of nation-building, arduous diplomacy and a second war with Great Britain. Yet by the time of the U.S. Jubilee celebration on July 4, 1826, the Constitution had inspired more than seventy new imitators, including the four French constitutions of the 1790s and those of Haiti, Mexico, the Netherlands, Poland, Switzerland, and Venezuela, to name a few. The world's admiration for the Constitution was clear. Whether the stakes of the constitutional experiment would be achieved remained to be seen. Indeed, it remains so still.

Chronology

1776	Second Continental Congress authorizes colonies to create republican governments (May)
1776	Eight states draft new constitutions (following months)
1777	Congress accepts Articles of Confederation
1780	Massachusetts ratifies state constitution
1781	States ratify Articles of Confederation
1782	States fail to ratify proposed Impost tax
1783	Newburgh Conspiracy thwarted

1784	Iroquois disclaim right to Ohio Country in Treaty of Fort Stanwix
1785	Congress passes Land Ordinance for Northwest Territory
1786	Annapolis Convention suggests second meeting to revise the Articles of Confederation (September)
1786	Shays's Rebellion frightens American leaders
1787	Constitutional Convention in Philadelphia (summer)
1787–1788	Constitution ratified by all states except North Carolina and Rhode Island
1791	Bill of Rights ratified by states

Suggestions for Further Reading

Chapter 1

For a general overview of African history prior to Portuguese arrival, see Basil Davidson, *West Africa before the Colonial Era: A History to 1850* (New York, 1998). J. H. Elliott provides a helpful overview of Spanish and English expansion in *Empires of the Atlantic World: Britain and Spain in America 1492–1830* (New Haven, 2006). For early European exploration, see Felipe Fernández-Armesto, *Before Columbus: Exploration and Colonisation from the Mediterranean to the Atlantic, 1229–1492* (Philadelphia, 1987). Ralph Davis, *The Rise of the Atlantic Economies* (Ithaca, 1973), explores the expansion of trade in the Atlantic World from the fifteenth century forward. An excellent recent reference work for further exploration of Atlantic World history is Joseph C. Miller, Vincent Brown, Jorge Cañizares-Esguerra, Laurent Dubois, and Karen Ordahl Kupperman, eds., *The Princeton Companion to Atlantic History* (Princeton, 2015).

The demand for dependent labor in America beginning in the early sixteenth century brought dramatic changes to African society and economy. Paul H. Lovejoy, *Transformations in Slavery: A History of Slavery in Africa* (Cambridge, 1983), provides a helpful overview.

North American history before Columbus is attracting a growing body of sophisticated scholarship. For a fascinating overview, see Brian M. Fagan, *Ancient North America: The Archaeology of a Continent* (New York, 2005). Fagan's *The Great Journey: The Peopling of Ancient America* (Gainesville, 2004) surveys the ancient migrations that populated the Americas. For a sweeping synthetic account of the North American environment from distant prehistory to the present, see Tim Flannery, *The Eternal Frontier: An Ecological History of North America and Its Peoples* (New York, 2001). Lyle Campbell, *American Indian Languages: The Historical Linguistics of Native America* (New York, 1997), reviews linguistic patterns in the New World and what they reveal about the movement of peoples and development of culture in the era before European contact. Frances Berdan explores the rise of the Aztecs in her *Aztecs of Central Mexico: An Imperial Society* (New York, 2004). Lynda Norene Shaffer explores the Mississippian origins of many Eastern Woodlands groups in her *Native Americans before 1492: The Moundbuilding Centers of the Eastern Woodlands* (Armonk, NY, 1992), while Bruce G. Trigger explores the archaeological and documentary history of an important Great Lakes nation in his *The Children of Aataentsic: A History of the Huron People to 1660* (Kingston, 1976).

Historical scholarship on the European background of exploration and colonization is vast. A good overview of popular responses to the Protestant Reformation is available in Euan Cameron, *Enchanted Europe: Superstition, Reason, and Religion 1250–1750* (New York, 2010). John Calvin exerted enormous influence on Protestantism on the Continent and the British Isles, and a good biographical treatment is available in F. Bruce Gordon, *Calvin* (New Haven, 2011). The rise of Protestantism in England is the subject of Peter Marshall's *Reformation England, 1480–1642* (London, 2012). Richard Helgerson, *Forms of Nationhood: The Elizabethan Writing of England* (Chicago, 1992), explores the beginnings of an English Protestant national identity. Nicholas P. Canny, *Kingdom and Colony: Ireland in the Atlantic World, 1560–1800* (Baltimore, 1988) explores Ireland's role in the development of English methods of colonization. Keith Wrightson, *Earthly Necessities: Economic Lives in Early Modern England* (New Haven, 2000), provides a helpful overview of the economic and social origins of colonization, while Lawrence Stone's *The Crisis of the Aristocracy, 1558–1641* (Oxford, 1965) offers a classic account of sweeping changes in English society from the reign of Elizabeth to the English Civil War.

The early modern encounter Atlantic peoples from Europe, Africa, and the Americas has become the subject of some of the most exciting and provocative scholarship of the past twenty years. For a succinct overview, see David Abulafia, *The Discovery of Mankind: Atlantic Encounters in the Age of Columbus* (New Haven, 2008). A good introduction to more than three centuries of encounter among Atlantic people groups may be found in Anthony Pagden, *European Encounters with the New World: From Renaissance to Romanticism* (New Haven, 1993). Stephen Greenblatt analyzes how early European visitors to the New World attempted to make sense of what they saw in his *Marvelous Possessions: The Wonder of the New World* (Oxford, 1991). Tzvetan Todorov offers a provocative interpretation of encounter in *The Conquest of America: The Question of the Other* (New York, 1984).

John Thornton explores the African impact on Atlantic trade and colonization in his *Africa and Africans in the Making of the Atlantic World, 1400–1800* rev. ed. (Cambridge, 1998). For

the beginnings of the slave trade, see Hugh Thomas, *The Slave Trade: The Story of the Atlantic Slave Trade, 1440–1870* (New York, 1997).

The process of encounter, conquest, and colonization between Spanish and Indians in the Caribbean and Mexico is treated in many recent studies. James Lockhart and Stuart B. Schwartz provide an excellent overview in *Early Latin America: A History of Colonial Spanish America and Brazil* (Cambridge, 1983). Inga Clendinnen analyzes the clash between Mayas and Spaniards in her *Ambivalent Conquests: Maya and Spaniard in the Yucatan, 1517–1570* (Cambridge, 1987). Good investigations of native peoples after the Spanish conquest may be found in James Lockhart, *The Nahuas after the Conquest: A Social and Cultural History of the Indians of Central Mexico, Sixteenth through Eighteenth Centuries* (Stanford, 1992), and Stuart B. Schwartz, *Victors and the Vanquished: Spanish and Nahua Views of the Conquest of Mexico* (1999).

An excellent starting point for reading about the European exploration of North America is Kirstin A. Seaver, *The Frozen Echo: Greenland and the Exploration of North America, ca. A.D. 1000–1500* (Stanford: 1996). David J. Weber's *The Spanish Frontier in North America* (New Haven, 1992), offers a thorough and fascinating account of early explorers from Ponce de León to Coronado and De Soto. W. J. Eccles, *The French in North America, 1500–1783* (East Lansing, 1998), treats early French exploration, while Neal Salisbury, *Manitou and Providence: Indians, Europeans, and the Making of New England* (Oxford, 1982) analyzes some of the earliest English encounters with North American peoples. For the Dutch in North America, see Jaap Jacobs, *The Colony of New Netherland: A Dutch Settlement in Seventeenth-Century America* (Ithaca, NY, 2009).

The variety of encounter among North American Indians and Europeans has been the subject of some of the most exciting and creative scholarship of the past thirty years. Bruce Trigger pioneered the use of archaeology and anthropology to reconstruct a carefully nuanced, culturally sensitive description of specific North American peoples in works such as his *Natives and Newcomers: Canada's "Heroic Age" Reconsidered* (Kingson, 1987). James Axtell's *The Invasion Within: The Contest of Cultures in Colonial North America* (Oxford, 1986) offers a comparative analysis of Franco-native and Anglo-native patterns of contact and exchange. Daniel Richter, *Facing East from Indian Country: A Native History of Early America* (Cambridge, Mass., 2001) explores native responses to European contact in the colonial period.

For the ecological impact of European exploration, see Alfred W. Crosby's pathbreaking study, *The Columbian Exchange: Biological and Cultural Consequences of 1492* (Westport, Conn., 1972), as well as his *Ecological Imperialism: The Biological Expansion of Europe, 900–1900*, 2nd ed. (Cambridge, 2004). For ecological change in New England, see William Cronon, *Changes in the Land: Indians, Colonists, and the Ecology of New England* (New York, 1983), and for the Southeast, see Timothy Silver, *A New Face on the Countryside: Indians, Colonists, and Slaves in South Atlantic Forests, 1500–1800* (Cambridge, 1990). For a comprehensive study of North America's historical geography, see D. W. Meinig's *The Shaping of America: A Geographical Perspective on 500 Years of History*, Vol. 1, *Atlantic America, 1492–1800* (New Haven, 1986).

Chapter 2

Over the past decade, historians have increasingly come to view the sixteenth-century Atlantic basin as a single vast theater of economic, military, and cultural interaction among the peoples who inhabited its rim. Two comprehensive treatments of the Atlantic World to date may be found in Thomas Benjamin, *The Atlantic World: Europeans, Africans, Indians and their Shared History, 1400–1900* (Cambridge, 2009) and John K. Thornton, *A Cultural History of the Atlantic World, 125–1820* (Cambridge, 2012). Philip D. Curtin explores one of the most important institutions in the creation of the Atlantic economies in his *Rise and Fall of the Plantation Complex: Essays in Atlantic History* (Cambridge, 1998).

The determination to view the Atlantic world as an arena of multiple initiative and interaction among its peoples has prompted recent historians to reexamine the role of Africans in the shaping of that world. John Thornton's *Africa and Africans in the Making of the Atlantic World, 1400–1800* (Cambridge, 1998) treats the various coastal peoples of sub-Saharan Africa as active participants in the shaping of that world through their control of commerce with Europeans. David Northrup, *Africa's Discovery of Europe, 1450–1850*, 2nd ed. (New York, 2008), provides a rich account of the varieties of African European encounter in the colonial period.

The history of the slave trade itself continues to attract much scholarly attention and generate a great deal of debate. An excellent synthesis of recent scholarship is available in Herbert S. Klein, *The Atlantic Slave Trade*, 2nd ed. (Cambridge, 2010). David Eltis argues that the slave trade developed as a result of African strength rather than African weakness in his *Rise of African Slavery in the Americas* (Cambridge, 2000). Patrick Manning traces the expansion of African peoples and cultures to the Atlantic World and beyond in his *The African Diaspora: A History through Culture* (New York, 2010).

James D. Tracy, ed., *The Rise of Merchant Empires: Long-Distance Trade in the Early Modern World, 1350–1750* (Cambridge, 1990) contains excellent essays examining the overall structure of Atlantic trade as well as the efforts of various European nations to develop transatlantic empires in the sixteenth and seventeenth centuries. For the international contest over Spanish treasure, see Stanley J. Stein and Barbara H.

Stein, *Silver, Trade, and War: Spain and America in the Making of Early Modern Europe* (Baltimore, 2000). For the Portuguese empire, see A. J. R. Russell-Wood, *The Portuguese Empire, 1415–1808: A World on the Move* (Baltimore, 1982). W. J. Eccles, *The French in North America, 1500–1783* (East Lansing, 1998), includes excellent chapters on France's sixteenth-century contest for a toehold in the New World. For England's efforts to establish a presence in the Americas, see David Armitage and Michael J. Braddick, *The British Atlantic World, 1500–1800* (New York, 2002). For English colonization in Ireland as a model of American colonization, see Nicholas Canny, *Making Ireland British, 1580–1650* (Oxford, 2001). Garrett Mattingly's *The Armada* (Boston, 1959) offers a classic account of the clash from an English perspective, while Felipe Fernández-Armesto's *The Spanish Armada: The Experience of War in 1588* (Oxford, 1988) attempts to balance Mattingly's largely pro-English narrative with an analysis more sympathetic to the Spanish. For Dutch activity in the New World, see Pieter Emmer, *The Dutch in the Atlantic Economy, 1580–1880: Trade, Slavery, and Emancipation* (Aldershot, 1998).

Chapter 3

The best single starting point for understanding the colonization of the Chesapeake and the development of English society there remains Edmund S. Morgan's *American Slavery, American Freedom: The Ordeal of Colonial Virginia* (New York, 1975), while Frederic W. Gleach's *Powhatan's World and Colonial Virginia: A Conflict of Cultures* (Lincoln, Nebr., 1997) provides a well-rounded treatment of Powhatan culture and Powhatan-English relations in the seventeenth century. Steven Sarson, *The Tobacco-Plantation South in the Early American Atlantic World* (New York, 2013), sets Virginia in a larger Atlantic context. For a tough-minded account of the ordeal of the first Jamestown colonists, see John Smith, *Captain John Smith: Writings with other Narratives of Roanoke, Jamestown,* and the *First English Settlement of America,* edited by James Horn (New York, 2007).

James Horn's *Adapting to a New World: English Society in the Seventeenth-Century Chesapeake* (Chapel Hill, 1994) analyzes how migrants to the Chesapeake adapted English institutions and cultural forms to their new environment. Excellent essays on many aspects of social development in the seventeenth-century Chesapeake may be found in two collections: Lois Green Carr, Philip D. Morgan, and Jean B. Russo eds., *Colonial Chesapeake Society* (Chapel Hill, 1988).

A provocative reassessment of social development in Virginia is Kathleen M. Brown's *Good Wives, Nasty Wenches, and Anxious Patriarchs: Gender, Race, and Power in Colonial Virginia* (Chapel Hill, 1996). The fluidity of race relations and the development of a free black community in seventeenth-century Virginia are explored in T. H. Breen and Stephen Innes, *"Myne Owne Ground": Race and Freedom on Virginia's Eastern Shore, 1640–1676* (New York, 1980). For an insightful account of how English law was adapted to the colonial Virginian context, see John Ruston Pagan, *Anne Orthwood's Bastard: Sex and Law in Early Virginia* (New York, 2002).

Insightful analyses of colonial development in early Maryland include John D. Krugler, *English and Catholic: The Lords Baltimore in the Seventeenth Century* (Baltimore, 2004), David B. Quinn, *Early Maryland in a Wider World* (Detroit, 1982), and Lois Green Carr, Russell R. Menard, and Lorena S. Walsh, *Robert Cole's World: Agriculture and Society in Early Maryland* (Chapel Hill, 1991).

Helen C. Rountree's *Pocahontas's People: The Powhatan Indians of Virginia through Four Centuries* (Norman, Okla., 1990) provides a good starting point for those interested in the history of native peoples of the Chesapeake before and after the English arrived. Her *Eastern Shore Indians of Virginia and Maryland* (Charlottesville, 1997) draws on archaeology as well as written records to reconstruct native life in that region, while her "Powhatan Indian Women: The People Captain John Smith Barely Saw," *Ethnohistory* 45 (1998): 1–29, analyzes the contributions of native women to Powhatan social life. For early Anglo-native contact in Maryland, see James H. Merrell, "Cultural Continuity among the Piscataway Indians of Colonial Maryland," *William and Mary Quarterly*, 3rd ser., 36 (1979): 548–570.

Chapter 4

The best starting point for further study of English colonization in the Caribbean is Richard S. Dunn, *Sugar and Slaves: The Rise of the Planter Class in the English West Indies, 1624–1713* (New York, 1972). Karen Ordahl Kupperman's *Providence Island, 1630–1641: The Other Puritan Colony* (Cambridge, 1993) provides a fascinating account of this often-forgotten Puritan enterprise. Good general overviews of Caribbean history include Kristin Block, *Ordinary Lives in the Early Caribbean: Religion, Colonial Competition, and the Politics of Profit* (Athens, Ga., 2012) and B. W. Higman, *A Concise History of the Caribbean* (New York, 2011). A sampling of writings by British colonists in the West Indies is available in Thomas W. Krise, ed., *Caribbeana: An Anthology of English Literature of the West Indies, 1657–1777* (Chicago, 1999).

The elusive histories of Caribbean native peoples are treated in Philip P. Boucher, *Cannibal Encounters: Europeans and the Island Caribs, 1492–1763* (Baltimore, 1992) and Peter Hulme, *Colonial Encounters: Europe and the Native Caribbean, 1492–1797* (London, 1986). Peter Hulme and Neil L. Whitehead, eds., *Wild Majesty: Encounters with the Caribs from Columbus to the Present Day* (Oxford, 1992) provides a revealing collection of firsthand accounts concerning European-native encounter in the Caribbean.

Early English efforts to establish a permanent presence in the seventeenth-century Caribbean are treated in Kenneth R. Andrews,

Ships, Money, and Politics: Seafaring and Naval Enterprises in the Reign of Charles I (Cambridge, 1991), and Robert Brenner, *Merchants and Revolutionaries: Commercial Change, Political Conflict and London Overseas Traders, 1550–1653* (Cambridge, 1993).

Eric Williams, *Capitalism and Slavery* (Chapel Hill, 1944) remains the classic account of the development of British West Indian slavery. Keith Albert Sandiford, *The Cultural Politics of Sugar: Caribbean Slavery and Narratives of Colonialism* (Cambridge, 2000) offers a provocative analysis of the links between sugar, colonialism, and the slave trade. A good selection of recent scholarship on slavery throughout the Caribbean is available in Hilary McD. Beckles and Verene A. Shepherd, eds., *Caribbean Slavery in the Atlantic World* (Princeton, 1999). For Barbados, see Hilary McD. Beckles, *White Servitude and Black Slavery in Barbados, 1627–1715* (Knoxville, 1989).

The development of African culture in the Caribbean has been the subject of innovative scholarship over the past three decades. Sidney W. Mintz and Richard Price, *The Birth of African-American Culture: An Anthropological Perspective* (Boston, 1992) draws from the authors' own work in Caribbean slave culture to provide an excellent introduction to the problems and methods of research into the field. Ira Berlin and Philip D. Morgan, eds., *Cultivation and Culture: Labor and the Shaping of Slave Life in the Americas* (Charlottesville, Va., 1993) includes essays discussing the role of labor in the development of African American culture among Caribbean slaves. For the experience of African American women in the Caribbean, see essays in David Barry Gaspar and Darlene Clark Hine, eds., *More than Chattel: Black Women and Slavery in the Americas* (Bloomington, Ind., 1996). For slave resistance and the development of maroon communities, see Alvin O. Thompson, *Flight to Freedom: African Runaways and Maroons in the Americas* (Kingston, 2006), and Nancie L. Solien González, *Sojourners of the Caribbean: Ethnogenesis and Ethnohistory of the Garifuna* (Chicago, 1988).

Chapter 5

Two of New England's most capable historians were William Bradford, *Of Plymouth Plantation*, ed. Samuel Eliot Morrison (New York, 1952), and John Winthrop, *Journal of John Winthrop, 1630–1649*, ed. Richard S. Dunn and Laetitia Yeandle (Cambridge, Mass., 1996). The most brilliant exploration of Puritan theology remains Perry Miller, *The New England Mind: From Colony to Province* (Cambridge, Mass., 1956), though more recent studies such as Michael Winship's *Making Heretics: Militant Protestantism and Free Grace in Massachusetts, 1636–1641* (Princeton, 2002) have questioned whether Puritans were as unified in their theology as Miller suggested. Popular religious belief is examined in such studies as David D. Hall, *Worlds of Wonder, Days of Judgment: Popular Religious Belief in Early New England* (1989) and Richard Godbeer, *The Devil's Dominion: Magic and Religion in Early New England* (Cambridge, Mass., 1992).

Excellent analyses of Puritan migration include Virginia De John Anderson, *New England's Generation: The Great Migration and the Formation of Society and Culture in the Seventeenth Century* (Cambridge, Mass., 1991) and Alison Games, *Migration and the Origins of the English Atlantic World* (Cambridge, Mass., 1999). David Grayson Allen's *In English Ways: The Movement of Societies and the Transferal of English Local Law and Custom* (New York, 1981) discusses the adaptation of English social and cultural institutions to New England.

Puritan political ideals and institutions are discussed in Francis J. Bremer, *First Founders: American Puritans and Puritanism in an Atlantic World* (Durham, N.H., 2012), and Michael P. Winship, *Godly Republicanism: Puritans,* *Pilgrims, and a City on a Hill* (Cambridge, Mass., 2012). Jane Kamensky offers a provocative analysis of speech, gender, and power in *Governing the Tongue: The Politics of Speech in Early New England* (New York, 1997), while Mary Beth Norton includes extensive consideration of New England in her *Founding Mothers and Fathers: Gender and Power in the Formation of American Society* (New York, 1996). Laurel Thatcher Ulrich examines women's roles more broadly in *Good Wives: Image and Reality in the Lives of Women in Northern New England, 1650–1750* (New York, 1982).

For analysis of economic development in New England, see Mark Valeri, *How Religion Shaped Commerce in Puritan America* (Princeton, 2010) and Stephen Innes, *Creating the Commonwealth: The Economic Culture of Puritan New England* (1995). The better New England town studies—and there are many—include Kenneth Lockridge, *The New England Town: The First Hundred Years* (New York, 1970); Philip Greven, Jr., *Four Generations: Population, Land, and Family in Colonial Andover* (Ithaca, 1970); Stephen Innes, *Labor in a New Land: Economy and Society in Seventeenth-Century Springfield* (Princeton, 1983); and John F. Martin, *Profits in the Wilderness: Entrepreneurship and the Founding of New England Towns in the Seventeenth Century* (Chapel Hill, 1991).

The past two decades have witnessed publication of a wealth of studies examining American Indian cultures and Anglo-Indian relations in New England. Neal Salisbury's *Manitou and Providence: Indians, Europeans, and the Making of New England, 1500–1643* (New York, 1982) explores contact from the time English and French fishermen dried their catch on New England shores to the closing years of the great Puritan migration. William Cronon explores environmental change accompanying colonization in *Changes in the Land: Indians, Colonists, and the Ecology of New England* (New York, 1983). James Axtell's *The Invasion Within:*

The Contest of Cultures in Colonial North America (New York, 1985) compares seventeenth-century French-Indian and Anglo-Indian relations. Alfred A. Cave analyzes one of the Puritans' earliest military campaigns against their native neighbors in *The Pequot War* (Amherst, 1995). For Puritan missionary efforts among New England Indians, see Dane Morrison, *A Praying People: Massachuset Acculturation and the Failure of the Puritan Mission, 1600–1690* (New York, 1995).

Chapter 6

Jan De Vries, "The Economic Crisis of the Seventeenth Century after Fifty Years," *Journal of Interdisciplinary History* 40, no. 2 (Autumn, 2009), 151–194, provides an excellent starting point for understanding the European context of the contest for Atlantic commercial empire in the later seventeenth century. For French imperial concerns, see James Pritchard, *In Search of Empire: The French in the Americas, 1670–1730* (Cambridge, 2004). For the Spanish, see J. H. Eliot, *Empires of the Atlantic World: Britain and Spain in America 1492–1830* (New Haven, 2006). For the Dutch, see Jonathan I. Israel, *Dutch Primacy in World Trade, 1585–1740* (Oxford, 1989). For developments in England in the later Stuart period, see Mark Kishlansky, *A Monarchy Transformed: Britain 1603–1714* (London, 1996). For the English Atlantic, see Carla Gardina Pestana's books, *The English Atlantic in an Age of Revolution, 1640–1661* (Cambridge, Mass., 2004), and *Protestant Empire: Religion and the Making of the British Atlantic World* (Philadelphia, 2010), and April Lee Hatfield's *Atlantic Virginia: Intercolonial Relations in the Seventeenth Century* (Philadelphia, 2007). For Anglo-Dutch conflict, see J. R. Jones, *The Anglo-Dutch Wars of the Seventeenth Century* (London, 1996).

The development of England's seventeenth-century Atlantic commercial policy is detailed in Charles M. Andrews, *The Colonial Period of American History*, vol. 4, *England's Commercial and Colonial Policy* (New Haven, 1938), Relevant essays in Peter A. Coclanis's *The Atlantic Economy during the Seventeenth and Eighteenth Centuries* (Columbia, 2005) set these developments in an Atlantic context. Michael Garibaldi Hall examines the development of English colonial policy through one of its most persistent and irascible agents in his *Edward Randolph and the American Colonies, 1676–1703* (Chapel Hill, 1960). For the problem of piracy and privateering in the seventeenth century, see John Latimer, *Buccaneers of the Caribbean: How Piracy Forged an Empire* (Cambridge, Mass., 2009).

Jaap Jacobs, *The Colony of New Netherland: A Dutch Settlement in Seventeenth-Century America* (Ithaca, 2009), explores the establishment of New Netherland, while Robert C. Ritchie, *The Duke's Province: A Study of New York Politics and Society, 1664–1691* (Chapel Hill, 1977), surveys the colony's history after 1664. For South Carolina, see S. Max Edelson, *Plantation Enterprise in Colonial South Carolina* (Cambridge, Mass., 2006), and for the emergence of North Carolina, see Noeleen McIlvenna, *A Very Multitudinous People: The Struggle for North Carolina, 1660–1713* (Chapel Hill, 2009). The standard account of Pennsylvania's early development remains Gary B. Nash, *Quakers and Politics: Pennsylvania, 1681–1726* (Princeton, 1968), while Brendan McConville, *These Daring Disturbers of the Peace: The Struggle for Property and Power in Early New Jersey* (Ithaca, 1999) offers a fresh examination of New Jersey's turbulent early history.

The ethnic diversity of the Middle Colonies has become the subject of many excellent and innovative studies in recent years. Donna Merwick's *Death of a Notary: Conquest and Change in Colonial New York* (Ithaca, 1999) offers an unsettling case study of the impact of English occupation on the original Dutch inhabitants. Cynthia A. Kerner's *Traders and Gentlefolk: The Livingstons of New York, 1675–1790* (Ithaca,

1992) explores the opportunities New York opened to one enterprising English family. Richard and Mary M. Dunn, eds., *The World of William Penn* (1986) contains essays on the diversity of early Pennsylvania settlement. For early Scottish settlement in New Jersey, see Ned C. Landsman, *Scotland and Its First American Colony, 1683–1765* (Princeton, 1985).

For a splendid analysis of the development of slavery and slave culture in South Carolina, see Peter H. Wood, *Black Majority: Negroes in Colonial South Carolina from 1670 through the Stono Rebellion* (New York, 1974). Daniel C. Littlefield explores the impact of African ethnicity on South Carolina slavery in, *Rice and Slaves: Ethnicity and the Slave Trade in Colonial South Carolina* (Urbana, 1981). Judith A. Carney, *Black Rice: The African Origins of Rice Cultivation in the Americas* (Cambridge, Mass., 2002) sets Carolina rice cultivation in a broader Atlantic context.

Daniel C. Richter's *Ordeal of the Longhouse: The Peoples of the Iroquois League in the Era of European Colonization* (Chapel Hill, 1992) includes an extensive analysis of New York-Iroquois relations after the arrival of the English. For the Delawares, while James H. Merrell, *Into the American Woods: Negotiators on the Pennsylvania Frontier* (New York, 1999) offers an insightful analysis of Anglo-Indian relations in that colony. For Indians in the Southeast, see Robbie Franklin Ethridge, *From Chicaza to Chickasaw: The European Invasion and the Transformation of the Mississippian World, 1540–1715* (Chapel Hill, 2011). For the Indian slave trade in early South Carolina, see Alan Gallay, *The Rise of English Empire in the American South, 1670–1717* (New Haven, 2002). For the Cherokees, see Tom Hatley, *The Dividing Paths: Cherokees and South Carolinians through the Era of Revolution* (New York, 1993). For the Choctaws, see Patricia Galloway's *Choctaw Genesis, 1500–1700* (Lincoln, 1995). James H. Merrell's pathbreaking *The Indians' New World: Catawbas and Their Neighbors from European Contact through the Era of Removal* (Chapel Hill, 1989) explores the emergence of this group and the history of their dealings with Carolina settlers.

Chapter 7

The best treatment of the Iroquois people during this period remains Daniel K. Richter, *The Ordial of the Longhouse: The Peoples of the Iroquois League in the Era of European Colonization* (Chapel Hill, 1992). For Bacon's Rebellion, see James D. Rice, *Tales from a Revolution: Bacon's Rebellion and the Transformation of Early America* (New York, 2012). For King Philip's War, see Daniel R. Mandell, *King Philip's War: Colonial Expansion, Native Resistance, and the End of Indian Sovereignty* (Baltimore, 2010), and Jenny Hale Pulsipher, *Subjects unto the Same King: Indians, English, and the Contest for Authority in Colonial Massachusetts* (Philadelphia, 2005). For Anglo-native diplomacy in the later seventeenth century, see Daniel K. Richter and James H. Merrell, eds., *Beyond the Covenant Chain: The Iroquois and Their Neighbors in Indian North America, 1600–1800* (Syracuse, 1987). For the Pueblo Revolt, see Matthew Liebmann, *Revolt: An Archaeological History of Pueblo Resistance and Revitalization in 17th Century New Mexico* (Tucson: University of Arizona Press, 2012).

Stephen C. A. Pincus, *1688: The First Modern Revolution* (New Haven, 2009), provides an excellent account of the Glorious Revolution and its consequences for the early modern world. Owen Stanwood, *The Empire Reformed: English America in the Age of the Glorious Revolution* (Philadelphia, 2011), provides the most comprehensive account of how the event reshaped empire in English America. For Atlantic Perspectives of the event, see Tim Harris and Stephen Taylor, *The Final Crisis of the Stuart Monarchy: The Revolutions of 1688–91 in Their British, Atlantic, and European Contexts* (Woodbridge, 2013), and Stephen Saunders Webb, *Lord Churchill's Coup: The Anglo-American*

Empire and the Glorious Revolution Reconsidered (New York, 1995).

John Brewer's *The Sinews of Power: War, Money and the English State, 1688–1783* (New York, 1989) remains a crucial starting point for understanding how the Glorious Revolution, international realignment, and war stimulated the development of an English "fiscal-military state." See also Ian K. Steele, *The English Atlantic, 1675–1740* (Oxford, 1986), and Thomas C. Barrow, *Trade and Empire: The British Customs Service in Colonial America 1660–1775* (Cambridge, Mass., 1967). On piracy, see Robert C. Ritchie, *Captain Kidd and the War against the Pirates* (Cambridge, Mass., 1986); Marcus Rediker, *Between the Devil and the Deep Blue Sea: Merchant Seamen, Pirates, and the Anglo-American Maritime World, 1700–1750* (Cambridge, 1987).

Treatments of the Glorious Revolution's impact on Anglo-Indian relations may be found in Kenneth M. Morrison, *The Embattled Northeast: The Elusive Ideal of Alliance in Wabenaki-Euramerican Relations* (Berkeley, 1984); Richter's *Ordeal of the Longhouse*, and Richard White, *The Middle Ground: Indians, Empires, and Republics in the Great Lakes Region, 1650–1815* (Cambridge, 1991); and Gilles Havard, *The Great Peace of 1791: French-Native Diplomacy in the Seventeenth Century* (Montreal, 2001).

There is no shortage of literature on witchcraft in colonial America. Richard Godbeer's *The Devil's Dominion: Magic and Religion in Early New England* (Cambridge, 1992) explores witchcraft as part of a struggle between folk belief and seventeenth-century Puritan religion. Carol Karlsen, *The Devil in the Shape of a Woman: Witchcraft in Colonial New England* (New York, 1987), explores witchcraft's gendered dimensions, while Mary Beth Norton, *In the Devil's Snare: The Salem Witchcraft Crisis of 1692* (New York, 2003), links the crisis to Anglo-Wabanaki conflict on the Maine frontier. Paul Boyer and Stephen Nissenbaum's *Salem Possessed: The Social Origins of Witchcraft* (Cambridge, Mass.,

1974) interprets the trials and convictions at Salem as expressions of deep social divisions in the community. Good collections of readings and primary documents include Boyer and Nissenbaum, eds., *The Salem Witchcraft Papers: Verbatim Transcripts of the Legal Documents of the Salem Witchcraft Outbreak*, 3 vols. (New York, 1977).

Chapter 8

A good general discussion of the varieties of European colonization in eighteenth-century America may be found in D. W. Meinig's *The Shaping of America: A Geographical Perspective on 500 Years of History: Volume 1, Atlantic America, 1492–1800* (New Haven, 1986). For the French in America, an essential starting point is W. J. Eccles, *The French in North America, 1500–1783* rev. ed. (East Lansing, 1998). For the French in the Great Lakes and central North America, see Robert Englebert and Guillaume Teasdale, eds., *French and Indians in the Heart of North America, 1630–1815* (Lansing, 2013). For French fur trading west of the Great Lakes, see W. Raymond Wood and Thomas D. Thiessen, eds., *Early Fur Trade on the Northern Plains: Canadian Traders among the Mandan and Hidatsa Indians, 1738–1818* (Norman, 1985). Daniel Usner, *Indians, Settlers, and Slaves in a Frontier Exchange Economy: The Lower Mississippi Valley before 1783* (Chapel Hill, 1992), provides an analysis of the economic and cultural life of French Louisiana during the eighteenth century. Carl J. Ekberg, *French Roots in the Illinois Country: The Mississippi Frontier in Colonial Times* (Urbana, 2000), provides an analysis of French settlement in the Illinois Country.

The best survey of the eighteenth-century Spanish borderlands remains David J. Weber, *The Spanish Frontier in North America* (New Haven, 1992). For the eighteenth-century culture of Spanish and Indians in New Mexico, see Tracy L. Brown, *Pueblo Indians and Spanish Colonial*

Authority in Eighteenth-Century New Mexico (Tucson, 2013). For Indians and Spanish in Texas, see Julian Barr, *Peace Came in the Form of a Woman: Indians and Spaniards in the Texas Borderlands* (Chapel Hill, 2007). For the Spanish search for La Salle in Texas, see Robert S. Weddle, *Wilderness Manhunt: The Spanish Search for La Salle* (Austin, 1973). Henry Folmer, *Franco-Spanish Rivalry in North America, 1524–1763* (Glendale, Calif., 1953), explores the imperial contest between France and Spain along the Gulf Coast.

The cultural zone among Indians, colonists, and, in many cases, slaves has become the focus of a growing number of studies. In addition to Usner's book on the lower Mississippi, Richard White has analyzed the succession of European and Indian interactions in the Great Lakes in his influential study, *The Middle Ground: Indians, Empires, and Republics in the Great Lakes Region, 1650–1815* (Cambridge, 1991), while Michael McConnell examines the Ohio Valley in his *A Country Between: The Upper Ohio Valley and Its Peoples, 1725–1774* (Lincoln, 1992). Kathleen DuVal argues that Indian peoples of central North America set the terms of exchange in her *The Native Ground: Indians and Colonists in the Heart of the Continent* (Philadelphia, 2007). Brett Rushforth's *Bonds of Alliance: Indigenous and Atlantic Slaveries in New France* (Chapel Hill, 2012) revises White's argument considerably by exploring the role of native slavery in forging alliance and limiting French expansion in the West. Andrew R. L. Cayton and Fredrika J. Teute, *Contact Points: American Frontiers from the Mohawk Valley to the Mississippi, 1750–1830* (Chapel Hill, 1998), treats a somewhat later period but contains essays that critique and offer alternatives to the "middle ground" as an analytical concept.

Queen Anne's War is treated in Howard H. Peckham, *The Colonial Wars, 1689–1762* (Chicago, 1964), and Douglas Edward Leach, *The Northern Colonial Frontier, 1607–1763* (New York, 1966).

For the "Sack of Deerfield" and its aftermath, see Richard I. Melvoin, *New England Outpost: War and Society in Colonial Deerfield* (New York, 1989), and Evan Haefeli and Kevin Sweeney, *Captors and Captives: The 1704 French and Indian Raid on Deerfield* (Amherst, 2006).

Chapter 9

The growth and migration of the colonial population, and the impact of colonial expansion on the lands between empires and Native American nations, have generated a growing body of illuminating historiography. The rapid population growth of England's thirteen mainland colonies is summarized in James T. Lemon, "Colonial America in the Eighteenth Century," in *North America: The Historical Geography of a Changing Continent*, ed. Robert D. Mitchell and Paul A. Groves (Lanham, 2001), 121–48. Good overviews of early migration patterns may be found in S. Scott Rohrer, *Wandering Souls: Protestant Migrations in America, 1630–1865* (Chapel Hill, 2010), and Alan Kulikoff's *The Agrarian Origins of American Capitalism* (Charlottesville and London, 1992). Internal migration to northern New England is discussed at length in Charles E. Clark, *The Eastern Frontier: The Settlement of Northern New England 1610–1763* (New York, 1970). Barry Levy discusses the development of Pennsylvania Quaker society in *Quakers and the American Family: British Settlement in the Delaware Valley* (New York, 1988), and Larry Dale Gragg explores Quaker migration from Pennsylvania to Virginia and North Carolina in *Migration in Early America: The Virginia Quaker Experience* (Ann Arbor, 1980). David Hacket Fischer and James C. Kelly discuss Virginia migration in *Bound Away: Virginia and the Westward Movement* (Charlottesville and London, 2000). For early Georgia, see Paul M. Pressly, *On the Rim of the Caribbean: Colonial Georgia and the British Atlantic World* (Athens, 2013). A. G. Roeber provides an impressively original interpretation of the transfer of German culture in *Palatines, Liberty, and Property: German Lutherans in Colonial British America* (Baltimore, 1993). For the Scots see Ned Landsman, *Scotland and Its First American Colony, 1683–1765* (Princeton, 1985), and for the Scots Irish, see Patrick Griffin, *The People with No Name: Ireland's Ulster Scots, America's Scots Irish, and the Creation of a British Atlantic World, 1689–1764* (Princeton, 2001). Marianne S. Wokeck argues that eighteenth-century immigration to North America from Germany and Ireland inaugurated a distinctly modern form of mass migration in her *Trade in Strangers: The Beginnings of Mass Migration to North America* (University Park, Pa., 1999). Roger A. Ekirch offers a thorough analysis of the convict trade in *Bound for America: The Transportation of British Convicts to the Colonies, 1718–1775* (Oxford, 1992). A general overview is available in David Hackett Fischer, *Albion's Seed: Four British Folkways in America* (New York, 1989).

Some of the most exciting recent historical literature deals with the formation of a multicultural frontier. Richard S. White's *The Middle Ground: Indians, Empires, and Republics in the Great Lakes Region, 1650–1815* (Cambridge, 1991) remains influential, but for a recent revision to his "middle ground" analysis, see Kathleen DuVal, *The Native Ground: Indians and Colonists in the Heart of the Continent* (Philadelphia, 2007). Michael N. McConnell explores the migration and interaction of native groups to the eighteenth-century Ohio Country in *A Country Between: The Upper Ohio Valley and Its Peoples, 1724–1774* (Lincoln and London, 1992). James H. Merrell's *The Indians' New World: Catawbas and Their Neighbors from European Contact through the Era of Removal* (New York, 1989) traces the formation and persistence of Catawba nation in western North Carolina through the eighteenth century. Merrell's *Into the American Woods: Negotiators on the Pennsylvania Frontier* (New York, 1999) explores eighteenth-century Indian-European relations in Pennsylvania through the experience

of Indian and Anglo-American interpreters and go-betweens. For native peoples of the Southeast, see Tom Hatley's *The Dividing Paths: Cherokees and South Carolinians through the Revolutionary Era* (New York, 1995), and Claudio Saunt, *A New Order of Things: Property, Power, and the Transformation of the Creek Indians, 1733–1816* (Cambridge, 1999). For developments in the trans-Mississippi West, see Pekka Hämäläinen, *The Comanche Empire* (New Haven, Conn., 2008).

Chapter 10

Jon Butler provides a general introduction to many topics addressed in this chapter in *Becoming America: The Revolution before 1776* (Cambridge, Mass., 2000), arguing that colonists developed a very distinct identity during the eighteenth century. In *The Marketplace of Revolution: How Consumer Politics Shaped American Independence* (Oxford, 2004), T. H. Breen argues by contrast that a distinct American identity emerged late in the colonial period. Brendan McConville traces the development of an Anglicized monarchial culture in eighteenth-century America in *The King's Three Faces: The Rise and Fall of Royal America, 1688–1776* (Chapel Hill, 2006). The most comprehensive overview of colonial economic growth remains John J. McCusker and Russell R. Menard, *The Economy of British America, 1607–1789* (Chapel Hill, 1991); but see also Cathy Matson, ed., *The Economy of Early America: Historical Perspectives and New Directions* (University Park, 2006). For a superb biography of Benjamin Franklin, see Edmund S. Morgan, *Benjamin Franklin* (New Haven, 2002).

On the Great Awakening, see Thomas Kidd, *The Great Awakening: The Roots of Evangelical Christianity in Colonial America* (New Haven, 2007) and Frank Lambert, *Inventing the Great Awakening* (Princeton, 1999). See also Timothy D. Hall, *Contested Boundaries: Itinerancy and the Reshaping of the Colonial American Religious*

World (Durham, 1994), and Christine L. Heyrman, *The Southern Cross: The Beginnings of the Bible Belt* (Chapel Hill, 1997). On black and Indian missionaries, see Edward E. Andrews, *Native Apostles: Black and Indian Missionaries in the British Atlantic World* (Cambridge, Mass., 2013). Two excellent treatments of women's experience in the revivals are Susan Juster, *Disorderly Women: Sexual Politics and Evangelicalism in Revolutionary New England* (Ithaca, 1994), and Catherine A. Brekus, *Sarah Osborn's World: The Rise of Evangelical Christianity in Early America* (New Haven, 2013).

On consumption and the cultural concerns of a rising middle class in the eighteenth-century colonial mainland, in addition to T. H. Breen above, see Carol Shammas, *The Preindustrial Consumer in England and America* (Oxford, 1990); David Jaffee, *A New Nation of Goods: The Material Culture of Early America* (Philadelphia, 2010); Ann Smart Martin, *Buying into the World of Goods: Early Consumers in Backcountry Virginia* (Baltimore, 2008); and David Hancock, *Oceans of Wine: Madeira and the Emergence of American Trade and Taste* (New Haven, 2009).

For the growth and cultural significance of communication and print culture in eighteenth-century America, see Ian K. Steele, *The English Atlantic 1675–1740: An Exploration of Communication and Community* (New York, 1986); Richard D. Brown, *Knowledge Is Power: The Diffusion of Information in Early America, 1700–1865* (New York, 1989); and Konstantin Dierks, *In My Power: Letter Writing and Communications in Early America* (Philadelphia, 2009). Print culture is explored in David S. Shields, *Civil Tongues and Polite Letters in British America* (Chapel Hill, 1997); Christopher Clark, *The Public Prints: The Newspaper in Anglo-American Culture, 1665–1740* (New York, 1994); and David D. Hall and Hugh Amory, eds., *The Colonial Book in the Atlantic World* (2000).

James A. Henretta advanced the classic argument for familial resistance to the growth of the market in his "Families and Farms: *Mentalité* in Pre-Industrial America," *William and Mary Quarterly*, 3rd ser., 35 (1978): 3–32, while James T. Lemon's *The Best Poor Man's Country: A Geographical Study of Early Southeastern Pennsylvania* (Baltimore, 1972) remains an excellent study of one agricultural region's robust participation in the Atlantic economy. More recent studies include Daniel Vickers, "Competency and Competition: Economic Culture in Early America," *William and Mary Quarterly* 3rd ser., 47 (1990): 3–29; Allan Kulikoff, *The Agrarian Origins of American Capitalism* (Charlottesville, 1992); and Richard Lyman Bushman, "Markets and Composite Farms in Early America," *William and Mary Quarterly*, 3rd ser., 55 (1998): 351–74. The shifting roles of women in eighteenth-century America and the Atlantic world are explored in Mary Beth Norton, *Separated by Their Sex: Women in Public and Private in the Colonial Atlantic World* (Ithaca, 2011). Barry Levy, *Quakers and the American Family: British Settlement in the Delaware Valley* (New York, 1988), treats the impact of prosperous farming on Quaker family life.

The impact of eighteenth-century cultural transformations on native cultures is explored in Jane T. Merritt, *At the Crossroads: Indians and Empires on a Mid-Atlantic Frontier* (Chapel Hill, 2003); David L. Preston, *The Texture of Contact: European and Indian Settler Communities on the Frontiers of Iroquoia, 1667–1783* (Lincoln, 2009); Gregory Evans Dowd, *A Spirited Resistance: The North American Indian Struggle for Unity, 1745–1815* (Baltimore, 1992), James Axtell, *Natives and Newcomers: The Cultural Origins of North America* (New York, 2001); Claudio Saunt, *A New Order of Things: Property, Power, and the Transformation of the Creek Indians, 1733–1816* (Cambridge, 1999); and Colin G. Calloway, *New Worlds for All: Indians, Europeans, and the Remaking of Early America* (Baltimore, 1997). On Indians and missions in the Great Awakening, see Richard W. Pointer, " 'Poor Indians' and the 'Poor in Spirit':

The Indian Impact on David Brainerd," *New England Quarterly* 67 (1994): 403–26, and Jane T. Merritt, "Dreaming of the Savior's Blood: Moravians and the Indian Great Awakening in Pennsylvania," *William and Mary Quarterly*, 3rd ser., 54 (1997): 723–68. On Indians and alcohol, see Peter C. Mancall, *Deadly Medicine: Indians and Alcohol in Early America* (Ithaca, 1995).

Chapter 11

A vast body of rich and highly sophisticated scholarship on slavery and early African American culture has emerged in the past thirty years. For an overview of slavery in the British empire before 1800, see Kenneth Morgan, *Slavery and the British Empire: From Africa to America* (New York, 2007). Ira Berlin and Philip D. Morgan have edited an excellent collection of comparative essays on New World slavery, *Cultivation and Culture: Labor and the Shaping of Slave Life in the Americas* (Charlottesville, 1993). The most comprehensive analysis of the slave experience in colonial North America is Ira Berlin, *Many Thousands Gone: The First Two Centuries of Slavery in North America* (Cambridge, Mass., 1998), while the richest comparative study of slavery in the Chesapeake and the Lower South is Philip D. Morgan, *Slave Counterpoint: Black Culture in the Eighteenth-Century Chesapeake and Lowcountry* (Chapel Hill, 1998). David Eltis explores the relationship between Atlantic economic developments and the slave trade in *The Rise of African Slavery in the Americas* (Cambridge, 2000). For a provocative analysis of the role of sugar in the Atlantic economy, see Sidney W. Mintz, *Sweetness and Power: The Place of Sugar in Modern History* (New York, 1985). On the relationship between the slave trade and culture formation, see Stephanie E. Smallwood, *Salt Water Slavery: A Middle Passage from Africa to American Diaspora* (Cambridge, Mass., 2009). On shifting patterns of the intercolonial slave trade and its influence on African American

culture, see Gregory E. O'Malley, *Final Passages: The Intercolonial Slave Trade of British America, 1619–1807* (Chapel Hill, 2014). Additional studies of slavery and African American culture in mainland British North America include Lorena S. Walsh, *Motives of Honor, Pleasure, and Profit: Plantation Management in the Colonial Chesapeake, 1606–1763* (Chapel Hill, 2010); Anthony S. Parent, *Foul Means: The Formation of a Slave Society in Virginia, 1660–1740* (Chapel Hill, 2006); and S. Max Edelson, *Plantation Enterprise in Colonial South Carolina* (Cambridge, Mass., 2006). For slavery in the colonial North, see C. S. Manegold, *Ten Hills Farm: The Forgotten History of Slavery in the North* (Princeton, 2010); Catherine Adams and Elizabeth Pleck, *Love of Freedom: Black Women in Colonial and Revolutionary New England* (New York, 2010); and Graham Russell Hodges, *Root and Branch: African Americans in New York and East Jersey, 1613–1863* (Chapel Hill, 1998). Leland Ferguson's *Uncommon Ground: Archaeology and Early African America, 1650–1800* (Washington, 1992) explores the material culture of North American slaves.

Studies of specific island societies include David Barry Gaspar, *Bondmen and Rebels: A Study of Master-Slave Relations in Antigua with Implications for North America* (Baltimore, 1985), Jerome S. Handler and Frederick W. Lange, *Plantation Slavery in Barbados: an Archaeological and Historical Investigation* (Cambridge, Mass., 1978), and Daive A. Dunkley, *Agency of the Enslaved: Jamaica and the Culture of Freedom in the Atlantic World* (Lanham, 2013).

Several recent studies explore specific themes in colonial black experience and culture. Two excellent collections of essays discuss aspects of sex, gender, family life, and women's experience in colonial African American communities: David Barry Gaspar and Darlene Clark Hine, eds., *More than Chattel: Black Women and Slavery in the Americas* (Bloomington, Ind.,

1996), and Catherine Clinton and Michele Gillespie, eds., *The Devil's Lane: Sex and Race in the Early South* (New York, 1997). Sylvia R. Frey and Betty Wood explore the incorporation of Protestant Christianity into Atlantic African American culture in *Come Shouting to Zion: African American Protestantism in the American South and British Caribbean to 1830* (Chapel Hill, 1998). Sylviane H. Diouf, *Servants of Allah: Muslims Enslaved in the Americas* (New York, 1998), argues that many Muslim slaves preserved their faith in the Americas, forming vital communities and exerting significant influence that endured for generations. Peter Linebaugh and Marcus Rediker explore the role of the African Diaspora in seafaring in *The Many-Headed Hydra: Sailors, Slaves, Commoners and the Hidden History of the Revolutionary Atlantic* (London, 2012).

Chapter 12

Eighteenth-century Atlantic political culture, in theory and practice, is the subject of an increasingly sophisticated literature. An excellent starting point for understanding the eighteenth-century contest for empire is Paul W. Mapp's *The Elusive West and the Contest for Empire, 1713–1763* (Chapel Hill, 2011). See also David Armitage's *The Ideological Origins of the British Empire* (Cambridge, 2000) and Anthony Pagden's *Lords of All the World: Ideologies of Empire in Spain, Britain, and France* (1995). On eighteenth-century Britain see Linda Colley, *Britons: Forging the Nation, 1707–1837*, 3rd ed. (New Haven, 2009), Lawrence Stone, ed., *An Imperial State at War: Britain from 1689 to 1815* (Abingdon, 1994); John Brewer, *The Sinews of Power: War, Money, and the English State* (New York, 1989); and Colin Kidd, *British Identities before Nationalism: Ethnicity and Nationhood in the Atlantic World, 1600–1800* (Cambridge, 1999). The relationship between Parliament and the colonial governments of the eighteenth-century British empire is explored in Mary Sarah Bilder, *The Transatlantic Constitution: Colonial Legal Culture and the Empire* (Cambridge, Mass., 2008), and Philip Lawson, ed., *Parliament and the Atlantic Empire* (Edinburgh, 1995).

How colonial British Americans perceived politics, both in their own assemblies and in Parliament, is discussed in Richard R. Beeman, *The Varieties of Political Experience in Eighteenth-Century America* (Philadelphia, 2004); Brendan McConville, *The King's Three Faces: The Rise and Fall of Royal America, 1688–1776* (Chapel Hill, 2007); and Bernard Bailyn, *The Origins of American Politics* (New York, 1970). The best study of how Indians and British colonists negotiated power within the empire is Timothy Shannon, *Indians and Colonists at the Crossroads of Empire: The Albany Congress of 1754* (Ithaca, 2000).

The impact of the contest for empire on Native American leadership is discussed in a growing number of excellent studies. For the contest in the Northeast and Ohio country, see Daniel K. Richter, *The Ordeal of the Longhouse: The Peoples of the Iroquois League in the Era of European Colonization* (Chapel Hill, 1992); Jane T. Merritt, *At the Crossroads: Indians and Empires on a Mid-Atlantic Frontier, 1700–1763* (Chapel Hill, 2003); and Eric Hinderaker, *Elusive Empires: Constructing Colonialism in the Ohio Valley, 1673–1800* (Cambridge, 1997). For the Great Lakes region, see Charles Beatty-Medina and Melissa Rinehart, *Contested Territories: Native Americans and Non-Natives in the Lower Great Lakes, 1700–1850* (East Lansing, 2012), and Richard White's *The Middle Ground: Indians, Empires, and Republics in the Great Lakes Region, 1650–1815* (Cambridge, 1991). Gregory Evans Dowd examines successive eighteenth-century efforts to form pan-Indian Alliances in the Great Lakes and Ohio country in his *A Spirited Resistance: The North American Indian Struggle for Unity, 1745–1815* (Baltimore, 1992), while his *War Under Heaven: Pontiac, the Indian Nations, and the*

British Empire (Baltimore, 2004) explores one of the greatest of these, which broke out at the end of the Seven Years' War. For the Southeast, see Tom Hatley, The Dividing Paths: Cherokees and South Carolinians through the Revolutionary Era (New York, 1995), and Claudio Saunt, A New Order of Things: Property, Power, and the Transformation of the Creek Indians, 1733–1816 (Cambridge, 1999).

Fred Anderson offers the most complete treatment of war and empire in Crucible of War: The Seven Years' War and the Fate of Empire in British North America, 1754–1766 (New York, 2000). For the removal of the Acadians, see Christopher Hodson, The Acadian Diaspora: An Eighteenth-Century History (New York, 2012), and Geoffrey Plank, An Unsettled Conquest: The British Campaign against the Peoples of Acadia (Philadelphia, 2001). For war in the eighteenth-century Caribbean, see Richard Harding, Amphibious Warfare in the Eighteenth Century: The British Expeditions to the West Indies, 1740–42 (Woodbridge, 1991), and Richard Pares, War and Trade in the West Indies, 1739–1763 (Oxford, 1936). For an analysis of Pontiac's uprising, see William R. Nester, "Haughty Conquerors": Amherst and the Great Indian Uprising of 1763 (Westport, Conn., 2000).

Chapter 13

The period leading up to the American Revolution has generated a rich historiography. Reliable surveys of the period include Edmund S. Morgan, The Birth of the Republic, 4th ed. (Chicago, 2012), and Peter D. G. Thomas, Revolution in America: Britain and the Colonies, 1763–1776 (Cardiff, 1992). Two books that transformed how an entire generation interpreted the Revolution are Edmund S. Morgan and Helen M. Morgan, The Stamp Act Crisis: Prologue to Revolution (Chapel Hill, 1953), and Bernard Bailyn, The Ideological Origins of the American Revolution (Cambridge, Mass., 1967).

The literature dealing with British politics on the eve of the American Revolution continues to grow and develop. John Brewer's Party Ideology and Popular Politics at the Accession of George III (Cambridge, 1981) remains a valuable starting point for understanding the period. Lee Ward, The Politics of Liberty in England and Revolutionary America (Cambridge, 2004), provides an analysis of differing American and British understandings of liberty and how these shaped divergent approaches to government and policy in England and America. For a reappraisal of leading British figures and their role in the growing rift between Great Britain and the mainland colonies, see Andrew Jackson O'Shaughnessy, The Men Who Lost America: British Leadership, the American Revolution, and the Fate of Empire (New Haven, 2013).

The variety of colonial experience in the Atlantic World after 1763 provides a rich field for ongoing investigation. For an excellent overview of the imperial situation in North America after 1763, see Colin Calloway, The Scratch of a Pen: 1763 and the Transformation of North America (Oxford, 2006). For divergent developments in the mainland colonies and the British West Indies, see Andrew Jackson O'Shaughnessy, An Empire Divided: The American Revolution and the British Caribbean (Philadelphia, 2000), and Eliga H. Gould, The Persistence of Empire: British Political Culture in the Age of the American Revolution (Chapel Hill, 2000). For Quebec after 1763, see Philip Lawson, The Imperial Challenge: Quebec and Britain in the Age of the American Revolution (Montreal, 1989), and Paul David Nelson, General Sir Guy Carleton, Lord Dorchester: Soldier-Statesman of Early British Canada (Madison, 2000).

Several rich studies explore the social and cultural aspects of political change after 1763. Three works by T. H. Breen on this topic include American Insurgents, American Patriots: The

Revolution of the People (New York, 2010), *The Marketplace of Revolution: How Consumer Politics Shaped American Independence* (New York, 2004), and *Tobacco Culture: The Mentality of the Great Tidewater Planters on the Eve of Revolution*, revised ed. (Princeton, 2001). Gary B. Nash, *Urban Crucible: Social Change, Political Consequences, and the Origins of the American Revolution* (Cambridge, 1981), remains an excellent study of colonial city life and the development of class tensions in this period. For the experience of women in this period, see Carol Berkin, *Revolutionary Mothers: Women in the Struggle for America's Independence* (New York, 2005).

The expansion of westward migration and the resulting explosion of Anglo-native conflict on the trans-Appalachian frontier is the subject of a growing number of studies. Daniel Richter provides an excellent overview from the native point of view in relevant chapters of *Facing East from Indian Country: A Native History of Early America* (Cambridge, 2001). Gregory Evans Dowd analyzes the emergence of early pan-Indian movements in *A Spirited Resistance: The North American Struggle for Unity, 1745–1815* (Baltimore, 1993). Colin Calloway surveys the variety of native experiences and actions during the period leading to the Revolution in *The American Revolution in Indian Country: Crisis and Diversity in Native American Communities* (Cambridge, 1995), while Walter S. Dunn analyzes frontier divisions during the Revolutionary period in *Choosing Sides on the Frontier in the American Revolution* (Westport, 2007).

Chapter 14

Engaging general overviews of the War for Independence may be found in John Ferling, *Almost a Miracle: The American Victory in the War of Independence* (Oxford, 2007); T. H. Breen, *American Insurgents, American Patriots: the Revolution of the People* (New York, 2010); and Patrick Griffin, *America's Revolution* (New York, 2012). A provocative view of the American Revolution and its outcomes may also be found in Alfred F. Young, Gary B. Nash, and Ray Raphael, eds., *Revolutionary Founders: Rebels, Radicals, and Reformers in the Making of the Nation* (New York, 2011).

An enormous volume of writing continues to appear annually on the Revolutionary experience of war. For the Continental Army, an excellent staring point remains Charles Royster, *A Revolutionary People at War: The Continental Army and the American Character, 1775–1783* (Chapel Hill, 1979). John Shy's *A People Numerous and Armed: Reflections on the Military Struggle for American Independence* (Ann Arbor, 1990) remains an excellent analysis of the larger military effort, including insightful treatment of the militia's role in the conflict. David Hackett Fischer captures the realities and myths of George Washington's leadership in his *Washington's Crossing* (New York, 2004). An excellent collection of essays edited by Alfred Young, *Liberty Tree: Ordinary People and the American Revolution* (New York, 2006), explores the manifold experience of ordinary Americans in the Revolution. The often-overlooked role of disease in the American conflict receives excellent analysis in Elizabeth Fenn, *Pox Americana: The Great Smallpox Epidemic of 1775–82* (New York, 2001).

The continental and Atlantic contexts of the American Revolution have gained much greater attention in recent years with the new approaches to Atlantic World history. For Quebec, see Philip Lawson, *The Imperial Challenge: Quebec and Britain in the American Revolution* (Montreal, 1990). For the borderlands of British Florida and Spanish Louisiana, see Gene Allen Smith and Sylvia L. Hilton, eds., *Nexus of Empire: Negotiating Loyalty and Identity in the Revolutionary Borderlands, 1760s–1820s* (Gainesville, 2010), and Robert V. Haines, *The Natchez District and the American Revolution* (Jackson, Miss., 1976). For the Caribbean, see Andrew Jackson O'Shaughnessy, *An Empire Divided: The*

American Revolution and the British Caribbean (Philadelphia, 2000). For the war at sea, see James M. Volo, *Blue Water Patriots: The American Revolution Afloat* (Westport, Conn., 2007).

The Declaration of Independence continues to attract robust scholarly attention. David Armitage sets the document in its Atlantic context and explores its global influence in *The Declaration of Independence: A Global History* (Cambridge, Mass., 2007). Pauline Maier analyzes the creation of the Declaration in *American Scripture: Making the Declaration of Independence* (New York, 1997). Jay Fliegelman explores the Declaration's rhetorical force in *Declaring Independence: Jefferson, Natural Language, and the Culture of Performance* (Stanford, 1993).

A number of excellent volumes have appeared in recent years on the British cause in the war along with the experience and fate of the Loyalists. For British leadership and strategy, see Andrew Jackson O'Shaughnessy, *The Men Who Lost America: British Leadership, the American Revolution, and the Fate of the Empire* (New Haven, 2013). For Loyalists at war, see Thomas B. Allen, *Tories: Fighting for the King in America's First Civil War* (New York, 2010). For the experience of exile, see Maya Jasanoff, *Liberty's Exiles: American Loyalists in the Revolutionary World* (New York, 2011).

The experience of African Americans and American Indians in the Revolution is the topic of many good studies, among them is Douglas Egerton, *Death or Liberty: African Americans and Revolutionary America* (Oxford, 2011). Cassandra Pybus captures several excellent narratives of African American experience during the Revolutionary period in her *Epic Journeys of Freedom: Runaway Slaves of the American Revolution and Their Global Quest for Liberty* (Boston, 2006), and Woody Holton, *Forced Founders: Indians, Debtors, Slaves, and the Making of the American Revolution in Virginia* (Chapel Hill, 1999). For American Indians, see Colin G. Calloway, *The American Revolution in Indian Country: Crisis and Diversity in Native American Communities* (Cambridge, 1995).

Chapter 15

Gordon S. Wood's *The Creation of the American Republic, 1776–1787* (Chapel Hill, 1969), along with his *Radicalism of the American Revolution* (New York, 1992), remains valuable starting points for anyone wishing to gain a deeper understanding of this period. Woody Holton has recently revised and updated an alternative interpretation of the period in his *Unruly Americans and the Origins of the Constitution* (New York, 2007).

The ferment of social change and the development of national identity during the 1780s have drawn substantial scholarly attention. An excellent starting point for investigation is David Waldstreicher, *In the Midst of Perpetual Fetes; The Making of American Nationalism, 1776–1820* (Chapel Hill, 1997), while T. H. Breen explores the development of American national identity in *Discovering America: George Washington's Journey to a New Nation* (New York, 2015). The response of women to Revolutionary-era rhetoric of liberty and equality is the subject of Rosemary Zagarri's *Revolutionary Backlash: Women and Politics in the Early American Republic* (Philadelphia, 2008). On social change and the development of political culture in the early republic, see also Douglas Bradburn, *The Citizenship Revolution: Politics and the Creation of the American Union 1774–1804* (Charlottesville, 2009).

Douglas Egerton explores the post-Revolutionary struggle for emancipation in *Death or Liberty: African Americans and Revolutionary America* (New York, 2011), as does Gary B. Nash, *The Forgotten Fifth: African Americans in the Age of Revolution* (Cambridge, Mass., 2006). Henry Wiencek explores one significant instance of the development of abolitionist sentiment in *An Imperfect God: George Washington, His Slaves and the Creation of America* (New York, 2003). For African American in the Atlantic World, see Jeffrey Bolster, *Black Jacks: African American Seamen in the Age of Sail* (Cambridge, Mass., 1997).

Of an overview of the development of the trans-Appalachian West, see Malcolm J. Rohrbough, *Trans-Appalachian Frontier: People, Societies, and Institutions, 1775–1850* (Bloomington, 2008). Erick Hinderaker analyzes the post-Revolutionary contest over the West in later chapters of *Elusive Empires: Constructing Colonialism in the Ohio Valley, 1673–1800* (New York, 1997). For the conflict with American Indians for control of the West, see David Andrew Nichols, *Red Gentlemen and White Savages: Indians, Federalists, and the Search for Order on the American Frontier* (Charlottesville, 2008), and Gregory Evans Dowd, *A Spirited Resistance: The North American Indian Struggle for Unity, 1745–1815* (Baltimore, 1993). For Spain in the Old Southwest, see Gene Allen Smith and Sylvia L. Hilton, *Nexus of Empire: Negotiating Loyalty and Identity in the Revolutionary Borderlands, 1760s–1820s* (Gainesville, 2010). For Britain in the Old Northwest, see Larry L. Nelson, *A Man of Distinction among Them: Alexander McKee and British-Indian Affairs along the Ohio Country Frontier, 1754–1799* (Kent, 1999).

The failure of Congress during the 1780s is the subject of Jack N. Rakove's *The Beginnings of National Politics: An Interpretive History of the Continental Congress* (New York, 1979). See also Benjamin H. Irvin, *Clothed in Robes of Sovereignty: The Continental Congress and the people Out of Doors* (New York, 2011). The most comprehensive treatment of the development of state constitutions remains Willi Paul Adams, *The First American Constitutions: Republican Ideology and the Making of the State Constitutions in the Revolutionary Era*, trans. Rita and Robert Kimber (Chapel Hill, 1980), while Peter Thompson and Peter S. Onuf, eds. further analyze their development in *State and Citizen: British America and the Early American States* (Charlottesville, 2012). See also Max M. Edling, *A Revolution in Favor of Government: Origins of the U.S. Constitution and the Making of the American States* (New York, 2003). Peter S. Onuf analyzes the development and passage of the Northwest Ordinance in *Statehood and Union: A History of the Northwest Ordinance* (Bloomington, 1987).

For the framing of the Constitution, see David J. Bodenhamer, *The Revolutionary Constitution* (Oxford, 2012), and David Brian Robertson, *The Original Compromise: What the Constitution's Framers Were Really Thinking* (New York, 2013). For the ratification debate, see Pauline Maier, *Ratification: The People Debate the Constitution, 1787–1788* (New York, 2010), and Jurgen Heideking, *The Constitution before the Judgment Seat: The Prehistory and Ratification of the American Constitution, 1787–1791* (Charlottesville, 2012).

For the global significance of the Constitution and the American Revolution, the classic analysis remains R. R. Palmer, *The Age of Democratic Revolution: A Political History of Europe and America, 1760–1800* (Princeton, 1959–64). Eliga S. Gould explores the early development of the United States as an independent nation in *Among the Powers of the Earth: The American Revolution and the Making of a New World Empire* (Cambridge, Mass., 2012). Eliga S. Gould and Peter Onuf explore the broader impact of the American Revolution in *Empire and Nation: The American Revolution in the Atlantic World* (Baltimore, 2005). For an Atlantic perspective on the Constitution and the British Empire, see Peter J. Marshall, *Remaking the British Atlantic: The United States and the British Empire after American Independence* (New York, 2012). For the subsequent global impact of America's written Constitution, see Linda Colley, "Empire and Writing: Britain, America, and Constitutions, 1776–1748," *Law and History Review* 32 (2014), 237–266.

Index

Text Credits

Chapter 1: p.1: Vespucci, Amerigo, quoted in Vespucci reprints : texts and studies. Princeton University Press, 1916; P. 4: Christopher Columbus, "Letter of Columbus on the First Voyage" in Cecil Jane (eds. and trans.), The Four Voyages of Columbus (New York: Dover, 1988); p.9: Olaudah Equiano, The Life of Olaudah Equiano, Or, Gustavus Vassa, the African. Courier Corporation, 1814; p.13: Bernal Díaz, The true history of the conquest of New Spain. Hakluyt society, 1908; p.14: Bartolomé de Las Casas, A short account of the destruction of the Indies. Translated by Nigel Griffin, Penguin Books, 1992; p.15: Miguel León-Portilla, Pre-Columbian Literatures of Mexico, trans. Grace Lobanov and Miguel León-Portilla, 87. Copyright (c) 1969 by University of Oklahoma Press. Reprinted with permission; p.19: Bartolomé de las Casas, History of the Indies, Harper & Row, 1971; p.22: James Axtell, quoted in Global Dumping Ground: The International Traffic in Hazardous Waste, Seven Locks Press, 1990; p.24: Jacques Cartier, Henry Percival Biggar, Ramsay Cook, Voyages of Jacques, University of Toronto Press, 1993.

Chapter 2: p.31: Samuel de Champlain, 1599, as quoted in Paul Butel, The Atlantic. Routledge, 2002; Richard Hakluyt, 1584; p.33: Sir Thomas Peckham, quoted in A selection of curious, rare and early voyages. R. H. Evans, 1810; p.40: David Eltis, "Free and Coerced Transatlantic Migrations: Some Comparisons," American Historical Review, Vol.88, No.2 (1983), 255; p.47: Sir John Davies in a letter to Robert Earl, 8 November 1610, cited in Morley, Henry, Ireland under Elizabeth and James the First. G. Routledge and sons, limited, 1890; p.48: Captain Arthur Barlow, quoted in The Trinity archive. Trinity College, N.C. : Literary Societies [of Trinity College], 1887; Kathleen M. Brown, Good Wives, Nasty Wenches, and Anxious Patriarchs: Gender, Race, and Power in Colonial Virginia. Institute of Early American History and Culture, 1996; p.49: Hakluyt, Richard, The principal navigations, voyages, traffiques and discoveries of the English nation [microform]. Edinburgh : E. & G. Goldsmid, 1885.

Chapter 3: p.51: Richard Hakluyt, A Discourse on Western Planting, Written in the Year 1584. J. Wilson and son, 1877; p.59: John Smith, The generall historie of Virginia. New York, Macmillan, 1907; p.60: John Smith, The generall historie of Virginia. New York, Macmillan, 1907; p.62: Edmund S. Morgan; p.64: Governor William Berkeley, 1646; William Byrd, The Westover Manuscripts. E. and J. C. Ruffin, 1841; p.65: Thomas O'Brien Hanley, S.J., Their Rights and Liberties: The Beginnings of Religious and Political Freedom in Maryland (Westminster, Md., 1959), p.77; p.67: Robert Beverley, 1705; p.72: James Merrell, "Cultural Continuity among the Piscataway Indians of Colonial Maryland; p.73: Governor Sir William Berkeley, 1671; Robert Beverley, Jr., The History and Present State of Virginia, National Humanities Center Resource Toolbox, 1705.

Chapter 4: p. 79: Sir William Courteen, 1626; p.85: Sidney Wilfred Mintz, Sweetness and Power: The Place of Sugar in Modern History, Penguin Books, 1986; p.85-86: Sidney Wilfred Mintz, Sweetness and Power: The Place of Sugar in Modern History, Penguin Books, 1986; p.88: Richard Ligon, A true & exact history of the island of Barbadoes. London: Peter Parker and Thomas Guy, 1673; Henry Whistler (1655), quoted in Richard Ligon, A true & exact history of the island of Barbadoes. London: Peter Parker and Thomas Guy, 1673; p.91: Richard Ligon, A true & exact history of the island of Barbadoes. London: Peter Parker and Thomas Guy, 1673; p.93: Richard Ligon, A true & exact history of the island of Barbadoes. London: Peter Parker and Thomas Guy, 1673.

Chapter 5: p.98: Anne Bradstreet, 1642; Letter from Deputy Governor Thomas Dudley to Lady Bridget, Countess of Lincoln, March , 1631, quoted in Collections of the masachusetts historical society, 1802; p.99: Jared Elliot, quoted in Collections of the Connecticut Historical Society (Vol. 3), 1874; p.99-100: John Smith, The trve travels, adventvres and observations of Captaine Iohn Smith, in Europe, Asia, Africke, and America. Franklin Press, 1819; p.100: Thomas Morton, 1622; Reverend Francis Higginson (1629), quoted in Joseph Barlow Felt, The Annals of Salem: From Its First Settlement. W. & S. B. Ives, 1827; p.101: The Mayflower Compact (1620), quoted in Henry Whittemore, The Signers of the Mayflower Compact and Their Descendants. Mayflower Publishing Company, 1899; p.103: John Winthrop letter to his wife, May 1629, quoted in Robert Charles Winthrop, John Winthrop, Life and letters of John Winthrop. Ticknor and Fields, 1864; Cambridge Agreement, August 26, 1629, quoted in Charles Sprague, An Ode Pronounced Before the Inhabitants of Boston, September the Seventeenth, 1830. John H. Eastburn, city printer, 1830; p.104: Francis Higginson, New Englands plantation. Printed by T.C. and R.C. for Michael Sparke, 1680; John Winthrop, "A Model of Christian Charity", 1630; John Cotton, God's Promise to His Plantation. Classic Textbooks, 1630; p.105: John Winthrop (1638), quoted in Winthrop's Journal, "History of New England," 1630-1649, Volume 7, Issue 2. C. Scribner's sons, 1908; p.106: John Winthrop, 1630s; p.107: Captain John Mason, may 1637; p.109: Anne Hutchinson, 1637; p.110: Benjamin Wadsworth, quoted in Edmund S. Morgan, The Puritan Family (New York: Harper and Row, 1944, 1966); p.111: Cotton Mather, "Elegy Upon the Death of Mrs. Mary Brown; Who Dyed in Travail, An"; p.112: Benjamin Harris, New-England Primer, 1690; p.113: Michael Wigglesworth, The Day of Doom, 1662; p.114: Anne Bradstreet, "To my Dear and loving Husband" 1678; John Winthrop, 1640s.

Chapter 6: p.130: Charles II, 1668; p.135: Ira Berlin, Many Thousands Gone: The First Two Centuries of Slavery in North America. Harvard University Press, 2009; p.137: The Charter or Fundamental Laws, of West New Jersey, 1676, in The Federal and State Constitutions Colonial Charters, and Other Organic Laws of the States, Territories, and Colonies Now or Heretofore Forming the United States of America Compiled and Edited Under the Act of Congress of June 30, 1906 by Francis Newton Thorpe Washington, DC : Government Printing Office, 1909; p.138: George Fox, Journal of George Fox: Being an Historical Account of the Life, Travels, Sufferings, Christian Experiences, and Labour of Love, in the Work of the Ministry, of that Eminent and Faithful Servant of Jesus Christ. W. and F. G. Cash, 1852; p.140: William Penn, "A Further Account of the Province of Pennsylvania.", 1685; Francis Daniel Pastorius, 1684; p.141: William Penn to the Kings of the Indians in Pennsylvania, October 18, 1681; p.142: William Penn, quoted in James Buchanan, Sketches of the History, Manners, and Customs of the North American Indians. Black, Young, and Young, 1824; Letter from William Penn to the Committee of the Free society of Traders, 1683; p.144: Richard Dunn.

Chapter 7: p.152: William Berkeley, quoted in George Chalmers, Political Annals of the Present United Colonies, 1780; William Berkeley, July 1, 1676; p.153: Lydia Chiesman, quoted in A narrative of the Indian and civil wars in Virginia: in the years 1675 and 1676, J. Eliot, 1814; p.154: Wampanoag sachem Philip, quoted in Proceedings of the Rhode Island Historical Society, Rhode Island Historical Society, 1877; p.157: Commission of Sir Edmund Andros for the Dominion of New England. April 7, 1688, quoted in The Federal and State Constitutions Colonial Charters, and Other Organic Laws of the States, Territories, and Colonies Now or Heretofore Forming the United States of America Compiled and Edited Under the Act of Congress of June 30, 1906 by Francis Newton Thorpe Washington, DC : Government Printing Office, 1909; p.163: Cotton Mather, Magnalia Christi Americana, London : Printed for Thomas Parkhurst, 1702; p.165: Increase Mather, Cases of Conscience Concerning Evil Spirits, Personating Men; Witchcrafts, Infallible Proofs of Guilt in Such as are Accused with that Crime, 1693; p.168: William III, quoted in Rapin de ThoyrasThe history of England, Volume 3, J. and P. Knapton, 1744; p.174: Cotton Mather, 1700.

Chapter 8: p.182: Peter Kalm , 1749, quoted in Thoreau, Henry David, A Yankee in Canada, : with Anti-slavery and reform papers. Boston: Ticknor and Fields, 1866; p.183: Nicolas Perrot, The Indian tribes of the upper Mississippi Valley and region of the Great Lakes : as described by Nicolas Perrot, French commandant in the Northwest; Bacquevile de la Potherie, French royal commissioner to Canada; Morrell Marston, American Army officer; and Thomas Forsyth, United States agent at Fort Armstrong ; translated, edited, annotated, and with bibliography and index. Cleveland, Ohio : Arthur H. Clark Co., 1911; p.184: Marquis de Denonville, quoted in Alberta Historical Review, Volume 17, Issues 2-19. Historical Society of Alberta., 1969; Peter Kalm, Travels Into North America. Translated by John Reinold Forster, The editor, 1771; p.187: Ramón A. Gutiérrez, When Jesus Came, the Corn Mothers Went Away: Marriage, Sexuality, and Power in New Mexico, 1500-1846. Stanford University Press, 1991; p.191: Cotton Mather, Ratio disciplinae fratrum Nov-Anglorum, Printed for S. Gerrish in Cornhill, 1726; p.194: James Axtell; p.195: Alexander Spotswood, quoted in London magazine or Gentleman's monthly intelligencer, Volume 26, 1757; p.196: Daniel K. Richter, The ordeal of the longhouse: the peoples of the Iroquois League in the era of European colonization. University of North Carolina Press, 1992; p.197: Richard White, The Middle Ground: Indians, Empires, and Republics in the Great Lakes Region, 1650-1815. Cambridge University Press, 1991; Peter H. Wood, Gregory A. Waselkov, Powhatan's Mantle: Indians in the Colonial Southeast, University of Nebraska Press, 1989.

Chapter 9: p.203: Colonial records of Pennsylvania. Published by the State, 1838; p.204: Sassoonan, quoted in Colonial records of Pennsylvania. Published by the State, 1838; p.206: Benjamin Franklin (1751), quoted in Benjamin Franklin, William Temple Franklin, Memoirs of Benjamin Franklin, Volume 2. M'Carty & Davis, 1840; p.210: Virginia clergyman Hugh Jones, 1724; p.211: Lieutenant Governor Thomas Handasyd, 1703; p.212: Benjamin Franklin, "Felons and Rattlesnakes", The Pennsylvania Gazette, May 9, 1751; p.213: Letters from General Oglethorpe, 14 may 1739; p.215: Gottfried Mittelberger, Gottlieb Mittelberger's journey to Pennsylvania in the year 1750 and return to Germany in the year 1754. Translated by Carl Theo. Eben, Philadelphia : J.J. McVey, 1898; p.216: Benjamin Franklin (1753), quoted in The Gentleman's Magazine, Volumes 155-156, F. Jeffries, 1834; p.220: Edmund Atkin (1755), quoted in Indians of the Southern Colonial Frontier: The Edmond Atkin Report and Plan of 1755. University of South Carolina Press, 1954; James Logan, quoted in Hazard, Samuel, Minutes of the Provincial Council of Pennsylvania, from the organization to the termination of the proprietary government. [Mar. 10, 1683-Sept. 27, 1775]. Philadelphia : Printed by J. Severns, 1851; Sassoonan, quoted in Colonial records of Pennsylvania. Published by the State, 1838; p.224: John Woolman, A Journal of the Life, Gospel labours and Christian experiences of ... J. W. ... To which are added his works, etc, 1824.

Chapter 10: p.226: Alexander Hamilton, Itinerarium, 1744; p.227: Alexander Hamilton, Itinerarium, 1744; p.230: Benjamin Franklin, William Duane, Memoirs of Benjamin Franklin, Volume 1. McCarty & Davis, 1840; p.235: Elizabeth Graeme; p.236: Benjamin Franklin, The autobiography of Benjamin Franklin. New York, E.A. Lawson Co., 1700; Benjamin Franklin, to the Author of the New-England Courant, July 23, 1722; Benjamin Franklin, The autobiography of Benjamin Franklin, Section Twenty Nine. New York, E.A. Lawson Co., 1700; p.238: Jonathan Edwards, The works of President Edwards, Leavitt & Allen, 1852; Psalm 118:23, New American Standard Bible; Jonathan Edwards, John Pye Smith, A narrative of the revival of religion in New England. W. Collins, 1829; Sarah Edwards, October 1740; George Whitefield (174-1770), quoted in Richard Hofstadter, America at 1750, Knopf, 1971; p.240: Charles Chauncy; p.241: Charles Woodmason, The Journal of Reverand Charles Woodmason, 1766; p.244: Joseph Park, quoted in Joseph Tracy, The Great Awakening: A History of the Revival of Religion in the Time of Edwards and Whitefield. Charles Tappan, 1845; David Brainerd, Memoirs of the Rev. David Brainerd. S. Converse, 1822; p.246: Neolin quoted in James Kenny and John W. Jordan, Journal of James Kenny, 1761-1763. The Pennsylvania Magazine of History and Biography Vol. 37, No. 2 (1913), pp. 152-201.

Chapter 11: p.250: John Cary, quoted in Richard B. Sheridan, Sugar and Slavery: An Economic History of the British West Indies, 1623-1775. Barbados : Caribbean Universities Press, 1974; p.254: William Byrd, 1726; p.258: Janet Schaw, Journal of a lady of quality; being the narrative of a journey from Scotland to the West Indies, North Carolina, and Portugal, in the years 1774 to 1776. New Haven: Yale University Press, 1921; p.259: Philip D. Morgan, Black Experience and the Empire. Oxford University Press, 2006; p.264: Life in the South, 1778-1779: The Letters of Benjamin West, ed. James S. Schoff (Ann Arbor. Mich: William L. Clements Library, 1963); p.265: Life in the South, 1778-1779: The Letters of Benjamin West, ed. James S. Schoff (Ann Arbor. Mich: William L. Clements Library, 1963); p.266: Olaudah Equiano, The Interesting Narrative of the Life of Olaudah Equiano, 1789; p.269: Josiah Smith, Jr., quoted in Michael Mullin, American Negro slavery: a documentary history. Harper & Row, 1976; p.269-270: Virginia Gazette, September 22, 1768.

Chapter 12: p.271-272: Captain Pierre-Joseph Céloron de Blainville, Fort Pitt and letters from the frontier. Pittsburgh, J.R. Weldin & co., 1892; p.274: Sir William Blackstone, Samuel Warren, Select Extracts from Blackstone's Commentaries ... With a glossary, questions, notes and introduction, by Rev. Samuel Warren. A. Maxwell, 1837; John Wesley, The Journal of the Rev. John Wesley. J. Kershaw, 1827; John Trenchard, Thomas Gordon, Cato's Letters. Printed for W. Wilkins, T. Woodward, J. Walthoe, and J. Peele, 1723; p.276-277: Independent Reflector, November 30, 1752; p.278: Benjamin Franklin, 1760s; p.280: Colonel Louise-Antoine de Bougainville (1757), as quoted in Alvin Finkel, Margaret Conrad, Veronica Jane Strong-Boag, History of the Canadian peoples: 1867 to the present, Volume 2. Copp Clark Pitman Ltd, 1993; Thomas Pownall, The administration of the British colonies: In 2 Vols, Volume 2. Walter, 1774; p.286: Hendrick, quoted in Pennsylvania Archives, J. Severns & Company, 1877; Letter from George Washington to John Augustine Washington, July 18, 1755; p.288: William Pitt, 1756; p.289: James Wolfe, 1759; p.292: James Wolfe, 1759; p.293: Rule, Britannia, James Thomson, 1740.

Chapter 13:   p.295: Thomas Paine, 1776; p.295: Declaration of Independence, 1776; p.298: Benjamin Franklin, The Works of Benjamin Franklin. Hillard, Gray, 1840; Declaratory Act of 1766; p.303: Thomas Pownall, 1776; Lord Hillsborough, quoted in Collections of the Massachusetts Historical Society. Massachusetts Historical Society, 1885; John Adams, Thoughts on Government, 1776; p.304: Connecticut Assembly, 1764; p.305: Sugar Act, April 5, 1764; p.306: Patrick Henry, 30 May 1765; p.307: The Declaration of Rights of the Stamp Act Congress; p.308: Andrew Jackson O'Shaughnessy, An Empire Divided: The American Revolution and the British Caribbean. University of Pennsylvania Press, 2000; p.310: George Mason to the Committe of London Merchants, June 6, 1766; p.311: Boston Gazette; p.312: Joseph Warren, Stories about General Warren, in relation to the fifth of March massacre, and the battle of Bunker Hill. By a Lady of Boston, 1835; p.316: General Thomas Gage, 1767.

Chapter 14:   p.321: George Washington's Address to the American Troops before the Battle of Long Island, Aug. 27, 1776; p.322: John Adams, Entry in Diary, December 17, 1773; p.323: Letter from General Thomas Gage to the Earl of Dartmouth, 1774; Edmund Burke, quoted in The History, Debates, and Proceedings of Both Houses of Parliament of Great Britain from the Year 1743 to the Year 1774. J. Debrett, 1792; p.324: Benjamin Franklin (1773), quoted in Benjamin Franklin, William Temple Franklin, Memoirs of the Life and Writings of Benjamin Franklin. H. Colburn, 1817; Letter from John Adams to Abigail Adams, 18 September 1774; p.325: George III, November 18, 1774; Hugh Percy; Thomas Gage; p.327: Rose Fuller, 1774; p.328: Thomas Paine, Common Sense, 1776; p.329: John Adams, July 3, 1776; p.329-330: George Washington, The Writings of George Washington, 1840; p.331: William Howe, quoted in Edward Pelham Brenton, ife and correspondence of John, Earl of St. Vincent, Volume 2. H. Colburn, 1838; p.331: Thomas Paine, The American Crisis, 1776; p.332: George Washington, John

Clement Fitzpatrick, David Maydole Matteson, The Writings of George Washington from the Original Manuscript Sources, 1745-1799, Volume 9. U.S. Government Printing Office, 1777; p.336: Henry Clinton, 1781; Lord North, quoted in Harper's New Monthly Magazine, Volume 67. Harper & Brothers, 1883; p.341: John Earl of Dunmore, November of 1775; State of Rhode Island and Providence Plantations, in General Assembly, 1778; p.344: Benjamin Rush, "On the Defects of the Confederation," 1786.

Chapter 15:   p.345: From Thomas Jefferson to James Madison, 22 July, 1789; From Thomas Jefferson to James Madison, 28 August, 1789; p.346: Thomas Jefferson, Memoirs, correspondence and private papers of Thomas Jefferson, 1829; p.351: James Wilson, Bird Wilson, The Works of the Honourable James Wilson, L. L. D, Lorenzo Press, 1804; Aedanus Burke, 1783; p.352: John Adams to James Sullivan, 26 May 1776; p.353: John Woolman, A Journal of the Life, Gospel labours, and christian experiences of..T. Hurst., 1840; Letter from Thomas Jefferson to Benjamin Banneker, 1791; p.354: Richard Randolph, as quoted in Facts and fancies for the curious from the harvest-fields of literature; a melange of excerpta, J.B. Lippincott company, 1905; p.355: Letter from Abigail Adams to John Adams, March 31, 1776; Letter from Lucy Knox to General Henry Knox, 1777; p.356: John Backus, 1784; p.357: Elbridge Gerry, Speech in the Constitutional Convention, 1787; p.359: Constitution of Massachusetts, 1780; Linda Colley; David Armitage, Foundations of Modern International Thought. Cambridge University Press, 2012; p.361: Timothy Pickering, quoted in King, Rufus, The life and correspondence of Rufus King; comprising his letters, private and official, his public documents, and his speeches. New York : G.P. Putnam's Sons, 1900; p.364: George Washington's Newburgh Address, 1783; George Washington, 1786; p.365: James Madison, Letters and Other Writings of James Madison: Fourth President of the United States. J.B. Lippincott & Company, 1865; p.366: James Madison to James Monroe, June 10, 1787; James Madison, Henry Dilworth Gilpin, Debates in the Congress of the Confederation, from February 19, 1787 to April 25, 1787. Langtree & O'Sullivan, 1840; p.367: James Wilson, quoted in James Madison, The Debates in the Several State Conventions on the Adoption of the Federal Constitution. J.B. Lippincott & Company, 1836; James Madison, July 14, 1787; P.368: Charles Cotesworth Pinckney, quoted in Edward Prigg, Richard Peters, Report of the Case of Edward Prigg Against the Commonwealth of Pennsylvania, Argued and Adjudged in the Supreme Court of the United States, at January Term, 1842, L. Johnson, 1842; James Madison, quoted in David Robertson debates and other proceedings of the Convention of Virginia. Enquirer-Press, 1805; p.369: Gouverneur Morris, Constitution of the United States ; James Madison, The Writings of James Madison: 1783-1787. G.P. Putnam's Sons, 1787; p.370: Samuel Chase, quoted in Jon L. Wakelyn, Birth of the Bill of Rights: Major

writings. Greenwood Publishing Group, 2004; p.371: Alexander Hamilton, The Federalist No. 84, 1788; James Madison, 1789; Tenth Amendment, United States Constitution; Thomas Jefferson, Memoir, correspondence, and miscellanies from the papers of T. Jefferson, Volumes 3-4, F. Carr & Co., 1829; p.372: Charles-James Fox, The Speeches ... in the House of Commons. - London, Longman 1815. Longman, 1815; George Washington, First Inaugural Address, April 30, 1789.

Photo Credits

Chapter 1: P. 8: Cahokia Mounds State Historic Site, painting by William R. Iseminger.

Chapter 2: P.42: Print Collection, Miriam and Ira D. Wallach Division of Art, Prints and Photography, New York Public Library, Astor, Lenox and Tilden Foundation.

Chapter 3: P.61: National Portrait Gallery, Smithsonian Institution/Art Resource, NY.

Chapter 4: P.86: Sugar Refinery, illustration from 'Histoire Generale des Antilles Habitees par les Francois Vol. 2' by Jean Baptiste Du Tertre (1610-1687) published 1667 (coloured engraving) (see also 177261), French School, (18th century) / Bibliotheque Nationale, Paris, France / Bridgeman Images

Chapter 5: P.103: Courtes American Antiquarian Society

Chapter 6: P.138: The Quakers Synod, The Historical Society of Pennsylvania

Chapter 8: P.186: The Newberry Library, Chicago

Chapter 9: P.205: Rare Book Division, New York Public Library, Astor, Lenox and Tilden Collections

Chapter 10: P.233: Andre Jenny/Alamy

Chapter 11: P.252: Abby Aldrich Rockefeller Folk Art Museum, Colonial Williamsburg Foundation, Williamsburg, VA

Chapter 12: P.282: Collection of The New York Historical Society

Chapter 13: P.312: Everett Historical/Shutterstock

Chapter 14: P.322: North Wind Picture Archives/Alamy

Chapter 15: P.356: Glasshouse Images/Alamy